# GREEN LIGHT!

## A Troop Carrier Squadron's War
## From Normandy to the Rhine

D1518690

**Center for
Air Force
History**

Washington. D.C.

Martin Wolfe

1993

**Library of Congress Cataloging-in-Publication Data**

Wolfe, Martin.
    Green Light! : a troop carrier squadron's war from Normandy to the
Rhine / Martin Wolfe. p. cm.
    New ed. of: Green light! : men of the 81st Troop Carrier Squadron
tell their story. Philadelphia University of Pennsylvania Press. c 1989.
    Includes bibliographical references and index.
    ISBN 0–8122–8143–8
    1. United States. Army Air Forces. Troop Carrier Squadron, 81st—
History. 2. World War, 1939–1945—Regimental histories—United States. 3.
World War, 1939–1945—Aerial operations, American. 4. Wolfe, Martin. 5.
World War, 1939–1945—Personal narratives, American. 6. World War,
1939–1945—Campaigns—Western. I. Center for Air Force History (U.S.) II.
Title.

D790.W559                                                    1993
940.54'4973—dc20                                          93–11739
                                                              CIP


Reprinted by arrangement with the University of Pennsylvania Press © 1989.

"Five (5) minutes out from the DZ [drop zone], the group leader will give the radio operator the preparatory order 'READY WITH THE RED.' The radio operator will then take the Aldis Lamp (C-3 Signal Lamp), attach the RED filter and take up position in the astro-dome.

"Four (4) minutes out from the DZ, the group leader will give the order 'SHOW THE RED.' The radio operator then pointing the Aldis Lamp to the rear, through the astro-dome, will turn on the lamp and swing the RED beam slowly to the right and left five (5) times, through approximately sixty (60) degrees.

"The group leader will then give the order 'READY WITH THE GREEN.' The radio operator will attach the GREEN filter to the Aldis Lamp. When the jump point is reached, the group leader will give the order 'SHOW THE GREEN.' The radio operator then pointing the Aldis Lamp to the rear in the astro-dome, will turn on the lamp and swing the GREEN beam slowly to the right and left five (5) times through approximately sixty (60) degrees.

"The GREEN signal will be repeated by the lead ship in each squadron in the group when the jump point is reached."

HQ, IX Troop Carrier Command, "Standard Operating Procedures for Troop Carrier-Airborne Operations." 2 May 1944

# Foreword

The history of air warfare is replete with accounts of derring-do and courage by fighter pilots, bomber pilots, and crews. Their exploits are exciting, often very colorful, and capture the imagination of the public. But air warfare does not consist of only fighter and bomber combat. It is a melange of disparate elements—fighters, bombers, airlifters, tankers, and a remarkable variety of ground support activities—combining to form an effective whole. For example, during the recent Gulf War, F–117, F–15, and F–111 combat operations received well-deserved praise; however, these operations would not have been nearly as successful had it not been for the extraordinary support of the U.S. Air Force's tanker and airlift fleet supporting these operations.

In *Green Light!*, Martin Wolfe tells the story of another organization in an earlier war whose activities never received much publicity yet had a great impact on various combat operations. During World War II, the 81st Troop Carrier Squadron, as its name implies, carried and dropped paratroopers onto the battlefield, often in the face of heavy enemy fire. Despite sometimes heavy losses in this hazardous and demanding job, the 81st TCS never wavered. This book relates the exploits of the 81st, which mirror the combat experience of all World War II troop carrier units.

The term "troop carrier" as an official organizational name is now obsolete, but the direct descendants of the troop carriers are still flying today. The new C–17, the older C–5 and C–141, and especially the workhorse C–130 of Air Mobility Command, the Air Force Reserve, and the Air National Guard fly troops all over the world. These airlifters and their forebears make possible today's "Global Reach—Global Power."


RICHARD P. HALLION
Air Force Historian

# Preface

Thirty-eight veterans of troop carrier squadrons other than my own, after reading the first edition of *Green Light!*, took the trouble to assure me—in almost identical words—"Change the names of the fellows and this history could have been ours!" Their approval of my efforts to show what troop carriers were all about means a great deal to me. In a very real sense, this is their book, too: the story of all troop carriers in the European theater of operations and not only that of the 81st Troop Carrier Squadron.

Like all troop carrier veterans—especially our glider pilots—I feel our part in World War II is one of the most overlooked features of that mighty struggle. We are extremely grateful to the Air Force historical program, therefore, for this chance to tell more readers about us through a new edition of our book. Particular thanks go to Dr. Richard P. Hallion, the Air Force Historian; to the Director of the Center for Air Force History, Jacob Neufeld; and to the chief of the Editorial Division at the Center, Anne Johnson Sachs. The complex work of seeing this project through to a successful conclusion fell mostly on the shoulders of Karen A. Fleming-Michael, an editor with the Center, and William T. Y'Blood, a historian at the Center. It was truly a pleasure to work with Mr. Y'Blood and the friendly and efficient team at the Center. Craig Kodera's striking cover painting is under copyright to the Greenwich Workshop, Inc., Trumbull, Connecticut 06611.

This new edition gave me the opportunity to correct some misstatements in the original book. I am grateful to Roger Airgood and Larry Camp of the 79th Troop Carrier Squadron, to Joe Harkiewicz of the 29th TCS, to Bill Horn, editor of *Silent Wings*, and to Ellery Bennett and Russ Carle of my 81st TCS for these improvements. My appeal for better photos—to twenty veterans who, I knew, had important souvenir albums—met with such a generous response that I can acknowledge only a few of those who loaned me their precious photos: Brig. Gen. Adriel T. Williams, our 436th Troop Carrier Group Commander, and Gale Ammerman, Thayer Bonecutter, Russ Carle, Roger Krey, and Ted Menderson, all of the 81st TCS Association.

When I first started work on *Green Light!*, way back in 1986, R. Cargill Hall–then chief of the Research Division of the USAF Historical Research Center at Maxwell Air Force Base–told me that I would derive more personal satisfaction from this project than anything I had ever written during my entire thirty-seven-year career as a historian.  He was right.

Martin Wolfe
Wynnewood, Pennsylvania
March 1993

# Contents

Party of the first part
On the glider line
Morale on the line

## 11. COMMANDING
### How to Run Combat Operations / 185

The TO of the TCC
The Operations Office
The motor pool
Communications
Intelligence

## 12. MANAGING
### How to Run a Squadron / 210

The Orderly Room
Sick Call!
Chow!
Quartermaster Supply

## 13. BREAKING OUT
### The Controversy Over Troop Carrier Freighting Potential / 226

Fighters or freighters?
Giving Patton the gas

## 14. SUNNING
### Italy and the Assault on Southern France / 247

From Membury to Voltone
Politics and strategy in Operation DRAGOON
The missions
"Champagne campaign"?

## 15. MARKET-GARDENING
### "Airborne Carpet" or "Hell's Highway"? / 273

Three names
"A bridge too far"?
The first two missions
Was there still a chance?

Hell on the ground
Assessing VARSITY

Repatriations
Adding up "points"
Last missions
Tag ends
Splitting up

Judging troop carrier
"A good outfit"
How our experiences changed our lives
Forgotten fields

# Maps

# GREEN LIGHT!

## A Troop Carrier Squadron's War
## From Normandy to the Rhine

# 1. Starting Up
## How to Put a Squadron Together

### Where we all came from

The 81st Troop Carrier Squadron was built from scratch. It was put together with civilians who had very little flying training, with a totally inadequate number of planes and gliders, all housed on pitifully inadequate airfields. It was dedicated to a daring new military concept: "vertical envelopment," that is, launching paratroopers and gliders into "airheads" behind enemy lines. For this new tactic there was only one important example, a Nazi one. Furthermore, this Nazi airborne assault (Operation MERKUR—the conquest of Crete in May 1941) had cost Germany frightening losses in men and aircraft—far too many, Hitler decided.

Yet only eight months after our Squadron activated (at Baer Field, Indiana, in April 1943) it was functioning well. We had become a highly self-confident group of specialists, convinced of the importance and feasibility of our mission and ready to run the risks associated with it. We had the capabilities, we had the tools, we had that indefinable but precious bonding which goes under the name of "esprit de corps." We had class—maybe less class than a fighter squadron, but class, nevertheless.

We came from every section of the country—from North Dakota to Mississippi, from California to Maine. Certainly the most exotic home background belonged to David Brack; born on an Indian reservation in Oklahoma, he commanded our 81st Troop Carrier Squadron. While the majority of us were WASPs (white Anglo-Saxon Protestants), there were fellows in the outfit from all major ethnic and religious groups—except blacks. Aside from a few token combat units, black soldiers those days could serve only in labor and transport groups.

Our family backgrounds, so far as I could tell, also represented a cross-section of America's white population—except for the richest and poorest classes. Some of us from farm or blue-collar families had certainly been poor, at least by today's standards; but the really dirt poor tended to have less schooling, and they were kept out by the Army Air Forces'[1] priority in the selection system. Fellows from wealthy families, on the other hand, were likely to go for the

Navy or for cushy administrative jobs. Only a few of us had university degrees, though many had a year or two in college. Almost everybody had finished high school—a greater accomplishment in the 1930s than in the 1980s.

With all this diversity, there was no one sort of person you could think of as typical. We did notice, however, that the majority of us came from small towns and not big cities. Considering the small proportion of our country's population in the South and Southwest, there seemed to be a lot of men from those regions. I hailed from Newark, New Jersey, a place which could not make up its mind whether it was a middle-size city or a suburb of New York.

What hopes and inclinations, what mysterious machinations of the military selection process, had guided us into this strange new branch of the service known as troop carrier? The prestige that attached to flying explained why some of us were there, especially those who had a chance to become pilots or crewmen. We came from the generation of children that would rush to the windows of our grade school classrooms to stare up at the sky whenever we heard that exciting new noise of an airplane. A Sunday treat for my family when I was a kid—as much appreciated as a movie—involved a drive out to the new airport just to watch planes arriving and departing. Charles Hastings, who was to become a pilot and whose hero was Charles Lindbergh, remembers carving balsawood models of Fokkers and Spads. I would bet virtually every person in the 81st also made model airplanes. John Hiles (radio mechanic) was president of his high school model airplane club.

In the beginning was the cadre: the small group of men selected to serve as the nucleus from which the Squadron would expand to its full strength.

HEADQUARTERS
436th TROOP CARRIER GROUP
BAER FIELD   FORT WAYNE   INDIANA,   4 April 1943

1. Major ADRIEL N. WILLIAMS, 0-22877 AC, having reported this date pursuant to par 2, SO 61, 10th Gp, AAF, Dunnellon, Florida, dated March 26, 1943, is asgd to Hq., 436th TC Gp, AAF. Prim. dy Commanding Officer.

12. CAPT. DAVID W. BRACK, 0-402316, AC, having reported this date pursuant to par 2, SO 61, Hq., 10th TC Gp., AAF, Dunnellon, Fla., dated March 26, 1943, is asgd to 81st TC Sq., AAF, as of April 1, 1943, and will assume command thereof.

14. The following named O, having rptd this date pursuant to par 2, SO 61, Hq. 10th TC Gp., AAF, Dunnellon, Fla., are asgd to organizations indicated and will report to the CO thereof for dy:

<u>81st TROOP CARRIER SQ</u>

1st LT JOHN J. BOHAN
1st LT CHARLES S. HASTINGS
2nd LT JOSEPH A. KONECNY
2nd LT HARLYN L. SEMAR
2nd LT CHARLES W. STEVENSON
2nd LT JOHN F. WALLEN, JR.
2nd LT BRUCE L. BARKER
2nd LT GEORGE J. RANKIN
2nd LT BENJAMIN J. DUCHARME
2nd LT FRANCIS E. FARLEY
2nd LT HAROLD W. WALKER

15. The following named EM, having rptd this date pursuant to par 2, SO 61, 10th TC Gp., AAF, Dunnellon, Fla., are asgd to organs indicated and will report to their respective CO's for duty:

<u>81st TROOP CARRIER SQ</u>

T/Sgt Edwin R. Harris
S/Sgt Leonard C. Lewis
S/Sgt John J. Shroeder
Sgt Edward F. Huff
Sgt Grover W. Benson
Sgt Carlisle A. Jordan
Sgt Ray C. Thomas
Sgt Michael (NMI) Hrycaj
Pfc Frank B. Schwartz
Pfc Irving (NMI) Bornstein
Pfc Joseph A. Raybits
Pfc Elmer F. Jespersen
Pfc Delma H. Montgomery

So read our very first orders (actually extracts from our 436th Group orders). We now had a legally constituted cadre of twelve "Os" and thirteen "EMs." The work of fleshing out the Squadron could begin.

For the rest of us, arriving at the 81st was mainly a matter of having been in the right cadet flight school graduating class, glider school, or technical school—or being in a replacement depot at just the time when the call came through from the high brass for additional men.

Our brass—that is, our chain of command—was structured like all Army Air Forces units into Command (ours eventually was to be the IX Troop Carrier

Command); Wing (ours already was the 53rd TC Wing); and Group (ours was the 436th TC Group). The 436th had three squadrons and a headquarters unit in addition to us. Groups were the Air Forces' "cells": the basic tactical units, the smallest bands that could function independently.

Arrival at the 81st TCS had taken some of us more than a year since we first put on uniforms in 1942—month after tedious month of being pushed around from one base to another, from basic training, to technical school, to the "repple depple" (replacement depots), to OCS (Officer Candidate School), flight school or glider school, to transition training airfields, to other squadrons that then decided they didn't need us. What a relief, having been shifted around like parts on a factory assembly line, to finally know we were in a regular outfit that could use us!

We now had "our" commanding officer, "our" administrative staff to tell us what to do, and for some of us, "our own" crew. By the late summer and fall of 1943, some of us got "our own" planes. This sense of belonging helped us to stop feeling like anonymous GI[2] pawns and to start thinking like individuals with a purpose, with a function, and with support in the form of others we knew and (for the most part) trusted.

A few of us were useful because of some civilian talent, such as typing, or because we had had experience as mechanics. Grant Howell, who ran a teletype for us, knew all about such machines since he had been an editor of a small-town newspaper. Many of us were very young and had not worked at all, except during summers. Most of the jobs the rest of us had had as civilians were of little value when we became members of the 81st. Delma Montgomery, our glider mechanic section chief, had worked as a switchboard operator and clerk in an Amarillo hotel. George Rankin, our Communications Officer, had worked as an apprentice machinist at ALCOA. James Ackerman, a pilot, had been a bank clerk. Don Skrdla, also a pilot, had run a cattle ranch.

Most of us, therefore, relied on our training in Air Forces schools. An instructor in radio school told me that we had been chosen because we had done well in tests for sensitivity to differences in musical tone and rhythm—and thus we promised to become proficient in receiving and sending Morse code messages. Others were selected for technical schools on the basis of their experience as well as their aptitude. Several crew chiefs had been farm boys; they had handled large and complex machinery and so were good bets for training as airplane mechanics. A very young Jerome Loving (crew chief) had waited until the fall crops came in in November 1942 to get his parents' permission to enlist.

Maybe other outfits were made up mostly of square pegs in round holes; but in the 81st the selection process seemed to work out well. There was also the negative incentive: we knew that if we didn't shape up we could be shipped out to the infantry. David Brack was famous for booting people that he regarded as shirkers, trouble-makers, or incompetents out of the Squadron.

Whatever our backgrounds, only a few had had any experience in or liking for military life. Middle-class attitudes during the 1930s held our tiny American peacetime army pretty much in contempt. It is true that two of the oldest men in the Squadron, Henry Allai (mechanic and duty roster clerk) and Theodore Slattery (airplane mechanic) had actually served as soldiers during World War I. Rip Collins, who became a pilot, had spent two years as a soldier in the Panama Canal Zone. Before he became an Eastern Airlines pilot, David Brack had been a sergeant in the horse-drawn Field Artillery; Leonard Braden (pilot) had served in the horse cavalry. Grover Benson, a flight chief (one of the top ground mechanics) had served four years in the regular army, including a stint as a 9th Division infantryman. Walter Ditto, our Squadron Adjutant, was the only regular army man among the officers; in the early days of our Squadron he liked to sport his big, round campaign hat from prewar days.

Louis Kramer, who came into our outfit as Assistant Operations Officer and ended up as our Intelligence Officer, was one of the few who came in via the tough three-months OCS—products of which also were called "ninety-day wonders." He likes to say he got into OCS because of his mother's pickled herring.

> I came from a very poor Jewish family on the Lower East Side of New York. In our house, instead of a cookie jar we had a big jar of pickled herring. When I enlisted my mother sent me a whole crock of pickled herring. I had to serve as an MP [military policeman] for almost a year in Sedalia, Missouri. The monotony there was terrible. I was nothing better than a night watchman. I was desperate to get into an outfit that was doing something about the war. Whenever I accompanied the OD [Officer of the Day] around the base I would fish him out some herring from my mother's crock. Now, when I was tested for OCS at Sedalia I came out with the highest score anyone had ever gotten there! This was a puzzle, since I was the kind of kid whose mother had had to give me apples for my teacher in order to get me graduated from kindergarten. But in thinking it over I realized that of the five officers at Sedalia who rated me, four of them had thoroughly enjoyed my mother's pickled herring!

We were "Depression babies." James Sindledecker and J. J. DiPietro (glider pilots) had worked for a few months doing forestry work in the CCC (Civilian Conservation Corps), one of Roosevelt's devices to fight unemployment. DiPietro, who graduated from high school in 1932, at the very bottom of the Depression, worked on a WPA project, split granite with a jackhammer, and worked in a gas station—when he wasn't helping out on his parents' farm. David Brack tried hard to pick up flying experience (and a little cash) as a barnstormer and cropduster. In spite of the Depression only a handful of us had chosen employment in the armed forces before Pearl Harbor.

Several of us who had some time in college before the war took ROTC (Reserve Officers Training Corps) classes, but only because they were compulsory in state colleges. When I was a freshman everyone wanted to get into the cavalry so we could ride those horses, wear those classy jodhpurs and boots, and come into classes smelling terrible. But there weren't enough horses to go around, or maybe somebody looked at me and thought I would never do, so I ended up in the infantry. When we showed up at infantry ROTC class, the drill sergeant looked at our sullen, disappointed faces and decided to give us a pep talk. Don't feel bad about being in the infantry, he said. The infantry is the only place in the whole goddamned Army where you can really kill a man!

At the time I was a confirmed pacifist.

## "What's your MOS?"

The silly Air Forces boast: "The difficult we will accomplish immediately; the impossible will take a bit longer," made us wince because of its bumptiousness. For troop carrier it was indeed reflected in the complex but smoothly functioning structure we achieved so quickly. The creation of the fully expanded 81st Troop Carrier Squadron—from scratch—is a good example of what our country could do when it had to.

Our airplane pilots and their abilities were the main reason the rest of us were also there. Pilots, however, were only the cutting edge of a large and complex operation. They amounted to fewer than one-tenth the total Squadron roster—forty out of about 420, when we were at maximum strength in Europe. We also needed navigators, glider pilots, crew chiefs, and radio operators. And neither pilots nor crewmen could have operated without clerks, motor pool drivers, mechanics, communications experts, cooks, supply managers, sheet-metal men (for repairing holes in a plane's skin), dope and fabric men (for repairing holes in gliders), and several other sorts of technicians.

When the flying personnel completed technical school and arrived in the Squadron, their training—and even their schooling—was far from finished. They had to attend Group and Squadron classes on "Renshaw recognition" (aircraft silhouettes on cards), navigation problems, and maintenance of the planes' engines and radios. Some of our crew chiefs, radio operators, and mechanics were sent on "DS" (detached service) to special schools in other parts of the country for advanced training in radar operation, instrument maintenance, and engine modification (as improvements came along that had to be plugged into the planes). Some of our glider mechanics were sent to school to learn the finer points of glider assembly and maintenance. Joseph Raybits (Intelligence clerk) went to Miami Beach for a course in calisthenics so he could become our physical education instructor. But we got out on the ramp to do some presses and sit-ups only once in a while.

During the summer of 1943, when a new batch of EMs arrived, some of them were given a chance to find what sort of job they were most willing and best fitted to take. Often this was done in spite of whatever "MOS" (military occupation specialization) they had originally been assigned. They would be ordered to the glider hangars for a few days, or the mess hall, or the Orderly Room, or the engineering part of the flight lines, to see where they would best fit in. Later on, as the shape of the Squadron firmed up, the only personnel accepted were those asked for to fill certain pre-specified slots.

Looking over our shoulders were the planners in our 53rd Troop Carrier Wing, seeing to it that we were fully manned in all positions before we went to our POE (port of embarkation). Some key figures in our Squadron joined us only shortly before we left for Britain (December 1943). David Britt, our Squadron Navigator, appeared on the scene at Laurinburg-Maxton, North Carolina, on October 21, less than two months before we shipped out. Darlyle Watters, our Squadron Glider Officer, came aboard even later, on November 1—though it is true that other glider pilots had been assigned previously.

Along with the job came the corresponding rank in the Air Forces TO (table of organization). A radio operator who was picked for a crew quickly made corporal and soon bounced up to staff sergeant. This was my grade, even though I came into the Squadron relatively late (October 1943) and as a private first class. For officers the procedure was more complicated, especially because many of them arrived as Flight Officers (this was the case for most of our glider pilots). Promoting them up to second lieutenant changed them into commissioned officers rather than mere holders of warrants; this meant that Squadron boards of high-ranking officers had to sit on each case and verify the promotion.

Almost all of us, directly after basic training, joined the Air Forces; but this is not true of several officers who came into the Squadron to take key ground-echelon positions. Our Adjutant and Supply Officer came already commissioned from other branches of the service. Some of our pilots—who might be outranked by these newly arrived, non-flying officers—labeled them, more or less in good humor, "paddlefeet."

Pay Day! Our first Squadron pay envelopes were distributed on May 31, 1943. Previously we had been paid by Group HQ. More than any other administrative action, Squadron payment affirmed that our outfit was really on the books. The arrival of a fully functioning 81st TCS was the end product of an extremely rapid process of organizational expansion: nothing called "troop carrier" had existed at the time America went to war. The first men to participate in the creation of this entirely new branch of the armed forces were taken, like Adam's rib, out of the Air Transport Command in July 1942.

This rapid begetting of dozens of higher- and lower-echelon units took place even while aircraft needed by the thousands were just beginning to be built, and the tens of thousands of additional men needed were just beginning to be trained. The process was further complicated by indecision in Washington and London over how much of this monstrously growing organization should eventually land in the various war "theaters": CBI (China-Burma-India), Pacific, MTO (Mediterranean Theater of Operations) or ETO (European Theater of Operations). Because the invasion of Nazi Europe had priority in the minds of high command, the greatest number of TC units by far would end up in Britain: three wings, fifteen groups, and sixty squadrons.

While our War Department attempted to sort out what shapes and sizes it wanted for troop carrier, the 81st Squadron moved to three additional posts after its beginnings in Dunnellon, Florida. After a week at Dunnellon we spent a few weeks at Baer Field (Fort Wayne, Indiana); and then, on May 1, we landed at our first main base—Alliance, Nebraska—of unhappy memory. After surviving three months of choking dust punctuated by periods of sickening mud at Alliance, we arrived at our chief American base, Laurinburg-Maxton, where we were to stay (August-December 1943) until we left for Britain. We came to Maxton by way of a six-day train trip in brutally hot weather over a ridiculously roundabout route (St. Louis, New Orleans, Atlanta). When we arrived at Maxton our Squadron, though far from completely trained, was pretty well formed up, and all its essential components were functioning. We were then just four months old.

Back at Alliance, Nebraska, our new organization's main job had been to absorb the men crowding in and swelling the ranks of our Squadron. These men were assigned to us by our brass at 436th Group and 53rd Wing HQ (both of which were also at Alliance). Only rarely would David Brack be consulted about the suitability of individuals assigned to us; but he had complete authority to kick out anybody he thought would not measure up, officers as well as men.

The Squadron's second biggest job at Alliance was to start working on becoming "operational," that is, to learn how to handle planes and gliders in combat. During the period that we were at Baer and Alliance, we never had more than four or five planes at a time to work with. These were planes left for us by other outfits on their way overseas. Some of them, Edwin "Pappy" Harris (Line

Chief, that is, head airplane mechanic) remembers, were truly tired-out, patched-up jobs, "real doozies." Our very first plane (April 18) was a commercial airlines DC-3; in spite of its age and lack of the modifications that made a C-47 out of a DC-3, it was put to work immediately.

> When we got our first airplane, its Form 41 showed it had just had a 100-hour inspection; so we made no inspection of our own. It was taken on a night training flight by two pilots who had had very little multi-engine training. They didn't notice that the cylinder head temperature was rising. Soon the oil pressure drop in the right engine forced them to feather that prop, but it kept on turning, and the engine heat melted parts of the engine. They just barely made it back to the field. That engine was a salvage job. Replacing it was our first big repair. (Carlisle Jordan, Squadron Airplane Inspector)

For a long time we had no gliders of our own. Finally, Harold Walker, our Squadron Executive Officer and a glider pilot, managed to get a badly worn-out J-3 Piper Cub airplane for "dead stick landing" practice, that is, landing with the engine off.

With so little to do concerning planes and gliders, the Squadron had time to take advantage of some advanced training courses and some schooling in general military organization. Six of our chief NCOs (noncommissioned officers) were sent to Fort Benning, Georgia, for a course in applied tactics—of real value, they reported, in learning how to run a squadron. A large number of men, especially those from the West and Midwest, received seven-day furloughs. Pappy Harris and some other airplane mechanics were sent to Long Beach, California, for invaluable experience working in the Douglas plant which was making C-47s. On the base more time was used up in enforced attendance at poorly presented lectures called "Army Orientation Courses," which were to tell us why we were fighting and "to fix in the mind of the American soldier a sense of the importance of his personal role and responsibilities in the current struggle." ("Propaganda!" we said.)

We also were put to work playing at being soldiers. This was another way of using up time. Some weeks we were taken on long hikes each morning, lugging full packs. We took our turns on the rifle range, under that broiling Alliance sun. In June we even had two bivouacs.

> Once some pilots came back and reported that they saw a nice lake with beautiful fields not too far away. Brack and Walker decided that it would be a nice place to spend a few days. We went full field pack. While we hiked

along, a couple of our planes flew overhead dropping small paper bags filled with flour. Anyone hit was a casualty—and got a ride the rest of the way in the ambulance or truck.

When we arrived at the site it was early afternoon. It was very hot, as usual, and we were told that after we set up our tents we could go swimming. While we were in the water, a deputy in a sheriff's car came along and said he was going to arrest the lot of us for swimming in the town reservoir. Major Walker convinced him we were all soldiers, not tramps; he said the tents were OK but there was to be no more swimming. (David Neumann, parachute rigger)

After the second bivouac at Alliance, the Squadron's first fully authenticated, bona fide false rumor surfaced: we were "hot to trot" and were about to be shipped out to the Pacific.

The excessive summertime heat could be a danger to machines as well as men. One day, when our crew chiefs at Alliance were learning how to taxi planes around the runways, the planes' tires became so overheated that they began to smoke; and when the planes were stopped at their hardstands, some tires exploded. The crew chiefs had to use fire extinguishers to cool the tires.

Another problem at Alliance was the food, stuff only a sadist would be glad to serve. It was there we learned the point of the marching song:

> The hot dogs that they serve you
> They say are mighty fine;
> One fell off the table
> And killed a pal of mine
> Oh, I don't want no more of Army life
> Gee, Mom, I want to come home!

This is not to say all our time at Alliance, for all of us, was sheer misery. Some were able to have our wives join us; it was "A-OK" to be able to take your wife to an Alliance steak house and have one of the superb pieces of beef for which this part of the country was and is famous. On May 8 Walter Ditto (Squadron Adjutant) gave us a better demonstration of what we were fighting for—he and his fiancée were married at the Alliance base chapel.

Group HQ tried to work up some interest at Alliance in a contest to design the 436th Group insignia—the winner was to get a seven-day furlough and ten dollars "in crisp new bills." Just before we left the base, our Squadron flew out a plane to pick up a piano for our newly decorated dayroom. There were movies at the base theater every night, with flicks like Abbott and Costello's "Hit the Ice," Buster Crabbe's "Western Cyclone," and "Once Upon a Honeymoon,"

Playing soldier: Rip Collins (pilot) on the way to a Squadron bivouac at Alliance, Nebraska.

Officers of the new 81st TCS pose for their official portrait. *Front, left to right:* Brack, Walker, Trellis, Bohan, Wolf; *second row:* Frye, Wallen, Hastings, Ditto, Coleman; *rear:* Farley.

with Ginger Rogers and Cary Grant. Sometimes you could hear the movie sound above the boos, whistles, and lewd comments of the audience—but not often.


## It was *not* a summer camp

Perhaps one of the reasons we remember so many bad aspects of Squadron life at Alliance is that our next base, Laurinburg-Maxton, was an improvement. Maxton had better food and better barracks, better runways, and—gradually— all the planes and gliders we needed. In September 1943, though, we suffered a real plague of gnats, the kind we could never get out of our eyes and ears or our food; and when those late summer winds blew across those sandy wastes near the airfield, sand could pile up an inch deep inside the barracks door.

In all our U.S. bases, and in our bases in Europe, the volume of complaining was enormous. It took essentially two forms: "bitching" about camp living and eating conditions; and "TARFU-talk," complaints when things went wrong with our work on the planes, the gliders, the equipment, or in flight training.

"TARFU" was our embellishment on "snafu." Snafu, already in use all over the U.S. and not only in the military, meant "Situation normal, all fucked up." You were supposed to say this with a resigned shrug of the shoulders, indicating that the submoronic people and junky devices you had to deal with would naturally fail. We in troop carrier, responsible as we were for immensely delicate and complex machinery and saddled with impossibly ambitious flying assignments, had to go beyond snafu; so we used "Things Are *Really* Fucked Up!" "TARFU Gazette" was the name of our Squadron newsletter; and we labeled the main road in our base "TARFU Boulevard."

Bitching explains the two logos on the masthead of the "TARFU Gazette"—a gremlin and a little square labeled "TS Card." One response to what sounded like a useless or unreasonable complaint would be "Gee, Tough Shit!" or even "Should I punch your TS card?" the latter supposedly the main activity of our Group Chaplain.

Some of the complaining came from the air of unreality that surrounded much of what we had to do. The shoe-shining, brass polishing, and the close-order drill struck us as playing at being soldiers, and not at all connected with our assignments as technicians and flyers. We sang "Roll Out the Barrel" and "I've Got Sixpence" as we marched in cadence; but we felt exceedingly silly doing this. How did "policing the area" (picking up trash and cigarette butts), or conforming to the "uniform of the day," or doing KP ("kitchen police"), or guard duty help us in our job of delivering paratroopers and gliders? Was it really important to make up our beds so tight that you could "bounce a quarter off the blanket?" Did it make sense for our Group and Wing inspectors to deprive us of our evening passes—or worse, to restrict us to our barracks—if there were some dust on the window ledges and we failed one of their stupid "white glove inspections?"

Reminders of how seriously we were expected to respect this paraphernalia of military life came when Captain John Bohan, our Intelligence Officer, assembled us and solemnly read out the Articles of War; this was a long litany of punishments—including execution by firing squad—for violating certain rules, such as striking an officer (a common temptation).

The most ignominious part of base life was "short arm inspection" for venereal disease. Most mornings, enlisted men would be roused out of bed by the barracks sergeant in charge, who might yell "Everybody up! Drop your cocks and grab your socks!" But once in a while—usually at 4:30 or 5:00 a.m.—there would be a surprise "Everybody up! Short arm!" and we would have to line up in our underwear in front of our bunks, while Jesse Coleman, our Flight Surgeon, and his assistant would go down the ranks ordering us to "milk it"—that is, squeeze our penises from base to tip. The presence of gonorrhea would be revealed if a milky substance was extruded.

During my two years in the 81st TCS, I heard of only a few men caught with what we called "the clap" during such inspections. But "short arms" went on and on. This is not to say there was no VD on the base. Probably the compulsory VD lectures we got from the Group Chaplain and the Group Flight Surgeon were well meant; but, through our yawns, we wished these lectures would be less sloppily presented and less boring.

The concern with VD was for the most part a hangover from regular Army days after World War I when soldiers, especially enlisted men, were expected to spend much of their free time with prostitutes. In our World War II "civilian army" this was just not the case for nearly all of us. That the concern was not entirely unjustified, however, was brought home to me by one episode just before we went overseas. Scheduled for a night training flight to the attractive city of New Orleans, I had to beg off because I had a bad case of flu. A fellow radio operator took my place. Three weeks later he was diagnosed as having contracted syphilis and he was hospitalized while we shipped out. This unlucky fellow could not rejoin us until several weeks after we arrived in England. One reason his treatment took so long is that, in those days, penicillin was still in short supply and was restricted to the treatment of officers. Enlisted men had to be satisfied with the other, slower, sulfa drug cure.

Today you hear a great deal about the problem of narcotics addiction in our armed forces. In the 1940s, this problem simply did not exist. In the 81st TCS we did not have any drug addicts I knew of. Alcoholism was another matter. The proper macho image for World War II soldiers required us to be heavy drinkers, and some of us were in fact alcoholics. One of my fellow radio operators was so afflicted that when he was "on a tear" he would spend all his cash and all he could borrow on booze and then steal and drink up any he could find in the barracks. When he was desperate enough, he would steal and drink hair tonic with a high alcoholic content. On the other hand, a few of us had never touched wine or liquor before enlisting, and continued to "teetotal" all through the war. Johnny Harris (crew chief) had his very first drink during debriefing after D-Day (the Normandy invasion). George Doerner (radio operator) wouldn't take his debriefing "medicinal shot" until much later, when our flight surgeon— observing that George was in a very shaky state after the second mission of the Holland invasion—ordered George to take it.

All our complaining did not mean we could not see how lucky we actually were. Most of the airplane pilots and those glider pilots who had "washed out" during cadet flight school of course were rather bitter at not making it as fighter or bomber pilots. The rest of us, including the enlisted men crew members who had to fly in the same planes as the pilots and navigators, had a strong sense of how much better off we were than the "dog faces" (infantry—we also called them "grunts" or "ground pounders"). Here, unlike the infantry, promotions came fast and often. Some enlisted men were bounced up three grades in as many months. All the flying personnel got a 50 percent addition to their pay. Perhaps most of all, we appreciated the fact that our outfit was not "chicken" ("chicken shit" was what we called giving unreasonable, overbearing, and demeaning orders to lower ranks).

One striking proof of the relative lack of "chicken" among us was the relaxed attitude officers took toward the formality of being saluted. Between the enlisted crewmen and the flying officers, of course, constant saluting or even the punctilious use of "Yes, Sir!" would have been a ridiculous annoyance. Our CO, David Brack, a former civilian pilot, so hated to be constantly saluted as he walked across the base that he would keep his eyes down to avoid being formally "recognized" by enlisted men walking past him. Our pilots, who set the tone in this matter as in everything else, saw themselves as flying technicians, not disciplinarians. Their informal style of dress and relaxed relations with enlisted men made our Squadron a place of relatively low pressure.

Several times the officers chipped in to treat the EMs to a beer bust, and the EMs reciprocated. Officers fielded a football team to play the EMs, and were pretty good-natured about losing. EMs and Os played together against a team from another squadron. While few real friendships developed between our Squadron Os and "other ranks," the relationship between them could best be described as a cross between the businesslike and the moderately friendly.

In fact, there were so many decent things about being in our particular Squadron and on our particular base that complaining often took on a mocking or even a humorous form, and could sometimes be interpreted (correctly) in a positive way, as a demand to work toward rectifying an unsatisfactory situation rather than an attempt to "bad-mouth" something or somebody. Sometimes, such as during an exceptionally good meal at Laurinburg-Maxton (fried chicken and ice cream, every Sunday), or while playing ping pong in the dayroom or picking up rations at the PX (post exchange), the strange feeling could steal over you that you were in a sort of summer camp for grown-up Boy Scouts. But spotting all those olive-drab C-47s lined up on the runway, ready for their next assault training mission, would bring you back to reality.

Officers and enlisted men alike certainly realized that there were worse fates than being part of the 81st TCS. Furthermore, we were all what President John F. Kennedy would later call "children of the Depression," born shortly after World War I: just old enough when the Crash came in 1929 to have strong feelings about mass unemployment, bread lines, and the sight of your father on relief. For us the jeering phrase "You found a home in the Army!" rang all too true. Regular chow, plentiful clothing, free amusements, and a chance to improve oneself through technical training, were not to be despised—though we all pretended to do just that to save our pride.

### Training crews

An 81st TCS pilot once told me bitterly, "Many are called, few are chosen, and the rest end up in troop carrier!" He may have been especially discouraged just then, since the two of us were watching in horror as a plane being flown by a recently arrived pilot who was practicing takeoffs and landings from the runway at Laurinburg-Maxton bounced in so hard that it seemed to go up again in the air some fifty feet; then it veered off to the right so dangerously it seemed inevitable its right wingtip would catch the ground.

By mid-1943 America's production of all sorts of combat aircraft had zoomed to heights that seemed downright miraculous. The production of pilots could hardly keep pace. It is difficult today to remember how small our base of trained flying personnel was in the 1930s and early 1940s. There were, of course, our commercial airline pilots, but these were only a tiny fraction of their present numbers; and most airline pilots had to be kept on in their civilian jobs because America's transport needs during wartime required a viable commercial airline system. We did have a small number of persons who had learned to fly on their own; some of them, like our Charles Hastings (who later left the 81st and flew with the 82nd TCS), volunteered early, soon after Pearl Harbor, and—once they had satisfied the requirements of cadet school—proved invaluable teachers for new pilots arriving in our Squadron in the summer of 1943. Most of our pilots (and glider pilots), however, had to get their training from scratch in flight schools.

Cadet flight schools were tough even for men who were sure they had "the right stuff" but who, before the war, had only dreamed of flying. Charles Hastings tells us that of the seven men in his quarters in cadet school all but he washed out. Perhaps those who went on to fighters or bombers did have marginally better nervous reactions and physical coordination than those in the 81st TCS; perhaps it was only Lady Luck who decided to which branch of the Air Forces new pilots were sent. But the splendid flying records compiled by our pilots, both in training and later in combat, stand as proof of their extremely high physical and psychological caliber.

In addition to learning how to get off the ground in small single-motored planes and come down again in one piece, cadets had to master the art of flight navigation, become familiar with aircraft engines and instruments, and survive a grueling regime of physical fitness. Having made it through cadet training and been awarded a commission attesting that they were now officers and gentlemen, would-be pilots were sent to a reception center (often this was Maxwell Field, at Montgomery, Alabama) for preliminary assignment to some branch of the Army Air Forces; while they waited they got in more flight training and usually some "transition flight training" to initiate them into the mysteries of handling two-motored planes. Many of the pilots who ended up in the 81st TCS did their transition training at Bergstrom Army Air Base at Austin, Texas.

Once they were assigned to us at Alliance (or later, at Laurinburg-Maxton), however, their flying education really began. Here our original Squadron cadre pilots, especially Charles Hastings, Francis Farley, Harlyn Semar, Charles Stevenson, and John Wallen (and, of course, David Brack) earned their keep by holding on to their patience while nursing along the newly arrived pilots. Starting as co-pilots, new pilots learned about C-47s and about the special requirements of flying this plane loaded with paratroopers or towing gliders. Nor were they excused from constantly refreshing their ability to handle flying problems with the aid of a Link Trainer. When the weather forbade flying, the rule was: Into that Link machine, or work over the airplane tech manuals, or master the names of all those Allied and Axis planes shown in silhouette on Renshaw recognition cards, or work out navigation problems with maps, slide-rule, and compass dividers.

Until the production of C-47s got into high gear, pilots had to learn two-motor procedures in other planes; they were lucky if they could get in some time on old DC-3s, the airlines' predecessor to the C-47. For months during the spring and summer of 1943 there were simply not enough two-motored planes of any sort to go around to permit all of our pilots the training required by IX Troop Carrier Command. Sometimes it took tight scheduling even to afford all pilots (and particularly the glider pilots) the four hours of flying time per month they needed to draw their flight pay. Many days you could locate quite a few pilots leaning over a desk in our Operations Office, trying to convince the Operations clerks to invent some way of getting them on the flight list.

Every flight, of course, was a different learning experience, but we tended to group them into a few categories. At the beginning, the pilots put in as much time as needed in practicing takeoffs and landings to demonstrate that they possessed at least this basic skill. Other types of flights included "triangular problems," in which a recently arrived pilot had to fly a fixed route and get back to the base at a predetermined time; and "contour flying," otherwise known as hedge-hopping—since we would be expected to drop parachute bundles at extremely low heights of 300 feet or even less.

Later, if he qualified high enough to be rated as a pilot (instead of a co-pilot), a new pilot could attempt a "cross-country flight"; that is, he landed at some base other than our own, sometimes with the additional duty of picking up a bit of freight we needed from a supply depot. Best of all were the RONs, flights that allowed you to "remain over night," preferably at some desirable location (within easy distance of your girl or family, or in a "fun city" like Chicago or New Orleans or San Antonio). Cross countries and RONs became so popular that pilots invented excuses to fly them. Soon the 81st TCS was found to be burning up an astonishing amount of gasoline—a rationed commodity during World War II. Orders went out to restrict all flying to purposes that were clearly for training only.

Inevitably, some pilots in training became overconfident and made critical mistakes. Although none of such mistakes in the 81st TCS resulted in tragedies, other squadrons were not so lucky. Charles Hastings reminds us of one "loud-mouth from the 79th TCS" who assured everyone he could outrun a thunderstorm threatening his flight plan. "After they had to scrape him off the North Dakota plain," says Hastings, "other pilots were more respectful of weather conditions." Virtually all crews, sooner or later, had anxious moments with weather that "became a little hairy."

> Once we sent all of our planes—three was all we had at the time—out on a long training flight to Texas and back. But in Texas the pilots ran into a bad hail storm. When they landed back in Alliance the planes were damaged worse than many planes later in combat. The de-icer boots on the wings were in shreds, the landing lights knocked out; there were dents in the noses of the planes, in the tail sections, and in many plates on the sides.
>
> One plane many of us remember crashing in Maxton [September 20, 1943] was the Wing shuttle. Vision that morning was bad; lots of fog and several layers of cloud. What happened was that when that plane was making a left turn the pilot saw another plane coming at him in the opposite direction, about to drop a tow rope. To avoid the tow rope, the shuttle plane

pilot made a very steep climb; but he began to stall out. We think that many of the passengers in that plane may have slid to the rear, possibly because they were sitting without their seat belts on. This would have thrown the plane further out of balance. We saw it make an almost full nose-up stall, then slide backward and fall off on the right wing side at about 1,200 to 1,500 feet. As it started to dive the pilot had full emergency power on trying to pull it out; but he never could get the nose up and it went almost straight down into a swamp near us. The plane's impact was so violent that we found the melted engines maybe twenty-five feet down through the mulch and the earth under that swamp. (Carlisle Jordan, Squadron Airplane Inspector)

Delma Montgomery, our glider mechanic chief, and George Britt, another mechanic, struggled for hours trying to help save the victims of this crash. They had to push their way through burning wreckage for some of the bodies. For this they were given the Soldier's Medal for bravery.

By late July in 1943, and even more during the fall when we were at Laurinburg-Maxton, we seemed to have planes heading for all parts of the country; Col. Brack took advantage of these flights to get many of us last-minute leaves before shipping out. Anyone in the Squadron who had a few days of leave coming could find out in the Operations Office if there was a plane scheduled to fly near his home and ask to be given a ride as a passenger. When we were at Alliance, Col. Brack favored men living in the Middle West or West; when we got to Laurinburg-Maxton men from the more eastern states got their turn. I remember getting a RON to Philadelphia, within easy train distance from my home in New Jersey, allowing me to see my wife and family for a few precious hours just one month before I flew to England.

A pilot, after he demonstrated his ability to fly a C-47, still had to come to grips with the function for which our outfit was created: delivering paratroopers and glider troopers to where they were needed. Now he had to move beyond individual pilot training and master the world of "formation flying," a term that covers a whole variety of complex, delicate, and dangerous skills. In fact, one could say, no formations, no troop carrier. Placing paratroopers or gliders on their drop or landing zones one planeload at a time would make no sense. Just after landing, airborne troops were vulnerable enough without depriving them of whatever support they could get not only from additional platoons but also from artillery and engineering units. Since airborne doctrine called for paratroopers to be able to hold out on their own for two or three days or even more until the line infantry could break through to them, they had to be landed in as large numbers as possible, and as compactly and as quickly as possible. The same applied to glider missions. Formation maneuvers called for the most rigid, most disciplined

Our first "glider-guiders." *Front, left to right:* DiPietro, Ryman, Hoshal, Chevalier, Robinson, Brewer, Miller; *rear:* Vancil, Steffens, Sindledecker, Cline, Fearn, Ward, McCann.

A picture-perfect glider formation: echelon to the left of four tugs and gliders. (Courtesy Smithsonian Institution)

flying possible. When the green jump light went on, a "stick" (planeload) of paratroopers hustled out through the jump door in a bunch, so as to be able to land all together and "roll up the stick" (reassemble, ready to fight) in less than five minutes. We knew that to drop troopers all over the countryside during combat was to condemn many of them to death.

We practiced various formations, more and more frequently, not only with other squadrons but also with additional TC groups. One formation was a "V-of-Vs," three planes in a V (two "wingmen" slightly behind each flight leader) and three flights of three planes each, nine planes to a "serial." Another was "Vs in trail," flights of three planes in line. "Vs" would never do for towing gliders, since gliders would then be so close they would be in terrible danger of colliding in the turbulent slipstream or wind gusts that made gliders swing all over the sky. For gliders, we usually flew in an "echelon of four to the left" (or to the right), with the flight leader followed slightly behind and to his left by his number 2, and the same relative position for numbers 3 and 4. The next flight leader would be directly behind the preceding one, also with his three wingmen strung out the same way. Each tow plane in a flight flew slightly below the preceding one so as to increase as much as possible the distance between gliders.

It is difficult to convey the sensations felt by C-47 crew members—some flying with rather green pilots—as their plane inched closer and closer to others in the formation and the formation leaders kept yelling radio commands at various wingmen to pull in even closer. I used to watch, my heart in my mouth, as the wings of the two others in our flight slowly inched in and finally were so close it looked as though I could open the door and step right out onto our left wingman's wingtip. After seeing a lot of this our hearts might pound a little less; we got used to the danger and could see our pilots getting better, but we could never ignore the terrible danger involved. Miraculously, we never had a mid-air collision in the 81st Squadron: not during training and not during all the formation missions we flew in Europe. Others were not so lucky. Troop carrier's losses from collisions during training were greater than all the losses we took during the invasion of Normandy.

"To pile on the misery," as the French say, toward the end of training we had to do all of this at night. As rough as this was on us, it seemed logical, since we were expected to pull most of our combat missions at night. Airborne doctrine held that such dangerous training exercises before we began to haul paratroopers and gliders were justified, since the safety of paratroopers and glider troopers took precedence over the safety of troop carrier crews. Gliders and troopers had to get down on the ground in as compact a bunch as possible, with the maximum of surprise, presenting a minimum target to enemy ground troops. This meant delivering troopers at night.

The only trouble with this impressive line of reasoning was that it was wrong. As we discovered during the invasion of Normandy, airborne soldiers could be delivered more safely and could assemble more quickly if the mission were accomplished during the day or at least at dusk. While we trained in the States, however, that was a lesson high command had yet to learn.

Night missions were thought to be so crucial that all the squadrons on our base tried out a procedure called "turning night into day." For a week at a time—once in May and once in October—we would sleep during the day, have "breakfast" around 4:00 p.m., and arrange our whole day accordingly. While at first we welcomed the novelty and accepted the logic of this arrangement, pretty soon it became apparent that all of us, ground personnel as well as crews, were functioning more and more sloppily in this topsy-turvy world. We were also becoming more and more irritable. Finally it was agreed that however we were to fly missions, night or day, it was better to keep meals and sleeping arrangements in their traditional time slots.

The final aspect of our stateside training came when we went on maneuvers with the airborne soldiers themselves. At first our contacts with paratroopers had been limited to providing them flying platforms from which to practice jumping. At Alliance we jumped a few sticks of 82nd Airborne Division troopers training to join the rest of their Division in North Africa. In Laurinburg-Maxton, however, we were paired with the new Airborne Division, the 101st, and it remained our chief paratrooper partner for the rest of the war.

There were essentially two kinds of airdrop maneuvers. In the first we learned how to jump troopers from a formation flight—night as well as day—and how to tow gliders as part of a regular war game. Our first large-scale maneuvers of this sort were based on Tullahoma, Tennessee, in early October 1943. This was a five-day operation simulating an invasion behind an enemy's shore; it included re-supply of the paratroopers, reinforcements with glider-borne troops—and a full complement of mosquitoes, lost tempers, and snafus. Now we experienced the dubious joys of eating "C-rations" (highly processed, canned food in individual boxes) away from our base. Says our Squadron diary: "Several men complained the biscuits contained a laxative, and the results speak for themselves."

We also had some training in "snatching," in which a C-47 in full flight would lower its tow rope and hook on to a glider on the ground. Snatching was expected to be very useful for extricating wounded GIs from a tight place where ambulances could not reach them. We also practiced "double-tow" flying: one plane tugging *two* gliders. Lifting two loaded gliders off the ground was desperately hard and dangerous work for airplane pilots. One of them described it to me as like trying to climb up a waterfall with your bare hands.

The 436th was the first outfit to try flying Wacos double tow. This was in Laurinburg-Maxton. We tried lots of things when we were there in North Carolina. We tried flying three gliders behind B-17s; we even tried flying a glider behind a PBY [amphibious plane]. And I remember we tried out a glider tow behind a fighter plane, a P-38. We tried to see if we could carry paratroopers in a plane that was towing a glider also loaded with paratroopers. We even jumped paratroopers out of gliders; but quite a few of them were badly hurt, and this was soon stopped. (Jack McGlothlin, glider mechanic)

The second major type of maneuver is best called a "demonstration maneuver." We did three of these: one in early October, one in late October, and one beginning on December 7, 1943, the second anniversary of Pearl Harbor.

These demonstration maneuvers served not so much to improve our skills as to convince the doubters among the high brass of the Army Air Forces—as well as among Washington politicians with some power over us—that troop carrier did indeed have the clout its enthusiasts promised. For each of these, distinguished visitors congregated in Laurinburg-Maxton to inspect, in person, full-fledged airborne maneuvers. Key generals in the War Department, including Arnold, Spaatz, and McNair, plus the high brass of the IX Troop Carrier Command and key Washington political figures such as Secretary of War Stimson, came to judge for themselves. If we had performed badly during these demonstration maneuvers we might have ended up without any large-scale combat role at all in World War II. Troop carrier might well have been restricted to moving freight, transporting troops inside non-combat zones, and providing a few small commando-type paratrooper raids.

For demonstration maneuvers, leaves were canceled, our base was restricted so that civilians could not enter, and everybody was kept on his toes. For one of these air shows, "Base security was being tested and guns were popping off all over the place. I don't think anybody slept in an upper bunk that night!" (Carlisle Jordan, Squadron Airplane Inspector). The strain was particularly hard on our flight chief mechanics (a "flight" was three planes) and crew chiefs (aircrew mechanics), who often had to work around the clock to keep the planes in good shape.

Fortunately, all the maneuvers went fairly well. Impressive armadas of gliders sailed over the observers' heads—on one occasion, a hundred gliders pulled in double tow. Once, as our Squadron diary admitted, "we released our troopers a trifle early." But for the most part the troopers and the gliders arrived right on the button, where and when they had previously been announced, and after being flown in a complex pattern to simulate an invasion of France.

The December 7 maneuvers delivered simulated attacks to points in both

North and South Carolina and included every contingency for a real invasion that could be imagined. By now we were getting fairly proficient at re-supplying the paratroopers by dropping them door bundles and "parapack" containers. It was the first time troop carrier showed it could handle such "re-supply" (for combat missions we always used the hyphen). This seemed to verify troop carrier's claim that with air transport alone paratroopers who had accomplished "vertical envelopment" of an enemy district could indeed be supplied by air for two or three days.

To the high brass and the government bigwigs, the December maneuvers demonstrated that troop carrier probably could be assigned a key role in the coming invasion of Europe. To us, it demonstrated that all would go well as long as Lady Luck was with us. Returning to base, somewhat bemused but still on the whole optimistic, we trooped into the Operations Office, submitted to debriefing, and accepted the "medicinal" shot of whiskey and the sandwiches that thenceforth became one of the established traditions of 81st TCS missions.

During November and December 1943 our TO filled up so fast that for a few specializations the Squadron was "over complement," and we were required to hive off men and ship them out to become cadre or replacements for troop carrier squadrons which formed up later. On one day alone we lost twenty-eight EMs who shipped out to form cadres of the 442nd Troop Carrier Group. We also lost many of the glider pilots originally assigned to us. If they had been able to foresee what was in store for them they might have become even more depressed; some were sent to theaters of war with few of the civilized comforts and halfway decent weather to be found in Britain, Italy, and France. Many ended up instead in the CBI, the Pacific, or North Africa. Some EMs were transferred because they did not measure up to the standards set by their immediate superior officers; these often ended up in the infantry. A few left in spite of their ability, because David Brack decided that their personalities made it difficult for them to accomplish all their assignments.

Thanksgiving Day, 1943: the Squadron got a chance to highlight the good esprit de corps building up among us. We were given a regular turkey dinner, complete with white tablecloths, pumpkin pie, and all the fixings. There were some speeches, half sentimental and half cynical. A few of us added our own hard liquor, got drunk, and gave some boxing demonstrations, with or without boxing gloves. Said the "TARFU Gazette": "A good time was had by all, and it is hoped that next year at the same time we might all enjoy this festive season at our own tables back home!" On Thanksgiving Day of 1944 we actually were all still in Britain, held there by the tragic failure of the invasion of Holland.

December 10, 1943: our Orderly Room was busier than it had ever been.

There were countless forms to fill out, since all paper work had to be completed before we could leave the States. There were last-minute demonstrations on how to fix up planes with litters for evacuating wounded soldiers. Everyone had to tramp over to the Squadron Dispensary and submit himself to all those "overseas shots"—some of which, administered in the customary undignified spot and accompanied by the customary bad jokes, hurt like the dickens. Not least, we had to pack our personal baggage—our "A-3" duffel bags and "B-4" valet packs, now jammed to the top by our heavy winter clothes and overcoats.

Everyone's insurance, medical records, allotments, flight records, and family addresses had to be brought up to date. Now the last contingents of navigators arrived so that we could have one for each plane for the long and dangerous trip—each plane on its own—across the South Atlantic. The TO was all in order. We had indeed shaped up. The time had come to ship out.

### Notes

1. Before World War II the air arm of our military was called the "Army Air Corps." After its enormous expansion in 1939–1941 its name was changed to "Army Air Forces," and not until 1947 was it detached from the Army, given its own Chief of Staff, and called "Air Force." Since the terms "Air Forces" (plural) and "Army Air Forces" were used all during the existence of our Squadron, I use them interchangeably in this book, but not "Army Air Corps" or "Air Force" though you do occasionally run across those two terms in the writings of 1943–1945.

2. During World War II "GI" had several meanings, most based on "government issue," that is, military supplies, clothing, and so forth. It also could mean "in accordance with military regulations" (as in "it was a very GI barracks"), or to designate an enlisted man rather than an officer (as in "off limits to GIs"). We also called intestinal disorders "the GIs" or "the GI trots." For other uses see Kennett, pp. 87–88.

# 2. Getting Blooded
## Airborne Operations Before Our Time

### Airborne combat begins

Three and a half years were to elapse between the first combat airborne operation of World War II—a German one (May 10, 1940)—and our Squadron's trip to Britain (December 14, 1943–January 28, 1944). The Germans launched this first airborne combat mission as part of their Blitzkrieg assault on Belgium and Holland. It was made up of only eleven gliders. Their objective was the great Belgian fortress of Eben Emael. These gliders, towed very high (about 6,000 feet), were able to fly silently after being released from their tow planes for some fifteen minutes before reaching the fortress. Surprise was complete. The paratroop engineers in those gliders, landing on the fortress grounds, began their deadly work of neutralizing the fort so as to clear the road for the great Nazi invasion of Western Europe. While the Belgian defenders controlled enough gun turrets to keep on fighting all that day, they were contained and finally overcome. Only six Germans out of the eighty-eight men in those eleven gliders were killed.

Meanwhile, other German airborne troopers had parachuted at key Dutch and Belgian bridges over the many canals and rivers in their path and in many cases captured them intact. One day later (May 11), the Wehrmacht was at the French border. Six weeks after that (June 22) France surrendered. Eben Emael marked a tremendous victory for the new technique of airborne warfare and gave the strongest possible signal to other countries: learn how to use combat gliders and paratroopers![1]

Later in the war the Nazis ran one large-scale glider and paratrooper operation (the conquest of Crete in May 1941) and several on a smaller scale. They tried—not very successfully—to use Luftwaffe transports to support hard-pressed Wehrmacht troops on the Russian front, and they used small paratrooper operations to attack Yugoslav partisans and French guerrillas. Their most famous commando-style airborne raid was the rescue of Mussolini from an Italian prison. After Italy surrendered and the new government imprisoned Mussolini in a mountaintop hotel (July 1943), Otto Skorzeny, the most daredevil German commando of them all, worked out a plan to land some gliders right outside the prison. Eight gliders committed to this stranger-than-fiction enterprise did manage to land in a rocky meadow near the hotel's car park; they overwhelmed Mussolini's jailers and spirited him away in a tiny plane on September 12, 1943.

In 1941 American military leaders faced a great question: should they develop an airborne arm committed to both small-scale and large-scale operations? They had to scrutinize each airborne experience, big or small, in training or combat, and whether undertaken by Allied or by Axis powers, in order to decide whether airborne forces should be developed only in a restricted way or in an all-out effort. Daring, small-scale airborne raids obviously could achieve gains out of all proportion to their costs, but they could hardly have an important bearing on victory or defeat in any major battle. Could the new airborne arm perhaps be used on a larger scale—for example, in combined operations during an assault on enemy lands?[2]

## The Germans conquer Crete

The world's first major airborne assault—in Operation MERKUR, Hitler's conquest of Crete—had a mighty impact on the way military leaders thought about airborne warfare potential. Hitler was drawn into that part of Europe out of impatience with Mussolini's humiliating defeats in the Balkans, which threatened to leave the Allies within bombing range of Germany's main gasoline supplies in Rumania. The Wehrmacht quickly smashed all resistance in Yugoslavia and Greece, forcing the British and Commonwealth troops to retreat to Crete across the scant hundred miles separating the Greek mainland from the island of Crete. They were accompanied by thousands of Greek troops anxious to continue the fighting and were joined by additional Australian and New Zealand troops from North Africa and by irregular soldiers from among the Greeks in Crete.

Now—as during the Napoleonic Wars—the chief European land power confronted Britain, the preponderant sea power. Hitler had a weapon that Napoleon never possessed: air power and airborne forces. To Kurt Student, Germany's airborne chief, the face-off seemed textbook perfect for a paratrooper and glider invasion of Crete that would simply hurdle the British fleet.

At 8:00 a.m. on May 20, 1941, JU-52 tow planes and DFS 230 gliders began to take off from several Greek airfields, headed for Maleme on the western tip of Crete and for three less important invasion points along Crete's northern coast. Before MERKUR was over, eleven days later, the German forces delivered the amazing total of more than 23,000 troops to Crete, as paratroopers, glider troops, or airlanded infantry. These soldiers were supremely self-confident; after all, Germany had been victorious in one smashing conquest after another and already dominated so much of Europe that at least some of the soldiers must have believed in Hitler's "Aryan blood" myth and the Nazi dream of a hugely expanded and racially pure nation of supermen dominating the world.

The Germans were about to be presented with a horrible shock. In that first day's fighting, almost 2,000 paratroopers died—more than the total in all of Germany's campaigns from the time war began in September 1939. General Student had vastly underestimated the number, preparedness, and spirit of the Allied soldiers on Crete. The defenders had a fair quantity of light antiaircraft and machine guns and were well dug in. When the Luftwaffe halted its bombing to allow the first German gliders to come in, the New Zealand defenders at Maleme airport were astounded at how easy it was to shoot the gliders out of the air. When the German paratroopers began their jumps thirty minutes later, the situation began to take on the proportions of a massacre. Smashed gliders, flaming JU-52s, and hundreds of dead paratroopers lay strewn around the Maleme airport. While the Germans managed to seize control of the runways, only about 600 remained alive and unhurt.

When the sun came up on the morning of May 21, JU-52 transports began airlifting troops from Greece into the far corners of Maleme airport, as far from the New Zealanders as possible. Dozens of these planes were also shot down; but the awesomely courageous German pilots continued to fly in more troops, some planes making several trips that day. The destruction of these planes proved to be an event that no military leader, Axis or Allied, could ever forget. Before the operation ended, nearly half of the JU-52s used in this operation had been destroyed.

For the world's military leaders, MERKUR afforded glimpses of the kind of tragic miscalculations and costly snafus risked in airborne warfare. Some German gliders broke apart and plunged to the ground because they could not resist the air turbulence around them, turbulence in some instances caused by supporting Luftwaffe bombers passing too closely. Entire sticks of paratroopers jumped too early and drowned in the Mediterranean. Other paratroopers and gliders landed virtually on top of disbelieving New Zealand defenders dug into a strategic hill overlooking Maleme airport ("Hill 107"), who picked off paratroopers almost as fast as they could pull the triggers. Whole German airborne units were wiped out literally to the last man.

At this point—today's military experts agree—a counterattack by the New Zealanders might have wiped out the Germans who remained. When German assault groups began to push toward Hill 107, however, they found, to their amazement, that the New Zealanders had evacuated it during the night. For whatever reason, the commander on that hill not only missed his chance for a counterattack but also bestowed on the invading Nazis a priceless gift. Worse, his own superior officers—perhaps with their minds on the chances of being evacuated to North Africa—did not prevent him from leaving Hill 107.[3]

While some of the defenders of Crete continued to inflict heavy casualties on the Germans—and the Royal Navy sank many of the small ships the Axis partners tried to sail to Crete—the German air build-up became so rapid now that the final issue of the battle was never in doubt. Thousands of British and Commonwealth soldiers were evacuated to North Africa on May 31, but almost 12,000 of them were taken prisoner.

To Hitler the terrible costs of MERKUR demonstrated that he should never again use airborne forces as major components of battles. He told his disappointed airborne chiefs that to his mind airborne assaults depended totally on surprise, and now that all the world knew how to defend against them, the surprise factor was gone. German paratrooper divisions never fought again as airborne forces in a major battle. Aside from a few small-scale commando operations, they were used as elite line infantry, often committed to the most dangerous battle assignments.

Ironically, the conclusions reached by British and American planners were quite the opposite, perhaps because they saw the final outcome, at least, of MERKUR as an airborne victory. It was precisely during this month of May 1941 that Major Bill Lee in the U.S. and General F. A. M. "Boy" Browning in Britain were given a very tentative and preliminary OK to prepare for massive increases in airborne personnel and to begin assessing the requirements for airborne operations on the scale of entire divisions.[4]

### Warming up

After Crete, the Germans could boast that a new military arm had been tested under fire and that the era of "three-dimensional warfare" had begun. Other nations lagged far behind. Germany had managed to get the jump on the rest of the world partly because of her reaction to the constraints imposed by the peace treaty after World War I. The Versailles Treaty forced Germany to surrender all warplanes still flyable; and, in fact, she had to agree not to manufacture any more military planes.

But there was a loophole. The treaty said nothing about gliders. Only a few years after the Versailles Treaty, gliding became the "in" sport in Germany; hundreds of gliding clubs sprang up in the 1920s in response to this wonderful opportunity for combining sport and national pride. Everyone understood that

increasing skills in gliding would go far toward keeping up interest and competence in all sorts of aircraft, powered and unpowered.

Hundreds of future Luftwaffe leaders trained themselves in these "silent
wings." Soon after Hitler came to power, of course, he tossed aside all the
restraints on military buildup imposed by the Versailles Treaty.[5] By 1936 Hitler
had formed up a *Fliegerdivision* of paratroopers and a *Luftlanddivision* for air-
landed and glider-borne troops. The Spanish Civil War (1936–1938) gave the
Nazis invaluable experience in the business of transporting troops by air; in
1936, when it looked as though the Loyalist supporters of the Spanish government might be able to crush the fascist and conservative rebels who supported
General Franco, the Luftwaffe airlifted 10,000 of Franco's Spanish Moroccan
troops from North Africa to Spain. Without that critical airlift the fascist cause
in Spain might have been lost.

While future American airborne divisions were to be part of our infantry,
German paratroopers and glider troopers from the beginning belonged to the
Luftwaffe. The German military transport workhorse, like our C-47, had proved
itself before the war as a reliable civilian cargo and passenger plane. Theirs was
the JU-52, a sturdy but ungainly looking tri-motor with none of the smooth lines
of the C-47. Unlike the C-47, the JU-52 mounted some armament: a machine
gun on top of the fuselage near the tail. The Germans, with a mixture of contempt and affection, called it the "Auntie Annie." In the days before MERKUR
it served Hitler well, not only during the Spanish Civil War but also during the
invasion of Norway in April 1940, when German paratroopers succeeded in disrupting the Norwegian defenses, and in many other small-scale operations besides the capture of Eben Emael.[6]

After the Blitzkrieg, when Britain stood alone against the Nazis, her interest
in parachute warfare soared to a fever pitch. Rumors of German parachute invaders ran riot through the land. Newspapers printed (false) reports of Nazi *Fall-
schirmjaeger* (paratroopers) disguised as London bobbies; there was the most
wild talk of assassination squads about to descend on Buckingham Palace; and,
more realistically, many British newspapers speculated that the Nazis might use
paratroopers to invade Britain.

In Britain, unlike Germany, dismayingly few people in 1940 had any good
knowledge about gliders, parachutes, jumping equipment, and jumping techniques. The British were still experimenting with different types of parachutes
well into the winter of 1940. They also took a long time to decide on the best
method of exiting from their planes—finally deciding to jump the troopers
through a hole cut in the bottom of the transport plane's fuselage. Until late in
1941 there were so few transports or converted bombers available for practicing

jumps that many British paratroopers trained by jumping from huge balloons, similar to the famous "barrage balloons" sent up to put obstacles in the path of Luftwaffe bombers. By 1942 some British airborne outfits began to receive exceedingly welcome American C-47s, which they called "Dakotas."

Before World War II, the only famous American general who predicted that future battles could be won with paratroopers was Billy Mitchell. He was the pioneer who, in 1922, tried to demonstrate that bombers could sink battleships; the junked ships he used indeed sank, but Mitchell was nevertheless contemptuously rejected as an "air power crank."

During the 1930s, the theory of airborne warfare attracted even less attention in the United States than the theory of tank warfare (we still relied on the horse cavalry). James Gavin, eventually commander of the 82nd Airborne Division, did try to piece together a theory of vertical envelopment while he was a cadet at West Point. The U.S. Air Corps Tactical School translated German articles on airborne warfare, speculated about the possible use of German air-landed troops and paratroopers in an invasion of Britain, and, in October 1941, prepared a study of the Nazi conquest of Crete. Most strategists, however, believed that to drop paratroopers or land large bodies of glider troops behind enemy lines was to court sure disaster. The harsh crack that "generals always get ready to fight the previous war" for the most part rang true for American generals in the late 1930s.

When the decision was made to go ahead with the development of a U.S. airborne arm with assault or vertical envelopment capabilities, therefore, concrete details of airborne equipment and tactics had to be worked out in a hurry. Although the C-47 was known and trusted, the Waco CG-4A glider was still not even on the drawing boards until the spring of 1941. Decision after specific decision had to be made: What was the best kind of parachute for static-line jumping? Was the "reserve" chest parachute worth the extra bulk it involved and would it open in time from the low heights our paratroopers used? Which weapons should the paratroopers carry down themselves, and which should be dropped to them in separate containers? Given that paratroopers could carry down only light weapons and would be provided with hardly any ground transportation, how might they defend themselves from counterattacks by tanks? How could they be re-supplied, and how many days could they be expected to hold out alone before ground troops could break through to them? Should their helmets be soft rubber, to protect them against head injuries when landing, or steel, to protect them on the ground from bullets? Could better jump shoes be devised to protect them against the ever-present likelihood of ankle injuries? Even basic terms like "DZ" (drop zones) for targets of paratroopers, and "LZ" for glider landing zones, had to be formalized and standardized so that everybody in the new fighting arm would talk the same language.

Most American military leaders continued to think of parachute jumping as a stunt. Who can blame them? In 1941 the rest of us, too, saw parachuting as a foolhardy gesture by daredevils who liked to thrill visitors at county fairs. Or it was something done in amusement park jump towers, like the huge tower at the New York World's Fair of 1939. More than any other person, it was Major Bill Lee, a disciple of Billy Mitchell's, who began to turn this situation around. In January 1940, Lee—after long and hard campaigns of persuasion—got permission to head up a single volunteer paratroop group named, significantly enough, the American Parachute Test Platoon.

Training paratroopers took time. It also took more transport planes than the Army Air Corps seemed willing to commit. The C-47s were not coming off the assembly line fast enough to be provided for airborne use until the end of 1941. For months, paratroopers had to train by jumping from towers. So far as records show, the very first military jump from an Air Corps transport plane by regular parachute soldiers occurred at Fort Benning, Georgia (the future home of the 82nd Airborne Division) on August 22, 1940. The man who would command our 436th Troop Carrier Group, Adriel Williams, was co-pilot on that plane.

After Pearl Harbor the pace of airborne development speeded up. In July 1942 Major Bill Lee was given the green light to begin plans for an entire airborne division. He was able to use the administrative structure of one already established division, the "All-American" 82nd Infantry; to this was amalgamated the already existing paratrooper regiments, and the new unit was entered into the books as the 82nd Airborne Division. The title "All-American," held over from the older outfit, explains the "AA" on the shoulder patches of the 82nd.

At about this time the CG-4A glider began to come off the assembly lines in large numbers. That forced a decision: Would the U.S. airborne forces airland troops in transport planes, as the Germans had during MERKUR, or airland them instead in towed gliders? The latter choice won out. Now a glider regiment was added to the units in the 82nd Airborne. And in July 1942 a cadre was split off from the 82nd to serve as the basis for the brand-new 101st Airborne Division. Matthew Ridgway took command of the 82nd and Bill Lee of the 101st. The European war had been going on for almost three years, but—better late than never—the main structures of the American airborne arm were finally all in place.[7]

## Troop carrier's baptism of fire: North Africa, Sicily, Italy

We in the 81st TCS had our baptism of fire in the Normandy invasion in June 1944. Before then, beginning in November 1942, American and British airborne forces invaded North Africa, Sicily, and Italy. These early operations served as parts of the Allied effort to open a "Second Front" against Hitler—the "First Front" being the gargantuan infantry and tank struggles then going on between the Nazis and the Soviets. British and American leaders knew that an attack against the well-defended Nazi positions in the north or west had to wait for a huge buildup of Allied (mostly American) soldiers and equipment in the British Isles. They decided instead to invade "the soft underbelly of Europe" (Churchill's phrase), that is, Italy. To do this, they first had to secure the other Mediterranean shore, North Africa, and then conquer Sicily so as to have a solid springboard into mainland Italy.

Late at night on November 7, 1942, thirty-nine C-47s of the 60th Troop Carrier Group carrying a single battalion of paratroopers set out from England on a recklessly long combat journey of more than 1,100 miles. The task force had as its mission the neutralization of airfields around Oran, Algeria, to help protect Operation TORCH, the seaborne invasion of the Allies into French North Africa. Included in TORCH was troop carrier's first combat assault. It was to prove a very shaky start to the kind of warfare for which we in the 81st TCS would be trained.

Epithets like "harebrained" and "suicidal" had been hurled at this airborne mission during the planning sessions. These planes were expected to fly an incredibly long combat course: ten weary hours, mostly at night. Then, paratroopers on board were expected to jump and cope with Vichy French troops in Algeria who were theoretically neutral but under pro-Nazi leadership. The mission's route would take it right over Spain, in fact, over Madrid itself, where the fascist dictator—also theoretically neutral—was actually a great admirer of Hitler. Little was known about the political climate around any one of the North African objectives except that they differed from one post to the other. For all we knew, when the time came the Vichy French at any one airfield might be doing their best to kill our troopers as they descended.

Storms over the Bay of Biscay and clouds and fog over Spain scattered the formation long before the planes reached the Mediterranean. Pilots were flying all alone or in groups of two or three. Unexpected strong winds blew them far to the west of their flight line. Almost all of them were hopelessly lost. Two planes landed 250 miles away from their target. Most were around fifty miles off course. Vichy French antiaircraft shot down two. French fighter planes forced down others. One desperate pilot landed his plane near a village and asked an astonished Arab to tell him the way to Oran.

The majority of the planes circled from one airfield to another, their gas gauges rapidly dropping to zero, trying to find a DZ where it would make some sense to give their paratroopers the green light. Only ten of the thirty-nine pilots finally jumped their troopers.

After it was over, the airborne parts of TORCH must have seemed like an exercise in futility, but the lessons learned were worth a great deal. Troop carrier planners now were forced to realize that targets should never be that distant; that training for formation flying and for navigation must be improved; that radar or other beacons must help the planes find their targets; that bad winds and bad visibility could ruin everything. What may have impressed the Allied commanders just as much, however, was the courage and determination those troop carrier pilots displayed. In spite of what must have been an overwhelming sense of frustration and bewilderment, not one of the planes headed back to England; and not one of the crews tried to land in friendly Portugal or get themselves safely interned in Spain.[8]

Between the time the first American paratrooper jumped into combat (North Africa, November 8, 1942) and our own 81st Troop Carrier Squadron's first combat mission during the Normandy invasion (June 6, 1944), other troop carrier units mounted five major assaults and several minor ones. Most of them produced results that were mediocre or worse. One of them, however, was a brilliant success; and one was a tragic failure of such daunting proportions that it occupies a somber place in the annals of military history. All were carefully scrutinized for what they revealed about troop carrier limitations and potentials; and they provided the basis for improvements incorporated into the training of our 81st TCS. These improvements not only made America's rapidly expanding airborne arm a great deal more effective but also made our own individual chances of surviving a great deal better.

That we in the 81st TCS learned at the expense of other Americans should be one of the permanent parts of our Squadron's collective memory. It seems fitting that we use our unit history to memorialize our debt to them. What we learned from their experiences undoubtedly was the reason many more of us were not killed.[9]

The Allied airborne invasions of Sicily are permanently engraved on the minds of all of us in the 81st TCS—even though none of us participated in these missions. We can never forget that on HUSKY II twenty-three troop carrier planes were shot down by our own U.S. Navy. Our 81st Squadron was just then being put together at Alliance, Nebraska, but we heard the news of what happened off the beaches of Sicily. This news ran through our ranks like a shock wave.

The conquest of Sicily, troop carrier's real baptism of fire in the European theater, involved four major airborne missions: two with British glider troopers and two with American parachutists. The British missions—run mainly with American C-47s and American aircrews—were called LADBROKE and FUS-TIAN. Their gliders supported the seaborne forces of Montgomery's British Eighth Army in its drives for the eastern cities of Syracuse and Catania. The American paratroopers in our HUSKY I and HUSKY II missions had the assignment of capturing the high ground around the town of Gela, in southern Sicily, to protect Patton's American Seventh Army as it stormed ashore.

The 51st and 52nd Troop Carrier Wings, the American 82nd Airborne, and the British 1st Airborne were readied for these invasions in an appallingly rash manner. For LADBROKE, American airplane pilots—who were themselves afforded just a few hours of night formation training—had to tow, through the formidable antiaircraft batteries at Syracuse and Catania, 136 Waco gliders. These gliders, furthermore, were given to British glider pilots with no training whatsoever in nighttime glider operations. There were also eight British planes towing Horsas, a heavy British glider.

For HUSKY I, the quality of preparations was slightly better: at least those pilots who served as flight leaders had some training in night formations. The 82nd Airborne troopers carried had the benefit (if that is the right word) of months of fighting in Algeria and Tunisia. General Matthew Ridgway, commander of the 82nd Airborne, kept forwarding highly optimistic estimates to General Dwight D. Eisenhower (commander of all the invasion forces) about the great potential of his airborne troopers. British General "Boy" Browning, who was Eisenhower's designated airborne advisor, forcefully supported Ridgway in these predictions. Troop carrier was to meet up with Browning later on, when he was put in charge of the disastrously overambitious Operation MARKET-GARDEN, an attempt to throw Allied paratroopers across the Lower Rhine (Holland, September 1944).

Troop carrier commanders now issued the famous "only crews will return" order. That is, pilots would not be permitted, for any reason, to abort their sorties on their own initiative, no matter what the hazards and frustrations. They would under no circumstances return from Sicily to North Africa with paratroopers on board or with gliders still in tow.

Only minutes after the planes of HUSKY I took off and assembled over North Africa, on that tragic evening of July 9, 1943, dangerously high winds scattered the formations for miles over the dark Mediterranean sky. Some planes were blown so far to the east that the pilots had to circle around and approach the Gela beaches from the east rather than the south. Of the 226 planes that set out, only one in six jumped its troopers into the DZ, or at least close enough to attack designated targets.

At about the same time that the winds scattered HUSKY I, gliders of the British LADBROKE mission were being towed toward the region of Syracuse, on the eastern shore of Sicily, mainly by American airplane crews. Again, high winds played havoc with the formation, but much worse was to come. The first few tugs and gliders went toward the LZ undetected. Soon banks of searchlights caught the planes in mid-air; a terrible barrage of antiaircraft fire came up at them from German and Italian defenders in Syracuse. The mission was reduced to chaos long before the planes were close enough to the shore to release their gliders. Many American pilots refused to fly further into that hell and turned back out to sea, meanwhile ordering their glider pilots to cut loose. Many glider pilots reckoned they were not close enough to make it all the way into shore—let alone to their LZs.[10] Some tugs and gliders made three passes this way, the C-47 pilots signaling for a cut-off and the glider pilots demanding to be flown closer. The air seemed filled with planes taking wild evasive action, loosed gliders frantically seeking a relatively safe way down, bursting puffs of flak, and machine-gun tracers filling the dark sky.

Of the 144 gliders in LADBROKE pulled to Sicily that night, seventy-two came down in the sea. High waves battered at the struggling men and smashed gliders. Some of the soldiers were picked up by British seaborne assault craft on their way in, but more than 200 were drowned. This horrible fiasco was made even more humiliating by debriefing reports given by American pilots when they got back to North Africa: virtually every one of them claimed "a good release," and XII Troop Carrier Command announced that at least half of the gliders had made it into their designated LZs. It was a preposterous claim, as anyone looking at the debris and bodies in the vicinity of Syracuse the next morning could plainly see.[11]

It is easy to understand why LADBROKE brought already existing tensions between British and American soldiers to the boiling point. Fights over this mission erupted not only in Mediterranean area cafés but also in British pubs. British paratroopers swore they would kill any troop carrier pilot they could get their hands on. They shouted that it was a lack of guts that made American pilots cut their gliders off so early. A stinging indictment in their argument: every single one of the American planes and crews involved in LADBROKE made it safely back to North Africa.[12]

Faced with two such ghastly disappointments, airborne commanders in North Africa postponed for one day the second mission designated for 82nd Airborne troops, HUSKY II. Like HUSKY I, HUSKY II was scheduled as an

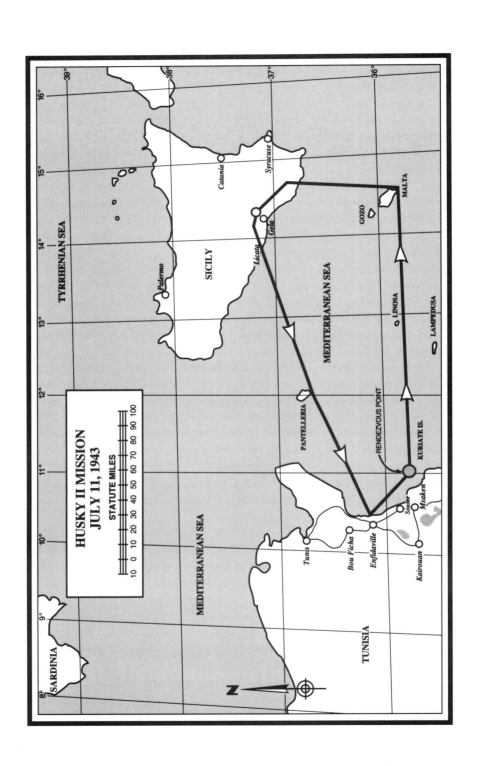

HUSKY II MISSION
JULY 11, 1943

STATUTE MILES

10  0  10  20  30  40  50  60  70  80  90  100

SARDINIA

TYRRHENIAN SEA

SICILY

Palermo

Catania

Syracuse

Gela
Licata

GOZO

MALTA

MEDITERRANEAN SEA

PANTELLERIA

LINOSA

LAMPEDUSA

RENDEZVOUS POINT

KURIATE IS.

Msaken
Sousse

Enfidaville

Bou Ficha

Tunis

Kairouan

MEDITERRANEAN SEA

TUNISIA

N

operation for paratroopers only. It seemed to be a real question, after this post-ponement, as to whether high command would soon announce that there would be no more large-scale combat operations for troop carrier. However, Patton was still calling for paratroop drops to help his advance into Sicily's interior by seiz-ing key roads and bridges. Both XII Troop Carrier Command and 82nd Airborne leaders were still willing to mount such operations. The one-day postponement gave crews and planners a welcome breather to review their assignments; and when HUSKY II did take off on July 11, crews and airborne troopers were confident that they would perform better and that they would have a relatively easy time of it—partly because the first waves of seaborne invaders now had worked their way a good distance off the beaches.

HUSKY II, in fact, flew toward Sicily in excellent order and seemed to be heading for a first-rate paratrooper drop when it was shot out of the sky by our own soldiers and sailors.

No one is sure who fired the first shot; possibly it came from American antiaircraft gunners with the 1st Infantry Division on land, in back of the beaches. In any case, after that first shot was fired, the heavens erupted. Every gunner in the invasion fleet, it seemed, blasted away at the low-flying planes. We know that most of the twenty-three C-47s shot down—six before they could drop their troops—were without a doubt victims of American naval gunners.[13] In addition to the twenty-three shot down, thirty-seven C-47s were badly dam-aged: a total of sixty planes out of the 144 in that mission.[14]

The last important airborne assault in Sicily, FUSTIAN, on the night of July 12, 1943, was a combined paratrooper and glider mission, the first in Allied airborne history. Aimed at the region of Catania, fifty miles north of Syracuse on the eastern coast of Sicily, it proved to be yet another frightening troop carrier disaster. Once again, "friendly fire" from ships raked the formation, shooting down two C-47s and causing two others to slam into each other in the confusion. To avoid "friendly fire" some planes went up to 6,000 feet, making them easy targets for the banks of searchlights in the vicinity of Catania. Next the planes had to make their way through a veritable wall of Axis flak all up and down the shoreline around Catania. Many planes headed off target, going inland where they hoped to find less murderous ground fire. They were then so hopelessly off course that several had to fly up and down eastern Sicily trying to find any reasonable DZ or LZ. Over thirty pilots gave up and returned with their troopers—in spite of having been given the gravest warnings against this. On the ground, small scattered bands of British troopers did manage to take some of their objectives, but they then had to yield them up in the face of Nazi counterattacks.

Apparently most troop carrier pilots, upon their return to Africa, claimed they had made good drops; but the British paratroopers later estimated that only one stick in three had landed within a mile or so of the assigned DZs.[15]

The American admirals involved in the "friendly fire" incidents only poured salt on the wound by trying to place the blame on troop carrier and airborne commanders. One of them brazenly asserted that the U.S. Navy always operated on the assumption that planes overhead were probably hostile; he also claimed that troop carrier planners should have known that antiaircraft gunners aboard ship tend to have itchy fingers. When queried as to whether the troop carrier planes had been in the designated invasion corridor, he admitted they were. When asked if he had received the teletypes to hold fire for a given time period, the U.S. Navy spokesman said yes—but this U.S. Army order had been forced on the Navy "unilaterally."

Whoever or whatever was to blame, the Navy was to get its way. Never again, in a major airborne mission, would troop carrier fly directly over a naval convoy. And—better late than never—for the next invasion (Normandy), troop carrier knew enough to paint those famous black and white recognition stripes on the wings of every C-47, every other kind of tow plane, every glider, and even on every bomber and fighter. Once again, the death of men in other outfits provided lessons that later helped spare many of us in the 81st TCS.

In the late summer of 1943, therefore, even while we in the 81st Troop Carrier Squadron began our intensive combat training at Laurinburg-Maxton Field in North Carolina, the airborne fiascos in Sicily suggested a big question mark about the entire nature of our future roles. For about three months the issue of large-scale parachute and glider operations hung in the balance. On the negative side, in addition to the battlefield results (or lack of them), were the revelations of how much could go wrong in the air. Eisenhower himself stated that airborne operations should never be attempted at more than regimental strength. After Sicily he remained dubious about the whole question of the airborne arm, just as Hitler had been after Crete.

Unexpectedly, just two months after HUSKY and LADBROKE, troop carrier got a chance to show that it could, with luck, produce results equal to the most optimistic predictions of its supporters. In July 1943, Italian opponents of Mussolini arrested him and overthrew the Fascist government. The "Rome-Berlin Axis" was breaking up. It soon became clear that Italy was going to surrender as soon as she could do so without too much damage to herself. On September 3, the British invaded the southernmost tips of the Italian mainland, its "toe" and "heel." On September 9, American and British Troops, under Mark Clark, landed at several points on the beaches of the Bay of Salerno, two hundred miles up the coast from the Italian "toe" and forty miles south of the great port of

Naples. That same day, the Italian government surrendered unconditionally, and even began to petition the Allies to join the struggle against Germany. The Nazis, though, were not about to give up on Italy. Instead of pulling out of the peninsula, as hoped, they poured more troops into southern Italy. In the hills in back of the Bay of Salerno, the Wehrmacht built up a strong defense line manned by crack German troops. The seaborne invasion of the Salerno beaches was in such desperate trouble that Eisenhower ordered Allied commanders near southern Italy to provide Clark with all the support they could.

After delaying to call in paratroopers until it was almost too late, Clark finally asked Ridgway to send in any elements of the 82nd Airborne that were ready. He asked that the right flank of the beachhead be protected by delivering paratroopers via an air drop. James Gavin's 505th and Reuben Tucker's 504th PIR, plus four groups of the 51st Troop Carrier Wing, were readied with amazing quickness, in just a few hours. Many of the pilots did not get any regular briefing but were shown the DZs on maps during hurried consultations by flashlight after they were already at their planes.

In two missions, on the nights of September 13 and 14, troop carrier delivered about one thousand sorely needed paratroopers to the Salerno beachhead defenses. This time no "friendly fire" brought down American planes, and this time the vast majority of the pilots jumped their troops either right on the money or not farther than two miles away. Gavin was able to assemble his whole regiment about an hour after he jumped.

The Salerno area jumps helped save the entire Bay of Salerno invasion. The 82nd Airborne troopers gave much needed support on an important sector of the fighting, and their arrival gave all the faltering American troops on the beaches a splendid psychological boost. Ridgway had not received the request for a rescue mission by the 82nd Airborne until September 12 and had not been able to assemble his unit leaders until 3:30 p.m. on September 13. Nevertheless troop carrier was able to get that mission into the air by 10:45 that night.

Now no prediction about the trouble-shooting potential of troop carrier and airborne divisions seemed too optimistic. The Salerno jumps certainly provided support for those arguing in favor of large-scale airborne operations in future battles. Furthermore, troop carrier planes were proving invaluable in evacuating wounded soldiers to hospitals in Sicily and North Africa, often from dirt runways only a few hundred feet from the German lines. General Clark said that without this evacuation many of the wounded would have died.[16]

The great port of Naples was now the big prize in the Italian campaign, but the roads to Naples still had to be won. The Germans had mined every road and dug into the top of every one of the countless Apennine hills. At the same time as the Salerno drops (September 13) General Clark tried to soften up the German lines before he drove on Naples by sending the 51st Troop Carrier Wing (carrying the 509th Parachute Infantry Battalion) to DZs near the town of Avellino, thirty miles east of Naples.

The paratrooper drop at Avellino was planned to prevent the Germans from reinforcing their troops near that city as the Allies advanced, and—so it was hoped—to convince them that they were in danger of being outflanked. If the Germans decided to fight inside the city of Naples it would take house-to-house fighting of the most ghastly sort, with terrible costs not only to the Allies but also to the civilians of that large and densely populated metropolis.

In spite of all the agonizing over "friendly fire" that had followed HUSKY II, there was more of it over Avellino. This time, mercifully, only two of our troop transport planes were shot down. A few planes went completely off course, became hopelessly lost, and returned to Sicily with their troopers aboard. Some who decided to jump their troopers scattered them so far and wide that only a few sticks of paratroopers landed within five miles of their objectives—none of which they captured. Many troopers came down more than twenty-five miles away. About 640 troopers jumped; almost a quarter of these were killed or captured, and some of the remainder needed weeks to find their way back to Allied lines.[17]

Eventually the Germans decided to pull out of Naples without destroying the city in house-to-house fighting, but the airborne operation itself had no effect on that decision. This operation was such a disappointment because it was the first large-scale American airborne operation in back of enemy lines. The two HUSKY missions and the jumps near Salerno had had the advantage of landing near Americans already on a beachhead.

An enormous shift in the location of airborne forces began to take shape during the fall and early winter of 1943. The reason, of course, was preparation for OVERLORD, the Allied invasion of Normandy. The 52nd Troop Carrier Wing moved from Italy to England, as did the 82nd Airborne Division. The 101st "Screaming Eagles" Division was on its way to England, and our own 53rd Troop Carrier Wing HQ and another new troop carrier wing, the 50th, were soon to follow.

Three months after the Avellino fiasco, in December 1943, we in the 81st TCS were heading for our "ports of embarkation," some of us bound for England by sea, some by air. What would be our role in the coming monumental struggle for Europe? No one could say; we in the 81st TCS, however, were convinced we certainly would be in the thick of the fighting. As 1944 began, however, it still was not clear whether our main function would be one of combat or logistics. High command was still wrestling with this question.

Crete and Sicily had been conquered in part with the assistance of large-scale airborne forces. But what was the exact contribution of these forces to victory in each case? Both the advocates of the "big airborne" approach (for major assaults) and the "little airborne" approach (for small-scale raids only) were claiming that the experiences of MERKUR, TORCH, and HUSKY proved them right. Others argued that troop carrier should be restricted altogether to non-combat work, moving supplies and troops.[18] In MERKUR, the cost in soldiers, gliders, and planes had been frightening. Hitler had scuttled all plans for large-scale airborne operations. In the late summer of 1943, American military leaders came within an ace of making the same decision.[19]

## Notes

1. Crookenden, pp. 10–23; Gregory and Batchelor, pp. 28–35; Devlin, *Silent Wings*, pp. 33–36.

2. For a good summary of the long genesis of airborne doctrine during the war, see Huston, *Blue*, pp. 49–82.

3. Crookenden, p. 48; Kiriakopoulos, pp. 289–94, 370–73, and 378. For MERKUR see also Comeau, *passim*.

4. See the highly optimistic critique of MERKUR circulated by the Air Corps Tactical School, Oct. 7, 1941.

5. Devlin, *Silent Wings*, pp. 29–32.

6. MacDonald, *Airborne*, pp. 57–68; Gregory and Batchelor, pp. 18–25.

7. Blair, pp. 26–32; Mrazek, pp. 52–63; Gregory and Batchelor, pp. 68–75.

8. For TORCH see Warren I, pp. 5–12; Breuer, *Torch*, pp. 43–48, 117–22, and 148–56; Huston, *Blue*, pp. 151–54; and Devlin, *Paratrooper*, pp. 150–61.

9. Some of these lessons were incorporated in a training circular of the War Department, "Employment of Airborne and Troop Carrier," Oct. 9, 1943.

10. Field orders for this operation called for releasing the gliders three thousand yards off shore and high enough to reach the LZ. Much later, American pilots claimed that it had been impossible to estimate heights and distances at night and under battle conditions. "Air Intelligence Contact Unit Report on Returnees," Dec. 18, 1944.

11. For HUSKY I and LADBROKE see Warren I, pp. 21–37 and 41–47; Devlin, *Silent Wings*, esp. p. 99; Breuer, *Sicily*, pp. 36–68; and Gavin, 1979, pp. 20–25.

12. "Red Berets" (British 1st Airborne troopers) carried their grudge against troop carrier on through the following year and the Holland invasion; some of them blamed their failure at Arnhem (see Chapter 16) on the failure of the Americans to drop adequate supplies to them while they were fighting there. Longmate, p. 103.

13. The 82nd Airborne observers believed it was naval gunners who fired

first. "Sicily, Italy, July 9, 1943, Sept. 13, 1943, Jan. 22, 1944." 82nd Airborne (mimeo) history, n.d., Ridgway papers, pp. 7–8, 37–38, in CBAMHI.

14. For HUSKY II see Warren I, pp. 37–41; Huston, *Blue*, pp. 158–61; Breuer, *Sicily*, pp. 138–45; and Devlin, *Silent Wings*, pp. 102–3. Some observers believe sailors mistook the pararacks under C-47s for torpedoes: see Moore, ch. 2, p. 38.

15. For FUSTIAN, see Warren II, pp. 47–54; Dank, pp. 85–90; Mrazek, pp. 98–101; and Devlin, *Silent Wings*, pp. 103–9.

16. For the drops near the Salerno beachhead, see Warren I, pp. 60–66; Blair, pp. 124–25 and 148–53; and Devlin, *Paratrooper*, pp. 300–303.

17. For the Avellino assault, see Warren I, pp. 66–69; Devlin, *Paratrooper*, pp. 306–328; and Blair, pp. 153–54. Clark later tried to defend himself by claiming that the troopers who managed to survive and who staged several raids disrupting German communications "paid off in big dividends." Clark, p. 206.

18. Moore, Ch. 3, p. 60.

19. Omar Bradley reports that "many of my infantry cohorts declared the paratrooper a dead dodo. There was a strong move in Washington to abolish the force. But I disagreed." Bradley, *Autobiography*, p. 184. See also Warren I, p. 54.

# 3. Traveling
## On the Road to Our War

### The trip

By the end of January 1944, the 81st TCS was fully established on its new base: Bottesford, England, otherwise known as Air Forces Station #481. We were in Nottinghamshire, smack in the center of England. We had been more than a month getting there: from December 24, 1943, when our first planes took off for their 11,000-mile trip across the South Atlantic, to January 30, when the rest of us arrived via the *Queen Mary* and a train from Edinburgh in Scotland.

When we arrived in Britain we were all exhausted; but we all had plenty to say about what we saw and did on the way. Our trip from Laurinburg-Maxton, North Carolina, to Bottesford began, in a way, only a couple of hours after we had completed our last "demonstration maneuver" on December 7–8, 1943. We had hardly caught our breath after this demanding exercise when we had to begin preparations for moving to Baer Field, at Fort Wayne, Indiana. Baer Field was to be our "final stage phase area" for those traveling overseas by ship, and our "POE" (port of embarkation) for those traveling by plane. A few of us managed to get last-minute leaves to see our families; but for most of us it was hard work every day, buttoning down everything as quickly as possible. One week later, on December 14, our planes began leaving for Baer Field. Most of us made the trip by train—a tiring two-day affair in crowded and dirty coaches.

For two tense weeks at Baer Field we continued the complex process of getting ready for the big trip. Officially, we still did not know where we were headed, but the absence of light weight clothing, insect repellent, and mosquito netting at Squadron Supply convinced the wiseacres that—unlike many other troop carrier groups—we were not going to the Pacific or the China-Burma-India theaters.

Meanwhile, we had to fill out more forms at Operations and listen to the Articles of War once more—this time with special attention to warnings that going AWOL from a POE was desertion, punishable by death. Our insurance arrangements were finalized—and it was with mixed feelings that we learned that our beneficiaries would receive $10,000 in case we did not make it back. This was a lot of money in 1943. Final arrangements, also, had to be made in our pay allotments to wives or families. Another source of worry was Supply— would we be able to take all we needed? Rumors (untrue) of how scarce things like razor blades would be in Europe sent us scurrying to the PX to load up on soap, cigarettes, writing paper, and candy. Supply clerks found they were not going to be allotted enough space in the boxes to be shipped with us to accommodate everything they had in Supply; they urged everybody with some room in duffle bags to squirrel away the shirts, pants, underwear, and socks which otherwise would have to be left behind.

Those who were to fly abroad were, of course, less limited in what they could bring along; but even they had to be careful not to put too much personal baggage on their planes. Because of the long flight over nothing but ocean, the planes were outfitted with four gasoline tanks ("ferry tanks") inside; these took up much of the room and added dangerously to the weight. The air echelon also had to carry the Squadron's parapack equipment, two bicycles in each plane, life rafts, boxes of emergency water cans and food packs, and numerous other heavy items (besides the men and their baggage). Inspectors from Group and Wing checked over each plane again and again and, where the weight seemed excessive, forced some men to return some of their stuff to the Baer Field Supply depot.

In the middle of all these hectic arrangements some of us managed to spend a few precious hours with our wives or other special people in downtown Fort Wayne. There were a lot of husky voices and half-suppressed tears. Our first planes and crews began their long trip overseas on Christmas Eve.

Those men who were to cross the Atlantic by steamer left Baer Field five days later. They headed for Camp Shanks, at Orangeburg, New York, temptingly close to the Big Apple. The trip to Camp Shanks required another two days on overheated and dirty trains. One of our Squadron's more "chicken" experiences occurred when it had to put up with a "dry run train formation"; obviously someone up at headquarters did not trust the men to get on and off a train. Or maybe this was a way of convincing them to pare down the loads of personal things they carried, a task easier said than done: in addition to the basic necessities like clothes, they had to carry that kind of military junk the orders called "full field equipment," including steel helmets, helmet liners, gas masks, "dubbing" (a greasy chemical to rub into clothing, supposedly to prevent poison gas burns), and other things that would prove of absolutely no use to us overseas.

When the ship echelon got to Camp Shanks they were told they could have passes and bring in the New Year in New York City itself! This was pretty grati-

Making friends: Ed Smith (communications) posing with an English sheep dog—a rare sight for Americans back in 1944!

Ye Olde English Charm: thatch roofed homes and swans on the Thames.

fying and many, on December 31 and later, took advantage of the opportunity to spend a few hours looking over Babylon-on-the-Hudson.

Not for the first or last time, the troops now experienced that old Army runaround known as Hurry Up and Wait. They had stretched themselves to the limit to get to the POE on time; now they were to cool their heels for another three weeks while someone found out how to put them on a ship. Camp Shanks, an old, established base, was pretty comfortable and had a good PX for last-minute purchases; besides, there was always New York City, an easy ferryboat ride away. Some who could afford it managed to make that trip three and even four times; though then, as now, money seemed to melt away faster in that city than anywhere else. The men who stayed on the base were liable to be assigned to clean up the filthy buildings left behind by previous outfits assigned there.

On January 22, 1944, it was "This is it, men!" (a phrase we never afterward used except in a self-mocking, disbelieving way). They boarded a train to the Weehawken Ferry Station in New Jersey, took a train to Manhattan, and there she was: the biggest and fastest thing in the water, the *Queen Mary*.

Now came the troops' first experience with that famous institution, Red Cross doughnuts and coffee, handed out as they waited to climb aboard ship; next came an Army band to serenade them as they staggered up the gangplank, loaded down with duffle bags. Everybody seemed to be going through the proper motions to cheer them as much as possible at this anxious moment. Until we entered the service, by far the greatest number of us had never even seen an ocean, let alone had an ocean liner voyage. The new experience had its draw-backs. Although the men on the *Queen Mary* weren't exactly crammed in like sardines, the crowding and discomforts aboard ship were just as awesome as its huge size and elegant decorations. Some enlisted men bunked six or seven to a compartment originally built for two. Others were worse off: some paratroopers had to sleep on deck, and because it was January, a few men came down with frostbite.

Nobody in the 81st TCS who made that trip can ever forget the constant battle against nausea. Russell Charlesworth, a glider mechanic, remembers:

> There were eight decks and about six of us to a compartment. For meals and for fire drills the ship was divided into three sections, red, white, and blue. During a storm or violent maneuvering to outrun subs, the ship would pitch and roll so much everything we hung from hooks on the wall would fall off; we heard once that there was six inches of water in one of the mess halls. The tables in the mess halls had sides to keep the food from sliding off one way but not the other; so that soon the floor would be covered with spilled plates and food.

The British crew was supposed to feed their American passengers only two times a day, but in rough weather only those with the strongest stomachs could manage anything at all. Breakfast might be sticky oatmeal mixed with prunes; even worse was the cabbage and mutton for the second meal. Several men lost a lot of weight by the time the trip was over.

> There were 7,000 or 8,000 men on the ship. One of the crewmen told me the ship raised up three feet a day in the water, just from the groceries that were used up.
>
> One day there was a sub warning, and they cut off the stabilizers and other electrical equipment such as radios. Just then we got caught in a storm; the result was a lot of broken arms and legs, mostly among the paratroopers. That day they couldn't even feed us. The ship sprang a bad leak; and when I opened the door to our corridor of F deck, the water was over my ankles. (Jack McGlothlin, glider mechanic)

There were movies and even a live USO (United Service Organizations) entertainment troop on board. Boat drills every once in a while were livened up by rumors about German submarine sightings. Unit commanders of troops going overseas were instructed to "arrange games and recreation for your men to divert their minds from the fact that they are on a hazardous journey," [1] but our men knew the *Queen* was so fast she could run away from anything, let alone a slow-moving sub. As it turned out they weren't the most crowded batch ever to make the voyage: on one record trip this ship, designed originally to carry 2,000 passengers and crew, carried 15,988 troops—twice as many as on our trip.

> On the *Queen Mary*, Harold Walker, our Squadron Executive Officer, handed out many assignments to us glider pilots. The one I drew was a nightly tour as Cigarette Watch on the sun deck. On this deck there were lots of colonels and lots of women officers. They would casually walk out on deck and light up a cigarette—practically a signal to any submarine that happened to be near us. My long hand was always there ready to grab that cigarette. (Darlyle Watters, Squadron Glider Officer)

On January 28 the *Queen Mary* dropped anchor in the Firth of Clyde, Scotland. The men were lightered by small boats to the docks of Gourock.

> We were welcomed in Scotland by the Scottish Home Guard. On the train we were told not to throw candy out of the windows; but in the towns the kids would run alongside the train and hold up the "V for Victory" sign.

So most of us did throw out candy, though it wasn't nice to see how they scrambled for it. After a while they stopped us so the kids wouldn't be hurt. (Russell Charlesworth, glider mechanic)

———

We docked in Scotland to the tune of bagpipes. There was a reception line of kind ladies who offered us tea plus what looked like what I would call tarts. I asked one lady for a tart; and she explained that in Britain "tart" was the word for a woman of ill repute. I liked the country right away! They had standards. (Darlyle Watters, Squadron Glider Officer)

The troops boarded a train first to Glasgow and then to Edinburgh; and then transferred to another train which took them to Nottingham. They stopped in Newcastle for a box lunch. Women in nearby houses opened their windows, though it was very cold, so they could wave. Worn out, but far from bored, the men finally arrived at Bottesford. Our CO, David Brack, met them at the train station, and trucks took them out to our new post.

The trip to Britain via the *Queen Mary* was a new experience for those who made it; the trip for the rest of us (including me), who flew the Atlantic, was even more dramatic. Men in the air echelon (46 Os and 48 EMs) got the better of the deal compared with the ship echelon—at least in this part of the war.

Back on December 24 the runways at Baer Field were covered with snow, and the air was very gusty; but the pilots had decided to put on a show when we left by getting up into a single V formation and doing a "grass-cutting job" on that field. Colonel Brack was in the lead and all the others strung out in echelon to the right and left.

We made a fast 180-degree turn to come back for "grass cutting." My plane was in a squeeze position; and our pilot couldn't change his speed during the turn, though it felt as if we were going so slowly we would stall out any second. Our pilot had to lower the landing gear, use more flaps, and open the engine cowl flaps to keep up his power while trying to go slow enough so as to avoid hitting the plane in front of him. I can tell you, things were pretty tense! It was a way of saying goodbye to the U.S.A. that was hard to forget.

Over the Atlantic we flew at about 16,000 feet because of the danger from German subs. At that height, if you walked around in the airplane, you had to breath heavily to take in enough oxygen. On one occasion we were darned lucky to be flying so high. Like all the planes, we had cabin gas tanks to supplement the main tanks. When we left Puerto Rico we were running both engines on those cabin tanks. All of a sudden both engines ran out of gas! The pilots had to take the plane down at a really steep angle in order to keep the engines turning over. We must have dropped about a mile before we could turn off the valves on the cabin tanks and switch on the main tanks. Meanwhile, we knew that our engines were rapidly cooling off. Would they fire up again when we switched tanks? They did; but we learned in a hurry that in the future we were going to use cabin tanks one at a time. (Carlisle Jordan, Squadron Airplane Inspector)

When the flight crews arrived at Bottesford we could say we had seen four continents, lots of islands, and too, too much ocean. We could show off the gaucho boots we bought in Brazil, describe the taste of mangos we ate in British Guiana, and tell about the real dangers from German fighters on the leg of the flight from North Africa to Land's End in England.

The aircrews and passengers touched down no less than ten times in nine different countries, but the entire trip lasted only two or three weeks, depending on the plane. At some stops we were rigidly confined to the base. At other bases, surrounded as we were by ocean or jungle, there was no place to go anyway, except the PX or the officers club. The rapid piling on of one strange experience after another, and the tensions we were all under, made for a confused jumble of impressions by the time we arrived in England:

The deep sense of loss at actually leaving the United States (after Baer Field we stayed overnight at Morrison Field, Florida). . . . The surprisingly clear green of the water that surrounded each Caribbean island, and the pretty white sand beaches and palm trees around Borinquen Field in Puerto Rico, with its plush officers club. . . . Christmas morning, in our planes ready for the next leg of the flight, Red Cross people brought out Christmas dinner in paper bags. . . . The endless green, menacing-looking jungle rushing up at Atkinson Field, British Guiana; the red-tiled roofs of Georgetown seemed the only break in that hot, suffocating scene for miles and miles around (in the jungle "a downed plane is a lost plane"). . . . The mighty Amazon River, that expanse of grayish, coffee-colored water, so big you would not see across it, even flying at about 10,000 feet. . . . The 900-mile flight over nothing but jungle to Belém, in northern Brazil, and the steaming hot and otherwise nasty barracks there. . . . The exhaustion everybody felt by the time we got to Natal, on the most eastern point ("the nose") of Brazil, and how grateful we were to learn we were to stay there for two nights. . . . Queuing up for hours to buy Swiss watches and gaucho boots the second day there. . . . The great surge of relief at spotting that tiny Ascension Island rising up out of the middle of the Atlantic Ocean. . . . The stunning realization that we were actually in Africa after the long stretch (1,020 miles) from Ascension to Roberts Field in Liberia. . . . First sights of Muslim women veiled head to toe, in Rufisque, near Dakar in Senegal, the most western

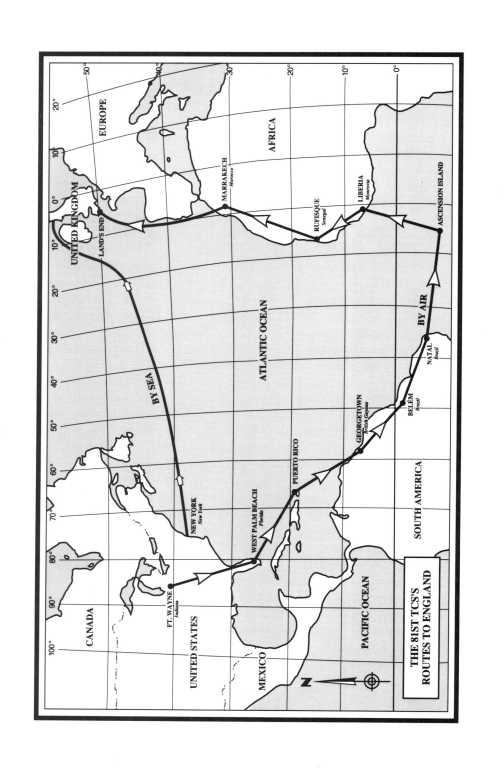

THE 81ST TCS'S
ROUTES TO ENGLAND

tip of Africa; the native guards in Rufisque, with their red fezzes and bare feet, eager to swap handmade knives for cigarettes. . . . The contrast between squalor in the Arab ghetto ("the Medina") of Marrakesh, in French Morocco, and the decent, wide streets and colorful houses of the "European" part of town—where some caught a glimpse of Winston Churchill and General Jimmy Doolittle, who also were passing through. . . . Bargaining for camels' hide wallets with Arab merchants on the streets of Marrakesh. . . . Being able to reach up and pluck an orange off the trees lining a city street in Marrakesh (they were too tart but a lot of fun). . . . And, finally, the green, manicured-looking farms we saw as we flew in to St. Mawgan, near the tip of Land's End, the southwestern-most part of England.

Most of our planes logged about 11,600 miles from Morrison Field in Florida to St. Mawgan in England. Taken all together, it was certainly the most demanding, tricky, and wearying assignment we had ever had. But—in retrospect, anyway—the technical aspects of the flight seem to have been accomplished, if not with ease, at least in good style. This happened partly because the Air Transport Command (ATC) in whose hands we were until we joined the Ninth Air Force in England furnished solid flight information and good plane maintenance facilities at its bases.

Air Forces headquarters, after much discussion, had decided our planes would fly across one by one and not in formation. This lowered the risk of losses if they were caught by a German fighter plane near Europe. Of course this also meant each plane had to be provided with its own navigator, and that it had to fly an empty sky—far away from help from one of our other planes. In fact, on each leg of the trip only a few of our planes saw anything at all in the air from the moment they took off to the moment they set down. Charles Hastings, however, had a close brush with a B-24 that suddenly zoomed out of the icy clouds near Britain and veered off only a few feet away from his wingtip; and Jack "Coach" Wallen reported another B-24 that seemed to be dropping bombs on what presumably was a German sub down below.

On the trip over, before each leg of the flight, ATC briefed the crews on what to expect ahead in the way of weather and what their best navigation aids might be. They also provided radio frequencies, recognition codes and flares, and reminders of how to handle ditching in the ocean. Sometimes they would also throw in advice. Don't drink the water! Stay away from those Arab women! Radio operators got the daily codes they used to transmit hourly position reports back to previous bases. At each landing the pilots, navigators, and radio operators turned in their logs and reported anything important seen on the way. It was the radio operator's duty to take the highly secret IFF radar ("identification, friend or foe") and see to it that this "black box" was locked up for the night.

Crew chiefs would report on what servicing was needed. Soldiers based on the field would gas up the planes and stand guard around them. It all seemed efficient, not to say cut-and-dried; but, of course, hundreds of planes like ours had already passed through, and the routine must have been firmly established before we took off.

Charles Hastings' plane lost an engine on the trip from Morrison Field; he "got to spend a great week in Puerto Rico." When he finally arrived in England our Group Commander, Adriel Williams, told him that if he had taken just one more day it would have meant a court-martial. Or, it may be that Williams had heard the story of how Hastings' crew had bought a fox in South America—for, presumably, a cool, Air Forces type of mascot. The fox made a pest of himself on board, however, and ungratefully chewed himself out of his bed, the plane's rubber raft; probably the crew was not too sorry when he was last seen "galloping away over the sand dunes at Marrakesh."

> On the leg of the trip to Ascension island, I asked our navigator, Edward Kozlowski, when we would be seeing the island; his answer was that it would be pretty soon. When I asked how come he knew it would be soon, he answered, "Because we have only fifteen minutes of gas left." That seemed like a good enough reason for me.
>
> At Ascension we had our first experience with being "de-bugged" by DDT. In those days people didn't know how harmful that particular insecticide could be. They came on the plane with their pressure cans of DDT, shut the door, sprayed everything in the plane, and made us sit there, choking, for three minutes. (Carlisle Jordan, Squadron Airplane Inspector)

Finding Ascension Island—five miles wide and seven miles long and in the middle of the trackless South Atlantic—seemed like a dangerous gamble to everybody but the truly fearless. If you missed it there was no turning back: you would have to head for Africa and pray you had enough gas to make it.

> I took a celestial fix that, according to my figures, would have made it impossible to reach Ascension because of tremendous headwinds. When I rushed to the cockpit to announce my findings and to beg the pilot, Jack Wallen, to return to Brazil, he astounded me by remaining totally calm. He merely asked me to take another fix! My second fix completely negated the first one; it indicated that we were in fact on course and making excellent time. After letting me squirm a while the pilots let me know that even before my first fix they had already tuned in the powerful radio station at Ascension and that we had already been riding the beam to our destination. (Bob Mac-Innes, navigator)

Ascension Island, barren and isolated as it was, in a way was the strangest experience of all. It felt peculiar to be able to walk some two miles from our own planes for a wonderful swim in the ocean. The constant cool and sweet sea breeze felt better than the best air conditioning imaginable. David Brack went fishing and pronounced it "the best fishing in the world!" But the sense of loneliness was fearful. Nobody in our crews would have traded places just then with the ATC and other soldiers fixed "for the duration" on that flyspeck of an island, with a single pass once every three months to Belém as the best they had to look forward to. There were only three or four trees on the whole island; no grass, in fact, no ground vegetation at all, just jagged mounds of volcanic rock with a few roads cut through and, of course, an airstrip.

The men in our crews had no way of knowing how safe and successful each leg of their transatlantic fight was to be; apprehension kept us company all the way, especially on the flights to Ascension Island and to St. Mawgan. The final Marrakesh-St. Mawgan journey, in particular, did seem to put us under the noses of German fighters based in western France. We had to fly ten weary hours up the Fourteenth Parallel, within easy range of enemy planes in France. The long flight past Spain, too, seemed dangerous; but there we had a rather bizarre bit of help from that pro-fascist country. The Spaniards had set up a radio beacon at Corunna, on the northwest tip of the country, expressly so Americans would not blunder into their air space. Theoretically neutral, they were not anxious to get involved in diplomatic disputes with the U.S. over interned planes and crews. During the Spanish Civil War in 1936–1938, Col. Brack had ferried over fighter planes for the Spanish Loyalists, the losing side. What reception would Franco, the Spanish dictator, give Brack if he were forced to land there?

### "It's rough in the ETO!"

There is an old Army saying that "an outfit that doesn't bitch is an outfit in trouble." Our Squadron must have been as right as rain in our new base at Bottesford, for we were bitching all the time. Rain! Rain was the main reason the month of February 1944 proved to be the most depressing time in the history of our Squadron. This was British rain: cold, windswept, foggy, incessant. Parachute riggers warned that some of the chutes were beginning to show signs of mildew. The only place to get warm was in bed. The barracks themselves weren't too bad (this had been a regular British air base vacated for us) and we even had an "ablutions hut" for washing and, if you were very brave, for showers.

We were pinned down by the rain. There never was enough coal for the pot-bellied iron stoves; actually, we didn't have decent coal but either coke or "briquettes"—spheres of compressed coal dust that were very hard to get started.

We used PX lighter fluid as well as paper and matches. Some of us demonstrated how little we worried about making friends with the British by chopping down the neighboring farmers' smaller trees for our stoves. This brought down the wrath of Group HQ on our heads, and we soon stopped.

It rained so regularly that we could fly only one-third as many total hours that month as we had each month during the fall of 1943 in the States. For one entire week, while we were sorting ourselves out and learning our way around the base, nobody got any leave, not even to nearby Nottingham. Boredom combined in an ugly way with the uneasiness we felt about our coming role in the invasion of Europe. Enlisted men not on flight crews seemed to be pulling a lot of KP and guard duty. The mail came too little and too late. It was easy to get a bad case of homesickness. One puzzling order upset us very much: the flight crews had to turn in all the small arms they had carried across the Atlantic—pistols, carbines, and submachine guns. Did this mean we were to become a non-combat outfit? No one bothered to explain.

And the food! The food was not only strange, it was sloppily cooked and unappetizing looking. We made the acquaintance of those dread scourges of war: powdered eggs; fried Spam; Brussels sprouts; and creamed chicken on toast, christened "SOS" (shit on a shingle). We learned that the British did not believe tea was strong enough to drink until you could float a spoon on it; and as for coffee—what we thought about British coffee is unprintable. There was no milk and precious little butter. But the worst was the mutton. Hours before chow, we would know that the mess hall was getting ready again to serve up sheep. Many of us were so nauseated by the smell that we couldn't even poke our heads into the mess hall to get some potatoes or bread (and that ever-present English marmalade) to keep us going. It was PX cookies, potato chips, candy—or packages from home—or starve.

> No wonder so many of us came down with dysentery those first weeks. It was so bad the worst victims couldn't make it out to the latrine; so we had to place "honey buckets" in handy places inside the barracks. . . .
>
> We used to snare rabbits. We would fry them up in the barracks at night. We would go up to the mess hall and beg, borrow, or—let's face it—steal something to go with those rabbits, especially some grease to fry them in on top of the barracks stove. We also needed something to fry some potatoes when we could get them. While the EMs in the mess hall would be trying to get us some grease, one of us would sneak back and try to get away with a sack of potatoes or some bread. When this worked we could have French fries, rabbit, and bread in the barracks.
>
> In addition to getting some good food, this sort of thing—and a lot of

it was going on—was pretty good fun. It was one of the fun things we did. (John Merril, glider mechanic)

Before many days at Bottesford, our sour mood began to color our assessment of the British people. Even before we had a chance to meet and talk with them, prejudices and clichés about life in Britain began to jell. For example: there were British workers on the base whose duty it was to maintain the taxiing strips and runways. One of them handled an ancient steamroller that became a kind of symbol of "Limey" ineptitude and addiction to moss-covered customs. Most of the time that steamroller would just sit there in the rain. Once in a while, when the weather cleared, you could see the worker who handled it up on the steamroller's seat, emptying out another mug of tea from his thermos. Then, whether he had actually driven it or not, he would carefully shine up the large brass manufacturer's plate on the boiler stack. This steamroller had a sort of Toonerville Trolley device for a pressure governor: two brass balls revolving in a stand near the gauge. When this British worker finished polishing his brass plate, darned if he then didn't polish up those brass balls. He and his shiny brass balls became the object of some pretty sarcastic comments.

Negative impressions like these clashed in a strange way with our universal admiration for the British countryside. The rich green color in the checkerboard fields, the neat hedgerows and fences, the stone farmhouses with their thatched roofs, and the soft, undulating hills and valleys looked like illustrations from a half-forgotten children's book. Many of us could identify with a remark by a soldier from another outfit who said he "felt he had passed out and awakened on a Hollywood movie set."[2]

Like all GIs transplanted to Britain we had been given a War Department brochure, *Guide to Britain*, that contained much advice. The booklet suggested we should not throw our money around, should refrain from boasting about the U.S. in ways that "put down" Britain, and should keep out of arguments about whether we were here to pull Britain's chestnuts out of the fire. A Briton is the most law-abiding citizen in the world, said this brochure, but one should not mistake civility for lack of guts. The majority of us, naturally, paid little attention to this War Department propaganda, and made up our own minds based partly on previous images and partly on our own experiences—but mostly from negative comments we passed to each other over poker tables or in the mess hall.

The easiest way to get a laugh was to imitate one of the British accents we heard—some of which, to tell the truth, were hard to understand. When the accent was no problem, however, most of us could appreciate their easy courtesy in conversation, especially their continual use of "please" and "Ta" ("thank you"). This politeness seemed to go together with their habit of queuing up rather than jostling for position at shop counters and at stops for those engagingly odd double-decker buses.

Only gradually, as we began to understand the privations the British were suffering because of the war, did our feelings toward them take a more positive turn. We had to admit, for example, that the dance hall at Nottingham was a pretty decent place after all. There it was easy to make a British acquaintance, since British girls, we found, were much more willing to chat than were older women—or men of any age.

> While we went right to work with glider training in our first base at Bottesford, we went right to play, too. I had a jeep that we could drive to dances at Nottingham. Dancing in England was fun. In Nottingham they had about a four acre floor so that people could go around and around—no "in place" dancing there! That was nice. What was not so nice was that coming back at night sometimes the fog and the blackout were so bad that the only way we could navigate was to follow along behind a bus. (Darlyle Watters, Squadron Glider Officer)

When the weather was decent, those of us with passes could use bicycles and visit Bottesford or other towns close by. Of course, those bikes became harder to manage on the way back from the pub to the base.

> I remember that at our first English base, Bottesford, somebody in high command got the bright idea to issue bicycles to all the flying personnel. After a week they could see this was a big mistake. The squadron was full of broken legs, sprained ankles, and so forth. You never saw such a nutty bunch of bicycle riders. When we got to Membury [our next base] we got no bicycles. The high command had learned its lesson. (Thayer Bonecutter, glider pilot)

We gradually realized that the scarcity of decent food and drink was not part of a devious British plot to make us feel miserable, but rather the outcome of their own desperate belt-tightening to save enough of the materiel needed for the war. It was easy to shake one's head over the harm English kids might be doing to their self-respect when they crowded around and demanded "Any goom, choom?" It made you more understanding to learn that strict British rationing meant that these kids were limited to one candy bar per week and that those five years old or younger had never seen an orange in their lives. Maybe the girls did look a bit dowdy, but the lamentable scarcity of women's cosmetics, fashionable clothes, and decent stockings (we couldn't help noticing how raw and chapped their legs looked) made it obvious they were not dowdy on purpose.

A pregnant phrase those days captured our feelings about our situation in Britain *and* our feelings about the people. "It's rough in the ETO!" You used it in response to what seemed like an unjustified bit of bitching. Full of sly double meanings, it was intended to convey "Quit your bitching, you might be in New Guinea!" as well as "Quit your bitching, think how rough things are for the poor Limeys!" This sort of more tolerant attitude, however, didn't become very general until we moved to Membury—and got better weather, better food, and increasingly vigorous training for D-Day.

### Notes

1. HQ, N.Y. POE, memo of June 22, 1943.
2. Howarth, p. 22.

# 4. Getting With It
## Training and Tourism in the ETO

### Training in England

A combination of planes, trains, and an ocean steamer had moved the 81st TCS from Baer Field, to Alliance, to Laurinburg-Maxton, back to Baer, and then to Bottesford; now we were to make our most important move of all, to Membury (known for code purposes as Air Forces Station #466). We would stay at Membury from March 2, 1944, to February 14, 1945. It was from there that we were to fly the Normandy, Holland, and Bastogne missions and the supply missions for Patton's divisions as they roared across France.

At Bottesford we had been in the geographical center of England, in Nottinghamshire; at Membury we were nearer the south of England, in Berkshire, directly west of London and 180 miles closer to the English Channel—and to France. Everybody knew we were being moved to lessen the distances over which we would have to haul paratroopers and gliders. This grim military reason aside, we were all grateful for the move.

In Membury some of us had to sleep or work in temporary-looking tar-paper shacks or galvanized-iron Quonset huts, instead of regular British RAF buildings. Everything else about Membury was a distinct improvement over Bottesford. We even had a pub, the Hare and Hounds, right on the edge of our base. The little towns around us, especially Hungerford and Chilton Foliat, were neater and cleaner than Bottesford, and the larger towns accessible to us—Swindon, Oxford, and Reading—had more to offer in the way of pubs, restaurants, and tourist-style attractions. Swindon was the town chosen for our evening shuttle run; while it was not as attractive as Hungerford or Oxford, it did have pubs, fish-and-chips shops, and a really enjoyable roller-skating rink. Unlike the often dour people we had met in the Midlands—from whom you sometimes could get only a grunt—these "southerners" were more open to a bit of conversation and to sharing opinions over a pint of "mild-and-bitter." Life in the 81st TCS suddenly became more open, less boring, and certainly better nourished: the mess hall at Membury was distinctly better. While essentially the same raw materials had to be used by our new cooks, they showed enough interest in their job to disguise the lack of so many basics (milk, butter, eggs, green vegetables) to turn out quite decent chow.

During March and April 1944, significantly large changes were taking place in our flying personnel rosters. Twelve additional glider pilots joined us in Membury, and nobody needed to be told that a combat glider mission was on the horizon. We also were joined by six additional complete aircrews, three of which did not as yet have their own planes and were referred to, ominously, as "attrition crews": in other words, replacements for those of the rest of us who might be killed in the upcoming invasion. We were now a squadron of twenty planes and twenty-three crews. On the other hand, half the navigators who had crossed the Atlantic with us or had been assigned to us in England were needed, we were told, for bomber squadrons in the Ninth Air Force. High command had made a decision to reduce troop carrier to only one navigator per flight (three planes). Some of these navigators, on their way out of Membury, were lost because of a horrible tragedy. The Wing shuttle pilot who was carrying them to their new base decided to buzz Membury airfield as he left; he crashed, the plane exploded, and the crew and all twelve navigators on board were killed.

During preparations for D-Day, the thought that some of us would not make it through this war began to push its way into our minds. While as individuals none of us truly believed that somewhere there was a German bullet with his name on it, the pace and character of our training in the early spring of 1944 made us at least face that possibility. The crews' guns were returned, and even the EMs were now issued Colt 45 pistols and shoulder holsters—weapons always regarded in past United States military tradition as to be worn by officers only. Flak suits to protect us from flying shrapnel were issued to each crew member.

Many other parts of the crews' training pointed in this direction. For example, one crew was sent for "TD" (temporary duty) on "DS" (detached service) to another base to train as a "pathfinder." Pathfinding was a new tactic developed after the Sicily fiasco for more accuracy in guiding our planes to their targets. Pathfinder crews were specially trained to handle ultra-secret radar navigation devices and were provided with pathfinder paratroop platoons; these highly specialized paratroopers' mission was to jump shortly before the main invasion armada would arrive and to place radar beacons and coded lights right on the DZs and LZs.

My plane and crew were selected to be fitted with radar. We were being trained for pathfinder work: dropping paratroopers by using only radar. Toward the end of our training period they scheduled us for a night drop of British paratroopers. When Kozlowski, our navigator, got us to the DZ, the troopers went out, and I thought this training mission had gone well.

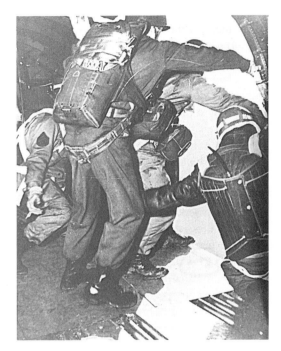

Stand in the door! Paratroopers practicing jumps from a C-47 in Britain. (Courtesy U.S. Army Military History Institute)

Paratroop specialists hook up pararack bundles under the belly of a C-47. (Courtesy USAMHI)

After a drop it was SOP [standard operating procedure] for the crew chief and the radio operator to pull in the shroud lines before we went back to normal flying speed. I waited for what seemed like an eternity for someone to come up from the rear and tell me we were all clear. Finally the crew chief ran up to the cockpit and told me that we had trouble, that one of the paratroopers was still hanging out there on his shroud lines. I said something to the effect that this was impossible and sent Eads [co-pilot] back to see what was wrong. He reported that indeed there was a paratrooper still on the line and banging like hell into the side of the ship.

Now four people began to pull on those lines to get that paratrooper back—crew chief, radio operator, navigator, and co-pilot. Several times they were able to get him in as far as the door, but then they would run out of strength and could not get him in all the way. We feathered the left engine and flew just barely above stalling speed. It was his opened chute that was making it so hard to pull him in. But finally they got him inside—a bloody banged up mess, unconscious most of the time and cold as well, but alive.

By the time they managed to pull that fellow in, I had not one single idea where the hell we were. This was during the time when England was in a total blackout—the Germans were still making regular nightly bombing runs over most of the country. And all the airfields down on the ground were blacked out—man, was it dark! The navigator was able to get us a pretty good fix, and I decided to call for help. This meant I had to break radio silence. I had to yell "May Day!" several times before we got a response. [The international distress call on radio telephone, "May Day," comes from the French "m'aidez!" meaning HELP!] Down on the ground they were very leary of our story; but we finally got them to turn on one of the runway lights on that base. When we landed and rolled to a stop and opened the door, we were greeted by a flock of MPs training their guns on us. We had to go to MP HQ where they checked our story by calling up home base at Membury.

After they checked us out they let us sleep overnight in their barracks. The next morning we went to the hospital to talk to that paratrooper. He told us his chute had opened OK but his foot had tangled with one of the shroud lines from one of the previous jumpers. He said he had resigned himself to the fact that we would have to cut him loose and let him fall. He thanked us over and over. I've often wondered whether that fellow made it through the war. (Ed Vosika, pilot)

One of our pilots, Art Feigion, who flew the Normandy invasion with us, was later permanently assigned to IX Troop Carrier Pathfinder Group.

We had a whole bunch of planes; and there wasn't enough for all of us to do for just leading invasions. I never got to drop paratroopers, myself. We worked as just another group under the IX Troop Carrier Command, flying a lot of re-supply missions for them, especially when the weather was so bad "even the birds were walking." Some of these missions had to be run on instrument, something other troop carrier groups didn't normally do.

I know that the radar sets and the beacons on the ground didn't work too well during combat; but this didn't matter all that much, since we flew in a V-of-Vs, nine ships across, and usually only the lead ship had radar working. In all the excitement over a combat target, the use of radar wasn't all that accurate, partly because of inadequacies in the sets themselves, partly because over a target, while the navigators were giving the pilots directions, the pilots had too much on their minds to pay them much attention.

A lot of us pilots fancied ourselves pretty much as navigators. I was the kind of pilot who was always a little antsy; and I always tried to keep track of where I was. And I've had navigators come up into the cockpit and say "Where the hell are we?" (Art Feigion, pathfinder pilot)

As the time for the Normandy invasion drew closer, we had to sit through two "Escape and Evasion" lectures by members of the Military Intelligence Department on how to protect ourselves and get help escaping if we had to parachute into France. Months before we arrived in Britain, fairly dependable escape routes for downed airmen had been set up by Resistance patriots across Holland to the Channel and through France to Spain. We had our pictures taken in civilian coats and ties to be used for forged identity papers which, it was hoped, would help get us to a neutral country (Switzerland or Spain), or even back across the Channel to Britain. These pictures went into a neat plastic "Escape and Evasion Kit," which also offered compressed chocolate, pep pills, a great little compass, halazone tablets (for decontaminating water), and even a little pouch in which the water could be treated—in case we would have to hide in a forest or a remote rural district. The largest item in these packets was an arm band with an American flag so we could identify ourselves to French people in the Resistance who might be out looking for us. Women in whorehouses, we were told, were known to be more likely to help downed Allied airmen than any other single element of the French population.

At this point one of the most serious bitches began to receive some attention: we were about to go into combat with gas tanks not provided with self-sealing rubber liners. Bombers and fighters had them, but not our C-47s. Our planes, we knew, were incomparably more vulnerable than fighters or bombers: we flew low and slow to accommodate paratrooper jumps and glider releases, we had no armor plating anywhere, and, of course, we had no mounted cannon or machine guns. We were so vulnerable, in fact, that we stood a distinct chance of being brought down by a single rifle bullet; certainly an incendiary tracer bullet penetrating a gas tank would turn a C-47 into a flaming trap. With a lot of expense and trouble, we knew, we *could* have been "retrofitted" with self-sealing tanks. There was a lot of talk about how desirable this would be, but only a few of our planes got them. Until the jump across the Rhine, most of us fought our war with gas tanks in each wing that were, in effect, potential bombs.

All these pre-invasion activities—including our experiences with British accents, beer, climate, and people—were only sidelights. On every day with decent weather we flew training missions in large formations, sometimes participating with paratroopers in regular maneuvers. When we trained with British paratroopers, some of whom wore hobnail boots, we had to lay down felt mats to keep them from sliding all over our aluminum flooring. Our glider pilots had to be checked out on the immense British Horsa glider; while at first we were really dubious about the handling quality of these huge wooden gliders, most of our glider pilots admitted, after only a few flights, that the Horsa flew fairly well, and, in some respects, was an even better combat aircraft.

The single most important part of all these advanced training experiences, during the early spring of 1944 was our nighttime formation flights. Because of the terrible risk of collision, these were flights that had to be handled with extreme precision and a very high level of pilot competence. They were spectacular demonstrations of how far we had come from Alliance, Nebraska. No one who was on one of these night maneuvers can forget the eerie sensation of looking out through the cockpit windshield and seeing indistinct black shapes in front and on the side, each plane illuminated by nothing but the pitifully dim blue formation lights near the top edge of the wings.

Once the night mission was on its way, we became involved in a simulated invasion flight, often out over the English Channel and back again. On these missions we sometimes would toss batches of aluminum strips out of the plane; these strips, called "window," were supposed to appear on enemy radar screens as huge assemblages of planes.

The first plane we lost in England was before D-Day, on a night training flight. Because of a German air raid in the vicinity [May 15] there was a red alert on our base; and the Membury control tower couldn't let the planes land. So they all had to circle around and around, wheels down, trying to keep in formation by following the dim blue formation lights of the plane in front. HQ was afraid the Luftwaffe would follow our planes in and bomb the hell out of the base. The pilot of one plane got confused by some bright stars and wandered out of formation. His plane ran up a hillside so hard the

C-47s on the runway for a formation training mission.

A good "V-of-Vs" formation over our barracks rooftops at Membury.

Close! Squadron planes closing it up during a formation training mission.

landing gear broke and the plane slammed to a stop. All these planes were loaded with five-gallon jerricans of gasoline to simulate a supply mission. The crew knew fire would break out at any moment. They tried to get out the cargo door; but it had been jammed by all those jerricans that had slid against it. So they had to climb out the escape hatch on top of the cockpit; and they all made it, just seconds before the plane exploded.

Next day Joe Konecny [Squadron Engineering Officer] and I drove a jeep to the area to see what was left. About all that was recognizable was two charred hunks that must have been the melted engines. (Carlisle Jordan, Squadron Airplane Inspector)

Each pilot had to sweat out routing his plane through the assembly pattern needed first for the Squadron, then our 436th Group, and finally our 53rd Wing. Then they had to jockey desperately in these formations for close but safe "Vs." In theory they were supposed to fly no more than a hundred feet from the wing of the nearest plane. Every rain squall, every sudden gust of wind, put us in serious jeopardy. Also on our minds, especially during the period of heavy training schedules in April and May, was the need to steer clear of other vast air fleets—fighters and bombers—on their way to or from the Continent. When the entire Wing assembled there would be more than 200 C-47s trying to make their way safely through that black and crowded English sky.

## Tourists

Just before D-Day, when the American buildup in Britain was at its height, over two million Americans were crowded into the island. When you thought about the Canadians, French, Australians, New Zealanders, and Poles, plus their tanks, trucks, planes, and so forth, you got the point of the joke about those "barrage balloons." Maybe these balloons, floating high above London and other ports, were not worth much as obstacles against the Luftwaffe; but if you cut them loose, the whole bloody island would sink under the sea.

In some British towns we saw as soldier-tourists, only the fact that there were uniforms everywhere reminded us a war was on. We biked into nearby Chilton Foliat, for example, and were struck by how marvelously peaceful it appeared and how it epitomized what we'd always thought of as "Olde World Charm": the snug-looking, ivy-covered brick or stone cottages with the occasional thatched roof; the one narrow, winding road that passed over a tiny stone bridge; the swans in the stream below the bridge; the yeasty smell of crumpets in the tea-room; the dart-board game in the Stag's Head pub; the tiny Anglican church, surrounded by its graveyard with ancient-looking stones and its air of having cared for many, many generations of worshippers. Inside, the church in Chilton Foliat seemed full of history, with its marble effigy of a knight in armor, its leaded-glass windows, its bronze wall plaques memorializing people who had died centuries ago, and its pews polished to a soft, dark glow by many years of use. In that little ancient church, even those of us who did not attend religious services on our Membury base still felt called on to offer up a prayer.

London, of course, was another story. Here the war was in plain sight on the ground, in the Underground (subways), and occasionally in the air above. Although the main Luftwaffe Blitz was three years in the past, the Nazis still made occasional night raids. In February 1944 some of us in London experienced the "Mini-Blitz" of fire-bombing that fortunately was only a short replay of the Battle of Britain. In some subway stations, even after February, you still had to pick your way carefully around women and children sleeping on the station floors for the night. Above ground the terrible devastation of 1940–1941 was much in evidence—huge piles of rubble, facades with no buildings behind them, tremendous basins of water carved out by "blockbuster" bombs, as large as swimming pools, ready for fire wardens to use.

We were in London primarily to escape the war. But being there and seeing what war had cost London made us less inclined to bitch about our own frustrations and annoyances.

> Sometimes it was hard to understand the English even when they were talking right to you. But one time the communication was clear enough. That was when the owner of a pub took four of us down into the cellar and showed us a dud bomb sitting there: it had crashed down right through the roof and through the first floor into the basement. I could sympathize with him when he said "That one was too blankety-blank close." Once, when I was in a London hotel room, a V-1 buzz bomb landed so close it shook the whole building and knocked big chunks of plaster down from the ceiling on me where I was lying in bed. (Ben Obermark, crew chief)

Meanwhile, the theaters, pubs, restaurants, museums, and other facilities of London town were there for us to enjoy. After D-Day, all the towns we visited were much less crowded—most of the infantry had left for France.

A few days after D-Day, the first V-1 flying bombs began to drop on London. These *Vergeltungswaffen* (retaliation weapons) were really small, pilotless ("robot") planes, each with a ton of explosives in the nose section. The first "V" product of Hitler's formidable collection of rocket scientists, they were not steerable toward any precise target, but rather were launched in the general direction of London; they would drop wherever they ran out of fuel. One of the frightening things about the V-1 bombs was that they seemed to come down at random, any place, any time. Once again, many of the weary London mothers and children took to spending the night on Underground train platforms.[1]

The distinct put-put-put sound they made earned them the name of "buzz bombs." The noise was unforgettable, partly because once you heard it close by—and then heard it *stop*—you knew it was time to slide under a bed. Many of us saw them streak across the London sky and heard the "crump!" when they blasted to bits another part of the town. I once saw one out of a bathroom window in the Hans Crescent Red Cross; I was emptying my bladder at the time and the sight had a peculiar effect on me—caught me in midstream, so to speak.

Happily, our invasion overran many of the V-1 launch sites that summer. Because the V-1s were relatively slow, fighter planes often could pick them off in the air. The V-1 menace was virtually licked by September 1944; but then began an even more frightening attack by the V-2s. Faster than sound, the V-2s were true rocket bombs, that is, ballistic missiles. The V-2 arrived without warning—so air raid sirens and shelters were useless. V-2 attacks on London lasted all the remaining time we were based in England.

One afternoon on leave in London I joined a long queue for a symphony concert at Royal Albert Hall. Once inside, I was handed a notice along with the program explaining that in view of the V-2 danger, "The Management" had placed two lights in back of the conductor's podium, one green, one red. As long as radar showed no incoming V-2s on its screens, the green light would stay on, but if radar spotted one of these rockets headed our way, the red light would flash.

"In this event," continued the explanation, "you are free to leave the Hall; but please do so as quietly as possible so as not to disturb the remaining Audience and the Orchestra." In the middle of the second piece, sure enough, the red light flashed on. I immediately rose in my seat and looked around nervously for the nearest exit. I soon sank back again, mortified; nobody else had so much as budged, and the orchestra did not miss a single beat. A few minutes later I heard the frightening crunch of the bomb—it had fallen (I learned later) only a few blocks away. I jumped at the sound but the audience remained riveted in their seats, probably observing the cowardly reaction of one of "those Yanks!" with cynical amusement. I had been treated to a perfect demonstration of that famous British stiff upper lip.

### Getting to know them

Every one of us in the Squadron was aware he was facing a new sort of challenge in learning how to get along with the British. Some of us were predisposed to like what we found, some not. Many of those coming from an Irish background arrived with real hatred of the British, based on centuries of mistreatment of their ancestors. Some of us, especially those from the predominantly isolationist Middle West, blamed the British for artfully backing us into a war that was none of our business. Such antagonism, latent or open, is probably why many of us never spoke of them as "British" or "English"—only as "Limeys," a term with more negative and condescending overtones than the "Yanks" they applied to us.

But none of us could ignore them. For example, since all of us had heard of Robin Hood, we laughed when we found that Bottesford was right up against Sherwood Forest; we were working where that mythical band of Merry Men once confronted the evil sheriff of Nottingham. Whether we realized it or not, we had been conditioned since childhood to a "special relationship" with Britain and the British people. Mother Goose nursery rhymes and unforgettable stories by Sir Walter Scott, Lewis Carroll, and Sir Arthur Conan Doyle were part of our heritage, too. Grant Howell (teletype operator) remembers that on his first trip to London, finding himself on Half Moon Street, he realized he was walking right through the locale of an Earl Derr Biggers mystery novel he had read when he was a kid. Much of the poetry we had to learn in school, the magazine pictures and the movies we saw, and our history books prepared us to have a large part of our thinking taken up by these people to whom we owed so much of our culture and our institutions and whose land we now inhabited.

Since 1939, in fact, when war began in Europe, American radio had been pouring out sentimental songs filled with admiration for the British, for their fight for freedom, and for the British longing for a better world. We had danced to tunes like "A Nightingale Sang in Berkeley Square," "When the Lights Go on Again All over the World" (a reference to the British blackout defenses against Nazi bombing), and "There'll be Bluebirds over the White Cliffs of Dover." Suddenly, here we were, among them! Some of us later got the chance, when returning to base in a training flight out over the English Channel with the sun at our backs, to see those very same white cliffs of Dover, highlighted against the dark green fields behind.

Like it or not, the wartime stage on which we were acting was a British one. A few of us chose to hang around the base when we were off duty, but most of us went to town as often as we could. Whole truckloads would be motored to neighboring towns, were we would be guests at a dance or could spend a few hours in the pubs of Swindon, Reading, or Oxford. Many of us got three or four three-day passes; some of us, especially the aircrews, got a full week's furlough after the Holland invasion, to be spent in a British resort hotel.

Under the circumstances, if most of us had picked up British tastes, mannerisms, and accents, it would have been easy to see why. If scores of us had worked up what today people might call "meaningful relationships" with British girls, no one would have been astonished. If dozens of us had brought back

British "war brides," our parents would have understood and our friends might have envied us. What stands out, however, is how little of this sort of thing actually happened. None of us in the 81st TCS "went native." Most of us kept pretty much to ourselves, and surprisingly few long-lasting friendships materialized with British girls or older people in British families who invited us into their homes.

One of the sorest points in British-American relationships was symbolized by that half-bitter, half-joking crack, "The trouble with you Yanks is that you are over-fed, over-paid, over-sexed, and over here!" How closely did we in the 81st TCS conform to this sour picture of American behavior in Britain?

One painful contrast between our treatment and that given British soldiers was the sheer quantity of food we had. In our mess halls, second helpings were the rule; and our garbage cans always filled up. British mess halls, I was told by British soldiers, served bad food and never enough of it. Much of the small amount of pay British enlisted men got went went to buy a bit more grub at fish-and-chips shops and at NAAFIs.[2]

Certainly we were overpaid by British standards. Since British style emphasized understatement not assertiveness, to them it seemed we were flaunting our wealth despicably. Some of us did indeed try to use our heavier wallets to get better treatment; for example, to urge a pub keeper to find us some gin or scotch when his "spirits" ration was used up. British officers in the rear of theaters we entered would mutter "Bloody Yanks!" as we EMs shouldered our way forward toward the more expensive seats.

The biggest exhibition of being overpaid came on pay day, or, as we said, "when the eagle shits!" Some of us on flying pay had so much cash that we allotted half our pay back home to our wives and families. For all of us, pay day was when we would pay off last month's debts, descend on the PX, or—if we had a pass—roar into town looking for souvenirs, restaurant meals, and, of course, girls.

Those who got more enjoyment staying on base and playing cards for money would sometimes run up the stakes on the table to impressive sums. Some of us were so consistently lucky at gambling that we bought postal money orders and sent home hundreds of dollars—or so the rumor went. Grant Howell remembers seeing a Communications sergeant, Fred Youngblood, walking across the base waving a thick wad of pound notes; when Youngblood spotted Howell he grinned and said, "It's rough in the ETO!" and he always claimed his real name was "GI Love-the-Army Youngblood."

> I've got sixpence, jolly, jolly sixpence.
> I've got sixpence to last me all my life;
> I've got sixpence to lend, and sixpence to spend

And sixpence to send home to my wife, poor wife!
No cares have I to grieve me, no pretty little girls to deceive me.
I'm happy as a king, believe me,
As we go rolling, rolling home!
Rolling home, rolling home by the light of the silvery moon,
Happy is the day when the airman gets his pay
As we go rolling, rolling home.

This sixpence, in our favorite marching song, was about the size of a dime and worth about ten cents back in those days when a British pound sterling exchanged for $4.20. A sixpence would buy you two pints of beer, or three cups of tea and cookies, or six days of the Armed Forces newspaper, *Stars and Stripes*. We were paid, of course, in British money; and once we got over the natural tendency to think of British coins and bills as "funny money," or as mere chips handy for playing poker or blackjack, we began to realize that we had substantial purchasing clout and not only in our base canteen. A staff sergeant, who was slightly above the middle of the enlisted men's pay scale, got $96 per month, plus a few dollars more for being overseas, plus 50 percent if he was on flying pay; an equivalent British rank would be paid around $48.[3]

Along with our boastfulness and too-ready cash, the numerous medal ribbons we sported on our tunics when we went to town became targets for British sneers. The American Air Forces were notorious for dishing out many times the number of decorations the British got; and we often got ours merely for participating in a battle.

Concerning the sort of behavior that most grated on British sensibilities, however, it seems clear the 81st TCS did better than the average GI unit. Certainly there were a few loud-mouthed show-offs among us; but most of us displayed decent enough manners. We therefore suffered from being lumped together with, say, paratroopers. Certainly none of us was ever court-martialed for mistreating British citizens; and, in fact, there were only a few court-martial proceedings against anyone, for any reason, all through the wartime history of the 81st TCS.

A great deal has been said in scholarly studies and in novels and movies, about the brash, persistent, and truly inconsiderate way American soldiers pursued British women—with the single-minded objective of what today would be called "scoring."[4] My recollections and those of others in the 81st TCS suggest this image is far from reality. Most of us did not have to worry about "refusing to take no for an answer," simply because we were too shy to ask in the first place. Or—in the old-fashioned way that seems so naive today, but was certainly a powerful deterrent back then—we did not chase women because we "wanted to keep ourselves clean" for our wives, fiancées, and sweethearts.

There was no end to *talk* about "shacking up," that is, staying overnight or for a weekend with a girl in her apartment or in a hotel. Even though we got many passes, however, most of us went on leave with one of our buddies and stayed in Red Cross hotels, where you could get a warm bath, an innerspring mattress, and sleep as late as you liked. It is true that one of our navigators, Eugene Davis, had what we used to call "a steady" in London; she was his mistress in the sense that he paid some of her bills and supplied her liberally with American rations. He had a wife in the States; and in some unknown way his wife learned of what was going on. But before things could come to a crisis between them he was killed during the drop over the Rhine. His wife had already obtained his mistress's address and written her, and, I'm told, the two later shared their grief in some amicable correspondence.

We know of one incident where one of us thought he was about to father a British infant. Since today nobody likes to talk about such problems, there may have been more of us in the same predicament. George Rankin, our Squadron Communications Officer, recalls that one crew radio operator came to ask his advice about whether he should marry the girl involved. Rankin advised him to consult the Group Chaplain.

Certainly a good deal of casual sex as well as dates were there for the taking. In big towns girls would saunter, two by two, in the vicinity of a Red Cross center and play the exciting game of "pick-up." We called these girls "chippies," a British term. It was notorious that at the biggest Red Cross hotel of them all, Rainbow Corners, on London's Shaftesbury Avenue near Picadilly, you could buy condoms along with your newspaper from the news vendors. Of course there were also prostitutes in the vicinity, and occasionally someone smuggled one into the base. Wherever these ladies came from, we called them "Picadilly commandos." But prostitutes were outnumbered by girls looking for amusement not pay.

Many of us recall getting dirty looks and a few curses from British soldiers when we walked down the street or into a pub with a British girl on our arm.

Let me tell you, some of those English soldiers hated our guts. Once I met a Jewish girl who invited me over to her house. I remember she talked about her boss as "the governor"—very English! Her brother, in the British Army, happened to be home on a furlough. He said, "What's that bloody Yank doing here? All the Yanks are doing here is entertaining the girls. I don't want my sister to be 'entertained' like that. Throw him the hell out!" (Irv Bornstein, Operations clerk)

One of the ways British and American authorities tried to reduce the dangers involved in relations between American soldiers and British girls was to encourage "mixers," that is, dances. The idea was that most of us were more curious and lonely than oversexed, and that these needs could be met conventionally and safely through dances. Most of these dances were Group, not Squadron affairs. In keeping both with Army traditions forbidding Os to fraternize with EMs and with British mores concerning the dangers of crossing class lines, there would be either officers' or enlisted men's dances but not combined dances. For a dance about one hundred girls would be brought onto the base, some from business offices in Reading and some who were serving locally as farmers' helpers in the WLA (Women's Land Army). Both EMs and Os paid for the food and drink out of their own pockets; but base motor pool provided the all-essential transport for the girls. On each truck was one of our officers to see to it that nobody got out of line; this duty was called "courtesy patrol." It was up to the American Red Cross or the British Special Service to "vet" these girls, that is, to affirm that they were of good character, a comforting protection for all concerned.

> Most of these dances were at our officers clubs. A lot of the officers, after the dances, would want to escort the girls back home, and we had trouble getting them out of the truck when we were on our way out of the base. Often one of them would sneak on the truck and make it back to town with his girl friend. One of the officers was a good friend of mine, and I sometimes let him get away with it.
>
> These girls were mostly from the little towns around Membury; but we got to go as far away as Reading to pick them up and deliver them. Sometimes we carried them in the "deuce-and-a-half" [two and a half ton truck]; the smaller numbers of girls would be transported in our weapons carriers. Of course I myself couldn't enjoy the dances; I had to go back to the barracks and be ready for any calls from the Orderly Room for any other transportation they might need. (Charles Parrish, motor pool)

Contrary to the romantic image of GIs in Britain, only two of us we know about—out of 420—married British girls during the war. Ted Menderson, our Assistant Adjutant until he moved to Group HQ, married a Scottish girl in the ATS (Auxiliary Territorial Service) he met at a Group dance. Bob Carney, a glider pilot, met his wife at a base dance: she had been trucked down from Oxford. She then invited him to her home, and he became a big favorite with her parents, who soon counted him as one of their friends. Before long he was spending most of his free time with this family, and the marriage took place before our Squadron left England. This marriage did not work out, however, partly because she seemed too interested in her family in Britain, some of whom she brought over to the States, and because she insisted on adopting an illegitimate British child of one of her friends. Roger Krey, another glider pilot, also married a girl he met in Britain, but later, after the war, when they met again in the States. This marriage prospered and is still going strong.

Gerald O'Shea, an Operations clerk, feels that we in the 81st TCS probably had more to do with British girls than we remember—or than we like to talk about.

> I was neither married nor engaged when I got to England. I made friends with an English girl from Nottingham soon after we landed. And her family often had me to dinner. Her father was in the Home Guard. In fact, he was a retired military man who served in the British Army in India. Her mother was an awfully nice person. And she had two sisters, one younger and one older than she was.
>
> Her name was Maureen Taylor. We were good friends; but neither of us took it very seriously, and of course it didn't last. But I value my recollections of my times with the Taylor family very much; I enjoyed knowing them—and of course her—tremendously.

Even more rare than having a girlfriend was finding a friend among one of the older British people. Very few of our officers were invited to have tea in neighboring "stately homes." When we did get a chance to exchange a few words with middle-aged people, usually what we experienced was not hostility, but rather a wall of highly cherished privacy, plus a feeling that they were nervously expecting us to commit some terrible social blunder. Those of us from the South and West of the United States, especially, found older British people cold and difficult to approach.

On the surface, at least, our relations with such people were perfectly decent, and some of them did unbend to a small degree for a few of us.

> [There was] a sweet old lady near our Membury base, who lived just beyond our officers club, and who found out that I loved to drink milk but couldn't stand to drink the stuff made from powdered milk. Every once in a while she would come up with a gift of milk. It was something I really appreciated, though at the time I remember a couple of qualms about the milk not being pasteurized! But I think of that as an example of the good relations we had with these English neighbors. (Adriel Williams, 436th Group CO)

Those of us who did consolidate real friendships with British families regarded this as a piece of exceptional luck and not the sort of thing any of us could expect. Sometimes an introduction from a relative in the States could help break you through the barriers:

> I was lucky to learn that my Dad's cousin had a close friend living in England. As soon as I could I got a pass and looked them up. They were a wonderful family and it was great to be treated as though I were an American relative of theirs. I'll never forget how they fed me in spite of the tiny food rations they had to live with. I visited them several times; and once they took me to their home farm in central England. For a farm boy like me, it was a real treat to learn how they handled things on a farm in England. (Jerome Loving, crew chief)

On the other hand, sometimes all it took was a lucky break during a chance meeting that turned the trick:

> One night, drinking in a pub in Swindon, I happened to meet an Australian officer who was visiting relatives in Swindon. When the call "Time, Gentlemen!" came, he insisted that I go meet his relatives, the Jeffrey family. But when we got there we fell into the middle of a conversation the family was having about Mrs. Jeffrey's birthday the following week. It was embarrassingly clear that they couldn't do anything else but invite me to the party, too.
>
> At Membury, I wracked my brains—what sort of present could I give Mrs. J? Finally I decided to bring along a pint of Southern rot-gut rye I had been cherishing on the entire trip from the States. I wrapped it up in brown paper—the only stuff available—and brought it along. At the party we passed the bottle around, and everybody waited until Mrs. J took the first drink. But instead of sipping it, she tossed the whole shot right back down her throat. She became red not only the face but right down her chest, and her eyes became distinctly glazed over. When she could speak all she said was, "I say, Yank, that's a bit stout!" Everybody roared; and that's how I became practically a part of the Jeffrey family. Never went to Swindon without stopping to say hello. It became my duty to escort their two daughters and daughter-in-law to the local dances and see to it they got home in time.
>
> It was clear to me that once accepted, for you the English family was a warm and understanding group. (Bill Westcott, pilot)

Especially after the Normandy invasion, when we were becoming more sure of the value of troop carrier, and a bit more confident of our ability to cope in a foreign environment, many of us would have welcomed the chance to have some

Celebrating the opening of our officers' club in Membury. Col. Williams, 436th TCG commander, is seated just to the right of the central post.

An 81st TCS enlisted men's party at Membury.

British friends (in addition to girlfriends)—if only we had been less busy and they had been less stand-offish. One very clear example of our good will toward the British people is the party we gave for 264 "war orphans" (evacuees as well as actual orphans) from local homes and asylums on Christmas Day, 1944.

> . . . this was during the re-supply missions to Bastogne; and the day before the party we were disappointed to learn that because of a mission on Christmas the party would have to be canceled. But that Christmas morning everything—the planes, the buildings, the runways—were covered with a heavy layer of rime ice. The mission had to be scrubbed until we could scrape and spray off that ice. This left enough time for the kids' party to go on again. We made frantic efforts to contact the orphanage and other places where they were staying and finally got through to them. I think the faces of those children when they were on the base that morning brought home to me more vividly than anything else the realization of why we were in the war. (Bill Westcott)

Around eleven o'clock a bunch of kids came to the Red Cross canteen. Jolly Alsdorf [radio operator] and I went up together. I picked out Zena, about five years old, as my little girl for the day. The girl Jolly picked out had had her father and mother killed in the London Blitz and was staying with Zena's parents—who also had been bombed out of their London home. At twelve we went to the mess hall for dinner. We had turkey and the works. The girls managed to eat the turkey and the ice cream but were too stuffed for anything else.

   I gave Zena the doll you sent me, and also the big can of mints, plus nine packs of gum to divide up with the other girls. When they left all the girls had a big box full of fruit and candy. And they saw Santa, who gave them each a book. We took our girls down to the barracks to show them off. (Ken De Blake, radio operator, written Dec. 30, 1944)

One of the reasons we remember those children so well is that everyone who had a camera, it seems, rushed to get it when they appeared and snapped photos—now to be found in so many of our World War II scrapbooks.

### Notes
1. In the first eleven weeks, the V-1s killed 6,200 civilians.
2. See Ambrose, *Pegasus*, p. 75. NAAFIs (Navy, Army and Air Force Institutes) were the British equivalent to our Red Cross canteens. NAAFIs were open to American GIs, too.

3. Average pay scales are hard to compute. These figures are for all branches of the U.S. and British Armies. The gap widened the lower the rank: for captains it was British, $101, Americans, $217 (more than double); for corporals it was British, $20, Americans, $77 (almost fourfold). Longmate, pp. 378–79.

4. There is much excellent material on this subject in Longmate, esp. chs. 23–25.

# 5. Assaulting
## To Normandy and Back

### D-Day: A day of revelations

There are two things one can say for certain about the paratrooper and glider operations of the Normandy invasion: they were the most critical airborne operations of the entire war and, in terms of their main purpose, they succeeded. Practically any other statement puts us in the realm of heated controversy, serious doubts, and unprovable claims.

Military historians provide mixed pictures of the value of Operation NEP-TUNE.[1] This may come as a surprise to those whose vision of paratrooper and glider fighting on D-Day comes from movies and television. Even today, troop carrier veterans are confused when they read criticisms of troop carrier in books based on reports made by paratroopers and glider soldiers. In sharp contrast, our own records, those compiled directly after each of the D-Day missions and on succeeding days, are permeated by such a strong sense of pride and accomplishment that a reader might wonder how the two groups of records could come out of the same war. How can different veterans of the same battle have such different perceptions of D-Day performance?

In those days, practically nothing was known about what a large-scale troop carrier operation *could* be expected to achieve. Today it is almost ludicrous to read about the contrasting expectations among planners of this battle. Some predicted overwhelming tragedy for all airborne troops and crews, and others could see on the airborne horizon nothing but "milk run" victories. The "doctrine" (theory) for airborne warfare was not yet formed. How could it be? Troop carrier itself was hardly six months old. No lessons drawn from experience were yet available for airborne missions that involved the transport and drop of three entire divisions. The combat paratroop and glider experiences before the tragic Sicily operations in 1943 were too small and too relatively uncomplicated to be truly useful to NEPTUNE planners. Sicily itself could be discounted by blaming it on a tragic change in the weather and on "friendly fire" by Allied vessels. Much of the complaints raised against troop carrier on D-Day and afterward, therefore, came from ignorance, that is, from inflated expectations of what the airborne arm *could* do. The "Longest Day" was to be a day of many revelations about the capabilities and problems of airborne warfare as it could be waged in the year 1944.

One measure of how little was known about the real possibilities of airborne warfare was a fantastically ambitious plan dreamed up in Washington by Army Air Forces staffers under the direction of no less than General Henry H. "Hap" Arnold, chief of the Air Forces, a plan sponsored enthusiastically by George C. Marshall, U.S. Chief of Staff. The plan proposed dropping the 101st and 82nd divisions, together with other Allied airborne forces, more than 40 miles inland from the English Channel, at Evreux, halfway between the French coast and Paris, where their mission would be to straddle the Seine River system and to block German forces in all of central France from counterattacking the Allied seaborne forces coming from Normandy. That such glider soldiers and para-troopers, equipped with light arms and no armor, supplied only from the air, would have to fight on their own possibly for weeks against armored and highly mobile German forces seems not to have fazed the generals who drew up and pushed what became known as "The Army Air Forces Plan." [2]

This proposal was not the worst example of ridiculously inflated expecta-tions. Some Allied planners actually suggested dropping airborne soldiers right in the heart of Paris, where—one must assume—the planners believed that the mere sight of such an awe-inspiring parachute drop would be enough to mes-merize Hitler into suing for peace.

At the opposite extreme from such optimism were the dire predictions of RAF Air Marshal Sir Trafford Leigh-Mallory, Eisenhower's head of OVER-LORD's air operations. On December 15, 1943, Eisenhower had removed opera-tional control (for both combat and training) from the Ninth Air Force and given it to the Allied Expeditionary Air Force under Leigh-Mallory. As D-Day ap-proached, Leigh-Mallory became more and more apprehensive about airborne casualties. After weighing what had happened in Crete and in Sicily, he decided that as many as 75 percent of the gliders and 50 percent of the troop carrier planes and their paratroopers would be shot out of the air before they reached their drop zones. He begged the airborne planners to cancel NEPTUNE com-pletely and to treat the 101st and 82nd as elite infantry, delivering them to the beaches by ship with other infantry divisions. To send them by air, he said, would be perpetrating "a futile slaughter of two fine American divisions." Leigh-Mallory insisted on presenting his case to Eisenhower personally, thereby straining to the utmost Eisenhower's ability to resist panic. [3]

Fortunately, Omar Bradley, head of the U.S. ground forces in OVER-LORD, told Eisenhower flatly that without the airborne assaults the beaches could not be secured; Eisenhower, fighting down a mounting tide of doubts and indecision, overruled Leigh-Mallory. By way of compromise, Leigh-Mallory got agreement for a plan to protect the first small glider missions and their tows by flying them at night, a few hours after the paratrooper drops (these operations, CHICAGO and DETROIT, arrived in Normandy around 4:00 a.m., June 6). Leigh-Mallory also refused to allow the main glider missions to arrive in full daylight, ruling that they had to come in just before dusk on June 6. This meant that paratroopers would have to fight *without* large numbers of gliderborne troopers and supporting artillery during all of D-Day.

The Cotentin peninsula of Normandy, the scene of Operation NEPTUNE's objectives, sticks out like a huge thumb from France's northern coast. At the eastern base of the thumb the beaches have a gradual rise, and the sand is firm enough to permit assault by the heaviest equipment needed by seaborne troops; here, also, the "Atlantic Wall" Field Marshal Erwin Rommel designed to thwart invasion was as yet less of an obstacle than elsewhere.

At the tip of the Cotentin peninsula, too, was Cherbourg—a good harbor, not as extensive as that of Calais (where Hitler believed invasion would come) but good enough to take the buildup in armor, men, and supplies the COSSAC planners (Chiefs of Staff, Supreme Allied Command) knew had to arrive quickly to protect the initial invaders against a massed German counterattack.

At our Membury base *five* squadrons (ninety planes) stood ready for our part in NEPTUNE. Our 436th Troop Carrier Group had borrowed the 85th Troop Carrier Squadron from the 437th TCG based at Ramsbury. The squadrons at Membury would have as their assignment dropping two complete battalions of the 101st Airborne Division: the first battalion of the 101st's 502nd Parachute Infantry Regiment and the 377th Parachute Field Artillery Battalion. Their drop zone, DZ "A," was about eight miles inland from the D-Day invasion beach that was code-named UTAH. The first thirty-six planes at Membury, those of the 82nd TCS and the 81st TCS, made up a "serial" committed to transporting the 502nd PIR's first battalion. The second serial's fifty-four planes—the 79th, 80th, and 85th TCSs—would carry the 101st's 377th PFAB, plus one plane with medics and five packed with ammunition. Much would depend on the twelve 75 mm howitzers (disassembled in pararacks under the planes and in door bundles inside the cabin) that were part of the 377th PFAB's equipment. Until the seaborne soldiers would be able to bring ashore their own artillery, the paratroopers' big guns would be the best protection available against counterattacking German tanks.

The five squadrons at Membury were to assemble into a formation over our base, join with others from the 53rd Troop Carrier Wing, and fly out over the English Channel. We were to fly southwest toward a turning point located about sixty miles west of the Normandy coastline. From there we would turn southeast, toward the west coast of the peninsula, and then directly eastward over the Cherbourg peninsula for about twenty-five miles.

All the squadrons from Membury made up the part of the NEPTUNE invasion that was code-named ALBANY, to be carried by the 436th and six other troop carrier groups. Additional troop carrier groups were committed to carry the 82nd Airborne Division; they were the part of the NEPTUNE operation that was code-named BOSTON.

Both ALBANY and BOSTON would be preceded by about half an hour by pathfinder planes whose troopers would try to locate the four DZs in NEPTUNE and set up radar beacons and lighted "T" signs. Each serial of thirty-six, forty-five, or fifty-four planes in ALBANY would be provided with navigators and be helped by beacon ships in the Channel and the pathfinder signals. Once the troopers jumped, our orders were to fly northeast out over the eastern coast of the Cherbourg peninsula, reassemble our squadron over the tiny St. Marcouf Islands in the English Channel, and return to Membury.

Just after midnight on the early morning of June 5, at the same time NEPTUNE and BOSTON were to be sent on their way, 6,000 British paratroopers and glider troopers of the 6th Airborne Division would head for the more easterly invasion beaches (JUNO, SWORD, and GOLD) in Normandy just north of the important city of Caen. General Sir Bernard Montgomery, in charge of all Allied OVERLORD ground forces under Eisenhower, believed he could capture Caen *in one day*—after which, he claimed, Caen could serve as the hinge for a huge Allied sweep up the Loire valley and on to Paris. In fact, Montgomery's troops needed more than forty days to take Caen, which by that time was more a heap of rubble than a city.

Three weeks before all the NEPTUNE plans were to be finalized as "field orders," bad news of nightmare proportions arrived. Allied intelligence, which had broken the German code, learned that the planned drop of the 82nd Division would be impossible. NEPTUNE had designated the middle of the Cotentin peninsula, near the town of St-Sauveur-le-Vicomte, as the drop area for the 82nd. The main idea (so impossibly ambitious in retrospect!) was to have the 82nd, driving east, connect with the 101st in a long line across the base of the peninsula, thereby preventing German forces caught inside from escaping south. But now intelligence knew that a body of first-class German troops, the 91st Division, had moved into the exact area where the 82nd was to be dropped. Requiring the 82nd Airborne to go through with the original plan was out of the question. NEPTUNE planning had to be wrung through some drastic changes. The DZ for the 82nd was moved ten miles east to an area close to that of the 101st, behind UTAH beach. New plans and objectives were hurriedly formulated for the 82nd troopers.[4]

Air Chief Marshal Sir Trafford Leigh-Mallory (hands on railing) addresses us, June 4, 1944, before the Normandy invasion.

John Webster, *far left,* poses with his D-Day crew: Whitney Brooks, co-pilot, Celar Obergfell, crew chief, and Harold "Shorty" Farr, radio operator. Three months later this crew was shot down over Holland.

As it turned out, the main task of both American paratrooper divisions was to backstop the seaborne invasion at UTAH beach, preventing—during the early invasion hours when the seaborne soldiers were clawing for a foothold—massive counterattacks by German forces stationed to the east and south. During the five hours or so between about 1:00 a.m., when they would jump, and "H-Hour" (dawn, actually 6:30), when the invaders hit the beaches, the paratroopers were ordered to capture certain bridges, destroy others, cut communication lines with interior Normandy, mop up pockets of German defenders, and capture the town of Ste-Mère-Eglise, a small but vital road center. Above all, the paratroopers were to seize control over four of the "exits" from the beaches, that is, roads headed west from UTAH that could take heavy traffic because they were built up on causeways over the sandy beach soil and the bogs and marshes behind them. It was at the western end of these causeways that the seaborne troops would join up with the airborne troops, once the Germans caught in the middle were overcome.

Some horrible flaws remained in NEPTUNE's planning. But (and there is always a "but" in D-Day discussions!) nobody can deny that the harassed and anxious planners at COSSAC did what they could to put together an operation that most of them thought at least had a good chance. They certainly intended to protect the extremely vulnerable troop carrier planes and gliders from a "friendly fire" disaster like the one in Sicily. "Friendly fire" was even more of a potential danger over Normandy: the NEPTUNE planes would have to fly over hundreds of Allied ships preparing to bombard the Normandy coast and deliver seaborne troops; and each of these ships, it could be expected, had its complement of nervous and itchy-fingered gunners. After some disgusting haggling with British and American naval commanders, COSSAC planners managed to obtain what looked like firm assurances that if troop carrier planes stayed within a ten-mile corridor along the designated air invasion route they would be in a "fire-free" zone, that is, one in which sailors would not shoot even if they suspected that some approaching planes were German. Furthermore, the invasion planners ordered that British bombers drop masses of shredded aluminum foil ("window") near Le Havre and Boulogne which would register on German radar as an invasion of a huge number of planes—far away from the true DZs.

Ironically, the OVERLORD planners were less worried at this time about Germans shooting down the transport planes than they were about British and American naval gunners. What a ghastly massacre it would have been if a few squadrons of German night fighters had been loosed inside the NEPTUNE skytrain, with its slow, unarmored, and unarmed planes lumbering along in tight formation! The planners had the right priorities here: by this time the Allies had won virtual air superiority over northwest France. With our own fighters patrolling overhead, we expected that relatively few German fighters could reach us.

## Securing the base

During all this planning and theorizing, we in the 81st TCS were bringing our-selves up to the highest possible level of preparedness. The more pessimistic fellows in our outfit were voicing their fears: compared with what we faced in the coming invasion, they said, missions of Eighth and Ninth Air Force bombers would look like Sunday School outings. This was only the wildest sort of guess-ing. What we did know was that we had benefited from fifteen months of the most thorough training: in tight formation flying, day and night, in glider tows (even double glider tows), in paratrooper drops simulating actual missions—some of which were reported as unqualifiedly successful—and in navigation and communication exercises. We were convinced that the entire outcome of the invasion, perhaps that of World War II itself, might well hinge on whether troop carrier succeeded in delivering the airborne troopers to where they could head off German counterattacks against the beaches.

All of our training, all of our indoctrination, and all of our pride in our own efficiency and dedication were on the line. No matter how devastating the ene-my's fire, we were told, our job was to drop the paratroopers and tow in the gliders. No matter how badly we were hit, as long as our planes were flyable, we were to keep on toward the DZs. We believed we could and would do just that.

Those of us in the 81st TCS regarded ourselves as expendable, in the best sense of the word. If any among us felt that it was unjust that we should be expendable, or that we could not live up to such high standards, he kept that idea to himself. We believed we were not only a good outfit but also a lucky one. We had lost not a single one of our crews during our training in the U.S. and in Britain. Our feeling that we were not only good but lucky was reinforced by many close shaves during the last months of training. For example, in Operation BUMBLE BEE, one of the invasion training maneuvers back in late May, Arthur Swasey crashed his plane while landing; his ship exploded and burned on the runway but none of the crew was hurt.

There seems no question about it: morale in the 81st Troop Carrier Squad-ron just before D-Day was high.[5] In his entries for the month of May, our Squad-ron diarist wrote:

> It is quite apparent that every man in the outfit is not only willing, but well trained for his part in things to come. It would seem that such a self-satisfied estimation of one's task would lead to a laxity in regards to further training; but the monotony has long since passed and it has now become more of a habit. Thus on D-Day nothing should be new or unexpected.

Certainly one additional reason for the aircrews' high morale was that on June 3 crew chiefs and radio operators were briefed together with navigators and pilots. After months of the wildest speculations about where we were to be employed in the invasion of Europe, the secret was out; and, like the officers, the rest of us in the plane crews were to be regarded as important enough to be given the whole picture and trustworthy enough to be keepers of that awesome secret. Officers and enlisted men of the aircrews of all four squadrons in the 436th Group trooped together into our briefing theater, where the long-secret maps were unveiled to all eyes; all the navigation, radio, and weather details were spelled out; and all the danger points were indicated. We were told exactly where we were going, exactly what we were doing. We knew about D-Day three days before Hitler did; and to be made recipients of such earthshaking news made the enlisted men in the crews feel even more proud of their coming role. In the face of the coming danger our individuality, our human equality, was recognized.

Such openness and trust, however, was not extended to the entire squadron. The 436th TCG base at Membury was completely buttoned up; no leaves, no outgoing mail, no personal telephoning. Combat crews were segregated from the rest of the squadron; non-combat personnel (including officers) moved out of the crews' barracks, which were then kept under twenty-four-hour guard and even surrounded by barbed wire. The combat NCOs were directed to eat with the combat officers in the officers mess: a perfect opportunity for sardonic cracks. "The condemned men ate a hearty meal." The day before D-Day, we had fresh eggs—a wonderful change from the powdered variety—and pancakes for breakfast; luscious roast chicken for lunch; and a big steak for supper.

Favoring the combat crewmen this way could not help but draw an irritating and, in many ways, unfair line between the aircrews and everybody else. However, the security precautions involved in this did work: most of the ground crew personnel had absolutely no idea of where NEPTUNE was headed until the planes were actually in the air.

> You moved from one building to another together, you ate together, all under the eye of the military police. I had a group of guys with me guarding one of the gates on the main highway running through our Membury camp. Suddenly a British car just zipped right through the gate without stopping or answering a challenge. So we telephoned and got a motorcycle MP to overtake that car and bring it back to the gate. When the driver of that car came back, it turned out he was a member of British intelligence; and he had been ordered by Eisenhower to do just that, with the idea of testing out our base security! I had a 45 pistol on me; and when this episode was over, John Bohan [Squadron Intelligence Officer] asked me how come I hadn't

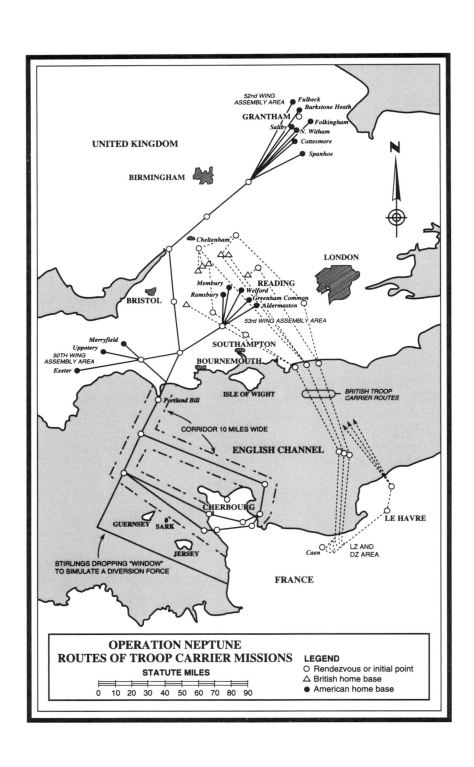

**OPERATION NEPTUNE
ROUTES OF TROOP CARRIER MISSIONS**

STATUTE MILES

0 10 20 30 40 50 60 70 80 90

**LEGEND**

○ Rendezvous or initial point
△ British home base
● American home base

shot at this guy. I had to confess that I had completely forgotten I had a gun. (Louis Kramer, at that time Assistant Operations Officer)

Another morale builder was the visit to the base by some high brass, particularly General Paul Williams, CG of the entire IX Troop Carrier Command (not related to our own Colonel Adriel Williams, head of our 436th Group). Two British Air Chief Marshals, Sir Arthur Tedder, Eisenhower's Deputy Supreme Commander, and Sir Trafford Leigh-Mallory, also visited. Leigh-Mallory gave us a veddy, veddy British harangue. Finally, on June 5, Eisenhower himself came to visit. Although "Ike" was there mainly to pump up the spirits of the 101st paratroopers we would haul, we nevertheless felt that some of the honor of his visit rightfully belonged to us.

Anyone who knows anything at all about D-Day knows that NEPTUNE almost did not take place. June 4, 1944, had been its designated "Departure-Day," but meteorological forecasts for June 5 predicted waves on the Normandy beaches so high that the landing craft would be swamped and winds so violent that paratroopers would be in danger of getting whipped right out of their chute shrouds when they jumped.

On June 1 the 101st paratroopers had already begun to arrive at our base—and they were promptly sealed off. They bivouacked in wooded lots away from the runways, and their tents were surrounded by barbed wire and guards. In Britain's ports, troopships were already being loaded with heavily equipped and mightily apprehensive soldiers. From the more northern ports some ships actually put out to sea on June 4—the waves in this rough weather adding to the misery of the soldiers.

In Membury, and at air bases throughout Britain, everyone became a painter, putting the famous D-Day stripes, three white and two black, around the fuselages and wings of every plane and glider. These were visual recognition signals—more protection from "friendly fire" from our naval convoys. Including bombers, fighters, transports, and gliders, some 10,000 aircraft were striped in a single evening.

Then, at 4:15 a.m. on June 4, only twenty hours before our planes were scheduled to take off, the bad weather forced Eisenhower to postpone OVERLORD—at least for twenty-four hours. Francis Farley, our Operations Officer, came around to our barracks to tell us NEPTUNE was off. That news was received with extremely mixed feelings. Meanwhile, the troopships already at sea had to turn around and steam away from Normandy.

No amount of imagination and sympathetic understanding can capture the agony in Eisenhower's mind at that time.[6] If he canceled the ponderous invasion, secrecy as to the actual landing beaches—given all the people who were now in the know—would have been impossible to maintain. He had been advised that the beach tides and other factors would not be favorable again for another two weeks. Battle commanders, whipped up to high levels of mental readiness, might have reacted negatively to a cancellation. The Soviet Union, pressing so stridently for a "second front" to take the pressure off her own armies and reduce her huge losses on the eastern front, might have concluded that the Allies were untrustworthy and even might have tried to work out a separate peace with the Nazis.

Six hours after its postponement, however, the invasion was back on. The beach landings would take place one day later, the morning of June 6. Meteorologists had been able to predict a definite but limited easing of the bad weather for the two days of June 6 and June 7, to be followed by another bad turn after June 8.

This foul-up because of weather may have had unexpected good results. Weather patterns in this part of Europe move from northwest to southeast; thus, while the weather was getting steadily clearer over southern England and the Channel, to the southeast, in Normandy and most of northern France, the weather on the night of June 5–6 was terrible. Most German garrisons relaxed in their barracks, confident that no invading planes or ships could be expected in the very near future. The Nazi commanders were caught with their Channel patrol boats at anchor and most of their reconnaissance planes in hangars. Our first troop carrier planes, undetected even by radar until they arrived, were able to follow the moving band of partially clearing weather right across from southern England into Normandy.

Our final briefing was at 2000 hours [that is, 8:00 p.m. British Double Summer Time], just a few hours before we were to take off. There were guards all around the Group briefing theater, and you had to show your credentials to get in. I saw how flushed and bright-eyed everybody looked— tense but not jittery. The bulletin board on the stage seemed covered with maps and photos. First to speak: Operations, with the essentials about mission objectives. Then Navigation: courses, beacons, turning points, our DZ. Then Communications: what frequencies to monitor, the recall message that would abort the mission and turn us around back to England. Absolute and unquestioned radio silence to be maintained; radar and radio aids; what to do if forced to ditch in the Channel. Then Weather: clearing, full moon, scattered clouds. Finally Intelligence, at the maps: "You can expect this sort of antiaircraft fire *here*, and *there*, but don't worry about German fighters; there are concentrations of Krauts *here* and *there*; use this road for a check point as you come in to the DZ; before you leave this hall you *must* turn in every scrap of identification you have on you except your dog tags; if forced down, retain your status as a soldier and fight your way to the Allied lines."

Thirty minutes to go: Colonel Williams on the runway at his plane before take-off for Normandy. In the plane's door is Major Bryan, our Group Intelligence Officer.

Loaded-down troopers are helped in the jump door just before the Normandy assault begins; the "invasion stripes" recently painted on all our planes and gliders show behind them.

We went directly from the briefing theater to our planes. The troopers, sitting on the runway near the plane door, looked sullen and resentful, and made a couple of bitter cracks to Obermark [crew chief] and me. We didn't blame them. . . . (Marty Wolfe, radio operator; written June 15, 1944)

The paratroopers had blackened their faces for the coming assault. When we walked up, the jumpmaster had them stand and strap on all their extremely heavy equipment. By the time a trooper had on all his weapons, his two chutes, and other equipment, he was so loaded down (with around 150 pounds) that we had to help push some of them up the stairs into the plane. Before they boarded, a few paratroopers gave away their British money—something of no value to them, they thought, in France.

### "This is it!"

No brilliant evocation of poetry, in fact, none of the arts, can convey the emotions we felt when the propellers of our Squadron's planes started to turn over. It was 2200 hours (10:00 p.m., British Double Summer Time), June 5, 1944, a moment fixed forever in memory. The immensity of our commitment was filling our minds, making each action, each thought, seem intensely meaningful.

The lead planes—those of the 82nd TCS—began to taxi down the runway. At their head was our Col. Adriel Williams. We in the 81st TCS followed the 82nd: these two squadrons made up the first serial from Membury, carrying the 1st Battalion of the 502nd PIR. The paratroopers on my plane seemed relaxed, almost sleepy; many of them had taken more than one Seconal tablet to ward off motion sickness. The rain had stopped but the runways were still wet. Looking out, we could barely see our dim blue formation lights—the sky was getting brighter as the moon began to push through the clouds. The roar of all those propellers filled the damp night air. At 2230 hours David Brack led the 81st TCS off. Our part in the invasion of Nazi Europe had begun.

Weeks of training in night formation flying paid off. In spite of the huge number of planes in the air and the terrible danger of collision in the darkness, we formed up a perfect V-of-Vs as we joined the rest of the airborne armada. Besides other groups in our 53rd Troop Carrier Wing, all carrying paratroopers of the 101st Division (Operation ALBANY), the invasion corridor was being traveled by the 50th Troop Carrier Wing, carrying the rest of the 101st paratroopers. The 52nd Wing, transporting three regiments of the 82nd Division (code-named Operation BOSTON) traveled the same route. This monstrous skytrain—both BOSTON and ALBANY—contained 821 C-47s carrying troopers and 104 more towing gliders. The British 6th Airborne Division was also headed out over the Channel, but on another route. All together, within the next two hours some 13,000 troopers were scheduled to jump or glide into Normandy.

Everybody in the two serials flying from Membury was headed for drop zone "A," an area about one and a half miles by two miles in the Normandy hedgerow country between Ste-Mère-Eglise and the marshes just in back of the UTAH invasion beach. Other serials were headed for five other drop zones south and west of ours.

Historians of D-Day agree that up to the point where we crossed the western shore of the Cotentin peninsula and headed toward the DZ, the pilots of AL-BANY flew a flawless formation under difficult circumstances: "It was a tribute to training that . . . the outward flight west of the Cherbourg peninsula was executed according to plan and without incident." This is the judgment of the official Air Forces history; other historians and journalists seem agreed on this point.[7]

As we turned southeast from our corridor over the Channel and toward Normandy the feeling grew that this monstrously complicated operation was clicking along perfectly. This feeling was strengthened when we saw that the anti-aircraft fire from the German-held Channel Islands (Guernsey and Jersey) was falling short—as we had been told it would.

A few minutes later, as we reached the western coastline, disaster loomed up. We slammed headlong into a dense cloud bank. Nothing had prepared us for this. The weather briefing had not foreseen it; our flight over the Channel had encountered only scattered clouds. The cloud bank was thicker in some spots than others. For some of us it was so thick that it was as if we had suddenly stopped flying through air and were now flying through grayish soup.[8] The pathfinders had also flown through these clouds; but because of strict radio silence imposed on all of us they had not warned anybody of this terrible danger.

Flying in almost zero visibility, practically wingtip to wingtip, pilots suddenly had to decide how to save their crews, paratroopers, and planes. Immediately, pilots flying in the number two and three position in each V pulled away back and to either the right or left to minimize the imminent danger of colliding with their leader. Some pilots climbed up, getting out of the cloud bank at about 2,000 feet. Some pushed their planes' noses down and broke out below the clouds at around 500 feet. A few bulled their way through at 700 feet, at the altitude they had been flying before hitting the clouds; and all miraculously escaped smashing into other planes. In a few tragic moments prospects for a concentrated paratrooper drop had been demolished. Meanwhile, our DZs were coming up in ten or twelve minutes.

A terrible responsibility now fell upon the shoulders of every pilot and (in planes that had them) every navigator. Although the murderous cloud bank

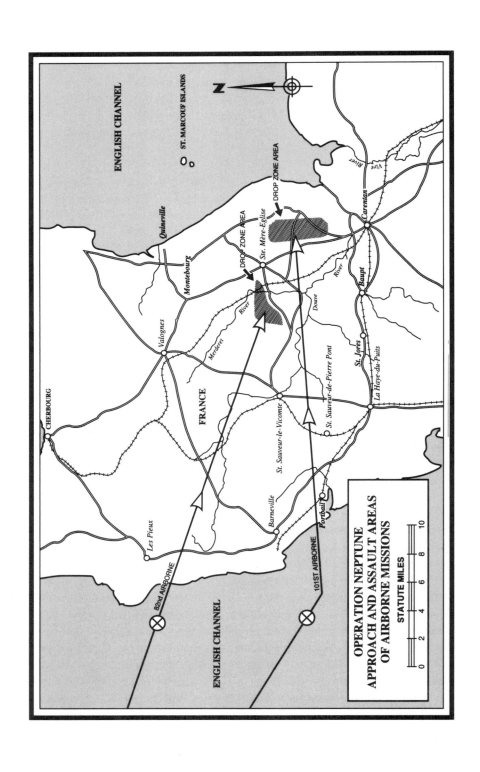

OPERATION NEPTUNE
APPROACH AND ASSAULT AREAS
OF AIRBORNE MISSIONS

STATUTE MILES

0    2    4    6    8    10

thinned out as we flew east over the Cotentin peninsula—so that soon we could begin to see some features on the ground—each pilot knew that in the preceding formation break-up he could have strayed many miles off course. The Cotentin peninsula was only twenty-three miles wide. We had about six or seven minutes before the DZ was supposed to come up. Decisions had to be made quickly, quickly! Each pilot—now essentially on his own—had to climb (or descend) to 700 feet, the best height for paratrooper jumping; and he had to slow down to 110 miles an hour to avoid putting too much stress on the opening chutes.

Looking down you could begin to spot a few landmarks—a town, a railroad, a river—that might or might not correspond to the check points you had been told to look for around your DZ. As if things were not bad enough, we now saw that the "Eureka-Rebecca" radar beacons were not working as they were supposed to in order to guide individual planes to the correct DZ; and crews of the few planes that had the more sophisticated "GEE" radar location device could not make sense of their readings. The pathfinders had not been given enough time to get down on the ground, find the right locations, and set up their holophane "T" lights and radar beacons. All that remained for most of the pilots and navigators was to try to recognize some landmark in the darkness—and give troopers the green light when there was a reasonable chance of their jumping close to our DZ "A."

And now, in my plane, the red light at the door is on: four minutes to go! The paratrooper jumpmaster yells out "Stand up! Hook up! Sound off for equipment check!" The troopers yell back, in sequence from the rear, "Sixteen OK! Fifteen OK! Fourteen OK! . . ." Then the jumpmaster screams out "STAND IN THE DOOR!" and the troopers squeeze forward against each other, their right hands on the shoulders of the man in front. One last jumpmaster yell: "ARE WE READY? ARE WE FUCKING-A READY!?" There is no answering yell; everybody is waiting for the door light to change from red to green.

Mercifully, up to this point the paratroopers had no way of knowing we were in big trouble. But now pilots in some planes, already badly rattled, began to see flak and small arms fire coming up at them. They dove and twisted under the upcoming arcs of tracer bullets while the heavily laden troopers struggled to stay on their feet. Some planes whipped around badly, forcing troopers down on their knees. "Barf-buckets" were knocked over and vomit spilled out, causing a dangerously slippery floor. Crew chiefs and radio operators in the rear of the planes screamed up at the pilots to keep the planes steady.

> Watching the tracers come up at us made the hairs on the back of my neck feel as though they were standing straight up . . . it's still hard to laugh about things like that.
>
> These things are stamped indelibly in my mind: the rattle of flak fragments against our plane; the sight of flak and tracers above us, some seem-

ing right on the mark for planes in front of us; the absolute stark terror in some paratroopers' eyes, their vomiting into their helmets and forgetting to empty these helmets out when it came time to "Stand Up! Hook Up!" as they prepared to make possibly their final jump. (Ben Obermark, crew chief)

When the pilots finally snapped on the green light it must have been a kind of momentary relief to the paratroopers, as they went out the jump door, heading for uncertain but presumably solid ground beneath.

After we were in those clouds a few minutes some bright searchlights came on; the way they lighted up the clouds almost blinded me. Flak and tracers were everywhere. One of our squadron's planes was taking such wild evasive action that he almost drove me into the ground. And that so-and-so wasn't even part of my flight—which shows how big a piece of sky he was using up! It took every bit of my strength and know-how, plus that of our co-pilot, Doug Mauldin, to prevent a collision. (Don Skrdla, pilot)

The instant before the lead trooper jumped, the heavy door bundles had to be pushed out. In the plane piloted by Don Skrdla the awkward bundles jammed the door space with fiendish perversity, thwarting every effort of the crew and the troopers to push them out.[9] There would have been no time for Skrdla to have dropped his troopers short of the English Channel. He flew out over the water, turned right, came back over land again, and made another pass at his DZ—but the door bundles were still malevolently stuck. Skrdla had to make yet a third pass before the bundles could be unjammed and his troopers could get out. For this exhibition of skill and cool judgment he was awarded the Distinguished Flying Cross, the only one granted to our Squadron for this mission.

Asked what was going through his mind at that time, Skrdla said, "Nothing much, apart from how scared I was"; and he claimed much of the credit should go to the crew chief, Dick Nice, the one who managed to unjam that door. Pressed further, Skrdla added, "It just wasn't in the book for me to go back with paratroopers in my plane." After his plane was headed home over the Channel, Skrdla got a shock when he looked back and saw one of his passengers still sitting there, but it turned out he was not a paratrooper but a newspaper reporter who had had no intention whatever of jumping.

Francis Farley [Operations Officer of the 81st TCS] was the leader of the second flight of nine planes. When we went through that famous cloud bank that hung over the Cherbourg peninsula, we were in a V-of-Vs of nine planes. Col. Brack was the leader of the other flight. As soon as Brack saw that cloud bank he went down so as to get through it; he figured he would still have enough altitude for the paratroopers underneath it.

But Farley, for some reason, thought he saw Brack turn to the left. So he also took his serial down under the cloud bank and turned our planes to the left. But we went too far north; and as a result we came out very near the top of the peninsula. We found ourselves only about five miles from the port of Cherbourg; and of course immediately we ran into heavy flak and other ground fire.

When we started to receive AA fire we were at a railroad junction some ten miles south of Cherbourg. Farley asked for a new heading to the DZ. When we turned to a 180 degree heading, we were over land; we did not fly over the coast, but sighted some burning buildings at Ste-Mère-Eglise and dropped our paratroop stick. By this time only our 3-ship "V" remained; the others had lost us in the descent through the undercast.

We had hits in our vertical stabilizer. There was a hole big enough for a man to crawl through, but fortunately none of the main controls were hit. We also took hits in one of the main gas tanks and lost a substantial portion of our fuel.

It was a close thing getting back to base. We were coming in with the indicator showing no fuel in the tanks. As we made our final approach, Lt. Greg Wolf, just ahead of us, landed and almost immediately went up on his nose because his tires had been shot out during the drop. We managed to pull up into the air just enough to clear his plane and immediately landed at a nearby base. When we got out the smell of gas was overpowering; it had sprayed over the entire fuselage. (Bob MacInnes, navigator)

---

In addition to the big hole in the vertical stabilizer in Farley's plane, we got our left wingtip shot off, and there was a really big hole in the fuselage where the door load had been before it went out. This must have been from one of those small explosive shells the Germans were using. It sure made a mess of the floor and a part of the side wall. I also got a little piece in my wrist, but I didn't know anything about this until two days later when it began to get sore and infected. Doc Coleman dug it out with a large hypodermic needle.

If those shell fragments had hit there *before* the door bundle went out, it would have been good-bye. The door load, all 1100 pounds of it, consisted of mortars and mortar ammunition. It had been resting on the floor directly above where the shell fragments came in.

The door load and the first paratrooper went out of the door as one. Everyone else in the stick went out in seconds. Major Farley acknowledged my yell of "All out!" and made a sharp turn to get away as I began to pull in the static lines. These were fifteen foot long tapes made of heavy webbing that were attached to the parachute rip panel and pulled open the chute when the paratrooper jumped. So there were eleven sets of static lines plus the two from the door load. Getting that sort of stuff inside the plane was not an easy thing to do. Before I got them half way in, the navigator, MacInnes, and Chick Knight, the radio operator, had to come back and give me a hand. (Howard "Pat" Bowen, crew chief)

---

After the drop we had some bad moments. Of course by then we were all alone. Out over the Channel I called "Darky" [a British direction-finding station on the coast] to get a steer home. The fix they gave me didn't seem right; but I figured they knew what they were doing. I made about a 180-degree turn; but pretty soon I saw all those lights and gun flashes, and, my God, I was damned near over Cherbourg again! So then I turned around again and headed back home. By the time I got in, they'd given us up for lost. (William "Rip" Collins, pilot)

In my plane, piloted by Jack Wallen, we began to yell and thump each other on the back as soon as the wheels touched the runway at Membury. The release from that frightful tension made us all a little giddy.

Crews walked in a glow across the field toward the Operations room. One plane after another came in, most with little damage. When the last plane's wheels touched down, about 4:00 a.m. (June 6), the crews all broke out in crazy yells and whistles. For this, our first combat mission—and a terribly dangerous one—we had sent out eighteen planes and returned eighteen planes. The contrast between what we had been led to expect in the way of "expendability" and what actually happened for this mission was stupefying.[10]

We got boisterous, almost hysterical, congratulations from the men who had been waiting for our return. While we were being debriefed we were given a medicinal double shot of rye by Jesse Coleman, our Flight Surgeon, plus the usual post-flight coffee and sandwiches. Later we all trooped over to the Group theater for a critique by Colonel Williams. He told us that *none* of the Group's ninety planes had been shot down, though three planes had been hard hit by bullets or flak. Colonel Williams told us he was proud of us. Who could blame us for thinking that the first D-Day mission had been a great success?

We were not alone in this delusion; the diarist of the 82nd TCS wrote, "The mission was successful—all planes dropped on or near the 'T' and there was very little opposition—some small arms fire and almost no flak." The diarist for the 79th TCS stated, "On this mission all planes discharged their troopers over, or at least very near the appointed 'DZ' and returned without loss of either personnel or aircraft."[11]

It wasn't until much later, when we heard rumors of complaints from paratroopers dropped far from their assigned DZ, that we began to question our performance.

## Notes

1. NEPTUNE was the code name for the assault phases (including the airborne operations) of Operation OVERLORD, the total invasion plan.

2. Craven and Cate, p. 71.

3. Ambrose, *Eisenhower*, pp. 406–7; Weigley, pp. 74–75; Howarth, p. 21. Hoyt Vandenberg, Leigh-Mallory's American deputy (later to become chief of the Ninth Air Force) was also opposed to the airborne operations. After witnessing a glider training maneuver, Leigh-Mallory relaxed somewhat his opposition to the use of gliders. Brereton, diary entry for May 6, 1944.

4. Why were airborne soldiers not dropped behind OMAHA beach, too? Primarily because much of the terrain behind that beach was just right for tanks, which practically would have invited the German armor to counterattack and overwhelm the paratroopers there.

5. General Brereton, commander of the Ninth Air Force, assured General Arnold that "morale could not be higher" for all of Troop Carrier Command. See his diary entry for May 20, 1944, p. 277.

6. Eisenhower, *Crusade*, 1948, p. 246. See also Ambrose, *Eisenhower*, pp. 413–18; Howarth, pp. 20–24.

7. Craven and Cate, p. 188.

8. James Gavin (at the time commanding a regiment of the 82nd Airborne Division) who was flying in another serial and standing in the open door of his plane, reports that he could not even see its wingtip. Gavin, 1979, pp. 113–14. We know now that the cloud bank was thick in some areas over the western half of the peninsula, that is, the first seven or eight minutes of our route across the peninsula, and that there were some fog banks over the Merderet River.

9. There were several other instances of door bundles hampering jumps: see Koskimaki, p. 258.

10. There were no serious 436th TCG crew casualties in this first NEPTUNE mission. The entire Troop Carrier Command lost only twenty-three out of its 925 planes on this first mission. This was a much smaller percentage of casualties than those suffered by the fighter and bomber groups of the Eighth and Ninth Air Forces, each mission, in the month before D-Day. The only casualties in the 81st TCS for *all* the NEPTUNE missions were four glider pilots who were wounded badly enough to be hospitalized.

11. 79th and 82nd TCS, hist. narr. for June 1944. The 53rd TCW report "D-Day: 53rd Troop Carrier Wing, 6 June 1944," stated: "Preliminary reports indicated that the 438th, 436th, and 435th units which participated in the paradrop, all dropped on the assigned DZ's."

# 6. Reinforcing
## Our Normandy Glider Mission

### Pre-dawn glider missions

Between 4:00 a.m. on D-Day, when we in the 81st TCS returned from Operation ALBANY, and 6:00 p.m. that same day, our aircrews were able to relax. Air Chief Marshal Sir Trafford Leigh-Mallory had ruled that glider missions must never be risked in broad daylight. Therefore our Squadron's second Normandy mission, part of Operation ELMIRA, had to wait until dusk began to settle over "the longest day." Other troop carrier groups, however, flew nighttime glider missions during the early morning of D-Day. These other groups, the 434th at Aldermaston and the 437th at Ramsbury, were releasing their gliders over Normandy around 4:00 a.m. on D-Day just when the last of our returning 81st TCS planes was arriving back at our Membury base after having delivered paratroopers. These pre-dawn glider missions were code-named Operations CHICAGO and DETROIT.

In airborne warfare history, glider missions such as CHICAGO and DETROIT are known as re-supply missions. But the term *re-supply* calls up images of more or less cut-and-dried transportation of goods from point A to point B. This gives an entirely inadequate picture of World War II glider re-supply missions. These were *combat* missions, that precipitated their airborne troopers and glider pilots into desperate battles. And these operations were awaited by the NEPTUNE commanders with the highest degree of apprehension. All the D-Day glider missions, both pre-dawn and dusk, were vital for the success of the invasion. During all of D-Day, and for at least one addditional day, it was not at all clear whether the 82nd Airborne and the 101st Airborne Divisions could hold their positions, let alone take the remainder of their objectives.

To make matters worse, Allied commanders in Britain, during most of D-Day, had no way of knowing what was facing the airborne divisions. Communication snafus prevented paratroopers from making radio contact with England. Fortunately, NEPTUNE's planners had assumed that the paratroopers certainly would need more medics, ammunition, and especially artillery.

One of the most important goals of all D-Day glider missions was to deliver

Thayer Bonecutter and Richard Farnsworth pose in front of their Horsa glider. They are showing their Thompson submachine guns.

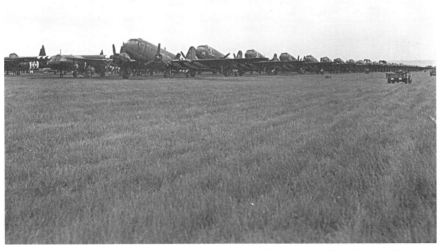

Planes and gliders lined up in Membury for our first glider mission into Normandy.

the 37 mm antitank guns and 75 mm pack howitzers. All that paratroopers had to protect themselves against German tanks were grenades, antitank mines, machine guns, and bazookas—bazookas which had proved to be pitifully inadequate against Panzer armor plate.

The timing of CHICAGO and DETROIT represents one of the more costly mistakes Air Chief Marshal Sir Trafford Leigh-Mallory saddled on IX Troop Carrier Command. Glider pilots in these operations were now to land in tiny fields surrounded by hedgerows, in the middle of a raging battle, with no longer any hope of surprising the Germans.[1] More serious was that many of the glider pilots now being ordered into battle had had no training whatsoever in night formation flying. Col. Mike Murphy, chief spokesman for the glider pilots, objected violently.[2] Leigh-Mallory kept insisting that to fly gliders in the daytime over German-held territory would result in at least 75 percent losses. Eisenhower felt he had to accept this verdict. About the only concession Leigh-Mallory made was to allow glider pilots in CHICAGO and DETROIT to use Waco CG-4As, with which they were more familiar, instead of the heavier British Horsa gliders (Horsas could carry about twice the payload of the Wacos).

Under these circumstances, the 434th's and 437th's CHICAGO and DE-TROIT operations during the early morning of June 6 proved marvelously lucky. Almost all of these gliders had to crash-land into their LZs rather than stop in a normal way, but amazingly few lives were lost.[3] The famous "Rommel's asparagus" (tall poles planted upright in fields Germans had guessed would be chosen as glider landing zones) were only the worst of the hazards facing these glider pilots. Gliders landed in trees, in swamps, or crashed into glider-trap ditches dug across the LZ; but artillery and supplies rescued from the crashed gliders provided precious help for the paratroopers.

### Operation ELMIRA

Fortunately for us in the 81st, we were assigned to operation ELMIRA, for which Leigh-Mallory had made the grudging concession that we could arrive over Normandy just before nightfall. He thought the gathering darkness would give glider pilots and their passengers at least some protection from the Germans. At the same time, presumably, there would still be enough light for the glider pilots to pick the least harmful landing sites.

As it turned out, glider trains coming in at dusk provided the Germans with excellent targets. For ELMIRA, the 81st TCS's first combat glider mission, we were going with heavy plywood Horsa gliders, not Wacos. The strain of tugging those heavy Horsa gliders turned the flame dampeners on the C-47 engines white-hot, making them stand out brilliantly against the darkening sky.

One welcome change was that in ELMIRA, instead of flying over the Cotentin peninsula from west to east, as we had on the paratrooper mission ALBANY, we were ordered to come in over the LZs from the east coast, directly over the UTAH beaches, in order to fly the shortest distance over German defenses. Both the 435th and the 436th Groups participated in ELMIRA; we in the 81st Squadron contributed eleven planes and fourteen gliders to the operation. ELMIRA was carrying the 82nd Division's 319th and 320th Field Artillery Battalions, including thirty-one jeeps, fifty tons of ammunition and other supplies, and two 75 mm guns.

> My co-pilot James J. DiPietro and I went to the flight line to meet our load of glider troops. Our "bird" was a giant glider, the British Horsa. We loaded up thirty troopers and their gear, plus boxes of anti-tank mines which were lashed to the floor in the aisle. I glanced back down the aisle into the blackened faces of the airborne troops, all looking so competent and confident, and I breathed a silent prayer. I made a last-minute check of my controls, and just as we started to roll, J. J. [DiPietro] gave me the "thumbs up" sign. As we reached proper air speed I could feel the positive responses. Picking up speed the rushing wind sounds increased. I eased back the yoke raising the nose wheel off the runway, and held it steady until reaching the ninety miles per hour take-off speed. Additional back-pressure of the yoke lifted the glider and we were airborne, but the tow plane was still running on the ground. We assumed our position behind and above him and at one hundred miles per hour he lifted off and began a slow climb. At five thousand feet we joined in line with the stream of other aircraft and headed for the English Channel. (Ben Ward, glider pilot)

As soon as we in the 81st TCS planes in ELMIRA passed over the English coast and headed south over the Channel, we were presented with a sight that was almost too stunning to take in. Ships and ships and ships crowding in toward the beach; as far as the eye could see, ships. Of every sort, size, and shape. The bigger ships were blinking furiously to each other with signal lamps. Before we could catch our breath, it seemed, it was 2250 hours (10:50 p.m. Double British Summer time), and we turned to the right toward our gliders' landing zone in back of the invasion beaches.

As we cut in to the Normandy coast, the Navy guns opened up—big puffs of blinding orange, followed by gushes of red on the land. LSTs (landing ships for tanks) were working on the beach. Big fires, houses burning—flashes of artillery fire along the beaches, long streams of tracers, apparently coming from a mile or so in back of the beach, arcing up into the darkening sky—and, in the distance, the green-lit "T" that was set up as the center of our LZ.

We were only 500 feet above the beach coming in; it was easy to see individual trucks and jeeps dashing about. Smoky black bursts of flak now seemed to be filling the sky. Practically uninterrupted arcs of tracers, red and yellow, came up toward us with fascinating deliberation and then fell away in graceful curves.

We were in echelons of four to the right, and our plane was an element leader. It was part of my job to signal back to the gliders with a red light four minutes out, and a green light over the LZ, where they would cut off. I climbed on the wooden stool in the companionway and poked my head into the plexiglass astrodome. To our right was the French coast coming up—still plenty visible in the gathering dark. Stretched out in front of me was an unbelievable panorama—hundreds and hundreds of ships crowding in toward the beach. Right then I wouldn't have given up my place in the astrodome for anything. Over Normandy, while the rational part of my mind was trying to take it all in, the emotional side was telling me that men were dying down there.

"Red Light!" I beamed the Aldis lamp back at my element and turned front again. I was mesmerized by the fire coming up at our planes—couldn't take my eyes off it. I could see the bullets finding the range of the leading elements. I felt right then that in a few moments I would be dead. No panic: just the mind-filling recognition of what had to be. I stood there rubbing my head with the Aldis lamp and hoping it would come painlessly and wondering how Dotty would take the news. One consolation: it seemed to me that most of the gliders from the leading elements were going to make it down near the LZ.

"Green Light!" and in that very instant I could hear bullets hitting the ship, a rather dry sound like peas being dropped into a pot. Our plane lurched forward on being released from the glider, and we banked sharply down and to the right, under the arcs of tracers. With the realization that we were still flying, I began to get really scared. Now that we had a chance for life I was afraid we wouldn't make it. But after that few minutes in the thick of battle all we had facing us was an uneventful, practically routine flight home.

No yelling, no rejoicing this time when we touched down at Membury. Just a quiet, heavy sensation: "Well, that's two out of the way." We went outside with flashlights to check on holes in our planes. I counted four in my plane and guessed that daylight would show more; we had one mean-looking hole in the faring about ten inches from our right gas tank.

Another critique at the Group theater: all gliders, we are told, "landed successfully," all the Group's planes back, though 31 of the 50 planes had been shot up, some badly. Fifteen minutes in the thick of battle—followed by a relatively safe, uneventful, practically routine flight home.[4] (Marty Wolfe, radio operator, written June 15, 1944)

### Over LZ "W"—and on it

In ELMIRA, in spite of the fact that most of the tug planes in our serial were hit, only two crew members were wounded.[5] For our glider pilots, ELMIRA was a different story. When they cut off from us and started downward, their war was just beginning.

When ELMIRA plans had been drawn up, it had been assumed that by the time the gliders got there, LZs "W" and "O," which straddled Ste-Mère-Eglise to the north and south, about two miles behind the UTAH beaches, would be firmly in the hands of 82nd Division troops. This was far from being the case, and the 82nd was unable to get word of its predicament back to England. In relatively small but desperate engagements, the Germans had pushed back into this zone, and they were only partially driven out again when the first gliders released their tow ropes and began, in the gathering dusk, to search out a good field for landing. In fact the gliders were descending into a no man's land. Americans on the ground tried to warn the gliders, but none of the signals they used were the pre-arranged warning signs, and the glider pilots ignored them.

As the gliders came in the Germans, who had been holding their fire, opened up with everything they had. Enemy fire was so deadly that the glider pilots broke out of their normal landing patterns and began to dive at excessive speeds into the dubious protection of the fields below.

I finally found three beautiful-looking fields side by side that seemed perfect for a 270-degree approach. I was all ready to cut—even had my hand on the release—when out of one corner of one of these very fields a lot of flak and machine gun stuff started coming up at us! If I had cut loose then I would have taken all of us right down into the middle of it.

By this time it began to look hopeless. But at last—a fair field. I cut, made one turn, slowed the glider, made my final turn, and headed into the field. Damn it! There was another glider cutting in front of me! I made a fast turn out of his way, another turn, and landed into the next field. All this happened very fast; and it happened at about only 400 feet up. Somehow on that pattern I had remembered to put down half flaps; but when I dodged the glider and headed for my alternate field I forgot to put my flaps all the

The huge British Horsa, the glider we flew to Normandy on our second mission (June 6, 1944); note the Y-shaped harness. (Courtesy Smithsonian Institution)

"You made it!" Adriel Williams, our 436th Group CO, greets the first glider pilots to return from Normandy.

way down so my air speed would be where it belonged. On this last approach I saw that the field had a line of trees that must have been fifty feet high on both ends, and in the middle a stump that looked as though it was forty feet high, plus a small pole that looked to be about a foot in diameter and twenty feet tall. Naturally, I opted for the small pole; I took it with my right wing while still in the air but it didn't hurt our landing in any way.

Wheels touched; put on the brakes; started praying. We did stop—with about fifty feet to spare. Through a kind of a daze I could hear my co-pilot saying: "I could kiss you for getting us down OK." (Darlyle Watters, Squadron Glider Officer)

For the glider pilots, coming to land on their LZ, it was every man for himself. Some gliders came down nearer to LZ "O" than to "W." As they slammed into the ground many of the gliders splintered apart; jeeps and artillery in some gliders were knocked loose, crushing some of the glider troops. Survivors had to chop their way out and jump for any ditch or other protection, while German bullets screamed over their heads. There was no possibility whatever of unloading cargoes until the field was covered in darkness. Fortunately, when night came the Germans pulled back.

Ben Ward remembers how his heart pounded while he was over his LZ, wondering where he could have a fair chance of a safe landing.

When the green signal light from the C-47 astrodome began flashing, I glanced down at the quilted patchwork of postage-stamp sized fields lined by hedgerows all around. I had only sixty seconds to decide and to cut off the tow line before I was cut off by the tow plane. If this occurred I would then have 300 feet of tow rope rushing back at us. If it missed me the rope would be dangling crazily beneath us and dragging dangerously through the trees and brush of the hedgerows below. So, taking a deep breath and thinking "Here goes," I reached up and hit the release mechanism with my right hand and the tow plane started to pull away.

Looking down upon the obvious hazards of landing on an obstacle course at ninety miles per hour with a cargo of thirty men, I wondered just how many invisible pitfalls awaited below. Were the hedgerows concealing Nazi soldiers? How about German machine gun nests? Tanks? Mines? No time to think now. Just hold the pattern, maintain my speed and rate of descent constant, and fly my ground pattern.

Just as our wheels touched down, our left wing dropped and hit the ground. This caused the glider to turn to the left, and we were now on a collision course for the trees. Now what? I am half out of field and haven't even started to slow down. I aim at the longest part of the field and set the brakes. Nothing happens. No brakes! Instant panic. Try the brakes again. I was not aware of any enemy fire; but during landing we had been hit several times by small arms fire that was probably responsible for the loss of brakes. Too late now to worry about anything except surviving.

J. J. [DiPietro], in the co-pilot's seat, looked across at me knowingly, no doubt saying his prayers. Here we were, fifty yards from the end of our field, moving at ninety and just slowing slightly. Trees looming ahead and nowhere to go but straight forward.

The glider pilot knows that in an emergency you land straight ahead. Don't attempt to turn suddenly. Just ride it out and try to miss anything in your path. This was that time. Was I ready for it? Just seconds remain. Two huge trees ahead maybe thirty or forty feet apart. Stick the nose right between them. As we slid into the open space, seemingly in slow motion, J. J. released his safety belt and pressed over beside me. Then we smashed through a hedgerow sideways, the sound of shattered plywood and crunching plexiglass filled my ears . . . then silence.

I was dazed by the impact. I groggily released my seat belt and staggered to my feet, wondering if I was still in one piece. The glider was a mass of wreckage. There seemed to be nothing left whole except my seat and my safety belt. Faintly I heard someone calling my name. Gradually, through the fog, I realized that it was J. J. asking if I was OK.

When we counted noses we found that we were short one man. It was a Greek soldier who had been telling J. J. how much he was going to do to the Germans for what they had done to his family. He was killed by the large tree that smashed through the fuselage just behind the co-pilot's seat. (Ben Ward, glider pilot)

———

The glider split open and rolled over the top of the trees and most of us landed in the next field. I had been thrown from the glider and when I quit rolling, about twenty-five yards from the impact, I noticed that my seat bottom was still attached to me. Much to my surprise I was not hurt, just a couple of scratches on my forehead caused by my helmet when I hit my head. Besides my seat remaining attached to me and my crash helmet, what prevented me from more serious injury was that the Mae West I wore under my flak suit inflated on impact and acted as a cushion when I landed and rolled on the ground.

After assuring myself that I was all in one piece, I surveyed the damage. Ben Ward was walking around in a daze, he must have hit his head; but he came to when I yelled at him. The team of medics took care of a few broken bones and other minor injuries, and the rest of us assembled on a nearby country road and proceeded toward Ste-Mère-Eglise, which was between us and the command post. (J. J. DiPietro, glider pilot)

Ten glider pilots (none from the 81st) in ELMIRA were killed by the landing impact or very soon afterward; seven others were later found to be missing. Survivors thought it a miracle so many of them were still alive. Two of our glider pilots, Henry Brewer and Clifford Fearn, had a bad scare: they were made prisoner by Germans—but not for long.

In our Horsa we had a doctor, some medics, and one of their trailers. After we landed that night a German infantry outfit came up so fast you couldn't say they captured us; they just sort of swept us up.

While we were prisoners we had to help lug German ammunition. Those shells were in metal canisters about two and a half feet high. We were forced to run with these cans over to a German half-track with a heavy gun. This half-track would go from one German artillery point to another and supply them with shells.

But not long afterward three American tanks coming up off the beach got behind those Germans that had sandbagged us, and started knocking them off fast.

While we were prisoners, I had been talking to one of the German boys. Now I walked him over to the American tanks to help the Germans surrender. I got the attention of the American tankers by handing this German soldier's P-38 pistol to the American tankers. It was a good souvenir. Later those tankers told me that previously they usually hadn't taken any prisoners until they killed off quite a few Germans with their hands up— that made the rest of them more ready to surrender. (Cliff Fearn, glider pilot)

Those glider pilots who could still function began to add to their already formidable reputation for guts, improvisation, and cantankerous independence. Besides helping unload the crashed gliders, they functioned as guards of German prisoners and even joined in establishing perimeter defense lines. Some of them, against orders, went along with paratroopers going out on patrol.

When we finally began our march toward the command post, the lieutenant in charge wasn't sure we were going in the right direction. I saw a farmer milking a cow in a nearby field. I went over to him and in my high-school French asked him if Ste-Mère-Eglise was in that direction as I pointed where we were headed. He said yes and volunteered the information that about an hour previously some German paratroopers had landed on a hill up ahead. I relayed the information to the lieutenant in charge, and he ordered the troops to spread out and be on the alert. There were about two hundred of us in all.

As we approached the hill we were fired on by burp guns. We hit the deck and looked around but couldn't see anyone. The firing ceased and we continued on. A short time later we heard the rumble of tanks. A bazooka team was dispatched to scout the tanks and we started to dig in. The bazooka team returned with the news that the tanks were American and that they had told the tank drivers about the German paratroopers on the hill. Soon we heard the tanks open up with their machine guns and they rumbled on. Under scattered sniper fire we finally arrived at the command post without casualties. (J. J. DiPietro, glider pilot)

---

We and the 82nd boys started to try to find our units. We ended up wandering around like chickens with our heads cut off. At the same time there were gliders crashing all around us, and the Germans were lobbing mortar shells in the field directly next to ours. I went down the road a bit to see if I could find somebody who knew where we were; but just at that time machine gun bullets, including tracers, cut through the hedge just in front of me. You can believe that I hit the ditch on the side of the road mighty fast. When the firing stopped I could hear Germans talking, and I figured it was only a question of time before one of them ran a bayonet through me.

I lay there quiet as could be; and every time I moved my head the steel helmet would rub up against the stiff grass there—to me the noise it made sounded like thunder. I stayed there until it was daylight; and boy, it was a great sight to spot only our attack bombers and fighter planes above me. Suddenly a paratrooper captain came by, walking down that road as if nothing special was going on. He looked down at me in disgust; but then he kindly took me back where some airborne troops and glider pilots were assembling, and told us to dig in. That was easier said than done. I dug away for about an hour and only got down about six inches. (Thayer Bonecutter, glider pilot)

---

The glider pilots' overriding responsibility now was to get the hell back to England and to Membury whatever way they could. For this they were given priority on cross-Channel transport second only to our wounded, since additional glider missions would have been needed if the battle had gone badly. Some got back on landing craft, some on bigger ships. We had six of them back in Membury on June 10; in a few days after that all the 81st glider pilots were back or accounted for; four of them were still hospitalized. On June 7, our glider pilot Joseph Graves, in a forward hospital recovering from his injuries, was killed when the Germans shelled the building.

> Late that afternoon [June 7] the major in charge gave us the bad news. He said that Ste-Mère-Eglise had been recaptured by the Germans. He gave us three options: (1) advance with the airborne troopers; (2) dig in where we stood and take a chance that the Panzer Division moving in our direction would pass us by; or (3) head back toward the beach for evacuation back to England, if we could fight our way back through Ste-Mère-Eglise, which was between us and the beach. We all opted to head for the beach!
>
> The wounded were placed in jeeps and trucks and were at the head of the column; and the rest of us, about 100 pilots, followed on foot. It was about 5:00 p.m. We marched with full pack, carrying our guns and ammunition which we never had a chance to fire. As we started our march, a German plane flew overhead at a low altitude; but it did not have a chance to open fire, because a P-51 was on its tail. We continued our march, and we could hear German 88 shells whizzing over our heads; one landed at the head of the column, putting a jeep out of commission. Apparently the Germans had zeroed in on the road with the intention of shelling it all night.
>
> As we approached the beach we encountered some GIs who had disembarked from landing craft; some had had to swim because their boat ran into some mines. They were wet and had lost their guns and ammunition. We handed them our equipment as they marched by; they were very grateful. Upon arriving at the beach and waiting to board a boat we were strafed by a couple of German night fighters. Now it was close to midnight. When I finally got on a boat I was so tired that I put on a life jacket and lay down on the wet deck and fell asleep. The next thing I knew we were back in England getting off the boat and waiting for transport back to Membury. (J. J. DiPietro, glider pilot)

Sixteen of our 81st TCS glider pilots who had not flown on D-Day were detached to fly June 7 with other squadrons in Operation GALVESTON, which flew the 82nd Division's 325th Glider Infantry Regiment to an LZ near Ste-Mère-Eglise. We were still on call; and some planes from the 436th Group did make six more re-supply glider missions between June 10 and June 13. But ELMIRA just about ended the 81st Squadron's combat experiences as a unit in Normandy.

### Notes

1. Some of the fields on our LZs were only 100 to 200 feet long and ringed about with fifty-foot trees. Warren II, p. 68.

2. Koskimaki, pp. 316–17.

3. However, General Don Pratt, assistant commander of the 101st Airborne, was killed riding a glider in this mission. Col. Mike Murphy, piloting that glider, was severely injured.

4. The Luftwaffe did shoot down one C-47 on the previous CHICAGO operation. On ELMIRA, in other squadrons, two planes were brought down by ground fire, but the pilots managed to crash land safely.

5. Warren II, p. 66.

# 7. Evaluating
## Second Thoughts About Operation NEPTUNE

### NEPTUNE worked

From the point of view of veterans of the 81st Troop Carrier Squadron, an evaluation of troop carrier's role in the Normandy invasion must proceed on several levels. First, did Operation NEPTUNE, the combined airborne components of the invasion—troop carrier and airborne together—succeed in its main task? Second, how do historians evaluate the performance of IX Troop Carrier Command in Normandy, both in its paratrooper and in its glider operations? And third, in particular, how are we to judge the work of our own Squadron?

General Gavin called Operation NEPTUNE "perhaps the most complex that had ever been attempted." [1] It could be thought of as an invitation for numberless demonstrations of "Murphy's Law"—whatever can go wrong, will. But in spite of its intimidating complexity and the daunting obstacles it faced, NEPTUNE scored many crucial successes. The time and place of the initial assault came as a complete surprise to the enemy. The Germans failed to push the seaborne infantry back down the causeways and into the sea. In fact, losses on UTAH beach of seaborne soldiers on D-Day through D-Day plus 2 were surprisingly light, compared to what might have been expected, and certainly compared with what might have happened if the 101st and the 82nd had not been thrust between the main German forces and the beach. Losses on UTAH beach also were much less than the terrible losses suffered by seaborne troops on OMAHA beach— behind which the American high brass chose *not* to drop airborne troopers. [2]

American paratrooper and gliderborne troops delivered during NEPTUNE did suffer heavy losses: perhaps 2,500 killed, seriously injured, or missing (for both the 82nd and the 101st Airborne Divisions); but the Germans did not destroy any single paratrooper battalion or any other large airborne unit. The UTAH beachhead held, expanded, and built up strength. The C-47 plane and the CG-4A glider proved their tremendous airworthiness under fire. Only forty-one planes and nine gliders were shot down out of a total of more than 1,500 plane and glider sorties in NEPTUNE. Only a handful of paratroopers, airsick and

scared as they were, refused to jump. Our own air superiority and fighter cover-
age reduced the Luftwaffe to a few raids on our skytrains.

And we learned a lot about how to manage massive airborne operations.
For example, because of the loss of almost all the 75 mm guns dropped from
airplanes on D-Day, airborne leaders decided future re-supply of artillery would
have to travel by glider.[3] We learned also about the toughness of the Germans.
Many of the Germans in Normandy must already have been convinced their war
was lost, but they fought on and fought very well after their initial confusion.
The British had a saying, "If you haven't fought Germans, you haven't been in a
war." NEPTUNE's success did not result in a quick collapse of Nazi Europe;
and this warned us about the tough fight that lay ahead.

After D-Day British Air Chief Marshal Sir Trafford Leigh-Mallory made an
interesting apology to Eisenhower in which he regretted having added to Ike's
burden of command decision before the Normandy invasion by his forceful demands that the airborne operations be canceled. He agreed that he had been
wrong to predict such an inflated rate of paratrooper and glider troop casualties.
Leigh-Mallory might well have apologized also for having been such a factor in
forcing two of the four main glider missions to land at night. The results of D-
Day glider operations showed that casualties among gliders landing when there
was at least a little daylight would be no greater than those landing in the dark.
This ended the debate over daylight versus nighttime glider operations. Never
again would a major glider tow in World War II be made at night. This was an
important change. Before NEPTUNE, even General Gavin believed night landing of gliders was entirely feasible.[4] In fact, demonstrating that gliders in daytime fared no worse gave weight to the argument that in future operations
paratroopers, too, should be allowed to jump only when they could see where
they were coming down.

NEPTUNE's airborne missions, it seems clear, were competently conceived
and bravely executed. They were tremendously important guides for planning
later airborne operations. We can conclude that NEPTUNE was more successful
than any rational observer had a right to expect.

### Troop carrier and NEPTUNE

Any balanced critique of NEPTUNE must start by making a sharp distinction
between troop carrier's performance in its paratrooper drops and in its glider
tows. Unlike the paratroopers, most gliders in NEPTUNE landed at or near
where they were supposed to land. Although terribly costly to glider pilots and
to glider troopers once they landed, the NEPTUNE glider missions are universally applauded as troop carrier successes.[5] In starkest contrast, during the para-

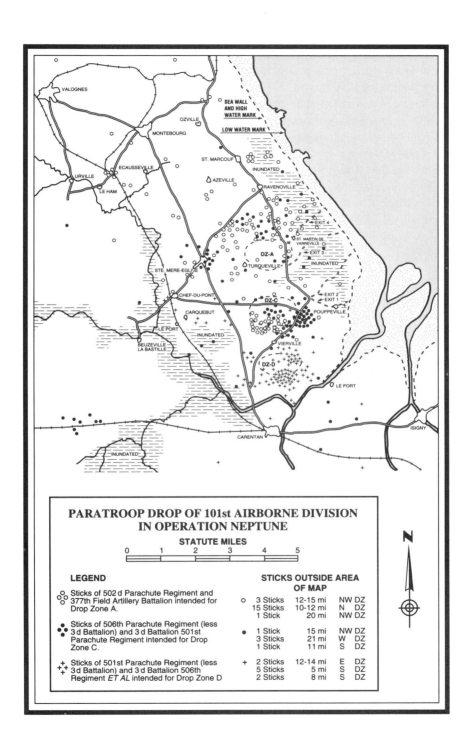

**PARATROOP DROP OF 101st AIRBORNE DIVISION IN OPERATION NEPTUNE**

STATUTE MILES

0    1    2    3    4    5

N

LEGEND

○○ Sticks of 502d Parachute Regiment and
○○ 377th Field Artillery Battalion intended for
    Drop Zone A.

•• Sticks of 506th Parachute Regiment (less
••  3d Battalion) and 3d Battalion 501st
    Parachute Regiment intended for Drop
    Zone C.

+  Sticks of 501st Parachute Regiment (less
+++ 3d Battalion) and 3d Battalion 506th
+  Regiment ET AL intended for Drop Zone D

**STICKS OUTSIDE AREA OF MAP**

| | | | |
|---|---|---|---|
| ○ | 3 Sticks | 12-15 mi | NW DZ |
| | 15 Sticks | 10-12 mi | N  DZ |
| | 1 Stick | 20 mi | NW DZ |
| • | 1 Stick | 15 mi | NW DZ |
| | 3 Sticks | 21 mi | W  DZ |
| | 1 Stick | 11 mi | S  DZ |
| + | 2 Sticks | 12-14 mi | E  DZ |
| | 5 Sticks | 5 mi | S  DZ |
| | 2 Sticks | 8 mi | S  DZ |

Map labels: VALOGNES, OZVILLE, MONTEBOURG, ST. MARCOUF, SEA WALL AND HIGH WATER MARK, LOW WATER MARK, INUNDATED, ECAUSSEVILLE, URVILLE, LE HAM, AZEVILLE, RAVENOVILLE, EXIT 4, ST. MARTIN DE VARREVILLE, EXIT 3, INUNDATED, DZ-A, TURQUEVILLE, STE. MERE-EGLISE, CHEF-DU-PONT, DZ-C, EXIT 2, EXIT 1, CARQUEBUT, POUPPEVILLE, LE PORT, VIERVILLE, INUNDATED, BEUZEVILLE LA BASTILLE, DZ-D, LE PORT, CARENTAN, ISIGNY, INUNDATED

trooper missions almost half the troopers landed more than two miles away from their designated DZs. About sixty out of the 432 troop carrier pilots in ALBANY seem to have given their paratroopers the green light more than ten miles away from their designated targets. Troopers placed this far away were forced to give up hope of overrunning their main objectives; they had to improvise whatever attacks against Nazi defenses lay in their path while they desperately tried to link up with others in their outfit.

The main source of information as to just where paratroopers may have landed are the "after-action reports" prepared by regimental and battalion head-quarters intelligence officers. When the airborne divisions could catch their breath—that is, about a month after D-Day, when the 101st and 82nd Airborne were pulled off the line—the after-action reports were used to compile after-action maps marking the observation, or the best guess, of unit leaders for each planeload as to where they landed. For historians, these after-action maps are conveniently summarized in two of the most basic texts on airborne warfare: the official USAF history called *Airborne Operations in World War II, European Theater*, written by John C. Warren (1956), and the official history of the 101st Airborne Division ("The Screaming Eagles," from their shoulder patch), *Rendezvous With Destiny* (1948, revised 1965), written by Leonard Rapport and Arthur Northwood, Jr. Rapport and Northwood's book gives us maps purporting to show not only the overall drop pattern for the 101st Airborne but also locations where each troop carrier stick (planeload) of troopers landed.

Taken at face value, these published maps certainly bear out the general impression historians give that during the early morning hours of D-Day, troop carrier was seriously off target. Very few sticks—for all of ALBANY and BOSTON—are shown as having come down precisely inside their designated DZ. Several sticks appear to have been dropped between twelve and twenty miles away. At least one stick is known to have been dropped in the English Channel (five other sticks of the 101st Airborne were listed as "unreported" and may have suffered the same fate). While many of the details shown on these maps are open to question, the overall picture they give must be accepted. It seems clear enough that, to put it mildly, the results of the 101st's paratroop drop during ALBANY were far below the hopes of those who planned these operations.

Some historians point out, rather patronizingly, that perhaps all the confusion on the ground in Normandy was worth the resulting losses; the Germans, they say, became so confused when paratroopers began dropping all over the landscape that they were kept off balance and did not throw up a major counter-attack until it was too late.[6] This grudging pat on the head ("we [airborne] did well in spite of you [troop carrier]") grates on the nerves of troop carrier veterans.

It certainly is true that all through the night of June 5–6 and until noon on

June 6, the Wehrmacht was unable to mount any coordinated reaction. German communications (mostly telephone and dispatch riders rather than radio) were cut to shreds by wandering bands of paratroopers. Troopers also managed to sever the main telephone lines from Cherbourg to the town of Carentan, near the base of the Cotentin peninsula. German dispatch riders on bikes or motorcycles were an easy mark. The commander of the German 91st Division, General Falley, frantic at the disjointed accounts and rumors coming into his HQ, jumped into his car to search out the answers himself; he was promptly cut down by a burst from a trooper's machine gun.[7] It is unfair and misleading, however, to imply that the main benefits from troop carrier in the paratrooper operations came from troop carrier mistakes.

## Judging the 81st Troop Carrier Squadron's role

As we saw in Chapter 5, we in the 81st TCS were part of the first serial out of Membury. The Membury serials were not the first in Operation ALBANY: two other serials, launched from Greenham Common—the four squadrons of the 438th TCG—preceded us in the skytrain headed for DZ "A." Our Membury serial was led into battle by our Group Commander, Col. Williams, at the head of the 82nd TCS; we in the 81st TCS were positioned behind the 82nd TCS. The 82nd and 81st TCSs carried the 1st Battalion of the 101st's 502nd Parachute Infantry Regiment. David Brack, our Squadron CO, led the first nine-plane element of the 81st TCS, and Francis Farley, our Operations Officer, led the second nine-plane element.

If we can believe the details of the ALBANY drop pattern maps prepared after D-Day—and, as we shall see, this is a very big "if"—none of the eighteen planes in our 81st TCS placed their troopers squarely inside DZ "A." Three sticks of paratroopers in Col. Brack's nine-plane element, according to these maps, landed close enough to be considered right on the money, that is, within a mile of the DZ; one other landed two miles away; and five more landed within three miles. Some of the nine planes of the 81st TCS led by Francis Farley—as we saw in chapter 5—wandered far off course to the north, found themselves near the tip of the Cotentin peninsula, turned around, and made their way back toward Ste-Mère-Eglise. Maps based on the paratroopers' after-action reports suggest that some of the planes in Farley's element dropped their troopers about seven miles northwest of DZ "A." Troopers dropped that far from their objectives were close to heavily defended German positions and in all likelihood were either taken prisoner or killed. They certainly could have been of little use in helping the 502nd PIR capture its primary objectives.

The second serial out of Membury carried the 101st's 377th Parachute Field Artillery Battalion, plus planeloads of ammunition and one planeload of parachute medics. These troopers were aboard the planes of the 79th and 80th TCSs from our 436th Group, plus one squadron—the 85th TCS—borrowed from the 437th Group at Ramsbury. John Warren's judgment of this second Membury serial is devastating.

> As for the 377th Field Artillery Battalion, only a handful of its men played a significant part in the fighting on D-Day, and only one of its 12 guns supported the operations of the 101st Division. Scattered many miles north and west of the drop area, the artillerymen engaged the enemy in innumerable little fights and showed great resourcefulness in regaining the Allied lines, but their actions had at best a nuisance value.[8]

Some of the 377th PFAB troopers landed in the marshy areas immediately behind UTAH beach. Unlike the 82nd Airborne Division's troopers dropped in Operation BOSTON into the terrible swamps of the Merderet River west of Ste-Mère-Eglise, none of the 377th PFAB men drowned. They had a nasty few minutes, however, before they could drag themselves out of the marshes; and almost all the heavy 75 mm pack howitzers dropped with them had to be abandoned. Guns that heavy could not be dragged along that soggy ground.[9]

## The airborne troopers' view

The after-action D-Day maps in Warren and in Rapport and Northwood seem so carefully drawn up, so conclusive, they leave little room for doubting the basic message: that in the early morning hours of D-Day, many planes from our 436th TCS did indeed drop their paratroopers far off target. However, we should not accept everything these maps show. This is especially the case concerning the *individual stick locations* on the maps.[10] There is reason to believe many troopers were only guessing about where they landed.

American paratroopers were the most gung-ho soldiers we had. They were convinced they could lick any bunch of lousy Krauts with one hand tied behind their backs. On that fearsome early morning of D-Day, however, many of them were isolated and bewildered, most often without their regular leaders, some of them having to drag themselves out of foul marsh waters. Troopers from the 101st Airborne found themselves fighting alongside equally bewildered troopers from the 82nd Airborne, so that instead of planned attacks, small-scale semi-independent ventures were the rule.[11] Many paratroopers were taken prisoner as soon as they hit the ground, further limiting their ability to give precise landing reports.

Only God and his recording angels know precisely where all the paratroopers landed who jumped from troop carrier planes in the awful morning darkness of June 6. We lesser beings have to rely on merely human observations and recollections. Once on the ground, that dark early morning of D-Day, many troopers reported seeing no recognizable landmarks, especially if they had landed behind hedgerows or in an orchard. Some lucky ones bumped into Frenchmen calm enough to give them good directions. Groups of two or three went searching for others in their stick, or for some officer to take charge— meanwhile nervously aware that German patrols, almost as bewildered as the Americans, were also on the prowl. Anything that moved was liable to be shot; the damage to cows and horses that night was considerable.[12]

Usually when the troopers began trying to find others in their units, they travelled in a sort of zigzag fashion, making it difficult to remember later where they had started. Some of them combined into larger groups and moved toward their mission objectives "in copybook style."[13] But others were so disoriented and jittery that, completely exhausted, they curled up under the protection of a hedgerow and went to sleep.[14] General James Gavin, who jumped with the 82nd Division, reports that even after daybreak he had trouble at first in getting the troopers he collected to obey orders quickly and to respond properly to enemy fire. One paratroop officer reported that he saw a group of paratroop engineers "too scared to move from a ditch."[15]

Such disorientation hampered even those sticks which reported having been dropped in or near their DZ. General Ridgway, CG of the 82nd Airborne, tells us that he had no idea where he was for thirty-six hours. General Maxwell Taylor, CG of the 101st, later judged that he had been dropped right on the button, but he reports that for half an hour he was totally alone, caught in an angle of a boxed-in meadow.

The 101st Airborne had decided to use toy crickets for re-assembling after the drop; they clicked these at each other before giving a password. The crickets brought some troopers together; others, however, after a few unavailing clicks, tossed their crickets away. The lush meadows and orchards and the tall, thick walls of hedgerows tended to absorb sounds past twenty or thirty yards.[16] By nightfall of D-Day, twenty hours after he had jumped, General Taylor knew the whereabouts of only 2,500 of his 6,000 men of the 101st Division.[17]

A deadly game of hide-and-seek was played out that fearsome night around the hamlets, marshes, roads, and hedgerows of the eastern Cotentin peninsula. Small groups of both 101st and 82nd paratroopers, those who were willing and able to fight but could not find a leader, moved out in what they hoped was a reasonable direction. The Germans were at a complete loss to piece together some picture of the paratroopers' objectives. Hitler was asleep and had left word that he must not be disturbed; the Wehrmacht leaders, meanwhile, had been ordered not to move their Panzer divisions without Hitler's express approval. "In this unique contest, writes Howarth, "the Americans knew what was happening, but few of them knew where they were; the Germans knew where they were, but none of them knew what was happening." [18]

In Lawrence Critchell's beautifully written book on the 101st Airborne, *Four Stars to Hell*, he raises the damning question: "*How the hell did the pilots know where they were?*" But in another passage on the same page he shows that the pilots may not have been responsible for at least some paratroopers landing off target:

> A K-ration bundle lay in front of Lieutenant Jansen [a jumpmaster]. He kicked it out the door. That was the last they ever saw of it. The second bundle weighed three hundred pounds. Before he and the crew chief could get rid of it, sixty seconds had passed. In that time the plane, going too fast anyway, had travelled almost two miles. [19]

Time after time, the same troopers who complained they were "widely scattered" also say that they went out the jump door quickly and in a tight bunch—only to find not a soul on the ground near them. George Koskimaki, author of *D-Day With the Screaming Eagles*, was the radio technician assigned that day to General Taylor; Koskimaki jumped immediately behind Taylor, but the two of them could not find each other until long after they hit the ground. [20] What explains this apparent contradiction? Donald Burgett, a 506th PIR trooper whose burning indictment of troop carrier is frequently quoted, says his stick jumped "in just fractions of seconds" but that when he got down he could not "find someone else, anyone else . . . . During this time I had no success in finding anyone, friend or foe." [21] Why were paratroopers so isolated from others in their stick, even though they jumped together? Was it the fault of flinching pilots—or of the hedgerows, the tree-lined meadows, and above all the disorientation on the ground resulting from that menacing darkness? *Serials* were "scattered" by troop carrier as well as by those Normandy clouds, though possibly not as badly as many historians and veterans believe; but *sticks* were "scattered" by the fortunes of war.

Unlike most paratroopers, glider pilots—whose landings in ELMIRA, the evening of D-Day, drew the highest praise—left some convincing evidence, the glider itself, to fix the location of their landings. This was especially the case for the heavier Horsa glider, which was virtually immovable once it landed on a battlefield. The lighter Waco, if its landing gear were still working, could be pushed and pulled by airborne soldiers to a convenient spot and serve as a dry and relatively comfortable command post. When Darlyle Watters returned to his Horsa after ELMIRA was over—because he was curious to see in the daytime what condition it was in—he could verify its position and its exact relation to his assigned LZ. No such highly visible marker was available to paratroopers.

One final warning should be raised about the reliability of the *details* (not the validity of the general picture) of the drop pattern maps, both those published and those in archives: the original maps were compiled long after the event. The original overlay map of the 101st Airborne drops I worked with at the National Archives, for example, is dated July 5—an entire month after D-Day. During the first few days after June 6, of course, the troopers were too busy to bother with pinpointing their landing on maps. Regimental headquarters did have "history sections," men authorized to question jumpmasters and unit officers for the purpose of compiling division histories and furnishing SHAEF (Supreme Headquarters, Allied Expeditionary Force) with an assessment of troop carrier performance. But such interrogation could only take place after the troopers were pulled out of the front lines.

We can gain some perspective on our 81st TC Squadron's experiences that night in learning how other units on paratrooper missions stand in today's military historians' evaluations. The 438th TCG, which carried the first two ALBANY serials to Normandy, experienced practically no ground fire from the surprised Germans. The 438th's drops were much more concentrated than ours, but on the wrong drop zone, DZ "C," three miles south of their target, DZ "A." Troop carrier planes that lifted the 82nd Airborne Division in Operation BOSTON, did manage to drop a higher proportion of their sticks in and near their drop zones;[22] but twenty-one of the 82nd Airborne sticks were reported to have been dropped ten miles away or more.

Worst of all, thirty 82nd Division sticks were dropped into the Merderet River marshes. Reconnaissance photos had seemed to show the Merderet River as narrow, with well-defined banks, but vegetation in the river's embankment marshes, sticking its tops just above the water, made the marshes appear in these photographs to be solid ground. In places the vegetation hid water six feet deep. Scores of 82nd Airborne troopers, weighed down by their equipment, were dragged below these slimy waters to a horrible death. Enough of the 82nd troopers, to their everlasting credit, managed to assemble to capture Ste-Mère-Eglise, their main objective. But their hold on it was so thinly maintained that the Nazis kept the issue in doubt for the remainder of D-Day and the entire day after.

Forty miles east of Ste-Mère-Eglise, meanwhile, some 6,000 paratrooper and gliderborne soldiers of the British Sixth Airborne Division were fighting on the left flank of the British and Canadian invasion beaches. British troopers quickly managed to achieve every one of their main objectives. The most important—the bridges across the Caen Canal, the bridges over two small nearby rivers, and the large and well-protected German battery at Merville—could have put the British seaborne landings in terrible jeopardy. The Caen Canal bridges were taken in what military tacticians call a coup de main, a spectacular surprise attack. A small party of British airborne soldiers, with pin-point accuracy, crashed their gliders into a tiny field only a few yards away from a canal bridge and overwhelmed the German guard before any warning could be given.[23] After the war, that bridge was renamed the Pegasus Bridge in honor of the emblem on the shoulder patch of the British Sixth Airborne.

Comparative judgments concerning the relative success of British and American airborne forces are hard to make. First, the land around the British drop zones was much less cut up by hedgerows. Second, the British Sixth Airborne suffered from many of the same foul-ups and planning errors that plagued the two American divisions. They also ran into clouds and were scattered; and their pathfinders also were unable to set up their DZ beacons in time. Their paratroopers and glider crews had benefited from much more extensive training and experience than the Americans, and most of their pilots had been under fire previously—in fact, the majority of the tow planes on this mission were converted Halifax and Stirling bombers (included were some 150 Dakotas, that is, British C-47s). Once exposed to German antiaircraft fire over Normandy, however, some of their pilots, like ours, took violent evasive action that threw their paratroopers onto the floor and sometimes entangled their gear.[24] Many British troopers also drowned in marshes. In this case, the marshes *had* shown up in reconnaissance photographs and so were known to British planners.

### Judging ourselves

Like the Americans, British paratroopers were inclined to blame their misfortunes on their pilots and navigators. Books on D-Day recollections give us examples of paratroopers' bitterness toward their plane crews, both British and American. These charges, often voiced much later to interviewing journalists or to intelligence officers, also appear in official USAF histories and, of course, in 101st and 82nd Division histories. Cornelius Ryan, speaking of the Holland invasion in September 1944, reports that "the standard 82nd Airborne Division joke was: 'we always use blind pilots.' "[25] Because such anecdotes seem to give a simple explanation for a terribly complex situation—and often provide a convenient scapegoat—they have become part of what we could call "airborne folklore."

Some airborne warfare histories pull out all the stops in blaming troop carrier for the crisis facing the American paratroopers. Donald Burgett, the 506th PIR trooper cited previously, reports that while on the ground he saw a plane come down to less than 300 feet in an effort to escape flak. Troopers in that plane had to jump from a height too low for their chutes to open. Burgett says he counted seventeen men hitting the ground "with a sound like ripe pumpkins

For those famous "three passes": Don Skrdla (pilot) receives the Distinguished Flying Cross from General Maurice Beach, CG of the 53rd TCW.

C-47s releasing Waco gliders in Normandy, June 7, 1944, the morning after D-Day; photo shows hedgerow obstacles and Horsas on the ground, some smashed, some whole, from the previous evening's missions. (Courtesy Smithsonian Institution)

being thrown down to burst against the ground. 'That dirty son of a bitch pilot,' I swore to myself, 'he's hedgehopping and killing a bunch of troopers just to save his ass. I hope he gets shot down in the Channel and drowns real slow.' " One lieutenant in the 101st who supposedly landed twelve miles away from his objective is reported to have "let loose a string of oaths, all of them directed at the U.S. Air Corps. 'They dropped us all over the whole Cherbourg Peninsula,' he raged. 'Who the hell's side are they on, anyway?' " [26]

My guess is that this messy problem of trying to decide *where* the paratroopers came down, and *why* so many drops were off target, is impossible to resolve. It is now encumbered with countless official but questionable records and with serious misinterpretations by military historians. We can never be sure about the troopers' reports as to how far they were dropped from their targets. We can never be sure *even in the case of some troopers who said they landed in or near the correct place.* For example, paratroopers who jumped from Don Skrdla's plane—on that famous third pass—later came to Membury to look him up and to tell that him they came down in the right place. Perhaps; but the drop pattern maps in Rapport and Northwood seem to show that not a single stick of the 502nd PIR's First Battalion landed inside the perimeter of DZ "A."

This night of wild terror and confusion, of muddle and fouled-up planning, therefore, has to be understood as the result of a large combination of factors— the clouds and the fog in Normandy, the pathfinders' problems with setting up radar beacons and lights in time, the glitches in the radar aids, the inability to orient oneself in a terrain boxed in everywhere by tall hedges and trees—as well as the inability of troop carrier crews to persevere through clouds and through ground fire, hold formation, and locate DZs.

No doubt some of troop carrier pilots—already sensing they were lost when they emerged from those Normandy clouds—flinched. We know that many pilots did try to escape that murderous-looking ground fire. No one questions that this was a serious mistake. But to assume that this action further reduced paratroopers' chances of arriving at their assigned DZ is only to indulge in speculation. Chances of most planes' hitting the right DZ together had already been lost because of the bad flying conditions and the fact that several of the pathfinders' beacons did not work in time. It must be emphasized that the troop carrier formations had already broken up—*before they were exposed to ground fire.* [27]

Why did many NEPTUNE pilots flinch that night? Some writers, especially British ones, attribute this performance to an American lack of nerve, and— referring to the previous tragic dumping of paratroops and gliders into the Mediterranean off Sicily—imply that this was all you could expect from those Yanks. These very same pilots, however, nineteen hours later (around 9:00 p.m., June 6), towed their gliders through ground fire that was just as deadly without flinching.

I can't remember who was my tow pilot on D-Day; but there is no doubt that our tow pilots did a good job. They stayed at the right heights, at the right speed, and brought us in at the right angle to those fields so that it was easy for us to cut off and make the 270-degree turn we needed—the three left turns—to go right on in. (Bob Carney, glider pilot)

We crews in the 81st TCS's part of ALBANY, after we returned and began to hear rumors that it had been far from a picture-perfect operation, felt that while some aspects of the pilots' performance in our Squadron may indeed have proved disappointing, the reasons for this situation were entirely understandable. The recollections of pilots in our Squadron are agreed that they were lost in that Normandy sky through no fault of their own, that they used pilotage and recollections of briefing information as best they could, and that they gave their troopers what they considered a good jump under the circumstances.

We were proud of our Squadron's performance during ALBANY as well as that during ELMIRA. An objective weighing of all the circumstances and of the available evidence reinforces our wartime convictions about the early morning of June 6, 1944: that we and troop carrier generally had done a good job.

## Notes

1. Gavin, 1979, p. 108.

2. See Devlin, *Silent Wings*, pp. 196–97. After the war, Maxwell Taylor, former CG of the 101st Airborne, stated he believed it was a mistake not to have placed airborne troopers behind OMAHA beach. Maxwell D. Taylor papers, CBAMHI, oral history interview of June 12, 1974.

3. Floyd Parks, Chief of Staff, FAAA, diary entry for Apr. 12, 1944. Floyd Parks Papers, CBAMHI.

4. Gavin, 1979, p. 85.

5. Craven and Cate, p. 188; see Koskimaki, pp. 321–22; see also General Ridgway's letter to General Beach (CG of our 53rd Wing), in "Ever First!" our 53rd TCW V-E Day souvenir brochure.

6. Craven and Cate, p. 188; Howarth, p. 87; Weigley 1981, p. 76; Warren II, pp. 29–30. Several divisional histories written for 82nd and 101st Airborne veterans repeat this interpretation: see, e.g., HQ, 101st Airborne, *History*, p. 12. Eisenhower believed that the fact the Germans had been misled by the airborne landings into grossly overestimating Allied strength prevented them from a possibly victorious counterattack against OMAHA beach. Ambrose, *Eisenhower*, p. 420.

7. Devlin, *Paratrooper!*, pp. 388–89.

8. Warren II, p. 40.

9. Koskimaki, pp. 249, 250.

10. I have checked the Warren and the Rapport and Northwood maps against an original drop pattern overlay map in the National Archives (Washington National Record Center at Suitland, Maryland). While there are several discrepancies between the published maps and the original, the general picture they present is about the same.

11. Cornett, p. 22.

12. Howarth, pp. 86–87.

13. Keegan, p. 99.

14. Keegan, pp. 91–92.

15. Critchell, p. 49.

16. The 82nd Airborne had learned in Sicily that toy crickets were of little use; and, unlike the 101st, the 82nd troopers did not blacken their faces. Gavin, 1947, p. 45.

17. MacDonald, p. 127.

18. Howarth, p. 86.

19. Critchell, p. 44.

20. Koskimaki, pp. 126–27.

21. Burgett, pp. 84–86. Cf. Critchell, p. 45: "Where we had expected to land in selected drop zones, to assemble as complete battalions, *each man* found himself alone" (emphasis added). There are several examples in Koskimaki of troopers reporting being entirely isolated: e.g., pp. 243, 252.

22. This comparison is disputed by troop carrier reports shortly after the war which held that the 101st Airborne drops were "good" and that the 82nd Airborne drops were "widely scattered." Moore, ch. 4, pp. 13–14.

23. Ambrose, *Pegasus*, pp. 88–105; Howarth, pp. 30–36.

24. Howarth, pp. 43–51; Ambrose, *Pegasus*, p. 109; here Ambrose uses the recollections of Richard Todd, later a famous British movie star, who was a paratrooper officer on this jump: "Quite a lot of people did fall out over the sea in fact [because of] evasive action."

25. Ryan, *Bridge*, p. 135.

26. Collier, pp. 100–102; Burgett, p. 85.

27. Some histories give an entirely incorrect version of the sequence of these events: for example, Critchell, p. 43, and HQ, 101st Airborne, *History*, p. 11. One of the paratroopers quoted by Koskimaki has the correct sequence: this trooper explains that all the planes in his formation "had vanished completely after the flight had broken clear of the fog and clouds and had begun to attract artillery fire." Koskimaki, pp. 259–60.

# 8. Flying
## Plane, Pilots, and Crew

### The C-47

Once in a great while a wonderful new piece of technology comes along so in tune with the times, such an obvious solution to society's hopes and needs, so much of an improvement over what is available, that it immediately dominates its field, serves for years and years, and sets the standard for all future rivals. The DC-3 (Douglas Commercial, third version) was one of these innovations. We in troop carrier knew this plane, somewhat modified, as the C-47. The DC-3 left such a massive imprint on both commercial and military aviation that a television documentary broadcast in December 1985, 50 years after the first DC-3 was completed, called it "the plane that changed the world." At the time of that television show about a thousand DC-3s were still flying all over the world in regularly scheduled flights—an incredible achievement for a fifty-year-old machine in an industry in which obsolescence usually comes fast.

The C-47 had what it takes—"the right stuff," we would say today. This is one of the main reasons that our pilots, who first may have been disappointed at not having made it into fighters or bombers, became pretty well reconciled to their job.

> Of course we all wanted to be fighter pilots. The next best thing was to be a bomber pilot, the way we were thinking back then. I'd never even heard of troop carrier; didn't even put it down on my application. I was highly disappointed at being assigned to a transport outfit. Of course I could recognize the good points of the C-47; I ended up with about 3,500 hours flying that thing. Even today I could still fly it and touch every dial and knob in the cockpit blindfolded. They'll never build another airplane that good. (Richard Wilson, pilot)

All the pejorative terms applied to the C-47, like "flying boxcar" and "Goony Bird," were always used in a half-patronizing, half-admiring way. Pilots could not help but approve the stable way it handled, the comfortable cock-pit, its remarkable freedom from breakdowns.

> I used to kid Jack Wallen and tell him he was the hardest man on an airplane of any of the pilots we had. Not that he was a bad pilot; he always knew where he was, he was a tremendous navigator. But he quit flying ten feet off the ground! He slammed that plane down so hard he could jam a set of struts like nothing. I was able to josh him about this; I was always putting the bad-mouth on him. Those struts could take 1,500 pounds of pressure, but Jack could bottom them out. That took some doing. (Edwin "Pappy" Harris, Line Chief)

Pilots told each other stories about taking off with impossible overloads and from impossibly small runways or fields. (The normal payload was two and one-half tons but it was common to have to carry three or even three and one-half tons; and the C-47 could take off and land on one-tenth the runway needed by a modern jet.) After we became operational (combat-ready) the ability of the C-47 to get us home safely—seemingly no matter how many hits from flak and bullets it sustained, or perhaps on only one engine—helped establish this great though unaggressive-looking ship as the stuff of which legends are made.

The DC-3 was not originally designed to become "the workhorse of the air" for World War II. It was so well adapted to that purpose, however, that it is almost as though its designers back in the early 1930s could have foreseen their country's future military needs. In 1942 many DC-3s were requisitioned by the Air Forces for training purposes; my first training flight was in an old DC-3, with its comfortable passenger seats still in place. Stripped of its comfortable seats, provided with a stronger floor (to support jeeps and other massive loads), given a larger door (for the paratroopers to jump through safely), much tougher landing gear (for handling bumpy arrivals on fields and dirt runways), fitted with para-pack racks underneath, the DC-3 became the C-47, the superb platform on which America launched its airborne warfare.

On paper, other planes may have looked like better airborne warfare vehi-cles. The Curtis C-46, for example, could carry almost twice as heavy a payload and had doors on each side of the fuselage so that paratroopers could get out more quickly. But we thanked heaven we were not assigned to them. I remember during the war always being able to tell whether C-46s had been on one of the airfields before us, even though there would be none in sight; there would be puddles of pink hydraulic fluid all over the field. Try as they might, the engineers working on the C-46 could never eliminate its tendency to leak hydraulic fluid. This stuff was dangerously flammable; as a result, a C-46 in combat that hap-pened to have leaking fluids or vapors could flare up like a torch when a spark was produced by a bullet passing through the fuselage—a hit that the C-47 could take in its stride. We called C-46s "flaming coffins." The C-46s had additional problems: observers noted they were too big to land easily on fields or dirt runways; and their doors were so high off the ground it was difficult to use them for transporting litter patients.[1] The names pilots painted on their C-47s were often marks of affection. Some of these names were the usual showoff or devil-may-care names like *My Shattered Nerves*, *Buzz Buggy*, *Shoo-Shoo Baby*, *Vivacious Virgin*, or *Black Sheep*. To many of us, however, our plane was a lady, our reliable protector, and deserving to be treated as such. My favorite name was *The Daly Express*, in honor of our Group Commander's wife, Mary Daly Williams.

Returning from our third mission during the invasion of Holland, September 19, 1944, David Brack's *My Shattered Nerves* took a bad hit in the tail.

> That hit completely severed the rudder cable. I had to make an emergency landing in Brussels. You can do this—if you know how—with the engines alone. But to get back to our base I had to leave the plane behind. I left Geary, my crew chief, with the plane. I told him "Now look, they're going to try to junk this thing. Don't you let them do it!" I gave him my gun, and told him not to let a single person on the plane. Back at the base I got Pappy Harris, our Line Chief—one of the best experts in the Air Forces on problems like this—and a few other mechanics, and I flew them back to Brussels in another airplane the very next day. I asked Geary whether anybody had tried to take the plane away and cannibalize it for parts; apparently three or four people had tried just that but he had prevented them. Pappy Harris and his crew rolled those rudder cable wires together and welded them, and I flew my plane back. Still the same old *My Shattered Nerves*! (David Brack, Squadron Commander)[2]

One particular honor paid to both the C-47 and to the 81st Troop Carrier Squadron came when Matthew Ridgway, CG of the 82nd Airborne Division, decided he would take a C-47 for his own plane to chauffeur him around the bases and battlefields. He was advised to get a crew from our Squadron.

> At that time [mid-December, 1944] the 82nd Airborne was being rushed up to help in the Battle of the Bulge. My first job was to get General Ridgway and his staff—and all their equipment and personal baggage—over to France and to their new base. When they finished loading the plane, every nook and cranny of the plane was jammed with luggage, stuffed musette bags, boxes of paper, and other boxed equipment—plus a jeep and a trailer. We were enormously overloaded.

Our liaison officer with the 82nd Airborne was a Major Forward, and he wanted to build up some flying time. He asked me to let him fly the plane. I was glad to give him the responsibility. It took every inch of the runway to get that plane off the ground. I would guess my plane was about 50 percent overloaded. But I'd heard about overloaded C-47s making it over the hump in the China-Burma-India theater, and I was pretty sure my plane would make it. The C-47 plane could handle much more than it was designed for. (Leonard Braden, pilot)

----

It was easy to have respect for Colonel Brack. He was a first-rate flyer. On missions, our planes often would have to land on short runways and even on cow pastures. Brack wanted to demonstrate the C-47 could do this. He had us mechanics measure off exactly half the standard landing distance for a C-47. Then he took off, circled the field, and landed within that half-distance. I flew with him on that trip. (Jack McGlothlin, glider mechanic)

The favorable things one could say about the World War II C-47 seem endless. It was easy to rig it up quickly as a stable flying hospital ship, with litters for wounded that clamped onto rings in the floor and ceiling. Its robust construction meant you could pull even two Waco gliders; and, amazingly, it also handled the heavy British Horsa glider well. C-47s might be shot out of the air, and you could crack them up, but nobody ever heard of one wearing out—give them rebuilt engines every 500 hours or so and they seemed to go on forever. Ditch a C-47 in the ocean and it floated—well, not exactly like a boat, but certainly long enough for the crews to get on their "Mae West" inflatable life jackets and throw out their life raft. In all its long and truly global history, there has never been an authenticated case of a C-47 or DC-3 in trouble because of basic structural failure or design faults.

During the invasion of Holland Judson Ball's plane got one engine knocked out, and the other wasn't turning over well; the crew chief had to get on the wobble pump, and by giving it hell, managed to get that one engine to keep the plane in the air. Judd managed to get it back across the Channel and to land at an RAF base at Dover. We had already started to put together a Missing in Action report on his crew when we got a call saying they were all right.

Brack was so impressed Ball saved his crew and whatever was left of the plane he had me put together a recommendation for a DFC. We sent it to Group; but Group sent it back, saying, sure, this man deserves a decoration, but flower it up a bit. So we flowered it up some, and the Old Man signed it again. But when it got to Wing, *they* forwarded it back to us and said, hey, flower this up more so that it will get through Command.

By the time we were through, that report had old Judd up there holding his crew up in the air with his bare hands and with nothing left of the plane but the wings and the stick. When *this* hit Command, they sent it back and said if this man endangered his crew that way by flying that plane back over the Channel he should be court-martialed!

So the Colonel called old Judd in and said, "Hey, here's this damn letter. Look it over and tell me what you want me to do. As far as being disciplined is concerned, just consider yourself as being dressed down for what you did."

Judd said, "Hell, I didn't want that medal anyway. I've had all the excitement and glory I need. When I get back to the States I'm going back to Mississippi and get me a model T Ford, take the tires off it and chain it to a stump; then whenever I get the urge to go traveling, I'll just chug that Ford slowly round and round that stump!"

But old Judd signed up again during the Berlin Airlift crisis [June 1948]. I kidded him some about that. (Walter Ditto, Squadron Adjutant)

The British, the French, and the Russians loved the C-47, and took all of them they could get, and begged for more. The Russians copied the design and, of course, pretended it was invented in Russia. By the end of 1943 our factories were turning them out at the incredible rate of two every hour of every day. After World War II, in Korea during the early 1950s, "Lightning Bug" C-47s dropped parachute flares for nighttime bombing and strafing missions. The French used hundreds of C-47s during the 1950s in their vain attempt to re-supply surrounded French troops and to hold on to northern Vietnam. And the U.S. used C-47s later in South Vietnam in the 1960s, not only for liaison and transport but also as ground attack aircraft: they were fitted out amidships with powerful guns that could fire through side doors both port and starboard. The idea of a C-47 gunship actually shooting at the enemy was so strange their crews called such a plane "Puff, the Magic Dragon"—after a kids' song of that era.

The C-47 was slow, even by the standards of 1944. It cruised at about 155 miles per hour, and 210 mph in level flight seems to have been the best it could do. It had the valuable capacity of remaining stable when throttled back to 100 mph, however, and it did not stall until down to 90 mph. This stability at low rates of speed made it trustworthy in maneuvering to keep a formation in order and that meant paratroops could exit in comparative safety. Other transports, especially converted bombers, generated a tremendous prop wash that could actually somersault the jumping paratroopers.

Bob Lough, one of our pilots, likes to tell about the time he had to shepherd a bevy of small single-engine planes from England to France. Since the designated landing field had been recently bombed out, Lough had to land in a field next to a château; this field presented a real problem, since it was just barely large enough for takeoff, and running right through it was a deep ditch. Nowhere was there a straight and level takeoff distance long enough to avoid that ditch.

You have to remember that the plane could begin to take off only when it got up to around 80 mph, even when it wasn't loaded down. You had to start at the other end of the field, give yourself quarter to half flaps, and hold there while you stood up on the brakes, and ran up those engines as fast as we could get them—until the whole plane would be vibrating like crazy. And then, let 'em loose!

That's the way we got across that ditch. When the plane was 60 to 70 mph you could lift it off the ground just a bit; but then of course it would slam back down to the ground. What we did was to bounce the plane over that ditch; in other words, we were on the ground when we reached the *other* side of the ditch before we could get up enough speed to take off into the wild blue yonder.

### "We were all a little crazy"

The World War II troop carrier pilot had to have a special combination of talents, training, and mental make-up. He was first of all an airplane commander, responsible for the safety of his crew and his passengers (especially the paratroopers). He was also responsible for his towed gliders and the glider pilots and all the airborne infantry they contained. In addition, he was a fighting commander authorized to commit all those who depended on him to attacks on the enemy. He made rapid life-or-death decisions for as many as thirty-three persons inside his plane, or even more if he was a flight, squadron, or group leader. He had to handle these responsibilities while performing complicated feats of formation flying. Finally, when on a combat mission he had to do all this in a slow, unarmed, unarmored plane that positively had to fly low and in an undeviating line to its target—no matter what or how much was being shot up at him.

Fighter and bomber pilots could fight back. It was the troop carrier pilot's job to stay in there and take it. Some of our pilots joked about what it would take to become a troop carrier "ace."

In that emergency landing in Brussels [September 19, 1944], I could see sitting off there toward the end of our runway a whole line of British Spitfires. I had no rudder to turn away from them: I also had no brakes—these had been shot away, too. We were heading right for that line of fighters. I said, "Well, looks like we're going to be aces now!" But by using the engines I managed to turn the plane just before there was a collision, just at the last possible minute. (David Brack, Squadron Commander)

One thing I do know is that I got really hot with frustration as the operation [the Holland invasion] went along. . . . On one of the missions I felt I just had to get some shots off at the Germans, just had to do something myself or go crazy. When we were flying over German territory I left Captain Wilson up there flying the plane by himself for a spell, picked up two submachine guns, and went back to the open door. This was during the run-in before we got to the DZ. I just let go with every bit of ammunition I had at the Germans who were shooting at us. It helped me a lot, psychologically; I didn't do it any more, but I got it off my chest right then. (Adriel Williams, Group Commander)

Today we hear a lot about the "right stuff" needed for difficult assignments, such as for test pilots and astronauts. To me (I was not a pilot) it seems that the right stuff needed to make a good troop carrier pilot—in addition, of course, to physical requirements like fast reactions—was a combination of a very strong sense of responsibility and, paradoxically, a taste for danger plus an ego that made you believe you could face that danger and win.

Sometimes the burdens and pressure involved became unbearable and a pilot would crack. In the first mission to Normandy, the CO of our sister squadron, the 82nd Troop Carrier, suffered a nervous collapse so severe he was unable to lift his leg and place it on the first step of ladder of the door to his plane. This happened while all the rest of us were warming up our engines on the Membury airfield, ready to take off. He had to be relieved then and there of his command. His plane was piloted on that mission by Whitman Peek, a pilot in our 81st Squadron who had previously been Operations Officer with the 82nd.

While most people knew about the 82nd CO pulling himself out of the Normandy invasion, what isn't well known is that this man was deadly afraid of flying at night and equally afraid of formation flying during our stateside training period. From the time we were training at Laurinburg-Maxton, I would always have to be in the left seat during nighttime missions or any formation missions. He always insisted on flying with me and would never take over as pilot during night flying.

Just before the 436th Group rotated overseas, I made an attempt to explain this problem to our Group Commander; but before I could get to him, the 82nd Commander told a bunch of lies about me and managed to get me transferred out of the 82nd and reassigned to the 81st TCS.

So it was poetic justice, if you want to think of it like that, that made this fellow faint dead away just before takeoff for the D-Day operation—and I was chosen to fill his shoes. (Whitman Peek, pilot)

If a pilot had even a slight undetected physical weakness, the stress of his job could lead to real danger for everybody concerned. For example,

On the second re-supply mission to Bastogne I was flying co-pilot. When we were over Bastogne and getting hit our pilot's entire face burst out in perspiration. He had developed a heart murmur. He and I talked it over and decided it would be best if he reported what had happened to our Flight Surgeon, Captain Coleman. Within a day he was on his way home. (Ellery Bennett, pilot)

It was his demanding military assignment, therefore, as well as the World War II public image of a combat pilot, that required troop carrier pilots to go through the war with a swagger. Once in a while this led our 81st pilots into a bit of exhibitionism. Buzzing control towers and cutting swaths across grain fields may not have been as spectacular as flying a C-47 under the Eiffel Tower arch in Paris (that was some other C-47 pilot) but it came out of the same basket. Occasionally one of the pilots would pull off a stunt just to show his friends or to thumb his nose at military discipline. "I guess we were all a little crazy," one of our pilots confessed to me.

On two occasions when I got a five-day pass I went up to a B-17 base at Somarket Airfield northeast of London, where I had quite a number of good friends. And on the first occasion I was permitted to fly with them in a rendezvous plane which had the duty of collecting the Group formation and then returning. I was able to check out in a B-17 and to shoot two landings. On the second visit I was permitted to fly as co-pilot for a mission over Essen in Germany. We returned without damage and that ended my B-17 career.

I suppose that if Colonel Brack had learned of this I would not have been permitted to take these two leaves. Had there been an incident involving injuries there would have been hell to pay for our Squadron's CO as well as for the B-17's squadron commander. (Bill Westcott, pilot)

Sometimes this sort of swagger would exhibit itself as nothing but kid's stuff. Rex Selbe, a pilot, admits that once in a while, during tight formation flight training, pilots in two planes would actually touch wingtips—"just as a stunt."

> Do you remember the urinal that was screwed into the back of the door at the rear of the plane? When nurses or WACs in our plane would go back to use that urinal, of course all they could do was stand up to it; and Lt. Anderson would have one of us give him the high sign. Then he would start snapping the tail of the plane. It was a kind of silly thing to do, but he got kicks out of it. The worst was that either Loving [the crew chief] or I would have the job of cleaning it up from being splashed around a bit. (Ken De Blake, radio operator)

Drinking while piloting a plane was a more serious business. During the war there was much talk about a few of our leading pilots who were thought to be virtual alcoholics; and several others—according to rumor—drank on the job. Today nobody likes to give particulars about this. However, Johnny Harris, a crew chief, admits having to help his drunken pilot out of the cockpit one day *after* the pilot had landed the plane. Johnny's plane was regularly detailed for the mission of mercy known as the "Scotch run" to Edinburgh; and the pilot always took Johnny along, knowing he was a teetotaler and was the only one who would stay sober enough to reload the jeep and trailer in the plane for the trip home.

One consequence of throwing forty or so men like our pilots together in close quarters was that quarrels and lasting animosities were bound to break out. In fact, few postwar life-long friendships seem to have developed among them, in contrast to the situation within our glider pilots' bunch.

To be a troop carrier pilot you had to believe you were as good as anybody else; so it hurt to see others gain more status and promotions because they happened to have seniority or some other advantage that had little to do with their flying skills. During the formation of the original cadre of our 436th Group, several pilots who had distinguished themselves in Aviation Cadet School and had temporary positions as squadron commanders or operations officers (second in command in a squadron) were relegated to lower positions in favor of airline pilots who volunteered later for the Army Air Forces. Thus Charles Hastings, who began in our 81st TCS and whose training and skills entitled him to hope for a command post, never really made his peace with David Brack, a former Eastern Airlines pilot. Hastings acted as Operations Officer of the 81st for a while, but before we moved overseas he transferred to the 82nd TCS where he served for a while as Operations Officer or as flight leader. Today Brack thinks of Hastings' transfer as motivated by a lack of the patience and leadership required in an operations officer, and he recalls that Hastings admitted as much to him. But Hastings feels he was unfairly treated.

Another source of frayed nerves among the pilots was the frustration experienced by those who arrived in the Squadron late and were stuck in the job of co-pilot. During a training flight or mission, a friendly pilot might allow the co-pilot to take over in order to log time as first pilot (the hours you spent in one capacity or another had to be entered in your flight log and could be one of the determining factors in getting a promotion). It was not unusual, though, during some flights, for relations between pilot and co-pilot to be damaged by jealousy on one hand and lack of esteem on the other.

> Another thing I never liked is that because both Roscoe Wilkins [a flight leader] and I were thin, they called him "Pencil" and me "Pencil Junior." I was never happy about those names. (Ellery Bennett, pilot)

However thorny their personal relations might be, pilots helped each other, and not only when flying. The older and more experienced pilots took care to teach the finer points of flying to the younger ones; Charles Hastings admits that in the early days of our Squadron he got many pointers from David Brack. And Hastings went on to teach more recently arrived pilots. Some pilots took on the task of keeping the more hot-headed among them out of trouble; one was "a real Mother Goose," who specialized in getting others back to base on time and in putting drunks to bed. Nobody wanted to "ground" any other pilot, since an even worse and certainly less experienced pilot might be brought in as a replacement.

Perhaps the most valuable service pilots could give each other was to prevent a fellow pilot from falling into a fit of depression out of sheer boredom. When that gray, cold, pitiless, ceaseless English rain fell, boredom was a real problem. Some pilots busied themselves redecorating the officers club and the dayroom. Others found ways to while away the time with food, drink, and of course playing cards.

> The first pilot I met when I joined the 81st at Membury was Captain Waterman. He was the only one of that barracks who had not gone out that night to see the movie. He challenged me to a game of gin rummy. This lesson cost me eighty-two dollars and was one I shall never forget. After the movie let out Doc Coleman came in, and his first words to me were "Have you had your penicillin shot this week?" "No," I said, "should I?" "Yep," he replied, "it helps keep VD down." And the next morning, at breakfast, I saw they had sulfa tablets on the mess hall line. But I later heard that regular use of sulfa pills could give you a problem with double vision. (Ellery Bennett, pilot)

---

I can't remember which day of the week beer was delivered to the local pub. I remember some of us taking a five-gallon jerrican to the pub and bringing it back full of beer together with a basket full of French fries to the barracks. When we found the mess hall was having chicken we would scrounge some giblets and bring them back to fry over our pot-bellied stove in the butter we saved from K-rations. I got interested in photography though it was hard to get film. I remember going to the latrine where it was dark, developing film, and making contact prints. This was the beginning of a hobby and also some activities as base photographer and official photographer for the officers club and other base functions. (Bill Westcott, pilot)

There was a lot of horsing around that relieved tension and boredom. In my barracks one of our pilots, Bill Bishop, always pretended that he was half Sioux; he liked to show us his knife and say to me—maybe because I was the youngest and greenest of the batch—"MacInnes, I'm going to get your scalp tonight!" His acting was so good sometimes I wondered if he really was a civilized American.

Coach Wallen, my pilot for several missions, helped to set good informal relations by pretending to pull rank on us. He was a captain and a good deal older than most of us. He would issue orders right and left—that nobody paid any attention to. In some strange way, this helped our morale considerably. (Bob MacInnes, navigator)

Navigators, like glider pilots, were often in that job partly because they had washed out of pilot training or because at the time they happened to finish there was no foreseeable opening for pilots. Navigators had about the same levels of rank as did pilots, and they lived in the pilots' BOQ (bachelor officers quarters). They started out as 2nd lieutenants, whereas glider pilots usually began as flight officers. (The flight officer rank, which no longer exists in our armed forces, was rated somewhere between a top sergeant and a "shavetail" 2nd lieutenant, about the same as a warrant officer. They were officers, all right, but they held "warrants" rather than the more exalted "commissions.")

In spite of their good training and impressive ability to handle the mathematical and cartographic calculations involved in their job, navigators were respected rather than obeyed in our squadron. Pilots thought of them as a kind of stand-by facility, to be used only when pilots could not handle a navigation problem themselves. During our briefings, therefore, navigators would carefully note down large amounts of seemingly important information: wind directions and velocities, map coordinates, weather conditions, compass variations, altimeter settings. The trouble was that the pilots were there at those same briefings. As a regular part of their training, pilots, too, had had to master at least some of the principles of navigation. Most important, during our days of training in the States, pilots had rarely had a navigator on board; the pilots, therefore, had gotten a lot of practical experience in mapping out and following their own routes. This was called "pilotage." Furthermore, the radio, radar, and beacon facilities were so plentiful in the ETO, and our maps were so good, that even if a pilot got lost the radio operator in the plane might be able to straighten him out. Even David Britt, Squadron Navigation Officer, mainly had to relegate himself to a sort of spectator's role while his pilot worked out his own course through approximate headings, "ground navigation" (that is, visual checkpoints such as towns and rivers), and radio aids. "Probably pilots could handle this sort of navigating even better than we could," he reports. "This is because they got in a lot more practical flying-navigating experience before we went into combat than we navigators could."

One of the big disappointments in World War II airborne tactics was that navigating with the brand new hush-hush radar navigation facilities turned out to be of little help. All our planes had the "Rebecca" receivers which were supposed to react to signals from the "Eureka" radar transmitters which pathfinder paratroopers carried down with them. When many planes in a large formation switched on Rebecca, however, the Eureka transmitters got swamped and tended to send out misleading signals, sometimes three or four miles away from the actual DZ.

Our flight leaders' planes, in addition, had the overly sophisticated, hard to interpret SCR-717, called the "belly-button radar" because of its exterior housing under the fuselage. The SCR-717 mapped out a crude image of the landscape over which we traveled and was practically useless for navigators except when we were passing over bodies of water like the Channel or large rivers. Finally, a few of us had the British GEE radar, meant to show through "triangulation" (three intersecting beacons) where you were. GEE was supposed to show, at nighttime, some features of the terrain over which we were flying, but it had been designed to pinpoint RAF bombing targets in Europe, since the RAF did most of its bombing at night. Because practically all of our flying after the Normandy invasion was during daylight hours, we did not find much use for it. All these sets sat on the desk in the navigators' compartment; but in actual flight you would usually find the sets turned off and the navigator standing behind the pilot, trying to match what he saw unrolling before him through the cockpit window with what he had in his briefing notes and what he read on his maps.

With all their equipment, navigators could get lost, too. I've had navigators come up in the cockpit and say, "Where in the hell are we?" A lot of pilots fancied themselves pretty much as navigators. I was the kind of pilot that always got a little antsy; and I always wanted to keep track of where I was myself. (Art Feigion, pathfinder pilot)

## Radio operators and crew chiefs

Picture a small space on the right side of the crew compartment behind the cockpit, about five feet by three. To your left is a bank of radio transmitters; against the plane's wall, a shelf with a Morse code transmitting key. In the chair, a radio operator, earphones on, a dreamy expression on his face. He is not working. In fact he has switched to a BBC news broadcast. He listens to BBC news this way pretty often. Sometimes he also listens to music on the American Forces Network and tells the pilots about it so they can listen, too. What really rivets his attention is the quality of female BBC news announcers' voices, coming in right after the chimes of Big Ben. The way they sound makes more of an impression than what they are saying. He finds their accents and phrasing very attractive: soft yet precise, and with a musical lilt.

Like the navigator, the troop carrier radio operator flew with his plane on a sort of stand-by basis and only seldom performed functions vital for the plane's mission or safety. On very long flights, such as those over the Atlantic, he called in position reports. He also got weather information and confirmed by radio the altimeter setting for the plane's next stop. Over a combat zone, his main duties involved listening for recall messages to abort the mission after it was in the air, and standing in the astrodome, Aldis lamp in hand, ready to give the planes and the gliders behind his plane the red light ("Four minutes to go!"), and then the green light. Even the green light signal to glider pilots was precautionary rather than essential as long as the intercom wire that snaked along the tow rope between glider and plane worked properly. Maddeningly, in the tightest combat situations the plane-to-glider intercom frequently did indeed malfunction.

Radio operators, like many others in our Squadron, would have preferred more important functions, and we often talked about how to cope with the sensation of feeling like fifth wheels. We knew that in certain crises we would really earn our keep; for example, if our plane had to ditch in the Channel, we were the ones trained to operate the hand-cranked emergency radio in our life-raft, to inflate the antenna balloon and send it up, and to get in touch with Air-Sea Rescue. Many C-47s in fact did have to ditch, but none in our Squadron. Every once in a while we were put through the routine of what was called "Dinghy Drill" ("dinghy" was a name for any little boat). The pilot would turn around and yell, "Dinghy, Dinghy! Prepare for ditching!" and I would have to jump out of my seat, haul the life raft to a position near the door, check to see if it had its radio and emergency food and water, and take my position, along with the crew chief, with my back against the crew compartment partition so as to minimize the severe shock when a plane landed in the water. Jack Wallen, our pilot, always had a big grin on his face when he yelled out "Dinghy, Dinghy!" because none of us really believed it ever would be necessary.

Hal Burrows is one of several radio operators who have admitted having had daydreams about saving their planes in some crisis through their radio expertise. On one occasion he and Pat Hart proved their usefulness—but not to the extent of being anybody's hero.

> Once I begged a ride on Hal Burrows' plane on some milk run. Our plane got completely lost on its way to deliver supplies to a German base. The glider pilot who was acting as navigator knew nothing about the plane's radar navigation sets. Hal Burrows and I were able to show what we knew. Like all good radio mechanics I had my tuning wrench along with me, and I was able to readjust the Rebecca radar and pick up the beacon from that German field where we were headed.
>
> Then, coming home in pretty nasty weather, we got lost again! So we set to work on the GEE radar. This British set worked by receiving signals from two ground transmitting stations; and after you lined up these signals on the screen, you could read off the ground coordinates for the plane's location on a chart. It worked; and before we got back to Melun, our French base, the weather cleared up and the pilot could see we had indeed pointed him in the right direction. (Pat Hart, radio mechanic)

A radio operator's job was pretty well done by the time he climbed on board. Early that morning he had already gotten his orders for the day either during briefing or directly from the Communications Officer, "Smiling George" Rankin (Captain Rankin was notorious for having the most serious face in the Squadron). Included were his "codes for the day" (for translating "clear language" into encoded Morse code); the correct calibration frequencies for his various sets; the "colors of the day" (recognition signals by Aldis lamp or "Very" flare pistols); and the "Pundits" (flashing codes identifying different airfields in England and the Continent). During pre-flight checks he saw to it that all radio sets were calibrated properly, that the radio compass was working, and that the radar set was in position; he also looked over the outside antennae to check whether they seemed to be in good shape.

According to our MOS (classification), we were radio mechanics as well as radio operators (ROMs), trained to maintain and repair radios as well as operate them; but Cecil Elder, our Communications section chief, and his crew of ground radio mechanics were more trained and more experienced at taking the gremlins

Bill Frye, pilot. Bill and his crew were shot down and all were
killed in our last main invasion mission, the drop across the Rhine,
March 24, 1945.

Cloyd Clemons, Bill Frye's crew
chief.

Ben Smith, Bill Frye's radio
operator. Williard Cooke, co-
pilot, also was killed on this
mission.

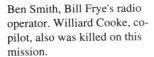

out of the radios than we were, so that all our equipment would usually be in good shape even before we "went out on the line" (to the waiting planes).

Once in flight, the crew chief had even less to do than the radio operator. The crew chief was the only crew member who did not have his own seat in the plane; he could use the navigator's seat (if a navigator was not on board), stand up behind the pilots, or—if we were not carrying paratroopers—try to rest on the hard bucket seats in the main section of the plane.

Nobody would have dreamed of calling the crew chiefs fifth wheels. They shouldered the responsibility for keeping the plane's engines and body in good operating condition. From the wheel tire under the tail to the windshield wipers outside the cockpit, every single bit of that plane, apart from radar and radios, was his responsibility. He did have support for the more demanding repairs from our Engineering Officer (Joseph Konecny), the Squadron Line Chief (Pappy Harris), the Squadron Airplane Inspector (Carlisle Jordan), and our ground airplane mechanics. For major overhauls the crew chief could call on the engineering departments of Group and Wing, but in the end it was the crew chief who kept the plane flying. For a radio operator, a gremlin in his sets was an annoyance and a black mark against him; for a crew chief an uninvestigated noise might mean the loss of the plane.

On easy days, our job was to get right out to the flight line after breakfast and to pre-flight the plane to see that everything was OK. We also were held responsible to be ready to fly along with our plane whenever it was given a mission. And we had to pull the fifty- and hundred-hour inspections. We kept records on each plane and turned them in to our Engineering Department. Tech Supply was there to provide us with the tools and small parts we needed; and our Line Chief helped out on complicated jobs and assigned us additional men when it became necessary. And then there were the specialists in hydraulics, electrical parts, and instruments in Group who would be there when we needed them.

We crew chiefs and the other airplane mechanics not only worked together; we also ate together, bunked together, and went to town together. I never really got to know the details of jobs the other fellows had. (Jerome Loving, crew chief)

Crew chiefs worked as though their lives depended on it—which was literally true. They worked all hours in that cold and rainy English climate while their fingers froze and their bellies churned with all the coffee it took to keep them awake on nights when the plane absolutely had to be made ready for the next mission. Several times I was startled to see Ben Obermark, our crew chief, treating a gash on his hand he got while working on an engine by just sucking it to draw out the grease, not even bothering to put on a Band-Aid. When I would try to urge him to get to the Dispensary to take care of the cut he would say "My Pappy, back on the farm, always told me the cheapest thing you could grow was skin."

> You better believe that the crew chiefs really looked the planes over after every mission to see if flak or shells had hit any vital spot. The ground crew mechanics worked with us—but maybe we were a little more interested in this line of work. When there were too many holes we took the planes over to the depot to have them patched; and after 500 or 600 hours the engines were replaced by new or rebuilt engines, just as they did for commercial planes in the States. (Ben Obermark, crew chief)

We radio operators, who tended to be a rather finicky and complaining bunch, always marveled at the good humor the long-suffering crew chiefs sported to sustain themselves at their difficult jobs. It was as if they appreciated the ridiculousness of entrusting themselves—after only some months in airplane engineering school—with the tremendous responsibility of maintaining and re-pairing that huge and complex piece of flying machinery. Ben Obermark, for example, had worked out a bit of philosophy for dealing hour after hour with that damned left oil pressure gauge that gave the wrong readings. "By God!" he would say, "All you have to know is that it's never the part you suspect that turns out to be doing the damage!"

Thinking back, I realize how much all the men in the crews looked up to their chiefs and appreciated their sense of responsibility and their (generally) good humor:

> I think it's plain that the crew chiefs had the hardest job of all. Not only did we have to cope with our own fears—like worrying about a shot in the gas tank that would blow us all to kingdom come. But we also had to take on everybody else's fears. First it was the pilots—they were always sure that the right engine or the left engine didn't sound just right. And I never could convince the navigator and radio operator that we needed both of them for some jobs.
>
> We also had the paratroopers' worries on our shoulders. It was hard to convince them they were better off on the ground than continuing to fly on in our airplane.
>
> Then there were the nurses—now, they were something else. They just

couldn't believe I was one guy that understood they, too, might have to use the plane's john. Neither would they believe I would be glad to clean it out for them, either. Well, they may have been right on this last score.

Once my pilot, Jack Wallen, made a believer of me when he claimed he could take our plane off safely although it was fully loaded down with a huge number of French POWs we were taking back to Paris. In addition he wanted to take on some captain who also needed a ride to Paris—plus a lot of that officer's equipment and duffle bags.

Well, we made it; and when Wallen left the plane he handed me a package and said, "That captain said this is for you!" When the plane was emptied out I opened the package; to my surprise it was a bottle of very good champagne.

This present gave me something else to worry about. Should I take it to my tent and share it with the other four crew chiefs there? Or should I try a little of it first?

I thought over this problem deeply while I was cleaning up the vomit the French POWs had left all over the floor. I decided to taste the champagne first. Wow! (Ben Obermark, crew chief)

Their complex and often exhausting responsibilities meant that crew chiefs stuck together. They also tended to relieve the tension with some pretty physical horseplay and, of course, with playing cards and drinking beer.

Recently I got to thinking about how much Flight Chief Vernon Sawvell meant to us back in those days. When we'd come back from a mission where we had taken some losses, we'd be pretty down in the dumps. Sawvell would come into our barracks and after a few words of sympathy he'd start complaining about something or other. The blankety blank cooks—or the ground mechanics, or the pilots. . . . That if the pilots tore up any more airplanes, hitting trees or each other, they'd have to get some kiddy-carts to get in their flying time! Pretty soon he'd have us all laughing. And then we'd all go out for something to eat. (Ben Obermark, crew chief)

One function radio operators and crew chiefs had to share was that of helping shove out the paratroopers' bundles. Some parabundles had to go out before the first trooper jumped; in this case it would be handled by the crew chief and the paratrooper jumpmaster. If they were careful types, the CC and RO would tie themselves to a hook near the door before a jump, since slipping and falling out that wide-open door, in a plane that often was violently slewing around, was a real danger. We also were required to wear parachutes while getting ready to manhandle door bundles during a jump. Seeing us this way, the paratroopers passing by us on their way out would often give us a taunting invitation to jump along with them, "just to see how it feels." None of us ever took advantage of such offers.

Whatever their rank, flying EMs and Os were in the same boat during combat. This usually tended to hold down the strict application of the rigid protocol and peremptory orders that still characterized other military units those days. It did not mean our officers broke the military tradition against fraternizing with EMs. There were exceptions. Captain Coleman was known to put on a sergeant's uniform and spend some time on leave in town with friends he had among the enlisted men—he claimed he had a more relaxed time of it with them than with some of our officers.

> Certainly I was not buddy-buddy with any officer. Those I dealt with were decent to me and I reciprocated. But I can't forget that once I let Captain Wilkins know that I would really like a pair of oxfords—you remember that enlisted men those days were issued only regular high-top shoes and were not allowed to buy dress shoes at the PX. Then, one day when I was coming back from the base theater, there was a pair of new dress shoes on my bunk. The fellows in the barracks told me that Captain Wilkins had brought them along for me. (Emmett Pate, crew chief)

As far as the entire Squadron was concerned, however, the old rules that put a social wall between EMs and Os still stood. For example, we had separate latrines. Even stranger, in July and August 1944, when part of the Squadron was in Italy preparing for the invasion of southern France, the nearby black sand beach was divided into officers' and enlisted men's sectors.

Everybody knew that all crew members shared the risk of death. Howard Walch, David Brack's radio operator, stood up at one point during the assault across the Rhine in order to take his position in the astrodome. At that moment a 20 mm shell passed right up through the seat he had just left. The message was plain: death was not segregated.

Recently Brigadier General Adriel Williams, who commanded our 436th Troop Carrier Group, told me he felt the 81st TCS was "the best in the ETO." Delighted with the way Williams had singled us out over his other three squadrons, I made a point of telling this to David Brack. I asked Brack why Williams had had such a high opinion of us. Brack's answer was that Williams thought of us as a thoroughly dependable unit, one where everybody knew his job and where the pilots were exceptionally well qualified. Williams always felt that whenever he gave us an assignment it would get done without quibbling, on time, and in good order. Part of the credit should go to the way almost all the flying personnel handled, in a relaxed and sensible manner, the very sticky problem of their relationships on and off the job.

## Notes

1. Moore, Ch. 1, p. 40.

2. Brack's plane survived additional ground fire during our jump across the Rhine (March 24, 1945); the plane made it back to the States and lived on until at least the Korean War era when "old serial number 42-100546" was spotted in Alaska by Johnny Harris (crew chief).

# 9. Gliding
## Our "Glider Guiders"

### *Whose* "return trip war"?

The fascination gliders hold for everybody is linked to man's eternal yearning for free flight.

> To me on the ground it was a beautiful sight, on a good day, to see a glider catching updrafts and staying there for what seemed like hours, soaring around and around, and even up and down. (Jerome Loving, crew chief)

All of us in the 81st TCS, whatever our job, have strongly etched memories not only of gliders soaring in the sky but also of gliders lined up on the ground taking on airborne infantry; gliders being towed in formation; gliders in hangars, their holes being patched up with a bit of fabric and glue. Our glider pilots, however, have a different set of glider images: gliders horribly smashed up on a field of combat, gliders smeared along a stone wall or a hedgerow, glider contents, including mangled bodies, strewn about the ground.

Combat gliders were an essential element of World War II. Their role in every airborne invasion was crucial. Yet they are the forgotten machine of this struggle. Later generations are not only ignorant of them, they find it hard to believe such a device, such a tactic, ever existed. Part of the reason is that "a glider," to most people, means an instrument of sport, a fragile-looking but beautifully sleek piece of adventure, a sailplane, exciting in the risks and new sensations it offers sportsmen who fly it. Even persons reasonably knowledgeable about the history of World War II are surprised, almost incredulous, when told there once were gliders that carried thirteen fully equipped infantrymen and two pilots on desperate missions behind enemy lines, and that the United States used hundreds of these gliders in a single operation.

Combat gliders went out of existence during the 1950s, replaced by the new combat helicopter and massive new assault transport airplanes.[1] Those combat gliders of World War II that were still flyable after 1945 were quickly scrapped.

You can find our American Waco and the British Horsa gliders in pictures and movies; and if you search hard enough you can find pictures of World War II German combat gliders, too. Still-functioning airplanes—the C-47s (in their DC-3 version) are a fairly common sight. If you want to get a look at a real American combat glider, though, you will have to go to the Air Force Museum at Wright Patterson Air Force Base in Dayton, Ohio. There are two others in rather out-of-the-way museums maintained by volunteer World War II buffs: the Silent Wings Museum in Terrell, Texas, and the museum maintained by the 101st Airborne Infantry Division at Fort Campbell, Kentucky. The fourth and last remaining CG-4A was put together out of scrap for use in the film version of Cornelius Ryan's *A Bridge Too Far*, but it was never actually used in that movie. It remains on view in the World War II museum at Ste-Mère-Eglise, Normandy. Not a single British Horsa glider is to be found anywhere.

When I first began work on this book, I anxiously fished around for a good title. I first hit on "The Return Trip War," hoping to underscore what made our troop carrier experience different from the rest of World War II outfits; one essential difference, I felt, was that while we were at risk during the relatively short periods over combat zones, if we and our planes survived we could be back at our comfortable base in a few hours, relaxing in our barracks or recounting what we saw over a beer in the day room or officers club, or over a hot meal in the mess hall. Glider pilots did not have a "return trip"—not, at least, until after having spent between a few days and a week heavily involved in the fighting on the ground.

If they emerged from their landed gliders in one piece, glider pilots were expected to grab their carbines and other weapons and make themselves useful. Often this meant fighting alongside the airborne infantry they had just landed in order to overwhelm a fortified German position on the perimeter of their field. When the dust of their assault battle settled down, they were expected to handle ammunition, guard prisoners, dig in and serve as perimeter defenses, or move along as the rear men in a squad of airborne infantry working toward some assigned objective. When and if the ground infantry linked up with the airborne— that is, when their mission was completed—glider pilots were expected to make it back to base as quickly as possible and by any reasonable conveyance, since they might be needed for a follow-up operation (reinforcement or possibly a re-supply) in case of a dangerous-looking enemy counterattack.

Even the best efforts of writers, poets, and artists fail when they try to convey to the rest of us what it feels like to be a soldier in combat. For the history of the 81st Troop Carrier Squadron, this is most true where glider pilots were concerned. Only by somehow getting inside their later nightmares could the rest of us realize what a glider pilot faced from the time he cut loose from his tow plane to the time he sank down on his bunk back in his barracks.

When pressure on glider pilots became too much to bear it could produce serious physical symptoms:

> Just prior to our mission across the Rhine River at Wesel [March 1945] several of us were sitting and jawing in our tent. I noticed that Herb Christie [glider pilot] was in terrible distress. When he tried to talk, only one side of his mouth and one side of his face would move. We rushed him to Doc Coleman. He explained that because of the accumulated stress from all our missions and the preparation for the Rhine crossing, Herb's central nervous system had simply rebelled. I learned later that one whole side of his body had been paralyzed. The doctors said that it was like an electrical system that had shorted out.
>
> But Herb recovered and went on the Rhine mission. He survived it and the rest of the war. After the war he flew a Super-Cub in Alaska. He was killed on one of these flights. (Gale Ammerman, glider pilot)

Perhaps the rest of us might possibly be able to understand at least one important point: in combat a glider could not be said to "land." It crashed, more or less successfully. Slow and easy targets, flying directly over enemy positions, gliders had to get down quickly. A skillful pilot might be able to stay up for five minutes or more—if he wanted to take his chances on the flak and bullets whizzing around him. It was life or death to reach the ground quickly, but often the question was, land where? When the Germans anticipated that a field or meadow might become a glider landing zone, they would "take denial measures" (militarese for loading the field with mines and deadly obstacles like "Rommel's asparagus"). Or, upon coming close enough to eyeball his assigned LZ, a glider pilot might suddenly realize that what had been reported in his briefing as a fourfoot hedge was really a twenty-foot row of Lombardy poplars with a stone fence behind.

> But of course during the actual operation [the invasion of Normandy] we could see that we were coming down in areas quite different from those pictures we had been shown. It was impossible to prevent the panic we all felt; lots of gliders began to cut off early and maneuver to get down on the ground and into those small fields as quickly as they could.
>
> I kept telling myself that when glider pilots are scared they drop the nose and try to get on the ground too fast. I told our co-pilot, Gephart, that according to our briefing, three minutes after crossing the coast would bring

us over the landing zone at just about the right place. I told him to check the time and watch the second hand. Three minutes at about 120 mph would put us into Normandy about six miles; this was how far from the coast our landing zone was supposed to be.

At about the same time that glider pilots were cutting loose ahead of us, ground fire started to come up; the tracers, like fireworks going off in the sky, were coming up at us with what looked like frightening accuracy. Pretty soon our tow plane was actually in the lead—all those in front of us had already peeled off and were heading back to England. But we didn't see anything recognizable on the ground; I said to Gephart that we would hang on for three minutes and then cut loose. To our relief, just as the second hand came up on three minutes we spotted a lighted "T" where the pathfinders had set up our landing. We cut off and circled to the left; we were already drawing some fire from the perimeter of the field.

We made a good turn and lined up to fly right into the corner of this field. But just as we were about to touch down, the left landing gear hit something and broke right off. A split second after that the tail hit the same obstacle; fortunately, the glider rolled straight ahead in spite of this. The glider stopped maybe two thirds of the way down this field—and there we sat, in the other pilots' way who were to be coming in after us! That worried us sick; but in a few seconds it became clear that, for a few moments at least, there was nobody that seemed to be about to crash into us.

When the tail hit, the glider's fuselage broke open at the bottom near the center. The opening was only some six or eight inches, and somehow we had to get out a jeep, its trailer with radio equipment, and seven or eight airborne troopers. But we couldn't get them out the cargo door, which had jammed; and we had to grab our fire axes and hack away at the fuselage.

Now other gliders started to come into our field. I had to yell at the men to get away and get away fast if they didn't want to get clobbered. Everybody ran out of the glider to see what was happening. Gliders were coming in crossways, at high speeds, hitting the ground and bouncing way up in the air. (Bob Carney, glider pilot)

---

Wriggled out of my flak suit and safety belt, grabbed my Garand, gas mask, and field equipment; got the hell away from the glider into a nearby ditch to use my Garand to cover the airborne boys while they were unloading. But I was so damned excited when I got down it took me a couple of minutes to load that gun. I had forgotten to load it before we took off from England!

And here we are in France. But where? The only noise we could hear was that of gliders coming in, most of them crashing. It was a nightmare to see those big gliders come in, hit trees and hedgerows and literally disinte-

A Waco glider taking off under tow. (Courtesy Smithsonian Institution)

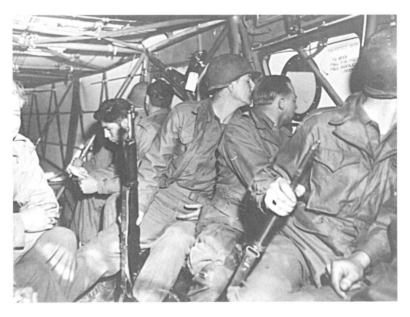

Glidermen on a practice mission trying to see out of the Waco's small portholes.
(Courtesy USAMHI)

grate. Some of them were in terrible shape. One of the boys in our Squadron went right by my glider at about 50 mph, hit the trees and hedgerows on the end of the field, tore one wing and the gear off, went on through the hedgerow, and hit the one across the road a hell of a whack. I felt: They're all dead. I stayed in my guard post. About five minutes later everybody crawled out of the wreckage. No fooling, it was the surprise of my life to see them.

Meanwhile, the airborne troopers weren't doing so well at unloading my glider. Because I wanted to get the hell out of there before things really began to pop, I took my equipment off and took charge of the unloading. We did it in about half an hour and then started to help the other gliders. But then all hell broke loose. Big shells started to go over and land in back of us about half a mile. Going the other way was smaller caliber stuff, but still damn noisy. We could also hear a low "whoosh" and then a small explosion every once in a while—these sounded like grenades. But it turned out to be mortar fire from Jerry in only the next field over—too damned close for comfort. We could hear firing on three sides of us—what were we supposed to do? Where were all the paratroopers who had jumped before us early that morning and were supposed to have cleared out the LZ for us and whom we were supposed to support with the glider troops?

Finally along came some lieutenant colonel who told us we were in a no-man's land and to lie still until ordered to move on. We lay there in that fire for five hours. (Darlyle Watters, Squadron Glider Officer, from a letter written in 1944)

## Doctrine and training

Might our glider pilots have been spared much grief if the American glider program had been less slow getting off the ground? While there is no way to be certain, the only reasonable answer must be *yes*. Would the invasion of "Fortress Europe" in 1944 have been even more successful if, by the time we entered the war in 1941, we had possessed *any* trained combat glider pilots to act as cadres for a glider program? Again, the answer has to be *yes*. But we had none, not a single combat glider pilot, not a single combat glider. To corrupt Churchill: never was so much accomplished starting from so little. You could even say the starting point for our glider program was not zero, it was negative, below zero. Prejudice against gliding in our armed forces during the 1920s had built up to the point where in 1931 sport gliding by any soldier had been banned—the excuse being that it was too risky. This ban remained in force right up until 1941.

The lesson of the Germans' earlier "silent wings" triumph in May 1940 with assault gliders at Eben Emael was too important to ignore. The implications of this lesson, involving as they did painful changes in American military doctrine, meant that few of our military planners were willing to advocate the changes that seemed needed. In March 1941 General H. H. Arnold finally succeeded in sending out invitations for bids for the construction of our first combat gliders. At that point more months had to be wasted because of the required procedures and traditions of American military procurement, which made it necessary to ask at least several firms to submit competing designs. To get going, Arnold had to agree to restricting the bid invitations to companies not already involved in the construction of powered aircraft. The winning design was submitted by the Waco Aircraft Company of Troy, Ohio—thus our name "Waco" for the CG-4A.

By July 1941 a few dozen military pilots had agreed to retread themselves as glider pilots. The only gliders available then for training were sport sailplanes; and any experience the pilots had in thermal soaring in these first military gliders had little to do with the kind of towed flying and troop landing later used in combat.

Slowly yielding to pressure from Arnold, who was strongly pushing for means to expand the program, the Army Air Forces let down the barriers a bit more and agreed to use civilian glider teachers on civilian fields on a contract basis. At a few airports such as Elmira, New York, and Lockport, Illinois, more attention was paid to glider training. During the late summer of 1941 a few more civilian training schools opened to glider pilots, and glider manufacturers were strongly pressured to manufacture two-place training gliders. In 1942 some trainers being used, however, were nothing but light planes with their engines removed. Removing the engine made room for another seat, flight controls, and an instrument panel, which turned the plane into a three-place glider. It was a fairly good glider to fly (and to teach others with); officially it was known as an Aeronca TG-5.

Even these TG-5s remained scarce for months, so much so that many glider pilots those days had no training in actual gliding except for "dead stick landings" in which a trainee would be taken up in a light power plane, allowed to kill the engine, and instructed in how to glide to a stop on the runway.

Many of the trainees had had previous flying experience; but this was the first time I had even been in an airplane. We had small planes—Piper Cubs, Aeroncas, and Taylorcrafts. After about eight hours of instruction, I was able to solo. When the instructor felt that we had enough confidence in our flying, he would tell us to fly up to about 8,000 feet and turn off the engine and make dead stick landings. After a few minor incidents we became quite proficient at landing the aircraft without benefit of propeller.

The next phase of our training was in Fort Sumner, New Mexico. Here we flew small gliders; they were like Aeroncas without an engine. We did some night flying as well. In our night flying training, all we had to land by was lighted smudge pots strung out to mark a runway. On one late night training flight, as I proceeded to lose altitude I became a bit disoriented; when I decided to look for the runway I spotted two rows of lights and flew in that direction until I saw a truck driving right along between those lights. It finally dawned on me that the lights were the street lights of the main street in Fort Sumner. Luckily I still had enough altitude to get back to the field—barely. (J. J. DiPietro, glider pilot)

Until the U.S. entered World War II, the glider program remained tiny and without much enthusiastic support among our military planners. There was a glaring inconsistency here, since already we were planning to reorganize entire divisions as airborne divisions (not formally authorized until August 1942). How could one deploy so many men without a sufficient number of combat gliders and glider pilots? Nevertheless, the Chiefs of Staff continued to channel pilot training into bombers and fighters; and until Pearl Harbor the suggestion that eventually we might need as many as a thousand glider pilots was dismissed as utterly out of the question.

The shock of Pearl Harbor changed all that. Revelations of how our country was being endangered by hidebound and outdated military doctrine weakened resistance to experimentation and innovation. By the end of December 1941, General Arnold was able to issue a country-wide appeal for volunteers for the Army Air Forces glider program from among our already trained military pilots and other officers. Officers not trained as pilots, who would have to begin all over again as glider pilot trainees, were promised that in the new program they could keep the rank they had previously attained.[2] The word went out that we would indeed be building our glider pilot corps up to 1,000, but the response to this appeal was disappointing. Practically every officer or cadet who wanted to be a pilot wanted to pilot a powered airplane, not a glider.

The British glider pilot program suggested a way out of this dilemma. The British had scuttled the traditional notion that every pilot should be a commissioned officer and were turning out enlisted glider pilots, "flight sergeants." During the first part of 1942 our Air Forces and the Civil Aeronautics Board cooperated in a strenuous effort to locate volunteers from among the many thousands of civilians who had at least a basic license to fly a power plane. The number of authorized glider pilots jumped from 1,000 to 4,200, and finally to

6,000. Few civilian pilots took advantage of the offer, however, since other options for them, in occupations exempt from the draft and in power pilot programs in the military, looked more attractive—or less dangerous.

In June 1942 the Army Air Forces took the one necessary step further and initiated a campaign for training glider pilots from among men who were not prospective power pilots, not officers, and who had no flying experience.

James J. DiPietro, whose first Army assignment early in 1942 was in a medical training unit, was "volunteered" for glider pilot training while peeling potatoes.

> On the second day of KP after finishing my chores, I went into the sergeant's office and told him I wanted a transfer. He asked me why and told me all the advantages of working in a nice comfortable hospital. I said, "I don't care, I want to get out of this chicken-shit outfit!" Next morning, while I was in the kitchen, knee deep in potatoes, old sarge came in and made his way around the mound of potatoes. He said, "How would you like to be a glider pilot?" I said OK, or something to that effect, as I studiously picked up another potato to peel. He put my name down on a pad he always carried around and disappeared. I was left wondering, "What the hell is a glider pilot?"

In a gesture as insulting as it was unnecessary, the new crop of glider pilot volunteers were termed "Class B students." Physical requirements were to be a bit less than those for conventional pilots, and even eyes that were not 100 percent perfect were accepted. A truly ambitious publicity campaign for more glider pilots was unleashed on college campuses, army bases, and in large towns. One recruiting brochure read, "Soar to Victory as a Glider Pilot in the U.S. Army Air Forces!" Army recruiters and top sergeants were told to be on the lookout for soldiers who might be attracted by the relatively elite appeal of being a combat glider pilot.

Today we can see that by the summer of 1942 the Army glider program was beginning to come into its own. One heartening symbol of its new status was the glider pilot wings awarded to graduates—like a power pilot's wings but with a large "G" on the central medallion.

The Air Forces, however, demonstrated just how low these glider cadets rated, placing most of them in the most barren, most out-of-the-way, grungiest bases in the country. There they sat and baked that summer—without gliders, tug planes, or glider instructors, deprived of any satisfactory training. In a heavy-handed attempt to keep them out of trouble, the Army Air Forces saddled them with "ground training": week after week of close-order drill, KP, tidying up the

base, target practice, and cross-country hikes. Morale reached rock bottom.
Many reacted by going AWOL (absent without leave).

> It was pretty disheartening; they actually put us into a Boy Scout camp! I
> got my bed assignment about 10 p.m.; and while I was sitting there a scor-
> pion ran right across the floor. I felt like the world had come to an end.
> After two weeks we were sent to Clovis, New Mexico, and billeted in a
> hotel—that was a real improvement. A few more weeks and there we were
> in the famous glider training school at Twentynine Palms, California. I
> would like you all to know that a Lt. Ronald Reagan sat in on one of my
> classes—but only as an observer. At the same school I saw Jackie Coogan
> but he looked like a sad case to me.
>
> After we finished light glider training we had to wait around until they
> had some heavy glider schools to send us to. I drew Dalhart, Texas, a new
> base, and what a mud hole! While we were sitting around in various bases,
> often they had nothing for us to do but ground training, that is, infantry. We
> were supposed to get so tough we could dive through a brick wall. Hah!
> (Thayer Bonecutter, glider pilot)

Gradually, during the fall of 1942, some glider training bases improved,
glider instructors became more plentiful, and glider cadets received more hours
of flight training. When this wasn't possible, commanders of the most-deprived
bases simply sent their glider cadets home on thirty-day furloughs. In November
1942 the whole program was put on a new basis, symbolically as well as materially. The Air Forces decreed that every graduate of a glider training program
who earned his wings was to be rated a flight officer rather than a flight sergeant.
The rank of flight officer was invented during World War II; it no longer exists
in the Air Force. A flight officer was not a commissioned officer. Glider pilots
called their blue-enamelled insignia of rank the "Blue Pickle," and many of
them stayed in that rank all through the war, never able to turn in the Blue Pickle
for the gold bar of a second lieutenant.

> We finally got army uniforms after being at Keesler Field with only the
> clothes on our backs for about ten days. My civilian clothes could stand up
> by themselves. From Keesler, we took a troop train to Columbus, Ohio,
> and Lockburn Air Force Base; we were about the first there. At that time
> we were just about all enlisted men; in fact, most of us were privates. We
> had a chicken second lieutenant in charge. He kept guards at the gates—
> although the rifles they carried were made of wood.
>
> At Lockburn . . . I never did fly, though I did get some rides. Then

some of us were shipped to Grand Forks, North Dakota, for training in light planes. We finished what they figured was half the required flying time for that level of training, and then shipped us to Randolph, Texas.

I believe that for some time we were actually lost from Army records. So finally we went to complain to the colonel; and shortly after that we were shipped out to Okmulgee Field, Oklahoma, to finish our light plane training.

We next were shipped to Stuttgart, Arkansas. We were the first ones there, and it was a mud-hole. We stayed in the kind of barracks that had one pot-bellied stove to warm the entire barracks. While the summer lasted this wasn't too bad; but when winter came it was hell. I got so cold one night that after putting as many newspapers as I could under my cot mattress, I actually put my gas mask over the top of my head so I could keep a little warmer.

At that time there were no airplanes on base, though later on it became a B-25 school. We went to Little Rock to get in our flying time. Most all weekends were spent either in Little Rock or in Memphis. These were pretty wild times. Then all of a sudden it was Hurry Up Time; we were sent to Lubbock, Texas, and there we flew CG-4As nearly all day long, even during the night.

We were graduated from Class 43-18 just before Christmas, and were made flight officers and shipped off to home. I was fortunate to be able to be home for Christmas. (Earl Goodwin, glider pilot)

Glider doctrine, as it developed during 1942 and 1943, envisioned a kind of one-two-three punch, in which paratroopers would land first, throwing the enemy into confusion and clearing out turf as landing zones for the next wave, the glider infantry. When needed, the third wave would be a re-supply glider mission, reinforcements of personnel and supplies. Possibly because we had overinflated expectations of what the first wave (the paratroopers) could accomplish, prevailing doctrine ruled that the gliders would be used as sparingly as possible and that the airborne mission would be over as soon as a link-up between infantry and airborne was made.

Some Army Air Forces officers—in the way common to all bureaucrats who try to build their own institutional empires—argued that since soldiers in gliders were brought into combat by Air Forces power pilots and accompanied by Air Forces glider pilots on the ground, they should therefore come under the control of the Air Forces. This point of view was indignantly rejected by the much more influential infantry generals in Washington. In fact, some infantry generals made strong counterproposals to have glider pilots organized as parts of infantry divisions, since they fought on the ground with the airborne troopers! There also was a good precedent, they thought, in the British practice of treating glider pilots as infantry soldiers, not RAF airmen. This proposal failed, too, and glider pilots remained Air Forces (in our case, the Ninth Air Force) while the glider troopers remained airborne infantry.

How we as individuals were affected by changing high command decisions about troop carrier is well illustrated by what happened to Darlyle Watters, who was our Squadron Glider Officer until he was forced down during the Holland invasion (September 1944) and captured by the Germans. His World War II career shows how by 1943 the Air Forces had to abandon the idea of training glider pilots in specialized schools and had to depend on on-the-job training.

From the time he was enticed into the glider training program, in June 1942, until American gliders were used to invade France, on June 6, 1944, it was never clear what kind of a war Watters would fight. First, gliders had to prove (in training maneuvers in the States) the capability of delivering airborne troopers behind enemy lines; then General Eisenhower had to be convinced that, in spite of the terrible losses and disastrous mistaken landings during the 1943 invasions of Sicily and Italy by the Allies, gliders were still feasible aerial assault systems.

Watters had his private pilot's license at age twenty, and fully expected to become a power pilot, but he repeatedly flunked the physical (he had 20-25 vision in one eye). He then volunteered for the glider program. By August 1942 he had gotten his glider pilot rating—as a staff sergeant. He became a glider pilot instructor just at the time when General Arnold began to push for a big expansion in glider training. The increased pace of glider production required Watters and other experienced glider pilots to help ferry Wacos all over the country from factories to bases where they were needed in training. This included flights with and without students from the largest CG-4A plant of them all, the Ford plant at Dearborn, Michigan.

Before he joined our 81st Troop Carrier Squadron, Watters was assigned to a squadron that did not have a single glider, the 68th TCS, supposedly on its way to the Pacific theater. As it happened, at the time the 68th was at Laurinburg-Maxton Air Base, soon to be the home of our 81st Squadron. Because there was nothing for him to do in the 68th, Watters joined friends who had taught beginning glider pilots and who were working with an experimental glider team, also at Maxton. This school was headed by the most famous American glider pilot of World War II—Major Mike Murphy, who, in his civilian days, had been a successful stunt pilot.

The glider teachers themselves, and, even more, the generals who anxiously surveyed the progress of the glider program in early 1943, seemed to feel that most of the signs were bad. Glider pilots in training maneuvers with combat

Glider assembly: CG-4As (Wacos) in wooden crates, foreground; fuselages out of the boxes, middle; assembled gliders at top. (Courtesy Smithsonian Institution)

A jeep trailer full of artillery shells is loaded by glidermen through the front end of a Waco.

loads came in too fast and broke up far too many gliders. Tragically, a large number of the airborne troops carried on these maneuvers were killed.

In July 1943 Arnold ordered Mike Murphy to find a cure for these problems or face the fact that the entire glider program, country-wide, would be closed down.

> Murphy was a convincing salesman for the program, however; and in July 1943 he managed to put on a two-day show that convinced Arnold and dozens of generals who came to watch that the program could deliver the goods.
>
> I was Murphy's administrative aide for this two-day set of maneuvers, and I also flew one of the gliders in a night tactical mission, where gliders had to land in short sand fields, some of which were cul-de-sacs, when they weren't in the pea patches around Maxton. We had live loads, flew double tow, and had only kerosene torches to mark the landing zones. The brass judged the show to be a great success, and the glider program was saved.
>
> Finally, the high brass began to realize that there wasn't time to put all the glider pilots they needed through this sort of tactical training school. They ordered some instructors transferred to individual troop carrier groups which needed that sort of training. (Darlyle Watters, Squadron Glider Officer)

Darlyle was assigned to the 436th at Maxton on November 1, 1943. There were four such glider teachers, one for each of the 436th squadrons. They were to report directly to Colonel Williams. Williams broke the news to them that now, instead of having five students each, they would have twenty-five! They were given full authority to transfer out any glider pilot if they thought he couldn't master the training. There were to be no appeals—and also no wasted time: Get the failures out and get a replacement fast! There were less than two months to do the job before the 436th TCG went overseas.

> The rush was on. We now had priority for the glider pilot training. No longer would our program get the hind tit when it came to personnel and supplies!
>
> "Graduation" for the GPs we were training included problems in which glider landings were made in Group strength, at night, with full combat loads, and with the ability to assess landing zones from photographs and from strip maps giving time, distance, and headings. We also had to put one hundred gliders down on the ground at Maxton AAFB at the same time. I remember that we didn't accomplish this until the third try. (Darlyle Watters, Squadron Glider Officer)

## Glider pilots and their status

All sorts of routes brought men to the novel job of glider pilot. Once on the job, however, they all accepted the aura that went with their rather peculiar line of work. Victims of relatively low status and mushy thinking by military leaders regarding their mission, glider pilots reacted by donning a defensive armor to guard their self-esteem and to allow them to function well in combat. This helps explain the dashing image of the World War II glider pilot: an unruly sort of a fellow who perpetrated reckless pranks, downed everything alcoholic he could lay his hands on, and who was known as the worst sort of obstreperous woman-chaser. His wildness, in keeping with this image, could be excused only on the grounds of the horrifying chances he took in combat.

Those of us in plane crews appreciated the recognition we were given for our supposedly perilous assignment—recognition in the form of high rank, high pay, and costly training. Still, glider pilots thought of themselves as badly undervalued, and as people from whom the military demanded everything but gave little in return. The airborne infantry tended to take them for granted.

I first came to Membury at about 10:30 p.m. on the night prior to the Holland invasion. The rest of my time before going on Operation MARKET-GARDEN was spent in briefings, drawing equipment, and getting ready to go. There was no time for me to get any sort of training with the 81st prior to the mission.

Just about the time my tow plane crossed enemy lines, a shell that we later guessed was a 20 mm went right through our tow plane's right wing without exploding. I yelled to the pilot of the tow plane that he had a hole in the right wing and that fuel was dumping. In a few seconds the fuel had caught on fire. The flame began to wrap around the fuselage of the C-47 and to travel down the tow rope toward us. We were able to tell this over the telephone wire to the tow plane pilot. He answered that he was going to have his crew bail out and he would continue to tow me to the landing zone as long as possible. His crew was successful in making a safe exit from his plane.

The pilot yelled that he was going to start to climb to give me all the altitude possible in the event that he would not be able to reach the LZ. Then the telephone between us stopped working. When the tow plane reached 3,000 feet I could figure that I would actually be able to glide to the LZ. I yanked the tow rope release; and as I watched, the tow pilot stopped the left engine and jumped through the emergency door behind his seat. But he didn't make it. His parachute streamed and never fully opened. I saw him hit the ground and bounce.

The Germans were sending flak at us with the fuses cut so that their bursts would be beneath us where they could do the most damage. It was obvious this was not an ideal place for any self-respecting person to be. I looked over at my right seat rider, a staff sergeant in the glider infantry. He was rolled up tight in a ball so his flak suit could protect as much of him as possible. I dumped the nose of the glider and headed for the LZ. Small arms fire followed us all the way down, and I was not able to slow down the glider for landing. I tore up a lot of real estate getting the glider stopped. The LZ was under intense fire and we had to evacuate the glider quickly. I never had a chance to find out how many of the glider infantry had been wounded. The next day I counted over 200 holes in the glider and quit counting.

I joined up with a squad of infantry. We were told to dig in because we would have to stay the night there. After digging a deep foxhole I wrapped myself in a parachute and went to sleep. I had not slept for two nights so I was really knocked out. The next morning when I woke, I found that I was all alone. I noticed tank tracks all over the ground and couldn't figure it out; apparently the noise of the tanks hadn't been able to wake me up. I found out later that German Tiger tanks had invaded the area and that our infantry had abandoned the place without bothering to take me along. (Bill Lane, glider pilot)

One worrisome feature of the relations between our twenty-six or so 81st TCS glider pilots and the rest of us was that when we began combat operations they tended to become a less tightly integrated element of the Squadron. After the Normandy invasion some of them were moved from one 436th Group squadron to another, and even to other groups, as the exigencies of succeeding missions demanded. Apart from Darlyle Watters and his successor, Curtis Steffens, who were our Squadron Glider Officers, and our Executive Officer, Major Harold Walker, himself a glider pilot, they had no visibly important duties; some of them served from time to time as ODs (Officers of the Day, that is, duty officer at Squadron HQ) or as mail censors, or in other not very prestigious capacities. They were prey to the feeling that, except during glider combat missions, nobody really wanted them.[3]

When we finally moved to Melun, in France, in some ways it was like England all over again—not much for glider guiders to do. For us it was either in the sack or in the officers club or in town on pass. I volunteered to help the Personnel Equipment Officer. But what I really did with my time was to build a softball field at Melun with the help of some engineers who were stationed near our base.

Darlyle Watters was in charge of the glider pilots; but as you know he kept us on only a very loose rein. We had a lot of sack time. I'm sure everybody remembers the blackjack games in the officers club. We didn't fly gliders nearly enough. (Earl Goodwin, glider pilot)

When the weather was bad and flying time was at a premium, glider pilots found it hard to get in the four hours per month necessary for them to get their flight pay. Often they could be found in the Operations Office, trying to convince Bert Schweizer or Gerry O'Shea, our Operations clerks, to assign them to flying duties. Several of them were good power pilots and they often volunteered to fly as co-pilots in our C-47s. From time to time an officer of the 101st Airborne would arrive to instruct them in infantry tactics. They also were expected to work out in physical training groups and to go on a five-mile hike with pack and rifle at least once a week.

For some pilots it was easier to act out their resentments by simply staying in the sack or getting passes and spending their time in town.

[Between missions] we were free to spend our time as we pleased. Except for some limited flying by a small percentage of us, we relaxed. We had many hours and days of standing down after each combat mission. The regular routine of the Squadron continued, with many chores that had to be done in keeping our aircraft working and to support the other necessary activities. But glider pilots were not expected to do anything but fly gliders. That is all we did except for a few who volunteered for some additional duties. The rest of us would sack out or take off for local pubs or catch a train into London for some sightseeing. Our next combat mission [after southern France] did not come until September. So we had a lot of idle hours to kill.

I would schedule myself to fly co-pilot on any desirable supply flight. Some were to Scotland for liquid supplies for the officers club. Some were to Paris for perfume and other niceties to bring home. (Ben Ward, glider pilot)

Glider pilots tried to minimize the distinctions between themselves and power pilots; and the power pilots, naturally, tried to maintain their more exalted professional status. Pilots of C-47s nourished their own resentments: they had to live with the fact that they had not made it into the even more prestigious ranks of bombers and fighters. The fact that one of their principal missions was to tow gliders rubbed a bit of salt into that wound. The tension between glider pilots and other pilots is best symbolized by the terms that glider pilots always used when referring to C-47 pilots: *tow pilots*, *power pilots*, or *tug pilots*, never just plain *pilots*. *Tug pilots* and *tow pilots* are terms suggesting that gliders were performing the more necessary function, that power pilots were aerial truck drivers. Today, some forty-five years later, former glider pilots still use the same terms.

Although glider pilots often expressed their resentment in a joking way, there is no doubt that the unfairness of their situation hurt them.

[After being trained in demolition work by the 17th Airborne Division] we carried some of the detonating devices used back to Membury with us. These were used to booby-trap various things by using a no. 8 dynamite cap. The power pilots were our primary target to be booby-trapped. We would put a device under their bunks so that when they sat on the bunk the device would be cocked and would explode when they got up. We booby-trapped the johns, barracks doors, and everything else we could think of. We had the power pilots very cautious, examining everything carefully before they would open it or pick it up.

All us glider pilots were called to a meeting and we were told that they knew we were installing those booby-traps. But we were also told that these pilots would soon be flying into France and would be landing in recently occupied enemy territory, and maybe, after seeing how easy it was to booby-trap something, they would be more careful about picking up souvenirs.

We were relieved to find we would not be punished for those booby-traps. One Saturday afternoon we went in the ladies' john in the officers club and booby-trapped all the commodes. When the 6 by 6 trucks arrived with the English girls of course they all immediately headed for the johns. In a few minutes there were several explosions. After that the English girls would never use the johns again. (Bill Lane, glider pilot)

Right across the street in "Tent City" [our base in France] from us, in France, were two flight officer power pilots. They were always bringing home enemy ammo and grenades. In our tents, one day, we heard some loud "chink, chink!" noises. Col. Brack came out of his tent at the end of the Squadron's street and saw that the two of them were in a bomb revetment about a hundred yards away from the tents. They had a hammer and chisel and were trying to pry off the cap of one of the dozen or so 500-pound bombs down there in that revetment.

When it came time to leave France, these two jokers threw some of their ammo into the burn barrel behind "Tent City." They added a batch of

Down easy: the hinged cockpit of a Waco is lowered into place. Visible to the right of the glider's wheel are its wooden skids. (Courtesy Smithsonian Institution)

A Horsa and a Waco glider down on a field surrounded by the infamous Normandy hedgerows.

paper and lit it. Talk about excitement when that ammo started to go off!
(Ellery Bennett, pilot)

So far as personal relationships were concerned, a few men in each group,
tug pilots and glider pilots, crossed that shadowy but important line and made
good friends of people on the other side. Some glider pilots even shared quarters
with power pilots and navigators, but they tended to bond tightly only to each
other. That bonding still shows up in the close relationships they maintain in
veterans organizations today, especially in the National World War II Glider
Pilots Association and in the periodical *Silent Wings*.

> When we arrived in England there were only a handful of us who had been
> together in the States. There are four of us who were close; and though it
> sounds funny, the reason is that our last names were close together in the
> rosters from which they had moved us around from one base to another
> during training. We were John Hampton, Ray Gephart, John Geary, and
> me. We were close buddies from the time we hit Membury. Johnny Hamp-
> ton and Ray Gephart flew together, so Geary and I flew together. John was
> closer to me than any person in the world except my family. (Earl Goodwin,
> glider pilot)

Because of a feeling that, for many purposes, they got the short end of the
stick, glider pilots tended to look for support and sympathy not to the pilots or
the CO of our Squadron but to officers in Group HQ, and particularly to Col.
Williams himself. Today our glider pilots are unanimous in agreeing that the
"glider guiders" in the 436th were particularly lucky in the concern and support
they got from their Group CO. They felt truly lucky in having Colonel Williams
as their Group CO. Among themselves, they always said that they were "Colonel
Williams' boys," meaning that there was somebody up there who would take
care of them in ways that were beyond the power of our Squadron CO.

> There were several occasions when it became obvious that Williams was
> worried about what would happen to us on missions—that he truly cared
> for us in a personal and emotional way. During the briefings for the Nor-
> mandy invasion, when he was explaining what the gliders would have to
> face, his voice broke and he had trouble talking, because he was so upset
> by the possible casualties among glider pilots.
> And when we made it back to southern England from the Normandy
> invasion, we were astonished to learn that Williams had flown his own
> personal plane down there to pick us up and take us back to Membury. I

don't know how many times he did this sort of thing; but I know that after Normandy I rode back on his plane. I'll never forget that tears were in his eyes—almost as if some of his sons were coming back home after he had about given up hope for them. I'll appreciate that concern as long as I live. I especially appreciated it because I never got to know Williams personally, never had anything to do with him socially. (Bob Carney, glider pilot)

---

You could respect and appreciate Colonel Brack; but he was a tough person to get to know. My favorite superior officer was our Group Commander, Adriel Williams. Recently, one of the men who used to be in our mess hall called me to say he had met General Williams; I was glad to learn Williams had asked after me. I always felt close to him and enjoyed thinking of him as a friend. This was one man about whom you could say, rank did not hurt him. He was a sweetheart! I think everyone liked him. (Earl Goodwin, glider pilot)

Recently, when he was told of the high esteem in which he was held by glider pilots, Adriel Williams explained his feelings about them in these terms:

I was terribly conscious of the dangers of their mission. This may explain why back in those days I seemed to be paying the glider pilots more attention. I don't mind telling you that today, when I get to talking about the way they had to run such awful risks, tears still come to my eyes.

After all, power pilots were in a different situation. Power pilots had pretty big egos. It goes with the job, with all the decisions they have to make and their need to trust their own judgment. They didn't seem to need or want special care from their commanders. But glider pilots were so vulnerable! Cut off from their tugs with no place to go but down, with every German in the neighborhood shooting at them. . . . And some of our power pilots, I suppose, couldn't help but show their feelings of superiority to every one else around. (Adriel Williams, 436th Group Commander)

### Notes

1. The U.S. Air Force did authorize a huge all-metal assault glider, the Chase Aircraft XG-20, which was produced in 1949. This glider was designed from the beginning to be fitted with engines, though, and after a few years it metamorphosed into the Fairchild C-123 B, an important assault transport airplane of the late 1950s and 1960s.

2. Much of the material on this and the following page is based on Devlin, *Silent Wings*, pp. 54–61.

3. Col. Samuel T. Moore, in an official survey of all of troop carrier, observed that for glider personnel "morale was always a problem." Ch. 2, p. 48. See also the advice of Major Frank J. Moore, a highly experienced glider pilot in the 51st TCW (MTO), who said his glider pilots felt like stepchildren until his wing commander pulled the glider pilots out of the individual squadrons and formed them into a separate "wing glider base." Air Contact Unit returnees' report of Dec. 18, 1944.

# 10. Engineering
## What It Took to Keep 'Em Flying

### Fly it or junk it?

If somebody asked me to describe the one event in the history of the 81st TCS that best epitomizes the kind of war we fought, I would choose the narrow escape of David Brack's plane from the junkyard (an episode referred to in another connection in Chapter 8). Brack's plane was hit heavily at least five times by flak, and the rudder and aileron cables were severed. He ordered his co-pilot to hit the release lever to cut off the glider he was towing, and with an extraordinary display of piloting skill he managed to turn his crippled plane around and get it safely back down on the ground at an airport near Brussels, which was in Allied hands. (The glider, however, had been cut off over enemy territory and its pilot suffered some terribly damaging experiences in a German prisoner-of-war camp.)[1] Rather than abandoning the plane in Brussels for salvage—something that would have been quite justifiable given the plane's condition—Brack arranged to have Pappy Harris, our Line Chief, flown from Membury to Brussels to see if he could get the plane in shape to fly back across the Channel.

> Brack always said it was his ambition to fly the same plane back from Europe to the States that he had flown from the States to Europe. My job was to get that airplane back in flying status. I got a couple of mechanics and we flew over to Brussels. As it happened, I was able to do most of the work by myself. But you have to put "flying status" in quotation marks. When we later got the plane to a depot in England, some officer there—maybe with tongue in cheek—said he was going to try to court-martial me for allowing that plane, in that condition, to be flown: the idea being that I had endangered the lives of the crew and passengers by permitting them to fly an aircraft that should not have been considered airworthy.
>
> In Brussels, when we stripped away what we had to in order to get at the severed cables, there was no floor left in the plane; I had to rip it all out and just junk it. To fix up the cables I took a welding torch and some spare cables and brazing rod. Since parts of the bulkheads that supported the cable

pulleys had been blown away, when the cables were spliced and rewired they were just suspended through the air from the cabin compartment clear back to the tail. (Pappy Harris, Line Chief)

Clyde Burkett, our Squadron welder, cut away the frayed ends of the cable and brazed in about two feet of new cable. He pulled the cables as taut as possible, turning them around the guides and clamping them down with vise grips. Then he wrapped the repaired section with wire and brazed the whole overlapped section again. The crew tested the repair by holding the rudder in the back and pushing down on the rudder pedals. Finally Harris wrapped the repaired cables with tape to protect the brazing against vibration.

That plane, I can tell you, was a shambles. Nothing but a great pilot's ability could have gotten that plane more or less in one piece down on the ground. And Brack was also very lucky, because there was no bad crosswind that day when he landed; he had no rudder, no brakes, and only one-half of an elevator. With a pilot having less than Brack's kind of skill, that plane would have wiped out when she got close to the ground.

Besides working on the "tail feathers" I had to take a hacksaw and cut off one end of a wing tip; and I did the same for one end of the right aileron. To cover these cuts I had some fabric and dope I had taken over with me, and I simply covered up the ragged spots where I had cut something off. I had some tin-snips with me, and I cut around holes in the fuselage which the shell fragments had made and covered them with dope and fabric.

Now, at that time there was a whole raft of people trying to get back to England from Brussels, and they wanted passage on Brack's plane. The whole airfield, it seemed to me, was covered with glider pilots who were supposed to return on the first available transport. They were anxious to ride with us, no matter what the condition of the plane.

The work took a couple of days; but we finally did take off with a batch of glider pilots. But there was nowhere for them to sit; they had to travel kind of standing up against the sides of the plane, or leaning up against what was left of the bulkheads. There was no floor at all. You could see right down through where the floor had been to where the cables were sliding along when they were worked from the cockpit. Now, wherever there were ragged sections of bulkhead there was a danger the cables—especially where I had spliced them—would snag. There was no tension on the cables because there weren't any of the regular pulleys left to take up the slack.

I told Brack: When you need a control—elevator or rudder—don't force it! If it hangs up, for goodness sake release it, and then try it again.

All the 81st TCS airplane mechanics swarm over a C-47—but only for a souvenir photo.

Pappy Harris (line chief) and the buggy he put together from salvaged parts.

The idea was that whichever glider pilot happened to be at that place where a cable was sticking could take a wooden pole I had previously handed out and hold up the cable with the stick until the control operated! (Pappy Harris, Line Chief)

In a blatant example of reverse boasting, Harris says of this episode, "It was all in a day's work."

Mechanics not working on inspections were not allowed to sit on their hands. Some of them, especially those not "on the flight roster" (accredited for replacing a crew chief), would have to take their turn at KP and guard duty. On the planes there was a constant volume of work aside from inspections: check the tire pressure, vacuum out the inside of planes, polish the cockpit and cabin windows, clean the wing lights, check the fabric on the ailerons and the tail surfaces, climb up into the landing gear wells and clean out any hydraulic fluid or oil that had collected dirt—there was always something.

In much of the work they did, our mechanics preferred coping with problems by themselves rather than waiting for strict and detailed orders. The working style of our 81st engineers and mechanics would be labeled today as "laid back." With little interest in dramatizing their problems or their achievements, they set up individual work centers, saw to it that all the necessary tools and parts were available, listened to the pilots' and the crew chiefs' complaints, diagnosed the problems, got help from other sections without going through channels, and usually accomplished their jobs very well.

This achievement is all the more remarkable when you realize that very few of our mechanics had had much experience in handling machinery as civilians. A few of our Engineering people worked as auto mechanics before entering the service. Johnny Hirtreiter, an assistant crew chief, had worked in the drafting department of Curtis Wright Aircraft in Buffalo, and had given up his deferment as a civilian in an "essential industry" in order to join the Army. The majority, however, had recently left high school or had held down jobs such as elevator operator or filling station attendant, or they had worked on farms.

Some troop carrier squadrons were plagued by gliders that malfunctioned in the air or had to be yanked off the runway during a mission takeoff. The 81st TCS had few such problems. Darlyle Watters, our Squadron Glider Officer, recalls that during his time in our Squadron he knew of not a single instance where a glider had to be pulled off the flight line due to a mechanical failure. The airplane side of our Squadron's Engineering sections ran up just as impressive a record: not one of our planes, throughout the entire war, had to abort any combat mission due to a mechanical problem.

## Our Engineering TO

The organization of our Squadron's Engineering sections was complex but far from rigid. According to our TO, all mechanics reported to Joseph Konecny, Squadron Engineering Officer. There were also Engineering specialties in both power plane and glider sections, each with a semi-independent chief: the propeller specialists, electrical specialists, instrument men, fabric and dope (varnish) men, sheet metal men, and hydraulic systems specialists. If our crew chiefs and clerk-typists were included, Squadron Engineering took up the work of between 100 and 120 men out of about 420 in our Squadron—more than any other single category.

Glider mechanics operated independently from the power plane mechanics, though on occasion they helped men in other sections. The men responsible for overseeing the glider mechanics were Delma Montgomery, glider mechanics chief, and Sam Green, a glider pilot who acted as unofficial liaison between the "glider guiders" and their mechanics. Chief of the airplane mechanics was Pappy Harris. Checking the quality of work done on the planes was the responsibility of Carlisle Jordon, our Squadron Airplane Inspector, and his assistant, Cliff Thompson. Keeping both plane and glider mechanics provided with parts was the responsibility of Mike Hrycaj, Tech Supply chief.

None of these men was a boss in the usual sense of that word, though. Rather, they allocated work by determining which of the mechanics were well suited for specific jobs and checked to see that the repairs and maintenance were the best possible. Informally organized groups of mechanics—some specialists and others not—worked where they could do the most good; and, as long as they produced quality work, they operated without much close supervision. Grover Benson, flight chief of "B" Flight in our Squadron, says, "There really was nobody who gave me what you could call orders. I always knew what I had to do the next day."

> My job wasn't easy; a lot of work and very little time off for play. There were a lot of inspections that had to be run on aircraft engines, especially when they were about to be changed. But we did get a couple of three-day passes to London. We did the usual there: ate fish and chips, had a few drinks, had a few women. But we put in some real work for the time off that we got. Often we had to get up at 5:00 in the morning and work right on through until 9:00 at night.
>
> But I was my own boss. I always had some of my own work to keep me busy, and the brass never bothered me much. (Grover Benson, flight chief)

Parachute riggers, too, were theoretically part of Engineering, but actually operated as an autonomous unit. It took eight weeks of schooling to learn to pack a parachute. More learning on the job was required to handle the different sorts of chutes: chest packs, seat packs, back packs, and cargo chutes big enough to float down a jeep.

> We would go to each plane and check each chute. Every member of a crew was assigned his own chute. When a chute was packed, the name of the packer and the date was put into a small booklet which was inserted into a pocket located at the bottom of the parachute pack.
>
> The rip cord and housing had to be inspected weekly to be sure that they hadn't come loose. The chutes were repacked monthly. Back packs on a combat chute had a lot of equipment in them—a machete, bandages, sulfa compressors for wounds, and morphine.
>
> We also inspected the life rafts and life preservers ("Mae Wests"). The $CO_2$ cylinders had to be checked. The life rafts had to be checked to see if they were equipped with a variety of provisions, such as cans of water, K-rations, fishing gear, and a "Gibson Girl"—a radio transmitter for sending out an SOS; it was curved in in the middle so a person in a life raft could grab it between his knees when cranking the transmitter lever. (David Neumann, parachute rigger)

The crews of only three of our planes had to "hit the silk" during combat missions. When a plane caught fire or got into trouble when it was too low, wearing a chute did not necessarily save the day. Ten of our crew members did survive jumps in combat and joined the "Caterpillar Club"—including three who parachuted into occupied Holland and were hidden by the Dutch Underground. One of our pilots who jumped found out later that David Neumann had packed his chute. On returning to Membury he made a point of going over to the chute riggers' hangar to thank him.

Everybody in our Squadron who knew our Line Chief called him Pappy. "Tough but always helpful" is the way most of us remember him. The nickname itself reminds us how important good personal relations were in establishing an environment where mechanics would be glad to put in a good day's work.

> I was out on the line a lot. I guess I was a sort of maverick officer in the sense that most of the time I just ran around in coveralls. I liked airplanes and the business of working on them very much. I started with airplane mechanics way back in 1939. So later on I was able to take some of the

fellows under my wing; showed them the way to use wrenches, spring compressors, all those tools which you get to know from the start when you get into the mechanics' business.

Another reason for the nickname may be because I wasn't the sort who left the base whenever I could. I hardly went anywhere but where we were working. When I went to an airbase I never went off it. The only leave I would take was when I could go back to my own home; but as far as taking a leave or a pass just to go to town, like everybody else did, that was not for me. I just had fun working with aircraft. But because I didn't go to town to spend my cash, I was able to loan the guys some money.

So the name kind of fell out from me helping some of the guys with their mechanical schooling and also with some money when they needed it. The name maybe came from the fact that I acted somewhat more mature than them—not from the fact that I was actually older; I wasn't older. Somebody might say, well, if you need twenty bucks, maybe you can go see Pappy. (Pappy Harris, Line Chief)

For some purposes, crew chiefs were responsible to Pappy Harris as well as to their pilots. Crew chiefs worked alongside "line personnel" (mechanics not members of crews) on inspections and minor repair work on their assigned planes. Each flight of three planes had a sort of assistant head we called a flight chief, with some authority (not much) over the other crew chiefs and assistant crew chiefs. Had there been quarrelsome personalities in a few key spots, such overlapping authority could have led to bitter controversy over turf, but we were fortunate in the five men who could be considered our chief chiefs: Konecny, Harris, Green, Montgomery, and Hrycaj. All of them cooperated in ways that helped the work of the Squadron go remarkably smoothly all through the war. None of them were nitpickers; none liked to demean the men who worked with them (we can't say "worked *under* them"). Our Squadron recollections agree that the chiefs ended up respected for their knowledge and for their decent natures. This is especially the case for Delma Montgomery, who everybody remembers as not only competent but also remarkably considerate, soft-spoken, and approachable—a handsome Southern gentleman.

Dwight Eisenhower once said that during D-Day in Normandy, from the time the airborne and seaborne men landed, "it was a soldier's war, not a general's war."

Except for the time we were actually in combat, our war was a *squadron's* war—not a group, not a wing, not Troop Carrier Command's war. Our Squadron handled its own engineering problems without much interference or assistance from higher echelons. Major Frome was our Group Engineering Officer, but his duties were essentially limited to furnishing engineering directives from Wing and Command to the four squadrons in the 436th Group.

> Our work, you have to understand, was done independently as a Squadron, not as part of the Group. The only guidance we got from Group was when an order came down from Wing or Command. It would be disseminated through the Group Engineering Officer, Major Jacob Frome, and he would get in touch with us. But we never saw much of him. His function was what you could think of as administrative inspection and handling of documents like our Tech Orders. TOs provided detailed illustrated procedures for maintaining the entire aircraft. They also specified what changes had to be made due to problems that might have been encountered by other outfits—either military or civilian—with the C-47.
>
> We learned as we worked, so we didn't have to reread these Tech Orders too often. We tried to highlight the problems ourselves and handle them ourselves. In this we were lucky to have Pappy Harris as our Line Chief. He was a real mechanical wizard. Harris was also a good organization man—serious, hardworking, and a good communicator. (Joseph Konecny, Squadron Engineering Officer)

One example of how higher Engineering echelons might leave even important decisions in a squadron's hands is the problem of engine changes before our last assault mission, the jump across the Rhine in March 1945. At that time the entire 53rd Wing was extremely busy flying planes from our bases in France back to England to pick up the new self-sealing gas tanks and ferry the 17th Airborne Division to its new French bases. Many planes were flown an extra hundred hours or so in these tasks, so some planes might have engines that were on record as having well over the usual 500 hours before replacement. Since replacement engines just then were hard to come by, Wing HQ had to rule that lower-echelon Engineering sections could use their discretion and allow engines to keep on being used up to 600 hours and even more—provided that the squadrons' Engineering chiefs could see that those particular engines were free of obvious problems.[2]

This autonomy in Squadron Engineering would not have been possible without a basic decision in troop carrier concerning the division of labor between large-scale repairs and smaller jobs. Unlike fighter and bomber outfits, which "owned" much of their own equipment for making major repairs, the squadrons in troop carrier were limited to jobs that could be done with hand tools and mobile equipment, did not involve important changes inside a large part—say, an engine—and did not involve working on that particular job for more than two or three days.

There was no sharp line drawn between jobs that could or could not be done inside the Squadron. According to formal Air Forces procedure, first echelon maintenance was primarily the job of the crew chief and consisted of preflight and daily inspections and minor repairs. Second echelon maintenance was understood to be performed by our line personnel, including inspections (called "preventive inspections" in the manuals) every twenty-five, fifty, and 500 hours and after engine replacement, and repairs that did not require massive equipment. Third echelon maintenance—major repairs and replacement of big parts— was done by the base service center, in our case, the 459th Service Squadron. Finally, if drastic, fourth echelon maintenance was called for, this meant the plane would have to be shipped to a IX Troop Carrier Command depot, often to be ruled beyond repair and "cannibalized" for parts.[3]

In practice, the line between first and second echelon maintenance was not a fine one. Our crew chiefs worked together with line personnel on inspections and some repairs, and often our Squadron mechanics worked along with those in our Service Squadron on a major repair, for example, in replacing metal gas tanks with self-sealing gas tanks. In marginal cases, Joseph Konecny made the decision about whether the job would be done by our Squadron mechanics.

> We didn't do much repair work on the engines or large plane parts themselves. In fact, one big theme of our work was "R and R," that is, Remove and Replace. We didn't fiddle with the internal parts of things; for example, when something went wrong with a generator, you removed the whole thing.
>
> The really big jobs, third and fourth echelon maintenance, went to the service centers or air depots where they did the major work. Our mission was to try to find the sources of problems. We put our efforts into investigating—listening for odd noises, trying to track down the sources of leaks, etc. When we found the cause of the trouble, and could repair it right then, we did so; otherwise we would pull it and put another part in. Besides that, we did fueling, oiling, preventive inspections, and cleaning and minor repairs. (Joseph Konecny, Squadron Engineering Officer)

When a plane managed to get back to base after being badly shot up, the squadrons were not supposed to keep it; we were directed to sign it over to some depot group, and they would try to restore it. Of course many planes like that were cannibalized—listed as being available for parts for any squadron or depot that needed parts. In return for a damaged plane, squadrons would be reassigned another, not necessarily a new one, but one that had to be certified as ready for active duty. (Pappy Harris, Line Chief)

## Party of the first part

Our Squadron was lucky in getting for its Tech Supply sergeant a man who knew his job even before he joined the Squadron. Michael Hrycaj (whose surname was later changed to Rickey) was part of our original cadre in Alliance, Nebraska. He had been transferred to us from the 32nd TCS along with Harris and Montgomery. While in the 32nd he worked in Tech Supply, and he had absorbed a lot of knowledge about the business. After he joined our Squadron he learned a good deal more about Tech Supply at AAFSAT, the Army Air Forces School of Applied Tactics.

Tech Supply had a big job: the issue and replacement of both tools and parts to crew chiefs, all the line personnel, and all the instrument specialists. Rickey handled both airplane and glider tools and parts. Tech Supply was also responsible for issuing and replacing flight clothing for both flight crew members (planes and gliders) and plane and glider mechanics who needed warm clothing when working out on the line.

> A good working knowledge of how to write up Tech Supply orders was a must in this job. There were no less than thirty different categories of supply classifications. Each item for aircraft and gliders had to be ordered by correct part number and in the right class. Wrong nomenclature—wrong item delivered! Everything was listed on a master list, by box and contents. In addition, each box carried a contents list. When an item was removed from a box it was taken off the master list and a slip was turned in to our man in the office who would then update the master list. All new items going into stock received the same treatment. We knew at all times what we had, how many of each, and where they could be found.
>
> One man took care of all typing, reports, tech orders, and correspondence. Two men worked the counter—that is, they gave out parts, got "returnables" ready for shipment, and kept the storeroom shipshape. The fourth man and myself would take old parts for exchange to the service depot.
>
> For our normal needs, I would get together with the Line Chief and flight chiefs to find out what their future requirements would be. Then I would be darn sure I had the parts on hand when that work started. I strongly believed in having the run-of-the-mill stuff ready and in the Supply

Ben Obermark, crew chief, about
to "pull the props through."

"We fix flats!"

At Mike Rickey's Place (Tech Supply): Lillard Mount (*left*), flight chief, and Carlisle
Jordan, Squadron Airplane Inspector.

Room whenever they would be needed. Of course the big items, like props, wingtips, and so on, I couldn't store.

There were times when we didn't have a part that was needed in a hurry. Then it was up to us to beg, borrow, swap—and yes, steal—that part, and get it "ASAP." If it was a real emergency I would get permission to fly to supply depots to get what was needed. The idea was to save time and not wait to get those parts through regular channels.

In England, besides getting parts from supply depots, we were able to cannibalize parts from downed and badly damaged planes that were in airplane graveyards. When we heard of one, we'd get together a few mechanics, grab a plane, and get there pronto! This sort of salvage got us a good many parts—electrical wire, tubing, cables, and different sorts of instruments.[4] (Michael Rickey, Tech Supply chief)

### On the glider line

Our glider mechanics worked independently of our airplane mechanics in a separate section; glider mechanics therefore had a TO parallel to that of power plane mechanics. This advantage meant higher rank for them as a group: since gliders had come into the AAF hierarchy late, if they had not been given their own department, glider personnel undoubtedly would have received the leavings as far as NCO stripes were concerned. As it was, the head of a separate section, according to AAF notions concerning rank, had to be at least a T/Sgt. (fivestriper), and so on down the line.

As soon as I hit the 81st I was amazed at all the rank. There was nothing like that in glider school. Sergeants everywhere—I couldn't believe it. Every other guy, it seemed, had sergeant's stripes. That's the pain of being the last guy to get into an outfit: you take what's left over. There are just so many tech, staff, and buck sergeants for each department. Of course for my job, rank didn't really mean much—we all were doing about the same job. But it did mean a little more pay. (John Merril, glider mechanic)

One big difference between power plane engineering and glider engineering was that planes were flown to us across the Atlantic; gliders, however, came to us in pieces, each one boxed up in six huge crates.

Another of our jobs was to assemble the Wacos when they arrived. Most would be shipped to Wing HQ; but others would arrive in Membury. They would come in huge wooden boxes maybe fifteen to twenty feet long. There was a lot of good wood in those boxes that we were able to use, especially when we moved to France and had to set up our "tent city."

Once the gliders were assembled, there never was much checking done on whether they were really flyable. We would give them whatever ground checks we could. Maybe some of them had been pre-assembled in the States and checked out there—we never knew. Then, of course, they would have to be disassembled and crated for the trip over the Atlantic. I've heard about glider test pilots; but we never had any. Usually our glider pilots simply got in the newly assembled glider and took them up themselves to check them out. (Jack McGlothlin, glider mechanic)

It took about 250 man-hours to assemble a glider. Inevitably, some crucial mistakes were made in putting them together—to be caught, one hoped, during the first tests. Sometimes it required good luck to uncover a grave problem. In July 1944 a new glider belonging to the 82nd TCS, one of our sister squadrons at Membury, caught fire during a minor welding adjustment to its metal skeleton. The glider fabric burned off completely, revealing that the right elevator was improperly attached. All gliders in the 436th Group had to be grounded while their elevators were checked out—but no other assembly mistakes were discovered.[5]

Waco gliders might look flimsy, and the tech manuals for assembling them might remind one of instructions for putting a kid's bike together, but nobody thought of these gliders as toys. Their mission was deadly serious, and the glider mechanics were very conscious of the responsibility they bore for the glider pilots and the airborne infantry.

A Waco possessed amazing lifting power, power that could be destructive if the glider was not handled properly. A violent wind blowing across the base could bring disaster.

In our Squadron we didn't have glider hangars, though there was one on the base. We would have to park gliders on a hardstand or in any available space. There were different ways we would tie them down; there were tie-downs on the wings and on the tail. When we got to England we tried out those English ties that look like a metal cork-screw. We would turn these into the ground and tie the gliders to them. In some other outfits I visited they would also dig holes and run the glider wheels right into the holes so the glider would actually be resting, not on its belly but on the skids underneath. (Joseph Hitchon, glider mechanic)

One day in England we had them all lined up ready to fly when the wind came up so hard there was no way these gliders were going anywhere. We even had to haul out sandbags to put in them to try to hold them on the ground. For a while it looked as though the wind would blow them all away before we could get them out of danger. One of the gliders being towed off the field by a weapons carrier headed into that strong wind and just took off in the air all by itself! It landed on the back of another weapons carrier. (John Merril, glider mechanic)

---

I also remember how we learned to respect the flying power of those gliders. Once Henry Bailey was pulling a glider with a tow truck; he was in a hurry because the weather looked so threatening. The faster he pulled, the more the glider tried to get up into the air; finally a gust of wind lifted that glider right up like a kite. And, since Henry and his truck kept right on going, the glider went so high the tow rope kept bouncing the back wheels of the truck right off the ground. The two glider mechanics inside that glider yelled themselves hoarse trying to get Henry to stop; he finally slowed down, but everybody was scared some. (Russell Charlesworth, glider mechanic)

The Waco looked small and light compared with the English Horsa glider; but the Waco, too, was a heavy, complicated machine that had to be handled with respect in order to avoid accidents. One terrible accident on the ground (not in our Squadron) everybody remembers happened when some airborne soldiers on our field were practicing driving a jeep in and out of a glider. To accommodate jeeps, the entire Waco nose section, including the cockpit with the pilots' seats, was hinged so that it could be swung directly up and back over the fuselage, allowing the jeep (or a miniature bulldozer) to get out and get into action quickly. During this training exercise the lifted nose section had crashed down on the two men seated in the jeep; one was hospitalized and the other killed.

Even the glider tow rope had to be handled with respect.

Once during training, after a glider had cut loose from its tow plane, the tow rope remained attached to the plane while that plane was coming in for a landing. The control tower fired off a flare to warn the plane; but it came in anyway, and its attached tow rope snaked around one of the gliders on the ground. This yanked the plane around like a big fish on a line. Finally the rope broke and the plane was released. (Russell Charlesworth, glider mechanic)

Unlike power planes, which were taxied into place for take-off, gliders had to be towed into position by glider mechanics, usually with six-by-six trucks. This was the glider mechanics' biggest job aside from assembling gliders and performing major repairs. What it called for was getting the gliders lined up right—and fast.

> We put in a lot of hard hours dragging gliders back and forth; we would have to get them lined up, then take them back, then line them up again. When there was no mission coming up this sometimes was just ground practice; they wouldn't even tow the gliders off the ground. They were trying to see how fast we could do it. And just before D-Day we had a tremendous amount of this sort of practice mission. I mean, there were really a lot of them. Every other day or so we were laying out ropes, picking up ropes, laying out the ropes again. (John Merril, glider mechanic)

Once aloft, a glider was a tricky thing to fly. Accidents during the early training days in the States were depressingly plentiful. In Membury there was a ghastly mid-air glider collision near our infirmary (see Chapter 16). We all were very conscious of the dangers that faced glider pilots and airborne troopers, not to mention what was in store for them once they landed and got into combat. The glider mechanics therefore assumed all the personal responsibility they could for seeing to it that the gliders were as safe as they could make them.

> One big problem for the glider mechanics was the D-rings, the fastenings on both sides of the nylon tow ropes. For a long time we couldn't get them to operate just right; gliders were coming loose during takeoff and even during tow in the air. We took it on ourselves to inspect the ropes and rings and to reject any that were banged up when they were dropped on the runways during training. Dragging the tow ropes, too, could cause a lot of damage. Once I rejected an entire rope, rings and all. There was a one-star general standing near at the time, and he ordered me to use it. I said I wouldn't unless he put that order in writing; and he backed down.
>
> One day five or six of us glider mechanics went on DS [detached service] to learn about the Horsa gliders. These gliders were built out of plywood; and in that wet weather there in England, that plywood was known to start rotting out. When we spotted this we would have to call it to the attention of the pilots. Often the pilots would say, "Would you yourselves fly this glider?" and when the mechanics admitted they wouldn't, the pilots also refused. There was plenty of reason for our pilots to be wary, even though they were being threatened with courts-martial for refusing to fly the Horsa. I remember that on one occasion two glider pilots in the 442nd Group took up a Horsa and it shed its wings. The pilots were killed. After that the threatened charges against our glider pilots were dropped. (Jack McGlothlin, glider mechanic)[6]

## Morale on the line

Carlisle Jordan, our Squadron Airplane Inspector, had one of the most intimidating burdens of responsibility. His job was to check on the quality of repair and maintenance work by crew chiefs, line mechanics, and Service Squadron mechanics and to see to it that the many forms recording airplane inspections were in good order. In each plane was a "Form 1A" that gave pilots the essential facts about the overall condition of the plane he was scheduled to fly. "Form 41B" listed dozens of particulars to be checked off; each serious problem had to be indicated by a red cross, a warning that the plane should not be flown. Each inspection, from daily checks through preflights, twenty-five-, fifty-, and one hundred-hour checkups, and engine changes, were checked off and initialed by the mechanics performing the work.

> Days when we had to pull inspections would start with us pushing the inspection stands up to the plane and yanking off the engine cowlings and the inspection plates. Two or four guys would work on the right engine and two more on the left. Inspection involved checking for leakage around the cylinders of the radial engines, checking all the fuel line and hydraulic line connectors, inspecting the hydraulic line bay, the air and water lines, the coolant lines, and anything else that went from some part of the aircraft to the engine. The accumulator had to be checked with a gauge to see if it was up to par. Specialists checked the instruments at the same time: gyros, compass, altimeter, radios. If the pilot had marked anything else down on the log, that also was checked out during inspection. We would work right on through the day until the inspection was finished. Then we would call the Squadron Inspector [Carlisle Jordan] over to OK everything. When he said things looked good enough, we would pull the props through [by hand] several times to clear the cylinders. Then: fire up the engines, let 'em run for three to five minutes, shut them down, and climb up on the inspection stands again to make sure there were no wet spots in any connections we previously had checked. Then: button up all the cowlings and the inspection plates, and we were through for the day. (Johnny Hirtreiter, assistant crew chief)

Each time a plane went up, thousands of things could go wrong, some with fatal consequences. When a flight revealed a condition that should have been caught during the inspection process, the buck stopped with Jordan. The recollections of our pilots and mechanics, however, produce virtually no criticisms of our airplane inspection process or the quality of repair, maintenance, and inspection work that kept our planes flying.

Common sense suggests there must have been plenty of anxious moments and bad situations. But today no one seems eager to fault others for shoddy work or for goofing off. Several mechanics agree that Pappy Harris was a tough taskmaster, although they say this more in admiration than in anger. Some mechanics criticize Desle Miller, who was our Assistant Engineering Officer, for rarely bothering to put in a day's work on the planes. But Joe Konecny points out that Miller's job was mainly administrative, that is, handling Engineering paper work. Nearly all the evidence points to a high level of morale and unit esprit on the 81st plane and glider lines. Even discounting the soothing effect of time's passage, no other conclusion seems possible.

> From what I could see, the men from other sections who used Tech Supply were decent and hard-working people. This includes practically everybody—The Line Chief, the flight chiefs, the glider and airplane mechanics, the prop men, the instrument men. When the Squadron needed it, they gave of themselves unsparingly. I'd shake their hand, every one of them, any day. I'm glad I was able to be a part of the engineering side of our Squadron. (Michael Rickey, Tech Supply chief)

One factor helped at least some mechanics feel good about their jobs. A number of them, both airplane and glider mechanics, were officially "assigned to regular and frequent aerial flights" as part of their duties. If any of these mechanics piled up the minimum of four hours flying time a month, they could draw the 50 percent supplement for flying pay. They could also wear flight crew wings on their tunics—a great source of satisfaction, especially when they were going to town on a pass. Recently Johnny Hirtreiter, an assistant crew chief, said, "Most of all, I loved to fly. I wouldn't give up my experience flying during World War II for anything in the world."

> It's true we had some free time and could go to town between operations and assignments. When we had a mission, whether a dry run for training, a glider tow, or a Squadron or Group flight, everybody had to pitch in. And when the job was done we were pretty much on our own. Most of our assignments were done during the course of our regular working hours.
>
> But the situation was different when something had to be done in a hurry. Then we simply worked from as soon as it was light until that job got done. When the job got done earlier, sure, we took things easy for a while.
>
> At times, we could have used more mechanics. Normally, this wasn't the case. But when we were building up for the big push before D-Day, our Squadron strength went up from about thirteen aircraft to around twenty-

seven. In times like that there was a strain on everybody. But I remember very little griping. We did get a few extra people sometimes. But the men who had the real know-how had to spread their effort around on to more planes; and then there would be the feeling that, hey, we were going to work right on through even if this meant working under the lights. (Joseph Konecny, Squadron Engineering Officer)

In late March 1945, at the time of the VARSITY airborne assault on Germany, our mechanics worked as hard as their tired bodies would allow. After VARSITY, too, there still was a disheartening amount of work to be done on battle damage: questionable engines, flak holes, broken hydraulic lines, wing flaps in shreds, ripped-up wiring, bent prop tips.[7] When a huge pile of work like this suddenly descended on Engineering, Harris drove our mechanics hard. As he says, he had a thing about seeing an airplane sitting useless out there on its hardstand just because it needed a minor repair or an inspection.

Unfortunately, there were a few who were unhappy with their lot and resisted efforts to get things done when we were being worked really hard. On one occasion, when we had been extremely busy, a group of mechanics refused to report to the line for work and declared that they were on strike! It was a real test of wills; but I was able to smooth things over. And as far as I know, Col. Brack was never aware that this occurred.

I'm sure that today some of those fellows think I was unreasonable. Part of the problem was that all my life I've had this ongoing love affair with airplanes; so I couldn't understand their attitudes. I failed to take into consideration that some of those fellows assigned to me were there by delegation and not by choice. (Pappy Harris, Line Chief)

## Notes

1. See the recollections of Darlyle Watters in Chapters 16 and 22.
2. 53rd TCW hist. narr., March 31, 1945.
3. *The Official Guide to the Army Air Forces*, n.p.: 1944, pp. 197–202.
4. The Air Force still follows this sensible practice; planes AGFP (aircraft grounded for parts) are called by today's Air Force mechanics "can-birds" or "hangar queens."
5. 436th TCG hist. narr. for Aug. 1944: report of the Assistant Engineering Officer.
6. In the winter of 1944–1945 the problem of rotting plywood and glue in Horsas became extremely serious. IX TCC hist. narr. for Jan.–Feb., p. 40.
7. 436th TCG hist. narr. for March 1945.

# 11. Commanding
## How to Run Combat Operations

### The TO of the TCC

Like Engineering, other functions of our Squadron tended to work through self-management and the dispersal of authority among sections and sub-sections rather than by strict control of everything from the top down. To a large extent, Communications, Intelligence, and the sections under our Operations Office and our Orderly Room all ran their own show. That is, they ran their own show *apart from combat or combat training missions*. Once a combat or combat training formation was launched, however, our "squadron's war" stopped short and the "generals' war" began. Then it was General Dwight D. Eisenhower, or RAF Air Marshal Sir Trafford Leigh-Mallory, or General Lewis H. Brereton, CG of the Ninth Air Force, or General Paul Williams, CG of IX Troop Carrier Command, or General Maurice M. Beach, CG of the 53rd Troop Carrier Wing, who controlled our every movement, not the officers and NCOs with whom we worked on a day-to-day basis.

In our Squadron we were a batch of self-reliant and, to some extent, self-governing technicians. In combat missions we were pawns on somebody else's very complex chess board. This sort of rigid constraint in combat was imposed on us by the very nature of troop carrier tactics. Bombers might have their "targets of opportunity"—some tactical flexibility in case the main objective was inaccessible. Fighter pilots, of course, made a large range of tactical decisions in the air, but a troop carrier mission—unless it was recalled in flight—had no flexibility whatever. It grew out of a large set of intricately interlocked combat plans, usually including deployment of Navy units and seaborne troops or tightly timed assaults by Army ground forces. Timing was everything. Once launched, troop carrier missions had to go where, when, and how the generals had sent them.

Of course our flight leaders had to be given a small amount of discretion; they could decide whether they were truly over the assigned LZ or DZ when the time came to give the paratroopers or the gliders the green light. But they could not choose an entirely different objective and—apart from the most terrible sort of emergency—neither could they choose to turn around and come home. This

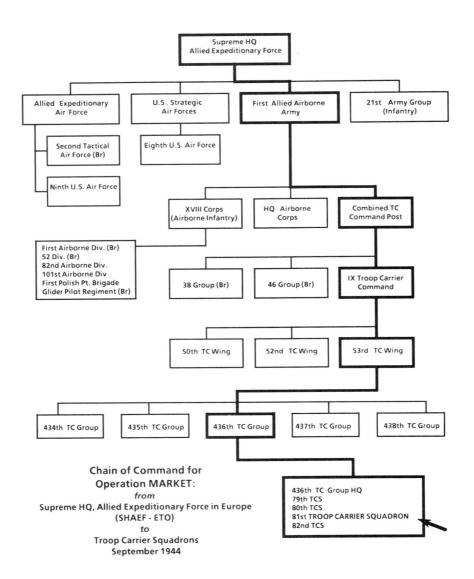

Supreme HQ
Allied Expeditionary Force

Allied Expeditionary
Air Force

U.S. Strategic
Air Forces

First Allied Airborne
Army

21st Army Group
(Infantry)

Second Tactical
Air Force (Br)

Eighth U.S. Air Force

Ninth U.S. Air Force

XVIII Corps
(Airborne Infantry)

HQ Airborne
Corps

Combined TC
Command Post

First Airborne Div. (Br)
52 Div. (Br)
82nd Airborne Div.
101st Airborne Div
First Polish Pt. Brigade
Glider Pilot Regiment (Br)

38 Group (Br)

46 Group (Br)

IX Troop Carrier
Command

50th TC Wing

52nd TC Wing

53rd TC Wing

434th TC Group

435th TC Group

436th TC Group

437th TC Group

438th TC Group

Chain of Command for
Operation MARKET:
*from*
Supreme HQ, Allied Expeditionary Force in Europe
(SHAEF - ETO)
*to*
Troop Carrier Squadrons
September 1944

436th TC Group HQ
79th TCS
80th TCS
81st TROOP CARRIER SQUADRON
82nd TCS

was borne in on us by the repeated warnings that to return with paratroopers still in your plane or a glider still stuck to your tail was a serious court-martial offense. After the Normandy invasion, we were also warned to take no "evasive action" (ducking flak and small-arms fire) from the moment we reached the IP (initial turning point). The IP was the point from which there was to be a straight run-in to the DZ or LZ, with no further course or altitude changes whatsoever.

Military historians often comment on the fact that troop carrier's war was different because we flew unarmed, unarmored, slow-moving aircraft into combat on a pre-set course. They should also recognize that the extreme tactical rigidity under which we operated marked us off from most other outfits.

We carried into combat our Squadron code (U5) painted on the fuselage near the cockpit, but we did not fly as *squadrons*, we flew as *serials*. A serial comprised the planes dedicated to one particular mission objective and numbered from a few to forty-five or more planes. It often had planes from two squadrons; even more often, the glider pilots from one squadron went into combat towed by pilots from another squadron.

When the troopers and bundles had left the planes and the free-flying gliders were making their 270-degree turn for a landing, the planes in our Squadron would revert to their "squadron's war," and the glider pilots and airborne troops on the ground would be caught up in a "soldier's war."

Where, then, did the 81st TCS fit into the U.S. Army Air Forces scheme of things? In simple terms, the 81st was one of four squadrons in the 436th Troop Carrier Group; which was one of the five groups in the 53rd Troop Carrier Wing; which was one of the three wings in the ETO's IX Troop Carrier Command; which at first was part of the Ninth Air Force, later part of the Allied Expeditionary Force, and finally a segment of the First Allied Airborne Army.

This simple table of organization does not begin to give a good picture of the complex and changing structure of which we were a part. At times our command relations interacted not only with other U.S. Army Air Forces and RAF units but also with those controlling certain airborne infantry forces, particularly our 82nd, 101st, and 17th Airborne Divisions, as well as some of the paratrooper and glider regiments and divisions of the British forces. This was most obviously the situation for the Holland invasion, when Brereton was made chief of the First Allied Airborne Army. Insofar as we had one fixed boss all through our combat experience, it was Paul Williams. Eisenhower tended to defer to the opinions of his airborne advisors, particularly Williams and Ridgway. Brereton—never entirely convinced that troop carrier performance justified its cost in terms of men and planes—for a long time was more wound up in his Ninth Air Force attack bombers and fighters than in his troop carrier groups.

Because troop carrier's main purpose was to work with airborne infantry soldiers, its chain of command was considerably different from other branches of the Army Air Forces. Inside the ETO, IX TCC's authority ran down from command to wings, groups, and squadrons—as with the rest of the Army Air Forces. But between October 1943 and August 1944, IX TCC was shifted from the Ninth Air Force to the Allied Expeditionary Air Force (AEAF), commanded by Sir Trafford Leigh-Mallory. After August 1944, IX TCC was taken from AEAF and given to Brereton's new First Allied Airborne Army (FAAA), together with the ETO's American, British, and Polish airborne infantry units (see diagram on p. 186).

Although several Air Forces as well as Army generals tried to limit the volume of materiel and the number of men flowing into troop carrier, our branch of the service zoomed upward in about two years from literally nothing in 1942 to a truly formidable array by 1944. Not until April 1942 did the Air Forces set up the Air Transport Command (ATC); and it was still later (October 1943) that IX Troop Carrier Command was activated in England. By May 1944, shortly before D-Day, IX Troop Carrier Command in the European Theater of Operations (ETO) alone sported three troop carrier wings; these included fifteen troop carrier groups. By D-Day, General Paul Williams had about 1,300 planes in his IX TCC. To put this figure in perspective: the number of *all* planes in the Eighth and Ninth Air Forces at that time was about 4,000 each. In the ETO alone there were fourteen airfields with a total of sixty combat-ready troop carrier squadrons; and there were five other fields that had troop carrier personnel (AA, engineering, communications, MPs, ordnance) under other commands. In February 1945, in our 81st TCS, we had 404 officers and men. On our airfield, Membury, in addition to the four tactical squadrons, we had a HQ Squadron and 173 other ("station complement") soldiers. Altogether there were around 21,000 men in the ETO's IX TCC, plus about 10,000 TCS personnel at other stations.[1] This is the personnel equivalent of two and a half infantry divisions.

After the war we found ourselves often correcting people who confused us with the Air Transport Command. Even during the war, *Stars and Stripes*, on occasion, had to remind its readers that "the TCC carries no bombs, but it does go into combat."[2] This was understandable: both TCC and ATC flew the same kind of planes. Between combat missions troop carrier also served the Army mainly as transport. To make matters more confusing, the Ninth Air Force had its own 31st Transport Group, in effect, its own airline for liaison and transport.

The most important difference, of course, is that TCC served in combat and ATC did not. The ATC was supposed to furnish transport *between* theaters of operation; for example, between the Americas and Europe, or between the ETO and the Mediterranean Theater of Operations (MTO). That is why the ATC was sometimes called "The Ferry Command." We in troop carrier, on the other hand, were responsible for transport (as well as airborne combat) *within* a single theater of operations. (Today, the Military Airlift Command separates its functions into inter-theater and intra-theater airlifts.)

The first combat theaters for troop carrier included North Africa, Sicily, and Italy. After preparations for the Normandy invasions began, XII Troop Carrier Command in the MTO lost its 52nd TC Wing, which moved to Britain. The 53rd and 50th Wings came to Britain from the States, giving IX Troop Carrier Command its full complement of three wings.

By March, 1944 ETO troop carrier strength dwarfed that of other theaters: there were only four troop carrier groups in Africa and the MTO, four in the China-Burma-India theater (CBI), and sixteen in the Pacific area, including Australia and New Guinea.


Of all the levels in our command echelon, that of Wing probably had the fewest direct effects on how we worked and fought. The 53rd Wing, under the direction of General Maurice Beach, transmitted commands from General Williams, CG of IX Troop Carrier Command, and briefed our Group officers for combat missions.[3] Apart from these functions, Wing worked mainly to coordinate the Group bases and Wing depots. The 53rd Wing depots had the duty of warehousing supplies and parts and seeing to it that these went to its squadrons on time, in good shape, and with a minimum of pilferage and spoilage.

Our 436th Group, on the other hand, on whose base we lived, was intimately enmeshed in Squadron affairs. In Air Forces parlance, Membury was our "tactical air station," the smallest unit able to sustain itself in combat and noncombat functions. Our Group CO, Adriel Williams, and his staff were our important "local brass," and complemented the work of our important "high brass" boss, Paul Williams.

Formally speaking, the men of 436th Group HQ constituted a headquarters squadron, but it was a coordinating and administrative body only. In his Group HQ staff, Colonel Adriel Williams had an officer for each important military function: Personnel, Intelligence, Operations, and Supply. There were also Group officers for engineering, glider operations, finance, weather, and so on. Occasionally, squadron COs would also sit with Group officers at staff meetings.

It was Col. Williams, and not Col. Brack, who was responsible to IX Troop Carrier Command for the satisfactory performance of our 81st TCS and the other three tactical squadrons at Membury. When we flew assault operations Col. Williams usually had the lead position in one of the 436th Group's serials. There were times, as we will see in Chapter 14, when Williams did indeed make crucial tactical decisions. But usually, once in the air, Williams had no more leeway inside a rigid troop carrier formation than did any other flying commander.

Many functions in our 81st TCS were duplicated—unnecessarily, I would

The Old Man: David Brack,
Squadron Commander.

436th TCG Commander Adriel Williams at the briefing for the
second Holland mission.

guess—at the Group level. For example, Group had an adjutant and so did each squadron; there was a Flight Surgeon at Group as well as one in each squadron; there were four squadron motor pools and another for the Group; Group had a Quartermaster Supply outfit and so did each squadron. All told, there were about 130 officers and enlisted men in the Group HQ Squadron at Membury.

Other functions, however, were reserved exclusively to Group: it was Group that handled the briefing of the chief squadron officers—who then went on to brief their own combat crews. And it was Group that ran base security, mounted guards, and controlled our small-arms ordnance; only Group had a chaplain; messages came into the squadrons from the Group message center; Group controlled the MPs and the airfield fire fighters, the weather observers, our base hospital (the 28th Field Hospital), the refuelling crews, the postal unit, and—a most important function—the PX, and, in England, the Red Cross Canteen. Most of the more formal forms of amusement, in addition, were Group functions, particularly the base theater and dances.

One example of how even direct orders from Wing or Group would be modified by Squadron officers comes from Darlyle Watters.

In England glider training missions usually were preceded by Squadron discussions between Brack, Farley, and me. Sometimes these discussions might get a bit warm when one of us tried to modify the flight plan we would get from Wing by way of Group HQ. The problem often was that Group and Wing glider pilots were not very experienced, and sometimes would propose dangerous patterns. They might want the takeoff to be on one runway, the tow ropes dropped on a second, and the gliders landed on a third. Brack would turn to Farley and me and order: "Set up your lines right away, and let's go!"

But I might say "Wait, wait! This will kill a lot of GPs and wreck a lot of CG-4As." Brack's usual reply would be "Explain yourself and make it fast!" I would point out that with the ordered pattern gliders would have to be landed down-wind and would need the whole runway to stop. For a good argument like this, Brack would call off or change the mission. I imagine that in this sort of case Brack had to face a lot of flak from Wing or Group—but he did it anyway. For this he received an "A-plus" in my book. (Darlyle Watters, Squadron Glider Officer)

## The Operations Office

The internal affairs of our squadron *could* have been run out of the Operations Office. Potentially, Operations had great sources of power. The Operations Officer, Major Francis Farley, was definitely Number Two in the Squadron, ranking just under David Brack. When flying orders came from Group (or from Wing or Command through Group), it was Squadron Operations that recorded those orders and arranged for their implementation. Besides acting as the conduit for orders, operations also supplied something that was greatly in demand: desirable flight assignments. In spite of this, Operations worked by arranging agreements rather than forcing compliance.

Perhaps the main reason for this was the personality of Francis Farley himself. He was respected as a fine pilot and universally liked as a fellow soldier. "A prince!" someone who worked in Operations has called him. But he was rather easy-going and inclined to duck embarrassing confrontations. Lt. Louis Kramer, who at first was our Assistant Operations Officer, also hated browbeating people; besides, since Kramer was not a flying officer, it soon became clear he would not be successful in forcing our pilots to behave against their inclinations.

The more gritty day-to-day decisions certainly could not be passed up to David Brack. Brack saw his main role in the Squadron as our chief pilot and combat leader, not as our manager. Therefore many decisions that threatened to stir up resentments among the officers tended to be settled by the clerks in the Operations Office itself, and more often than not by Gerry O'Shea, the number two NCO in that office.

Here again an issue of personality helps explain how our Operations worked. O'Shea was not our Operations chief; this rank was held by Irving Bornstein. But Bornstein hated the service; he was in his mid-thirties when he was called up, and he resented soldiering at that stage in life. Quick to take offense, he found it hard to get along with several officers and NCOs who had business with Operations. Therefore many of these men tended to bypass him and to get a ruling from O'Shea—a situation that both Farley and Bornstein, for different reasons, found convenient.

Sometimes it was impossible for O'Shea to resolve some of the thorny issues that cropped up. For example, when the weather was bad for long stretches, some of the power pilots and glider pilots found it difficult to fly the necessary four hours per month needed to get their extra flying pay. They would turn to Farley, who tended to lend them a sympathetic ear rather than to back up O'Shea's arrangements. A few times, when this sort of situation repeated itself, Brack would have to intervene and tell Farley in no uncertain terms to exercise his authority. More often, our other chief pilots, the flight leaders, would step into the argument and arrange things by themselves; this was particularly true of Stevenson, Wallen, Peek, and Wilkins, who were all captains.

There were occasions when Brack showed he could crack the whip. Usually he didn't have to; his impressive presence and gruff manner of speaking made people steer clear of antagonizing him. Once in a while, however, the sparks would fly.

> When I came into the 81st I was a young guy, and kind of an assy pilot like everybody; and I wanted to get around right away and see the sights, especially London. But when they started giving leaves, they worked alphabetically; they would get up to the "Fs," and then they would get an invasion scare, and cancel all leaves. Then, around a week later, they would open up the leaves again; but this time they would start from the *end* of the alphabet! They would come up to my name again, and then stop. I would get screwed again!
>
> I was out shaving in the latrine one morning, explaining my gripes to somebody standing next to me; and I said Brack was to blame for all this. I guess my language wasn't too nice at the time. Then I turned around, and there he was! His face got real red; then, without saying a word, he spun around and walked out. Pretty soon the Squadron Exec. came around to see me and said, "Feigion, pack up! You're going to Pathfinders!"
>
> I was left wondering what or who Pathfinders could be—first I'd ever heard of them. (Art Feigion, Pathfinder pilot)

One reason the complex balance of power in our Squadron worked well is that while the pilots and crew members might maneuver to get favors, they did not duck important responsibilities. When Operations arranged its line-up for the next day, the flying personnel did not refuse dangerous or boring assignments. We, too, responded to the famous "military peer pressure" that makes soldiers perform under fire even when terrified because they are even more afraid of risking their buddies' contempt. For us, this kind of pressure was particularly strong, since Operations tried to keep the same people in the same plane as much as possible. Neither Gerry O'Shea nor Bert Schweizer (assistant Operations Clerk) remember any cases of pilots or crew members refusing to fly their assigned ship unless they happened to be seriously ill. One exception was a radio operator who became so overwrought during the Holland invasion that when his plane landed in Membury he was found curled up tightly in a ball under his desk in the radio compartment. He literally had to be pulled out. He was relieved of flying duties and quietly shipped out of the Squadron.

However uneasy our fellows in Operations might feel about some aspects of their jobs, none of them ever complained that he was overworked.

> To put it mildly, we did not have to keep our noses to the grindstone. For example, when part of the Squadron was shipped to Italy for the invasion of southern France, I was the only enlisted man from Operations to go

along. And I ran Operations out of our HQ tent that whole month, all by myself. This seems to suggest that we were pretty well overstaffed in England, where there were eight of us in the office. (Gerry O'Shea, Operations clerk)

———————

In fact, there were too many of us for the job that had to be done. There were eight of us—four of us could have done it just as well. So some of the guys in Operations and other sections—like the other Squadrons in the 436th—were sent over to Belgium to fight as infantry during the Battle of the Bulge. This happened when the Nazis broke through and they needed so many more foot soldiers to patch up the line. The persons they took from our outfit were the few that had fouled up and got themselves into real trouble, the real screw-ups. But usually *these* screw-ups were people who did not have important MOS numbers like *you* guys who were flying!

I have to admit that even though the burden of work was not all that great, it was possible to make mistakes in the Operations Office. For flights that were not combat, but those, for example, in which gas would be ferried into France or Germany and wounded soldiers brought back, we would get calls from Group Operations late at night. The designated crews would have to be notified and ready at the flight line at just the right time next day. An order might read: "Get eight crews ready to fly to strip no. A-48 at 0645 tomorrow." Now, usually there would be only one man on duty in the Operations Office at night. Once, when the phone call from Group came down to me, I wrote down the wrong number of the French air strip to which supplies were to be carried! I had no idea of what I'd done; and at 0800, when the rest of the Operations guys came on duty, I went to the barracks for some sleep. At around 1030 some officer began to tug at my shoulder with the bad news. I really got eaten apart for sending those airplanes to the wrong field. I tried, as they say, to cover my ass; and I always contended that it was some guy from Group that had given me the wrong number. I don't remember what the devil happened to those supplies! (Bert Schweizer, assistant Operations clerk)

The Number Three man in our Squadron was Major Harold Walker, our Executive Officer. He was a vigorous, disciplined man who obviously would have become a much more powerful figure in the Squadron if he had not operated so much in Brack's shadow. It was his job to see that the Old Man's orders concerning our officer personnel were carried out, just as Captain Walter Ditto (our Adjutant) and Luman Fason (our First Sergeant) had to see to it that the Squadron functioned the way Brack wanted so far as the enlisted men were concerned.

Walker was one of the few "spit-and-polish" men in the Squadron; he spent a lot of time on his appearance, hated the fact that he had to wear a toupee, and worked out hard in athletic games and exercises. He had been some kind of an acrobat before the war. He got a lot of respect in the Squadron because he was a glider pilot; many execs in troop carrier were ground officers. But he came in for a certain amount of resentment because every once in a while he had to enforce an order by Brack that was resented by one of the officers.

Now, Brack was not comfortable in his CO position. He was a complex personality, who hated having to go through some sort of pretense about being a "good fellow" to cajole the officers into doing something he wanted. At the same time, he couldn't stand what he saw as unreasonable resistance. When he heard that Major Walker was being called a "brown-nose" for enforcing his orders, Brack would react furiously. This is the reason he eventually threw Lt. Trotman, our Assistant Intelligence Officer, out of the Squadron.

But when you come right down to it, there wasn't that much for Walker to do. Keeping the officers in line didn't take up that much of his time. Most of them were intelligent and cooperative guys who knew their jobs and their responsibilities. And most of the sections in our Squadron also knew their jobs and functioned pretty well without constant directives. We really had too many people in every department, so that nobody had to feel harassed from overwork. You know, if we had been a private organization instead of a military outfit, half of us would have been fired! (Louis Kramer, Squadron Intelligence Officer)

## The motor pool

Another section of our Squadron that was neither undermanned nor overworked was our motor pool. Operations, which was in control of most motor pool duties, found itself with so many drivers that some of them were regularly loaned to Group and others were sent off on DS to different bases.

On the other hand, we had to be ready to go any time they wanted us. They could—and they did—call us out in the middle of the night to bring pilots or crew members out or back to the flying line or to handle any other transport Operations or the Orderly Room wanted. The call from Operations was usually like this: be at the hangar within the next fifteen minutes; or, be ready to get out to the flight line at 0645.

Another reason things in the motor pool worked so well is that all of us were the kind of people who could take good care of our equipment. For greasing and oil change and small stuff like that, we handled the maintenance ourselves; for changing parts, like carburetors, there was a special crew. Before the war I had always felt I should take good care of my car and my truck; and we were pretty good in the motor pool about things like that. For the big trucks, the deuce-and-a-halfs [two and a half ton truck], there actually were two of us assigned to one truck. So that when I wasn't available, Sgt. Russell, for example, would always drive my deuce-and-a-half. It was pretty easy for us to know our equipment and keep all that stuff in good shape.

Our main town shuttle was into Swindon. Those days the best thing you could find to eat there was fish and chips. You could eat better and have a better time in Nottingham and in Oxford. Some of us made runs to Oxford, too; but for most of the guys what you had to do was catch a train at Swindon or some other place to get to Oxford or another big town.

Gas may have been a problem for civilians during the war; but not for us. There always seemed to be enough gas for everything we needed. Usually other outfits would bring in tanker trucks of gas right onto our base, to what we called "fueling points." Then we would take our trucks, jeeps, and whatever to these fueling points to gas up. It was there, also, that we loaded the jerricans when the planes had to ferry gas across the Channel.

I learned about driving English style pretty well; in fact, for a couple of months it was my job to drive one of those English two-decker buses. This was when I was on DS down in Torquay, which was a Rest and Rehab station for air crews. Those double-deckers could kind of scare you sometimes, because they were so high off the road and because you worried about all the people in them maybe shifting to one side when you were making a turn. Sometimes I carried a bunch of drunks on top who would try to make life interesting by throwing all their weight around from one side of the bus to another. This is the kind of danger that truck drivers call "swinging beef." I saw several double-deckers dumped; but I never dumped one myself.

Some people think it was our job to get jeeps and trailers into the gliders for combat missions; but this is wrong. As a matter of fact, it was the Airborne division men themselves—they must have had their own motor pool units. It was their job; but they did it under the supervision of our glider pilots, of course.

Col. Brack, you know, had his own personal jeep and his own driver to get him out on the flight line and wherever else he wanted to get. I forget the driver's name; but I remember we called him "Little Boy Blue," and I think the Colonel did, too. I'm not sure why; but I think it was because he was so young and so small and because he may have looked like the boy in that picture *The Blue Boy*. The Colonel himself was not allowed to drive a jeep—he had to use an assigned driver. (Charles Parrish, motor pool)

## Communications

One of the striking feature of our Squadron was that large and complex streams of information were devoted to running it. Every day, almost every hour, orders, news, tech data, and "how-to" manuals poured in. Besides "non-classified" (open) information, some intelligence of various grades (Confidential, Restricted, Secret, Top Secret) came our way. Receiving, processing, and transmitting these communications was the business of a surprisingly large number of us, not only in our Communications and Intelligence sections but also in the Operations Office and the Orderly Room. Depending on when one does the counting, between fifty-three and sixty of us were under the orders of the Squadron Communications Officer (George Rankin) and the Squadron Intelligence Officer (John Bohan, later Lou Kramer)—in other words, one out of every seven of us had as his primary duty the processing of information in some form. Adding the many clerk-typists in other sections, plus some equivalent time spent in censoring the mail by officers outside of Communications and Intelligence, the proportion is up to one out of every six—excluding the rumor-mongers!

Back in that pre-computer age, processing information jobs did require large numbers of people. Even so, our recollections emphasize that Communications and Intelligence—like some other sections our Squadron—housed more men than were needed.

One example of overabundant information personnel was my own department, the crew and ground radio operators. Those of us assigned to flying duties had been given several months of very good training both in wireless receiving and transmitting and in maintaining radios. In fact, our official MOS title was ROM, that is, radio operator *and* mechanic. But in addition to us the Squadron had six radio mechanics who were not assigned flying duties. We crew radio operators were forbidden to have anything to do with maintaining or repairing our own equipment. And the other radio men—including our top NCO, Cecil Elder, one of the best radio men in the business—were refused regular flying duties.

Communications was also assigned six radar mechanics—a considerably inflated number considering the amount of work they performed. And that is not all. We also had three telephone linemen, four teletype operators, three ground radio operators, and two control tower operators—each sub-section with its "complement" of specialists, and each with its high-ranking NCO ("chief").

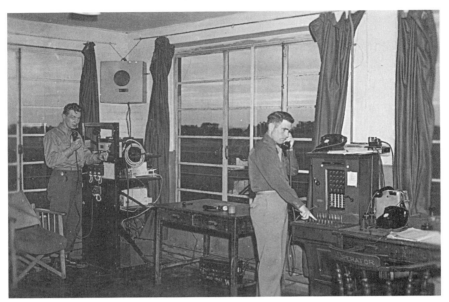

Inside our Membury control tower.

Key pounders: crew radio operators pose. *Front, left to right:* Franklin, Burress, De Blake, Alsdorf, Olmstead, Minder; *second row:* Rohan, Holmes, Zifka, Doerner, Salisbury, Dennis, Sheldon; *rear:* Burrows, Walch, Knight, Wolfe, Thomas, Sheehan.

Both Communications and Intelligence had two commissioned officers: George Rankin and Vito Capuco for communications and (after February 1945) Lou Kramer and Joseph Garcia for intelligence.

One of the problems we faced working in Communications and Intelligence was that much of the information received, processed, and transmitted was stupifyingly dull. Even during combat, most of the messages we received and sent were cut-and-dried and quite unimportant. For many of us, the hardest part of the war involved staying awake on duty. I have located only three messages that partook of high drama: the one received by Grant Howell at Group teletype signifying that the Normandy invasion was on after all those delays; the "CHINA BOY" recall message we got while flying the invasion of southern France (see Chapter 14); and the message of July 2, 1945, telling us in what order we were going to be shipped back to the United States. Many of us, therefore, had to cope with the realization that while our Squadron as a unit was playing an important role in the European war, our own individual contributions seemed pretty marginal.

Such a view of how we felt about our jobs cannot be obtained from an overview of official records that deal with information personnel and show long and impressive lists of functions we fulfilled: erecting telephone poles, setting up and manning switchboards, servicing radio and radar sets, installing radio beacons to identify our base, operating mobile radio stations (vans).

Neither would you get the impression that we were doing anything but working ourselves to a frazzle if you looked over the lists of complex equipment for which we were responsible. Inside the planes alone, Communications had to care for the command radios, the liaison radios, the intercom system, the radio compass, the two radar sets, the IFF "Black Box" transponder, the Morse Code transmitting keys ("bugs"), junction boxes, voice mikes, and so on. Further long lists cover handling equipment in ground radio operations, the teletype network, and the control tower.

Our recollections of what we as individuals and groups did, however, give an entirely different impression. For example, even during the most hectic days of combat operations, there are no memories among us of working right through a night to help set up an operation or make a crucial repair of our equipment—as our buddies occasionally did in Engineering.

Dan Bonica, one of our radio mechanics, gives one explanation. Troop carrier's supply of radio equipment was so plentiful that our Squadron radio mechanics were limited to first echelon maintenance, that is, only the simplest sort of repairs and replacements. More delicate work was turned over to other specialists, often at Wing electronics depots. Most of our own Squadron radio repairs and maintenance could be done with screwdrivers, wire cutters, and long-nose pliers. When a component seemed to be giving trouble it was yanked out and a new or rebuilt one plugged in. Bonica remembers that most of the regular fifty-hour radio inspections consisted of merely checking the glass and metal vacuum tubes (the 1940s were pre-transistor days), verifying the calibration of some of the receivers and transmitters, and looking over the antenna to make sure they were connected properly and not showing signs of wear.

Radar mechanics, like their counterparts, the radio operators, were hardly stretched to their limits. They did have much more complicated equipment, such as the relatively sophisticated oscilloscopes they used to calibrate some radar sets. They also were in charge of the VHF (very high frequency) crystals plugged into some of the plane radios to prevent frequencies from drifting.

As long as hopes lasted for using radar to pinpoint the delivery of paratroopers and gliders, our radar men were given updated instructions and training on new devices or procedures—none of which provided dramatic improvements in bad weather or at night, and none of which turned out to be vital during good weather. However, our radar sets still were regarded as so important that the IFF and the Eureka were retro-fitted with detonators to prevent their falling into German hands. The gradual disillusionment of these hopes for radar did not result in any decrease in radar personnel or training. Cecil Elder was sent on DS as late as March 1945 to learn new radar techniques.

Several of our Communications people partly earned their salt by working in the Group message center rather than on Squadron assignments. This is particularly true of our teletype and control tower specialists, for these were functions that were handled by Group not Squadron. We also loaned telephone linemen and radio mechanics to Group, but only on an "as required" basis. We had four teletype men, and so did each of the other three squadrons in our Group. The pressure of work on the teletypists, therefore, was, to say the least, rather light.

"Generally Dullsville!" reports Grant Howell, a teletype operator. One aspect of the teletypist's job that still rankles a bit is that Grant was not allowed to encode or decode restricted messages: this was a job handled by Group cryptographers only. There was plenty of time while you were on duty to kid around with other operators hooked into the teletype network, some of whom were British women.

In addition to the tactical disappointments we experienced with our radar equipment, there was one other aspect of communications that proved a constant headache: the maddening tendency for communication between a tug plane and a glider to fail.[4] In an effort to prevent the stretching and flailing of nylon tow ropes from snapping telephone lines, we tried other kinds of lines, including one that was really field telephone wire loosely looped and taped around the tow rope. We also tried other kinds of telephones, and finally hand-held walkie-talkie radios, but nothing seemed to work well or consistently. Glider pilots were

Communications characters. *Front, left to right:* Harrison, Clohosey; *center:* Promis, Baum, Ruffini, Koelbl, Elder, Lukasceski; *rear:* Bonica, Carasco.

Howard Walch, radio operator, receives his Air Medal from Col. Maurice Beach, commanding the 53rd Troop Carrier Wing; our Col. Williams is to his left.

warned not to abort their flight by cutting off from the tug if the intercom failed. We were left with the simple but unsatisfactory device of having the crew radio operator signal to the glider pilot with his Aldis lamp from inside the plexiglass astrodome of the C-47.

Some minor headaches were caused by pilots rather than by us or our equipment. An example was the tendency of pilots to mishandle their radio compass controls and so damage the delicate circular antennas of this vital equipment. Such mishaps were the exceptions. In all else that counted, Communications functioned very well. With all their equipment and their plethora of trained men, it was not difficult for George Rankin and Cecil Elder to get what was needed from their Communications people. It's true that in spite of Elder's obvious competence and somewhat intimidating manner, the crew radio operators sometimes showed signs of ignoring his authority over them after combat operations began. One of us, Warren Runyan, is remembered for ignoring Elder's injunctions to reel back in his trailing antenna before his plane landed. The trailing antenna was reeled out from the bottom of the fuselage and was weighted with a very heavy steel ball; if it dangled out the bottom of a plane that was coming in for a landing it could be a real danger to life and property.

Nearly all of us in Communications admired Cecil Elder for his great radio skills. And while George Rankin may have been the most shy officer in the entire Squadron, who found it hard to adopt informal relationships with his enlisted men, we all respected him for his obvious fair-mindedness, his dedication to his job, and the way he kept a tight grip on his temper when things went wrong.


## Intelligence

Our Squadron did not have a chaplain; in troop carrier chaplains were provided only at the Group level. We did have John Bohan, our Squadron Intelligence Officer, who did what he could in that capacity. That is, he satisfied *one* of a chaplain's chief duties: bolstering morale. Bohan was a man you could go to with your troubles and expect not only an attentive audience but a person who could carry a good deal of weight in acting on what you told him—to correct injustices, protect the less powerful against harassment, and ease resentments. Our Squadron newsletter once called him "Trouble shooter super deluxe—now to be known as Mother Bohan, because he is always taking someone under his wing."[5]

Bohan had many advantages in his role as adjudicator-protector. He was more mature than most of us (in fact, he had four children before entering the service); he had been a lawyer; and with his captain's bars he had some clout. Unlike most of us, he did not seem reluctant to stand up to our CO when some issue of fair play was involved. Not only did he have a ready sympathy for people who needed help, and an upbeat outlook on life in general, but also he was knowledgeable and willing to argue about the great political and military issues of the day—and to give advice on one's personal problems.

During the time Lou Kramer was Assistant Operations Officer in charge of censoring mail, he worked very closely with Bohan, whom he replaced as Squadron S-2 (Intelligence Officer) when Bohan left the Squadron. Lou neatly summarized Bohan's role as "a kind of stabilizer, a fine man who was able to prevent the clashing personalities and drives among our officers from causing serious resentments."

Concern with morale was not just a matter of John Bohan's engaging personality. It was also one of his principal jobs—though in a way not usually understood. "S-2" (unit-level intelligence) is not at all the same thing as "G-2" (command-level intelligence) on a reduced scale. It was only G-2 that produced and communicated the vital secret information involving combat and troop movements. By the time secret information came down to our level, it had been disseminated so widely that giving it to the enemy would probably have caused little damage. There were exceptions, of course: our combat crews and others among us knew the secret of the D-Day invasion two days before it was launched. One of Bohan's jobs was indeed to guard against men who might turn out to be security risks in the sense that they would blab—for whatever motives. Another part of his job involved protecting us against men whose anger at having been forced to be soldiers might affect Squadron esprit.

As it turned out, however, only a small handful of men were security problems. Much more of Intelligence's time was taken up with the question of Squadron morale: complaints about food, for example, or mistreatment, or anxieties about one's family at home that might spread to the point of weakening our ability to function. Information on such potential trouble spots was picked up from both direct complaints made to Intelligence and written complaints spotted while censoring our mail.

The job of censoring mail was a big one; and it ran so thoroughly against American traditions of free speech and privacy that it was thoroughly despised, by both those who did it and those who had to endure it. The officer in charge, Lou Kramer, had to dragoon highly unwilling lower-ranking officers (often glider pilots) into helping with this unsavory chore. Each enlisted man's letter had to carry on its envelope the signature of the censoring officer, though an Intelligence NCO might do the actual work. Officers' mail was only spot-checked, and by officers only.

Beginning when we were still in Laurinburg-Maxton, we had a secret agency inside the Squadron that was supposed to keep track of everybody. There were about five of us; we were supposed to keep our eyes open and, once a week, to write a letter summarizing our observations on who might be the questionable characters in the Squadron. These letters went to what was supposed to be an insurance company in North Carolina. Of course this "insurance company" was just a fake, just a post office box for collecting this sort of intelligence. But some clerk in the Maxton mail office—not a smart guy, but smart enough to be worried about all those letters going to an insurance company—went on leave one day, tracked down that address, and found there was no such company. Then he came back to Intelligence to tell us what he had found; and I had to confess this was secret work, and to ask him not to let on what he knew.

Of course we realized a lot of the mail we looked at would have sentimental and personal stuff for wives and girl friends. But it was our job, anyway, to skim through them and to see if they mentioned important names or locations. What we in particular were looking for was some clue that the person writing a letter might be deliberately giving away secret information that could be a danger. Rather than cut out that part of the letter, we would call in the letter writer and try to figure out his intention. Then our office would discuss the situation and decide whether the writer had just made an unfortunate slip or had actually been wanting to pass on harmful information.

With a real problem letter, we simply didn't send it on. But there weren't any great security risks that I knew about in the Squadron. I don't recall that we ever actually brought charges and prosecuted anybody. (Francis Lester, Intelligence clerk)

---

Our Squadron censorship was based in our Orderly Room; and I was the officer in charge. It was a monotonous job, sometimes to the point of being downright nauseating. Sometimes a letter would come along a bit out of the ordinary. I must say I enjoyed reading Marty Wolfe's letters to his wife Dotty; that's why I almost felt I knew her already when I finally saw her when we got back to the States. And I remember, also, that Sgt. Haney [parachute rigger chief] wrote letters that were well composed and had good descriptions of his buddies and of what was happening to him. But some of our guys' letters were awful, not only because they were silly and boring, but also because sometimes they were boastful to the point of being outright lies—like that fellow who kept saying we were constantly under enemy attack, practically living in the trenches. (Louis Kramer, Squadron Intelligence Officer)

The setting in which actual combat intelligence would be communicated to us, of course, was at our briefings. There were various sorts of briefings, some simple and quick, especially those involving single-plane missions for bringing supplies up near the front and evacuating wounded. Orders would be phoned in during the night from Group. For such a single-plane mission pilots would come to Squadron Operations and pick up their packet of maps, coordinates, weather, and radio information and some last-minute advice from Brack or Farley. Then the pilots would go directly out to their planes, where the rest of the crew would be waiting. Only then would the others in the crew learn about their destination or the nature of their mission.

For formation flights, especially those that involved full-fledged assaults against the enemy, on the other hand, briefings would be more formal and more comprehensive. This sort of briefing would be organized in two stages. First would come a 436th TCG briefing, at Group Operations: only a small group of men, for the most part our Squadron CO and his flight leaders, would be at this briefing, together with the other chief pilots of the 436th Group. Even our Squadron Communications and Intelligence officers would be excluded from these Group briefings. Colonel Adriel Williams and his aides, themselves previously briefed by Wing officers, would explain the main purpose of the mission and the chief problems the Squadron leaders would face. When needed, Group Navigation, Intelligence, Communications, and Weather Officers would give their advice and their warnings. After this sort of Group briefing, our top Squadron pilots would return to our Squadron Operations room and hold another briefing, this time including others in the crews who might need some of this intelligence: the co-pilots, navigators, and the Squadron Communications and Intelligence Officers.

After the CO told us there would be a Squadron briefing, it was our job to assemble all the information and tell him when we were ready. The maps, orders, and codes would arrive from Group Intelligence. These would be classified as secret and would be carried to our Squadron by two dispatchers, one to handle the documents, the other to protect the dispatcher.

We would place maps on the wall showing the targets and which places to avoid as far as ground fire was concerned—"the safest way in and the safest way out." This information would be based on the most recent aerial photographs and the most recent Air Forces maps. And the maps would show all the landing zones and drop zones for the mission.

Then it would be my job to point things out on the maps that were being referred to while Captain Bohan was talking. We would also announce all the important time checks: take-off, RPs, [rendezvous points], and IPs. Much of this information would be copied on sheets which would be handed out to each flight leader. But of course all these times and other orders were predetermined by IX Troop Carrier Command: at the Squadron level we had nothing to say about this. (Francis Lester, Intelligence clerk)

Briefings could be anxious and wearisome affairs, especially for flight leaders. Some of them, not wanting to rely only on their memories or on the packets of intelligence they got, would carefully jot down details of the briefing in little notebooks they could keep handy in their flight jacket pockets. Then, after sweating through a briefing and getting all wound up for a mission, they would often learn from IX Troop Carrier Command HQ that Allied ground troops had already smashed through and past the area where we had been told to drop our Airborne troopers. The mission would be scrubbed. Between the Third Army's breakout near St-Lô and the invasion of Holland (July 25–September 17, 1944) seven major airborne invasion missions were planned and canceled.

Four of our invasion mission briefings were staged in an atmosphere of high drama. These were the missions regarded as so crucial and so dangerous that we were all called in: co-pilots, glider pilots, even crew chiefs and crew radio operators. The first such was the briefing for D-Day. There were two other briefings for all combat personnel during the Holland invasions, one for the "southern route" to Eindhoven which took us over much of German-held Belgium, and the second for the "northern route," which took us to Nijmegen over as much water (the North Sea) as possible. The final all-crew briefing was for the double glider assault across the Rhine.

These larger briefings were held out in the open, directly in front of our base control tower. We would squat down on the turf and look up at the control tower balcony where our Group CO—already in his flight clothes—and his aides would explain the situation. Adriel Williams, using large maps, would point out routes and emphasize the danger spots. He would also give us stern reminders about our responsibilities for getting the airborne troopers to their destination without regard for our own safety. These were unforgettably dramatic moments. The presence of such a large mass of highly keyed-up men, all committed to what we understood to be a vital and dangerous enterprise, filled the air with tension.

All of us, and not only the crew members, would certainly have appreciated being involved in all briefings that touched on any aspect of our Squadron's role in the war. The fact that before D-Day all the combat crews had been let in on the secret was a tremendous boost for their morale. Looking back at the total Intelligence situation, however, it seems just as well that most of us—including most of the crew members—were excluded from almost all Group briefings. Intelligence security at Membury was not good, and probably could not have been made really secure without the place being run like some sort of a prison.

Even restricting all the 1,900 or so of us in the Group to the base would not have solved the problem, since there were too many of us with acquaintances among the civilians at the Red Cross canteen and the local pubs; and telephoning outside the base was almost impossible to control.

> To show you how loose Intelligence could be, we were having a drink in Jim Knott's [our Supply and Transport Officer] room with the civilian superintendent of the base—I think his official title was Clerk of the Works. He told us he had heard that our outfit would shortly be shipped across the Channel to France, that we would have one more major mission in France, and that then we would go home, re-group, and get ready for the invasion of Japan. We were intrigued; but we thought, what the hell does this civilian know? About an hour later, I met Brack at the officers club and I told him this rumor. He answered, "I'll be damned! That's exactly what I just heard at a top-secret Group briefing!" (Louis Kramer, Squadron Intelligence Officer)

Like everybody else involved in information processing, the men in Intelligence had to contend with the boredom resulting from monotonous jobs and with responsibilities insufficient to bolster a man's ego. But they did have one of the more satisfying jobs in the outfit: greeting our crews coming back from missions. This was the function we called "de-briefing." As each crew landed and left its plane, they all would amble over to Operations; there "Doc" Coleman would given them a shot of rye while looking them over for bad cases of jitters; John Bohan, Lou Kramer, and our Intelligence clerks would congratulate them for coming back in one piece; pilots would excitedly explain how things had looked on the ground when the green light went on for the paratroopers or glider troopers; navigators and pilots would give their guesses as to how closely they had come to the assigned LZs or DZs; and the radio men would turn in their logs. Then Intelligence would collate this information and send it along to Group.

For Intelligence, as for all of us in the information business, the moments when we could be really satisfied with what we were doing came along all too seldom. Of course there were other ways of making the time pass besides going to John Bohan and having him "punch your TS card." There was always "sacking out": some of us could snooze the hours away in our cots no matter what the barrack's noise level. Other reliefs were cards, dice, "pub-crawling," and sightseeing in London or Oxford. A few of us started Army correspondence courses; but I know of nobody who actually finished his course and got his certificate. Many of us remember Horacio Romo, a ground radio operator, who was marvelously clever at carving up bits of plexiglass (often from junked astrodomes) into attractive pendants and paperweights—he would polish them up and sell them to us for a small price. He also learned to take British sixpence, florins, and half-crowns—in those days made of almost pure silver—and beat them into rings and bracelets, taking care to work the coin so as to leave the legend ("George V [or VI], by the Grace of God, King of England") showing on the outside of the ring. Cecil Elder managed to connect up an old phonograph to a public address system. Harold Read (wire chief) and George Doerner (radio operator) played in the Group band for officers' dances. Some men in Communications managed to beg unauthorized rides, or actually stowed away, on some of the less dangerous missions; and John Bohan and Lou Kramer each went along on an invasion as official observers. Lou Kramer remembers that he flew the Rhine mission (he was not ordered to go) principally because he was ashamed to refuse; John Bohan, on the other hand, seemed so happy and excited at the prospect that Kramer wondered if, for all his relatively advanced years, Bohan still had a lot of the kid in him.

Sadly, the part of John Bohan's personality which sought out enjoyment even in military life resulted in his falling foul of Army regulations. He had an almost uncontrollable yen for souvenirs. We were all subject to that famous American souvenir craze; after all, didn't they say "Germans fight for their Fatherland, British for King and Country, Americans for souvenirs and for the hell of it?" Many of us stepped over the line of Army regulations (and of good sense) with Axis souvenirs; for example, we illegally shipped home Italian and German pistols, especially the highly desired P-38s and Luegers. But Bohan filled whole boxes full of souvenirs, including, it seems, many guns and other questionable items.

Then, toward the end of our stay in Britain (February 1945), he was transferred to a new duty at a Scottish base, where, as a former lawyer, he would assess and terminate military contracts when the need for certain products tapered off as the war (we hoped) wound down in Europe. When he left Membury, he required a small trailer to accommodate his baggage and souvenirs. The authorities at his new base, examining the items he brought with him, decided he had not acted in accordance with "conduct becoming an officer." They confiscated all his souvenirs, and he was shipped back to the States.

One of John Bohan's jobs in the last few months before his discharge was giving the standard Escape and Evasion lectures to new pilots. Ironically, he was stationed at Laurinburg-Maxton, North Carolina, our main Stateside base back in 1943.

### Notes

1. IX TCC, hist. narr. for Nov. 1944; Moore, Ch. 3, p. 3 and Appendix "Station List and Strength Report, July 1, 1944." Moore estimates there were about 50,000 troop carrier people in all theaters other than the ETO.

2. *Stars and Stripes*, April 4, 1944.

3. Wing also controlled the final stages of inspection: airworthiness of planes and gliders, proficiency of plane and glider pilots.

4. One glider pilot reported that his communications line snapped in all three of his missions: to Normandy, southern France, and Holland. Air Intelligence Contact Unit, "Reports of returnees," Jan. 1945.

5. "TARFU Gazette," Sept. 29, 1943.

# 12. Managing
## How to Run a Squadron

### The Orderly Room

The Squadron *could* have been run from the Orderly Room, where our Adjutant and our First Sergeant wielded great power over the lives of enlisted men and even over some officers. It was the Orderly Room that kept personnel and performance records and controlled furloughs and passes. Promotions for enlisted men, pay day, and sick call (reporting to the Flight Surgeon) also came under its control. And—who can forget?—it was the Orderly Room which parceled out those functions that were such necessary and such despised parts of a soldier's life: KP, guard duty, and "latrine orderly." In a general way, you could say the Orderly Room oversaw all Squadron matters not connected with flying and combat. Insofar as we had a Squadron HQ, the Orderly Room was it. Like other key Squadron offices, the Orderly Room functioned autonomously, free of narrow control by Group. One clear indication of such autonomy is that personnel records were definitely a Squadron, not a Group responsibility: at one point all S-1 (personnel) officers at our Membury base discussed consolidating all records in the Group office but decided in favor of keeping them within the four squadrons.

Three men were in charge of the Orderly Room and all it managed: Walter Ditto, Squadron Adjutant; Edgar (Ted) Menderson, Jr., Assistant Adjutant until August 1944 when he transferred to the Group Adjutant's office; and Luman Fason, First Sergeant. These three men maintained the delicate balance between forcing us to perform as we should and helping us keep up our spirits. Military fiction and nonfiction both give us accounts of outfits controlled by vindictive martinets who used their power to churn up such massive resentments that hostilities inside the unit seemed more important than any hostility marshalled against the enemy. All our recollections agree that this was definitely not the case in the 81st. Today we are almost unanimous that Squadron power was exercised in a manner that was as decent as it was effective. Those who suppose that men at war must act like a cage full of snarling tigers are, in our case, completely wrong.

Long before we moved to Britain, the NCOs in charge of our Orderly Room gained the reputation of being a reasonable and decent bunch. This reputation stuck throughout our entire wartime experience.

I joined the 81st after they were in England. Now, I had a brother in the service in England I hadn't seen for a long time. I went into the Orderly Room and asked for a three-day pass to get to Ipswich, where my brother was with the 358th Fighter Group. They gave me a pass right away—no problem. It was then I became convinced I was in a good outfit. (John Merril, glider mechanic)

Walter Ditto's chief explanation of why our Squadron functioned well was that "the Old Man" (Brack) made sure all officers and NCOs in important management positions measured up to Brack's own sense of competency and teamwork.

Now, Brack was ruthless when it came to getting good men. He would tolerate a mistake, especially if you went to him and explained how it happened and showed you could get it straightened out. But if somebody made a mistake and tried to hide it, he was *gone*. We had two Operations Officers before we wound up with Farley. We had two or three Supply Officers before we wound up with Oliver Semmes. Brack's first Adjutant didn't last twenty days. (Walter Ditto, Squadron Adjutant)

One of the effective personnel changes was in the post of First Sergeant itself. In the early fall of 1943, when we were still at Laurinburg-Maxton, our First Sergeant was Leonard Lewis. Lewis, who had been a commercial fisherman in civilian life, was baffled by the complexities of paper work, and he asked to be moved to another job. Our next First Sergeant was Fason, at that time personnel and payroll clerk. Fason's qualifications for the promotion were impressive: when drafted, he had been an administrative assistant at Maxwell Air Force Base, in Montgomery, Alabama, in charge of supervising several hundred clerks and workers.

One reason our Orderly Room functioned so well was the abilities of our First Sergeant. Luman Fason was assigned to us after we arrived at Alliance, Nebraska—he was a Pfc., as I remember it. We gave him the duties of Orderly Room Clerk. Now, I had been a First Sergeant myself and it didn't take me long to see that Fason was a natural. One of the things a First Sergeant has to do to perform well is to know everything that is going on in his outfit. Fason was so good at this I am convinced he would have made a great newspaper reporter! I moved him up to First Sergeant as fast as the Old Man would allow. He was the best I ever saw. As a First Sergeant, I wouldn't have made a mole on his nose. (Walter Ditto, Squadron Adjutant)

Once Brack became convinced he had the best possible man for a job, he let him perform pretty much on his own—as long as everything went well from Brack's point of view. Ditto refers to himself as "the Old Man's paper shaker"; but in a way this gives the wrong impression. Many important personnel decisions had to be made without consulting Brack—in fact, Brack would have resented others leaning on him instead of doing their job. "In this position," says Ditto, "you'd better get to the point where you thought like Brack did; because there were lots of times you had to do something fast, and then hope to God it would be all right with Brack."

The Orderly Room had many of the outward and visible signs of office management: typewriters, file cabinets, telephones, and most important, a mimeograph machine for duplicating and distributing "Special Orders" (personnel orders). It was in the Orderly Room, also, that we had our bulletin boards for posting the duty rosters, the orders for the "uniform of the day," and other directives all of us were supposed to eyeball regularly—but seldom did. On the other hand, when somebody banged on our barracks door and yelled "Mail Call!" you can be sure we zipped over to the Orderly Room fast enough.

Besides mail call, good news out of the Orderly Room came in the form of passes to town and pay at the end of the month.

> Leaves and passes for flying personnel were granted when recommended or approved by Colonel Brack or the Operations Officer. I granted them to enlisted ground personnel on the basis of need, workload and existing conditions. Of course, a man's attitude and performance record did affect our decision. But there was no set pattern for granting passes. It was our policy to grant passes whenever possible, consistent with keeping enough personnel available to do the job under existing conditions. You will possibly have some who will dispute this; but even today I do feel that this was the method we followed. You must bear in mind that there were those who requested very few passes, and others who were ready for one every day; and we did have to weigh the merits of these requests at times. (Luman Fason, First Sergeant)

Bad news out of the Orderly Room was in the hands of Henry Allai, our duty sergeant, and Alfred Carifa, our duty roster clerk, who had to decide who did the dirty work. The fact that Allai was the oldest man in the Squadron helped

The Orderly Room bunch at TARFU Boulevard. *Front, left to right:* Lodge, Johnson, Menderson, Elrod; *rear:* Carroll, McCoy, Fason, Bates. Ted Menderson was our Assistant Adjutant at this time, and Luman Fason was our First Sergeant.

Off to Edinburgh: Loading a jeep onto a C-47 for the officers' club's "Scotch run."

us accept his decisions. Allai had actually served as a soldier in France during World War I.

The chief records kept and updated by the Orderly Room were our "201 files," covering every administrative aspect of each man's military career. The "Form 20" and the "66-1" forms described each man's background: his education and other important features of his civilian life. There were other forms for military training, efficiency ratings, and pay records.

## Sick Call!

One section that functioned smoothly—perhaps in part because it had responsibilities that were almost too easy for its personnel—was the medical unit. Jesse "Doc" Coleman, our Squadron Flight Surgeon, had a long list of responsibilities in addition to being what today would be called our primary care physician. He supervised our immunization shots and boosters; cared for the injuries our Engineering people suffered on the line; made sure all our medical records were up to date; checked on our water supply and "sanitary facilities" (latrines); tried to guard against venereal disease; and decided when one of us had to be hospitalized. But he had three medical assistants, one of whom was qualified as a medical technician and the other as a surgical technician. On one occasion, when we had just moved to our new base in France, Jesse Coleman asked our CO for a detail of men to dig the latrine trenches; Brack brusquely recommended the medics do it themselves, since they seemed to have so much time on their hands.[1] If we had been victims of those famous scourges of war (cholera, typhus, tetanus) or infectious diseases or many injuries, our medical section would have had its hands full. We were so healthy (apart from VD), though, that our medical people were not any more overworked than the rest of us.

However, we did have a few exciting medical moments.

One night after D-Day we missed the last truck back to the base. We walked back; it was only about five miles. When I got back to the base, I felt like I'd been kicked in the stomach by a horse. The medics came over shortly and took me to the base hospital. The medic there thought I had a little flu or something. But then the doc found I had a ruptured appendix, and things started happening pretty fast. They put me in an ambulance and took me to another hospital about fourteen miles away. They had to put me on the floor because there were so many wounded infantry guys back from the front. I did what I could for them after I could walk around: brought them water, played cards with them, tried to cheer them up. (Johnny Hirtreiter, assistant crew chief)

Anybody who imagines that in troop carrier squadrons our medical section operated somewhat like the frantic medics in the famous "M*A*S*H" television series has the wrong idea. For our medics, duty was pretty well confined to the routine known as sick call, when we all had the right to carry our complaints to the Dispensary first thing after reveille ("Take two aspirin and see me in the morning") and to occasional (and always unannounced) "short arm inspections" at around 4:00 a.m.

Jesse Coleman remembers that when the Squadron was still forming up at Baer Field, Indiana, a few men (and their wives) came down with pneumonia in that cold and damp winter weather of February–March 1943; but for the rest—again, apart from VD—few of us were obliging enough to make life interesting for our medics.

> We stayed at the POE for about a week. The weather wasn't too good; I remember we had some snow. Just as we were getting on the *Queen Mary* one of our men passed a kidney stone. He was in a hell of a state, in terrible pain, and passing blood. We had to put him in a hospital; and he came over in another ship and rejoined our Squadron later. Then—all the time we were in Europe!—I myself did not have to deal with another single case of serious illness until we were boarding our planes to come home. (Jesse Coleman, Squadron Flight Surgeon)

It was obvious that if they had been given the opportunity, our medics would have coped very well indeed with more serious problems or even a succession of crises. Doc Coleman was obviously exceptionally competent as well as kind and caring; "a *gentle* gentleman as well as an officer!" one of us remembers. And his top NCO, George Trumbo, was universally popular in spite of the fact that he gave us most of our shots.

Another job of our medics was to make sure the first aid kits in our planes and gliders were complete and in good shape. This last duty turned up one of the most disgusting problems our Squadron ever faced: while we were in France, somebody repeatedly stole morphine ampules from our airplane aid kits— morphine we needed for combat wounds and injuries. Why? Because this thief had become an addict, or because he was selling to the French black market? Nobody knows; and nobody was formally charged for the crime. But some of us are pretty sure it was one of the officers Col. Brack booted out of our Squadron at about this time.

One puzzle is why our medical team was not put to more use in medical evacuation missions when the invasions started: they were not only qualified for such work but they had some experience with it. Maybe our Squadron medics would have had more to do with evacuation during combat if we had been assigned any nurses; it was required, in those days, for a registered nurse to be on each medical evacuation flight. In troop carrier nurses were assigned only to special Medical Evacuation Units.

> The first months we were in England, medical evacuation was about all the hard work we did. Most of the patients we flew were cases of psychological problems, people (not those in our Squadron!) who had gone sort of bonkers before the invasion of Normandy had even started, just sitting around and kind of worrying themselves sick. We flew them over to hospitals in Ireland, practically a plane load of such cases every day. They kept them there in Ireland until they got in good enough shape to be shipped back to the States. This was good training for our Squadron pilots, too, for the medical evacuation they would have to do later on. (Jesse Coleman, Squadron Flight Surgeon)

One of the standard bits of Army humor concerned "section 8s." A "section 8," so called because of its number in the regulations concerning discharges, was a release from the military for reasons of psychological illness. One of Jesse Coleman's duties was keeping his eyes peeled for signs of psychological problems among our pilots that might make them dangerous for the rest of us as well as themselves. On only two occasions did he have to intervene and yank a pilot off duty. The first was Herb Christie, a glider pilot, in circumstances already described in Chapter 9. The other was a power pilot, embarrassingly suspected of malingering by other officers in the Squadron, but who, says Coleman, "only needed to rest up awhile."

For all the "short arms" he oversaw, for all the kindly advice he gave, and for all the pills he dispensed, Doc Coleman could not solve the constant problem we had with venereal disease. He was aware that Horacio Romo, a ground radio operator, had somehow gotten a batch of sulfa pills and was giving them to men who did not want to report that they suspected they were infected.

One of the reasons syphilis was such a problem for us concerned an enterprising prostitute in Bristol. Bristol was the town many of our cooks and motor pool people often visited to pick up food and other supplies. When this prostitute learned they were on the premises, she got over the fence that surrounded the military base in Bristol where they spent the night, led them in a group to a haystack, and gave them all something to remember her by.

For troop carrier as a whole, during the spring of 1944, VD rates rose to forty out of every thousand men per annum in April and increased alarmingly to sixty per thousand in June. General Paul Williams then ordered all his station commanders to launch "an active campaign" against it. During the summer and fall campaigns of 1944 VD became less of a problem, but in the spring of 1945 it rose again.[2] At one time the Group Flight Surgeon reported to Brack that—to judge from the medical reports—the 81st Troop Carrier Squadron had the highest percentage of men with some form of VD in the entire Ninth Air Force! Brack was furious, and he swore that the next man who came down with VD would immediately be shipped out to some infantry outfit. This threat, of course, led some men to try even more desperately to hide their problem, or to rely on Romo's pills.

In addition to the famous sulfa pills, Romo seemed to have an endless supply of condoms, which he freely distributed to his buddies going to town. Another individual who enjoyed Romo's condoms was our Squadron mascot, the black Labrador retriever named Trixie, who belonged to Jesse Coleman. Like most Labs, Trixie got along well with everybody, but Romo was her special favorite. He would blow up condoms like balloons and throw them up in the air for her. It was her special treat to chase them as the wind took them and to grab them in her teeth. Those of us watching would laugh until our sides ached. The fun ended when Trixie chewed up and swallowed one of the condoms she caught. Some very strong medicine was needed to ream out her insides.

> Trixie was surely a dog that loved to fly. She would look around for a plane that was getting ready, with its door open and steps set in, and if she could she would just jump right in!
>
> While we were in Membury we bred Trixie to a golden Lab. She had her puppies just as we were unloading the plane she flew on when we came over to our new French base. She just jumped out of the plane, went over to an old dog house that some German had built there before us, and had her pups. (Jesse Coleman, Squadron Flight Surgeon)

## Chow!

Everybody who has ever been a soldier knows that one of the important ways of rating one base against another is the quality of its PX (Post Exchange). Today a BX (Base Exchange) on a large base can be spectacular: a department store, drug store, and supermarket all in one. Our World War II PXs were tiny and poorly stocked, but to the people they served they were very important. We had few alternatives to buying at a PX. It was there we got many necessities (soap, toothpaste, shaving equipment, handkerchiefs) and semi-luxuries (candy, cookies, tobacco) at low prices. We were rationed, but the rations were so generous few of us could complain. Cigarettes were untaxed. They cost one dollar a carton and we could usually get one carton a week. This was much more than many of us used; some of us didn't smoke at all. I traded mine for candy or sold them to French black market operators. Sometimes candy, 3.2 percent beer, or soft drinks would be scarce, but we could usually buy all the gum or cookies we wanted.

In fact, the PX (and in Britain, the Red Cross canteen) was one reason we could afford to turn up our noses, once in a while, at what the mess hall had to offer. Some barracks would even send out a runner to report back on whether, compared with the candy in your barracks bag, the food available on the chow line was worth getting out of the sack for.

> Sometimes I really depended on food from the PX to get me through. It was that and packages from home. The first salami I got in a package from home was spoiled. It was all covered with mildew. But one of our guys, when he saw me getting ready to throw it away, grabbed it; he wiped it off, washed it good, and sat right down and ate it.
>
> I remember the PX would give you a ticket for a prize; and if you had the lucky number, when you bought your rations you were entitled to buy a box of candy—I think it was Fanny Farmer chocolates. I used to buy those chocolates from fellows I hung around with; and I would eat that when I couldn't eat the junk they had at the mess hall. (Irv Bornstein, Operations clerk)

It was understandable why much of our food in Britain was far from delicious: some of our cooks, former truck drivers who had been pushed out of the motor pool because they frequently got into accidents or because they were general FOs (fuck-offs), had had no training for that job. Another constant problem on the chow line was the tendency of KPs who cherished a grievance against Army life to slop food down anywhere on your tray, making an ugly-looking scramble out of items that often were not appetizing looking in the first place. Lower-ranking enlisted men (under buck sergeant) had to serve as KPs once a week and hated it. John Hiles, who came into the Squadron late and was only a Pfc., was often put to work cleaning out the kitchen grease traps; he feels this was partly because he never got along well with Cecil Elder, our Communications chief.

Sgt. Mullen, a "KP pusher" (mess hall chief), occasionally tried to get those dishing out food to spoon it into the proper tray compartment, but when a sour-tempered KP was behind the counter it was a minor triumph to get to your table with food that didn't look as though it had been scraped out of the garbage pail.

At first most of the 1,800 men of the four Squadrons and other units in Membury ate together in one huge consolidated mess hall—officers on one side,

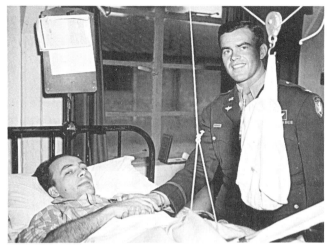

Group Commander Adriel Williams visits a wounded crewman in our base hospital; a Purple Heart medal is on the window sill.

Chow time! 81st TCS cooks pose in front of TARFU Country Club, the fine new mess hall at Melun, France, which they and our glider pilots built.

EMs on the other. Certain outfits on our base, including the Service Squadron, had their own mess halls in smaller buildings, and counted themselves lucky. In the consolidated mess hall, cooks and KPs didn't know the men they served and consequently were sloppy and inconsiderate. During the last few months of our stay in Membury, officers in each squadron were able to organize small improved messes of their own, to their great relief. EMs continued to eat "consolidated." When we moved to our new "Tent City" base in France and each squadron got its own mess hall, the quality of the cooking and of service in the chow line improved dramatically.

Officers messes, of course, had better service and somewhat better food. Officers also had first crack at deliveries of beer and soft drinks. When hard-to-get items like butter became scarce, these disappeared first from the EMs' mess. When there were fresh eggs and good bacon, they went to the officers, who could order them cooked the way they liked, whereas the EMs always got powdered eggs, served scrambled. Once the officers took all the condensed milk from the EMs' mess to make ice cream; a few NCOs got a can or two of this ice cream.

William "Rip" Collins, a pilot, figured out an ingenious way of deciding whether the walk to the officers' mess was worthwhile. In England he bought a push-button radio and converted it to an eight-station intercom. Then he could call up and find what was on the menu. He connected his other channels to the Squadron dayroom, the Operations Office, and a telephone on the flight line; after that, on rainy days he and the others in his quarters didn't have to venture out of doors at all to find out what was happening.

Pretty often, it seemed to me, the cooks in the EM mess would get pretty sloppy, the complaints would build up, and our brass would have to put on the pressure. Once when Colonel Williams was coming through, making a surprise inspection of the barracks, he saw that on practically every bunk in the glider mechanics' barracks there was a little pile of C-rations.[3] He wanted to know where we'd acquired all those. He also wanted to know why we had them. One of our fellows answered that the food up in the mess hall wasn't good. Knowing what C-rations were like, the Colonel had to think maybe we were right. He said, "You mean to tell me you'd rather eat C-rations than the food in your own mess hall?" Some of us yelled "Yes, sir!"

The very next day, at noon, Williams came through the EM mess, mess kit in hand. The Mess Officer hurried to get a tray for him and started to pick up some food to take up to him. But the Colonel told the Mess Officer he was going to eat what he had on the mess kit, just like the rest of us. He sat down at a table and called the Mess Officer over and said "Do you expect these men to eat this garbage?" Those were the exact words he used. He added, "This stuff isn't fit for hogs to eat." And he finished by saying "I'm going to be coming through this mess hall periodically from now on; the food system better be changed around here! These men have earned better food than you are making for them." (John Merril, glider mechanic)

Grousing about mess hall food was more a way of passing time waiting in a chow line than it was an indicator of serious discontent. Today we are inclined to agree that most of that food—even that dished out to enlisted men—wasn't all that bad. Johnny Hirtreiter, an assistant crew chief, remembers that for him the problem was not quality but quantity: not mess hall food but rather how hungry he got between chow times. He and other mechanics would carry K-rations into a plane on which they were working and gobble them down when their stomachs began to growl.

Remembering how we upped the quality or at least the variety of food we ate occupies a pleasant niche in the recollections of each of us. I can never forget the great chunks of bulk chocolate my Aunt Jennie sent me every month— enough for half my barracks. Bill Westcott remembers that whenever the mess hall was having chicken, he would scrounge some giblets and fry them over his barracks' pot-bellied stove, with butter saved up from C-rations. On the day beer was delivered to the local pub, he would fill up a jerrican with beer and bring that plus some "chips" (French fries) back to his quarters. Those of us who could beg or bribe the cooks and KP pushers could nicely supplement their bill of fare. Do-it-yourself cooking—even in the summer when stoves were not working—was no great obstacle: in fact one of us did it with a welder's torch borrowed from Tech Supply.

In England the opportunities for supplementing chow were less plentiful than in the States and therefore even more important. In Membury some of us could drop into a Group NCO club when our schedules permitted; there we could sometimes buy beer and Cokes and even hard liquor, and we could always get tea and rather tasteless sandwiches put up by the English civilian employees there. On the base in England, in addition to a PX we had a Red Cross canteen, with less variety but still plenty of necessary items to serve; and in some towns we could buy tea, scones, and sandwiches from the British equivalent of our USO, the NAAFI (Navy, Army, and Air Force Institute).

There was also some food to be had in town when we got passes. Our American appetites were too sharp to be satisfied by just one of these poorly cooked and severely limited British meals; so—if the money held out—we went directly from one restaurant to another. In July and August, when many of us were in Italy for the invasion of southern France, we took our K-rations into restaurants and got back good Italian cooking from our miraculously transformed boxes of rations. In France, especially, we could trade rations for wine, good bread, and even an entire meal in somebody's home.

> I used to have me an egg deal going for myself alone. I found haystacks that a lot of chickens must have liked; I carried my helmet over there and came back with it full of eggs. And I was able to bribe Sgt. Mullen with those eggs, too. In turn he'd give them to Col. Brack or Capt. Knott or whomever. But even though we had to divide with these fellows, we ourselves always had plenty of eggs. We'd get that old mess kit out and boil them over the stoves in our barracks. Or we'd get some butter and fry them ourselves.
>
> I remember we used weapons carriers for transporting small stuff or only a few people; and I remember that we drove weapons carriers to Newbury where they had a bakery that supplied the base with our bread. We used to trade pound boxes of butter for extra bread; this is one of the reasons I always liked to get that run to Newbury. I bribed Sgt. Mullen by telling him that if he put me on that run I would bring him back a fresh loaf of bread. We got that bread actually hot; and we could keep it pretty warm all the way back. That bread was so good we used to rip the package open and eat some of it right on the spot. Maybe the reason butter sometimes was scarce at the mess hall—and the EMs would have apple butter or marmalade—was that we traded so much of our butter for that good hot bread. (Charles Parrish, motor pool)

Marmalade instead of butter was hardly an insufferable burden. Between parcels from home, the PX and the Red Cross canteen, and the mess hall, we had so much to eat it is no wonder the British thought of us as hopelessly coddled and soft.

> The first meal we had at our first British base [Bottesford] was typical English Army and RAF mess. Our meal consisted of a strong smelling goat stew with some horrible, bitter boiled greens. . . . We had to hold our noses to swallow it. We Americans were spoiled by the American military always serving up decent food. The British people eating with us could not imagine why we were not enjoying that meal. (Ben Ward, glider pilot)

Those of us who found ourselves at British bases at meal time came back with horror stories that made our own chow, at least by the time we got to Membury, seem pretty good. Once when we flew down to St. Mawgan on the southwestern tip of England we landed with a flat tire and stayed in the middle of the runway for half an hour before the English could pull us off. We had to stay overnight; in the British officers' mess the next morning at breakfast I remember being upset at seeing the beady eyes of a kipper staring at me from the plate—and having nothing to drink but a cup of lukewarm tea. (Bill Westcott, pilot)

## Quartermaster Supply

Later on, after the war, a historian, David Potter, wrote an influential book called *People of Plenty* in which he argued that Americans were different from everybody else because of our country's overflowing abundance of food and commodities. It was this that made us, as a nation, so generous and so confident of the future compared with other nations—but also so wasteful. This interpretation was certainly borne out as far as our own Squadron's experiences are concerned. Sometimes one of us would refer to "scrounging" for this or that, but the fact is that considering wartime needs and considering how other Allied soldiers lived, we had an almost embarrassing surplus of decent food and supplies.

No, we never had any serious shortages. I remember that other squadrons at first had some. That was when we first got to England. I really loaded us up when we left the States. I made sure we had enough of everything; even heavy stuff like generators and batteries. Adriel Williams found out other squadrons were running short; once he called Brack and me and asked if we couldn't help the others out. That was fine with me; we kept them supplied with a few things for quite a while.

I was lucky to have two damn good NCOs helping out in QM and Tech Supply. Mike Rickey, especially, was a sharp man. He had friends in other outfits over in Europe before we left the States; he wrote to them to ask them what sort of supply they were short on, and then he and I went to work on this and got just those items in our stock and shipped on over.

We never had much of a problem with our whole logistical situation. The flow of materials over to Europe was about all we needed. And what we didn't have we somehow managed to get pretty easily. I remember that when we moved to France our mess sergeant and a fellow we called "Frenchie" went out to local towns and scrounged up enough wood and other stuff to help build us our new mess hall. (Oliver Semmes, Squadron Supply and Mess Officer)

Gasoline, in Europe, was even more plentiful than it had been on our American bases. Usually the Red Ball (Army truck line) would bring in our gas;

sometimes we had our own men drive to a depot and load up our own 6,000-gallon trailers. Gas was often desperately needed at the front lines, but behind the lines, on our bases, gas for planes, jeeps, and trucks was never a problem. We thought nothing of using high-octane aviation fuel to wash down our planes and trucks.

It's only human: the details we tend to remember now are not our cornucopia of supply goods, but rather this time or that when we had to wait a week for a new pair of shoes or for laundry to be returned. All the clerks complained there were never enough typewriters. The KPs complained that the British soap they used would not suds up in the hard water, making it impossible to get grease off cooking utensils. Sometimes when crews came in late there was nothing to eat but corned beef or C-rations. I remember that all the flying radio operators were promised wristwatches—sharp looking, GI (government issue) black Walthams given to the flying officers and often promised but never obtained for the rest of the crew members. There were similar complaints about those classy-looking aviator's sun glasses many of us never got.[4] As a radio operator, I really needed a good watch, but I didn't get one until our Operations Office managed to buy a whole batch of civilian watches to *sell* to us, though admittedly at very low prices.

Supply was basically a Squadron function, not a Group (base) or Wing function. This was true of both Quartermaster and Tech Supply. There was a Group Supply Officer, but his main job was to coordinate Supply for squadrons. In November 1944 he reported that truck and plane tires for all squadrons were in short supply, that not all enlisted men crew members had bedrolls as yet, and that for a few weeks an adequate amount of de-icer fluid had been hard to find. Such shortages either were not crucial or were cleared up in a few weeks or less.

It seems obvious that by making each squadron responsible for its own supply, instead of trying to handle supply through one central department for all the squadrons on our base, the Army Air Forces made a wise decision. Squadron-level supply officers and NCOs were in a much better position to check on supplies and see that they got promptly to where they were needed. By keeping supply at the squadron level, the Air Forces induced a healthy element of rivalry that could spice up duties which were essential but hardly glamorous.

> While we were being moved from Bottesford to Membury, I and a few other officers and EMs were assigned to stay behind for a few days to see to it that some of our equipment was being made ready for shipment—and to act as guards. I had full run of the field; and I had a jeep. I had to know where our own supplies and parts were; but I found out where other material was being held, too. Once I located a building that was full—and I mean full—of brand new CG-4A nylon tow ropes. Now, some time soon there

would be a new group assigned to that base; but meanwhile it was empty except for us and a few MPs. We flew to Membury, flew back with a six-by-six trailer, and loaded our plane from top to bottom with those ropes. We went back to Membury with no one the wiser.

It was a classic case of a "midnight requisition."

Our glider training sessions at Membury were notable in that fine new ropes were always in evidence, while the other three squadrons were using dirty and frayed ones. But Captain Brown, the Group Glider Officer, learned of this and had a serious talk with me. The invasion of Normandy was coming up. Soon—thanks to the generosity and enterprise of the 81st—the other three squadrons also had nice new ropes to drop on the Germans. (Darlyle Watters, Squadron Glider Officer)

People of plenty we were, and Americans still are, but it pays to remember that in other ways we have changed mightily. One of the few really sour incidents involving our mess hall serves to remind us that there was not a single black man in our Squadron and in fact, practically none in the entire Army Air Forces.

One day the Red Ball [Army truck line] brought up a load of gasoline. There was a black fellow who was driving that six-by-six. Our top NCOs felt it would cause trouble to let him eat in our mess hall. Our brass felt I shouldn't contradict a decision by my superior NCOs. I still argued it was funny not to give this guy who had brought us that gasoline something to eat. Finally I had to take his mess kit into the mess hall myself and bring him back some food. (Irv Bornstein, Operations clerk)

### Notes

1. When the Group Flight Surgeon heard about this and similar situations in other squadrons, he ruled that no medical personnel had to dig latrines, though they did have to instruct those doing the work on how to construct proper latrines. 436th TCG hist. narr. for Feb. 1945.

2. IX TCC HQ, hist. narr. for April and June 1944, reports of the office of the Surgeon.

3. C-ration boxes, small enough to tuck into a pocket of your fatigues, contained unappetizing canned meat (Spam) and canned vegetables, plus dried crystals for making a dreary-tasting lemon drink; the later K-rations were better. They contained that brand-new invention, instant coffee, and often also provided a rather decent-tasting prize, an "emergency" (D-ration) compressed bar of chocolate.

4. 81st TCS hist. narr. for May 1945.

# 13. Breaking Out
## The Controversy Over Troop Carrier Freighting Potential

### Fighters or freighters?

David Brack's plane, *My Shattered Nerves*, was housed for a while at Hunter Field, Georgia, after our part of the war was over. There some enterprising reporter spotted a story in all those unusual-looking symbols he saw painted on the front left side of the fuselage. By this time (July 1945), everybody had become familiar with the mission symbols displayed by bombers and fighters. The C-47s, of course, had neither "kills" nor bombing missions to show. Instead they depicted tactical achievement with a whole variety of mission symbols. Brack's plane had stenciled on it three parachutes, six gliders, four parachuted bundles, a locomotive pulling no less than ninety-five little railroad freight cars (plus eight more for passengers), and, finally, forty-one red crosses for medical evacuation missions. The reporter who snapped the photo of this display may have been thinking that if all those little stenciled pictures could only talk, what a huge number of different kinds of war stories they could tell![1]

Those mission stencils on our planes symbolized one of the least understood but most important features of the war on the western front—not just our part of the war, and not because our missions individually or collectively determined any great battle. Their very variety signifies how unsure high command, including Eisenhower himself, was about what role we would play. Would troop carrier continue to place airborne troopers behind enemy lines, as we had in Normandy? Or should it use the superb ability of the C-47 to land practically anywhere with a load of fuel or ammunition? Would troop carrier's main destinations be primarily hastily improvised supply dumps far in advance of any place trucks could reach? Or would it continue to be directed toward DZs and LZs? Would troop carrier serve primarily as freighters or as fighters?

This controversy was no sideshow. After mid-July 1944, when the American Third and First Armies began to break through the German defenses in Normandy and Brittany, SHAEF was presented with a very hot troop carrier potato. Troop Carrier Command and the British transports together could not provide all the planes that infantry commanders in the field demanded for *both* combat airborne operations and logistical (freighting) support.

In late August 1944, Field Marshal Sir Bernard Montgomery's convictions hardened around the idea that all British and American airborne divisions and carriers should be used to spearhead one massive, concentrated assault across the northern tributaries of the Rhine and to penetrate through Holland into northern Germany. He wanted Eisenhower to stop the U.S. Third Army in its tracks; this would allow much more gasoline and other supplies to be delivered to Montgomery's own command area. At the same time Bradley and Patton, headed straight toward the middle reaches of the Rhine and central Germany, were almost beside themselves with frustration as their advancing tanks—so close to the French-German border!—began to run out of gas. They hounded Eisenhower with demands that all C-47s (and whatever bombers could be converted to carriers) be used for forward fuel delivery. At one point, on September 10, 1944, when Montgomery and Eisenhower were arguing this point, Montgomery flew into such a rage that a serious breach might have been made in the very fabric of British-American cooperation. Montgomery calmed down only after Eisenhower agreed to a compromise that seemed to give Montgomery most of what he wanted. Unfortunately, out of this compromise came MARKET-GARDEN (the invasion of Holland), with all its terrible consequences.

Very little of this impending storm over the use of troop carrier was visible in the weeks after Normandy. This was a time of agonizing over how slowly the beachheads were expanding and how terrible were the casualties our troops on the ground were suffering. Couldn't some way be found to use airborne assaults and break out of that ghastly fighting, yard by yard, through those Normandy hedgerows?

Back on June 7, 1944, two additional glider re-supply missions had been dispatched by other troop carrier groups to the airborne troopers fighting in back of the Normandy beaches. These missions suffered heavy losses, and few of their gliders reached the targets. On June 10 our own Squadron sent out two separate glider missions, six planes each, to Normandy; these re-supply missions were so successful and so free from enemy fire that the delighted pilots called them "milk runs."

Johnny Harris, one of our crew chiefs, suffered a bizarre accident on this flight: his plane was flying over the battleship *Texas* when the ship let go an enormous broadside. The concussion hurled the plane up in the air and down again. Johnny was thrown up at the plane's ceiling, and a girder there cracked his neck so hard it crushed one of the spinal vertebrae.

For the most part, these weeks of middle and late June, our Squadron was only marking time. The rest of our glider pilots who had participated in the Normandy mission made it back to Membury to a heartfelt welcome by the rest of us. Landings for glider pilots towed into France after June 10 became more and more safe, almost routine: some of the pilots were able to make the trip back by ship and to arrive in Membury the following day.

> Back in Membury, I wasn't yet settled in my barracks when another call came. Another trip to Normandy! This time I flew pilot, with Sam Green at my right acting as co-pilot. We led a small group of gliders in and landed on a strip that was still being prepared. They were rolling out those steel mesh mats to make a runway. All the men on the ground left in a hurry when they saw us coming; but we had plenty of room left and stopped well short of the rolled-up mats. Sam Green and I were, I believe, the first people to land on a strip in Normandy during the D-Day invasion. So I racked up two extra "combat" missions during the Normandy operation! (Earl Goodwin, glider pilot)

Most of us felt that the main business of the war was passing us by.

The British, during June, were debating authorizing smaller airborne assaults ahead of their stalled lines near the key city of Caen in Normandy; one such plan did develop far enough to be given a code name (WILDOATS). On June 14 it had to be canceled because the Germans had recaptured the DZ grounds on which the British and Polish troopers were supposed to jump. A few not-very-serious schemes were broached to drop paratroopers on some Channel port, perhaps St. Malo or Cherbourg; but because of the massed German defenses in those ports, these were vetoed by troop carrier and the British airborne commanders as practically suicidal. At that time the Allies still had not captured a single major French or Belgian port, so that shiploads had to be either handled on the artificial concrete harbors ("Mulberries") hauled across the Channel after D-Day or actually lightered down off the ships onto small boats and so to the beaches. A terrible and prolonged Atlantic gale beginning June 19 wrecked most of the Mulberry installations; and for three crucial days most of the desperately needed ammunition and supplies had to be delivered by air.[2]

One heartening evidence of troop carrier's multi-purpose efficiency came on June 14: our Squadron used three planes that day on a supply and evacuation mission. This time we actually landed our C-47s on a tiny airstrip carved out for us on the Normandy beachhead. We in the C-47 crews had been over France several times; now, at least momentarily, we were in France. We landed there thanks to the engineers who had leveled a runway and covered parts of the more soggy sections with "Marston strips," interlocking steel matting that kept our wheels from sinking in that sandy soil.[3] The mission went off like clockwork:

An early medical evacuation mission: a nurse and medics carry a
stretcher from a C-47. Notice that both jump and cargo doors are open,
and that the plane is seated on "PSP" (pierced steel planking) used for
dirt air strips.

For the record: Colonel Williams, Group CO, poses near his plane's
"mission symbols": so far, two combat paratrooper drops, three combat
glider missions, five combat resupply missions, forty-plus freight hauls,
and four med-evac missions (Red Crosses).

ammunition and medical supplies in, wounded soldiers out. In fact, we returned only five hours after we started out from Membury.

Strong emotions gripped all of us on that June 14 flight as we landed in France and climbed out of our planes. It meant a great deal to me that at least for a moment I was planting my feet on French soil—even though I was in fact standing on American-made Marston strips. The only sour note on this mission came when we saw that some of the wounded soldiers we were transporting back to England were German POWs. George Doerner (radio operator) remembers a frantic nurse who pounded on the crew compartment door, yelling for help: together Doerner and the nurse had to hold down an American paratrooper, one who had only a bloody stump where his left leg had been. Coming out of his sedation, this trooper had seen a German prisoner (who had a massive chest wound). The American trooper began to crawl out of his litter to get at that German. We could sympathize with that paratrooper. Even today, in spite of the close relationship between Americans and West Germans, our recollections show that, back then, all of us hated giving any humanitarian consideration to our enemies, let alone giving them a nice ride to a comfortable hospital.

All through the rest of June and the first part of July 1944 little attention was paid by SHAEF to the IX Troop Carrier Command. As yet we were not even important as freighters, since the beachheads were enlarging so slowly they could hardly contain all the materiel arriving by sea. Enough equipment continued to flow in right across the beaches to satisfy even the most demanding commanders in the field.

Just another mission to France. We took off with rolls of tar-paper matting. These fit under the steel mats on landing strips, and hold down dust and mud. Out again over the Channel. I stayed in the astrodome, looking for enemy planes. No formation this time—we travel singly, to facilitate traffic handling on the landing strips.

Over France—the east tip of the Cherbourg peninsula. You can just see the town off to the right. It's already in our hands. Wonder how long before they can be using its port?

Our landing wheels are lowered while we are in the air to show American fighters our good intentions—that is, to avoid "friendly fire." Now we come to Isigny. You can see the long, long lines of trucks moving out in all directions to the front lines. The center of the town is battered to hell. Deep shell holes all around it. In the canal leading to the town, overturned barges.

We pass over one, two, three landing strips. You can see them for quite a distance, because of the dust raised by landing planes. They say that the Germans use that dust to zero in their artillery. The matting we carry should help take care of all that. At last we come to our strip. It's very close to the beachhead, and hundreds of ships are still clustered around. Barrage balloons everywhere.

We call in for landing directions. It seems a very small strip to land a loaded airplane on! Down we go, bouncing along the strip. But the fools have landed us down-wind! Wallen [pilot] has to stand up on the brakes. We finally come to a stop right at the very end of the strip. A truck parked there—fellows tumbling out of the truck as soon as they see our predicament.

The field master has decided not to give our plane any wounded soldiers. Instead they fill our plane with big empty blood-bank containers, to be refilled. Each container is marked "Vital—Urgent."

We have a passenger on our return trip. An older fellow—a T/5 in the medics. His brother is dying in a hospital in England, and the Red Cross got him permission to go back. They took him right out of the fighting around Cherbourg. Didn't know they could do that. Chalk one up for the Red Cross.

A *real* milk run. In half an hour we're ready to return. Don't even need radio to get home—the navigator knows the way so well. Total round-trip tour: three hours, including the time on the ground.

A ship takes a *whole day* to get from Southampton to the French beachhead. Quite a contrast. For the life of me I can't see why they don't have us do this more often. It isn't much, but at least a guy feels he's helping out a bit. (Marty Wolfe, radio operator; written July 4, 1944)

On July 16, SHAEF pulled the wraps off plans for an entirely new sort of command: the First Allied Airborne Army (FAAA). This command consolidated tactical control over both airborne infantry and troop carrier units: *all* the American and British airborne divisions and *all* the American and British combat troop transport planes. Finally, it seemed, a rational command structure had been forged that could weld together the separate components in this new form of warfare. The disruptive effects of having airborne infantry commanders who were not talking the same sort of language as Air Forces commanders would be ended by integrating both into a single army independent of either Army or Army Air Forces high brass and answering only to SHAEF. FAAA, "this sky army," activated on August 2 and was heralded as "the greatest military innovation of World War II." [4]

Command over the FAAA was given to an Air Forces man: General Lewis H. Brereton, who was strongly committed to using Troop Carrier Command for airborne assaults rather than restricting it to freighting. [5] General Matthew Ridgway became head of the U.S. XVIII Airborne Corps: the 101st, 82nd, and 17th

Airborne Divisions. Ridgway's 82nd Division was given to General James Gavin. General F. A. M. "Boy" Browning was Ridgway's British counterpart, commanding the 1st British Airborne Division and the 1st Polish Parachute Brigade.[6] Additional parts of the FAAA were our IX Troop Carrier Command and the RAF's 38 and 46 Transport Groups. We in the 81st were no longer under the tactical control of the Ninth Air Force—though we remained tied to the Ninth Air Force for maintenance and supply needs. We were now part of the First Allied Airborne Army. And we received new shoulder patches to prove it.

Finally the terrible stalemate in Normandy began to dissolve—in our favor. The ground slugfest continued; the British had won so little ground that their sector looked as though it was in danger of becoming an area of trench warfare resembling World War I. The Americans, on the other hand, were learning how to take advantage of their increasing control of the air and massive superiority in supplies. The 101st and 82nd Divisions were pulled off the line and sent back to Britain to rest and regroup. Early in August Patton's new Third Army began to probe westward out of Normandy toward Brittany, greatly widening the scope of action for our armored units. Reporters on *Stars and Stripes* began to speculate hopefully about when we would finally crash through the German lines and begin the dash toward Paris.

By the end of July, American armor was ripping huge holes through the German lines in Normandy and Brittany, and tanks of the First U.S. Army were pouring through in an apparently irresistible surge. There was hardly any effective German resistance in front of them. It was a Blitzkrieg in reverse. American infantry commanders now had every hope that they could throw their forward units across both the Loire and the Seine rivers before the Germans could regroup behind effective new defense lines. Finally—one would have thought—the full weight of the new FAAA would be hurled into an effort to trap and crush the German armies in northern France. But we in the 81st, instead of getting ourselves prepared to fly in troopers to new Allied airheads in back of the German lines, were told that twelve of our planes and crews were going to be flown to Italy! In Italy we would become part of an invasion of southern France (operation DRAGOON; see Chapter 14). A full third of all IX Troop Carrier Command's planes were to be pulled out of Britain and, for the time being, to have no part in aiding the rush eastward of the First and Third American Armies.

## Giving Patton the gas

During the slow progress of Allied infantry in late June and early July, there was plenty of time for us to get the hang of things in our capacity as freighters. We learned how to run cords through the handles of those wonderful jerricans and tie them down securely to the plane's floor rings.[7] Jerricans were sturdy, slab-sided steel containers Americans copied from the Germans. They could be lifted and stacked easily. They were filled with diesel fuel or gasoline, depending on which kinds of tanks or trucks needed them.

We also learned how to help the loaders move ammo boxes up ramps into the airplanes; when the radio operators and crew chiefs should help with the loading; and when it was wiser to stand back and let the truckers handle everything. There was also plenty of opportunity to demonstrate, once again, that fully loaded—even overloaded—C-47s were capable of making safe landings on short, bumpy, improvised airstrips with no ground radio or beacon assistance.

By the time armor of the First and Third American Armies broke out in late July 1944, the portion of our Squadron left in Britain was highly expert in loading, landing, and unloading freight. Those crews also learned what needed to be done when taking on wounded soldiers for the return trip. Most of our training was on the job; in 1943 and early 1944 the Air Forces had given little thought and less effort to transforming troop carrier from a combat to a supply function when the need should arise.

There was no such thing as a typical freight run to the Continent. We called them "gas runs" because the most important items were five-gallon jerricans. We might also have on board drums of oil or grease. The British supply people called this category of freight "POL": petrol, oil, and lubricants. Sometimes we flew single missions; sometimes we went out in groups of two, three, or even four or five. We might also have a load of medical supplies, with or without an accompanying pair of medical technicians, or cases of K-rations.

For command purposes (since Col. Adriel Williams, our 436th CO, was in Italy from July 18 to August 23, 1944) the 81st planes that did not make that trip were under the control of the 437th Troop Carrier Group at "Station 474," Ramsbury. Their cargo might come to Membury, or to Ramsbury, or to an entirely different station in another part of Britain. Often, after unloading supplies in some part of France or Belgium, we would be ordered to a different airfield on the Continent, where we might find a nurse, a medical crew, and a group of wounded (either walking wounded or litter cases) waiting for us to take them to a hospital base in Britain.

Usually we never knew where we were going until just before takeoff. The purpose of most of my flights was to supply General Patton's tanks with gasoline. We could carry between 5,000 and 6,000 pounds each trip [100 or 120 jerricans]. Sometimes we landed on hastily-cleared and recently evacuated German airfields. Sometimes it was nothing but a hayfield, without even a windsock to tell us which was the best direction to land. Maybe fifty percent of these flights finished by evacuating wounded men back to England. After off-loading the diesel there always was a scramble to install the litters and get the plane ready to receive the wounded soldiers. (Bill Westcott, pilot)

As Patton's breakout expanded and our freight destinations were set further and further away from Membury, the danger from Luftwaffe fighter planes increased dramatically. Some earlier flights, those with five planes each, had Allied fighter escorts they could count on, but when we flew single-plane missions we were on our own. As the Germans began their headlong dash to escape from France, we would often have to fly over areas without any clear battle lines, and we would find ourselves setting down in a field in a no man's land, ahead (that is, east) of our own tanks and west (we hoped!) of the retreating Germans.

When we were hauling plane loads full of jerricans of gas for Patton's big tank push, we were supposed to fly inside very narrow flight lanes, lanes supposedly protected by fighters above us. Much of the trips took place over land still held by Germans. A mistake of a degree or two would put us right over their ground fire. (Jerome Loving, crew chief)

Still, we were surprised to learn these freighting trips counted as "combat operations" on our records. The Presidential Unit Citation we (and other troop carrier outfits) received on August 23, 1944, dwelt on the dangers of such flights, almost putting them in the same category as the invasion of Normandy. Col. Brack assembled the whole Squadron on August 31, 1944, to read us the wording of this Presidential Unit Citation.

In spite of the obvious possibility of heavy losses from the Luftwaffe, from ground fire, or from poor navigation and landing facilities, not a single plane in the 81st Troop Carrier Squadron was lost on freighter flights. Praise should go not so much to our pilots' "braving enemy fire" as to their admirable ability to navigate and to handle heavy planeloads in conditions that would have fazed barnstorming pilots of the 1920s.

We are given map coordinates for a field someplace near Rheims. We lead in a flight of five or six of us. The runways are full of bomb craters; but we manage to land. Up comes a jeep and we are told that the field hadn't been secured yet. And sure enough, when our engines are shut down, we can hear heavy artillery going over our heads. We leave in somewhat of a hurry. Later we find we have been given the wrong map coordinates. ("Rip" Collins, pilot)

Sometimes we used well-equipped fields, such as those outside Paris or Chartres; but the same day might see us, on another leg of our flight, landing in a cow pasture ringed about with fruit trees and crisscrossed with drainage ditches. Some pilots reported having to buzz a field to scare off horses before landing. Since the wind direction and velocity information we got in Ramsbury might turn out to be useless or even harmful in eastern France or Belgium, pilots often had to figure out wind direction by doing a figure eight over the strip and estimating wind drift. They sometimes found themselves landing with the wind at their tail pushing them along, rather than at their head slowing them down. Pilots learned to keep their eyes peeled for smoke from house or factory chimneys so they could judge how to land upwind.

Other troop carrier outfits did not have the luck of the 81st.

At the time we were all carrying jerricans of gasoline that had to be very securely tied down on the floor of our plane's fuselage. I was coming in to one of the steel mesh airstrips, right behind the Operations Officer of the 80th or 79th Squadron—which, I'm not sure. We were supposed to land about three minutes apart. Now, that pilot may have been one of those frustrated people who had always wanted to be a fighter pilot. Upon turning on the final approach, he made a real sharp bank which must have been pretty close to ninety degrees. Anyway, his wing tips looked to me as though they were practically vertical. The load inside the plane must have shifted as a consequence.

The way those jerricans were tied down with rope through the handle openings, coupled with the angle of bank, makes me think the load obviously shifted—and the poor fellow lost control of the airplane. The plane went straight down near the runway approach-end, but did not catch fire. Of course, all the crew members were killed. (Whitman Peek, pilot)

Another danger was our old enemy, north European weather. Sometimes we would take off in rain though with decent visibility, find unclouded blue sky over our Continental destination, and return to encounter English pea-soup fog. Art Feigion's Pathfinder Squadron, also pressed into freight service, was better equipped than most of us with radar navigation aids to handle weather, but sometimes tragedy struck anyway.

We had one radar set that warned you about getting too low. It had red, yellow, and green lights, and was about the size of a matchbox. It sat on the panel right between pilot and co-pilot. Once when we were coming back from the Continent we Pathfinder planes fell into formation (we didn't have to, but we usually did anyway). The weather began to get really lousy; and the leader of this flight started to creep down and down to get below the clouds. Finally I couldn't see at all where we were going, so I pulled over to the right of the formation. I had hardly got there when right in front of us there was the most god-awful explosion you've ever seen. Our cockpit lighted up like a bonfire.

What had happened was that the other three planes, those which were flying in formation to my left, had plowed into a hill in England. I found out later that this was the only 800-foot high hill in that whole part of England. The crash killed everybody in all three planes except one navigator; his plane split in two and he was able to climb out of the front. I met that navigator in a Pathfinder reunion we had in Texas in 1986.

Seconds before the collision, my co-pilot had seen that the radar panel light was switching back and forth from red to green; so I hauled back on the stick just as hard as I could—darn near stalled the plane out.

When we got back to my base we found some leaves and small branches in one of our air scoops. (Art Feigion, pathfinder pilot)


Today's military historians mainly agree that even if troop carrier had put 100 percent of its effort into freighting gas, this still would not have been enough to enable Patton's forces to crash through. The resources we possessed for forward air delivery were simply not up to this gigantic task. Back in those days, however, many of us did believe we could have helped turn the trick and "end the war in '44." Today, honesty compels us to admit we were thinking that way not so much because of an objective analysis of what was militarily possible, but because of our need to blame the lack of victory that September on British arrogance and obstructionism.

In mid-August Montgomery's British forces, bottled up in Normandy for three months, finally broke through. The British began to move east at almost as fast a clip as Patton's divisions. The big prize for the British and Canadians was the great Belgian port of Antwerp, so close to northern Germany. Antwerp was captured with its huge harbor facilities fairly intact. Means for ending the gasoline supply crisis seemed within our grasp. But the British high command, in an unforgiveable display of overconfidence and poor planning, neglected to take the east bank and several islands in the Scheldt estuary (the Scheldt is the long waterway that connects Antwerp to the North Sea). Somehow, the Germans managed to scratch together enough defensive units on the Scheldt to stave off the British for three months. Antwerp itself was ours, but our vessels could not reach it.

American supply lines, which had to originate in England (by air) or in Normandy (by truck), were being stretched longer and longer. The British and Canadians, close to some tiny ports in north France, were not seriously hurt by

Mud Alley: 81st TCS planes, freight now unloaded, wait for a break in the weather to take off from a very soggy forward air strip.

Flying in the gas: jerricans tied down in a C-47.

the lack of gas. Some units in our Third Army sector had to stop in their tracks for a while—although the still-disorganized Germans were fleeing before them. If it had not been for Patton's capture of two large stores of German gas, his divisions would have ground to a complete halt. As it was, on August 18 he was able to convince Bradley and Eisenhower to allow him to continue on toward the Rhine until he used up every drop of gas.

For Patton's and Bradley's staffs, and at supreme headquarters, the most bitter pill to swallow was Eisenhower's siding with Montgomery against Patton's Third Army. Patton, after all, had stormed eastward for four hundred miles in a little over five weeks and was rapidly nearing the German border on the Rhine. Eisenhower, who formerly had seemed to favor Bradley's idea of full support for the Third Army's drive, now was saying that the northern sector (Montgomery's command) gave the best chance of crashing into good tank-maneuvering country, the flat lands of Holland and northern Germany. He had given control over several American units (mainly General Hodge's First Army operating north of Patton's Third Army) to Montgomery; and it was the British plus the American First Army that received priority in gasoline supply.

Eisenhower's hope was that once Montgomery had crashed across the water barriers of the north Rhine and its tributaries, his forces would be able to encircle the Ruhr, the industrial heartland of Germany, and choke off the flow of armaments to the Wehrmacht. Montgomery believed that in view of the increasing shortage of fuel, most Allied resources should be channeled into one "full-blooded thrust" along a narrow corridor. Bradley and most American field commanders, on the other hand, were pushing the doctrine of "advance along a broad front." Their aim was to keep the retreating Germans constantly off balance by pushing through as many gaps as possible while moving toward the central reaches of the Rhine and getting across that last important barrier in not one but several places.

Now more and more of our gas runs were to Belgium for the British and for Hodge's First American Army rather than to eastern France in support of Patton. Even the Red Ball trucking system was channeled in Montgomery's favor, several of its routes now diverted to the Brussels area. When we in the 81st learned of this change, it touched off furious condemnations of "those Limey bastards!" We blamed "politics," that is, the apparent need of Eisenhower to favor the British by depriving Americans of their own resources. The "Montgomery or Patton" dilemma was not the only cause of confusion over how to use troop carrier. The "fighter or freighter" dilemma was even more complicated. A third of IX TCC's planes, which could have been ferrying gas to British or American armor in northern France, were in Italy in July and August, preparing for an airborne assault in southern France. The combat assault potential of troop carrier had run head-on into its freighting function. Each time high command authorized

Brereton to begin planning a paratrooper operation, troop carrier would begin training and planning for it, and the gas runs slowed down. They did not stop completely: usually some troop carrier outfit (or a few of each squadron's planes) was delegated to continue ferrying supplies. The rest of us had to switch gears in a massive way. Charles Hastings' briefing notes for the 436th TCG planes at Membury show that at least two of these canceled missions, LINNET I and TRANSFIGURE, were all ready to go. They were called off only hours before takeoff. Brereton complained bitterly to Eisenhower about the difficulties of calling off assault missions on such short notice.[8]

An airborne assault mission was nothing that could be put together and sent off in a matter of hours. Besides time for planning, FAAA needed time to marshal planes, bring in gliders, get the paratroopers on the airfields, and put together at least some minimum intelligence package for the flight leaders. Some of the more complicated proposals required feasibility tests: that is, going through a practice aerial mission in Britain, which required even more time. Time was also needed to service planes and load them up. Seven major FAAA operations in August 1944 were pushed almost to the point where everybody involved thoroughly expected they would be run; but in each case, either Montgomery or Patton induced Eisenhower to call it off because it appeared too dangerous or because our ground forces had already overrun the objectives in question.

Each time the gears for planning an aerial assault would be put into motion, less gas would be air freighted to the advancing Allied infantry.[9] Somewhat unreasonably, Eisenhower demanded that the 101st and 82nd Airborne Divisions ready themselves for assault missions but that "there should be no interference of the air support of the present ground effort in France."[10] Bradley estimated that the time lost in shifting troop carrier from freighting to preparing for an airborne assault in one of these canceled operations (LINNET I) cost Patton's troops the equivalent of six days' gasoline. No wonder Bradley, in his memoirs, grumbled that the main function of troop carrier seemed to be devising a whole flock of useless missions.[11]

By the time the invasion of Holland began on September 17, 1944, the 81st Troop Carrier Squadron—together again since August 24—was at the very peak of its wartime efficiency. We were a unit of confident, competent, blooded veterans who could find our way all around the map of all Europe west of the Rhine, deliver anything from crates of C-rations to gliders with jeeps in them, dress up picture-perfect aerial formations—and do this day after day. Besides working well, we showed we could work hard and long.

We all remember late August and September as "the time we worked our asses off." The invasion of Holland failed; and that was the end of our combat flying until the Battle of the Bulge in December 1944. But until well into October, we continued other sorts of work at an unremitting pace.

We set out from Membury, went to Kimble, loaded up 5,000 pounds of gasoline, and took it to Brussels. Landed—finally!—in bad soup. On our first pass for a landing we got a red flare and had to pull up and go around. Flew around for some twenty minutes. We landed, unloaded our gas, and Earl Hein and I went over to look at a Focke-Wulf 190 that had been strafed. Took off again for Verdun. We overshot the field, a grassy and wet one, where our brakes were of little use. We finally got stopped four feet from a four-foot trench hard up against the tail assembly of an old ME 410; this punched a couple of small holes in our right wing. A half-track had to pull us out.

There were no wounded for us there. We could hear the big guns up at the front. We went over to Nancy and picked up twenty-five walking wounded. But flying them back we were forced down by bad weather and a lack of fuel. We had to land on an emergency field and stay there overnight. When we landed there was only about 40 gallons of gas left. We had to buzz that field to get the horses there out of the way. Fortunately, we landed near an ordnance outfit. They were very accommodating, and used their trucks to take the casualties to a general hospital at Carentan.

I slept in the plane, had a good breakfast courtesy of that ordnance outfit. Then off for airfield A-25 [Le Bourget, near Paris] at 2:10. We had to snitch some oil there for our engines. Some fifteen minutes after we took off we were flying over the DZ where we had dropped paratroopers on D-Day. We landed at Ramsbury at 3:30. We let the nurse and medic out and came back to home base at Membury. That was a long, long twenty-four hours. (Howard "Pat" Bowen, crew chief, journal entry for September 24, 1944)

On this one trip Pat Bowen's plane landed at eight different fields or strips.

Some of us in the 81st had come from farm backgrounds or had worked hard at manual jobs before joining up, but for all of us these weeks in the late summer and autumn of 1944 were physically exhausting and nerve-wracking. This was especially true for crew chiefs and radio operators, who often helped with the loading and unloading; a few times even the pilots and navigators would help. If it was a matter of wrestling jeeps, or pack howitzers, or artillery shells, we had no choice but to wait for engineers or ordnance people to do the job. For the jerricans or anything in crates, crew members were expected to help load and unload, and often we were it—the only men available for the work.

We would land on dirt roads or cow pastures just as fast as we could, unload the gas cans, and get out of there to make room for the next planes coming in. On some of these fields there would be men to help us unload; I remember once when the unloading was done with the help of a rhythm tune the unloaders were singing. But on another trip the unloaders were so engrossed in their crap game we couldn't get any help from them at all. (Jerome Loving, crew chief)

---

HEADQUARTERS TWELFTH ARMY GROUP
G-4 Section, APO 655

11 September 1944

SUBJECT: Supply by Air
TO: Commanding General, Troop Carrier Command (Through Channels).

1. In connection with the rapid advance of our Armies your command has rendered valuable aid in transporting by air to our forward areas, 80 octane gas and other critically required supplies. . . .

2. Your pilots and crews, waiving all formalities regarding their place in this particular supply picture, dug in most cheerfully and furnished much of the labor of unloading the planes. On 5th and 6th September, the first two days, your air crew personnel did 90% of the unloading. On 8 September, with more Ground Force troops having arrived, your personnel were still performing 50% of the unloading labor. . . .

/s/ R.G. Moses
Brigadier General, GSC
AC of S, G-4

Of course, we were young and strong; the actual lifting, stacking, and tying down of the cargo was in itself not all that rough. It was exhausting to perform this kind of work, though, when we were already tuckered out from long hours of flying and from worrying over whether that damn dirt road we were about to land on had anything at all to do with this particular point on our map of Belgium marked as our destination. Lugging two jerricans at a time up the steps and through our cargo door did give many of us muscles where we'd never suspected any; but it was the continuous sensation of fatigue from this combination of working, flying, and worrying that finally ground us down.[12]

Sometimes, after sleeping on the plane, I would wake up so stiff and numb it was more than I could do to find out whether there was a mess hall in the neighborhood where I could get a cup of coffee. I would break open a box of

K-rations for breakfast, stagger off the plane, stretch out on the ground (if the sun was out), and fall asleep right there until the pilots came back with information about our next stop. Pilots usually had a better time of it. If there was a military base in the vicinity, they could get the local soldiers to provide them with a cot and breakfast in the officers' mess—if there was one. But when we took off, I would see the pilots, just as exhausted as the rest of us, taking turns to snatch a bit of sleep in the cockpit as we droned on toward our next destination. After a few days of this sort of work it was a real relief whenever the Squadron would have to stop freighting in order to participate in a training flight for a (usually canceled) combat operation. However much the interruptions might have slowed Patton, to us this was a decidedly restful change of pace.[13]

One compensation of freighting missions was that they often provided some opportunity to indulge that unquenchable American yearning for souvenirs. If a stopover meant we would be near a battle zone for several hours, and if we were not too sleepy, we could scour buildings recently abandoned by the Germans to pick up something interesting. These forays were seldom very rewarding, since usually such forward areas would already have been picked over by our own infantry. Ken De Blake (radio operator) brought back a copy of Hitler's *Mein Kampf* and a handsome beer mug—which we felt said it all about Germany and our mission there. The rest of us were less lucky. Once I did find an impressively solid-looking German wireless transmitting key ("bug") which—being a radio operator myself—I thought a perfect souvenir. Another time I found a German World War I vintage rifle which, I was assured, would make a good hunting gun if I could mail it home (I did—but it wasn't). Once, slightly ashamed of myself, I even bought a "liberated" German camera from an American infantryman. The saddest souvenir I found was a Wehrmacht passbook made out to one Walther Kreck. Because the photo had been torn out, I wondered whether Kreck had thrown it away because he wanted to desert and needed that picture for forged papers.

> Often the planes to France on these non-combat missions would come back with a "liberated" motorcycle in them. I remember very clearly that several of our pilots sported German motorbikes around our base in Membury. Stroup, Collins, and many other pilots had bikes. There were so many of them on our base that Wing HQ finally had to put a stop to it. There were cases of pilots wrecking themselves on their liberated motorcycles and then not being available for their missions the next day. (Bert Schweizer, Operations clerk)

By far, the souvenirs we were proudest of from these gas runs were liquid rather than solid. General Patton made a real effort—on the occasions when we delivered POL to his sector—to reward us with cases of liberated wines and harder stuff. This "thank you" not only was a marvelous way to uplift troop carrier spirits, but it also provided that publicity-conscious general a way to dramatize his opposition to Eisenhower's decision to give logistical priority to Montgomery.

> After our supplies were unloaded the infantry troops in the neighborhood would give us some liberated spirits to take back. This included Calvados, wine, champagne, and schnapps. They would put cases of this stuff down near our planes and we could help ourselves.
>
> Later, when we moved to France, we found that Calvados would burn with a blue flame; we got some gallon cans from the mess tent, placed sand in them, added a quart of Calvados, and got a nice hot light. We used this to cook a bit and also to heat up the tent. (Bill Lane, glider pilot)

> A friend of mine, another pilot who also was delivering gasoline to the tanks in France, actually saw Patton there. When he set down, a truck pulled up alongside with a load of booze, and what looked like a middle-aged soldier stuck his head out and said "Give this to your CO with my compliments." My friend answered, "And who the hell are you?" The answer came back "My name is General Patton." It took my friend quite some time to come out of his brace. (Art Feigion, pathfinder pilot)

Those of us not lucky enough to have cases of wine or spirits to put on our planes nevertheless got some taste of this booty. Back in Membury we were called over to Operations and given some bottles out of cases others had brought back. Usually officers took the Calvados, brandy, and schnapps and left the bottles of wine for the EMs.

In addition to gasoline and other desperately needed supplies, a few of our planes carried boxes of maps for Patton's commanders, who had moved so fast they had run right off the eastern edge of the maps of western France that had been issued a month previously. Troop carrier flew in ten tons of maps at this time.[14]

George S. Patton, Jr.—the most quoted general in World War II—once said "Give me enough gasoline and I will go through Germany like shit through a goose!" In mid-September 1944, many of us were inclined to believe him, or at least to argue that his spectacular dash across France had earned him the right to have that chance.

What are the realities behind those 1944 hopes? Countless World War II veterans and scores of military historians have been chewing over this bitter issue made particularly bitter when Montgomery's alternative to Patton failed. As far as specialists in military history are concerned, there seems to be a consensus on three points: first, if all our air transport facilities had been directed toward Patton, they would still not have been sufficient by themselves to sustain his drive; second, even if truck freight could have been added to bring Patton's supplies up to what he needed in September, his Third Army probably would have been stopped at the Rhine or, at the very best, would have made only slow progress upon crossing the Rhine; and third, German targets in the path of Patton's proposed drive were much less important, in industrial or strategic terms, than those before Montgomery. Given our feelings back in 1944 about Montgomery and his partisan, counterproductive down-playing of the American role in the fighting, it hurts today to admit that Eisenhower was right to put his money on Montgomery.[15]

It is difficult to imagine how supply, through troop carrier, could have been made much more effective. There was talk of converting "war weary" B-24s which could carry much more cargo than C-47s; but these heavy, awkward planes could not possibly have set down on the tiny dirt or grassy fields we used to get C-47s close enough to the front lines. Once a converted B-24 was brought into our base and several pilots checked out in flight orientation rides. Afterward, they were grateful none of them ever had to fly a payload of gasoline to Patton in those heavy, unstable B-24s.

Certainly we in the 81st TCS were being worked for all we were worth. The month of September 1944 (which included the Holland invasion) was our record month for the entire war. We freighted around 790 tons of gas and other supplies, carried 710 troopers (in planes and in gliders), and evacuated 381 patients.

The Red Ball trucks were not the answer—yet. Their lines were stretching further and further, forcing more delays through accidents and other foul-ups. The truck routes originated either at the port of Cherbourg in Normandy or from recently conquered Marseilles, in the south of France—both about the same distance from Patton. The Red Ball Express was also plagued by a pilferage problem: some of its drivers sold their cargoes to amazingly efficient French black marketeers.

Total available truck delivery of gas and other supplies has been estimated at about 7,000 tons a day during September. Of course not all the gas could go to Patton; there were two other American armies to be supplied (the First and the Seventh)—in all, a total of forty American divisions, some of which were engaged in desperate battles elsewhere. For example, General Middleton's forces were locked into a costly fight to overwhelm the surrounded but stubborn German defenders of the port of Brest back in Brittany.[16]

This analysis should also include the supply needs of the British and the Poles. A division of Free French soldiers had also come into the field, and they, too, needed to be supplied by the Americans. Finally, while the liberation of Paris on August 25 thrilled us all, the millions of Frenchmen there also had to depend to some extent on American supply. But there always remain the tantalizing "ifs." *If* all other field commanders could have been persuaded to give up their supplies to Patton; *if* the weather had been perfect, allowing us to fly every day; and *if* we could have used not only all British transport planes but also all the bombers capable of being converted; then perhaps the amount of gas that could have been delivered to Patton would have been about doubled. Yet this still would not have been nearly enough for his needs.

## Notes

1. "The Staging Wing," Hunter Field, July 20, 1945.

2. Moore, Ch. 4, pp. 26–30.

3. Also called PSP (pierced steel planking).

4. FAAA, "The First Allied Airborne Army, Commanded by Lt. General Lewis H. Brereton," n.d. (Dec. 1944?).

5. See Brereton, pp. 333, 339, 365.

6. On July 18, 1944, twelve planes in our Squadron flew to Italy for the invasion of southern France. The aircrews that did not go to Italy for the invasion of southern France—the "rear echelon"—flew several training missions with Polish paratroopers in England in addition to their very demanding freighting work.

7. There is a good account of the unsung but indispensable jerrican: "The Little Can That Could," *Invention and Technology*, Fall 1987, pp. 60–64.

8. Diary of Floyd Parks, Chief of Staff of FAAA, Aug. 17, 1944, in CBAMHI.

9. Nobody those days worried about the gas troop carrier planes burned in order to deliver those jerricans; nevertheless, it required on the average one gallon of gas consumed by a C-47 to deliver two gallons to the front.

10. Floyd Parks Papers, Aug. 13, 1944.

11. Bradley, *A Soldier's Story*, p. 402. An extended but inconclusive evaluation of the problem, made after the war by Bradley, is in "Effects of Air Power in Military Operations," in IX TCC "Final Stages," pp. 1–5.

12. Before the war, safety rules for civil aviation restricted pilots to a maximum of eighty-five hours flying time per month, but most of our pilots and crews flew well over 200 hours per month during July–October 1944 and again in March–May 1945.

13. For our entire year at Membury, the 436th TCG flew a total of almost 3,000 supply/evacuation sorties from England to "the far shore." 436th TCG history written by Captain John E. Kerney.

14. 436th TCG hist. narr. for Aug. 1944.

15. This is the conclusion of Russell Weigley, pp. 282–83, in his *Eisenhower's Lieutenants*, a book I feel is the most competent and judicious account we have of the European war from the point of view of high command. There is a good discussion of this problem in Charles B. MacDonald, "The Decision to Launch Operation Market-Garden," pp. 429–42, in Greenfield, *Command Decisions*.

16. Persisting in this assault on Brest was one of Bradley's worst blunders: see his *Autobiography*, pp. 305–6; see also Weigley, 1981, pp. 284–86.

# 14. Sunning
## Italy and the Assault on Southern France

### From Membury to Voltone

Among the honors bestowed by America upon soldiers who risk death in combat is an award known as the "oak leaf cluster." It is a tiny representation of leaves made so that you can pin it onto the ribbon of a medal you have already received. It signifies that you have twice won the award connected with that medal. The eighteen aircrews—eighty-three officers and men—and the thirty-four glider pilots in the 81st Troop Carrier Squadron who had flown in NEPTUNE, the Normandy invasion, all received the Air Medal, not as prestigious as the Distinguished Flying Cross (given for bravery or truly outstanding service), but widely recognizable as a "combat medal." [1] As a combat medal, the Air Medal was to be distinguished from a theater service medal (meaning, for example, "I served in the European Theater of Operations") or the Good Conduct Medal (meaning nothing whatsoever). In August 1944, our aircrews and glider pilots who participated in the invasion of southern France earned an oak leaf cluster to pin onto the Air Medal awarded for Normandy. We were glad to get it—but not at all sure we deserved it.

In fact, some of us remember the airborne parts of the invasion of southern France as "milk runs." [2] Even the airborne troopers we delivered called it the "champagne campaign," epitomized by officers who bedded down in the most opulent hotel in Nice, the Negresco, went off by jeep in the morning to lead attacks up in the hills against the weak and retreating Germans, and returned in the evening to another few bottles of champagne at the Negresco. [3] Once the airborne soldiers moved north out of the Riviera and toward east-central France, however, it became a different story: "long, weary forced marches over the jagged trails of the Maritime Alps carrying backbreaking loads, pursuing the enemy that was responsible for those still, silent forms of American paratroopers that lay scattered in the hills and along the roads." [4]

"War is hell"? Perhaps not always, or not for everybody, so far as this little piece of the war was concerned. For those of us in the 81st TCS, as it turned out, our part of the airborne invasion of south France was a sort of extended vacation with a good deal of not-very-dangerous excitement thrown in.

It is true that during the invasion—code-named Operation DRAGOON—eleven glider pilots were killed (none from our Squadron) and many others badly hurt. Mechanical failures and the fact that many of them had to crash-land under terrible conditions caused these casualties, not German ground fire. Out of some 385 C-47s, which flew a total of almost a thousand sorties, only one was shot down, and the crew of this plane managed to ditch it safely in the sea. Not a single power plane crew member was hurt as a result of DRAGOON, and only a few airplanes returned to base with a couple of bullet holes. Most glider pilots, after they landed, had an uproariously good time in southern France and came back so pleased with themselves that we got the impression they would have been glad to do it over again.[5]

Only about a quarter of us in the 81st Troop Carrier Squadron were privileged to travel to Italy for DRAGOON. Our Squadron sent twelve of its planes and a skeleton support group of communications specialists, clerks, and mechanics—just ninety-six officers and men in all. The other three squadrons of our 436th Group also sent twelve planes each. A total of 413 planes were moved for this operation from Britain to Italy, from both the 53rd and the 50th Wings, and from some pathfinder squadrons. We were leaving the ETO and entering the territory run by the MTO, and we would use the MTO's service and support personnel. Only our more experienced crews were picked; each plane would have two first pilots, one of whom would serve as co-pilot. Others in the Squadron remained in England, embedded in SHAEF's "fighters or freighters" controversy (discussed in Chapter 13).

It was to be a long trip: 1,400 miles from Membury to Marrakesh, Morocco, and 900 more from Marrakesh to Voltone, a tiny hamlet with a dirt and grass airfield near the shore of the Tyrrhenian Sea, about fifty miles north of Rome. The nearest town of any size was Tarquinia. To make that flight—with its extra weight of ground personnel, supplies, and parapack equipment—we all installed four "Bolero" auxiliary gas tanks in our aircraft cabins.

On July 18, 1944, we flew from England south to North Africa, traversing the same route we had followed eight months before in the opposite direction, to Europe from the States. By this time there was less worry about the Luftwaffe, and we traveled in small formations rather than singly. This time, however, there would be no chance to get a pass to town and see strange North African sights and people. The airfield in Marrakesh where we stayed overnight was totally buttoned up, but we were able to enjoy its good PX, which served all the cokes you wanted.

Our planes in the 81st TCS traveled from England in formations of three. I stayed up all night so the other two radio operators could sleep. They returned the favor on the leg from Marrakesh to Italy, when I didn't have to go near my radios. Three of our passengers wanted a fourth for bridge in the cabin of the plane, and we played bridge for five solid hours. Once in a while one of us would drop out and the pilot or co-pilot would fill in. I kept wondering if my folks back home knew what a tough war I was fighting.

At Marrakesh we were awakened at 3 a.m. for chow and a briefing. At 4:30 we flew east over the Mediterranean, turned north when we passed the southern tip of Sardinia, and landed at Ciampino, one of the main airfields near Rome. After a few hours we left Rome for Voltone. It had been a long flight (2,300 miles) but it was executed perfectly—no glitches, no accidents, no sweat.

On July 26, 1944, nine of our planes and crews were sent on detached service from Voltone to Ciampino. Their job was to train with the 64th Troop Carrier Group, of the XII Troop Carrier Command, for the invasion. Only three of the 81st airplanes and aircrews stayed at Voltone with the rest of our 436th Group.

The 64th TCG was badly in need of combat training. Since the ghastly miscarried airborne invasion of Sicily the previous year, the 64th had done very little besides freighting. The 64th TCG had become so involved in single-mission supply flights, air evacuation, and liaison work that its aircrews were completely out of practice in flying formations or towing gliders.[6] For the task of bringing them up to snuff, our Group CO, Adriel Williams, decided that of his four squadrons at Voltone, the 81st had the best record of safe and efficient flying, and should help train the 64th TCG. This was a most gratifying honor conferred on the 81st Troop Carrier Squadron.

Our landing strip at Voltone was just a leveled farmer's field, basically, just a hunk of flattened dirt. When the Italian wind blew that dry, hot summer, the dust was so thick that the pilots had to stop taxiing—you couldn't see ten feet in front of you. Nasty dust was in and on everything.

It took two days before our tents arrived. Most of us, meanwhile, lived in our planes. Finally we got our tent city set up, complete with mess tent, medical tent, and trenches for latrines. For several days we lived on C- and K-rations, which we soon learned were very good items to trade with the Italians for chores like clothes-washing and treats like fresh fruit.

We were only a few hundred yards from the sea, and the black-sand beach, very close to our tent area, was mighty pleasant. The sky was a brilliant blue, the waters in this part of the Mediterranean a fantastic blue-green—topped here and there with blobs of oil from ships that had gone to the bottom. Most of us managed to get the suntan of our lives. Quite a contrast to life in England! About

81st TCS planes in Italy training with the 64th TCG for the invasion of southern France. (Courtesy Smithsonian Institution)

A flood washes out our tents at Tarquinia, Italy. Colonel Williams is on the left.

the only fly in that ointment was the segregation of our beach into one area for enlisted men and one for officers. Such "chicken" procedure, especially under these makeshift circumstances, seemed really silly.

One day at Voltone, on August 10, 1944, the heavens opened up, the rains came down in a tropical deluge, and in minutes our entire tent city was awash in a foot of muddy water. Shoes left by the side of a bed just floated away downstream. In that balmy Italian weather, though, the flood was more like a happening on a hiking trip than any real bother; we paddled around in our bare feet, laughing at those fellows whose tents had more water in them than ours.

Another contrast between Membury and Voltone was our relations with the citizens. In Britain we were barely tolerated guests; in Italy—it is embarrassing to admit—we regarded the people patronizingly, and some of us, with contempt. Just one year ago Italians had been our enemies. We could not forget that after the American defeat in February 1943 at the battle of Kasserine Pass in North Africa, American prisoners had been paraded through the streets of Naples, where the Neapolitans spat at them and pelted them with filth.

Back in July 1943, when the Allies invaded south Italy, Italian opponents of Mussolini organized a coup d'état, overthrew the Fascist government, imprisoned Mussolini, and joined the Allied war against the Nazis, who were still in control of much of central and all of northern Italy. The Germans rescued Mussolini from prison in the most famous small-scale airborne operation of the war. In September 1943, Otto Skorzeny, a daredevil German commando, worked out a plan to land airborne troopers right outside Mussolini's prison. When our Squadron arrived in Italy, in July 1944, Mussolini was supposedly still in control of Italy from Florence on north, but it was obvious he functioned only as a puppet for the Wehrmacht.

Was Italy being "liberated" or "occupied" by the Allies? The distinction was a fine one. The new Italian government in Rome, though allowed to join the war against Nazi Germany, was not our full-fledged ally. She was only a "cobelligerent." In practice this meant that we used Italians as day laborers or in various service jobs. Until the winter of 1944–1945 we did not allow them to fight as soldiers on our side.[7]

On the other hand, even the more prejudiced among us were sensitive to Italy's importance in America's cultural and religious heritage. Every one of us made a sort of soldier's pilgrimage to Rome, where we took in the great sights. Since the Germans had decided to leave Rome an open city, very little in its central districts had been damaged by artillery or bombing. The same Italian tourist guides who, the year before, had undoubtedly been showing German soldiers around were now pleased to show Americans the Coliseum, the Roman Forum, and St. Peter's.

Our training schedules often took us to Rome and every once in a while to

Naples. It was easy to get a pass for a day in either city. The misery suffered by Italians in this war was most forcefully brought home to us when we toured Naples. What struck us was the despair of the people more than the devastation of the buildings and streets. In Britain we had never experienced begging, apart from the kids who, rather impudently, pestered us for gum and candy. But Naples in 1944 was a hungry city. People here were begging for their lives. Unlike the Romans, Neapolitans seemed sullen and afraid. Food was so scarce we had to take K-rations into town with us; we brought the rations into certain designated restaurants and the waiters would take them off to the chef who would heat them, add spices and Italian know-how, and bring back pretty tasty dishes—plus a glass of cheap wine (the sort we called "Dago red").

The dirt, desolation, and hunger in Naples was enough to spoil any of our tourist interest in that city. Although we rode around in picturesque horse-drawn carriages, it was no fun. I can never forget the desperate tension on the face of the violin player who sidled up to our restaurant table, playing beseechingly until we gave him some money, and then instead of leaving, insisted on playing on and on in gratitude, thereby thoroughly spoiling our lunch.[8]

One image each of us brought back from wartime Italy is of people rooting around in garbage cans. We saw this not only in Naples, but also in our tent city at Voltone, and even in Rome.

> Small kids were always around our camp's garbage cans, digging for bits of food. We gave them scraps from our plates. But there were so many of them! Boys and girls six to ten years old. What was going to happen to them? Why couldn't their government or we do something better for them?
>
> I saw Italian women taking up with American men to get food for their families. Who could blame them? It's often that way after an invasion. Food becomes scarce; what there is belongs to the armed forces. Civilians have to do without. This could happen to American women, too. The way to prevent it is to fight on the enemy's home ground, not yours. (Ben Ward, glider pilot)

Most of us liked Italians, some of us pitied them, some despised them—but we all took advantage of them. The Army Air Forces had a service corps of Italians, some of whom were former POWs flown in from Africa, who worked to improve the nine dirt airstrips carved out along the western Italian coast for DRAGOON. After a while at Voltone (but not at some of the other airstrips) Italians were employed to spread crude oil on the airstrip in order to hold down the choking dust that made takeoff and landing so slow and so dangerous. Poor visibility from that dust caused two planes of the 82nd Squadron to collide when landing. Today Ciampino is a great airfield, but those days our 81st TCS's nine planes based there had to eat dust. On some training missions it took more than a minute apiece to get planes off the ground.

Peasant women from nearby villages would hang around our tent area, anxious to trade fruit and eggs for supplies we got from QM or the PX. In return for one bar of soap (soap, it seems, always gets scarce in war-torn lands) they would wash a whole week's laundry. Some of us traded our GI (khaki-colored) undershirts to the local Italians, and soon such undershirts could be seen in this balmy summer weather on Italian men all around Voltone. One item the villagers needed even more was shoes, but most of us had no extra shoes to trade.

It was in Voltone that some of us first had the stomach-wrenching experience of having a little boy sidle up and, in broken but very understandable English, offer to sell "my sister, real virgin, very nice!"

### Politics and strategy in Operation DRAGOON

The invasion of southern France was born in controversy. Even in early July 1944, when those of us assigned from the 81st TCS were already preparing ourselves for the flight from Membury to Italy, the British kept insisting that the men, materiel, and ships required would be better used in northern Italy or in Yugoslavia. Churchill tried every trick in the book to get the forces being considered for this operation reassigned for what he wanted. After failing to persuade the American generals in London, he turned his very considerable powers of persuasion directly on President Roosevelt—but in vain.

Just before the final green light was given to this invasion, its name was changed from ANVIL to DRAGOON: it had been on the boards for so long that its planners, with good reason, believed its security had been breached. Also, they liked the new name because Churchill had had to be "dragooned" into it. The seaborne invasion phases of DRAGOON were code-named BIGOT.

Plans for ANVIL/DRAGOON had been argued over at the very top during the three summit meetings of 1943 between Roosevelt, Churchill, and Stalin. It was first put forward as a part of the second front Stalin sought against the Germans. At the Quebec summit in August 1943, the Americans had argued that the coming invasion of France would have the best chance of success if it could be organized as a pincers assault, with one arm thrusting into Normandy from Britain and the other into south France from Africa. The Russians liked the concept, and—at this time—Churchill raised no important objections, although he always insisted that the invasion of mainland Italy (then scheduled for September 1943) should really be considered as the second front. For several months the chief Allied strategists had assumed that OVERLORD and ANVIL/DRAGOON would be launched simultaneously.

For the remainder of 1943 most planning was focused on Normandy and OVERLORD. A few planners (known as "Force 163") were attached to the American Seventh Army in Italy to begin working up the details for DRAGOON.

Instead of giving up in southern Italy, the Nazis put together a dogged, brilliant defense, making the Allies pay for every additional mile northward. In May 1944 the picture changed. The Allies broke out of the stalemate around Anzio and, on the fourth bloody attempt, overwhelmed the bombed-out rubble that had been the Monte Cassino monastery and town. The Germans abandoned Rome on June 4, 1944, and retreated to a stronger defense line south of Florence. Now, the Allied front lines were close enough to southern France for an airborne assault based in central Italy. Therefore as soon as the Combined Chiefs of Staff could see that the Normandy invasion was going well, they gave DRAGOON's planners the green light to go ahead and complete their ideas.

On July 10, 1944, David Brack told us that the 81st TCS would indeed be going on detached service to another theater of operations; but for four weeks thereafter—all the while that this ponderous effort was actually getting under way—Churchill continued to lobby almost frantically against it. He finally gave up, grudgingly and almost insultingly, less than a week before the operation was launched.[9]

Our controversy with the British over DRAGOON remains one of the ugliest episodes in the Allies' relationships during World War II. It was this sort of disagreement that kept Hitler hoping he could split the alliance and negotiate a separate peace with one power. To this day some British writers treat the American preference for DRAGOON, instead of an assault in the Balkans, with irritating condescension. On the other hand, some American writers remain extremely bitter about the British attempt to use our men and resources to promote British postwar interests in the Balkans and the eastern Mediterranean.[10]

The military argument for invading southern France was so compelling that it makes the British objections and counter-proposals seem rather strange. Eisenhower knew that he needed Marseilles, the biggest port in France, to handle the huge amounts of transport and freight needed for our forthcoming invasion of the Nazi homeland. Corsica, a French island close to the Riviera, had been retaken by the Free French from the Germans; it would be invaluable as a support base for the invasion. It was known that German forces in southern France were relatively weak and could not be easily reinforced.[11] There were also very large Free French forces in north Africa—men the U.S. had equipped and supplied. They could be expected to make their best fight for France, their homeland.[12]

Hostile rumors of Churchill's "Balkan option" circulated so widely that they came down into the ranks of enlisted men in our 81st Squadron. Until 5:30 p.m. on August 14, when we were briefed the day before DRAGOON's first assault, I still believed it was a tossup as to whether we would be headed for southern France or some region in north Yugoslavia, perhaps the Istrian peninsula south of Trieste.

When DRAGOON received the final OK on August 9, the troopers, planes, gliders, ships, and seaborne infantry had to be scraped together in a hurry. Only six days remained before the invasion would begin. The need for haste and improvisation was reflected even in the names given the new airborne HQ units: troop carrier forces would be run by the Provisional Troop Carrier Air Division (PTCAD), and the paratrooper and glider soldiers were to be under the First Airborne Task Force (FATF). PTCAD was given to General Paul Williams (who, before the Normandy invasion, had also been made head of the IX Troop Carrier Command). The FATF commander was General Robert Frederick, from the First Special Service Force (commandos), a general who had gained fame in North Africa and Italy when he was wounded nine times *after* he attained the rank of general. The overall commander of DRAGOON was General Alexander Patch, whose Seventh Army divisions would storm the Riviera beaches (Operation BIGOT).

DRAGOON's glider and parachute troopers were assembled out of a mixed bag of outfits. Several smaller American units that had stayed in the MTO after the Italian invasion were included. The biggest paratrooper unit was the veteran British 2nd Independent Parachute Brigade, then fighting as ground infantry in Italy.[13] Among the American glider-borne outfits was the famous antitank Japanese-American 442nd Combat Team. The pioneer 509th Parachute Infantry Battalion was detached from the 82nd Airborne Division and given to PCTAD. There were also several agents of the Office of Strategic Services (OSS, the forerunner of the CIA), who would parachute deeper into France to work with the French Resistance, the French Forces of the Interior (FFI), and the French Communist groups known as the Maquis. We would have no regular French Army paratroopers with us; in a fit of pique, Charles de Gaulle refused to allow two Free French paratroop battalions to be used in DRAGOON because British and American brass rejected his harebrained scheme to drop and air-land an entire French division in the interior of France, far behind German lines.[14] Finally, about a thousand troopers of the First Special Service Force would participate in DRAGOON. These were the commandos who were to give the "Champagne Campaign" much of its boisterous reputation. All told, DRAGOON would have about 10,000 airborne soldiers, something less than the equivalent of one division.

In addition to handling this hectic improvisation, Generals Frederick and Williams had to deal with resistance on the part of commanders in other zones who resented lending DRAGOON any of their men. Some SHAEF generals, even in the face of Washington's strong support for DRAGOON, resisted allowing the 50th and 53rd Troop Carrier Wings to ship any airplanes to Italy; this problem was solved only when SHAEF was assured these planes would fly "on loan" only and be returned to Britain within a month or so. The British generals in Italy also made it clear that as soon as the airborne parts of DRAGOON were completed, the British 2nd Independent Parachute Brigade would be shipped back to the front lines in Italy.[15]

By far the most frantic rush job in DRAGOON was assembling enough gliders. It was hard enough work pulling together the paratrooper units for DRAGOON, but the airborne assault would call for both paratroopers and glider-borne troopers. There were only a few dozen gliders available in all of Italy. Fortunately, some of the high brass in Washington took the responsibility of shipping 346 gliders off to Naples from the United States long before they were sure DRAGOON would ever become a reality. It was a long sea voyage; had they waited on final confirmation from London there would have been no airborne operation.[16]

When the Allied freighters carrying gliders finally arrived in Naples, it took strenuous work on the part of General Patch to cut through naval red tape and get these ships priority treatment at the jammed-up port and on the docks. Even then, the gliders had to be unboxed, assembled, tested, and flown to their bases. Glider mechanics and other engineers were flown in from several districts to help with this herculean task. By working around the clock and cannibalizing parts from wrecked planes and gliders, these men put all the gliders together—just four days before DRAGOON was to begin.

## The missions

As if Mother Nature intended to demonstrate once again that airborne operations need calm weather and clear skies, the early paratrooper and glider missions in DRAGOON were hurt badly by a high, dense ground fog that settled into the river valleys of the mountains in back of the Riviera. The weathermen had expected some fog. But we at our two 436th briefings—at Ciampino for the pathfinders and paratroop missions, and at Voltone for the glider mission—heard little mention of it. Later we learned that PTCAD leaders had decided that the value of these first missions for the total invasion of south France was worth the risk the fog presented.

The main objectives of all DRAGOON's airborne operations were three areas around the town of Le Muy, about fifteen miles north of the little Riviera port of St. Tropez. In this part of France the land is cut up by the foothills and mountains of the Maritime Alps, truly an unlikely looking place for paratrooper and glider operations. DRAGOON's planners had located a few stretches of

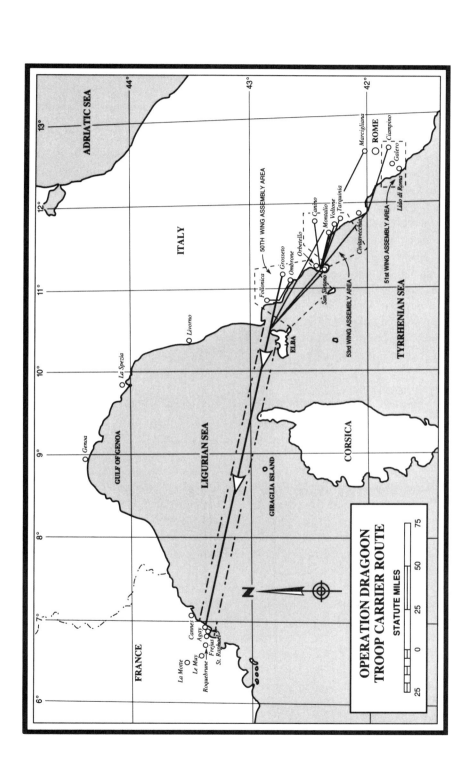

OPERATION DRAGOON
TROOP CARRIER ROUTE

STATUTE MILES

25  0  25  50  75

ADRIATIC SEA

ITALY

FRANCE

La Motte
Le Muy
Roquebrune
Fréjus
St. Raphaël
Agay
Cannes

Genoa

GULF OF GENOA

La Spezia

Livorno

LIGURIAN SEA

GIRAGLIA ISLAND

CORSICA

TYRRHENIAN SEA

ELBA

Follonica

Girosseto

Ombrone

Orbetello

50TH WING ASSEMBLY AREA

San Siano

Montalto

Volbne

Canino

Tarquinia

Civitavecchia

53rd WING ASSEMBLY AREA

51st WING ASSEMBLY AREA

Marcigliana

ROME

Ciampino

Galeri

Lido di Roma

N

6°    7°    8°    9°    10°    11°    12°    13°

44°    43°    42°

country around Le Muy that had just barely enough flat fields for airborne requirements. This region also had the much more important feature of lying athwart the routes the Germans would have to use if they decided to divert their armor from central France to counterattack the seaborne landings in the south.

Because the countryside chosen for DZs and LZs was so rugged, PTCAD gave all the glider and parachute infantry men scarves printed with a map of the Riviera and the mountainous region (the district known as Provence) in the Riviera hinterland. On August 14, the day before we were to begin our part in DRAGOON, we were all called out on the field and told about the serious shortage of glider pilots for this operation. For many gliders there would be no co-pilot. That right-hand seat would have to be occupied by one of the glider troopers, who could not be expected to be much help in handling the spoilers or the brakes, let alone land, in case the pilot was hit by ground fire. Since many of the enlisted men who were power plane crew members (crew chiefs and radio operators) had at least some casual "stick time" in their planes, they were asked to volunteer—presumably on a better-something-than-nothing basis.

The only person to volunteer from the 81st TCS was Vernon Sawvell (flight chief). He had washed out of glider pilot school, so we had to admit he was a good choice, but the rest of us did our best to talk him out of it. After all, it was a one-way trip for those guys. Secretly, we were all proud of Sawvell and a little envious of his guts.

Sawvell was assigned to number 2 glider in our 436th TCG glider serial. He had a major on board, a chaplain who the night before had named his glider *The Leakin' Deacon*.

The first airborne operation of DRAGOON was not the Voltone glider mission but a paratrooper operation code-named ALBATROSS. It left the Rome area airfields at about 3:00 a.m. on August 15 and was slated to arrive in France just as the sun came over the mountains. ALBATROSS carried about 5,600 paratroopers in 396 planes. Included in ALBATROSS were the nine planes of our 81st Squadron that had been sent on detached service to Ciampino to help lead in the MTO's 64th Troop Carrier Group.

About the only simple feature of ALBATROSS was its routing. This paratroop mission flew north up the Italian coast until it hit the island of Elba—an easy landmark. Then it turned northwest until it passed the northern tip of the French island of Corsica. It continued on the same course until it made landfall at the little Riviera port town of St. Raphael, not far from the great resort city of Cannes. DZ "O," just north of Le Muy, was only fifteen miles further inland. It had been about a 500-mile nighttime trip.

The first light of dawn, reflected back from the top of that morning fog bank, made the overcast that covered this part of Provence seem all the more dense and impenetrable. Down on the ground the fog was so thick and so unusual for that time of the year that residents of the Riviera believed it to be artificial, manufactured in some way by the military.[17] Up in the air, only the tallest mountain peaks jutted above the fog. ALBATROSS was flying on dead reckoning and on the hope that the pathfinder paratroopers had somehow located the DZ and set up their radar beacons.

The official Air Forces history of World War II describes those pathfinders as having been "dropped with great accuracy."[18] But we know some pathfinder planes had to make five passes before they could spot anything through that fog, and some of the pathfinder paratroopers were dropped about fifteen miles away from their target.[19]

One serial in ALBATROSS was not in this dilemma: to their credit, the 442nd TCG had used their relief model ("sand table") of the Le Muy area very well. The Group's leader, in the air over that fog bank, recognized the peculiar shape of one mountain peak above the fog, with the result that the 442nd had the most accurate and compact drop of that day. But all pilots in ALBATROSS had to drop their paratroopers right through that dense fog bank. Many paratroopers, seeing what they were jumping through, were convinced they were coming down over the sea.

The pathfinders who had been headed toward DZ "A," west of Le Muy, jumped miles away from their objective and could not set up any beacons until long after ALBATROSS was over. At DZ "O," however, pathfinders were luckier: they reached it in time and set up their Eureka radar homing beacon. Therefore the MTO's 62nd and 64th TC Groups—led to DZ "O" by elements of the 435th and our 436th TC Groups—had moderately successful jumps in spite of the fog. Of the two, the 435th's was more accurate and more concentrated—fortunately, since General Frederick, CO of the airborne ground forces, jumped with them. Frederick was inside DZ "O" and setting up his command post five minutes after he jumped.

The paratroopers in our 81st Squadron planes were part of the British 2nd Independent Parachute Brigade. Some of these troopers later complained that about a quarter of their men landed outside the drop zone. But this was looking at the hole instead of the doughnut, considering the difficulties under which the operation had to work. Military historians are agreed that the drop of this outfit was one of the very best of all the airborne operations during World War II.[20]

Other serials were not that lucky. Two C-47s of the 441st Group became hopelessly lost and separated and dropped their sticks of paratroopers into the sea.[21] Some serials gave their troopers the green light more than twenty-five miles away from any DZ. In one bizarre incident, the nervous leader of a planeload of troopers lost his head and jumped when the *red* jump light came on, four minutes ahead of time, and he was immediately followed not only by all the troopers in his plane but also by those in nineteen other planes in that serial. Some of these men, who came down near St. Tropez, fifteen miles away from their objective, decided to redeem themselves. They stormed St. Tropez, overwhelmed the German garrison there, and gave the town as a present to the American seaborne troops of the 3rd Division who had been sent from the beach to attack St. Tropez.[22]

The three planes of the 81st Squadron that had been based at Voltone were part of DRAGOON's second mission, an all-glider mission code-named BLUE-BIRD. Together with the rest of the 436th TCG, we had forty planes towing forty Waco gliders, slated to arrive at LZ "O" about an hour after the early-morning paratrooper mission (ALBATROSS). BLUEBIRD was carrying glider troopers from the British 64th Light Artillery Battalion. Just ahead of those of us in the 436th TCG was another part of BLUEBIRD, the 435th TCG, towing thirty-five Horsa gliders piloted by British glider pilots. Both groups were ferrying artillerymen and their guns from the British 2nd Independent Parachute Brigade. Both groups had unnerving experiences.

The 435th TCG planes and gliders had just reached Corsica when an emergency recall message turned them right around again. PTCAD had decided that the ground fog in the LZ valleys was still so thick that any attempt to land gliders there would be to commit mass murder. Two planes of the 435th, on their way back to Italy, had to release their gliders over Corsica, where they landed on a Free French airfield. Pulling those heavy Horsas back was consuming so much gas that it was very chancey for the rest of the 435th to take them all the way back to their base on the Italian mainland; but they all made it back. Later that same day the 435th delivered their gliders to south France as part of Operation DOVE.

Meanwhile, the three 81st TCS planes participating in the 436th TCG glider mission, took off from Voltone at 6:00 a.m. Out over the sea and on our way to France, we saw the planes of the 64th TCG returning from the earlier paratrooper mission (ALBATROSS) scattered all over the sky—singles, doubles, rarely in a formation of three. But then, passing us to our left, came the nine paratrooper ships we in the 81st had loaned to the 64th TCG! We could see plain as day our Squadron identification, the big "U5" painted on their sides. They came, all nine, in a classy V-of-Vs. I felt a surge of pride go right through me. The pilots yelled congrats and good luck back and forth on the interplane frequency. This was strictly against the rules—but who cared?

Fifteen minutes later, however, we saw the 435th TCG C-47s heading back to Italy, Horsa gliders still in tow! What had gone wrong?[23]

I was one of the radio operators in the planes leading an element (four planes). It was the job of radio operators in element leader planes to monitor the HQ control station near Rome for messages. Suddenly I heard our mission call sign coming across in Morse code. But there was no "go ahead" ("K") response from our planes. Another call. Still no response. Finally someone in the formation radioed back to HQ to go ahead with the message. Hardly believing what I heard, I made out a recall message, beginning with the secret recall code "CHINA BOY." What sort of a disaster would make them want to turn this skytrain around and send us back home?

Then it came: "CHINA BOY LZ COVERED WITH GROUND FOG RE-TURN GLIDERS LAND IN CORSICA IF NECESSARY WILLIAMS CHINA BOY." ("Williams" was General Paul Williams, CG of the IX Troop Carrier Command and of all troop carrier operations in DRAGOON, not our Colonel Adriel Williams who at that very moment was having to decide how to turn around the skytrain he had been leading toward France.) At that point I realized the message had been sent "in the clear," in Morse code dots and dashes making words in clear English, rather than the words being encoded into other letters according to the code sheet we had been given. This was breaking radio silence with a vengeance. We were too far away from Rome for PTCAD to have sent us a recall message by voice, that is, by radio telephone; it was in Morse, which travels much further. For a few heart-stopping minutes we kept heading toward France, though the message in my hand indicated our mission should be aborted.

But now we were turning! The entire air armada of planes and gliders in our serial of BLUEBIRD was slowly veering around and heading back to mainland Italy. Listening on the ground station frequency I could hear another radio operator (Adriel Williams's?) calling back to HQ for additional verification. "QJC" (stand by) came the answer. Headquarters kept on sending QJCs at five-minute intervals, while we kept wondering what our fate would be.

We finally received another HQ message, also "in the clear:" "CHINA BOY PROCEED TO DESTINATION RETURN GLIDERS ONLY IF REPEAT ("IMI") IF FUEL INSUFFICIENT." And back we turned: another 180-degree turn, this time toward France. We had lost an hour's flying time; but Jack Wallen, our pilot, told me we still had plenty of gas to get the gliders to France and get ourselves back to Italy again.[24]

The French coastline loomed up on the horizon. Soon we could see the famous Riviera shore. It was beautiful—just what I had expected. Majestic mountains right near the water, pleasant little villages with red tile roofs in the valleys. Just before we reached the French coast we saw a grim event. One Waco glider's wings folded back in flight, and the whole aircraft came to pieces. It was a horrible sight. Bits of debris and cloth bobbed around in the air for what seemed like a long time, kept up by the prop wash of the formation's planes.

We flew about twenty miles inland. Ground fog? Hardly a trace of it. It must have burned off during the time it took us to circle. Our LZ "O," north of Le Muy and east of the little village of La Motte, was plainly visible. The pathfinders had done their work well—there was a big red "T" in the center of the field and green smudge-pots burning to show wind direction. It was about 9:30 a.m. when we released our gliders.

The reason our approach went so easily soon became apparent: no flak! As far as I could see, there was not a shot of any kind being fired up at us. We could see plenty of pill-boxes and flak towers, but no sign of any Germans. We all felt a little silly, sitting there in our flak suits.

Geary and I flew this mission together. We had British soldiers in our glider. Out over the Mediterranean we saw coming at us a flight of planes towing Horsa gliders; they were coming back to Italy without having released their gliders!

Later our power pilot came on the horn and yelled "We're going back! Ground fire!" But after we circled for a while he came on again and said "Fasten your seat belts! We're going on in!" It turned out that the trouble had been "ground fog" and not "ground fire."

We landed in a grape vineyard. The stakes in the vineyard took off our wings; but nobody was badly hurt. We went toward a farmhouse and found it was loaded with good wine. As you can imagine, we got loaded, too. (Earl Goodwin, glider pilot)

The next missions were a paratrooper operation (CANARY) and an immense glider operation (DOVE). These afternoon missions had dramatically contrasting fates. The 437th TCG, which ferried the 551st Parachute Infantry Battalion, scored an almost perfect jump into DZ "A," west of Le Muy, for CANARY. But DOVE turned out to be a wounded bird—because the operation failed to achieve the delicate precision required by large-scale glider missions, and because somehow the last remnants of German resistance near DZ "O" managed to put up a good deal of ground fire.

DOVE involved four and a half times as many gliders as our morning BLUEBIRD operation: 332 CG-4As compared with our forty CG-4A's and thirty-five Horsas. DOVE carried more than 2,000 glider troopers plus an immense amount of equipment and supplies. No less than six troop carrier groups were needed to tow all those gliders.

Trouble plagued DOVE from the start. Clouds of thick dust were stirred up at some of the airstrips in Italy when planes and gliders took off. This made several groups dangerously late in forming their skytrain. Because of this delay, the lead group, the 442nd, forced planes in back of it to stack up dangerously in their efforts to maintain a safe towing speed. Some planes ended up towing their gliders twice as high as the designated 1,500 feet. Three gliders of the 441st had to ditch in the sea. Then the leader of the 442nd had to free his glider because it

One of the gliders towed by the 81st TCS down on the LZ near LeMuy. British glider troopers are checking to see if any more supplies are salvageable. The pole in the foreground is one of the infamous "Rommel's asparagus" (obstacles planted in an expected glider LZ).

had developed trouble in its stabilizer controls. In the process the C-47 pilot turned away from the proscribed flight path and, for a few very confusing moments, all the rest of the planes in the 442nd TCG followed him, possibly expecting to be sent back to Italy!

By the time the 442nd got back on track, at about 6:00 p.m. of DRAGOON's D-Day, DOVE was hopelessly jammed up. One of our Navy's cruisers added to the chaos by firing at a segment of the glider train which had been navigated slightly off course and out of the clear channel guaranteed as "fire free."[25] As each following serial approached the LZs, it found other planes arriving there out of sequence, still releasing their gliders.[26] The congestion at both "O" and "A" was frightening. There were several layers of gliders desperately maneuvering over the same turf. One horrified glider pilot said the only comparison he could imagine was "Picadilly Circus at high noon with the traffic being directed by an insane policeman."[27] It seemed a miracle there were only two collisions in the air.

Both LZs had had some areas planted with "Rommel's asparagus"—tall poles connected with trip-wire for detonating land mines. Some glider pilots, diving any which way to get out of that traffic before they ran out of air, opted to glide into other fields a few miles away. Others took the "Rommel's asparagus" head on. Fortunately, some of the French who planted these poles had deliberately installed them only a few feet deep; also, the Germans had not been able to install the mine fuses in time.[28]

The main danger to the gliders was not these obstacles but each other. Glider pilots coming into impossibly small open areas on these LZs at ninety miles per hour were, as it turned out, lucky to have their wings hit these poles: this helped slow them down with only minor damage. Those not so lucky stopped only when they crashed into other gliders on the ground. DOVE looked more like a demolition derby than a milk run.

We crossed the coast and flew inland up a mountain pass bordered on each side by high rocky ridges. It was like flying through a tunnel. The ridges on each side of me were higher than I was, and so close I felt I could almost reach out and touch them. If I ever locate that tow plane pilot I am going to shake his hand for safely getting us through that long and dangerous trip and right to our LZ.

As we broke out of the mountain pass we had to fly through some ground fire. Holes appeared as if by magic accompanied by the "pop pop!" sound of bullets ripping through the canvas. Miraculously, no one was hit. Once we were past those Germans we had clear sailing. I adjusted my approach pattern and followed other gliders into my final approach over the edge of the field. As I sailed over the field boundary I brushed the top of an olive tree. This caused me to land short. My landing gear caught in a drainage ditch and was torn off. The glider skidded on its belly into the field which was more like a sea of mud. We slid to a stop and everyone spilled out of the door and hit the ground running to escape being hit by the oncoming gliders behind us.

We moved into an adjoining field and dug in. Our job was to help block off the Germans' escape route. By this time it was dark. That night the hours passed by very, very slowly. Gunfire and other explosions ebbed and flowed all around us. We could identify the spatter and crackle of small arms fire and the heavier boom of artillery, probably 88 mm guns. We also listened to the whine of the missile launchers and to men shouting at each other. The worst of all that horrible din was the sound of voices calling for medics.

Finally that frightful night was over. Morning dawned. "The sun also rises." We puny humans had not changed the course of nature one iota. As I think back on it, forty-five years later, I could cry over the futility of war.

We deployed to guard the perimeter of our area, waiting for an enemy counterattack that never came. I never even fired my weapon, not once. Never even so much as glimpsed a German soldier. Seventy-two hours after our landings it was all over. American tanks reached our position. The path from the beachheads to our position was now secured. We glider pilots were free to be evacuated to the coast. (Ben Ward, glider pilot)

The airborne part of the invasion of southern France went down in histories—including our own Squadron history written right after the war—as a milk run.[29] This is an oversimplification. It was not a milk run to the glider pilots who had to ditch in the sea, even though most of them were picked up by Air-Sea Rescue vessels. It was not a milk run for the glider pilots in Operation DOVE, several of whom were killed in those nightmarish landings. What misled some historians into thinking everybody involved must have had an easy time is the accounts of some glider pilots who, once down, made the most out of the enthusiastic reception they got from the French people and the holiday atmosphere the Riviera always provides. Some glider pilots stayed in a Riviera town for as long as they dared, living it up. None of them, even those who sought transportation back as soon as they could, arrived at base without wonderful stories.

We went into a town and were shown a German payroll office that had been captured. Francs were lying around all over the place. We picked up quite a few and later used them in poker games. We thought they must have been fakes, worth nothing except as "funny money."

But on our way back to Italy we first put in to Corsica. Corsica is a

French island. Just for fun we tried to change those francs into Italian lire we could take back to base with us. To our surprise people in Corsica were entirely willing to give us lire for those supposedly fake francs! We were sick—it would have been easy for us to have picked up a lot more money from that payroll office. (Earl Goodwin, glider pilot)

Later, in Italy, we were lying on our bunks when we heard a motorcycle put-putting outside. It stopped right in front of our tent—and there was Sawvell, back from being a glider pilot, with a bike he had swiped from a British officer. Although he looked pretty tuckered out, we made him tell all his stories right then.

One of the most futile combat missions we ever flew occurred on the day after DOVE, August 16, 1944; it was code-named EAGLE. This was a re-supply mission with pararacks and door bundles. By then our planes were equipped with what we always called "Limey rollers," a track of cylindrical steel rollers down the center of our planes ending up near the cargo door. In theory these rollers allowed us to push the parachute bundles out much more quickly, but often they didn't work: in going around the curve just before the door the bundles would fall off and jam the exit.

For EAGLE, the rollers worked well. At first everything else seemed to work well, too. We had good weather, had an easy trip to the DZ, and went back saying "just another milk run!" When we landed at Voltone, however, we saw that one part of the mission, at least, had fouled up. The Service Squadron people hadn't cocked the racks properly, and several of us came back to Voltone with some pararack containers still caught under the plane.[30] This didn't make anybody too angry, since by then we all knew how relatively smoothly the whole invasion was proceeding. Not for the last time, we asked ourselves, "Was this trip really necessary?"[31]

## "Champagne campaign"?

One week after our last DRAGOON mission, the twelve planes of the 81st Troop Carrier Squadron were on their way back to England. Our route was slightly different from our trip to Italy: we stopped overnight at "the rock"—Gibraltar. Seeing that famous and awesome shape rising up out of the Mediterranean as we approached provided an additional tourist bonus for us. And some excitement was added by the very tricky piloting needed to land on its short runway with its dangerous crosswinds. But there was no chance to see the town of Gibraltar; we were restricted to the airfield and had to take off early the next morning. By early afternoon of August 24 we were back in Membury, showing off our great coats

When in Rome: Pilots enjoying a bar
in the Eternal City. *Left to right:*
Berryman, Vosika, Wolf, Skrdla,
Eads, Frye.

Squadron planes on the way back
from Italy to England land at
Gibraltar.

of tan and our souvenirs.[32] The long and difficult flight had been accomplished—once again—without a hitch.

Only one day after our return to Membury, DRAGOON was driven off the front pages by the liberation of Paris and the wild celebrations that followed. The campaign in southern France now became a kind of sideshow. We could read in the back pages of *Stars and Stripes* that the Seventh Army was driving rapidly up the Rhone Valley toward a junction with Patton's Third Army. But most attention was focused on the retreat of the main German forces out of northern France. Many of us began to feel that to "end the war in Forty-four" was a real possibility.

Had DRAGOON-BIGOT been a success? Or had the British been right to oppose it? And if it was a success, were its airborne features an important part of that success?

One problem in assessing DRAGOON is the significance of the relatively weak German defenses. DRAGOON was not "a success" in the sense that NEPTUNE (the airborne parts of the invasion of Normandy) and VARSITY (the jump across the Rhine) were judged successes; in the latter operations our airborne forces had to overcome the strongest resistance the Germans could offer.

The question becomes clearer if instead of asking whether DRAGOON was "a success" we ask whether "it worked," whether it accomplished most of its objectives. Examined in this light, DRAGOON certainly succeeded. Within two weeks the Allies cleared the entire south coast of France of the enemy. The ports of Marseilles and Toulon were quickly opened, and a precious supply line consolidated between the Mediterranean and eastern France. The Americans and the French bagged 79,000 German prisoners—though they failed to cut off the escape of even larger numbers of German soldiers. And, perhaps most important, the rapid advance of Patch's Seventh Army prevented the Germans from attacking the thin and extended right flank of Patton's Third Army armored forces, where they were vulnerable.

Toward the end of the war, HQ of our 53rd Troop Carrier Wing distributed a small history of our campaigns in the form of a little brochure obviously intended to be kept as a souvenir. In this, the 53rd TCW claimed that in southern France its forces had been "99% effective."[33] This, of course, was only a silly piece of boasting. But assessments by General Frederick's top intelligence officer of where the paratroopers and gliders came down—as unsatisfactory as such assessments must be—maintained that probably only fifteen percent or so of the airborne troopers landed so far from their assigned drop zones that for two days or more they could not function effectively in the battle.[34] Some airborne histories portray DRAGOON as having had the most accurate and the most concentrated drops of the entire war.

When you consider that many of the pilots involved had had very little combat formation training, the proportions of accurate drops looks very impressive, even if it can be explained partly by weak German resistance. The airborne trooper casualty rate, also, was the lowest of any major World War II airborne operation: 434 killed and 292 injured (both by enemy action and in landing accidents) or four percent.[35]

In a way, the most striking airborne achievement of DRAGOON was in its preparation rather than in its execution. Scraping together in a few weeks the C-47s, gliders, pilots, and troopers from several war zones was a major accomplishment. It has been called "an administrative miracle."[36] It highlighted the marvelous flexibility troop carrier could provide. We were plucked up out of southern England and, in two days, set down in central Italy, intact and ready for anything.

Some strategists, as a consequence of these good results in DRAGOON, became very optimistic about what you could do with an armada of troop carrier planes—perhaps too optimistic, as our failure in Holland would show.

Finally, were the airborne missions in DRAGOON essential to its success? That is, would the seaborne forces (Operation BIGOT) have been able to storm the Riviera beaches, consolidate their beachheads, and work their way north through Provence without the support of these airborne missions? This, of course, is a "what if" complex question about a highly controversial situation. The consensus of military historians seems to be that *as the situation developed from about August 13 onward*, the seaborne landings probably would have succeeded without the airborne operations. DRAGOON was perhaps the worst-kept secret of the war.[37] Given Allied air superiority and the lack of strong German armor available—now that the invasion of Normandy was the main Wehrmacht problem in western Europe—there was little Hitler could do to crush an Allied invasion of southern France. His only option was not to counterattack the beachheads and airheads but to organize as successful a German retreat as possible.

But this is not at all the same as saying that if DRAGOON had been planned and executed without any airborne features at all the invasion would have been as successful. The obvious presence, after mid-July, of an Allied airborne force being pulled together in central Italy, surely encouraged the Germans not to waste scarce resources, that is, not to send some of their divisions from north or central France down toward the Riviera.[38] There was a Panzer division nearby in south-central France; but it was used to cover the retreat rather than to mount a counteroffensive.

The main objective of DRAGOON's airborne missions was to prevent a German counterattack down the Argens Valley against the BIGOT beachhead. That counterattack never materialized; but we can never be sure whether or not it might have, in the absence of nearly a division of airborne troopers north of the beachhead. Certainly the Force 163 planners had no right to believe they were betting on a sure thing.

Later Hitler showed that, against all odds, he could scrape together effective fighting forces and move them with amazing rapidity and stealth over large distances. When we think of the Ardennes campaign (the Battle of the Bulge) in December 1944, we have to realize that if he had chosen, he might indeed have organized a counterattack against DRAGOON in August.

We do know that the DRAGOON airborne landings disrupted any chance the Germans may have had to organize a more effective resistance against the BIGOT sea landings. The airborne troopers behind the Riviera thoroughly confused local German commanders about where the main Allied effort would be directed. The troopers cut communications, knocked out radar installations, set up roadblocks, and—with the enthusiastic help of French Resistance fighters in the district—sought out and attacked German garrisons.[39]

We also know that the Seventh Army advanced much more rapidly up the Rhone River Valley than its planned timetable had indicated. Its movement has been described as "one of the fastest deployments of a major American force ever executed."[40] By September 11, 1944, it had advanced 400 miles northward and joined up with Patton's armor in northern Burgundy. Would this rapid an advance have been possible without the work of the airborne forces down near the Riviera?[41]

### Notes

1. HQ IX TCC hist. narr. for Aug. 1944.

2. Why the term "milk runs?" Because supposedly such missions were as uneventful as a milkman's rounds—back in the days when bottled milk was still delivered to your door.

3. Adelman and Walton, esp. pp. 209–35.

4. From a history of the 517th PCT, quoted in Devlin, *Paratrooper*, p. 463.

5. Some glider pilots prolonged their trip back for several weeks—none of those from the 81st, of course! Dank, p. 165.

6. Warren I, p. 89.

7. By the end of the war General Mark Clark had approximately 100,000 Italian troops under his command. Clark, pp. 418–19.

8. For a vivid account of American soldiers' reactions to poverty and degradation in Naples during 1943–44, see Kennett, pp. 203–5.

9. Wilt, pp. 59–60.

10. Weigley, 1973, pp. 331–33. The Germans began to withdraw from Greece one month after DRAGOON; three months later the British became

deeply involved in a ghastly civil war between Greek Communists and Greek Royalists. See also Weigley, 1981, p. 219.

11. HQ PTCAD, plans for DRAGOON, July 29, 1944.

12. Weigley, 1973, pp. 329–30.

13. This outfit had been part of the 1st British Airborne Division, which was now in England.

14. Warren I, p. 82.

15. General Frederick was glad to see them go, and even expedited their departure—mostly because, after landing, they seemed more interested in minimizing casualties than in storming their main objective, the town of Le Muy. See Adelman and Walton, pp. 135–40.

16. Warren I, p. 89.

17. Robichon, p. 132.

18. Craven and Cate, p. 428.

19. Devlin, *Paratrooper*, p. 448. Warren I, p. 95, calls this pathfinder effort "less than 50 percent effective."

20. Warren I, pp. 99–100; Robichon, p. 135.

21. Warren I, p. 99.

22. An official U.S. Air Forces study concluded that ninety percent of the troopers landed close to their proper DZs. USAFETO, "Organization, Equipment, and Tactical Employment of the Airborne Division."

23. Apparently PTCAD at Lido di Roma had decided to abort the Horsa serial because of pathfinder reports from the LZ that the fog bank was still thick and was about 500 feet high. Moore, Ch. 3, pp. 75–76.

24. The official report states: ". . . a Command re-call was sent as groups approached far shore. [436th] Group circled over the Tyrrhenian Sea for approximately one hour awaiting further orders. Command advised them to take a look at the LZ and release gliders if feasible or return with gliders if not feasible. 436th Group went in and released gliders successfully." HQ, 53rd TCW, "Historical Report . . . [on] Operation DRAGOON," Sept. 10, 1944, pp. 2–3.

25. Dank, pp. 152–53. Dank, a glider pilot with the 439th TCG, suffered "friendly fire" that tore away his right horizontal stabilizer; he was able to land only through good luck—and great skill. See also Warren I, pp. 84,90.

26. Warren I, pp. 106–7.

27. Dank, p. 156.

28. Robichon, p. 135. Some glider pilots reported that the loosely set poles proved a real advantage in helping them to slow down. Moore, Ch. 3, p. 72. See also the report of a 99th TCS glider pilot in Air Intelligence Contact Unit, "Report on Returnees," May 15, 1945.

29. The sketch history of the 81st TCS by Frank Lester and Grant Howell said of DRAGOON: "Our task was as easy as a practice mission."

30. Pararack failure was common throughout troop carrier and throughout the war: see, e.g., the Air Intelligence Contact Unit returnees report for March 6, 1945, and IX TCC, "Operation VARSITY," p. 2.

31. Weigley, however, believes that the re-supply on August 16 (and another the following day) were important to keep the unexpectedly fast Seventh Army breakout moving along. 1973, p. 233.

32. The Group diarist wrote that the men returning from Italy made the rest "look like sick call." 436th TCG hist. narr. for Aug. 1944.

33. "Ever First! The 53rd Troop Carrier Wing," pp. 16–17.

34. Adelman and Walton, p. 272, fn. 11, "HQ Allied Force G-3 Section Report on Airborne Operation in DRAGOON, September 16, 1944."

35. Wilt, p. 91.

36. Adelman and Walton, p. 69.

37. Base security for our Italian fields would have been just about impossible to attain because of the many Italians who had to be given entry into the areas. And in fact at Voltone, unlike Membury, no attempt was made to put the base under guard just before the assault began.

38. Wilt, pp. 76–79, 115. See also the extremely cautious intelligence report by 53rd TCW HQ, annex #1 of the DRAGOON-BIGOT field order, Aug. 11, 1944.

39. Adelman and Walton, pp. 109–25.

40. Adelman and Walton, p. 154.

41. See HQ, 53rd TCW, "Historical Report," p. 6. This report credits DRAGOON "with providing the surprise which made possible such a rapid advance of the 7th Army following their landings between Marseilles and Nice."

# 15. MARKET-GARDENING
## "Airborne Carpet" or "Hell's Highway"?

### Three names

Like most Americans, we of the 81st Troop Carrier Squadron Association are not good at pronouncing the names of unfamiliar European towns. But of the hundreds of towns we encountered on freighting or combat missions, there are three names we will always be able to say correctly: Eindhoven, Nijmegen, and Arnhem. These three Dutch towns were the main targets of the Allied invasion of Holland in September 1944 code-named MARKET-GARDEN. This was the greatest airborne operation of the war—probably, of all time. It was also the greatest failure of combined American-British action. "MARKET" was the code name for the airborne half of the operation; "GARDEN," the name for the ground forces mission.

These three towns were on a north-south line that ended on the other side of the Lower Rhine, across the bridge at Arnhem, the famous "bridge too far" in the movie of that name. The plan: starting from the stalled British lines along the Albert and Escaut Canals in northern Belgium, British armor would punch across the border into Holland and race some twenty miles to Eindhoven, the southernmost of these three towns. At the same time, American and British parachute and glider troopers would drop into the Eindhoven, Nijmegen, and Arnhem districts, seize the bridges and road junctions, and provide a corridor up which the British Guards Armored Division would push, headed for Arnhem and the crucial bridge across the Lower Rhine.

This was the invasion calculated to break the back of German defenses in the west. It was on MARKET-GARDEN we counted to "end the war in Forty-four." After traveling over the "airborne carpet," the British armor—moving along with massive British and American infantry support—was supposed to have an easy path through the lightly defended northern tier of Holland all the way to the North Sea somewhere in the region of the Zuyder Zee. The many thousands of Germans caught to the west of this Allied line would have to surrender. And from new Allied positions across the Rhine, Montgomery and the American forces under his control would then swing southeast across the flat plains of northern Germany—so well suited for rapid tank movement—cut south to surround the Ruhr, and make it clear to Germany's generals (if not to Hitler) that further resistance was useless.

The Ruhr, and not the Netherlands, was the real goal of MARKET-GARDEN. It was the prospect of cutting the rest of Germany off from its industrial heartland that induced Eisenhower to go for Montgomery's plan of a British-led thrust along the northern route into Germany. But the decision was not an easy one, since Eisenhower's American advisors pushed him hard to choose instead Bradley's idea of an all-out American push straight east into the German lines along the central reaches of the Rhine.

MARKET-GARDEN was a brilliant plan. It might have worked. Therein lies its special tragedy.

## "A bridge too far"?

Unlike the almost nonchalant piecing together of DRAGOON, MARKET-GARDEN was launched in a crisis atmosphere. Its final plans were not ready until just one week before we took off on our first mission to Eindhoven.

SHAEF was able to launch MARKET-GARDEN in so little time because it had plans made for many airborne campaigns during the Allies' rapid advance across France—campaigns that invariably were canceled. Planners of those operations during late August and early September were able to modify some available intelligence data, maps, routing, and command organization already on the boards, and apply the data to the needs of MARKET-GARDEN. Some of those canceled operations called for using precisely the same routes and airborne forces eventually employed in MARKET-GARDEN.

The invasion of Holland could begin only if Eisenhower ordered that the IX Troop Carrier Command and the rest of the FAAA be placed in Montgomery's hands. Meanwhile General Lewis Brereton, CG of the First Allied Airborne Army, was trying to interest Eisenhower in an American-led alternative plan to use FAAA in an assault in front of General Courtney Hodge's First American Army in the region around Aachen near the German border (code-named LINNET II). But Bradley insisted that troop carrier planes should be used to continue to feed gas to Patton, and at this point he was not at all willing to support any sort of large-scale airborne operation.[1] On the other hand, ever since DRAGOON, the FAAA—with all its veteran airborne troopers in Britain and with its vast armada of trained C-47 and glider crews—had been like coins burning a hole in SHAEF's pocket.[2] Since Eisenhower was under strong pressure from Hap Arnold and George Marshall to use the FAAA in some bold operation, he was left with plans based on Arnhem not Aachen. This meant he would have to go

along with Montgomery's British-based ideas.[3] Another incentive for Eisenhower—always anxious to do what he could to strengthen good Anglo-American
relations—was that the fearsome V-2 missiles, now crashing down on London,
were located along Montgomery's planned invasion path, not Brereton's.

Eisenhower was probably already tilting toward Montgomery's concepts,
therefore, when Montgomery learned of a conference between Eisenhower and
Hodges in which Hodges got the impression (not without some justification) that
Eisenhower still hoped the First American Army could support *both* Patton's and
Montgomery's drives across the Rhine. He also had heard about Brereton's
planned LINNET II for the Aachen area. To Montgomery this meant Eisenhower
was going back on his agreement to give logistical priority to a British-led drive
across the Lower Rhine. British General F. A. M. "Boy" Browning, in charge
of ground operations for FAAA, slapped his resignation on the table in an effort
to convince Eisenhower he had to back Montgomery or forfeit the cooperation
of British military leadership. So, after flying into one of his famous rages,
Montgomery got Eisenhower to cancel LINNET II and repeat his pledge of
priority support for the British plan. To his chagrin, Brereton learned that
the FAAA "would be made available to the Northern Group of Armies [i.e.,
Montgomery] until the Rhine is crossed." Browning quickly withdrew his resignation.[4] On September 10 Eisenhower confirmed his prior assurances to Montgomery that FAAA could indeed be used in the British-led northeastern drive.

There now was less than a week before the invasion was to be launched.
And haste was really needed. The Allied push toward Germany was rapidly
running out of steam. All the Allied forward lines, so far away from their English
and Normandy supply bases, were stretched to the point that getting adequate
supplies was an increasingly serious matter. Furthermore, the Germans now had
shorter supply lines and, with their backs to the wall, could be expected to fight
with increasing determination to defend their Fatherland.

Were we facing the possibility of fixed battle lines along the Rhine, something like the trench warfare of World War I? Most Allied commanders believed
this was not a real possibility, since they believed—or hoped—that the German
forces were so disorganized and disheartened after their headlong retreat out of
France that only one more solid blow was needed to open the road all the way to
Berlin. But they also had to take into consideration that there might be time
enough before winter set in for only one major invasion strike; and this had to
be launched before the Germans redeployed their remaining forces into an effective defensive system.

After September 10 the American commanders—a few of them haunted by
a foreboding of failure—sat down with the British to work out the final plans. In
addition to Brereton, the most important MARKET (air assault) decisions were

in the hands of Generals Matthew Ridgway, Maxwell Taylor, Paul Williams, and Browning. General Sir Miles Dempsey, head of the British Second Army, was in charge of planning for GARDEN (ground assault). A previous, relatively modest plan of Montgomery's for the Arnhem area, code-named COMET, was available as a rough outline for the new, greatly augmented assault plan. What emerged was an enormously complicated set of interlocking plans, each segment of which had to work. If British armor failed to punch through to Arnhem—a matter of sixty-three miles through German-held territory—all the airborne endeavors in MARKET would be in vain.

On one point there was no debate: all the MARKET-GARDEN missions would go in daylight. Decisions on two other vital points were made on September 12, 1944, just five days before the Holland invasion began. Everybody realized that it would be preferable to bring in all glider-borne troops as soon as possible after the paratroopers were dropped. There were enough gliders on hand, but not enough C-47s for each glider; therefore to bring all the gliders in on D + 1 would mean a double tow, two gliders per plane. While we in the 81st had trained for double glider tows as far back as our stay in Laurinburg-Maxton, Brereton and the IX Troop Carrier commanders ruled this out. This invasion would involve too long and too dangerous a flight over too much enemy territory. Brereton insisted that the glider-borne troops would have to be brought in on two different days.[5] Second, two separate routes to Holland were laid out, a "northern route" directly across the North Sea, and a "southern route" across Belgium. The 81st TCS, part of the 53rd TC Wing's mission to carry the 101st Airborne Division paratroopers to Eindhoven on the first day, would fly the southern route. This meant that for the first mission we would be over enemy-held territory only about half as long as the 50th and 52nd TC Wings headed for the Nijmegen district over the northern route with the 82nd Airborne Division, and the British troop carriers headed for Arnhem with the British First Airborne. The "northern route" called for troop carrier planes to fly over about eighty miles of enemy-held territory; but reconnaissance intelligence seemed to show flak along this route was not prohibitively dangerous.

By September 14 the airborne troopers had arrived at Membury and our base was sealed off. The weather predictions were favorable. Nothing could stop Montgomery's big gamble now.

Our crews were briefed for this first Holland mission not on the day before the mission but on September 17, the very morning of D-Day. Takeoff would be around 10:30 a.m., so there was plenty of time. The entire 436th TC Group was briefed out in the open under the Membury control tower. On the outside balcony of the control tower stood Adriel Williams and his staff. In back of him was a huge map with the invasion routes marked. Williams explained the mission's

Our first briefing for the invasion of Holland, at Membury control tower. The maps display the "southern route" to the drop zone (Eindhoven) and the best flight pattern to take after the drop.

Faces of pilots and crewmen at the Holland briefing.

objectives and pointed out the landmarks and radar locations near our turning points. I looked around at the rest of us staring up at him. At this briefing there was no kidding around, no grinning to be seen among the watchers. Tension and care marked every face.

One of the problems on our minds at this dramatic moment was the fact that our C-47s still did not have the self-sealing gas tanks that we had been promised. Not enough of them were yet delivered; therefore only the squadron and group leaders had them. The Eighth and Ninth Air Forces in Britain had enough self-sealing tanks for us; but they refused to give them up on the grounds that they would be depriving their own planes. The glider pilots may also have been thinking that very few of them would be piloting gliders with the new "Griswold nose," a simple but clever arrangement of metal bars in front of the glider cockpit to help gliders absorb the shock of impact against hedges and similar obstacles. Furthermore, though everybody realized the value of drogue chutes in helping gliders to stop quickly upon landing, only about a third of the gliders had them. Troop carrier would go into Holland with essentially the same equipment we had used in Normandy.

Hanging over plans for MARKET-GARDEN were two enormously important question marks: Would the weather be good for the three days needed in order to mount three airborne drops? And would the leading elements of the British 30 Corps be able to overcome German defenses in the region quickly enough to reach Arnhem and consolidate the hold of the British First Airborne over that bridge? Pouring over the invasion maps with Montgomery, counting up all the rivers and canals to be crossed, "Boy" Browning asked Montgomery how long he thought it would take Brian Horrocks, commander of 30 Corps, to get to Arnhem. "Two days," was the reply. "They should be up to you by then."

"We can hold it for four," said Browning. "But I think we may be going one bridge too far."[6]

### The first two missions

The worst nightmare IX Troop Carrier commanders could face was the very real possibility of utter operational failure—either because of snafus in timing resulting in formation jam-ups or because of unacceptable losses to crews and planes. In MARKET, this nightmare did not materialize. But almost every other possible terror did. About the only absent horror was "friendly fire:" there would be no Allied naval armada for us to fly over while invading Holland.

The military annals of the Holland invasion are full of unstinting, even extravagant praise for C-47 pilots, glider pilots, and aircrews who delivered their

Paratroopers and their equipment near our planes at Membury before a drop during the Holland invasion.

Paratroopers being helped into our planes for a drop during the Holland invasion.

airborne troopers to their objectives.[7] It needs to be said, emphatically and repeatedly, that troop carrier squadrons did everything that was asked of them—and paid heavily for it. Flying MARKET was not a milk run: it was more like running an exceedingly deadly gauntlet.

But neither at that time nor today does the realization that we performed excellently ease the feelings of frustration and guilt that came when MARKET-GARDEN failed to get the Allies across the Lower Rhine.

> I remember three things about the Holland missions: first, the lousy weather. It was near-instrument conditions with low clouds and poor visibility. Second, I remember Ed Griffen. His glider either cut loose or broke loose and ditched into the sea. I learned that all the glider troopers got out and were saved; but because of some strange accident, Ed was killed. This was a bitter blow to those of us who lived in his barracks and liked him very much. Ed was a good-natured lad who came from the South. He was our local barber: I don't know whether he had actually done this work before or just had a natural gift for it.
>
> The third thing I remember was our feeling that General Montgomery's armor more or less just sat there for two days and didn't do much of anything to break through to Arnhem. (Bill Westcott, pilot)

On our first mission in MARKET, on September 17, 1944, our Squadron was to deliver 390 troopers and their equipment from the 506th Parachute Infantry Regiment of the "Screaming Eagles" (101st) Airborne Division. This was a full-strength operation for our Squadron: twenty-two planes. We were headed for DZ "C," about seven miles north of Eindhoven and just north of the little town of Zon. This DZ was close to one of the key bridges MARKET had to seize, the one over the Wilhelmina Canal. In fact, the 101st Airborne was ordered to take that bridge even before it turned to assaulting the town of Eindhoven. This was to be the first major bridge the British infantry (Guards Division) would have to cross on its way past Eindhoven and Nijmegen and on to Arnhem.

Along with the rest of the 436th TCG, we were part of a huge and meticulously orchestrated air armada. Col. Robert Sink, commander of the 506th PIR, would parachute from Adriel Williams' plane. The 436th and the other four Groups in the 53rd Wing were flying 424 planes and seventy gliders to the Eindhoven area. Aboard the C-47s in these five groups was a total of 6,700 troopers from the 101st Airborne, more than half that entire division's strength. At the same time the 50th and 52nd TC Wings were carrying about the same number of troopers from the 82nd Airborne to DZs and LZs just south of Nijmegen; and the British troop carriers (plus some American planes) were flying the British First Airborne Division to MARKET's single most important objective, the

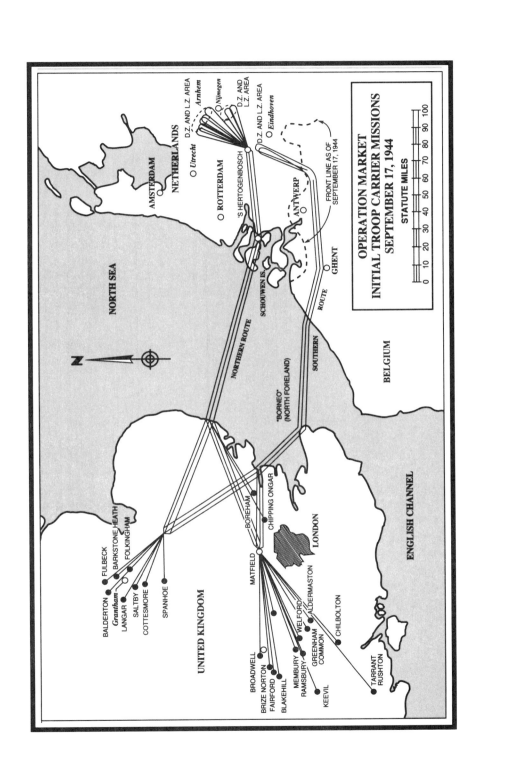

OPERATION MARKET
INITIAL TROOP CARRIER MISSIONS
SEPTEMBER 17, 1944

STATUTE MILES

0  10  20  30  40  50  60  70  80  90  100

bridge over the Lower Rhine at Arnhem. Altogether, troop carrier planes from twenty-five British airfields "had to converge like tributaries joining a river until they should fly evenly and punctually into the landing fields of Holland." [8]

We left Membury at about 10:30 a.m., flew to the Wing assembly point, and joined the skytrain along the "southern route" across the Channel and the parts of northern Belgium now in Allied hands. The weather was decent. Some clouds and haze, but not enough to obscure the Channel and the Belgian countryside over which we were passing. Nary a Luftwaffe plane in sight; we could see P-51s off on the horizon flying perimeter patrol for us. Once past Antwerp we swung north and headed straight for Eindhoven. For about the next twenty miles past this point we were over German held territory—ten of the scariest minutes we as a Squadron had ever experienced.

One of our pilots, Rip Collins, reported that there was no problem navigating up that corridor toward Eindhoven: in an earlier serial, one of the new Luftwaffe ME 262 jet fighters had successfully penetrated our fighter cover and had shot down a C-47, so that our route was all too plainly marked by the smoke at the crash site. For me, looking out through the cockpit windshield over the pilots' shoulders, the scene after we crossed the front lines seemed not entirely real. Down below, the neat and peaceful-looking Dutch countryside, criss-crossed with little waterways and dotted with doll-house towns and charming church spires. We were flying so low it was easy to see individual Hollanders out in the streets, heads tilted up at us in open-mouthed wonder. Some crew members spotted Dutch civilians holding up two fingers in the "V for Victory" sign. But soon, we were flying through apparently endless bursts of mean-looking little flak clouds, some grey, some yellowish-white. I asked our navigator the number one stupid question—how much longer we would have to fly through that crap. "Only a few more minutes," he said, never taking his eyes off the map he was gripping. Just then came the rattle of flak hitting someplace back in the plane. It was time for me to climb up on the stool under the astrodome and get ready to signal "red light" (four minutes out); then "green light!" and the paratroopers in our plane went out in a rush. Ben Obermark (crew chief) and I pushed out the last parabundles while the formation was turning left to get back onto the same course we had used coming in. It was on such wide turns over enemy territory that C-47s were most vulnerable; but, unlike other planes in our Squadron, this time our plane took no more hits from ground fire. Our Group formation closed up and we headed back for Britain. By about 4:00 p.m. we were on the ground in Membury.

The 101st troopers, after this first mission, were unanimous in agreeing that from their viewpoint the drop was almost perfect. Their division history records

Bill Westcott's remarkable photo of an Eindhoven drop, taken from his co-pilot's seat.

it as "a parade-ground jump."[9] The 53rd TC Wing's groups delivered more than 85 percent of their parachute and glider troopers either right on target or within two miles. Some parachute units were dropped so compactly they didn't bother to wait for an SOP assembly ("rolling up the stick") but simply grabbed up their equipment and immediately went off toward their unit objectives.

All of us in the 81st Squadron made it back. It was a close thing, though, for the plane piloted by Jim Ackerman: he had his left engine and a tire shot out, and two large holes in the elevator. But this would be the last time our Squadron would fly a major combat mission without casualties. And on this day, others in the 53rd TC Wing had not been so lucky. Sixteen planes were shot down and fourteen badly damaged. Two of those lost were from our sister squadron, the 79th TCS. Many crew members, unable to jump in time, were dead; others were missing.

This Holland mission must be remembered as one in which several troop carrier pilots deliberately sacrificed themselves to jockey their damaged planes to the DZ and deliver their paratroopers. Troopers already on the ground stared up in disbelief as at least four planes, on fire, stubbornly headed for the DZ, jumped their troopers, and crashed almost immediately afterward. This was the case for one of the 79th TCS planes, piloted by Robert Stoddard, and one in the 80th TCS, piloted by John Gurecki.[10] In the lead plane of the 435th TC Group the regimental commander, standing in the door, was so appalled by the sight of flames spreading over a nearby C-47 that he didn't see the green light come on until he was prodded by General Matthew Taylor, CG of the 101st, standing in number two position.[11]

The two glider serials of the 437th Group that followed us to the Zon area shortly afterwards were sitting ducks for German small-arms fire. Six of their sixty-four planes were shot down and forty-six damaged, some beyond repair. Nine gliders were lost, two when they collided. But even on this glider mission, about 80 percent of the troopers, jeeps, and trailers made it close enough to the LZ to enter the battle right away.

On this D-Day in Holland a member of our Squadron became a party to one of those events that truly try men's souls; this episode, also, epitomizes everything troop carrier stood for. The person involved was Gale Ammerman, one of our glider pilots, being towed on this mission by a plane of another group.

> I was flying at various times through clouds so thick I could see only about fifteen to twenty feet of tow rope in front of me. Then we would break out into the clear for a minute or so, only to find ourselves back in the clouds again. Try as I could to judge the altitude of the glider in relation to the tug, it was not possible to maintain normal position. After prolonged flying in that soup we broke out with the C-47 tow plane almost straight down under

my glider. A near panic dive was absolutely essential to get back into some kind of a normal position. After several repeats of this we did finally break into the clear and had a good flight until we passed over the German lines.

Then all hell broke loose. My tow plane took ground fire and started to lose a thick stream of gas from the right fuel tank. I got on the phone line with the tow plane and told the pilot he had a stream of gasoline as big around as my arm coming from the right tank. After a slight pause, his answer was, "Stay on; we'll go on as long as the fuel holds out." He took me right down the pike to my drop zone. I cut off and landed in what seemed to be a thousand acres of flat Dutch fields. I didn't even break a tail wheel on that landing. (Gale Ammerman, glider pilot) [12]

The drops of the 82nd Airborne in the Nijmegen area, too, were near perfect. General Matthew Ridgway, former head of the 82nd Airborne and now CG of the XVIII Corps, was flying overhead in a bomber as an observer and remembered:

The drop was beautiful, the best we'd ever done. Despite the fact that planes were being lost to AA fire, those magnificent pilots of the 52nd Troop Carrier held formation perfectly, and hit their drop zones on the nose. As we circled wide, watching the skies fill with thousands of colored chutes, we could look down into the streets of the little villages. The people were all out in their Sunday best, looking up as the great sky train, five hundred miles long, went past. The little houses were all intact, and I felt a great pang of regret knowing that these fine Hollanders were all unaware of the tragedy that was soon to strike. [13]

By the time D-Day in Holland was ended, the Allies had sent 1,545 paratrooper planes and an additional 451 plane and glider combinations to begin nailing down that "airborne carpet."

September 18, 1944, D-Day + 1: The second Holland mission was also huge: 1,700 troop carrier planes (British and American) plus 1,200 gliders and 250 bombers converted to deliver parabundles. The air over southeast England was again crowded with three parallel skytrains, one headed for Eindhoven, one for Nijmegen, and one for Arnhem. We in the 81st were sending twenty planes to Eindhoven, this time to LZ "W" between the towns of Best and Zon. We were part of the 53rd TC Wing's assignment to deliver 2,700 troopers of the 101st Airborne Division (the 327th Glider Infantry Regiment and the 326th Battalion Engineers and Medics). These men had the assignment of mopping up in the Eindhoven region and getting the bridges in that district ready for the British armor. Jumping this day was General Anthony McAuliffe, the 101st's artillery general, destined three months later to create an enduring legend at the battle for Bastogne.

Up to a few hours before we took off, we were slated to fly the "southern route," the same as the previous day, though this time, presumably, the Germans in that area would be waiting for us. Ominously, the weather over Belgium was deteriorating rapidly; a route mostly over land would force the glider pilots (many of whom had no co-pilots) to fly virtually blind for most of the way. IX Troop Carrier Command reversed its orders at the very last minute and sent us along the "northern route," that is, across the North Sea and the Scheldt estuary, where we could expect to run into plenty of light flak and small-arms fire.[14]

This four-hour delay, from 7:30 to 11:30 a.m., while we had waited to see if the weather over the "southern route" would improve, amounted to a serious blow for the 101st Airborne. The 502nd PIR was fighting against stronger German units for one of the bridges across the Wilhelmina Canal, and the troops and vehicles in our gliders were badly needed. From our point of view, however, the delay was essential, not only because of the deteriorating weather, but also because the Germans had launched a counterattack in the area around Best and Zon, and it took hard fighting on the part of the 101st paratroopers to clear out the fields into which our gliders would be coming.

Traveling the "northern route," as it happened, solved nothing. Bad flying weather now became a terrible threat to the whole MARKET operation. Flying conditions over England were not bad; but over the Channel and the North Sea it was a different story.

> On the Holland invasion I flew in on September 18. My co-pilot was a 101st Airborne trooper. By the time we hit the English coast on our way over, the fog was so bad there really was *no* visibility. The tow pilot had to fly so low over the sea that if a ship had been in our path I am sure we would have hit it. The visibility improved a bit as we approached Holland; but I could tell from the way our tow plane was changing course that the pilots were lost. They flew on until they spotted a town; then they were able to get their bearings and turn us toward the LZ.
>
> We had been told we would have to be over enemy territory for about fifteen minutes before we reached the LZ. I want to tell you that the small arms fire and 20 mm flak was pretty bad. But we did make it to the LZ; we landed intact and with nobody hurt. (Thayer Bonecutter, glider pilot)

Fog over the water also set in motion a train of events that was to force J. J. DiPietro, one of our glider pilots, to experience another troop carrier terror: having to ditch in the sea.

All at once, as we flew over the water, the weather really socked in. There were only short periods when I could see my tow ship and correct my angle of flight. For a long time all I could see in front of me was a couple of feet of tow rope. By the angle of the rope it looked as though I was not in level flight and was not in proper tow position. Suddenly I saw a clearing in the fog and the outline of a C-47; it was below and to the right, and far enough ahead so that it looked as though it could have been our tow-ship. I dived down to get behind that plane; and as I did the tow rope broke like a piece of string. I was in free flight half way across the North Sea.

The plane I had seen was somebody else's tow plane.

I looked over at the 101st Airborne trooper sitting next to me in the co-pilot's seat. His face was turning green. I was scared, too; but it helped that I had a job to do. He said, "What do we do now?" I answered: "Pray."

The rest of the troopers were quiet; apparently they had not yet realized our predicament. I looked at my altimeter: 2,000 feet. I had to pick up speed to make a good ditching approach. My thinking was that if the fog went all the way down, and we hit the water before we broke out of it, we would never know the difference; and if we did see water at a decent altitude, I would be able to level off and attempt a ditching. While all these things were going through my mind, I turned around to the troopers and shouted out ditching instructions: "When we hit the water we will land tail first. You will feel two jolts. Release your seat belts after the second jolt and punch holes through the top of the glider. Get up on the wing of the glider when you get out! Keep your eyes open for a dinghy which will be dropped by the tow pilot!"

Meanwhile, I was paying good attention to the airspeed indicator and the altimeter. We were doing a dangerous 150 mph and the altimeter was soon at 500 feet; still couldn't see the water! Now I was too busy to be scared.

Finally, at 200 feet, there was the water. It was a good sight. I began to level off and make my final approach. When the tail hit the water I was doing maybe fifty mph. The first shock slowed the glider a bit. On the second jolt, as the undercarriage hit the water, the glider came to a stop.

I looked back into the fuselage—but there was no one there! The troopers had already scrambled to the top of the wing. The fuselage was quickly filling up with water. I was alone in the glider with water up to my neck. I grabbed for my seat belt release and reached for one of the holes they had punched in the roof. A couple of the troopers grabbed my hands and pulled me up.

The glider was floating sweetly in the water. There had been no injuries. In a short time we spotted a low-flying British plane. It made a turn over us to let us know he knew where we were. About an hour later a British Air-Sea Rescue launch picked us up.

On the launch they gave us dry clothes, a shot of brandy, food and hot tea. They also informed us that we were the third glider batch they had fished out; and that some others were not so lucky as us.

When we landed in England I said goodbye to my troopers and turned them over to an airborne captain. I took the next train to London. From London I caught a train to Hungerford, the nearest train stop to home base. From Hungerford I phoned the base and asked for transportation. When I told them who I was, they said, "What! You are supposed to be missing in action!"

By now it was late at night. When I got back to the barracks, David Brack and a few buddies were waiting up for me. I told them my story. They told me that when my tow-plane returned to Membury, the pilot had said it looked as though I was nosing down head-first into the sea and that there could be no survivors; that is why he decided to go with the rest of the formation to Holland rather than circle back and drop us a dinghy. (J. J. DiPietro, glider pilot) [15]

Another searing experience this glider mission brought us was the loss of our first plane in combat. On the run in to the LZ, John Webster's plane was caught by a flak burst and set on fire. Webster cut his glider loose, put his plane on automatic pilot, ordered his crew to bail out, and jumped himself right after them.

From the other planes in that formation we could see all four of the chutes from Webster's plane opening safely. But we were over German-held territory; would they be picked off by ground fire as they came down? Lady Luck dealt them a mixed hand. They all hit the ground safely. They ripped off their chutes and made a mad dash to get the hell out of there before any Germans arrived. But they scattered in different directions; and Webster ran right into the arms of a German patrol. The other three, however, were picked up and spirited away by Dutch patriots. Webster had to spend the rest of the war as a POW; but the co-pilot (Whitney Brooks), the crew chief (Celar Obergfell), and the radio operator (Harold "Shorty" Farr) were kept in hiding by the Dutch Underground for thirty-seven days until they could be shipped back across the Channel to England. We were spared the need to sweat them out. Only a few hours after we ourselves had landed in Membury, we learned that the superbly well-organized Dutch Underground had sent us a radio message that Farr, Obergfell, and Brooks were safe.

Another of our gliders, besides J. J. DiPietro's, did not land in Holland. It was the one piloted by Ben Ward. Much of the agony and frustration that was MARKET-GARDEN is contained in his experiences.

Luck of the 81st: Jim Ackerman's plane, its tires shot out, slammed into an 82nd TCS plane landing back at Membury. No one was hurt.

I was seated on a bar stool in town when suddenly over the BBC radio came the news that the Allied forces had begun dropping paratroopers in Holland. I knew that my part of the mission, the glider assault, was scheduled to begin shortly after the paratrooper drop. I was about twenty-five miles from the base; so I took off from my bar stool and started toward the base. But I had to walk the entire twenty-five miles—I didn't see a soul and didn't get a single lift.

I arrived at the base early in the morning; and by the time I got there the glider pilots were all dressed in their combat gear and headed for the flight line. In a few minutes I changed clothes, hustled down to the flight line, got my glider assignment, and went over to the glider. When I started up my check list I realized I didn't have my flak suit. So I yelled out the window to one of the ground crewmen to run and get me a flak suit. He said OK; and he took off. That was the last I ever saw of him.

As we climbed to join the formation of the entire 53rd Wing, which had been circling, we picked up our place in a formation of forty-seven other aircraft and headed for the Channel. At the Channel the weather became cloudier and cloudier; and as we crossed over the open sea it wasn't long before we ran into a tremendous fog bank. We plunged into that fog bank; almost immediately, I was flying blind. The only thing I could see was about six feet of tow rope. So I flew by the seat of my pants—watching the tow rope and hanging on as best I could, knowing that I had no other place to go but down into the sea. I was able to hold a relatively normal flight pattern behind my tow plane as we slowly climbed through the cloud bank. I flew blind that way some forty minutes until we broke out. Lo and behold—we were all alone! I had no idea where the other forty-six airplanes had gone; but we continued and pressed on toward Holland.

As we approached the Dutch coastline the weather got worse; we finally had to drop to a lower altitude. We were just about 500 feet across the tossing, churning waves of the North Sea. The weather was beginning to close in again, and we were scooting in and out of cloud banks. When we crossed into Holland we were in really marginal weather. As a matter of fact my first glimpse of any habitation was a church steeple sweeping past my left wingtip.

That entire, flat land of Holland was spotted with clumps of woods; every time we would fly across a clump there seemed to be a German anti-aircraft battery located there, and they would blast away at us. At first—as far as we could tell at that time—they only seemed to be managing a few scattered hits on the glider. But while crossing one woods I watched, fascinated, as a wall of fire ball tracers swept up at us. German gunners were aiming at the tow plane, and this wall of tracers came up to the left of the tow plane and swept back toward me. It swept past, but not before it blew off my left wingtip.

We were actually so low now that the Germans had a hard time zeroing in our aircraft. Only once, after this, were we hit with more than isolated shots: a German gunner let loose a burst of machine-gun fire at the tow plane, but his mark was off slightly to the left, and the stream of tracers raked back along my fuselage and ripped through the last three feet of my left wingtip. For perhaps three seconds I just watched, fascinated, as the red balls of tracers swept back from slightly ahead of and through my wingtip—then were gone, leaving only a tattered hole and waving fabric where my wingtip had been a few seconds before. Instinctively, my first act was to turn my control wheel first left then right to test my aileron response. Everything worked. I was able once again to concentrate on the task of maintaining my proper position on tow.

Now the weather was getting even worse. Cloud cover was descending lower and lower, reducing visibility to patches of cloud banks. Once through a hole in the low cloud bank I caught a glimpse of a glider burning on the ground, about 500 feet below. For a moment I thought my tow pilot had found the landing zone were I could cut off and land; but that was not the case—nor was it destined to be. After frantically searching back and forth over Holland without success, the tow plane was so low on fuel there was nothing for it but to head back to England—some three hours flying time away.

Just before we reached the white cliffs of Dover we burst out of the murk and saw the tranquil, green countryside below. In the space of a few seconds we swept from murk and angry seas to a peaceful, serene countryside basking in the autumn sun—seemingly a million miles away from turmoil and war.

In a few minutes we were down at our base. My human cargo deplaned and left—no doubt thanking their lucky stars for their safe return.

My Group commander zipped out to the flight line and up to our glider. I told him my tow plane pilot couldn't find the LZ. He just looked at the tattered wingtip, shook his head, and walked off. The salvage crew came and looked over my bird—and found that in addition to the shattered wingtip, it was full of bullet holes from small arms fire. They just towed it off to the junk yard. (Ben Ward, glider pilot)

In spite of terrible weather and the German defenses, all the squadrons in the 53rd TC Wing performed very well indeed on this second Holland mission. When the final count was in, it showed that 428 out of the 450 gliders dispatched made it either in or very close to the 101st Division's landing zones.

If any of us needed convincing that the Holland invasion would not be a pushover, the Germans' ability to shoot down so many of our planes and gliders on the first two missions certainly erased all remaining overconfidence. The Wehrmacht were not about to give up and fall back again. While our own part of the operation at first seemed to be succeeding better than ever, the main objective, getting British armor across the Rhine in strength, began to slip from our grasp.

The first premonition of disaster we had came when we learned on September 18 that Horrocks' Guards Division had advanced only about six miles into Holland that first day, and was still six miles from the Eindhoven area when it stopped. For their tea break? we asked. It took them an entire additional day to travel six more miles; they did not join up with the 101st Airborne until the evening of D + 1. As yet we did not realize the problems that faced the British tanks working their way north up the narrow main highway—a road often banked by soft or even marshy shoulders that would not support their weight.

## Was there still a chance?

Before MARKET-GARDEN was a few hours old, it became obvious the British had made a terrible mistake in dropping their 1st Airborne Division too far away from the Arnhem bridge. British General Robert Urquhart, chosen over American objections as the commander of the British 1st Airborne, had no experience in airborne warfare. He let himself be talked into establishing his DZs and LZs six to eight miles west of Arnhem, near the little town of Oosterbeek, mainly because the RAF feared flak concentrations at Arnhem and at the Deelen airport would be more than they could handle.[16] Urquhart, it seems, vaguely understood that his troops might have a difficult time getting through Oosterbeek and over the seven or so miles to the Arnhem bridge before the Germans could consolidate a defense or blow the bridge; but he counted on his gliders bringing in enough armored jeeps to drive at least one battalion quickly into Arnhem.[17] It was a bad gamble. Because of unstable loading, the tow ropes of twenty-three of those gliders snapped shortly after takeoff, and seven more snapped before reaching the LZ, leaving Urquhart's reconnaissance troops the task of getting through Oosterbeek and reaching Arnhem on foot. Only about 500 British paratroopers made it into Arnhem on the north side of the bridge before the Germans cut the road between Oosterbeek and Arnhem.

South of Arnhem, the Dutch terrain itself favored the Germans. The British Guards essentially had to push all the way up from the Belgian border behind a "one-tank front"; all the Germans had to do was disable the leading vehicle and the whole column would grind to a halt while the tank or truck in trouble was

Re-supply: ammunition and supplies dropped at Nijmegen. (Courtesy USAMHI)

Richard Farnsworth and "Bull" Ryman with Dutch kids in Eindhoven.

pushed off the road. German flak units could lower their really formidable 88 mm flak guns—perhaps the most versatile big gun in use during World War II—all the way down to fire at tank and troop targets and, as artillery, could send their shells to distances as much as a mile away.

By D + 2, September 19, on many parts of the invasion route, the Germans were actually able to deploy a heavier weight of tanks and artillery than the Allies. Working either from the east or the west, the Germans cut all traffic in several places. Now the 101st and 82nd Airborne troopers—who had little artillery of their own—had to help the British 30 Corps infantry fight off the Germans on either side of the road. This was in addition to consolidating a hold on their own bridges and clearing the LZs and DZs for later airborne missions. Casualties to our airborne divisions began to mount at a ghastly rate. The worst aspect of "Hell's Highway"—as the airborne troopers now called the Eindhoven-Arnhem road—was that no amount of pleading on the part of our airborne liaison officers working with the British troops could convince the British commanders to push ahead regardless of casualties.

After MARKET-GARDEN ended, when accusations about who or what caused it to fail flew thick and fast between the British and the Americans, stories appeared claiming that the Germans knew where and when we were coming, and thus were able to mount such an effective defense. That also explained, we supposed at first, why the 9th and the 10th Waffen-SS Panzer Divisions, which were supposed to be far away, turned up within a few miles of MARKET-GARDEN objectives. But we know now from German sources that these veteran German armored divisions, battered and depleted after their retreat from France, had been sent into central Holland precisely became this was supposed to be a quiet zone where they could recuperate and refit. It was not lack of surprise that lost this battle. Certainly there were no massive German reception committees waiting for our paratroopers and glider troopers to land. Several of the key bridges were lightly defended.

There is a consensus among military historians that MARKET-GARDEN could be judged to have failed by the morning of D + 2, if not before. This was not the way it appeared to American soldiers and military leaders at the time.[18] On September 19, General Bedell Smith, Eisenhower's chief of staff, and General Floyd Parks, Brereton's chief of staff, were exchanging congratulatory messages.[19] We in the 81st TCS were about to set out on our third mission, another glider operation. At least some British troops, we knew, had won control of the north end of Arnhem bridge. While we were more and more apprehensive about the overall chances for MARKET-GARDEN (and for our own individual chances of survival), we certainly all believed that if the British Guards armor could reach Arnhem in time, the operation would be worth its costs.

It was only after the complete collapse of our own assault mission on that "Black Tuesday," September 19, that mentally, at least, we in our Squadron were defeated. But the Allied invasion of Holland, and our less and less significant part in it, was to persist for another six days.

## Notes

1. Devlin, *Paratrooper!*, p. 232.

2. McKee, p. 116.

3. Weigley says Marshall still believed airborne force was the trump card in the war, and "would not rest nor let Eisenhower forget his desires" until some test of deep vertical envelopment was launched. 1981, pp. 288–89.

4. Blair, *Ridgway*, pp. 319–21. See also Floyd Parks Papers, Sept. 9, 1944.

5. As it happened, D + 2 turned out to have such terrible weather that practically none of the gliders could be delivered. Brereton would not make the same mistake again; in the jump across the Rhine in March 1945 most of the gliders were carried double tow.

6. Farrar-Hockley, p. 36.

7. For example, Warren II, pp. 103–6. (Warren does not mete out praise uncritically.) See also Devlin, *Silent Wings*, p. 260, Huston, *Blue*, pp. 3–4, and many others.

8. Anstey, p. 33.

9. Rapport and Northwood, pp. 260, 272, 279.

10. Stoddard was killed; Gurecki miraculously survived his crash landing. Warren II, p. 103, mistakenly has Gurecki dying in that crash.

11. Warren II, p. 103; Ryan, *Bridge* p. 213; Rapport and Northwood, pp. 279–81.

12. Ammerman's exchange with his tow pilot on this mission is probably the experience that made the biggest impression on journalists and military historians of anything that happened to any member of our 81st TCS. It is recounted in Collier, 181, Dank, pp. 174–75, and several other works. It bothers Gale Ammerman very much that he never learned the name of his tow pilot.

13. Ridgway *Soldier*, p. 109.

14. These "northern/southern" route options can be confusing. Blair, *Ridgway*, pp. 336–37, mistakenly puts us on the "southern route." Cf. Warren II, p. 118.

15. Gliders did not have dinghies (inflatable life rafts); glider pilots and troopers were provided only with "Mae West" life jackets.

16. Collier, p. 179. Weigley, 1981, p. 306, also blames our General Paul Williams for arguing that the flak concentrations close to Arnhem were too dangerous for the troop carriers.

17. As it happened, the main problem for British 1st Airborne Division troopers in Oosterbeek was working their way through the overjoyed Dutch citizens who were convinced that their liberation was at hand and wanted to show their gratitude to the British soldiers.

18. Evidence of SHAEF's hopes that MARKET-GARDEN would bring about the collapse of the Wehrmacht is the ultra-secret plans for Operation TALISMAN, drawn up by mid-September, and slated "at very short notice" to use FAAA for planting airheads deep in Germany—at Berlin and the naval base of Kiel—in order to prevent chaos "by seizing control over the Nazi machinery and its records." SHAEF, "Operation TALISMAN," letter to General Brereton dated Sept. 26, 1944.

19. Floyd Parks Papers, Sept. 19, 1944, CBAMHI.

# 16. Falling Short
## The Tragic Outcome of the Holland Invasion

### An aborted mission

On the morning of D + 2, Tuesday, September 19, 1944, *two* MARKET-GARDEN crises had to be resolved immediately. At Nijmegen, the Germans had to be driven from the crucial bridge they still held over the Waal; and at Arnhem, the British paratroopers at the north end of the bridge somehow had to hold on until the larger force of paratroopers eight miles west (around Oosterbeek) forced their way through to them and to the tiny band of paratroopers who were inside Arnhem and trying to fight their way toward the southern end of the bridge. By nightfall, neither of these objectives had been won. And elsewhere, while some big Allied gains were registered, the German defenses were proving that they were building up enough force to be able to cut across "Hell's Highway" (the road from Eindhoven to Arnhem) in many places.

Unfortunately for MARKET, British 30 Corps commanders had determined not to risk high casualties; they inched their way forward whenever they ran up against any real (or even suspected) German resistance. They were thinking more about minimizing casualties than capturing objectives. Therefore everything depended on the ability of the American 101st and the 82nd Airborne units scattered along the invasion route to keep the main highway open for much longer than planned, while the British Household Cavalry and the Guards Armored troops made their cautious way northward toward Arnhem. In turn, this depended on troop carrier's ability to keep on operating day after day—and troop carrier depended on the weather. But the weather, already disappointing on D + 1, was turning worse and worse. On some of the airfields of the 50th and 52nd Wings in central England, the ceiling was down to a few hundred feet early in the morning, virtually suicidal for any glider formation assembly. For us and other squadrons on 53rd TCW airfields, further to the south in England, the weather was not quite so bad—but definitely not at all good. And reports of deteriorating weather over the Channel and the North Sea, and even over Belgium, made the outlook for operating successfully on D + 2 very, very doubtful.

In the 81st Squadron, on September 19, we were already on edge because of the loss of John Webster's plane and crew the day before. We were slated to tow gliders loaded with artillery and supplies (mainly ammunition) into the Eindhoven area. Takeoff, originally slated for the morning, was postponed in hopes that flying conditions would improve. They did not. Our Group briefing was short and scary. We learned about the fog and clouds over the Channel and about the build-up of German flak batteries. We would fly the "southern route" as on September 17; but this time, instead of going over Belgium via the shortest route to the Eindhoven area, we would fly to the British-held salient at the Albert Canal and then, turning straight north, fly right up "Hell's Highway" toward LZ "W." This would keep us as far as possible from areas controlled by the Germans.

Now Adriel Williams, our Group CO, addressed the glider pilots. Most of them, again, would be without co-pilots. In view of the worsening weather, Williams said, he would not compel any man to pilot a glider who doubted his ability to make it to Holland under these conditions. But only a few of the Group's glider pilots took advantage of this disquieting offer.

Nine of our planes were scheduled to fly in our Group's first serial, and nine in the second. We all took off and managed to meet up at the assembly point in fairly good order. But the weather closed in rapidly even before we could reach the Channel. By the time the nine planes of our second serial took their place at the tag end of the 53rd TCW's formation, they were flying through a virtually solid cloud bank all the way. The pilots persisted, nevertheless, until they were some distance over the Channel. There IX Troop Carrier Command, learning that the weather over the Lowlands was also deteriorating dangerously, sent this second serial a recall message.

It was with mixed feelings that the tow plane crews and glider pilots of our second serial began to turn around and come back to Membury. Since we were the last serial in this invasion, we knew that the odds had been that we would suffer the worst from German flak and small-arms fire. At the same time we had to live with the thought that we were letting down the 101st Airborne troopers who were fighting a very tough battle.

Only nineteen of the eighty-one gliders in all of our 436th Group reached the LZ that day.[1]

We had to wait until several hours after we landed before we learned about the frightful flying conditions that had faced our first serial—and about the tragic loss of several of our men.

In spite of terrible flying conditions, most of our first serial bulled its way through the clouds over the Channel and into Belgium. But by the time they got to Belgium, the weather had turned so rough that six gliders had to cut loose

Darlyle Watters and Herb Christie pose near Watters' glider *Jeanie II* before our third mission into Holland.

Gliders, their tow ropes snaked along the ground, wait for hookup to the tow planes. Notice the ties fixing the telephone cord from plane to glider onto the tow rope.

right there; and one was brought all the way back to England. Only two of our gliders in this serial reached LZ "W."[2]

Ed Vosika was one of several tow pilots that day who did their best to pull their gliders to LZ "W" in spite of the fact that their planes were badly hit or even burning. After turning his burning plane back into Belgium to try jumping his crew over friendly territory, Vosika changed his mind and turned back toward Holland. As we shall see, however, at this point the glider pilot, Adelore Chevalier, reckoned he had had enough of this nonsense and cut off from Vosika's burning plane.

> At the time of our third mission during the Holland invasion, the front lines on the ground were very fluid; on our flight you would pass over friendly areas to enemy held territory and back again. We took our first hits before the drop zone. Our wing man [pilot flying on Vosika's wing] told us we were on fire. I made a 180 [degree turn] to get back to friendly territory; but then I decided that since the gliders were still on, they needed to get to the landing zone—and I made another 180. We started to turn back when I got the report the glider had released; but our wing man told us to get our asses out—the fire was getting worse.[3] The navigator, crew chief, and radio operator jumped. My co-pilot [Martin Jacobson] got out of his seat; but, bless him, he said he was not going to jump until he saw me coming back toward the open door. The first three men were taken prisoner. But my co-pilot and I landed among some Dutch people who got us over to an area controlled by British soldiers. On the way to the ground in our chutes we had been clay pigeons for Germans on the ground. We saw our plane explode before it hit the ground.
>
> The British were very nice to us, and gave us tea every afternoon, while they stopped the war for a while. They told us we would have to wait to be evacuated till things settled down a bit. Finally we were able to hitch rides back to Brussels, where we stayed a few days trying to arrange rides to our base in England. We arrived ten days after we jumped. (Ed Vosika, pilot)

The three men in Vosika's crew captured by the Germans were Howard Johnson, navigator, Willis Shumake, crew chief, and Warren Runyan, radio operator.

> On September 19 I flew my glider by myself. The weather on that day wasn't fit for a dog. The haze and soup were so thick that planes ahead and to the sides of us disappeared completely. Then even our tow ship faded from sight.
>
> The weather cleared somewhat when we neared our target. But not a

single fighter escort did we see. Antiaircraft and machine guns started banging away right under us. What an awful racket! I pulled myself into the smallest space possible and just waited for the shock. And I prayed. I had a prayer just six words long, and I kept saying it over and over. . . .

Just then I saw three men diving out of our tow ship door, right down into enemy hands. I found out later there was a fire in that plane's cabin. From the glider, I could see the tow-ship get hit again. A shell (20 mm, I think) tore a big hole in its right aileron. But the two pilots stuck to the ship—thank God. They poured on the coal full blast, and went into a climb and a turn away from our target LZ.

At last, we were far enough away from the battleground so that the shooting stopped. Those good old tug pilots had pulled us to safety.

Then the tow-ship burst into flame. Two men, obviously the pilots, went out the door. That's all, brother! That airplane was not only on fire, it was empty. No use hanging on any longer! So I hit the release, the rope popped away, and I whipped that glider around in a U-turn, setting a compass course southwest, away from enemy lines. I just kept on going; the further I could glide, the better.

I was doing a free glide in the general direction of Paris. If I had been high enough, I might have landed on the Champs Elysées, or something. As it was, with the help of a tail wind, I did about eleven or twelve miles.

The heavy flak suit was cramping my style, so I jerked it off. When I had put it on half an hour before, it was a warning to the eleven men with me that things would soon get hot. Now that I was taking it off, they could see they were in a different kind of danger. They were eleven tough fighting men; but right then they were as helpless as babes. Everything depended on the glider pilot.

Eventually our altitude did run out. Now was the time to pick a landing spot. There was a little town just below with a church steeple poking up rather high. I picked a likely spot right alongside the town and proceeded to make a landing pattern, doing a 360 degree turn right over the town. It was easy to see the many faces turned up to watch us. I've made better landing patterns and better landings; but we eventually ended up in a good spot.

Doors and emergency doors in the glider popped open; and twelve men piled out like all hell had busted loose. People standing nearby were pretty scared! I waved the "come here" sign at the nearest man. He came over, a little slow at first. Indicating the whole neighborhood with a sweep of my arm, I asked, "German, German?" A smile spread across his face, and he came back with a shake of the head, saying "Belgique, Belgique!" By this time the people and kids were coming on the run from all directions. Some of the airborne GIs then proceeded to shake my hand and congratulate me on a good job of flying. (Adelore Chevalier, glider pilot)

In our Squadron's first serial of nine planes and gliders, disaster overtook four of our pilots, three glider pilots, two navigators, two crew chiefs, and two radio operators. Of these thirteen, eight were casualties: one pilot and one navigator were killed; one glider pilot was cut off over hostile territory, wounded, and thrown into a German POW camp; the navigator, crew chief, and radio operator in Vosika's plane also were captured; one glider pilot was killed at Eindhoven; and another died ditching in the Channel. Eight men had to bail out of burning planes.

Killed in action were Charles Stevenson, one of our flight leaders, and his navigator, Kenneth Okeson. Soon after Stevenson's plane was hit, other pilots spotted three men jumping and reported that they could see three chutes opening. Then a fourth man jumped out, either Stevenson or Okeson; but this chute did not open in time. Several days later, a glider pilot returning to England reported that while he was guarding German prisoners set to work digging graves, he had seen the graves of Charles Stevenson and Kenneth Okeson. The three men from this crew who jumped safely—Robert Moore, co-pilot; Clinton Perry, crew chief; and Lawrence Borland, radio operator—were listed as missing in action. These three all landed on Allied-held territory, and within a few days they were back in Membury.

Darlyle Watters, whose glider in this first serial was being towed by our Squadron commander, David Brack, was cut off over Holland. Watters was captured by Germans. This was another serious loss to our Squadron, since Watters was Squadron Glider Officer and had important responsibilities for handling glider operations.

My glider is named *Jeanie II*, after my wife; *Jeanie I* had been the Horsa we took into Normandy on D-Day. Brack taxies out slowly, and I line up carefully behind him. He applies power, the rope comes up off the ground, stretches, and up comes my glider tail. I get good rudder control; just a short roll on the runway and our glider is in the air.

During our briefing, weather had been discussed: some clouding was reported, but it did not sound too bad. And all the way to the English Channel there were no surprises. But when we got up to the Channel: Oops! Lots of clouds. No change of heading: we go right into that cloud bank. Surely it will clear up soon! Brack disappears; I fly according to the "angle of dangle" of the eight or ten feet of tow rope still visible. Twenty or thirty seconds later Brack shows up without having deviated. Damn, he is one good pilot! Hurry up and line up neatly behind him. Into the clouds again.

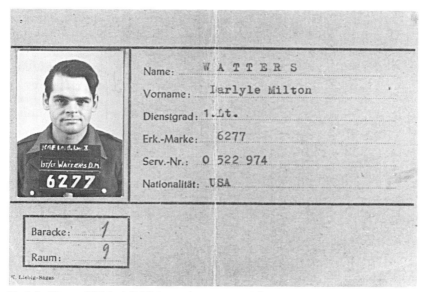

Darlyle Watters' "Kriegie" (*Kriegsgefangener*) or POW card, issued when he was captured during the Holland invasion.

The tow plane's view of gliders and parachutes down on the invasion fields near Zon, Holland.

A minute or two and Brack once more appears. Line up carefully again. The weather is getting worse. Brack climbs ever so gently then disappears, to appear again two minutes later. Now we go down, down, down, gently; now we can see water—we're right on the deck! But clouds this low over the Channel are no better, just more dangerous. A gentle climb, then Brack apparently decides to toughen it out, go straight through the clouds.

Did Brack turn off our intercom? Haven't heard a peep from him since the phone was checked prior to takeoff.

My "co-pilot" is a 1st Lt. from the 101st Airborne. He hasn't said a word; and it's always too noisy to hear what the airborne kids in the cargo area are saying. No doubt those glider troopers all think this is just another flight to us, and not the most difficult one I have ever been in, by far.

Now we are over Belgium and miraculously, the cloud bank disappears. Just like that—no clouds! It is a clear day: not bright, but clear enough. I think: Probably I could not spit right now. All that concentration had really drained me dry.

Now we are crossing the enemy line at around 500 feet. Fifty miles to go. Looks like we have it made!

But now, about twenty-five miles to go, Brack's plane is beginning to catch flak. He takes two hits in his left wing, and then I count at least three more in his fuselage from front to back. I notice that both his engines, however, are still running—thank God! That German gun zeroing in on us is in a patch of woods right ahead. Where the hell is our fighter cover? Gone back home, I guess. I push my steel helmet lower over my eyes and hunch forward in my seat.

All of a sudden the tow rope comes off Brack's plane and snaps back at me! An abort! The rope must have snapped, or been hit by that flak, I think. I automatically hit my rope release and the tow rope disappears. We are now in free flight somewhere over German territory.

Just when I begin to slow down I receive a direct hit from that gun in those woods. The flak comes up from an angle to my right and it slams straight into the airborne lieutenant in my co-pilot's seat. He slumps over and I see he is either badly wounded or dead. A piece of that explosive shell grazes my neck: the burning sensation really wakes me up, and I realize that straight and level flight just then is not what the doctor ordered. I do everything but loop in slowing the glider down. I make two turns, put my approach leg parallel to a deep ditch where maybe we can hide. Although my evasive actions saves us from more direct hits, I can hear exploding flak continually, quite close to *Jeanie II* all the way to the ground.

Everyone out! Two steps, and here we are in that ditch. My idea was to go up this ditch to another, then down toward those woods where that flak gun was still working over our other planes and gliders. But according to the book I am now nothing but a private. The S/Sgt. squad leader is in charge. The order is, "Dump packs, be prepared to fight!" We bob and run across an open field toward another ditch, with me taking up the rear. Safe in that ditch, I glance back toward the glider. I see a German beginning to look it over. But just as he comes into my gun sights I decide not to shoot. Maybe that airborne lieutenant in the co-pilot's seat is still alive and can be saved by German medics.

We are in the ditch for about ten minutes, the S/Sgt. at one end and me at the other. Then we hear the command: "Surrender!" We all look up; nothing but Luegers pointing straight down at us from ten or fifteen feet away! I notice the Germans who took us are wearing their garrison caps, not their steel helmets—that's how far behind the front lines we are! Out of the ditch and get searched for weapons.

Back at our Membury briefing we had discussed whether we should wear paratrooper boots. We were told not to wear them. The logic was that Germans were known to shoot paratroopers on the spot. We were issued rough leather boots with two buckles on the side so we could blouse up our pants.

Now the Germans march us up to a brick wall—are we headed for execution? But they lead us right on by that wall, then stop—another search, this time for souvenirs. They get my watch and Zippo lighter, but not my 45 pistol—I had buried that in the mud of the ditch when we surrendered. And I did manage to hide the gold ring my wife Jean had given me. (Darlyle Watters, Squadron Glider Officer. For other aspects of Darlyle's experiences at this time see Chapters 10 and 22.)

Darlyle ended up in Stalag Luft no. 1; and there he found our John Webster, captured during the previous day's mission.

The second glider pilot lost was Emory Fry, killed somewhere near Eindhoven—none of us are sure just how. The third glider pilot we lost was Edward Griffen, who was killed this day of disasters when he ditched in the Channel. In some ways this death was the hardest of all for his friends in the Squadron, since it was a misfortune that turned into a tragedy.

I happened to be one of the glidermen in our squad who was forced to ditch in the Channel on our way to Holland. Our pilot told us something was wrong. Our glider and tow rope were ahead of our tow craft. Somehow due to clouds and fog the flight had slowed down to 100 miles per hour and our glider was still moving along at 120. The pilot tried everything he could to get us back of the plane because he thought the towline would catch in the propellers; and then there was silence until we were told to start heaving our equipment out and prepare for ditching. The pilot estimated we were about forty miles from the coast. As we circled, God must have been with us, because the pilot and our squad sergeant saw an Air-Sea Rescue ship coming toward us. The pilot brought us down tail first and the glider plopped down to the nose and wings when the English boat handed out a boat hook to us. We started counting heads and one was missing. It was the pilot. He was found in his seat and brought to the wing. A medic on the rescue boat said he was dead and thought the pilot had died of a broken neck. He saved our lives by proper ditching procedures and yet lost his life in doing so. God bless his soul! (Pfc. George Kempf, 327th Glider Infantry Regiment, 101st Airborne Division)[4]

The most ghastly disaster of that "Black Tuesday," September 19, happened not to our Squadron but to our sister Squadron, the 82nd TCS. And it happened at Membury, not over Holland. Two 82nd Squadron glider pilots, Kenneth Hinkel and Adolf Riscky, previously good friends, allowed the tensions of the time and "a fairly large bottle of Beefeater gin" to entangle them in a vicious brawl. They became the worst of enemies. On D + 2, when the second serial of our 436th Group had to abort and return with its gliders to Membury, these two were maneuvering for a landing dangerously close to each other. Suddenly they slammed their gliders together and plunged to the ground not far from our base infirmary. Hinkel and Riscky killed each other—and six glider troopers too.[5]

Serials that left earlier than our two did somewhat better. Taking all the 53rd Wing's planes together (for this operation the 442nd Group, from the 50th Wing, was attached to the 53rd), our Wing had started out with 385 gliders. In addition to our own recalled serial, several gliders had to cut loose over the Channel near the English coast but made it back to England. No less than seventeen, however, had to ditch in the Channel. Miraculously, Air-Sea Rescue picked up most of these ditched pilots and their passengers. Of those which made it as far as Belgium, more than thirty gliders broke loose or had to cut loose. But the troopers, jeeps, and supplies in the remaining 209 gliders that managed to land someplace near the Eindhoven region amounted to a godsend for Maxwell Taylor's harassed 101st Airborne troopers.[6]

Once again, several pilots of the 53rd TCW sacrificed themselves to bring their gliders into the LZ area. A total of seventeen 53rd C-47s were shot down. Thirty-six gliders were confirmed as either shot down or missing.

Meanwhile, in the Nijmegen area of Holland, which was the responsibility of the 50th and 52nd TC Wings, the situation was even more desperate than around Eindhoven. One of General Gavin's 82nd Airborne regiments had failed to take the Waal River bridge the previous day. But September 19 started well: British tanks near Eindhoven crossed the patched-up Zon bridge and, finding the road in front of them free of Germans, made a dash for the town of Grave, about three-fourths of the way to Nijmegen. But from there on only a few tanks, using back roads, were able to reach the Waal River and begin operations with 82nd Division troopers to capture that bridge. Tragically this attempt, too, failed.

On September 19, Gavin got practically no help from airborne operations. All of the gliders and tugs dispatched by the 50th and 52nd Wings were turned back by impossibly dense clouds; they all landed in England. In Gavin's mind, the shortage of troopers caused by the bad weather required him to put about 450 glider pilots into the line, "an expedient," he reports with masterful understatement, "that aroused no one's enthusiasm." [7] A few re-supply sorties were made by planes of these Wings from 53rd Wing airfields where the takeoff weather, at least, was slightly better; but four-fifths of the bundles they tried to deliver to the 82nd Airborne ended up in the hands of the Germans.

In one of the few errors the Germans made during the Holland invasion, they failed to blow up the Nijmegen bridge over the Waal River even after this second attempt. But the Allies were not able to seize the bridge until D + 3, Wednesday, when a heroic band of 82nd Division troopers rowed across the Waal River in the face of a hail of machine gun bullets and attacked the bridge from the north. [8]

Around Arnhem, the situation for the British 1st Airborne Division on D + 2 was turning from bad to hopeless. British paratroopers at Oosterbeek failed to force their way through to the rapidly dwindling remnants of their comrades inside the town and north of the Arnhem bridge.

This was the day British General "Boy" Browning and General Louis Brereton, CG of the First Allied Airborne Army, had planned to drop the Polish Independent Parachute Brigade on the south end of the Arnhem bridge. One hundred fourteen planes were lined up in Britain ready to go on that mission— which everybody could see represented possibly the last chance we would get to storm across the Lower Rhine.

But the weather on British airfields was so bad, on September 19, that there was no way the planes for this Polish paratrooper mission could get off the ground. The entire mission had to be scrubbed. A re-supply mission did fly that day to Arnhem but succeeded in getting only a tiny fraction of its bundles to the British.

## MARKET-GARDEN falls to pieces

On Wednesday, September 20, D + 3 in Holland, FAAA ordered another huge delivery of troopers and supplies—weather permitting. But the weather turned worse. Once again, the airfields of the 50th and 52nd TC Wings in central England were almost completely socked in. Their operations were postponed; and, as the day wore on, it became obvious the clouds and fog were going to get even thicker right through the evening. Once again, the crucial flight of the Polish Brigade to the Arnhem area was postponed twenty-four hours. Once again, the glider missions to the Nijmegen area were postponed twenty-four hours.

But on the airfields of our 53rd TC Wing, further to the south in England, the weather was slightly better. We had been scheduled to re-supply the 101st Airborne, dropping our bundles to the same DZ "W" as before; but because the 82nd Airborne was in much more danger, we were sent instead to DZ "O," in the 82nd Division's region. Though it was hardly any consolation, this mission of ours went down in the records as "a complete success." The 436th Group sent out eighty-four planes, eighteen from our Squadron; for the most part our Squadron was carrying ammunition. The weather was so bad that it was impossible to maintain formation; but, singly or in small groups, we all made our IP south of Eindhoven; and we all delivered our door bundles and pararacks to the 82nd troopers in the Nijmegen area. All eighteen of us in the 81st TCS came back, most with only minor damage. But unknown to one pilot, a tire of his plane had been shot out; and on landing he careened across the runway and slammed so hard into another plane that his left engine was knocked clean off. By great good fortune, the planes involved in this collision did not catch fire.

Later reports on this re-supply mission on D + 3 bore out our feelings that we had done well. Since none of the British supply trucks had yet gotten through to the 82nd Airborne, our parachuted bundles were desperately needed. It was true that only 60 percent of the TC Wing's bundles landed right on the money (the problem here was that door bundles, as usual, took more time to push out than was required to drop the pararacks from underneath the planes). But the 82nd Airborne's observers reported that eventually about 80 percent of the 53rd Wing's drop was recovered, some with the help of the truly admirable Dutch Resistance.

When September 21 dawned, it became obvious that the weather in the Netherlands would remain just as bad as ever. And now, to add to the general misery, the fog and clouds were thicker around our 53rd TC Wing airfields as well. The weather over the Lowlands was reported as improving; but in our own area of south central England, even if we had been able to take off and assemble, returning and landing safely would have been impossible. In the 81st Squadron, we did no flying at all either this day or the next (Thursday and Friday).

By now the increasingly well-organized Wehrmacht defenders were able to cut across "Hell's Highway" virtually anywhere they chose to mount an offensive, including the areas we held most strongly in the southern part of the salient.[9] The 101st Airborne was now completely on the defensive, performing like a fire brigade threatened by one flash point after another. On Thursday, September 21, the FAAA launched a desperation mission by the 314th and 315th Groups. They were ordered to deliver at least some of the Polish Brigade paratroopers to a point south of the Rhine, near the beleaguered British 1st Airborne. This day not only bad weather plagued the mission. In the 314th Group over the North Sea, a radio operator on a flight leader's plane received a coded message he was unable to decipher; his pilot, assuming (incorrectly) it was a recall message, turned back to England—followed by ten other C-47s in this serial.

Meanwhile, at the Spanhoe base of the 315th TC Group, the clouds were so thick that the planes had to climb up to 10,000 feet before they could assemble—an astonishing operational altitude for a troop carrier mission. Many of them, unable to find their formations, gave up and returned to base.[10] The rest did drop their Polish troopers fairly close to the target, a skillful as well as a courageous performance.

Also on D + 4, some British Dakotas and converted Stirling bombers of the British 46 and 38 Groups set out on another desperation mission to re-supply the British 1st Airborne. This time the Luftwaffe, dodging fighter escorts, demonstrated what might have happened to all of us in our slow and unarmored transport planes if we had not had overwhelming air superiority. A Luftwaffe fox got right in among the chickens; of ten planes in one string of Stirlings, seven were shot down. In all, twenty-three out of 117 planes sent out on this re-supply mission did not return, and many others were so badly damaged they were good for nothing but salvage.

In sharpest contrast to the brave performance of British airmen over Arnhem, British tank commanders down on "Hell's Highway" during D + 3 and D + 4 refused to move until their supporting infantry could clear out German antitank guns that menaced them.[11] Even more agonizing was the performance of British 43rd Wessex Division truck drivers, who refused to pull over onto the shoulders of the highway when priority traffic needed to come through: the drivers claimed they were in too much danger from German mines planted beside the roadway.[12]

On September 22, D + 5 in the Holland invasion, decent flying weather finally returned to northwest Europe. A huge glider mission with almost 3,000 troopers made it into the 82nd drop zones. The 436th TC Group sent forty planes to re-supply the 101st Airborne (none from our Squadron). This re-supply mission counted as a combat mission; but nobody reported seeing even a single burst of flak or a single tracer bullet. Next day, Saturday, the British trucks and tanks began, finally, to pour up the road from Eindhoven and dash across the Nijmegen bridge. Apparently one more effort would be made to reach the British 1st Airborne Division airhead north of the Rhine. But we all had the feeling the high brass was only going through the motions, unable to admit that MARKET-GARDEN was dead.

As if to underscore what harm can come from a combination of bad luck and poor planning, the assault boats supposed to take the forward British and Polish troopers across the Rhine could not make it up that accursed highway. And the weather turned bad again. But "it's an ill wind . . ."; the pouring rain that fell Sunday night enabled the pitiful remnants of the British 1st Airborne north of the Lower Rhine to slip back across to safety—leaving their wounded behind them.

In spite of great feats of courage by individuals in the British 1st Airborne, it had been so decimated—and so humiliated—that the British Army did not re-equip it and decided to break up its remaining units.

And after Holland, "Boy" Browning was removed from FAAA and sent to India. It's a good guess the high brass in our American airborne forces were not sorry to see him go.

### Did troop carrier fail the test?

Before the end of September 1944, in fact, only a few days after our last MAR-KET-GARDEN mission, we were again flying evacuation missions. Once again, as during late August, we flew all over the map. These flights were so different from one another there were really no typical "evac missions." They signaled the fact that we were out of the invasion business. We were back in the air transport business. In fact, FAAA now "withdrew its commitment" to MAR-KET-GARDEN. All that remained was to argue over what it all had meant. For weeks afterward, the main topic of conversation (besides girls and home) was what Adriel Williams called "that son-of-a-bitch operation."

> We took more casualties than we did in any other operation—not so many as some other Groups, but it was pretty rough. In Cornelius Ryan's book *A Bridge Too Far*, he describes the way Colonel Robert Sink, commander of the 506th Parachute Infantry Regiment, was standing in the jump door and saw some flak take off part of the wingtip of the plane—and leave the rest of the wingtip dangling there.[13] Well, that was my plane. I led all my Group's Holland missions. They got worse every day.
>
> I don't know why the British didn't try harder to get up that "airborne carpet" to Arnhem; I've heard that at one point they delayed because they

were busy drinking tea. Maybe so. One thing I do know is that I got really hot with frustration as the operation went along.

Even though I was just a young Air Force officer at the time, with no high command experience, I knew—really knew—that stopping Patton's sweep toward Germany and getting ready for MARKET-GARDEN was a terrible mistake. I talked with some of Patton's staff; in fact, before the Holland invasion Patton's G-4 [supply chief] was on one of those forward airfields when we were bringing in the last of that gasoline we freighted to him. He and I had a long conversation and he told me that Patton was absolutely livid and was convinced that this bad decision would prolong the war.

But it was a political decision. The British seemed to think it was necessary to go along with Montgomery's egotistical need to invade on the front he controlled. This meant we had to fly in our airborne to areas in which, we found out later, many Panzer units had been moved. (Adriel Williams, 436th Group commander)

Arguments over the failure of the Holland invasion continued all through the rest of the war and many years thereafter. British Field Marshal Bernard Montgomery, overall commander of MARKET-GARDEN, put the main blame on the weather. We blamed Montgomery (for terrible weaknesses in the plan) and British Generals Miles Dempsey and Brian Horrocks, in charge of British 30 Corps GARDEN forces (for its weak execution on the ground). More objective military historians have compiled long lists of factors that contributed to the failure, trying to demonstrate that no one cause explains the final result.

MARKET-GARDEN is a well-analyzed, not to say over-analyzed set of events. There is no need to rehash all the sophisticated arguments that have been made in support of one analyst's position or another's.[14] But from our own Squadron's point of view, two essential points should be made. First, whatever faults certain writers find in troop carrier's performance, the overwhelming consensus is that when you take all the circumstances into consideration, troop carrier not only performed well, it performed brilliantly.[15] Second, any excuses made for the failure of British 30 Corps armor and foot soldiers to reach Arnhem in time are more than overbalanced by the many reports of over-cautious, self-serving actions on their part.

One particularly damning example comes from Matthew Ridgway's autobiography, *Soldier*. Ridgway, who was overall commander of the FAAA airborne soldiers, flew to Eindhoven on D + 2 and tried to make his way up the main highway to the Nijmegen area to the 82nd Airborne, which he had commanded until promoted to head XVIII Corps.

A few miles up the road we came up with the advance elements of British armor. There a junior officer stopped me and told me I could go no further because the road in front was swept with small-arms fire. So we stopped a minute to watch how our good British comrades would take out this resistance. They had the muzzles of their tank guns pointed down the road toward where the enemy was supposed to be, but not a shot was being fired. . . .

Having no command responsiblity for this operation, however, I couldn't order this tank commander to move on down the road. So, after waiting about forty minutes, and seeing no visible effort being made to outflank this resistance. . . . I took Dan Faith [Ridgway's aide] and Casey [his bodyguard], and we started walking down the ditch along the side of the road. We went a mile and a half, perhaps, with every sense alert, but not a shot was fired at us. . . .

We moved until we found General Max Taylor, at the CP [command post] of the 101st Division. I then sent back . . . for my jeep, and went on for another couple of miles until I found General Gavin [now the CO of the 82nd].[16]

After September, with our most recent combat assignment behind us, we began to come to grips with the fact that there was no longer any hope the war soon would be over. This unhappy prospect, plus the loss of several of our men, made the atmosphere in the Squadron much more grim than during the previous spring and summer. On rainy October days, grousing and arguing in our barracks, we could not help but wonder whether part of the failure could be laid at troop carrier's doorstep.

During the fall of 1944, both British and American commanders who had had some responsibility in MARKET-GARDEN, responding to questions from high command, gave their assessments of the campaign, and added their suggestions of how we could take advantage of our experiences in Holland to improve future airborne invasions. What was at stake here, of course, were the possible uses of the airborne arm in the coming invasions not only in Germany but also in Japan. Many long and carefully detailed statements on troop carrier performance were compiled, plus suggestions for possible reform of its structure and tactics. At first top secret, these critiques later were deposited in military archives, and they are now open to military historians—who, of course, have continued the arguments begun right after the end of MARKET-GARDEN.[17]

The most chewed-over aspect of such critiques concerns the possibility of the better use of glider pilots once they got down on the ground. This is a point I shall examine in some detail in the next chapter. Another important question raised in these critiques was whether we had been forced to fly too long a distance during MARKET-GARDEN. From Membury to Eindhoven you needed three hours each way—three and a half to four hours if you had a glider attached to your tail. If the distances had been shorter, every troop carrier outfit might have been able to pull two missions per day during the first two days when the weather was decent.

By the same token, could at least some troop carrier groups have been moved to recently liberated airfields in France during August? Perhaps—but this, of course, would have been difficult if not impossible for those of us just returning from the invasion of southern France. And besides, the relatively few airfields available in France were all being tenaciously preempted by fighter and fighter-bomber groups, which wanted them for protecting bomber formations on their way to Germany. Only Hap Arnold could have put troop carrier in France before running MARKET-GARDEN; and he ruled otherwise.

A host of other, more minor criticisms and suggested improvements surfaced during the fall of 1944. Several observers severely criticized the RAF Second Tactical Air Force for not giving more support to troop carrier missions by blasting German flak positions. Everyone chided Brereton for gambling on three consecutive days of flyable weather. Rather superfluously, everybody demanded more reliable weather forecasting. Many observers wanted tighter and better communications between liaison officers on the ground and arriving troop carrier mission commanders, so as to divert the transports away from unexpectedly hot flak concentrations.

There is one significant point in the analysis of MARKET-GARDEN that was easier to accept after the war than during it. This is the truly outstanding performance of German soldiers in Holland—in what most of them, by that time, must have realized was a losing cause.[18] Both Montgomery's dashing but faulty plan and Patton's aim of going through the Siegfried Line "like shit through a goose" were based on the assumption that the forces Germany could muster in September were tired, poorly supplied, dispirited, and few in number. This was a gross miscalculation. Today, unlike 1944, it is possible for us to admit that the Germans outfought, out-maneuvered, and out-generaled *both* the heavily armored British Guards Division and the three lightly-armed airborne divisions—not to mention the other infantry in Horrock's command. To be blunt about it, MARKET-GARDEN was a great German victory.[19]

One of the most intriguing speculations about MARKET-GARDEN concerns the capture by the Germans, on D-Day, of a complete set of operational orders for MARKET-GARDEN. These orders were retrieved from a downed glider close to German General Kurt Student's HQ; and General Walther Model soon had a copy. Some historians believe the capture of these documents—an incident so effectively dramatized in Ryan's *A Bridge Too Far* and the movie based on it—was crucial, because this allowed the Germans to anticipate the major Allied thrusts and so helped to foil them. Others believe this piece of luck in no way helps explain the Germans' success; we know now that Model placed very little faith in these captured documents and even suspected they might be a "plant"; and in any case, the direction and goals of the Allied push were so transparent as soon as MARKET-GARDEN began that no such captured documents were needed to show the Germans what they had to do.[20]

It goes against the grain to admit that German soldiers fought so long and so superbly in defense of a despicable regime like that of the Nazis, and at the bidding of a fanatical dictator who, by late 1944, was half mad. Some military historians therefore try to explain away German performance during MARKET-GARDEN by emphasizing the lucky movement of the 9th and 10th Waffen-SS Panzer Divisions to the Arnhem area.[21] But many other German units also fought well. These included bits and pieces of broken regiments wearily making their way back from France, and a few battalions recently returned from the Russian front, as well as groups of sailors, Luftwaffe airmen, military and civilian police, and even construction workers, conscripted teenage boys, men in their forties and fifties, and barely convalescent soldiers. These units were scraped together, put under the command of a small number of fit, battle-hardened, first class troops, and hustled off to the Arnhem region and to "Hell's Highway."[22] One U. S. officer on the scene was reported as saying "We've seen everything now except the Hitler Maidens."[23] The generalship of this defensive effort, the work of Walther Model and Kurt Student, must be characterized as brilliant.

One story coming out of MARKET-GARDEN concerns Brian Horrocks, commander of British 30 Corps, just before D-Day in Holland. Addressing his assembled officers for the main briefing, Horrocks said, "Gentlemen, this is a tale you will tell your grandchildren!" Then, sensing from the embarrassed reaction of his audience that he might have sounded too pompous, he tried to pass it off as a joke by adding, "And mighty bored they'll be!"

Would this great operation, with all it meant to us, have succeeded if Horrocks' officers had been less concerned with trying to make sure they would indeed have grandchildren? Would the assault have gotten us across the Lower Rhine if it had been launched two weeks earlier—while the Germans were still hopelessly disorganized? Would the bloodshed of the massive battles yet to be fought in the late fall and winter of 1944–45 have been spared us if Urquhart's men had dropped close to Arnhem bridge instead of seven miles away? Would the revenge the Germans visited on the pro-Allied Dutch, and much of the extermination work in the death camps, have been cut short if the weather had been fair on D + 2? These are matters about which we can only fantasize. What we know for a fact is that after D + 2 the initiative on the battlefield went over to the Germans.

At the end, the Allies pulled back completely from Arnhem and erected defensive lines north of Nijmegen. All that MARKET-GARDEN had brought us was a 50-mile-long bulge into Holland—going nowhere.

One aspect of MARKET-GARDEN's aftermath that particularly grated on our nerves were the statements, publicized in *Yank*, the American Forces Network radio, *Stars and Stripes*, and many civilian newspapers, that tried to put the best possible face on our defeat. Montgomery brazenly declared that the operation had been "90 percent successful." General Brereton said that the 101st and 82nd, at least, "had fought their hearts out and whipped hell out of the Germans." The 500 or so men of the British 1st Airborne Division were virtually treated as heroes, their stand trumpeted as "a great drama of which all of us should be proud." Such statements were so beside the point that they were greeted with bursts of well-deserved obscenity.

Frustration, grief, fear, anger—all these sensations come boiling to the surface when we in the 81st TCS, once again, argue over the agony that was MARKET-GARDEN. It is not easy, even today, to know how this campaign should be viewed. I feel the best summation was proposed way back in 1956 by John Warren, who wrote the official—but far from partisan—history of airborne warfare in World War II.

When all is said, it is not the monumental size nor the operational intricacies of MARKET that linger longest in the memory. It is the heroism of the men who flew burning, disintegrating planes over their zones as coolly as if on review and gave their lives to get the last trooper out, the last bundle dropped. It is the stubborn courage of the airborne troops who would not surrender though an army came against them. In the sense that both troop carrier crews and airborne troops did all that men could do, there was, as Gavin said, no failure in MARKET.[24]

### Notes

1. The recalled second serial numbered forty-three out of the Group's eighty-one planes. 436th TCG hist. narr. for Sept.–Oct., 1944.

2. Four planes and gliders from the 79th TCS made it to LZ "W."

3. After the war, in a letter to Vosika, Adelore Chevalier, the glider pilot Vosika was towing, reported that Vosika's plane "started burning like a torch under the fuselage. I also saw them knock a hole in your right wing about three feet in diameter. Those 20 millimeter slugs were mean" (written Aug. 31, 1984).

4. From a recollection kindly shown me by George Koskimaki; this recollection will appear in his forthcoming book on the Holland invasion, *Hell's Highway*.

316    *Falling Short*

5. Dank, pp. 170, 187–88; see also Devlin, *Silent Wings*, pp. 266–67.

6. "Graphic History of the 101st Airborne Division," Annex no. 4, p. 2. See also HQ XVIII Corps, "Report of Airborne Phase 'Market'," Dec. 4, 1944.

7. Gavin, 1979, p. 313. Warren II, p. 133, also reports that on the night of D + 3, 185 glider pilots had to be hurried into the line to support the 505th PIR around the town of Mook.

8. This is the episode so brilliantly narrated by Cornelius Ryan in his book *A Bridge Too Far*, pp. 428–33 and 456–64. See also Gavin, 1979, pp. 197–200.

9. "Graphic History of the 101st Airborne," p. 4.

10. Brinson, p. 65.

11. Weigley 1981, p. 315.

12. On the 43rd Wessex, see the correspondence of June 1973 between Cornelius Ryan and Matthew Ridgway, Ridgway Papers, CBAMHI.

13. Cf. Ryan, *Bridge*, p. 215.

14. For example, Weigley 1981, pp. 317–19; Farrar-Hockley, p. 159; Blair, *Ridgway*, pp. 337–43; Huston, *Blue*, pp. 38–46.

15. This is Warren's conclusion; see his vol. II, p. 154. Observers from the 101st Airborne Division agreed; see, e.g., the report of one 101st captain to the effect that the glider landings on LZ "W" were "splendidly executed." IX TCC HQ, "Report on Operation MARKET," Oct. 1, 1944, p. 2. See also the letter of Oct. 6, 1944, from General Urquhart, Commander of the British 1st Airborne, saying to General Paul Williams that "no formation could have had a better start than the one you gave us at Arnhem." In IX TCC HQ, hist. narr. for Nov.–Dec., 1944.

16. *Soldier*, pp. 110–11.

17. These critiques are summarized in Craven and Cate, p. 608.

18. For a different interpretation—that the 101st Airborne's successes in the Eindhoven area can partly be explained by the fact that compared to German troops later used in the Ardennes campaign, those in Holland were "second-rate troops"—see the oral history interview with Maxwell Taylor, dated June 12, 1974. CBAMHI, Maxwell Taylor papers.

19. A symbol of how hard it is for Americans to believe that any campaign in World War II ended in defeat was the ad in *TV Guide* of May 20, 1986, for a showing of the movie "A Bridge Too Far" and headed "The Drama of Final Allied Victory—and its Terrible Cost!"

20. Dank, pp. 204–5.

21. Today we know that the Dutch Underground earlier had warned Montgomery and Browning of these armored divisions and that Montgomery dismissed the intelligence as probably only a rumor and in any case unimportant. See Warren II, p. 115. We at Membury certainly were unaware of this danger;

Charles Hastings' preliminary briefing notes for MARKET-GARDEN, September 16, show our Group Intelligence believed there were no armored units in the vicinity.

22. Weigley 1981, pp. 294–95.
23. *Stars and Stripes,* September 18, 1944.
24. Warren II, p. 155.

# 17. Reassessing
## Glider Potential and Performance

### The Waco and the Horsa

Two contrasting images our glider pilots retain from their experiences demonstrate how hard it is to judge the validity of the glider program as far as the dangers of landing are concerned. The first image is that of a downed glider with its nose crumpled into the earth, its tail sticking up in the air. Inside such a glider you could see the wreckage of a jeep that had been torn loose from its mooring by the impact and smashed forward against the two glider pilots.

An entirely different sort of combat glider image is one several of our pilots report: a glider smashing in, shearing off its wings against trees, bouncing up several feet in the air, crashing down against a hedge, and skidding sideways to a shuddering stop. The tail would end up twenty feet away from the fuselage. Then, just when you had given up the troopers and pilots inside for dead, they would all climb out of the wreckage—bruised and badly shaken up, but with few serious injuries.[1] In certain kinds of impact, it seemed, the tubular steel framing of the glider was able to give its occupants more protection than anyone would have dreamed possible.

Even some contemporaries during World War II found it hard to believe that there was such a thing as a military glider. One of the stories about gliders in *Yank*, those days, tells of a glider in England that had to cut loose and make an emergency landing in a farmer's field. The farmer's wife came to her door to watch the excitement; and as the airborne troopers piled out of the glider and sat down near her, she was heard to say "I never knew they used men in those machines!"

To outsiders, the term "combat glider" could even seem like a contradiction in terms; to them it seemed incredible that an unpowered contraption made of plywood and cloth fabric draped around a simple skeleton of steel tubing could be flung into battle in the face of heavy anti-aircraft fire and desperate enemy ground troops fighting on their own home grounds. But to us who worked with them, gliders—for all their fragile appearances—looked like exceedingly potent weapons of war. To us, their functioning seemed effective, their assignment seemed credible, and the men associated with them—airborne troopers and glider mechanics as well as glider pilots—seemed thoroughly capable of performing their jobs along the lines promised by the Army doctrine of glider tactics.

In theory, glider soldiers stood a better chance of quickly entering into battle together than did paratroopers. In a Waco, thirteen airborne infantrymen landed all together in one spot; in a Horsa, up to twenty-five soldiers stepped out of one glider. And it made sense that glider pilots, who had to ride down with their troopers and perhaps enter combat with them, would be even more careful than C-47 pilots with paratroopers aboard. The C-47 pilot had the right to give his paratroopers the green light at a time and place fixed during his briefing instructions. This was true whether or not the C-47 pilot could see if the ground situation looked safe at the moment he arrived at the DZ or LZ. The glider pilot, on the other hand, after cutting loose, constantly had to reassess his chances of getting out alive as he came closer and closer to some field at his LZ where he could eyeball the actual situation and decide, if he was lucky enough to still have some altitude, to choose a safer-looking field. No matter how much concern power pilots might feel for paratroopers in their planes, there is no denying that glider pilots had a more pressing incentive to see to the safety of their passengers.

Gliders ready for a formation flight looked as though they meant business. The sight of gliders being hooked up was more than impressive: it was awesome. Covering the main runway from side to side and halfway down its length, with the noise of the C-47 engines filling the air, a glider mission in the making was one of the unforgettable sights of World War II; in a way, more monumental than the sight of the same aircraft in the air above you.

In the center of the runway would be two lines of C-47s flanked left and right by two lines of gliders. Just off the runway would be two lines of glider mechanics with jeeps and trucks, ready to hook up to the gliders and help out in case of trouble. Snaked out on the ground in front of each glider would be its 300-foot long, thickly braided nylon rope. Each C-47 would inch forward to a position in front of its designated glider and cut back its engines. Glider mechanics would dash forward with the rope and attach its front clasp to a hook on the plane's tail. A glider officer in a jeep would motion the C-47 slowly forward until the towrope stretched taut; then the power pilots would get a green light from an Aldis lamp in the jeep, a signal to push throttles forward hard.

You could see a glider pilot fighting the tendency of his glider to fishtail from one side to another as it picked up speed. A speed of sixty mph was enough to lift the Waco glider up in the air; airborne, it could not go more than a few feet above its tow ship, which was still on the ground. Relieved of the glider's drag, the C-47 picked up speed, and at about 85 mph the tow plane lifted off, slapped up its landing gear, and cleared the field while banking slowly up and

Some Horsas had cordite explosives installed around their midsections to break them in two after landing; this made for easier exiting and unloading after a hard landing.

Thayer Bonecutter and an unidentified glider pilot in combat gear. Bonecutter is wearing paratrooper boots—a practice thought to be dangerous if you were captured by Germans, who had the reputation of slaughtering paratrooper prisoners.

off to the left. Long before this plane and the glider reached tree-top level, the next C-47 would be throttling forward down the runway towing the next glider.

During hook-up and the beginning of taxiing, plane or glider might turn up some mechanical problem; it would call in its trouble to the control tower and abort its takeoff. Plane and glider would be whisked off the runway, their pilots and infantry quickly transferred to stand-by planes and gliders, and they would take their place at the rear of the line-up. A scant half hour from the time the first plane began to turn over its engines, an entire group of four squadrons—perhaps forty-eight planes and forty-eight Wacos—could be aloft in formation and on its way to a training exercise or to an invasion LZ behind enemy lines.

Because gliders had no noisy engines, those of us who never rode in them imagined they provided a quiet flight. But for most of its flight a CG-4A was every bit as noisy as our power airplanes, which was to say pretty noisy. On the runway, after hook-up, all the roar of the tow plane's engines shot right back into the thin-skinned glider. The increasingly loud roaring of the tow plane as it fought to pick up speed on the runway built up the noise inside the glider to deafening levels. The prop wash forced back against the glider made it shake alarmingly and caused the struts and braces to vibrate, adding to the din. Even in the air, a CG-4A was not a peaceful place. Under tow, the impact of the slipstream rushing by at some 120 mph made the glider so noisy that the men inside had to shout at one another to be heard. But once cut loose and on their own, the men in the glider enjoyed a blessed release from all that racket. Over a battlefield, of course, noises of a different sort were added. Glider pilots often report that when they were coming down toward their LZ it could be so quiet that the only thing you heard was the "pop!" of a bullet as it tore through the fabric of your craft.

It seems unfair; but a person could work up a large-sized prejudice against the Waco simply because of its appearance. It looked so slab-sided we thought of it as a long box with wings. It had none of the smooth, streamlined look of our C-47, let alone the aerodynamic lines of a fighter. Its blunt nose added to its overall squat and ugly appearance. The box-like appearance made it easy to understand that several of the Waco's manufacturers had been furniture makers in peacetime. Among our glider mechanics, Wacos manufactured by the Steinway Piano Company held the reputation for being the most trustworthy of them all.

It was hard for us to reconcile the Waco's dumpy look with its impressive size and abilities. It was almost fifty feet long, and its wings spanned eighty-four feet—only ten feet less than those of the C-47 itself. Just in back of the cockpit area were landing wheels that looked ridiculously small for a craft of that size.

Of course we knew that these wheels would be little help in coming down anywhere but on a fairly smooth field or a runway. And, in fact, during combat the glider's main landing aid was not its wheels—designed to snap off at any substantial impact—but a pair of wooden skids under the glider between the wheels. It was a sensible arrangement for a "controlled crash."

The Wacos were regarded as entirely interchangeable with each other and not endowed with any particular individual characteristics. Therefore no glider pilot had "his own" glider. If they featured names, the names were applied in chalk just before a mission. At the same time, gliders received the "chalk mark" numbers on their noses, indicating their place in line during hook-up. Painting gliders with names seemed pretty pointless, since the chances were ninety-nine out of a hundred you would never see "your" glider again after a combat mission.

Inside, a Waco looked minimal but efficient. Pilots liked its spacious cockpit and the limited number of uncomplicated instruments on the instrument panel. Several of the controls—the ailerons, tabs, elevators, and "spoilers"—were simple manual cranks or levers. The nose was virtually all plexiglass, giving good visibility all around.

It is true that since the fuselage of the Waco was nothing but steel tubing covered with fabric it gave a somewhat insubstantial feel to those inside. The passenger seats were solid enough: they were made of light but strong plywood. Smallish plexiglass holes in the fuselage fabric gave the infantry seated there a bit of visibility to the outside.

The sturdiest feature of a Waco was its floor, which had to be capable of supporting a jeep or a heavy field artillery piece or even a downsized Caterpillar tractor. The floor was made of strong plywood set in a honeycomb pattern. The wings, also, were made of plywood with solid wooden ribs, covered by fabric, and they had extremely strong spars.

Gliders had an ingenious sort of air brake, the "spoilers."

> Many people reading about World War II gliders wonder about the term "spoilers" glider pilots were always using. Spoilers were really extendable, rigid flaps that could be pushed upright on top of the wings and worked to "spoil" the air flow coming over a portion of the wings. This canceled the lift effect of the air flow and made it possible to land much sooner by losing altitude more quickly. Spoilers were pushed up by a lever in the cockpit that let you adjust the amount of "spoilage" you got. (Leonard Braden, pilot)

The Horsa glider was a huge affair, sixty-seven feet long, and made entirely of hardwood and plywood. It could carry *two* jeeps, or a jeep and its fully loaded trailer, plus several glider troopers; this in spite of its own great weight when

Hard-nose glider: Tazewell Sanderson (glider mechanic) displays the "Griswold Nose" modification to help Waco glider pilots deal with hedges and other obstacles when landing.

The huge Horsa glider seems to dwarf its tug plane, a C–47, in the background.

empty (more than 8,000 pounds). Frequently it was loaded up with 9,000 additional pounds. A C-47 could not pull a fully loaded Horsa along the runway fast enough to get the glider into the air *before* the tug ship lifted. Since, in this case, the C-47 would have to lift up the Horsa while the glider was still on the ground, the tug pilot had to use all his skill to maneuver his plane carefully so as not to unbalance the glider.

Originally the Horsa was slated to be towed only by four-engine planes such as the British Halifax bomber. But before the Normandy invasion tests showed that our twin-engine C-47 could tow it—with a lot of huffing and puffing, to be sure.

> One fine day [in May 1944] the CO of the 436th [Col. Williams] decided it was possible to fly an English Horsa from a C-47. The example chosen was "old horseshit Charlie" [Hastings] and his *Black Sheep* plane from the 82nd Squadron.
>
> As we were burning 145 mag. at full RPM to get that huge cigar of a glider off the ground, Col. Williams (without a parachute, as I later found out) jumped into the Horsa and took over as pilot. Well, we chugged up to five thousand feet and we overheated. I went over to a single engine to see how we would make out. Williams saw us sink down on that one engine and, in a panic, cut the glider loose from the tow. Down, down for a landing he had to take that big, black, bastard of a Horsa! I started up my feathered engine and landed. Williams slapped me with a reprimand and made me a co-pilot for I don't know how long. (Charles Hastings, pilot)

The Horsa might look impossibly heavy; but it was actually faster than the Waco. It could be towed up to 160 mph, compared to 130 for the Waco. While of course its great weight meant it could come down in a hurry, it had huge flaps, worked by cylinders of compressed air, and so could come down at a steep angle but at fairly safe speeds. Its brakes, also, were air-pressure assisted; but, like the Waco, the Horsa landing gear often snapped off in combat and the Horsa rode to a stop on its skids.

By the time of the Holland invasion, the Horsa and the Waco were supposed to have either a drag ("drogue") chute to slow down their landing speed or a reinforced Griswold nose of steel bars to protect the glider when it had to smash up against hedges or other obstructions. But many gliders had neither.

> D-Day I flew a Horsa. They had a very ingenious way of getting out of that craft if the nose section was jammed and wouldn't swing out of the way when it was on the ground during combat. It had a prima-cord [explosive] wrapped around the fuselage; and, when safely on the ground and out of

the glider, the pilot could set off the prima-cord and blow the glider's two main sections apart.

Billy Hart [co-pilot] and I carried 7,200 pounds of artillery ammunition to Normandy on D-Day. Before reaching the landing zone, shell-fire punctured the air tanks; so we had no brakes or flaps. We came in hot, sailed across the field we had selected, and managed to slow down by putting the fuselage between two trees. When we stopped, Billy Hart had a broken leg. But I think that load was still usable by the artillery. And Billy got back to England safely. (Gale Ammerman, glider pilot)

---

It was Col. Brack who taught me to use flaps. He said, "Watters, you ever fly a ship with flaps?" I had to say no. Brack: "OK, let's talk about flaps." And for a solid hour he pumped me full of invaluable info on the use of flaps. He had things to say about both good and bad usage. One thing still really vivid in my mind is the way he said, "Maintain the same attitude of the ship when the flaps are first applied: that is, keep the nose up in spite of the flaps. With the flaps down you should at first keep the nose up and maintain your air speed. This will keep you in control and safe from excessive air speed."

When applied to the Horsa, this turned out to be very good advice. The Horsa's flaps could take two positions—forty and eighty degrees. On the approach leg we would use only the forty-degree position. Then at the right moment we would drop the flaps down the other forty degrees and try to come in at about a forty-five-degree angle with a uniform air speed—then level it off and pop it on the numbers. Just as if we'd been doing it all our lives.

We were finding that we sometimes were better off not using the aileron to keep the wings level on tow. When we did use them they caused the wing on one side to stall and the wing on the other side to flop violently. It was better to use opposite rudder. And we found that, especially with full loads, Horsas came off the runway more easily and more safely if we used the trim tab and did not pull back on the wheel. But many times this meant we would have to run all the way down the runway and find ourselves on the gravel at the end before we could lift off. Very hairy! On the other hand, since it took every bit of our skill, it made us feel more like pilots than when we were in a CG-4A. (Darlyle Watters, Squadron Glider Officer)

## Assessing the glider's role

The most devastating criticism of any aspect of troop carrier doctrine and tactics came from General James Gavin, commander of the 82nd Airborne Division.

This happened in late September 1944, after the terrible shock we all suffered when MARKET-GARDEN failed to put the Allies across the Rhine. At that time the air was full of angry accusations and denials, all seeking to lay the blame for this ghastly defeat on somebody else. It was in such an atmosphere that Gavin chose to single out troop carrier glider performance during the battle as "in most urgent need of correction." It was just as well we were far away from the high command levels to which this secret blast was communicated.

"Despite their individual willingness to help," said Gavin, "I feel [glider pilots] were definitely a liability to me." He criticized them for lack of proper training in infantry skills, for arriving at the battle without blankets, rations, and other items needed to perform as infantry, for causing confusion by "aimlessly wandering about" after landing, rather than "moving via command channels" toward 82nd or 101st Division command posts, and in general for acting more like tourists than disciplined soldiers. He finished by asking that glider pilots be detached from troop carrier and from the Air Forces and assigned to airborne infantry units, that is, placed under his command and that of other airborne infantry generals.[2] This critique was turned over to General Matthew Ridgway, Gavin's superior and the head of the XVIII Airborne Corps. A few months later Ridgway decided that while the glider pilots' performance on the ground needed improvement, this was a secondary consideration. Their main job was to fly gliders; and as pilots they belonged with the Air Forces not the infantry.[3]

But Ridgway's decision hardly ended the argument. From that day to this, a bitter and complex debate has centered on whether the performance of the glider arm of troop carrier was equal to its potential. It may seem strange that such passion still rages concerning a military tactic that essentially disappeared in March 1945, with the last massive airborne assault into Nazi Germany. The reason: improvements in glider operations seemed desperately needed during that fall and winter of 1944–45 to end the war successfully—and not only in Europe, but also for application later in the Pacific.

## Their critiques and our experiences

Criticisms of the glider's role in World War II can be grouped under the following headings: (1) the airworthiness of the gliders themselves; (2) whether gliders were excessively dangerous to the airborne troops they carried; (3) glider pilot training, especially as this concerned their commitment to fight alongside the airborne troops once on the ground; and (4) the tendency of some glider pilots to take their own sweet time in returning to their base after fulfilling their duties in support of the airborne infantry.

Critics of the Waco's airworthiness summarized their view by labeling it an "unforgiving aircraft." They meant that if it was not flown just right, a vicious circle of reactions might be set off, escalating the possibility of a crash. For example, if a glider pilot overcorrected while he was bringing his ship down to its proper "high-low tow position," a few feet above the C-47, the glider would sink precipitously below the tow plane; and an unskilled glider pilot might then overcorrect in the opposite direction, until finally the glider would be flailing up and down like a yo-yo, putting such pressure on the nylon tow rope that the rope might snap. About the same complaint was made concerning the Waco's tendency to fishtail in increasingly dangerous swings from side to side during take-off. British glider pilots, who sometimes had to fly Wacos, hated them.[4]

We also heard that the Waco's ailerons might lock up if the glider banked too steeply, causing the glider to bank over further and further until it went into a spin and crashed. Some glider pilots even reported that they had been yawing so violently that their ship was actually in danger of flipping over on its back while in tow. Another criticism of the glider's basic design was that when it was put under stress, such as when bucking a strong headwind, its struts, braces, and fuselage would vibrate so violently that there was a grave danger that portions of the wings would snap off. All of us who flew the invasion of southern France could see what might have been an example of this last fault: during that mission one Waco's wings snapped off, and the glider slammed down into the Mediterranean right in front of our eyes.

But was it design faults or other problems that brought about such disasters? Today some glider pilots argue that, while in training Waco loads were kept at or under the weight limit, in combat these rules were ignored and gliders were seriously overloaded. We know that in strong winds, if a glider carried a massive load—such as a jeep or barrels of gasoline—a dangerous situation could result if the load started to shift around on its moorings. But such problems were hardly the fault of the glider's engineering. Supporters of the Waco pointed out that the newness of the entire program meant that much of the grief would disappear with experience. Mishaps did tend to come less often during the last months of 1943 and even less once we were in England; but even very occasional disasters kept us all on edge.

Did flying a Waco require just too much skill? Was it unflyable by all but the most experienced glider pilots? To judge from our own experience, this was far from the truth. Pilots arriving in our Squadron long after we arrived in England, such as Roger Krey, seemed to handle their gliders in combat just as capably as those who had started with us all the way back in Alliance, Nebraska. Glider pilots with no previous flying experience before the war, like J. J. DiPietro and Thayer Bonecutter, managed to handle their combat assignments admirably right on through the war. Some of our power pilots, with no experience in flying CG-4As, found they were able to ferry them across the English Channel when we moved from our English to our French base.

On balance, however, piloting a glider did seem to take more out of a man than piloting a C-47. A "glider guider" had to be on his toes all the time, unlike a C-47 pilot who, under some circumstances, could relax and almost let his ship fly itself. The glider pilot had to engage in a sort of nervous aerial dance with his tow plane, his eyes constantly on the tow line so he did not drift right or left, carefully following every movement of the tow plane, and keeping just the right amount of stress on the tow rope. In fact, explains Darlyle Watters,

> We almost never looked at instruments when flying. The C-47 tug plane was our flight instrument. When its wings changed in a turn, we changed. When the C-47 climbed, we held the best position we could and climbed with him. In straight and level flight, we trimmed the glider, and then kept constant watch on two things: (1) the tug ship; and (2) an emergency field in case!

The glider pilot was totally dependent on the tow plane pilot, who always had to be careful not to change direction spasmodically, since this could result in flailing the glider around at the end of its rope. Some glider tragedies during combat happened when power pilots reacted to the sudden appearance of heavy flak by putting their plane into a dive, thus snapping the tow rope. Fortunately, in our Squadron we never suffered the terrible accidents that happened to others when a taut tow rope snapped and the loose end shot back at the glider with such force it smashed a piece of plexiglass right out of the cockpit windshield.

All through training and combat, our glider pilots had experiences that suggested the Waco was hardly a dangerously fragile craft that would fly apart at the least sign of abuse.

> We were at a satellite base one day where we were making takeoffs and landings all day long. One day a windshield popped out of a CG-4A. When the time came to return to Maxton, I volunteered to fly the damaged glider home. As soon as I got up to 2,000 feet I heard a loud noise toward the rear. I looked back and saw that the horizontal stabilizer on the right side had snapped in two and was hanging down at about a sixty-degree angle. I felt a very strong urge to get back on the ground; so I immediately hit the release and got loose from the tow plane. I started to establish some sort of normal glide. When I pulled back on the control column, the glider responded only sluggishly. When the nose did come up and I tried to level off, the controls stayed sluggish. This is what you might expect, with one

intact horizontal stabilizer and elevator and the other broken and causing drag. I dropped almost the whole 2,000 feet, going from high speed to very near stalling speed, and then into a long glide which brought me up again to an unnervingly high speed before I could bring the glider out of the dive. Luck was with me that day. A good open field was there and I was just coming out of that dive when my altitude ran out. The big bird stalled out just as I was a few feet above the ground; but the landing was near perfect. Needless to say, the palms of my hands were wet and my pulse rate was up a bit. Most importantly, I have never again flown a windshieldless aircraft. (Gale Ammerman, glider pilot)

Time after time, between half and two-thirds of the gliders on a mission would sustain bullet or flak hits, but somehow would manage to reach their LZ areas. Even incendiary tracer bullets which could set the plywood Horsa aflame almost always tore right through the fabric-sided Waco without causing much damage. Of the some 906 Wacos that started out during the immense glider assault across the Rhine, only about half a dozen were shot down.[5]

The second set of criticisms of the glider program centers around the conviction that during the crucial five minutes or so between cut-off from the tow plane and entry into actual combat, the dangers run by airborne infantry troopers were simply too great. Asking even the tough men of the 82nd, 101st, and 17th Divisions to capture their objectives immediately, after the appalling experiences they had to suffer during the tow, the descent to the battlefield, and the landing itself, was asking too much. Subjected to such demoralizing pre-battle experiences they were licked before they started.

As far as we in our Squadron could see, glider troopers certainly were subjected to terrible shocks in the air, on the way down, and during the landing itself. The insubstantial feeling of that Waco glider itself was something they could get used to during training. But the nausea which they suffered in flight was hard to avoid, no matter how many airsickness pills they took. A conscientious glider pilot could reduce tension by explaining to his passengers before takeoff what they could expect once airborne. Some glider pilots reported that having glider troopers vomit during flight was one of the facts of life; and gliders carried cardboard "barf boxes" on a shelf.[6] On the other hand, our own Squadron Glider Officer, Darlyle Watters, says he never had a vomiting problem in his glider in his hundreds of training and combat flights.

Paratroopers in a C-47 could tell themselves that even if their ship was badly shot up they might be able to bail out before it crashed. But for glider troopers there was no way to get down but to sweat it out all the way in your glider. This inseparable connection between the fate of glider troopers and the fate of their glider was made all too obvious by the fact that glider troopers were not allowed

Down hard: glidermen look through the wreckage of a *Waco* (its cockpit and wings) during the Holland invasion. (National Archives)

to wear parachutes. They could take whatever comfort there was from the fact that glider pilots were in the same boat; glider pilots were not allowed to wear parachutes in combat either.

And after arriving weak and nauseous over the LZ, a glider trooper had even more traumatic experiences awaiting him. The trip down to the ground was likely to feel like one insanely dangerous maneuver after another. All our glider pilots report that on the way down, it was "mayhem in the air." This was true even during the so-called milk run glider mission into southern France. Under fire, the theory of proper glider landing tactics simply flew out the window as each pilot desperately jockeyed for a relatively safe landing spot and tried to keep from colliding with others doing the same. Landing in the rigid order they had learned during training would have been suicidal. As soon as one pilot realized he had to break out of a "normal" landing pattern and dive for his life, every other glider pilot in the vicinity had to react in order to protect himself and his troopers. This was not "pilot panic"; it was the best way of handling an appalling situation.

Surely airborne glider troopers had to shoulder one of the worst assignments in all our armed forces. And yet, perhaps because of the doubts that clouded the glider program, glider troopers were not given the recognition they deserved. The glamorous publicity went to paratroopers. Unlike paratroopers in the same division, who from the beginning were volunteers, soldiers were ordered into glider units at first. Even when their status was changed and only volunteers were accepted for gliders, the troopers for a long time were not given the "hazardous duty" pay that went to paratroopers. Fortunately for their morale, just after the invasion of Normandy glider troopers were given the same hazardous duty pay as paratroopers.

The third set of criticisms—and the one about which General Gavin seemed most anxious—concerned what he saw as the inability of glider pilots to function in support of the airborne infantry once they landed. He attributed this failure to a lack of training and a lack of command discipline in the LZ.

The notion that the glider pilots received inadequate ground combat training, however, seems to have not a shred of truth in it. On the contrary, not only did our glider pilots go through extensive and repeated weapons training programs, but once in combat they certainly did demonstrate that they could handle infantry duties. As we have seen, those who entered the program early did little *but* infantry training for months at a time while they waited for instructors, gliders, and tow planes on their bases. And in England our glider pilots received additional training—comprehensive and rather rugged—that lasted weeks at a time.

Before we left England for France, all the glider pilots were ordered to report to the 17th Airborne Division. Upon our arrival, we were told that we would be taught infantry tactics and the use of hand weapons. This training was supposed to enable us to become qualified to fight alongside the troops after landing. We were told that we would fire rifles for the record and after we had completed the training we would fire for the record again to see how much of an improvement we made. We all qualified with a high score. We were again assembled for a briefing. The commanding general there told us that we had received more training in the use of small arms and infantry tactics than his Division troops. We were also told that if we wished we could return to our outfits; or we could stay and learn the use of antitank weapons and demolition. We all stayed and received the additional training. (Bill Lane, glider pilot)

Clay Blair, a well-known military historian, is one writer who still today seems anxious to blame part of the difficulties of airborne missions on glider pilots. In the fights around Ste-Mère-Eglise during the Normandy invasion, Blair describes an 82nd Airborne officer attempting to flank one German position "with a reluctant, ragtag group of glider pilots, some of whom had to be coaxed into the assault at pistol point. About half the glider pilots 'bugged out' for UTAH beach, and the attack failed."[7] But on the same page Blair acknowledges that before that particular position could be captured, three airborne battalions supported by tanks and infantry had to be brought up to do the job—suggesting that the glider pilots' "reluctance" was well founded.

Some glider pilots, once on the ground, did abandon their airborne troopers; but sometimes, as we have seen, it was the troopers who chose to dispense with the glider pilots' services.

The most horrible accident I ever saw—one that has haunted me ever since—was a Horsa glider that came in so hard it bounced, literally bounced, at least thirty and maybe forty feet into the air. The center of its fuselage landed in a thicket of Lombardy poplars. Its wings were sheared off, and it hung up there, up in the air maybe thirty feet off the ground. Now, [Jim] Gephart and I were supposed to follow along after the infantry who had come down in our own glider. They went down the road past where the glider was hung up; and of course they all had to see that terrible sight. We were to follow along as a sort of rear guard for these troopers. I remember them saying they were going to check up on all the wounded around that glider, and that they would then come back. When they didn't come back for about half an hour, we started down the road toward where they should be. We moved as we had been taught in basic training—one of us would advance about twenty-five feet, on the run, and the other would cover him. When we got to where this glider was, the infantry had all gone! No men, no jeep, no trailer, no one at all.

But on the ground there lay a wounded man. He was moaning—he obviously was in terrible pain even though he seemed to be unconscious. To us it looked as though he had been positioned there.

One of my most painful memories of World War II is the decision we had to make right then. Should we stay and try to help that wounded man, at least until we could get some medics? Or should we move on toward the assembly point as we had been instructed? It was clear that so far as the safety of the unit we had landed with was concerned, we should join up with them at their rear. I asked Gephart his opinion; and then we together decided that we had to go on and try to find our unit and the assembly point.

We went straight down the road—as carefully as we could—but we found nobody at all. We had to spend the night by the side of the road hidden in the hedgerow.

Every once in a while we would hear somebody going by; we would strain to hear whether they were talking German or English. For a long time we heard nothing but German. Finally someone stringing telephone wire for the airborne came by and we realized we were in an area now more or less free of Germans. That fellow was able to direct us to the assembly point, which turned out to be only about half an hour away.

But ever since then I have worried about whether I should have stayed with that poor guy lying wounded on the road and should have tried to minister to him. This has been a bad source of anguish to me; I can't help wondering what finally happened to him. (Bob Carney, glider pilot)

All that we know about our Squadron combat missions shows that when airborne officers delegated a job to our glider pilots, it was done. In spite of the fatigue resulting from getting the glider down to the LZ, our pilots immediately shifted gears and became infantry soldiers. Our glider pilots certainly understood that in fighting alongside airborne troopers they also were fighting to save their own necks.[8] Sometimes this meant giving covering fire to the airborne troops while the gliders were being unloaded. Sometimes it meant acting as perimeter guards or POW guards.

On D-Day + 2 several of us 81st TCS glider pilots were detailed to guard forty or so German prisoners. There were maybe six or seven of us on this job, including Thayer Bonecutter, Bob Carney, perhaps also Robinson Crobie, and myself. One German who, we suspected, was an SS officer trying to incite the other prisoners to escape, bothered us a great deal. We kept warning him by making threatening motions with our M-1s and carbines; he would stop for a time and then start in again. Because of him, we put in a very uneasy night. Next day we were ordered to escort the Germans to the beach. From time to time we came under sniper fire; each time this happened the prisoners became very agitated. And this officer would again begin to harangue them—we suppose to get them to make a break. We warned him two or three times; finally Bob Carney got tired of all this. Bob stuck a bayonet into the German's ass about two inches. Needless to say we had no more trouble with him; and we delivered him and all the other prisoners to the MPs at the beach. (Gale Ammerman, glider pilot)

Criticism of glider pilots that implies they were not sharing the risks of the airborne infantry seem far from the facts.

I remember that when we landed our airborne troopers in Holland, safely and in just the right spot, the troopers were practically ecstatic. On the flight they had taken a flak jacket off the trooper who was acting as co-pilot—who was a member of their group—and had bundled me up in the jacket because they figured if I got shot they would be in bad trouble anyway. (Bob Carney, glider pilot)

The final set of glider program criticisms centers on evidence that some glider pilots acted too independently—to put it mildly—on the way back to their base. From evidence we have concerning our own Squadron, this seems true enough, at least for the invasions of southern France and Holland, though not for the invasions of Normandy and of Germany.[9] Partly because of a feeling that they were no longer needed, partly because they felt the wringer they had just been put through entitled them to blow off some steam, some of our glider pilots did interpret rather liberally their directives about using their own discretion on how to get back to home base as quickly as possible.

One glider pilot (not in our Squadron) reported as MIA, spent a whole month substituting for somebody in an airborne antitank gun team. The fact that his court-martial acquitted him when he returned suggests that inside IX Troop Carrier Command, at any rate, post-mission goofing-off by glider pilots was viewed with some sympathy.[10]

The field we landed in was larger than the whole world; we were really lucky. I got one lonesome bullet hole in the wing. We landed close to Eindhoven, and I hooked up with the outfit of airborne infantry we had flown in. I stayed with that infantry outfit right up to Nijmegen. Before we reached Nijmegen, we camped in a field. Mortar shells were landing everywhere. Because the Germans had been there and knew the ground, we knew sooner or later they would be able to zero in on us, and that the next batch of mortar shells could get some of us.

In Nijmegen, we took over a German motor pool. There was a German bike there. I had never ridden a motorbike in my life. But some captain said, "If I were you, I'd take that bike and get the hell out of here." So I did. Rode the thing all the way back to Brussels. Rode it right onto the airfield; and here was a plane all ready to ride back to our base. But I said, "The hell with that; I'm going to town!" I sold that German bike for 740 Belgian francs. You can imagine what we did with the money. As it turned out, it took me seven days to get back to Membury.

They were beginning to send in a "missing in action" report on me just at the time I reported in. (Earl Goodwin, glider pilot)

It certainly made sense to order glider pilots to use their own judgment on how to return. Take the Holland mission as an example. The Eindhoven-Nijmegen area was a long way from England. Over the three days in which we were involved there in glider missions, our glider pilots were widely scattered. And they were in no frame of mind to wait passively at the nearest airborne divisional assembly point while somebody organized some transport back to Membury.

Glider pilots had impressed on them that they had *priority* in returning home whatever way seemed feasible. During the Normandy invasion they were told they had priority over everybody except the severely wounded in getting back to the beaches and to England. And some of them were indeed permitted to cross the Channel in hospital ships.

British glider pilots—whom no commentator I have read accuses of inadequate commitment to the airborne infantry—also carried special orders to return quickly and "by the most expeditious means." Field Marshal Montgomery himself signed that order. And the CG of the British 6th Airborne Division is reported to have said "Whatever you do, don't let those [glider] pilots get into combat. They are much too valuable to be wasted. Get them back here." [11]

This is not to say our glider pilots were model soldiers. Their recollections show them as men who certainly were independent-minded and who possessed a rather impudent sense of humor—in addition to the kind of guts needed to take desperate chances. But this, after all, was the type of man we needed in glider combat.

Glider pilots were used as ferry pilots to take small liaison aircraft to Chartres, France. . . . One time as we were going across the Channel we encountered a terrific headwind and our fuel was low when we got to France. We had to land at Le Havre to refuel. F/O Reed clipped my rudder with his right wing on landing. With damaged airplanes we were not able to go on with the rest of the group. I began to make telephone calls to request permission to remove and replace the rudder from the plane having a damaged wing to my own plane.

A general in COMZ HQ in Paris finally gave me permission. After making the exchange, Reed and I went to Chartres. But by the time we got there, they had been snowed in. I managed to land the plane and was told the field was closed for at least three days. We hitched a ride to Paris with the Red Ball Truck Line. The driver dropped us off at an officers mess and we went in. As we were sitting there eating, a couple of colonels came in and came to our table. We were in our flying coveralls so one of the colonels asked what we were doing in Paris. I told him we were P-51 pilots and had been shot down over northern France and were being evacuated back to England. The colonel said he was the Provost Marshal for Paris. He also informed us that we were in a Field Officers Mess and that Paris was off limits to all Americans. But then he said that the P-51s were doing a great job and he would help us. He gave us a pass for Paris and told us where we could get billets and mess facilities; and he wished us good luck. We were able to spend three days in Paris before the airfields were cleared of snow. (Bill Lane, glider pilot)

### Notes

1. More than 80 percent of the CG-4As that came into Normandy on D-Day are reported to have landed with their trooper passengers uninjured. Moore, Ch. 4, p. 15.

2. IX TCC, HQ, and 53rd TCW, hist. narr. for Sept. 1944, pp. 20–21 (letter dated Sept. 25, 1944); "Report on MARKET," Oct. 20, 1944, pp. 7–8; Devlin, *Silent Wings*, pp. 278–81. See also Dank, p. 205; Huston, *Blue*, pp. 39–40 and 42–43; and Adelman, 1966, pp. 105–6.

3. This decision was later supported by Ridgway's survey of opinions of a score of high-ranking officers from the Air Forces and the Army: "Airborne Future," Ridgway papers, CBAMHI.

4. Ambrose, *Pegasus*, p. 55.

5. Warren II, pp. 182, 184.

6. The problem was equally bad in Horsas: see Ambrose, *Pegasus*, p. 48.

7. Blair, p. 259.

8. In discussing this problem as it involved MARKET, Warren concludes

that 90 percent of the glider pilots "obeyed orders and did their best." II, pp. 152–53.

9. This is also borne out in the report of a 91st TCS glider pilot: see the Air Intelligence Contact Unit "Report on Returnees," May 15, 1945.

10. "Ever First! The 53rd Troop Carrier Wing," pp. 21–22.

11. Ambrose, *Pegasus,* p. 84.

# 18. Re-Supplying
## The Battle of the Bulge

### A dreaded winter war

In October, 1944, one month after the German victory at Arnhem, we in the 81st TCS received a token of things to come from Quartermaster Supply: winter flight clothing. At the time these arrived the weather was still beautiful: mostly crisp, clear days and nights with just enough zip in the air to make you glad of your bed roll when you had to sleep overnight in your plane on some French or Belgian airstrip.

Those winter flight clothes were designed for nastier weather. They had lambswool lining almost half an inch thick, and were wonderfully warm—though the leather exteriors were so thin and insubstantial you could poke a hole in them with your fingernail. When November rolled around, with its incessant, cold winds that never let you relax, we wore our winter clothes gratefully, especially those fleece-lined boots; and by December the airplane crews felt their warm outerwear was absolutely essential to their being able to function. Winter flight clothes were also a blessing for glider pilots, since there was no way of heating up their gliders. (In C-47s there were good heaters that ran off the engine exhaust system.) And before long Supply managed to find at least some winter flight clothes for non-flying mechanics and others who needed them—or who had friends in Supply.

To me this clothing, perhaps more than anything else in World War II, symbolized the contrast between how well Army Air Forces soldiers fared during the dread winter of 1944–45 and the suffering that had to be borne by our infantry—not to mention the German soldiers, dependent on donations of warm clothing from civilians. Sure, there were times when we worked out on the line, or when the pot-bellied stoves in our barracks failed, that we were miserably cold; but we should never forget that the causes of many thousands of infantry casualties that winter were chest infections brought on by exposure, trench foot, and severely frost-bitten hands.[1]

As long as those clear fall days of October continued, the 81st TCS certainly earned its keep in logistic if not combat functions. In fact, we remained just as busy then as we had been during the summer when we freighted gas to Patton. There were only two days during all of October when the weather became so bad we could not fly either practice paratroop or glider missions, or carry freight "to the far shore" (any place in Continental Europe). Our Squadron diary shows the long list of different kinds of freight to be found on our manifests: medical supplies, blood plasma, signal corps wire, clothing, PSP matting, "dubbing" (for treating clothes against poison gas), tires, binoculars, 45 caliber pistols, even an occasional jeep and trailer—in addition to the usual ammunition, bazookas, pack mortars, and jerricans of gas.

During October, in elements of from two to twelve, we flew to at least seven different forward airstrips, plus large airfields such as Brussels and Paris. And on the return flights, increasingly we carried wounded infantry boys (sometimes including German POWs): everyone from the walking wounded, able to give you a cheerful smile of relief at being "fucking well out of it!" to troopers strapped in litters and all too obviously headed not for home but for a death bed in some British hospital.

On several supply-evacuation missions we ran into yet another reason to resent "those Limeys": on Belgian fields, where the British were in control, they would not allow us to land together ("in trail") as we had been trained; they insisted on taking us in only one or two at a time, while the rest of the flight—sometimes as many as ten planes—wasted time circling the airstrip, anxiously eying the horizon for signs of those newfangled ME 262 Luftwaffe jet fighters.

You might think that the failure of MARKET-GARDEN would have ended once and for all the arguments over whether troop carrier should be "freighters or fighters," in favor of the former; but this was not the case. While our infantry, at terrible cost, was slugging through icy mud toward the Rhine, we were flying practice combat missions that seemed to have little to do with the "meat-grinder" battles on the ground. We flew four practice paratroop drops, two glider tows, and one double glider tow during October alone. Only a few planes at a time were involved in these practice combat missions. The crews on such training missions usually were "attrition crews" recently arrived in Britain. The old-timers were mostly involved with supply and evacuation assignments. The 81st TCS was now at our peak airplane strength: twenty-seven planes and crews.

In combat training missions, however, we could not practice with our regular airborne infantry partner, the 101st Airborne. Most of the troopers in our planes and gliders these days were from the 17th Airborne Division, recently arrived in Britain. They worked with us so we could "familiarize them with some conditions and terrain of the European Theater of Operations."[2] The 101st and 82nd Airborne Divisions, incredibly, were still out there fighting as line infantry in eastern France, held at the front by Montgomery's paranoid refusal to let go of any troops and supplies he had gotten his hands on. In spite of Montgomery's repeated promises that he would allow the 101st and 82nd to be pulled back for R & R (rest and replacements) right after MARKET-GARDEN, the 101st was not relieved until November 23, and the 82nd not until November 27! Then the two divisions were allowed to fall back to the Rheims area. They had only three short weeks to make good their terrible losses with replacement troops and refit before being yanked out of R & R and rushed to the front again in mid-December—to bear the brunt of the Battle of the Bulge.

On November 7, 1944, Shorty Farr, a fellow radio operator, returned to Membury after the Dutch Underground hid him for thirty-seven days. On September 18, D-Day + 1, Shorty and the rest of John Webster's crew had jumped from their burning plane after releasing their glider at the time of the 81st TCS's first glider mission into Holland. Shorty could not stay long in Membury; rules of U.S. Intelligence held that any person in his position must never again be exposed to the risk of capture by the Germans since he might then be tortured into revealing the Underground system that spirited Americans through German lines back to Britain, or disclosing the names of Dutch patriots who had taken him under their wing after he parachuted from the burning plane.

So Shorty was here in the radio operators' barracks only overnight; he picked up his things and next day shipped back to the States. We clustered around his bunk while he packed, but there was little he would tell us. Webster, his pilot, had ordered the crew to jump soon after their plane was hit; but Webster himself stayed at the controls until his crew was out. Jumping a minute or two later than the others, Webster landed in sight of the Germans and was captured. He remained a prisoner for the rest of the war—in the same prison camp as Darlyle Watters, our Squadron Glider Officer, who was captured during our second glider mission in MARKET.

When we asked Shorty Farr just how he was feeling when he, his crew chief Obergfell, and his co-pilot Brooks had to jump, Shorty only said that when he stood frozen for a moment in the open door—with the airplane cabin rapidly filling with smoke—the crew chief in back of him yelled, "When you gotta go, you gotta go!"

Right then, for just a second, all of us around Shorty's bunk were inside his skull, staring down at the ground from his burning plane. We had all been on that mission. It was a moment of empathy only those who had repeatedly flown through German flak could share.

We trained with the 17th Airborne because we were slated to drop them across the Rhine in the next airborne assault. But during that winter of 1944–45 the next invasion seemed very far away. The weather worsened steadily, and the ground troops bogged down in ice and mud. Eisenhower, we know now, had sworn he never would again be caught in a logistic crisis like the one that slowed Patton's tanks the previous August. Until Antwerp was cleared, he ruled, both American and British infantry would push ahead toward the Rhine only cautiously, while enormous supply depots for the coming invasion of Germany were built up. Of course everyone was hoping the Germans' morale would crack; but the continued heavy losses they still were able to inflict on us in eastern France, Luxemburg, and Belgium made it likely that there would have to be another airborne invasion some time next spring.

Meanwhile, the freighting missions we ran seemed thoroughly useful. The Scheldt estuary, waterway to the great port of Antwerp, remained closed. It could have been secured back in early September by the British and Canadians. But they had let this chance slip through their fingers; and after MARKET-GARDEN, they began the nasty job of clearing away all the Germans who had dug themselves into the banks and islands of the Scheldt. Even after this was done, it took two additional weeks, until the last week in November 1944, to clear the Scheldt of mines the Germans left behind.

Some progress was made in the massive repairs needed to get the French railroad system going; but until the end of 1944 the main forward supply deliveries depended on Red Ball Express and on troop carrier. And the more the weather worsened, the less supplies we could carry. Squadron and Group records show that there were only seventeen days in November when the weather permitted supply missions "to the far shore." On the best days Group dispatched very large numbers of our planes to France, Belgium, and Luxemburg: between forty and sixty-five per day, out of the 436th TCG's total of around 100.[3] Total freight for Group in November was around three and a half million tons, down by a third from October; and in December we shipped much less than that. However, we were already in the business of ferrying units of the 17th Airborne across the Channel to their new French bases; and on December 5th the 17th's CG, General William Miley, along with his jeep and trailer, traveled to his Brussels HQ that way. Meanwhile, troop carrier groups in the 52nd Wing practiced with the British 6th Airborne Division. Paratroopers of the 17th, still untried in battle, had been deliberately trained to act mean and gang up on men from other outfits. Whenever we were with them on airfields they always acted the role of gung-ho bullies and paraded their contempt for us "lily-livered fly babies." Some commanders, it seemed, had funny ideas about what it took to make a good paratrooper.

Ironically, while our Squadron's combat know-how and general proficiency in the fall of 1944 were better than ever, combat in the near future was not on the books. Meanwhile, high public praise was being heaped on our performance in MARKET-GARDEN. (General Gavin's criticism of our glider program was still secret.) Articles in *Yank* and in *Stars and Stripes*,[4] as well as in home-town newspapers, showed how much the rest of the world had begun to appreciate troop carrier. On October 6, the entire 436th TC Group assembled at Welford Park, where General Paul Williams, CG of IX Troop Carrier Command, presented us with the Presidential Unit Citation; during the same ceremony General Lewis Brereton, CG of the FAAA, gave those who had flown in the Normandy invasion our first Air Medals.

The frustrations we in troop carrier were experiencing, of course, can in no way be compared with the misery and danger facing the infantry. But our frustrations, nevertheless, were real. We would have been glad to have been of more use during this winter war. But while high command refused to recommit the FAAA to another airborne assault, we were stuck in our role of training and freighting.

Symbolic of how we were being out-maneuvered by "General Winter" was the danger we all ran from ice. November and the first two weeks of December 1944 brought little snow in Britain, but almost constant fog and drizzle. In these conditions a temperature drop of only a few degrees would coat our runways—and the planes—with ice. More and more of our time was spent scraping ice off the cockpit windows and the wings and stabilizers of our grounded planes. Not only crew chiefs and airplane mechanics but also radio operators and glider personnel had to be enlisted in this never-ending task of keeping the planes operational in spite of the ice.

Once up in the air, ice presented a much, much more serious problem. Altitudes at which we could expect icing to occur on the planes now became a regular feature of our WXR (weather reports). Usually we could expect icing at about 5,000 feet up; but often icing would strike at much lower levels. Looking out, you could see the menacing coating beginning to form over the wings, and the pilots could feel their planes beginning to sink under all that weight. Then it was up to the rubber de-icer boots on the leading edges of the wings; these were inflated with hydraulic fluid. The trick was to let the ice coating form up well enough so it would shatter under pressure—without letting it grow thick enough to withstand the de-icer boot expansion. When the de-icer boots worked, you could see chunks of ice fly off the wings; when they didn't, it was time to get down on the ground as fast as you could.

### Hitler's Ardennes offensive

My plane was grounded in Chartres, the great cathedral town a bit southwest of Paris, when we first heard of Hitler's break-out in the Ardennes region. Our crew and another had been kept there for four days, caught by a snowstorm that closed the airfield down tight. By the time we could return to Membury, two days before Christmas, the 81st had already flown the first of its four re-supply missions to the surrounded 101st Airborne troopers in Bastogne. We peeled off our raunchy underclothes and washed off the accumulated grime; meanwhile Jack Wallen, our pilot, trotted over to Operations for our assignment in the second re-supply mission to Bastogne, on December 24.

The fact that the Squadron had allowed Wallen, one of its most experienced pilots (he was leader of A-Flight), to be away on a supply and evacuation mission at the time of Hitler's offensive demonstrates how successful the Germans had been in keeping advance knowledge of this massive attack from Allied intelligence. The Germans had begun planning for this offensive almost as soon as MARKET-GARDEN ended. Driven by a mad scheme to push a wedge all the way through the American and British lines to the Meuse River and eventually to Liège and Antwerp, Hitler would gamble the reserves he certainly would need when the inevitable Allied offensives began the following spring.

Twenty-two newly refitted German divisions, led by some of Hitler's most fanatical SS units and followed by almost a thousand tanks, tore through the thinly deployed Allied lines west of the Ardennes forest on December 17. The Nazis picked areas to attack that were manned by inexperienced American troops; the 106th Infantry Division, for example, was only a few weeks off the ship from the States. Some of our infantry managed to slow parts of the German offensive down; but thousands of men in other units were overrun and captured, and whole regiments in the 28th and 99th American Infantry Divisions began a panicky, disorganized retreat—virtually a rout.

Now began the month-long Battle of the Bulge, destined to be the largest single battle on the western front in World War II, involving eventually more than one million soldiers.

The surprise was complete. Matthew Ridgway, CG of XVIII Corps, and Maxwell Taylor, CG of the 101st Airborne, were away from their commands—Ridgway in England, Taylor in Washington. After some agonizing, SHAEF released the 82nd and 101st Airborne Division to Hodges, whose First Army (especially Troy Middlelton's VIII Corps) was in serious disarray under that attack. Anthony McAuliffe, deputy CG of the 101st, rushed his 501st Parachute Infantry Regiment immediately into Bastogne, a key road center in the German path; the rest of the 101st, following as quickly as it could, formed up a defense perimeter around Bastogne with pickup combat teams from splinters of infantry, armor, and artillery broken off from overrun American outfits. The 82nd Airborne was bundled into ten-ton trailers and trucked into the town of Werbomont, in the St. Vith area of Belgium, on the northern shoulder of "the Bulge." Together with some battered remnants of other infantry divisions around St. Vith, the 82nd Airborne tried to slow down the German assault. Some of the last

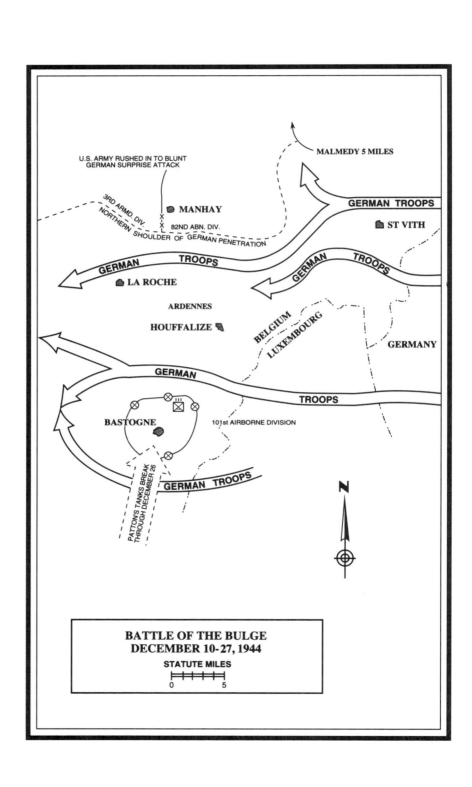

U.S. ARMY RUSHED IN TO BLUNT
GERMAN SURPRISE ATTACK

MALMEDY 5 MILES

GERMAN TROOPS

ST VITH

3RD ARMD. DIV.

MANHAY

82ND ABN. DIV.

NORTHERN SHOULDER OF GERMAN PENETRATION

GERMAN TROOPS

GERMAN TROOPS

LA ROCHE

ARDENNES

HOUFFALIZE

BELGIUM

LUXEMBOURG

GERMANY

GERMAN

TROOPS

BASTOGNE

101st AIRBORNE DIVISION

N

PATTON'S TANKS BREAK
THROUGH DECEMBER 26

GERMAN TROOPS

**BATTLE OF THE BULGE
DECEMBER 10-27, 1944**

STATUTE MILES

0                    5

arrivals from the 101st and 82nd Airborne Divisions were flown in by troop carrier planes. The 53rd TC Wing was placed on thirty-minute alert; a plan was being organized for us to carry units of the 17th Airborne and the British 6th Airborne to the Ardennes area.

St. Vith is not as famous in World War II histories as Bastogne; but to the Germans it was just as important a road center. On December 21 the Germans overran St. Vith in the face of a valiant defense. Unable to get to the town in time, all the 82nd Airborne could do was protect the defeated infantry units retreating out of St. Vith. Meanwhile, as everyone knows, Bastogne held out, surrounded, for a week—which is why the 101st got all the glory from the Battle of the Bulge.[5]

This was troop carrier's chance to show what it could do to re-supply surrounded American soldiers. McAulliffe forwarded a remarkably restrained request for ammunition and blood plasma to be supplied by air to his surrounded forces. Troop carrier then proceeded to perform just as airborne warfare enthusiasts had always argued we could, supplying the 101st troopers in Bastogne with the ammo, gas, food, and medicine needed to hang on until elements of Patton's Third Army could break through the shoulders of "the Bulge."

But these troop carrier missions to Bastogne could never have been launched without a great, great gift from Mother Nature: four days of clear skies from December 23 to December 26, the greatest possible contrast with the unceasing dense clouds, drizzle, and heavy snow that had dominated the rest of the month.

In movies and novels about the Battle of the Bulge, the break-up of those solid, low December cloudbanks and the advent of decent flying weather on December 23 is hailed as a miracle. Certainly all of us were praying for just such a miracle. And "miraculous" is an understandable way of thinking about it: during some years in this part of Europe, you hardly get to see the sun at all between mid-November and mid-February. At the beginning of his offensive, Hitler had had every right to expect that the solid overcast keeping fighters and fighter-bombers as well as troop carriers down on the ground would continue right through the winter.[6]

On December 23, the first day of aerial re-supply, 260 troop carrier planes, including seven from our Squadron, flew in 334 tons of supplies to Bastogne.[7] This and our subsequent re-supply missions into the Bastogne area were so straightforward they seemed ·almost cut and dried—except that, unlike non-combat supply missions, we now flew as part of large formations, dropped our supplies with pararacks and parapacks instead of landing them, and came back with a mess of bullet holes. No fancy tactical planning, no elaborate flight paths this time. Just straight on in, jettison your loads over the position markers west of Bastogne, and get the hell out of there.[8] In our Squadron we carried mostly ammunition, but also K-rations and signal corps equipment. We took off from

Membury shortly after noon each day and flew the long (three-hour) trip to Belgium at 1,500 feet.

The first thing you saw, coming toward Bastogne, was a large, flat plain completely covered in snow, the whiteness broken only by a few trees and some roads, and, off in the distance, the town itself. Next, your eye caught the pattern of tank tracks across the snow. We came down lower and lower, finally to about 300 feet off the ground, our drop height.

> When we were flying over the Bastogne area I couldn't believe an army of men could be trapped down there in what looked like nothing but wide fields of snow. At first I couldn't see any men at all. We pushed out the parapacks through the open door and then I lay down on the floor, looking out the door, and sort of squinting against the glare of the snow; that way I could see men running toward the stuff we had dropped and dragging it away to their still invisible foxholes. (Ben Obermark, crew chief)[9]

There was little flak coming up at us; but every plane was tracked by machine gun fire. At the height we were flying, it almost seemed the Germans could hit us by throwing rocks. None of us were shot down—an additional tribute to the airworthiness of those C-47s. But some of us came back so full of holes that the sheet-metal men were kept up till all hours riveting on patches. The plane piloted by Richard Wilson probably scored an 81st TCS record:

> I got caught in machine-gun fire just at the time I was making my turn. That gave the gunner on the ground a long time to fix his sights on me. He raked me back and forth; but fortunately he wasn't good enough to lead me properly, or he would certainly have brought us down. He blew up the radios and other things inside the plane; but he didn't wreck any vital part. When we landed we got out and counted up the bullet holes: there were ninety of them! It was a miracle nobody in the plane got hit. (Richard Wilson, pilot)

As usual, the most vulnerable part of most of our planes was our gas tanks: still metal, still not replaced with those desperately needed self-sealing tanks.

> Returning to England, I noticed that the gas gauge on one of our tanks was dropping down very fast. We knew we had been hit by some bullets; must have caught one of our tanks. The white cliffs of Dover never looked better when we came in off the North Sea. We made it back to Membury OK and spent all night changing that fuel tank to get ready for the next trip. (Jerome Loving, crew chief)

Washing the ice off our planes after the ice storm that cancelled our Christmas Day mission for the relief of Bastogne.

Bill Westcott's dramatic shot of the snowy fields around Bastogne as we flew in to supply the surrounded 101st Airborne troopers. The descending supply chutes are visible below the planes.

On Christmas morning we woke up to see that we were going to be grounded by a freak of nature. Fog and cold and high winds on Christmas Eve had combined in just the right proportions to produce a true ice storm. It was the coldest Christmas Day on record in England. Buildings, wires, trees glistened in the sun under a thick coat of ice everywhere. You could skate on the runways—but you sure couldn't taxi planes on them. The C-47s themselves were coated with a thick rime that had to be scraped off or washed away with gasoline. There was no way any re-supply mission could be run that day, not only from Membury, but from any of the 53rd and 50th TC Wing bases. Seventeen troop carrier planes did try to transport units of the 17th Airborne that day; but icing was so dangerous only five made it to France.[10]

This ice storm meant that our plans for the Christmas party for local war orphans and evacuee children which had to be canceled when we entered the Battle of the Bulge on December 23 were hurriedly put together again on Christmas morning (see Chapter 4). This mission postponement was a source of great satisfaction to everybody but the troopers in Bastogne. On December 26, however, and again on December 27, we delivered the goods by air to the 101st Airborne—for the very last time in World War II.

Our Squadron engineers cherish a recollection—never confirmed and possibly just a bit exaggerated—that when the last of us came back from the fourth Bastogne mission our planes sported so many holes that Tech Supply ran out of aluminum sheet, and the sheet-metal specialists, who had anticipated this very problem and had hoarded up a batch of tin can lids, had to rivet on those lids instead.

In addition to the groups in the 53rd and 50th TC Wings that re-supplied Bastogne, some Pathfinder Group planes also were involved. Only a few of them had been needed to drop the pathfinder paratroopers who set up markers and beacons in the Bastogne area. Others were set to work delivering parachuted supplies like the rest of us. Art Feigion, formerly in our Squadron but now a pathfinder pilot flying out of North Witham, was able to share in this experience—for the Pathfinder Group, a costly one. On their mission of December 23 the weather was still so bad that four of the planes crashed coming back to England, and nine others were forced to land on the Continent.[11]

I like to think that my crew was among the first eight planes into Bastogne. We took off from England in instrument weather. In Pathfinder, we flew a lot of our missions on instrument, when the weather was so bad "even the birds were walking." We handled our formation by time and altitude separation. And believe it or not, we all broke out of the weather over France and within sight of each other.

We went in pretty low over the snowy fields in France. Before we got to Bastogne we must have flown over some German areas; we were all hit by small-arms fire, but nothing serious. One of those bullets came up through the belly of the plane, right through the navigator's seat, and missed his dinkus by about an inch. The bullet then buried itself in the radar control box. We didn't find out where the bullet had ended up until we got back to England. (Art Feigion, pathfinder pilot)

By any standard, the air re-supply of Bastogne was a hugely successful operation. Everything worked. The pathfinder paratrooper teams placed their markers well. A swarm of P-47 fighters hammered the German infantry with bombs and napalm, and IX TAC fighter-bombers kept at least some German tanks at a distance. The 101st paratroopers at Bastogne, whose ammunition had run so low that shells for their guns had to be severely rationed for "lucrative targets," now had enough to protect themselves. Some of the parachuted ammo boxes were needed so badly they were rushed immediately to the field artillery and tank destroyers, to be fired off only minutes later. Estimates of the accuracy of our drops sound almost incredibly high: between 90 and 95 percent of the bundles are thought to have landed where the troopers could recover them.[12] This time the Germans got only a small percentage of American supplies.

The most threatening aspect of the Bastogne re-supply operation after December 23 was the critical shortage of medics and medicine. On December 19, a German raiding party overran an entire medical company in the area, and only a few surgeons escaped.[13] On December 24, the medical situation seemed so desperate that a Piper Cub plane was flown in with a surgical team and a load of penicillin. Medics, of course, could not be asked to parachute into Bastogne— they would likely have ended up litter cases themselves. But they could volunteer to be taken in in gliders. Messages urging them to do just that arrived from Bastogne. On December 26, eleven gliders were towed in (not by our outfit) and successfully landed with surgical teams and 600 jerricans of extremely welcome gasoline. Some of these gliders landed with dozens of bullet holes, including some through the jerricans but, probably because of the absence of gasoline vapor in cans that were hit, none of the gliders was set on fire. The following day, however, another medical glider mission suffered frightening losses. Fifty gliders were towed by the 439th TC Group to Bastogne, but only thirty-five of them made it. The Nazis shot down fifteen gliders, killing or capturing the glider pilots; thirteen C-47s were shot down.

The fabulous luck of the 81st TCS was holding up. We did not lose a single plane during the entire Bastogne operation. Even on the first day when the re-supply mission caught the Germans by surprise, other outfits in troop carrier lost a total of eight planes. And on December 27, we in the 81st TCS were treated to another piece of good fortune. While we were flying back from Bastogne, the weather turned extremely threatening. Our Group commander decided not to return to England but to take us into "landing strip A-41" (Dreux in France); and we all landed there safely. This turned out to be an exceptionally wise decision. The weather over Membury on December 27 was socked in, and we could not return to our base for two days.

As if to point up the magnitude of our re-supply successes, the Germans failed utterly in a re-supply attempt of their own. By Christmas Eve, Jochen Peiper, the ruthless SS Colonel who had spearheaded the breakthrough of the Sixth Panzer Army on December 17th—and whose troops massacred at least 117 Belgian men, women, and children plus at least 105 American prisoners of war in cold blood (most at Malmédy)—was hard pressed by American counter-attacks. And he was short of supplies. The Germans tried to re-supply him that night by parachute; but their mission failed almost completely. Most of their parachuted containers floated down into areas controlled by Gavin's 504th and 505th PIRs.[14] Peiper had to abandon his position, leaving his wounded and many of his tanks and trucks behind.[15]

The Battle of the Bulge also saw one last German use of combat paratroopers. At the beginning of the German assault, Otto Skorzeny—the same tough commando who had rescued Mussolini from prison in a daring glider raid on September 12, 1943—mustered a brigade of German paratroopers and gave them the assignment of capturing key bridges and road junctions in the German path. Another of their objectives was maximizing confusion among the Americans. But this mission also failed. Only ten German planes out of 105 dropped their troopers in the correct zones, and most of the German paratroopers were captured or killed immediately. A few, those who spoke fluent English and were dressed in American uniforms were sent in as saboteurs; these men did cause the wildest kinds of rumors to be spread among the disheartened Americans—including one that they had been sent out to assassinate Eisenhower. But the most harm these saboteurs caused was to scare American military police into setting up extraordinary security checks on the roads, which slowed the flow of our own traffic. The saboteurs had no real effect on the battle.[16]

Thus ended, ingloriously, the hopes of those in the Third Reich who had pioneered airborne warfare in the 1930s and early 1940s.

On the evening of December 27, a few tanks from the 4th Armored Division, shepherding some fifty supply trucks, penetrated the southern shoulder of the German line around Bastogne. The Germans desperately attempted to pinch off this penetration, and even launched another frontal attack against Bastogne. The ground fighting in the Bastogne area would continue for three more weeks; but on December 28 ambulances and trucks were able to drive unimpeded into Bastogne. For troop carrier, the Battle of the Bulge was over.

By that time our squadrons in the 436th TCG had flown in more than half a million pounds of supplies at an amazingly minor cost: although 40 percent of the Group's planes had been damaged, we had not suffered a single casualty![17] The situation on the ground offers a grim comparison. The 101st Airborne, alone, sustained more than 1,000 casualties.

The 101st kept fighting in this area until January 19, 1945. While no one day can be used to designate the end of Hitler's Ardennes assault, effectively it was all over by mid-January. The sixty-mile salient the Germans had won was eliminated, and the front lines were close to those of December 19. No reliable figures are available for German losses; estimates run between 100,000 and 120,000 killed or captured.

At the end of December, the diarist at 436th TC Group HQ wrote,

It was the opinion of this Group that they had seen everything in the way of bad weather during the month of November, but after the run of cold fog-freezing weather of December, including a snow storm, with everything blanketed with a thin coat of ice, including the runways and planes, November [in retrospect seemed] very mild compared to December.

In February, the same diarist had to admit that while nobody would have believed it possible, January had turned out even worse than December. This generally dismal stretch of time was hard to take.

We were winding up things in Britain and getting ready to move closer to the action on the Continent. Meanwhile, the weather was so rotten that there were only seven days during January when any flying was possible. On January 21 a plane from one of our sister squadrons, the 79th TCS, crashed on our base, killing the pilot and co-pilot and seriously burning the other crew members. Soon the good feelings of the days after Bastogne had completely evaporated.

The weather was so unceasingly bad that it was difficult for many of our power pilots and glider pilots to pile up the four hours of flying time they needed to get their supplemental flight pay. During all of January, our 436th Group's squadrons flew about the same number of sorties to the Continent we had flown during the short stretch of only five days in December, when we were flying the Bastogne missions. The total for January (206) was less than one-third the number of total Group flights in December (625). Before the month was out, the glider and airplane crews were becoming moody, restless, and noticeably sloppy—in our barracks, planes, and personal habits. Some weeks we got no mail at all from home. The level of bitching escalated, and foul language threatened to become the standard form of communication. Ken De Blake, a radio operator and a conscientious letter writer, wrote his mother, "If we didn't cuss each other out, we would die of boredom."

Desperate for ways of coping with "General Boredom," men in the radio operator barracks took to playing bridge. Gambling no longer held much interest. In this bone-chilling weather, tourism had lost its charms; men were known to return from an overnight pass before nightfall. Some fellows helped others by involving them in crafts. Many of us tried our hand at making rings and bracelets out of British silver coins. Alton Benson, an Intelligence clerk, introduced friends to the fun of making jewelry boxes and ornaments out of wood from the seats of wrecked gliders; this wood was high-quality plywood with mahogany or maple veneer. Some fellows learned how to make decorative pillow cases out of scraps of parachute nylon. Benson also showed us how to make napkin rings from discarded aluminum flare gun shells and how to decorate these rings with troop carrier insignia.

Our pilots used up excess energy by redecorating their lounge. Some enlisted men began planning a new dayroom for EMs out of wood from the huge boxes used to ship gliders; but we left for France before this project materialized. (An even better use eventually was found for that wood: floors for the tents in which we were housed on our French base.)

One way Group HQ thought it could prevent everybody's spirits from sinking even lower was to give furloughs to as many of us as possible to get us off the base. Anybody not needed for day-to-day affairs of the Squadron could get a three or even a five-day furlough. Operations and the Orderly Room worked together to get plane crews out of their hair by pretending we were all about to collapse from combat-induced nervous exhaustion. This meant we could apply for seven or even nine days of Air Forces-style R & R: rest and rehabilitation. We were sent to various British vacation resorts, usually at the seaside. There the hotels—grateful for any business in such a season—opened up and took us in. But we tended to come back from such R & R more depressed than ever.

Together with two other radio operators, I went to Blackpool, a resort town near Liverpool. Today I remember it looking like the dismal setting for a movie by one of those "angry young men" of the 1950s, whose main ambition seemed to be to show up life as thoroughly despicable in every respect. "Seedy" is too kind a word for the resort facilities of Blackpool at that time. EMs were paid $3.50 extra per day while on leave—plus a free hotel room—but there was little to spend it on. The food there made Membury mess hall chow seem better than ever. The heat in our hotel room was so scanty I had to wear my socks in bed and pile my overcoat on top of the blankets before I could fall asleep. The promenade along the beach was barren and filthy, and the cold winds blowing in across the Irish Sea made walking along the water a form of self-punishment. Worse,

Delivering blood bank containers.

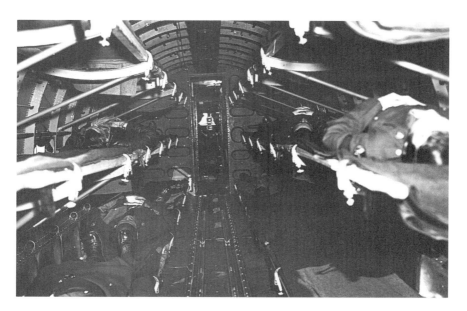

How we transported a load of litter patients.

the dreary-looking gulls that waddled along the beach looked more friendly than the women in the pubs.

Another way Group HQ coped with boredom was to force as many of us as possible to attend "orientation meetings" under the control of Squadron Intelligence.[18] The report from our 81st Squadron suggests how futile these were:

> 8 January—1400 to 1600 hours [2 to 4 p.m.], 300 Officers and E.M.s from this Squadron attended a news orientation film and a VD film at the Base Theater.
>
> 9 January—0900 to 1000, 150 Combat Crew members attended a P/W [prisoner of war] lecture on Interrogation of Troop Carrier Personnel by Germans, given by Lt. Col. D. W. Brack, CO.
>
> 1000 to 1045, 150 Combat Crew members attended a lecture on Identification of Deceased Personnel, given by Maj. Francis E. Farley, S-3. Both of these lectures were given in the 81st Pilots Lounge.
>
> 15 January—1400, approximately 100 members of this Squadron attended a news summary and orientation lecture given in the 81st Pilots Lounge by Sgt. Hoffman, Gp S-2.
>
> 22 January—1330 to 1415, approximately 150 Officers and E.M. attended a showing of a combat film at the Base Theater.
>
> 1430 to 1530, 126 Officers attended a lecture on Single Engine procedure, given by Lt. Col. Brack and Maj. Farley in the 81st Pilots Lounge.
>
> 23 January—1330–1530, 75 Officers attended a news summary and round table discussion of the news, held by 2nd Lt. Garcia, 81st Asst. S-2, in the 81st Officers Lounge.

By mid-January, signs of malaise were so plentiful that Group HQ stepped in with a new effort to prevent us from going entirely flat. We were now to experience a series of all-out inspections. Every department of the Squadron was subjected to surprise visits by Adriel Williams or a member of his staff. On January 16, Williams suddenly appeared in our Squadron's motor pool—which had managed to get warnings of the wrath about to descend on them, and had quickly washed every single vehicle in their charge. (To their relief Williams admitted that at least our Squadron's motor pool was in better shape than those of his other three squadrons.) On January 17 Williams "poked into unusual places," says our Squadron diary, including nooks and corners of the mess hall, departmental offices, and Tech Supply, and "found them not above average."

The following day it was the turn of our planes, the interiors of which Williams complained were downright filthy. Furious at his crews for letting him down, David Brack ordered us (including the pilots) to scrub floors in every part of the planes, to take up the seats and clean underneath them, to clean up the johns in the rear of the planes, and to put every single piece of personal stuff we customarily left around in the plane (notebooks, manuals, clothing, food snacks) either in the garbage or in its proper place.

One of us, at least, did manage to enjoy a temporary change of jobs during this dispiriting post-Bastogne season—a new position where he was afforded the feeling of being more useful.

> After the Battle of the Bulge they ordered every Flight Surgeon off his own airfield and to the nearest base hospital. The one I was sent to had mostly convalescent cases, soldiers with casts and crutches, walking around though not yet ready to be evacuated to hospitals in the States. I was able to give about half of those guys passes for visiting some nearby city; but several of these never did come back to that hospital. They took off for the high country; and when I was ready to come back to Membury, three or four of them still had not returned! (Jesse Coleman, Squadron Flight Surgeon)

While the rest of us were waiting for spring and possibly for a more active role in the coming assaults on Germany, up in high command the debates were still proceeding over how best to use troop carrier. The first day the 101st was surrounded, FAAA had tried to resolve the "fighters or freighters?" dilemma by doing everything at once. FAAA was still using parts of troop carrier to train paratroopers in the 17th Airborne Division and the British 6th Airborne. For a while FAAA believed it could continue this training while using other troop carrier planes to re-supply the 101st Airborne surrounded at Bastogne. FAAA also wanted still other units in troop carrier to continue ferrying those units of the 17th Airborne still in Britain into France, where they could be trucked up into the endangered Ardennes region.

More than the insufficient number of crews and planes, bad flying weather ruined this attempt to continue all sorts of troop carrier operations. On December 22 SHAEF ruled that re-supply of Bastogne had to take priority, but that moving the 17th Airborne to France could take priority over all other sorts of operations (that is, practice formations and bringing up supplies to other front line troops).[19] An order to our 53rd TC Wing to switch from ferrying the 17th Airborne to re-supplying the 101st Airborne came down to us only hours before our Squadron's first mission into Bastogne.[20] Units of the 17th Airborne which eventually were transported into the Ardennes area and used as line troops there at first experienced the confusion and failures most green troops suffer;[21] but later this division performed well in helping to contain "the Bulge" and then eliminate it. When we next met up with the 17th Airborne in March 1945 for its jump across the Rhine, however, the troopers proved just as bumptious, just as contemptuous of troop carrier, as in December 1944.

Our main airborne partner, on the other hand—the 101st Airborne—seems to have decided that troop carrier's performance at Bastogne had earned us their somewhat grudging acceptance. The official history of the 101st Airborne says, "The troops saw a number of C-47s shot down, but these losses had not made other planes take evasive action." [22] A formal letter from McAuliffe to Paul Williams on February 15, 1945, expressed

> the admiration all of us in the 101st Airborne feel for the grand job of air re-supply you furnished us during the siege of Bastogne. . . . Despite intense flak, the much-needed ammunition and medical supplies were dropped just where we wanted them. Needless to say, Bastogne could not have been held without this excellent support. [23]

Other evidence suggests that polite communications between generals did not reflect the complex feelings about troop carrier held by the men of the 101st. This was spelled out in Critchell's *Four Stars of Hell*, published soon after the war (1947) and certainly one of the best books ever written on the experiences of infantry during World War II. One of the key paragraphs in Critchell's book displays a somewhat patronizing willingness to forget the supposedly bad job troop carrier had done in Normandy.

> We were not bitter about the pilot error that had scattered us over a wide area of enemy territory and taken the lives of so many of our comrades. Having succeeded in our own missions despite the error, we were scornful, but it was not until late in the following winter, under slightly unexpected circumstances [that is, at Bastogne], that the Troop Carrier Command entirely redeemed itself in our eyes. [24]

Critchell had been a captain in the 501st Parachute Infantry Regiment of the 101st Airborne. In the chapter where he takes up the Bastogne episode in detail, he talks about the "great surge of relief and pride" he and his troopers felt when the first C-47s came into view that December 23 afternoon, and how he observed that "Flak [was] heavy, but not a single plane took evasive action." [25]

Perhaps all soldiers facing death relieve some of their feelings by cursing men on their own side whom they blame for part of their dangers—and who are not as much at risk as themselves. U.S. airborne soldiers sometimes seemed to hate troop carrier more than they did the Nazis, and we in troop carrier tried to cope with our own frustrations by cursing the British. Another wave of anti-British feeling arose among us at this time: Montgomery told the press in January that the German break-out in the Ardennes was the fault of American command failures. He also made truly insulting insinuations that our inexperienced (we read, cowardly) troops had broken and run in the face of the German attack. He claimed that it was mainly British intervention in the battle that contained and reduced "the Bulge." (He was in nominal command of the American First Army, as well as the British forces north of "the Bulge.")

The plain fact is that Montgomery deliberately held back British troops from this battle until near its end.[26] Eisenhower was livid when Montgomery's remarks were approvingly reported in British and some American newspapers. He decided that in spite of political risks he would force Montgomery to leave his command by threatening to resign himself.[27] Montgomery's staff managed to get Montgomery to send a rather abject letter of apology to Eisenhower only hours before Ike had determined to send off a cable (already written out) to get rid of that British hair shirt once and for all. Churchill helped smooth things over in a major address praising American performance in the battle and pointing out that thirty times as many Americans as British soldiers had been committed to this battle, while American losses in the Ardennes campaign outnumbered those of the British about seventy to one.

The excitement of our forthcoming move to France helped us fight off depression in the last weeks of January. The news, also, was full of the achievements of the vast Russian armies, which were starting their spring offensive early and advancing rapidly in Nazi-held Poland and Czechoslovakia. We knew that now the Nazis were doomed: Hitler could never replace the men and tanks lost during the Battle of the Bulge and on the Russian front.

In early February the diarist of our 436th Group HQ wrote:

> . . . a new hope for the speedy conclusion of this war appeared on the horizon of desire brought on by the swift moving and onrushing Russian offensive . . . as the personnel of this organization queued up for their pay, an atmosphere of optimism was very much in evidence as [they] waited for the materialization of their hopes, "finie la guerre."

And the diarist for our own 81st Squadron noted that some fellows were thinking so hard about home that they had resolved "not to use certain habitual vulgar words" so as "not to shock the folks back home whom they expect to see before the year is over."[28]

### Notes

1. John Eisenhower, *Bitter Woods*, pp. 86–87. Eight thousand of the 27,000 casualties sustained by Hodge's First Army alone came from exhaustion and exposure.

2. 436th TCG, hist. narr. for Oct. 1944.

3. 436th TCG, hist. narr. for Nov. 1944.

4. October 3, 5, 7, 14, and 23.

5. McAuliffe's wonderful one-word "Nuts!" reply (in writing) to the elaborate and almost courteous German demand to surrender, was made December 22. The German demand is reproduced in Rapport and Northwood, p. 511.

6. The weather actually got worse December 19–22; on December 20 and 21, even the Luftwaffe could not operate from its nearby fields. Rust, p. 132.

7. Huston, *Blue*, p. 206.

8. Retroactively, however, IX Troop Carrier Command gave the Bastogne re-supply missions the code name "Operation REPULSE."

9. Americans in forward posts wound sheets around their uniforms and even wore their long johns outside their uniforms to help camouflage themselves against the snow; many Germans, on the other hand, were provided with regular white winter uniforms.

10. Huston, *Blue*, p. 207.

11. HQ Squadron, IX TC Pathfinder Group, hist. narr. for December 1944.

12. Marshall, *Bastogne*, p. 137.

13. Rapport and Northwood, pp. 467–69.

14. Gavin, 1979, p. 263.

15. Weigley, 1981, pp. 512–13.

16. HQ FAAA, "German Paratroopers and their part in the Ardennes offensive," March 12, 1945.

17. 436th TCG, hist. narr. for Dec. 1944; see also the 436th TCG history by Captain Kenney, p. 5.

18. Intelligence in the 81st TCS then was under Lt. Thomas E. Trotman, who had replaced Captain John Bohan. But soon Trotman and David Brack fell out with each other over; Trotman was shipped out and replaced as head of our Squadron S-2 by Lt. Louis Kramer, until then Assistant Operations Officer.

19. "History of HQ, FAAA," pp. 44–45. Before the Ardennes campaign was over, troop carrier would ferry 13,000 soldiers of the 17th Airborne to France and evacuate 4,264 casualties.

20. "Ever First! The 53rd Troop Carrier Wing," pp. 24–25.

21. Blair, p. 413.

22. Rapport and Northwood, p. 531.

23. Conveyed to the 436th Group by a letter from HQ, IX TCC, dated February 15, 1945.

24. Critchell, p. 96.

25. See also the condescending remarks in Burgett (of the 506th PIR), pp. 191–92.

26. Blair, pp. 381–84; Weigley, 1981, pp. 538–41.

27. Weigley, 1981, pp. 543–44.

28. 436th TCG hist. narr. for Jan. and Feb. 1945.

# 19. Camping Out
## The French Connection

### Setting up at Melun

The mood around the Squadron on New Year's Day, 1945, was still pretty high, partly because we were pleased with our part in the Bastogne operation. These good feelings evaporated quickly, however, during the early days of 1945. A few of us had managed to attend New Year's Eve dances in nearby British towns, but those affairs were reported to be pretty forgettable, compared to American celebrations. The rest of us were left with whatever booze we had hoarded to help bring in the New Year. Somebody noticed that January 2 marked the anniversary of our Squadron's first landings in Britain; but that didn't seem to be any occasion for rejoicing.

The weather in January 1945 was truly depressing. We were told we were living through the worst winter Europe had experienced during the past forty years. And the news from the front lines in eastern France and Belgium made discouraging reading: nothing but costly, inconclusive slugging matches in icy mud. It took the American armies until the end of January to get back the territory they had lost during the Battle of the Bulge. The silver lining in all those gloomy British clouds was the news that we soon would be moving to France. Aside from a few of us who had British girl friends or strong attachments to British families, the only thing wrong with this announcement was that it hadn't come sooner.

Our new base was to be "Strip #A-55." It was to be very close to Paris— only thirty miles south-east of that very special city. This was a big plus. The nearest sizeable town to A-55 was Melun, six miles away and on the Seine River; but there was a little village, Villaroche, even nearer. Therefore a few of us remember it as "Villaroche," but most of us think of it as "Melun Airfield."

We made this move in accordance with the usual procedure of first sending an "advanced echelon." (See Appendix 2: The Roster.) On February 14 and 15, our first planes—fifteen of them, carrying thirty-two passengers as well as crews— flew to Melun. The advanced echelon's first job was putting up tents for both living quarters and for the Squadron's various departments. The tents in our living area were large, four-sided pyramid tents, intended to house six enlisted men or four officers.

The advanced echelon's biggest problem: trying to keep from freezing. That first night—which several of us remember as the coldest night of our lives—we were sheltered in a bare, empty building near the base. It had no sleeping accommodations besides a few chairs and the hard floor. Some of us managed to round up some straw to keep out the worst of the cold; others tried to get what sleep they could in their planes. All of us slept in the warmest clothes we had; some of us kept on our fleece-lined flying boots and pitied those without them.

It took about a week before we could get our quarters decently warm. There were no regular beds or mattresses, only folding canvas cots. We had only two blankets per man; and we quickly learned that it was better to have one blanket underneath, preferably on top of some straw. We waited for several days for delivery of pot-bellied stoves intended to heat the tents; even after stoves arrived the cold coming up from the frozen mud floor struck upward through the thin canvas of our cots like an icy dagger.

Meanwhile, the rest of our Squadron was ferried over, a couple of loads at a time, by our own C-47s. By February 23 we were all together again. Soon, the weather improved, and so did conditions in our tents. The plane crews soon became very conscious of how much more stable the French weather was: often, at the same time weather around Melun was quite decent, our planes there could not make the shuttle because Membury was closed down on account of heavy ground fog. Quartermaster Supply, meantime, received a vast shipment of sleeping bags for enlisted men. To get one you had to turn in one of your blankets. It was still cold enough in the tents to appreciate those sleeping bags very much indeed.

Our move from Britain to France represented more of a logistical achievement than did our move from North Carolina to Britain. In Britain we had moved onto an RAF airfield, vacated specifically for our Group and provided with decent runways, hardstands, regular barracks, and a few hangars, in addition to important amenities like running water, electric lighting, and telephone lines. In France we were plunked down on a former Luftwaffe base so thoroughly bombed out that an aerial view taken before we arrived showed the field with as many bomb craters as a Swiss cheese has holes. Most of the airfield structures were heaps of rubble piled around twisted steel girders. Only a few buildings were still standing, and Group appropriated all of these, for supply storage, vehicle maintenance, parachute rigging, and for a briefing building. For the first time since we activated we had no base theater.

But by February 26, just twelve days after the first of us got there, Melun was "operational," that is, ready to take on any of troop carrier's tasks. And our

David Brack, Squadron CO, in Melun.

Climbing into our rather makeshift control
tower at Melun.

living quarters were conspicuously improving—to the point where they became not only tolerable but in some ways more comfortable than our barracks in Membury. Fixing up our Melun tents as ingeniously as we could became our main preoccupation for weeks, until the weather turned almost balmy and the ban against going to Paris was lifted. One reason this transition from Membury was so effective is that we made it with the aid of our own transportation. And it was the best in the business: twenty-seven capacious, dependable, and well-maintained C-47s. The distance was an easy two-hour flight, with a chance to spot the Eiffel Tower and some other famous landmarks in Paris on the way. Ken De Blake, a radio operator, reports that on one of these trips his plane buzzed the Arch of Triumph.

Our shuttle service brought back from Membury not only the rest of our personnel, but also load after load of equipment and supplies. In our collective Squadron memory these are called "the lumber runs," because aside from people, the most notable item we hauled was wood. Somebody (it's not clear who) had the truly brilliant idea that the boxes in which disassembled gliders had been crated to Membury would make perfect floors for our tents—floors that would keep out cold as well as mud. Without any formal permission from headquarters, the men still at Membury fell to work sawing up those crates into pieces that could be knocked together into just the right size for tent floors. When we flew this fine flooring into Melun we were greeted like heroes.

More basic and less pleasant work also had to be done at Melun. When we arrived in February dozens of French construction workers were filling in the worst of the bomb craters and repairing taxiing strips and hardstands. The runways had to be strengthened and widened: for this, Army engineers had to be brought in. The job took tons of concrete, macadam, steel mesh, and gravel. More work was needed on vehicle roads running through all the Group areas and giving access to the maintenance lines and the runways; for this we were able to use the German landing mats left behind. Also useful were the beams and girders we recovered: with these we built a bridge across a ditch that cut one of our roads. Joe Konecny (Squadron Engineering Officer) and his crew worked on several of these massive improvements. Even before the streets and runways were in good shape, our engineers erected our Membury street sign, "TARFU Boulevard," out on the road running between our mess hall and our Operations Office. By the time our main echelon arrived (February 19), most of the tents had cots and stoves, the mess tent was working well—and we were becoming more and more pleased with the results of our handiwork.

Our medics, too, had some basic responsibilities for improving our new base. They opened up a new dispensary, conveniently placed near our tent area. And since there was no running water on the base, they set up huge canvas "Lister bags" in a few positions around the tent area. These bags dispensed treated water—safe but nasty-tasting—through a spigot on the bottom. It was the medics under Jesse Coleman, too, who took responsibility for providing facilities for latrines and garbage disposal under the "sanitary survey" system. The latrines were nothing but slit trenches of the "straddle and squat" variety; later these were replaced with "Chic Sales" fitted with seats but, for some silly reason, not with doors. The urinals were shielded from view on only two sides by a couple of yards of canvas supported by some stakes.

> In front of the officers' pots was a big sign that said, on one side, "Big-Ass Birds," and on the other, "Little-Ass Birds." One day Waterman and some other guys were sitting on the pots when a whole bunch of nurses coming into our "Tent City" walked right by. But you could tell the nurses could care less; they'd seen much worse. (Ellery Bennett, pilot)

Not everyone at Melun was housed in tents. The enlisted men of Group HQ were billeted in fairly decent stone houses in Villaroche; and the Group HQ officers used a really comfortable building in the nearby village of Réau. There was an officers club in Melun, "by far the most beautiful the [436th] officers have ever had"; and Melun also provided a rather more modest Red Cross Club for enlisted men. We had a Squadron shuttle truck that ran to the Red Cross Club every hour after 7 p.m.[1]

## At home in "Tent City"

By the second week of March 1945 our "Tent City" was becoming a pretty comfortable place. Once in a while the early spring rains would send rivulets of mud into the tent area. But there were compensations, even for those too contemptuous of (or too suspicious of) those "Frogs" (Frenchmen) to venture on our evenings off into Melun or the neighboring villages. Every one of us got a great deal of satisfaction out of refusing to surrender to the potentially minimal conditions of life at our base. We all set about transforming those bare tents and bombed-out buildings into accommodations as luxurious as our own ingenuity and zest for scrounging would permit. One neat improvement had come when we found that a bombed-out building near our mess hall had a boiler in it that was mostly intact—this building had been the German's power plant. A few repairs, some piping located in a nearby scrap heap, and that building became a pretty good shower room. It was available to enlisted men as well as officers, according to a posted schedule.

> I remember that we got a two-and-a-half gallon bucket of coke for our tent stoves that was supposed to last a week. When the coke got low we would

take a jeep into the nearby woods and cut ourselves a load. But our pile of wood outside our tent had a way of disappearing each time we went off to fly. So we took down that little old heater in the middle of the tent and dug us a hole about four feet deep. Then we filled the hole up with wood, and put our stove back on top of it. After a few days a fellow living close asked us what we were doing with all that wood he saw us bringing back in the jeep. We never did tell him we had a cellar under our tent. (Emmett Pate, crew chief)

Some of the transformations we wrought in our tents were pretty gratifying. In my tent we had large cans on our stove for hot water, and a "liberated" German radio that got BBC and American Forces Network broadcasts as well as Radio Berlin. Outside, we built a vestibule to shield the tent entrance from cold blasts of air—complete with a plexiglass skylight scrounged from a junkyard; and we also hammered together a washstand with holes for our inverted steel helmets that functioned very well as basins for shaving or washing.

But this was nothing compared with what other tent-dwellers were able to contrive.

We finally got tent stoves; then we got a stainless steel coil and put it inside the stove. We used drained and discarded aircraft engine oil for fuel for that stove. As the oil traveled through the coil it would be preheated and would burn exceptionally well. Next we put another coil in the stove; and when we wanted hot water, we would allow water to travel through the second coil. We had two fifty-five-gallon barrels outside the tent for a water supply. We got a wash basin out of a wrecked plane and used this to wash and shave in. (Bill Lane, glider pilot)

I served as Gas Officer; so I had at my disposal a large tank (the decontaminating tank) to carry water. We went out to one of the empty châteaus in the neighborhood and borrowed a sink; and we also found a container for a bomb that could serve as a water tank inside the tent. Every morning I would have water poured from the decontaminating tank into our tent tank—and we had running water! Later, everybody had electricity in his tent; but we were the only ones that had our own running water. (Louis Kramer, Squadron Intelligence Officer)

Electric lights in tents? Why not! Hal Read, our wire chief, supplied the necessary wiring not only to our department buildings but also to each and every tent. Read and other Communications fellows (especially Frank Ruffini)—with the assistance of Thayer Bonecutter, a glider pilot who had been a telephone

"Tent City": Officers' tents in our camp at Melun, France.

Fresh air chow: Thayer Bonecutter (glider pilot) and friends escaping the dingy mess hall tent we used before our new Melun "TARFU Country Club" was built.

lineman before the war—also found ways of hooking up our little PE-110 generators, supplied for electric power to Operations and to plane and glider mechanics working on the line. Other squadrons at Melun, too, managed electric lights: Charles Hastings, now in the 82nd Squadron, at first wrote his wife for a gasoline tent light, but soon wrote again to cancel the order, since his tent had acquired electricity. When our own generators failed to provide all the light and power we wanted, the French power plant engineers in Melun obligingly hooked us into their own system.

And we were more than pleased with Group facilities on the base. American and French construction engineers rebuilt several of the bombed-out Luftwaffe structures; and they also put together some "Romney huts" and "Butler hangars" out of parts crated over from Britain. By mid-March the parachute riggers, tech and QM supply clerks, and 459th Service Squadron engineers had more than adequate structures for their use. James Knott, who was our Squadron Supply Officer until he was transferred up to the same job at Group, reported that "the supply set-up on this field is excellent."[2]

Some of us had the time of our lives in France; others were hostile to everything French and couldn't wait to leave. But none of us can deny that eating anywhere in France—on or off the base—was conspicuously better than in Britain. We had neither the money nor the interest to try "haute cuisine" in the better French restaurants; we were happy enough with the tasty food at Red Cross hotels in Paris and other towns. But the biggest change in food was in our own mess hall situation. Back in Membury we had had a consolidated mess hall for all four squadrons in the 436th; at Melun we had our own small Squadron mess hall. Both the officers and men of the 81st TCS ate here (on different sides of the hall). And here we had our own 81st TCS cooks rather than Group cooks as at Membury. Sergeants Maguire and Mullen now were feeding only their own officers and buddies and they reacted by preparing chow more carefully and ladling it out into our trays less sloppily.

Of course it took several weeks before all the problems of setting up good chow in an attractive mess hall could be solved.

> For a few days in France there was no bread at all. I remember that every time I was about to fly one of those shuttles back to Membury, everybody would come running to give me money to buy bread in England. And I bought as much bread as I could carry. (Emmett Pate, crew chief)

At first we ate in one huge tent; but soon our glider pilots, helped by a lot of other volunteers, took over a small bombed-out hangar and turned it into "TARFU Country Club," a relatively attractive place complete with a welcoming sign, fresh paint, and comfortable tables and benches. (Squadron Operations and Intelligence moved into our vacated mess hall tent.) When Colonel Adriel Williams, our Group commander, had visiting dignitaries interested in seeing how his men ate, he always took them around to the 81st TCS mess hall.

The Squadron diarist summed it all up:

> The morale of the Squadron appears very high. Everyone seems pleased with the present living conditions and the general location. The attendance at all meals is almost 100%—no better barometer of conditions could be obtained.[3]

## Operations before the Rhine assault

In France we did much less gambling; in fact, there was much less card-playing altogether. The cramped quarters in those tents did not encourage indoor amusements. Later, when the weather got better, you could play volleyball, pitch horseshoes, or get into a softball game on the Squadron's own diamond. But most days there was just too much work to allow for poker or bridge. Very few of us had time enough on our hands to attend French language classes offered in the Group briefing room. And we had a bare month to do it all; as we soon learned, the assault across the Rhine was set for March 24.

Meanwhile, those do-it-yourself amenities we put together were always needing improvements or repairs. The wires that Hal Read and his crew strung all over the place for our field telephones were always getting chewed up in somebody's wheel when a vehicle ran over them: "It was an ongoing battle," he reported.

Some of the best improvements presented us with some novel problems.

> Those wooden floors we had were great. But we must have brought some rats along with all that junk, because pretty soon the rats were getting into our rations. Some nights you would wake up to the sound of someone in your tent pounding on the floor to kill a rat. One day we organized The Great Rat Hunt. We brought in some weapons carriers, put hoses on their exhaust pipes, and put the hoses under our wood floors. When the rats were driven out we were waiting with clubs. But many of them got away running right between those swinging clubs. (Jerome Loving, crew chief)

Our planes were as busy the month of March as during the hectic days of the past September. There was some rain; but compared with England much less fog and low-lying clouds. Only three days after transporting all our own personnel and equipment across the Channel, we were put to work running supply-evac missions all over the liberated parts of the Continent. We also transferred litter patients from base hospitals in France to hospitals in England. Some of our supply flights were to fighter bases in the eastern parts of France (near Nancy and Strasbourg) and a few even to bases in occupied German territory west of the Rhine (around Aachen). Ken De Blake, a radio operator, stayed overnight on one former German base and was struck by the differences between their accommodations and our own Tent City: they had had two-story concrete barracks with stoves in every room and attractively painted walls with some coats of arms—but no pin-ups!

And we had to provide planes for several airborne training missions. One of these (Operation DEWDROP), on March 10, was a huge Group mission aimed at giving the 17th Airborne more practice in jumping from formations. We performed only one glider training mission, aimed at familiarizing glider pilots with the hazards of double-tow gliding. Another purpose of this glider training mission (Operation TOKEN) was to check carefully on the rate of gas consumption in a C-47 towing two fully loaded gliders.

And we were still ferrying some units of the 17th Airborne from Britain to France. When the weather was exceptionally good several of our C-47s could chalk up two missions a day. Soon there were a lot of C-47 engines with more time on them than the maximum of 500 or 600 hours; and the doubtful engines had to be changed in a hurry.[4] This meant that out on the engineering lines the pace of work speeded up beyond anything we had experienced. Besides all the regular work, we had twelve new self-sealing gas tanks (finally!), and these had to be installed quickly. The glider mechanics had a big job in checking over all the newly assembled gliders now crowding onto our field, and in installing important "up-dates"—including the enthusiastically welcomed arrester chutes in the gliders' tails that could check your speed after landing. The burden of work on the plane and glider mechanics became so fatiguing that, for the first time, bitching became a really serious problem; Pappy Harris, our line chief, had to step in and work out some new arrangements in order to deal with the grievances. Col. Brack showed that he appreciated the strain our mechanics were under by ordering that they be served first on the chow line; the mechanics at least got hot food; the rest of the enlisted men came later.

On March 21 the reason for all this hurry-up work was made clear to all. The units of the 17th Airborne we were to ferry across the Rhine moved into Melun and were put in tents on our field. The airborne assault on Germany was about to begin.

Our "TARFU Airlines" Operations tent in Melun. In the foreground: Louis George *(left)*, Roscoe Wilkins *(center)*, and Joe Berryman, pilots.

Cecil Elder *(left)*, communications chief, and John Sheldon *(center)*, and Marty Wolfe, radio operators, pose in front of their Melun airbase tent—more comfortable than it looks.

Pilot Ellery Bennett and his elegant tent.

## The first time I saw Paris

"How're Ya Gonna Keep 'Em Down on the Farm, After They've Seen Paree?" That song was a hit just after the First World War. The half mocking, half serious question it raised had no message for us in the Second World War—our generation was not a batch of "innocents abroad," whose lives might be transformed just by exposure to a city of great culture and (relatively) uninhibited sex. But the "City of Light" was still a powerful magnet. And, after a second gloomy winter in Britain, we were more than ready to try it out. Feeling that the war was about to end (at least, the war in Europe), we were anxious for a few experiences— tame or otherwise—to take home with us.

Some of us in the plane crews had already had a chance to visit Paris while still based in Britain, thanks to supply-evac missions nearby. A few of us numbered among the lucky ones who made it to Paris when the tremendous exhilaration that followed the expulsions of the Germans was still in the air. By the time our whole outfit arrived in Melun, however, seven months had gone by. Not for us, the jubilant kisses of August 1944 bestowed on "les libérateurs!"

Paris in March 1945 looked shabby, though there were none of the ruins we saw in London. Paris certainly held more attractions than nearby Melun—not to mention the tiny villages clustered around our airfield. Still, some of us found it worth the risk, after work was through for the day, to walk out an unguarded rear gate and stroll a short distance to the villages of Villaroche or Lissy. In Lissy, Gerry O'Shea remembers, there was a charming French barmaid by the name of Suzanne.

When the weather became milder, some officers liked to stroll into Melun and sample the *vin blanc* there. But the pressure was great to ignore these more local attractions and to invent any excuse at all to get a pass to Paris. Some glider pilots sent over in our advanced echelon managed to do this even before our tents went up. The majority of our enlisted men had to wait until their turn came to board the "liberty run" truck that set out for Paris three times a week at 0800 hours and returned at 2200 (10 p.m.). The passes we got at the Orderly Room were accompanied by stern warnings to make that return truck or face the court-martial that would come for anyone picked up late in Paris by the MPs and tossed in the "Stragglers Barracks" for the night.

Basically we found three things to do in Paris. We could stroll along the boulevards and perhaps ride the buses or the Métro (subway), with no particular aim aside from sampling the sidewalk cafés and restaurants and taking in the general atmosphere; on the way we could wait in those long lines in front of Chanel or some other famous shop to buy a bottle of perfume. Or, we could "do the sights," the great Paris landmarks. Or, we could go looking for girls (or prostitutes).

So far as sex was concerned, most of us confined ourselves to looking (and to talking about it). We may have made a beeline to the Rue Pigalle (the "Pig Alley" of World War I fame) to see the famous red-light district, but for the most part we were there to gawk rather than to sample. As Ben Ward (glider pilot) reported, "I saw many strange sights while visiting Paris, including ladies with purple hair." It certainly was true that the classy style of those prostitutes, their boldness, and the sheer quantity of them, was something about which we were all very conscious. Prostitutes were everywhere GIs were likely to stroll. I remember the shock a bunch of us felt when we emerged from a Métro stop in front of the Paris Opera to be accosted by one who advertised her specialty by asking "Suckee, suckee?" We were even more startled when one of us took her arm and went off with her.

None of the fellows with whom I walked around Paris bought any of those famous "feelthee peekchures" ("French postcards") offered on every corner. For most of us sex in Paris was confined to visits to the Follies Bergère or the Casino de Paris—grandly presented and satisfactorily naughty spectacles. These visits are now memorialized in the playbills we all kept and put in our scrapbooks.

What took most of our time in Paris was not sex but—as with all first-time visitors to Paris—the famous sights of the city. In fact, we took decorous, organized Red Cross bus tours that started on the Boulevard de la Madeleine (there was a Red Cross hotel here labeled, after the famous one in London, "Rainbow Corners") and showed us the Place de la Concorde, the bridges over the Seine, the Arch of Triumph (where we dutifully waited in line to file by the tomb of the Unknown Soldier), the Eiffel Tower, Notre Dame, and the Tuileries gardens. We all took pictures of ourselves standing in front of the Arch of Triumph. Some of us even poked our heads into the Louvre museum; but the Louvre was dismayingly bare. We felt less than daring spending our time in Paris doing this sort of thing, but it was safe, and it was at least partially satisfying.

In France we were poorer than we had been in Britain—not because our pay was less, but because the exchange rate of the French franc was pegged artificially high. At first we were paid in "occupation currency"—notes printed in the U.S. that had to be accepted by the French as legal tender. This infuriated General Charles de Gaulle, who saw it as a slap at French sovereignty, partly because this money had the phrase "occupation currency" printed right on it, in English. He soon forced the American government to pay us with regular francs printed at the Banque de France.

Whatever francs we got were set at the rate of two cents per franc; in terms of what we could buy, however, a franc was worth only about a cent or even less. This deal—which De Gaulle forced on Eisenhower—was a way of having

American soldiers support a high exchange value for the franc. We were provided, however, with one way of jacking up our purchasing power: the famous French black market. The French faced shortages of almost every kind, and they were avid buyers of things we could get (at low, untaxed prices) in our PX: candy, soap, gum, and especially cigarettes. Black marketeers were everywhere: they would hang about in the cafés or converge at spots where "liberty run" buses would stop. And when they spotted someone carrying a stuffed musette bag they would sidle up and ask, "Anything to sell?" They would whip out a thick wad of notes and pay high prices: for example, 100 francs ($2.00) for a single pack of cigarettes that cost us a nickel. This was all illegal; but it was universally tolerated, by both French and American authorities. We would feel slightly squeamish doing it. But this feeling would be more than overcome by the thought that we could load up with a bundle of PX stuff we didn't need which paid for our whole day in town—and in a sense compensated us for the unfair exchange rate of the franc.

A less questionable deal was to trade your PX rations, not sell them. This way you could get fresh eggs, wine or cognac, and delicious French bread. Several of us developed connections in Melun where this could be done easily and to everybody's satisfaction. Johnny Harris (crew chief) had some unusual trade goods; he had located an unguarded box of stockings intended for MAES nurses: "Sure was good bartering material!" You could also trade for a bottle of the local potato vodka, guaranteed to make your eyes water, made by farmers around Lissy who had emigrated there from Poland during the 1920s.

Much more dangerous was the black market trade in U.S. dollars. Every black marketeer in Paris would begin by asking if you had dollars or British pounds; for this they would pay three times the official exchange rate or even more (if you wanted to engage in tough bargaining). But we all knew that black marketeers had connections through the French underworld with Nazi espionage networks that wanted those dollars to pay their spies in America and in Britain. At one time we were ordered to turn in all our remaining American dollars and take in return "gold seal certificates," dollars with a yellow rather than a blue seal on the face which would not be usable in the United States. We were all involved in the French black market one way or another. But several of us in our Squadron have told me that they drew the line at trading in U.S. currency.

Later in France, toward the end of our stay, black market operations involving American troops grew to such proportions that American counter-intelligence and military police specialists had to be brought in to fight it. By then it had expanded to include GI clothes, silk stockings and other items mailed to soldiers from the United States, and even gasoline and rubber tires stolen from quartermaster supply depots. There were no criminal black market cases involving the 81st TCS. But a gasoline truck was stolen from the motor pool of our sister squadron, the 82nd. Eventually the soldier who engineered this heist (not one from our 436th Group) was caught; but the truck and the gasoline were never recovered.

We did have one 81st TCS vehicle stolen at this time; but it turned out that this was not a black market affair.

While the 81st was at Melun I used the jeep that was assigned to Engineering, and that way I got to visit Paris occasionally. Since Melun was only thirty miles from Paris, we were able to drive in, have a short visit, and come right back. One time I was there with George Rankin, our Communications Officer. On our return trip that night we stopped for a snack and drink at a café half-way between Paris and Melun. When we came out the damn jeep was gone!

Only a few civilians were in sight and nobody knew anything. So we had to start walking about fifteen miles back to base. It was just after dawn when we came in, took a shower and a cup of coffee, and went right to work.

Later, after we had informed the MPs about the theft, we found out that the jeep had been taken for a joy-ride and banged up by an escapee from a nearby military mental hospital. It took about two weeks to get that jeep repaired and returned. (Joe Konecny, Squadron Engineering Officer)

Our Squadron recollections about the French people in general are pretty complex and not easy to interpret. Before we moved to France, and before we had much to do with the French, you could hear many expressions of pity for all that these people suffered under the German occupation.

We stayed in France last night—a lot of French people came out to the field to see us. All the kids wanted to shake hands. I really felt sorry for those poor devils. I doubt if they know what a full stomach is. One of our guys opened a box of K-rations and ate it right in front of them. I thought those kids would stare it right out of his hands before he finished. I don't know why he ate it in front of them anyway. (Ken De Blake, radio operator; from a letter written November 6, 1944)

But after we had been there for a few weeks, our impressions of the French became contradictory. Many of us remember the French (at least, the French at that time) with a certain amount of contempt. We made fun of their *pissoires* (enclosed street urinals) and their primitive "squat" (no seat) toilets, where you ran the risk of getting your shoes drowned if you didn't get out of the way fast after you pulled the chain. Seeing men and women in café and restaurant lavatories using the same facilities made us feel pretty uneasy.

> Once I visited the Jockey Club de France in Paris at the invitation of a fellow officer stationed at SHAEF Headquarters. I was surprised by the lifestyle of French society, especially at poolside. The ladies wore pretty scanty bathing suits—the kind we later called bikinis—and children up to the age of five were "déshabillés." Drinks and hors d'oeuvres were plentiful. I'm still teed off because my mini-camera, with pictures in it taken at this Club, was stolen from my tent at Melun. (Joe Konecny, Squadron Engineering Officer)

Many of us called them "Frogs" (because they ate those nasty-looking frog legs). Yet we all admired the great monuments of Paris and other cultural achievements so abundantly displayed. I remember visiting a jazz *boîte* with George Doerner, a radio operator who played trumpet in our 436th TCG dance band, and being astonished at the virtuosity of the musicians there, who seemed to have the American jazz idiom down pat.

Certainly many of us were made uneasy by all those prostitutes: Hal Read, our wire chief, was accosted by one of them right on our base, in fact only hours after our advanced echelon landed in Melun; and this one had a young girl (her daughter?) in tow, whom she also offered for sale.

"*Voulez-vous couchez avec moi?*" ("How about going to bed with me?") was the first French phrase many of us learned; a few of the more obnoxious fellows in our Squadron did indeed try this out on French girls strolling by, though it plainly was an inexcusable insult. On the other hand we all remarked on how chic French girls looked: even though they were no prettier than British girls, they took a lot more care with their make-up and clothes. Many of us begged French girls to let us take a picture with our arm around their waists: a nice, safe souvenir.

Another fine souvenir we collected was the street and subway map of Paris handed out at Red Cross hotels. It folded up into a handy size for your shirt pocket, and had useful phrases for asking directions—complete with pronunciation guides ("Ah kel stas-iong foh tiel desandr?"). It listed and located the chief "Places to See." But the most evocative feature of this souvenir was its back: it was printed on the backs of captured German war maps—good quality paper! The back of my Red Cross map shows enormous details ("*Masstab* 1:50,000") of the southern Ireland area in the Kilkenny-Waterford district ("*Anschlussblaetter* 168"). Military historians have engaged in a long and inconclusive debate over whether the Nazis truly had intended to invade Britain after their conquest of France. These maps show that at least some Germans considered it seriously.

After we had been at Melun for a few months, whatever feelings of compassion we may have had at first for the French seem to have vanished. We were curious but not particularly sympathetic. We were interested to see that they could run their buses and trucks on gas (not gasoline) made by heating coke in what looked like large boilers perched on those vehicles. The hardships that made such devices necessary, however, bothered us not at all. We noticed that the outskirts of Melun had been hurt by bombing, undoubtedly by British or American planes; but this seemed not nearly so bad as the bomb damage we had seen in Britain. And central Paris had not been bombed at all. Several of us remarked that if you didn't know any French—but spoke a little German—you could get around well in Melun, where many people seemed to know that language. This suggested that at least a lot of people had not found things too terrible under the Nazi occupation.

We realized they suffered from many scarcities; the scarcity of soap was all too plain when you rode a bus or a subway car and were surrounded by overpowering body odors. On the other hand, everybody seemed to have some connections with farmers or black marketeers. And we found the French attitude toward the black market compared very unfavorably with the British, who—to us at least—seemed to be obeying the rules that were laid down in the interest of the common war effort. We also were bothered by the pushing and shoving in French crowds, so different from the sort of politeness we had found in Britain. In Paris nobody waited in a queue.

### Notes

1. 436th Group, hist. narr. for March 1945.
2. 81st TCS, hist. narr. for March 1945.
3. 81st TCS, hist. narr. for March 1945.
4. This was a general problem throughout the 53rd Wing squadrons; the Wing historical narrative for March 1945 says that when no less than sixty engines had to be changed in five days, this was "the largest commitment [Wing] had ever faced."

# 20. Supporting Montgomery
## Preparations for the Last Assault

### Summitry

The end of this war was coming, everybody knew. But how? and—for God's sake—*when*? Soviet armies were grinding their way forward, inflicting savage reprisals on a Nazi Germany that for four years had been butchering and exploiting conquered Russians as though they were cattle. German troops on the western front were weakening; but they still fought desperately—and competently—as they were pushed back toward the Rhine.

The Allied air forces continued to pulverize German cities, many of which were already heaps of rubble; but the inhabitants somehow managed to dig out, keep factories going, and maintain order under these nightmare conditions. In spite of all the promises of British and American air commanders who had advocated victory through air power, an end would not come either through a collapse of civilian morale or the mass surrender of German armies in the face of strategic bombing.

Nazi fanaticism seemed to increase as the noose tightened around Germany. We learned that if shot down we should surrender to regular army (Wehrmacht) units and not to SS troops; and once in prison we were to forget about the duty of imprisoned officers to attempt escape. Hitler announced that any German commander who lost a Rhine bridge would be shot. The Nazi propaganda machine insisted that civilians as well as soldiers would be forced to fight Allied advances street by street and house by house in every city. Joseph Goebbels, the Nazi propaganda minister, circulated accounts of how Nazis were building up a "redoubt" of hundreds of thousands of elite troops dug into the mountain sides of the Bavarian and Austrian Alps where they would defend impregnable positions to the last man. (This "Nazi redoubt" was a hoax, but many Allied generals believed it.)[1] Incredibly, Nazi leaders still held the German people and the Wehrmacht in a tight grip. The war would end only when all of Germany was overrun by "ground pounders," the Allied infantry.

But the end *was* coming. And with its approach came the problem of how the superpowers would deal with a conquered German nation. Though there was no way for us in troop carrier to know it, this political problem, even more than any military question, determined for the next three months how we would operate—as freighters or fighters, in combat or in non-combat.

We soldiers, of course, wanted to "get it the hell over with!" We wanted to get back to our families, to regain control over our own lives—in a word, to become civilians. ("Call Me Mister!" was the name of a smash hit musical comedy that opened in early 1946.) Military commanders and statesmen, as a group, also wanted the war to end quickly. But they fell to quarreling over the *manner* in which the war should end, a manner they hoped would reflect glory on their own particular country, repay their own nation's sacrifices, and (especially as far as the top generals were concerned) insure public recognition for their own particular military accomplishments. By early 1945, maneuvering over how to divide up honors and benefits seemed to become more important than the fighting itself.

At the same time that our Squadron was learning how to operate out of "Tent City," the Combined Chiefs of Staff and the superpower statesmen were meeting to determine which Allied power would rule what parts of Germany and Austria. An even more pressing problem: How and where Allied armies would advance until victory was complete. Out of these meetings, as everybody knows, came the Yalta accords (February 3, 1945) which fixed the Elbe River as the military frontier between the American and British troops on the one hand and the Russians on the other—a boundary which would leave the great prize of Berlin surrounded by Soviet-occupied Germany. Berlin itself, however, would be divided up among the occupying powers.

The first part of our Squadron's involvement in these great decisions came with our participation in Operation VARSITY, the airborne jump across the Rhine.

From that day to this, weighing the significance of Operation VARSITY has perplexed historians. VARSITY was a model airborne assault: everything worked as planned, demonstrating that the troop carrier-airborne team was now honed to perfection; but then, instead of using this weapon for assaults further into Germany, troop carrier was restricted to supply and evacuation exclusively.

## Planning VARSITY

Planning an airborne invasion somewhere across the Rhine began way back in September 1944. At that time the Lower Rhine was the only stretch of the river where Allied forces were close enough to make an airborne assault seem feasible.[2] Further south along the river everything depended on Americans breaking through to the Rhine across the system of German defenses called the "Siegfried Line."

The Battle of the Bulge, of course, put all such airborne planning on hold. In February 1945, however, the rapid advances of the Soviet "steamroller" revived hopes for an early end to the war, and FAAA pulled its sketch for VARSITY out of the files and began detailed planning.

Some features of the plans for VARSITY were brilliant. These plans also amounted to a truly courageous departure from past airborne operations. VARSITY showed that FAAA planners knew they would have to take chances to avoid the mistakes of previous airborne operations. The most startling change was that the established sequence of airborne warfare was to be abandoned. From HUSKY through MARKET, this sequence always started with paratroopers landing behind enemy lines and starting to carve out an airhead. Then gliders, bringing in reinforcements and heavier equipment, would land in areas secured by paratroopers. Finally, the combined airborne troopers would punch through enemy encirclement and link up with a land- or sea-borne infantry launched in their direction some hours after the airborne attack began.

This time, however, parachutists and glider-borne troopers would be landed virtually on top of each other, or at any rate at just about the same time; in other words, the gliders would *not* wait until paratroopers cleared out their LZs. Furthermore, this time the land forces were to fight their way across the Rhine *first*, eight hours before the first troop carriers took to the air. This was supposed to insure that the British would have at least a small bridgehead across the Rhine *before* the airborne troopers came in, which would greatly increase the chances of an early linkup between airborne and land infantry. (The amphibious infantry portion of the invasion, mostly a British affair, was code-named PLUNDER.)

But the biggest and most risky change of all was that the entire operation was to be squeezed into the shortest time frame possible: VARSITY was to place two entire airborne divisions—about 21,700 paratroopers and glidermen—into German-held fields east of the Rhine in a bit more than two and one-half hours. This would mean "double-tow": most of the gliders would have to be pulled two to a tug plane.

The decision to put everybody across the Rhine together was a reaction to one of the causes of MARKET's failure. VARSITY planners were haunted by the conviction that if all the airborne troopers could have been dropped or landed together during the invasion of Holland, the Allies could have broken through in September 1944. Planners also hoped that the all-at-once feature of VARSITY would deny the Germans time to move in effective supporting defenses. By gambling everything on one gigantic airborne lift, the Allies might be losing something in tactical flexibility; but this would be more than offset by not running the

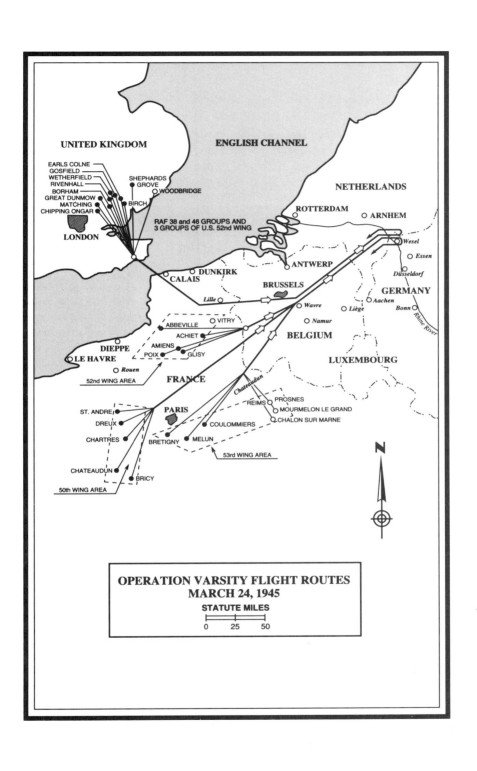

UNITED KINGDOM

ENGLISH CHANNEL

EARLS COLNE
GOSFIELD
WETHERFIELD
RIVENHALL
BORHAM
GREAT DUNMOW
MATCHING
CHIPPING ONGAR

SHEPHARDS
GROVE
WOODBRIDGE
BIRCH

LONDON

RAF 38 and 46 GROUPS AND
3 GROUPS OF U.S. 52nd WING

NETHERLANDS

ROTTERDAM

ARNHEM

Wesel

Essen

Düsseldorf

DUNKIRK

CALAIS

ANTWERP

BRUSSELS

GERMANY

Lille

Wavre

Aachen

Bonn

Liège

Rhine River

ABBEVILLE

VITRY

Namur

BELGIUM

ACHIET

AMIENS

POIX

GLISY

DIEPPE

LE HAVRE

LUXEMBOURG

Rouen

52nd WING AREA

FRANCE

Chateaudun

ST. ANDRE

REIMS

PROSNES

MOURMELON LE GRAND

CHALON SUR MARNE

PARIS

DREUX

COULOMMIERS

CHARTRES

BRETIGNY

MELUN

53rd WING AREA

CHATEAUDUN

BRICY

50th WING AREA

N

OPERATION VARSITY FLIGHT ROUTES
MARCH 24, 1945

STATUTE MILES

0    25    50

risk of unexpected bad weather on successive days, such as had helped wreck MARKET.

NEPTUNE and MARKET, like VARSITY, had also called for delivering two divisions by air, but over two or three days. The number one concern of VARSITY planners, therefore, was that by delivering everything at once they faced a traffic problem of gigantic proportions. The armada they proposed to put up—more than 1,550 planes and 1,300 gliders—was going to be crowded to-gether into a tight air corridor.[3] All these planes and gliders had to arrive at invasion sites in the most rigorously orchestrated sequence. Therefore everything depended on each branch of troop carrier doing its job perfectly and on schedule. The ground crews, for example, would have to meet the most exacting timetables for getting planes and gliders into shape and into position. The operation also was totally dependent on the most demanding sort of formation flying FAAA had ever imposed on its pilots.

From tip to tail, VARSITY, once airborne, would measure more than 200 miles.[4] It would also be very densely packed from side to side. To prevent jam-ups in such a gigantic airlift, VARSITY planners relied on two traffic control devices. They arrayed the aircraft in parallel lanes, three abreast, plus a fourth flying above the other three. And they positioned the more slowly moving planes very carefully in the armada lanes so as not to slow those that were faster. Plans called for seven different prescribed air speeds in VARSITY, depending on the plane and its load: British converted Sterling and Halifax bombers towing Horsas and Hamilcars;[5] Dakotas (British C-47s) tugging Horsas; C-47s carrying British paratroopers; C-47s carrying American paratroopers; and C-47s towing either one or two Wacos. And there was a new American transport on the scene larger than the C-47: the Curtiss "Commando" also known as the C-46.

Our Air Forces and airborne leaders were enthusiastic about the C-46. It was supposed to be more ruggedly built than the C-47, and it had *two* jump doors, one on each side of the plane, allowing paratroopers (twice the number of those carried in a C-47) to get out quickly. On paper, the speed and lane controls set up for VARSITY seemed capable of handling all these different sorts of planes in one airlift; whether this complex marshalling would hold up in com-bat was another matter.

The VARSITY armada would be heading for DZs and LZs just north of the Rhine town of Wesel, some fifty miles upstream from Arnhem. It would be ferrying the British 6th Airborne Division from fields in southeastern England, and the American 17th Airborne Division from several fields in France. All of IX Troop Carrier Command's 50th and 53rd Wings would be committed to car-rying the 17th Airborne. Part of the 52nd TCW also would be needed to ferry the 17th Airborne. The remaining groups in the 52nd TCW would be loaned to the British, where they would help the RAF's 38 and 46 Groups transport the British 6th Airborne.

It was one of the 52nd Wing's groups, the 313th, that won the honor (!) of flying the new C-46s.

The DZs and LZs in VARSITY were all within a five-mile radius, for the most part butted up against the western fringe of the key airborne objective, the Diersfordter Forest. This clump of woods, so close to the Rhine, occupies the only high ground in the region. It was thought to be positively thick with German troops, flak guns, and heavier artillery. General Miles Dempsey, commanding the British Second Army—which was to lead the amphibious assault—believed that unless the Allies could silence artillery in that forest, the Germans, from their protected high ground, could destroy any pontoon bridge British engineers might be able to throw across the river; and, no bridge, no tanks.[6]

A second objective of VARSITY troopers was to prevent German forces in the town of Wesel itself from joining in a counterattack against the British infantry. Once a link-up had been made between airborne and ground infantry, they would try to overrun Wesel; then they would work their way across the smaller Issel River, a few miles to the east of the Rhine and the last natural barrier from which the Germans might conceivably hold up a big break-through by the British armor in Operation PLUNDER.

Working up VARSITY's final details took until March 16, just a week before it was scheduled to go. Some high-pressure negotiating was needed before Brereton (head of FAAA), Ridgway (head of XVIII Corps, that is, the airborne troopers) and Dempsey (head of the British Second Army) could agree on all the complex innovations.[7] But they managed to settle all disagreements quickly and in a faily cooperative atmosphere.

At higher command levels, however, jealousies and recriminations between British and Americans were building up to a dangerous pitch. Bradley and Patton—who had favored an airborne drop across the Rhine back in November, when this was planned for the American sectors—now regarded VARSITY as just another example of Eisenhower's knuckling under to the British.[8] Americans at SHAEF, and American commanders in the field, believed Ike was subordinating military necessity to political expediency. Eisenhower's arrangement with Montgomery not only meant VARSITY would be dropped in front of British rather than American armies; it also meant that at this crucial time Montgomery would get priority for delivery of scarce supplies.

American generals were particularly irritated at Eisenhower's decision to take some divisions away from Bradley's forces and assign them to General William Simpson's Ninth (U.S.) Army. This transfer was intended to assist Montgomery's awaited sweep into Germany north of the Ruhr, rather than to aid the

American armies south of the Ruhr.[9] SHAEF expected American armies south of the Ruhr to limit themselves to "aggressive defense."

Recriminations began to boil over toward the end of February, when Simpson's men broke through the Siegfried Line in their northern sector and reached the west bank of the Rhine just across from Düsseldorf, south of Wesel. Simpson demanded Montgomery's permission to take advantage of the confusion among the retreating Germans and punch a quick bridgehead across the Rhine. But Montgomery refused; he had no intention of taking chances with any of the U.S. land and airborne forces Eisenhower had assigned to him.[10] And even when the Germans in front of Dempsey's 2nd Army retreated across the Rhine on March 10, Montgomery allowed his forces only a very cautious advance toward the river. His only concern seemed to be building up his men and supplies into an overwhelmingly superior assault force. The American generals harbored a well-founded suspicion that Montgomery wanted to insure that the honor of crossing the Rhine first would fall to the British and not the Americans.[11] By now Bradley was calling Montgomery "an arrogant egomaniac."

But the fortunes of war favored the Americans. On March 7, a spearhead unit of General Courtney Hodge's First (U.S.) Army reached the west bank of the Rhine in the central sector and found to their astonishment that the Germans still had not blown the Ludendorff Bridge at Remagen (just south of Bonn). Furthermore, it appeared poorly guarded. To their still greater amazement, a patrol sent dashing across that bridge reached the other side before the Germans set off the explosives planted there. The exultant American generals near the Rhine rushed reinforcements and tanks across the bridge on their own authority.[12] Two weeks later, troops of Patton's Third Army managed to force another breakthrough and crossed the Rhine further south, near Oppenheim. On March 22 the delighted Patton was able to plant his feet on the east bank of the Rhine—while VARSITY-PLUNDER was still more than a day away and Montgomery was still west of the Rhine.

### Preliminaries at Melun

The whole world knew we in the 81st TCS had been moved to France to take part in another airborne assault against Germany. Security at Villaroche was almost impossible to maintain; anybody in the nearby villages or Melun could figure out what all those airborne troopers, extra planes, and huge truck convoys meant. Dozens of French civilians worked right on the base.

We all realized that Hitler could have more tricks up his sleeve: perhaps the "wonder weapons" which, he boasted, would soon turn the tide of the war in Germany's favor. Headquarters at IX Troop Carrier Command had gotten wind of a supposed German plan for a preemptive sneak attack on troop carrier outfits expected to lead the coming Allied assault across the Rhine. So, on March 5, all of us were put to work digging zigzag lines of slit trenches in back of our tents; "and by late evening," said our Squadron diarist, "the Squadron area looked something like the Siegfried Line."

But we knew better. We had been making flight after flight to eastern France, Belgium, and Holland, very near Germany, with nary a sign or even a rumor of the Luftwaffe—except for the Nazi planes we saw smashed up on the ground. While we were being ordered to dig trenches as though our lives depended on it, we were also being told that in two days enlisted men would start being eligible for passes to Paris.

Radio Berlin was assuring airborne troopers in our sector that the Wehrmacht knew all about why they were there, and that they could leave their parachutes behind because they could slide down the solid curtain of flak that would be coming up at them.

> We had supper with the airborne boys the night before the mission. They gave us a good one. Spam and Vienna sausage were prohibited from this mess. They gave us steak. I had no appetite that day and even steak had to be pushed in. After supper a priest said Mass outside. There was good attendance, everybody kneeling on the grass. The feeling surrounding that service was different from anything you will ever experience. It was mighty solemn. The men—boys, I should say—were all in battle dress, Indian haircuts and all, but during that Mass they knelt and bowed their heads more reverently than I'd ever seen it done before. They were going over the Rhine the next morning, and they weren't all coming back.
>
> I didn't sleep well that night; in fact, I didn't sleep at all. (Adelore Chevalier, glider pilot, from a letter written March 31, 1945)

Our Melun airbase now was stuffed to bursting, not only with paratroopers, but with gliders, ammunition, and supplies. In the event that VARSITY would require a second major mission, scores of extra planes and gliders were standing by. More than ninety planeloads of supplies were stockpiled on the base against the possibility of re-supplying airheads that might become surrounded by the enemy east of the Rhine. Several of our veteran glider pilots were in reserve. They were not slated for VARSITY unless a second mission should become necessary. This meant that in order to provide each glider with a co-pilot, 124 glider pilots from the 434th and 438th Groups (groups that would be flying paratroopers, not towing gliders) were transferred to our base. And a number of power pilots—some volunteers, some not—had been retrained as glider pilots.[13] Some of these "throttle-jockey retreads" were now on our base.

Our plane crews could relax a bit on one score: finally, all sixteen of our planes going on this mission would have self sealing gas tanks. Twelve planes had gotten them just in time for VARSITY.

> We had from six to eight people for that job on each plane. We would start early in the morning, taking out the hundreds of screws that held the bottom panels underneath the wing tanks. Then we would lower the panels, remove the brackets and straps that held the old metal tanks up, and uncouple the piping that went into the filler hole in the wing. Trying to get those doggone metal tanks out was a heck of a job, I can tell you. They must have built the C-47 *around* those metal tanks. But we finally finagled them out. Getting the rubber tanks up was easier, because they were somewhat flexible, and we could get them around obstructions. I think it took a good seventy-two hours, stopping only for going to the john or getting a bite to eat or a cup of coffee, to replace the tanks in a plane. We had to get those self-sealing tanks in there in a hurry. We didn't get much sleep. (Johnny Hirtreiter, assistant crew chief)

Our glider pilots finally had much of the equipment so greviously lacking on previous missions: entrenching shovels, good compasses, sleeping bags, and canteens. For once, all glider pilots had enough good maps and photos of their LZs. Those who wanted them could carry bazookas rather than carbines into battle. Even more important improvements were the protective steel bumpers (Griswold noses) and arrester parachutes fitted to almost all our gliders.

On the other hand, glider pilots had to listen to stern lectures aimed at insuring that they would be of maximum use to the airborne infantry once landed. Glider pilots still had high priority for being evacuated; but until it was certain they were no longer needed on the battlefield, they were to report to assigned command posts and remain under the strict orders of a senior glider pilot from the 53rd Wing. Once assembled, glider pilots would serve, in effect, as provisional infantry companies; they were not to let themselves be enticed singly or in small groups into volunteering for some sideshow by junior airborne officers who might need help.

In addition to slit trenches, our Melun base now displayed another new defensive feature: antiaircraft guns. High command seemed to be taking the threat of a Luftwaffe incursion quite seriously. A few batteries of AA artillery soldiers now were in position around the base. Nobody paid them much attention. A much more intriguing new feature of this invasion: for the last few days our glider pilots had been invited to attend German language classes.

No amount of improved preparations, however, could make us forget that getting all those double-tow planes and gliders up into the air without collisions would require enormous skill, hard work, and good luck on everybody's part. Around the gliders, the vastly increased prop wash stirred up by all those planes straining to pull two gliders would be so dangerous that both pilot and co-pilot would have to exert all their strength to keep their glider from turning right over. Tow pilots would have to fight much harder against being swayed from side to side by their double burdens. Merely getting their planes into the air before reaching the end of the runway—especially for the first planes in line—would be an accomplishment in itself.

Double-glider tow! Of all the extraordinary features of airborne warfare in World War II, having *one* C-47 pull *two* Wacos—each almost as big as itself—seems the most dangerous. But it was something we in the 81st TCS had practiced many times; in fact, we had first tried it out at Laurinburg-Maxton during the fall of 1943. We knew that having one glider tow rope shorter than the other—given good pilots, the absence of too much air turbulence, and a bit of luck—would help prevent mid-air entanglements. But apart from one disastrous attempt in Burma, double tows in combat were unknown.

Our gliders would transport elements of the 17th Airborne: the 194th Parachute Infantry Regiment, beefed up with artillery and engineers and, therefore, formally a "Regimental Combat Team."

March 23: Tension was building up fast. Base restrictions were now in effect: no more passes; in fact, no unauthorized entries or exits at all from the base. Extra guards against saboteurs were posted on both the north-south and east-west runways where the planes and gliders were already lined up. After lunch, David Brack and Harold Walker, accompanied by Colonel Williams, went through the Squadron on a fast inspection of every department. At 1:00 p.m. all glider pilots attended a Group briefing and were given new "escape and evasion" kits. Finally, at 4:00 p.m., Brack briefed all our combat crews in front of the Operations tent.

One thing must be said for Montgomery's ponderous buildup: beginning during the night of March 23 the first phases of carving out a bridgehead across the Rhine cost the British Second Army only thirty-one casualties. First, Allied planes and artillery subjected the Germans on the other side of the river to one of the most concentrated and sustained bombardments of the war. Then, Montgomery laid down a thick curtain of smoke to cover the commandos who moved across the river in "Buffalos" (speedy assault boats). Dazed German defenders could do little to prevent the British from reaching the other side.

The stage was finally set for VARSITY.

## Notes

1. Breuer, *Rhine*, pp. 12–14.
2. The Germans were still tenaciously holding on to Arnhem.

3. Several historians give slightly lower totals, possibly because they subtracted the planes and gliders that aborted or were lost on the way from the total that were planned to go. On the other hand, MacDonald, *Airborne*, p. 148, finds a total of 1,696 transport planes; but this must be too high.

4. Breuer, *Rhine*, p. 206, has this figure as 150 miles; Brinson, p. 83 has it as 420 miles, following the figure given in IX TCC "Final Phases," p. 76.

5. Hamilcars were huge British gliders, even larger than Horsas. The Hamilcar had a wingspan of 110 feet, compared with 88 feet for the Horsa; and the Hamilcar was capable of carrying a light tank.

6. Warren II, p. 160.

7. Additional innovations included abandoning the use of special pathfinder planes ahead of the main serials, and placing "combat control teams" on the ground, provided with powerful radio equipment, to warn incoming serials of especially dangerous flak.

8. No less than three sets of plans were on the boards for drops in front of different American armies; and one drop (Operation ECLIPSE) was planned for Berlin itself.

9. Bradley, *Autobiography*, p. 394. As chief of the XXI Army Group, Montgomery commanded not only the British and Canadians in the northern tier or armies, but also Simpson's Ninth Army.

10. Bradley, *Autobiography*, p. 400; Gavin, 1979, p. 307 and fn.; Breuer, *Rhine*, pp. 83–84, 89–90.

11. Bradley, *Autobiography*, p. 394.

12. When he heard of the Remagen coup, however, Eisenhower was delighted; and he was quick to send his approval and encouragement. Bradley, *Autobiography*, pp. 405–9; Gavin, 1979, pp. 304–6; Breuer, *Rhine*, pp. 118–45.

13. 53rd TCW hist. narr. for March 1945; 436th TCG hist. narr. for March 1945: report by S-4. See also Devlin, *Silent Wings*, p. 309. IX Troop Carrier Command had persuaded the U.S. Air Forces to assign 50 percent of power pilots coming into the ETO between November 1944 and January 1945 to glider retraining. The RAF also had to provide power-pilot retreads for its own VARSITY gliders. Warren II, p. 158.

# 21. Storming Germany
## The Drop Across the Rhine

### Our Rhine journey

Saturday, March 24, 1945—a bright, sunny, early spring morning, and only a few clouds flecked a pale blue sky. Most of us had been up for hours. After breakfast—for those who could choke something down—we had a final weather briefing in front of the control tower, plus good luck wishes and a short prayer from the Group Chaplain. Our sixteen C-47 crews, our thirty-two glider crews, and the airborne troopers, were on board by 0730 hours. Fifteen minutes later it was: engines on! Our Group's lead plane, with Adriel Williams and his two gliders (one piloted by Group Glider Officer William Brown, the other by the 81st's Purl Stockton) took off at 0754 hours. Col. Williams, in the lead plane with the shortest runway takeoff distance, had to bounce his plane in order to get enough altitude before he ran out of runway. Forty-three minutes later our entire Group was off the ground and maneuvering over Melun into formation.[1] We were headed for LZ "S," just three miles north of Wesel.

> Even with full power, it seemed to take forever to get to takeoff speed. We literally staggered into the air, just above stalling speed, because of the tremendous load we were pulling. Even maintaining full power, it seemed to take forever to get up a hundred feet off the ground. If, during the first few minutes of flight, one engine would have merely faltered, we would have bored right into the ground. Only after we got up to 500 feet or so was the danger from engine failure reduced; we then could slack off the power somewhat and know that in an emergency we could cut the gliders loose, since they would now have a chance to pick a safe landing spot. (Rex Selbe, pilot)

No collisions; only one glider aborted; no planes down with engine failure! A good beginning for what we hoped would be our last assault mission. We circled Melun once, the usual airman's goodbye. Flying in echelons of four to

Squadron planes and gliders lined up just before our double-tow mission to Wesel.

Two gliders on one C–47's tail. Taken through the astrodome of a plane on the way to our jump across the Rhine.

the right, our plane-glider tandems headed northeast toward Brussels and a rendezvous with the rest of the huge air armada named VARSITY.

For a while nothing indicated that this mission would be rougher than the last—certainly not the vast British formations passing to our left with their four-motored planes and huge Horsa and Hamilcar gliders that carried over thirty men or even armored cars. To me it simply spelled invincibility. (Roger Krey, glider pilot)

From the ground it must have been an awsome sight. World War II histories describe the amazement of people in Brussels, staring up at that gigantic aerial procession—far longer than the eye could see. From my place in the astrodome, the sky seemed thick with aircraft. In that air armada were C-47s from all our 53rd TC Wing fields and others from the 50th TC Wing around Chartres. Part of the 52nd TC Wing, up around Amiens, fell into line when we passed Brussels. Off to the left of our double-tow formation, and far above us, were the British formations; to our right were other C-47s carrying paratroopers.

For the first two hours of this flight, our main problem was air turbulence generated by all those planes—"Worst I've ever experienced!" reported Adriel Williams. Glider pilots had to spell each other fifteen minutes at a time because of the sheer physical exertion required to keep from colliding with the other glider on their tow.

The picture worsened quickly after about 10:15. We had been pushed along by an unexpected tail wind, and our Group was too close to the serial in front of us. Colonel Williams tried to slow us down by "S-ing," that is, maneuvering in large curves from right to left. But such curves were limited by the columns of planes to our left (the British) and our right (the paratrooper planes). We crossed the Rhine when the serials in front of us were still launching their gliders over Wesel. To avoid a jam-up, Williams had to take us up over the prescribed height. This meant our gliders would be released higher than planned—and therefore subject to more flak on the way down.

To make matters worse, the British commandos who had crossed the Rhine some hours earlier had been protected by a thick chemical smoke screen; this was still in the air, and it, plus the bombing of Wesel, raised so much dirty smoke that it was really hard to make out our landing zone.[2] And it was not encouraging, either, to be looking ahead and to see that several tow planes already were in trouble and seemed about to crash. (Thayer Bonecutter, glider pilot)

We sailed over the Rhine at 1300 feet. Where was the war? I asked myself as I peered down through smoky murk, seeing only some British assault boats on the river and more burning plane wrecks on the ground. In seconds the Kraut gave me my answer: four or five heavy reports from a big flak gun below is enough to tell anyone he is in a war. Bill Lane [the other pilot] gave me a grin: "That's us they're shooting at!" he said. (Roger Krey, glider pilot)

---

The Krauts knew when we were coming and they knew just exactly where and they were ready. They had machine guns, antiaircraft, and rifles set up in every house, barn, pillbox, and slit trench, all over the area. So when our gliders started coming in we caught hell all the way down. A heckuva lotta nice guys died right there in their seats before their gliders touched the ground. Some got it as they were piling out the doors. Some came in on fire and got roasted. I never thought a glider could catch fire from an incendiary bullet, but some did.

My glider was one of the very few that didn't collect a mess of lead, even though I flew right through a whole potful of the stuff making my landing pattern. I had to come in over a high tension line, side-slip like everything, and plop it down hard to stop before I went ramming into a woods. Even then a telephone pole got in the way and chopped off ten feet of wing—that was nothing, we hardly noticed it. Then I lay down in a ditch and watched the show. It was the show of a lifetime—I kid you not. (Adelore Chevalier, glider pilot)

Looking back, it seems a miracle any of our glider pilots got out of LZ "S" alive. Practically every glider coming into this landing zone was hit by flak or machine gun fire. German "flak wagons" of 20 mm guns held their fire until gliders rolled to a stop; so enemy fire, deadly enough as the gliders were coming in, was even more murderous once the troopers tried to get out of the gliders and unload their equipment.[3]

The next second we saw smoke coming out of the left engine of our tow plane. The prop slowed. That engine was gone. But even though that plane could have exploded any minute, the crew—on one engine—continued to pull us and the other glider deeper into Germany. But all three aircraft were losing altitude rapidly.

Bill Lane of course was anxiously scanning for a place to go down; but the smoke was blocking any clear view. He did know that we were far enough beyond the Rhine to be able to hit our landing zone. And if the

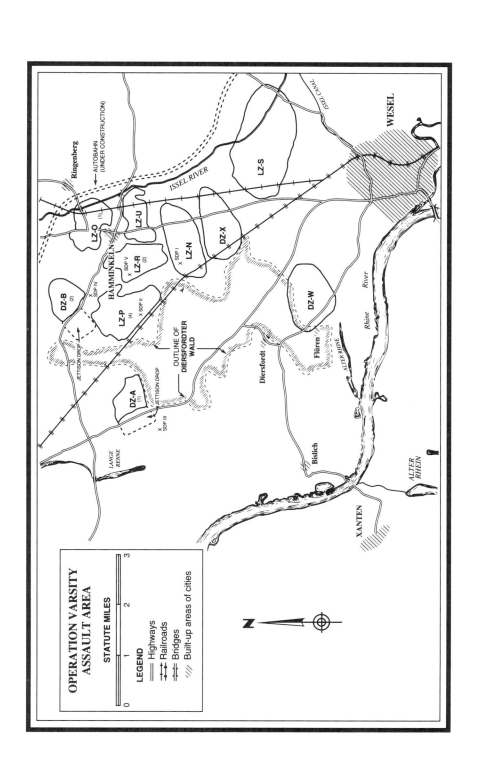

OPERATION VARSITY
ASSAULT AREA

STATUTE MILES

LEGEND
Highways
Railroads
Bridges
Built-up areas of cities

WESEL

Ringenberg

AUTOBAHN
(UNDER CONSTRUCTION)

ISSEL CANAL

ISSEL RIVER

LZ-S

LZ-O
(1)

LZ-U

HAMMINKELN

x SDP V
LZ-R
(2)

x SDP I
LZ-N

DZ-X

DZ-B
(2)

x SDP IV

LZ-P
(4)

x SDP II

JETTISON DROP

OUTLINE OF
DIERSFORDTER
WALD

DZ-W

Flüren

ALTER RHINE

Rhine
River

Diersfordt

DZ-A
(1)

JETTISON DROP

x SDP III

LANGE
RENNE

Bislich

XANTEN

ALTER
RHEIN

N

gliders got off right away the tow plane crew might have a chance to stay airborne. With a mild curse, Bill hit the rope release. I relaxed my hold on the controls and he took over in a beautiful peel-off. The other glider cut, too. A quick look backward gave me a last look at our tug as it disappeared westward into the haze with the tow ropes still attached. They looked as though they might make it.

Now we began to have glimpses of the ground through the smoke. The Kraut, of course, had glimpses of us, too. We were gliding silently at eighty miles an hour; we seemed to be able to hear every crack, crack of rifles and every pup-pup-pup of machine guns aimed at us. You could see the gun flashes, too. Later I heard that sight described as like flying over a junk yard with hundreds of tin cans glistening back at you in the sun.

In our glider, our eleven airborne glider troopers began to sing, very loudly, "Hail, hail, the gang's all here!" and I joined in. But after the second series of "hails!" a 20 mm shell exploded right in front of the glider—and the singing had to stop. Shell fragments got me in the head, face, and neck, and Bill was hit in the foot. The glider troopers thought we had had it; but the glider wasn't badly hurt, and the two of us were still fully effective.

The smoke now was gone. The sunshine seemed brilliant. My God: there, directly in front of us, was a tall transmission tower and all its wires. No way to go over it at our airspeed; Bill dove the glider under the wires and swept around the tower. This increased our airspeed—something we truly did not need, now that we were about to land. But I yanked the red handle for the arrester chute, and our speed once more was under control. I pulled the yellow handle to release the chute as Bill flattened the glider for a landing. We skimmed half across a large field—and we were in. We were under fire; but there was no panic as all thirteen men on that glider piled outside in an instant. (Roger Krey, glider pilot)

---

Just as I was circling for my final approach my glider was hit by flak. I was able to land OK; and we came down in a freshly plowed field, which kept us from rolling too far. But when we came to a stop the airborne troopers there were just frozen in their seats. I yelled, "Get the hell out!" and the glider emptied quickly—except for one lad who was dead. That flak had exploded right underneath him. And the same shot had wounded the troopers seated to his left and his right.

We got the dead and wounded out and did our best to make things easier for the wounded until the medics arrived. (Thayer Bonecutter, glider pilot)

## Casualty lists

Among the ties that bind our 81st TCS Association are painful memories of those whose luck ran out on this Rhine journey. In the somber theater that was the airborne battle for Wesel, several of us had to be spectators of that most terrible drama—seeing some of your buddies facing death in front of you. Gale Ammerman had to watch while Gephart's and Hampton's glider was riddled by machine-gun fire; no one, neither pilots nor airborne troopers, got out of that glider alive. Several of us saw Ed Vosika's plane with one engine on fire. (One of the gliders this plane tugged was piloted by Bill Lane and Roger Krey.)

### NARRATIVE OF EMERGENCY LANDING
by Capt. Edward J. Vosika, O-677345

The flight was normal from take-off to the IP. The run-in was started at the IP and proceeded uneventfully until we crossed the paratroop drop zone. About 800 yards after crossing the DZ we were fired upon and hit in the left main tank and left engine. The left engine wasn't giving very much power, and I didn't feather it, as it would be an invitation to more fire from the ground. The gliders hung on and with absolute full power I pulled the gliders to the LZ. My gliders cut in the same spot as did the three ships in front of me. It was the LZ, as I saw the canal in front of me. I made my turn and at that time my crew chief told me that we were burning underneath. I told him to watch the fire's progress, and told the co-pilot to pull the fire extinguisher on the left engine. At this time I feathered the left prop. When I had reached a heading of 240 (the reading out) I put the ship into a steep dive so that I could regain my air speed and also if anything worse should happen, we would be on the west bank of the Rhine. Just as we crossed the Rhine at low altitude, the crew chief reported that the fire seemed to be out as the smoke had stopped; but that the gas fumes were strong in the cabin. I had remembered the field at B-100 as we went by going in, and I headed for it. Landing was single engine with wheels down. None of the crew was injured.

Looking over the plane upon landing I found the following damage:
Left engine: out and burned, and covered with fire extinguisher fluid.
Left prop: had a bullet hole.
Left main tank: bullet went through tank, floor boards in cabin, and through top of ship.
A couple of holes in left wing.

Holes in tail, and horizontal stabilizer.

A hole in the right engine but don't know where it came out.

> (signed) Edward J. Vosika
>
> Capt., A.C.

We saw the agonies of Bill Frye's plane when it climbed skyward and then plunged straight down.

81st TROOP CARRIER SQUADRON

OFFICE OF THE INTELLIGENCE OFFICER

APO 133 U.S. Army

24 March 1945

Report on plane lost in combat. Piloted by Capt. William M. Frye, Jr., O-800341

1. Plane #42-100674 took off from this station (A-55) at 0804 hours on 23 March 1945 [a mistake: the mission was run on March 24] with fifteen (15) other planes from this Squadron, in Serial #A-10 of Mission VARSITY. Destination—LZ S (51 40' N—06 38' E)

2. The following statements made by 2nd Lt. Harry W. Zimmerman, O-766139, co-pilot in plane #504, last plane in the preceeding element, and 1st Lt. Stuart J. Anderson, O-806770 AC, pilot of plane #723, flying Capt. Frye's right wing.

Lt. Anderson—"I was pilot of plane #723, flying on Capt. Frye's right wing. We split for the 'run in' and I was flying parallel with him at a distance of about 400 yards, when I noticed flames coming from one of his engines. I called him and told him he was on fire, but there was no reply and he kept on flying his course. The gliders released over the LZ and he immediately started a steep climb. I watched him in his climb until he was out of my line of vision due to my forward flight. The last attitude I saw him in was this vertical climb."

Lt. Zimmerman—"I was co-pilot for Capt. Wolf in plane #504. Capt. Frye was behind us leading an element. We had cut our gliders and climbed up 400 to 500 feet to make our turn. During the turn I looked out the right hand window and saw a ship pull straight up in a vertical climb. The gliders cut loose when the ship went into this climb. The ship was going over on its back and started to drop. I saw two men jump at this time but can't be certain whether the chutes opened or not. The ship was falling down, tail first, and gradually the nose came down and it went into a dive. The ship pulled out of this dive and started into another climb. It was going up as in a chandelle when it fell off on one wing and went straight down. I saw the ship crash and burn, and saw no one else bail out. In my opinion the ship was out of control at all times indicating a hit in the cockpit."

> (signed) Louis G. Kramer
> 1st Lt., A.C.
> S-2, 81st TC Sq.

The preliminary casualty list compiled the day after VARSITY showed two known dead, thirteen missing in action—several of whom were later found to be dead—and eight known to be wounded and in hospitals. Fourteen of our Squadron's sixteen planes, though, had made it back; four of these suffered major damage and four others only a few bullet holes.

Of all our losses, the ones we talk about most today are those of Frye and his crew, partly because shocked witnesses had different interpretations of the eerie performance of his C-47 after it was hit.

The Wesel mission shook me up badly. Lt. Cooke, who had been my co-pilot all the way through transition training and for the flight overseas, was shot down on this mission. [Cooke was Frye's co-pilot on VARSITY.] I was looking out the navigator's window at the time to keep track of any hits we might get in or behind the engines. Lt. Cooke's plane, apparently, took an incendiary hit, or anyway, I saw a fire starting up right by one of his engines. I had to sit there and watch while the fire must have melted off some of the control surfaces on that side, since the plane went into a dive. The pilots pulled it out, though, and they followed through with their approach pattern, going right straight ahead toward the landing zone. Then they must have gone into another dive, since I lost sight of them. (Ken De Blake, radio operator)

---

Going over the Rhine we saw at least three British bombers used as tow planes and five Horsa gliders going down out of control in front and to our left. . . . Bill Frye was right in front of us. I watched him get hit. That plane must have caught it right in the cockpit. In his death agonies a pilot probably would pull back on the wheel; and that plane just went straight up, turned over on its left wing, and then went straight down. It didn't look as though it went into any spin whatever. (Ellery Bennett, pilot)

---

As we were coming in for the glider release I could see the British planes getting hit one after the other. Just as we crossed the river, one of our own flight leader's planes [Frye's] was hit and one of its engines caught fire. We called to him on the radio to tell him that fire was streaming out behind him. We were worried he couldn't see it. After cutting off his gliders he snapped his plane up and down trying to blow out the fire; but on the third attempt he went down and crashed. (Jerome Loving, crew chief)

---

I could see that Captain Frye's plane was on fire. I knew that Eugene Davis, who had flown with us several times as navigator, was on that plane. I heard somebody yelling over the radio to them: "Whip it! Whip it! The fire will blow out!" As if in answer, the plane started a steep climb. But suddenly it broke off, flipped over on its back, and plunged down. I could see the cockpit escape hatch on top of the plane pop open; but nobody got out that way. (Hal Friedland, radio operator)

The luck of the 81st TCS had deserted us. Among our glider pilots, Ray Gephart and John Hampton were known dead; John Kearns, Tom McGrath, Pierson Metoxen, George Pittman, and John Sweeney were all missing in action; and Chauncey Clapp, Lee Personius, Jim Pritchett, Rex Cook, Roger Krey, Bill Lane, Fred Tuck, and Harry Zonge were either wounded or injured. Glider pilots of the 81st TCS accounted for 7 percent of those sent by the 53rd TC Wing into LZ "S" that day; but they took 14 percent of the 53rd's glider pilot casualties.[4]

## Hell on the ground

Hell in the air over Wesel, that day, had lasted about fifteen minutes for our airplane crews; for our glider pilots, hell coming down and hell on the ground lasted another twelve hours. Those who came through with only minor injuries carry the emotional scars of those terrible hours.

With a load of infantry in your glider, it is the pilots who leave last. The glider's doors are in the rear. Pilots have to unbelt and pick up their weapons before running for those rear doors.

But this can have its advantages. With a glider on a landing zone, the enemy may wait to fire until they see men pouring out the doors. Another matter of luck is—which is safer, the right or left door? That depends on which side is facing the enemy. In our case, the door on the right was the lucky one—that's the one Bill Lane and I used. German rifle fire did not get either of us.

I was last out and went through the doorway in a flat dive, clutching my submachine gun. I hit the ground and looked around. What I saw was bad. Three or four of the airborne men had been hit. Their lieutenant and sergeant were taken out of the fight right beside the unlucky left door; neither could move. All the lieutenant could do was yell at us not to draw any more fire. Bill and I could do nothing but keep very flat along with the infantry and hope that the fire would remain over our heads. Nobody could spot where the Germans were shooting from. It seemed as if the two or three gliders now down in this field had the whole Wehrmacht to contend with.

But soon the situation changed. As more of our big birds floated in, the Germans' fire seemed to get more dispersed and confused. One of the airborne men near me thought he could make it to a safer place. He shouted my way: "Lieutenant, wanna get out of here? I'll try if you cover me. Follow behind with your grease gun, and every time you see me hit the ground and roll back up, you do the same!"

"Let's go!" I yelled back.

"OK, but first I gotta get back into the glider for mortar ammo!" I saw this guy had been hit; but he was not about to give up. He went back in, crawled out of the glider with a bag of mortar rounds, slung the bag over one shoulder, and took off. I followed about fifteen feet behind, and we both made it to a nearby patch of woods. I never saw that airborne guy again; but I may well owe my life to him.

Bill Lane also made it somehow out of that German fire. I was glad to see him the following day in the same field hospital where I ended up. That field hospital, by the way, had itself been brought in by gliders. (Roger Krey, glider pilot; from a letter written May 15, 1945)

---

As soon as I took off my boot to see what damage that piece of flak had done, my foot started to swell up. It was a small wound but I could not get my boot back on. We walked out along a ditch, looking for an aid station. Then, standing on top of the ditch, we saw the same lieutenant and his squad who had been in my glider. Back in Melun, when they had been loading up, I had noticed some equipment I never saw before; but when I asked about it the lieutenant had told me it was classified. Now that we were down on the battlefield he could explain: it was a new recoilless rifle just arrived in the ETO. This would be the first time it would be used in combat. He and his men were watching three German Tiger tanks they knew were behind a farmhouse. The tanks, just then, started to move out; and the troopers got all three tanks with just four shots. (Bill Lane, glider pilot)

The most graphic account we have of what might happen to a glider pilot once he joined the battle on the ground comes from Sherman Ryman. A rather heavy man with a build like a wrestler, he was "Bull" to our other glider pilots—a nickname they still use.

Several of our troopers were hit on the way down. The Germans were still firing at us after we got out of the glider; but we were able to haul out the wounded and dive into a nearby empty canal. Pretty soon we were able to get the wounded men to medics.

When all of us glider pilots showed up at a rendezvous point, we were given an assignment to go down a road and set up a roadblock at a railroad crossing. The road went into Wesel. Down the road we could see a German tank half up a sidewalk: it was on fire, looking as though it was about ready to blow. There was no way to get around that tank by going in back of the buildings, because the Germans out in the woods behind the buildings then would see us. Those stone and brick houses were separated by alleyways about ten or twelve feet apart; so we had to run by the alleyways, one at a time, to stay out of the field of fire from the Germans behind the town. By the time I got by that tank I could feel the adrenaline pumping pretty good. Sure enough, after we all got by, the tank blew up.

Further down the road things got more quiet—too quiet to suit us. As much as we could, we kept behind the scattered small houses and trees while we kept on going. Around here some houses had white sheets hanging out of the windows—what did all that mean? Pretty soon we realized the people were showing they wanted to surrender, or maybe that they didn't want their houses shot up. By now it looked as though we had gone too far, past the perimeter we were to set up. We stopped and got out the maps; and sure enough, we had walked too far! We could spot ourselves by a railroad track running parallel with the road.

We decided to walk back along the railroad instead of the road; this was safer, out of view of the houses. It was then we saw how the Germans had coped with the endless bombing of their railroads by Americans and British. On one side of the track they had dug a continuous trench—in a zig-zag pattern to protect themselves as much as possible from strafing—so that when bombers or fighters came along everybody on those trains could scramble into a trench. Most of us were walking along the track on the side of that trench; but Tommy McCann and I were on the other side.

All of a sudden machine gun and rifle fire started to come our way. The guys on the other side of the track jumped into that trench. Mac and I hit the ground. Luckily, the path we were on had a slight rise beside it; but this rise was only about a foot high and about fifteen or twenty feet long, and after that the land flattened out. When I looked to my left I could see bullets hitting the top of that rise and chewing it up. The dirt was showering down on us, and that rise seemed to be getting smaller and smaller. We moved forward about six feet; but they must have guessed what we were doing, because they started to work on us again in the new position. The same thing happened when we moved back again.

Now we were really pressing our faces into that dirt. The thought flashed through my mind: this is it. I remember thinking "So long, Ma." The machine gun that seemed so anxious to make our acquaintance wasn't firing continuous bursts, but rather with pauses in between—I suppose to prevent it from overheating. During one pause we heard this loud clanking— and there through the bushes we could see a tank coming down toward us. It had to be a German—our people didn't have any tanks around yet.

The way he was going, if that tank crossed the road we would have seen my big butt lying on the other side of the tracks. Now we could see it was a Tiger tank with a big 88 gun on the turret. We yelled at the guys in the trench to give us some covering fire; they did, and the machine gun stopped. Mac and I jumped up, dashed across the track, and dove into that trench.

When the tank reached the tracks, not far from where we had just been, it stopped; they must have realized there was trouble around. But the tank was tightly buttoned up; and they couldn't really see too much. They turned that turret down toward the trench where we were, but they couldn't see us; then they straightened out the turret. Finally the tank and the rest of the Germans moved on up the road. (Sherman "Bull" Ryman, glider pilot)

Our glider pilots were committed to help hold a defense perimeter between LZ "S" and Wesel. This was aimed at repelling an expected German attack from the direction of the town toward that landing zone. The same LZ might have to be used by gliders the following day.

During the afternoon, several hundred American glider pilots from several squadrons moved into this perimeter and did what they could to prepare for what the night might bring. From where they were digging in they could see the Diersfordter Forest, and hear the scattered fire still coming from that direction. Much of that fire came from Schmeiser submachine guns that always fired in long bursts—which to Americans sounded like an enormous "Burp!" The central part of this perimeter was near a fork of two roads coming together and leading toward Wesel. An engagement now known as "the Battle of Burp Gun Corner," a fight won by glider pilots (not ours—they were mainly from the 435th TCG) against German infantry supported by tanks, was about to begin.

First, the Germans sent out patrols:

Mac and some of the others said they were going to sack up in an abandoned building. But [Julian] Hoshal and I decided that a better bet was a two-man foxhole. We found a nice spot hidden by a couple of bushes. In front of the bushes was a huge bomb crater that gave us a good field of fire. It was getting dark. We broke out our K-rations and tried to get comfortable. It had been a long day.

The next thing I knew I was waking up with a hand across my mouth. Hoshal's face was inches from mine and he had a finger across his lips. "Krauts!" he whispered. Now I could hear them, maybe three or four. I slipped my 45 out of my holster and felt for the handle of my trench knife strapped to my boot. But before long those Germans moved off. (Bull Ryman, glider pilot)

---

We dug in around a German house. To our left there was another group of glider pilots. During the night those fellows had to beat off a German attack with tanks. By now glider pilots had enough fire power so they could give a good account of themselves. During that attack I kept thinking that if it moved over in our direction I would have to use my bazooka. But, thank God, I never had to fire it, because—as I found out later—I had positioned its batteries the wrong way! Geary, another glider pilot, fixed up my bazooka the next morning. But I never had to use it at all. (Thayer Bonecutter, glider pilot)

---

When morning came the Germans let fly what we called "screaming mee-mies." These were mortar shells with a whistle or a screamer attached that made them sound as though they were coming down right on top of your head. They kept this up for about twenty minutes. Pretty soon some of the shrapnel from those mortars were coming right down into our foxhole. Hoshal reached down and picked up a good-sized piece; luckily for him he had leather gloves on, because that piece of lead was so hot it sizzled on his hand. Meanwhile, there wasn't anything to do but lie there in that hole and take it.

Finally, the barrage stopped. Thank God! Hoshal and I just sat there looking at each other. He said, "Bull, I don't know how you can be so calm!" I said, "Hosh, I was thinking the exact same thing about you!" We broke out laughing—pretty hysterical, I guess. (Bull Ryman, glider pilot)

---

The next day—a Sunday, I remember—we were relieved and ferried back across the Rhine. There we saw a field with lots of tanks lined up, waiting to cross the Rhine on a pontoon bridge British engineers had just put down. But above the other side a German plane, a lone JU-88, kept trying to knock down that bridge while our artillery, time after time, sent up a cone of fire around him without knocking him down. That Luftwaffe plane finally had to leave without getting that pontoon bridge. (Thayer Bonecutter, glider pilot)

---

Now, every once in a while, that whole scene comes back to me; I can hear those screaming meemies, and see that tank turret revolving around in our direction. It's not a good feeling. It can wake you up in the middle of the night. (Bull Ryman, glider pilot)


## Assessing VARSITY

Some of our most experienced glider pilots did not fly gliders to Wesel; they were kept back in case a second mission would be needed. There also was a possibility that those who did not fly in VARSITY would be used for entirely separate troop carrier drops in support of American armies around Mainz, Koblenz, and Cologne; there was even one proposed drop on the city of Berlin, Operation ECLIPSE.[5] But, as J. J. DiPietro explains it, "just before takeoff we were informed that General Patton had crossed the Rhine and that he 'didn't need any more of our damn gliders.' So I went back to bed."

Everywhere on the western front, aside from a few pockets of fanatical Nazi defenders, German soldiers were either surrendering or fleeing. The FAAA canceled contingency plans for further airborne drops near the Rhine. Fighting was being replaced by chasing. Some elements of the motorized American infantry and armor that had crossed the Rhine were able to move ahead as much as thirty miles a day. Large regions of Germany, therefore, were being added to troop carrier's areas of responsibility for freighting and evacuating wounded soldiers. We set to work on "sub-operational" missions immediately.[6] In fact, we were the first Squadron in the 53rd Wing to fly regular "supply-evac" missions to Germany.

It was just as well for us that we worked so hard and had little time to brood about the losses we took in VARSITY. Today, in our Squadron recollections, those supply-evac flights in Germany remain only a confused blur. What we do remember, clearly and in detail, is the shock and sorrow involved in the loss of all those glider pilots and of Bill Frye's plane crew. Before long it became clear that Ben Smith and Cloyd Clemons had not managed to jump safely from Bill Frye's plane, and that John Kearns and George Pittman also were dead. As the days went by, and the status of one after another was changed from "missing in action" to "killed in action," the thought that these men had had their lives snuffed out during our very last combat mission became harder and harder to

Our Group Commander, Adriel Williams, in the cockpit of his plane, named in honor of his wife, the former Mary Daly.

Gephart and Hampton, in front of their glider, just before they took off for Wesel, where they were both killed.

bear. It still hurts. Each of the men in Frye's plane is remembered when we talk these things over at Squadron reunions.

> I was very close to Bill Frye and had tremendous respect for this kind, soft-spoken gentleman. He had left his wallet, ring, and other personal items with me that morning. But that was to be his last flight. Bad as I felt, I couldn't even write his wife at the time. Everything had to "go through channels." I remember she was from Kelly Lake, Minnesota. (Bert Schweizer, Operations clerk)

We talk so much about Frye's crew partly because several of us saw them go down; probably, also, some of carry what psychologists call "survivors' guilt." For one of us, this is explicit.

> As you know, flight chiefs like me were supposed to take the place of crew chiefs in our flight when a crew chief became sick before a mission. The crew chief on Captain Frye's plane was sick and I was to take his place. I had all my things in the plane ready to go. But he came down to the line and said he felt better, and that as it probably would be our last combat mission he wanted to go. And I let him go. Then he never made it back. I can't remember his name. (Grover Benson, flight chief. This crew chief was Cloyd Clemons.)

At every reunion, navigators and pilots talk about Eugene Davis; of course he had been the subject of much discussion back in 1944–45 because he was the only one of us, as far as we knew, who had an English mistress. And we radio operators can never forget Ben Smith; we called him "The Brush" because of his elegant moustache. Smith was a handsome North Carolinan, more mature and much more poised than the rest of us; and from what I could see he was the best bridge player in the Squadron. Lou Kramer (Squadron Intelligence Officer) remembers the good conversations he and Smith had about their similar prewar jobs: they had both worked in men's haberdashery stores.

Perhaps the recollection concerning this plane's crew that haunts us the most involves Willard Cooke, Frye's co-pilot. Cooke had a brother, J. R. Cooke, also in our 81st Squadron, and he too was a power pilot. When it became obvious that Willard Cooke's plane was overdue, J. R. waited anxiously in front of our Operations Office, asking crew members coming in: Did they see that plane actually crash? Did they see any parachutes coming out? Were they sure it was Frye's plane they saw on fire? Ellery Bennett sorrowfully remembers telling him that he wasn't sure whether this plane's tail letter was "O" or "Q."

I had the chance to fly with Bill Frye in our last mission. I had flown with Frye on one of the Holland missions, the one to Eindhoven. But this time Colonel Brack didn't want me to go; and it's a good thing, since that's the mission Frye's plane was shot right out of the air.

His co-pilot was a fellow named Willard Cooke, Jr.; when I learned his name I asked if he was related to the Dr. Willard Cooke who had taught me in medical school in Galveston—and it turned out it was his father!

I thought the world of young Cooke. I guess we tend to feel that the fellows who got shot down were the best ones of the batch. It's only human to feel that way. (Jesse Coleman, Squadron Flight Surgeon)

Still, we knew, we numbered among the relatively lucky ones. The 315th TC Group, ferrying British paratroopers from England, had ten planes shot out of the air in the few minutes after they had dropped their sticks and were making their turn;[7] seven others were damaged so badly they had to make forced landings west of the Rhine. Squadrons of the 313th TC Group, which had been given the task of flying those dreadful C-46s, proved only too tragically that these planes deserved the label "flaming coffins" that we pinned on them. One of these C-46s crashed on takeoff. Nineteen of the seventy-two C-46s in those four squadrons that made it to Wesel were shot down; and out of these, fourteen went down in flames.[8] British tug planes also suffered a high rate of casualties; and a higher proportion of British glider pilots were killed in VARSITY than during NEPTUNE or even MARKET.[9]

Was it worth it? At that stage in the war, should Eisenhower have granted Montgomery the right to launch VARSITY?

Many of us would say no, that VARSITY should never have gotten off the ground. Some military historians agree. Ridgway's biographer believes that the capture of the Remagen bridge more than two weeks earlier meant "that the whole course of the war was going to change, that the real push would now come in the center, and that Montgomery's Rhine crossing—and VARSITY—would become an overstaged side-show."[10] Russell Weigley argues that the planners of this operation should have realized that the amount of ground to be gained by this assault could never be "commensurate with the men and resources [committed]." In judging this battle, says Weigley, you have to take into account not only troop carrier losses, but also those of the American 17th Airborne and the British 6th Airborne Divisions, and the losses suffered by Allied bomber and fighter groups sent in to protect the airborne craft and men. "It is hard," says Weigley, "to discover a proportionate return, for VARSITY did not much hasten the Allied advance; the 30th Division on its own had already given the bridgehead [across the Rhine] as much depth as VARSITY added in the British sector."[11]

American and British infantry who crossed the Rhine in the amphibious assaults suffered proportionately much smaller losses than the airborne infantry and Allied troop carrier losses in VARSITY.

But other military historians—including John Warren, author of the official USAF airborne history—emphasize instead that during the fighting in the weeks prior to VARSITY the Germans were able to inflict very heavy casualties on Ninth Army troops pushing toward the Rhine.[12] With a purely amphibious assault there would have been no diversion, no airborne troopers directly attacking the Diersfordter Forest high grounds that still had the potential to direct deadly artillery fire down on the Allied assault bridges across the Rhine.[13] If it had not been for the concerted efforts of British ground troops and VARSITY airborne troopers, the fighting around Wesel and north of it might well have lasted much longer. And we also have to take into account the demoralizing effect that that awesome display of aerial power in VARSITY must have had on the Germans. Without VARSITY, we can guess, German defences all along the western front might not have collapsed the way they did.

One of the most sensible analyses I have seen of VARSITY's significance was jotted down in a letter from Adelore Chevalier, one of our glider pilots, only a few days after the invasion.

> The thing that whipped the Krauts was the suddenness and the size of the attack. Each C-47 was pulling two gliders, and that was a lot of gliders. They came in so thick and fast that the Krauts were swamped. All of a sudden, a pin-pointed section of Germany was swarming with Yanks who weren't there five minutes before.

Caught up as it is in questions of Anglo-American rivalries as well as tactical significance, VARSITY probably will remain a topic of controversy among military historians as long as they remain interested in airborne warfare. But for us veterans, some partial satisfaction comes from realizing that whatever you say about VARSITY's *significance*, its *performance* was truly excellent. General Paul Williams, right after the operation, called it "the most successful [airborne] delivery ever completed." Even historians who question the value of VARSITY agree that both RAF and troop carrier crews showed enormous competence in piloting this colossal formation as well as enormous courage in taking their paratroopers and gliders straight in to their targets.[14]

After VARSITY, there was no airborne trooper complaining about "evasive action." Many of us coming in to LZ "S" had to face the spectacle of ships—who had been ahead of us—returning on fire. James Gavin (whose 82th Airborne Division was not in this battle) was flying above VARSITY as an observer; he counted twenty-three aircraft on fire at one time, all trying to make it back to the west bank of the river.[15] Nobody questions that apart from the doomed formation of C-46s, most of the paratroopers were dropped on target; and it certainly is clear that the gliders were landed with almost pinpoint accuracy—even though some of the fields they had to use were only 200 feet long.

American glider pilots, after VARSITY, were showered with praise for the disciplined accomplishment of all their assignments—and especially for fighting, right along with the airborne infantry, in the "Battle of Burp Gun Corner" and elsewhere. "Magnificently courageous!" said Brereton; and the commanders of the 17th Airborne and the British 6th Airborne Divisions agreed. Glider pilots were also praised for making it their business to get back across the Rhine quickly when their services in maintaining defense perimeters and guarding prisoners were no longer needed; this time, all of them were back in their base camps by March 28, four days after the mission.[16]

A notably self-satisfied analysis drawn up by 53rd Troop Carrier Wing HQ made the point that as far as gliders were concerned, "practically every operational criticism or objection raised during previous missions [was] satisfactorily overcome in VARSITY."[17] Gavin called VARSITY "the highest state of development attained by troop-carrier and airborne units."[18]

For once, every aspect of an airborne mission seemed to work as well as the most enthusiastic proponents had predicted. Everybody was delighted with the new 57 mm recoilless rifle, the "superbazooka," which for the first time gave airborne infantry a respectable chance to knock out even heavily armored German Tiger tanks. And while German flak hurt us badly, analysts agreed that the supporting fighters and bombers had done all they could to hold it down— and paid dearly in casualties while performing this service. Troop carrier was also pleased that, for the first time, a substantial number of gliders were recovered in good enough shape to be repaired and made ready for possible future operations. Vandals and souvenir hunters, it is true, had taken their usual toll of all gliders, including those which had landed more or less intact. But 148 gliders on the LZs were prepared by recovery teams and "snatched" by C-47s in flight right off the ground and brought back to a depot in France. (None of us in the 81st TCS were involved in this exciting work.)

Glider pilots in our Squadron like to talk about another small but highly appreciated improvement: flak protection under their seats. IX Troop Carrier Command had finally realized the danger to glider pilots from flak exploding directly under their cockpits—and indeed it was known that Germans tried to fuse their ack-ack shells to explode just below the gliders rather than level with or above them.[19] Glider pilots were provided—finally!—with enough 14-inch square flak pads to sit on: some glider pilots used two of these. Some went even further and managed to scrounge from fighter or bomber depots squares of scrap armor plating that could be installed to really protect their behinds and their legs.

When Chauncey Clapp went on the Wesel mission, he caught a burst in the legs and the back; but he had a piece of metal under him, a sheet cut out of the kind of armor plating they have in fighters. I finally found out he was in a hospital in Paris and a batch of us went up to see him. When we walked in, the first thing he said was: "Well, they didn't get my family jewels!" (Ellery Bennett, pilot)

## Notes

1. 81st TCS, hist. narr. for March 1945; 436th TCG, hist. narr. for March 1945.

2. Glider pilots had been given no advance warning they would have to contend with Montgomery's smoke screen. Dank, pp. 243, 246, 249.

3. Dank, pp. 245, 250–51; Crookenden, pp. 102, 133.

4. 53rd TCW, "Report on Operation VARSITY," April 1945.

5. These planned drops were on the books well before VARSITY was launched: see IX TCC, hist. narr. for Jan.–Feb. 1945, pp. 18–19.

6. For a few more weeks, however, since we had to fly over German regions that were either no man's land or still under German control, we were given "combat credit" for each flight into Germany—something we already knew would be important in deciding which of us would go home after the Germans surrendered and which of us would be shipped to the Pacific.

7. Brinson, p. 84.

8. The C-46s did not yet have self-sealing gas tanks. In a later investigation, angry survivors blamed the planes' vulnerability on their leaky hydraulic systems; the 52nd TCW inspectors, however, believed the fatal flaw was the positioning of the plane's wing tanks: once pierced, these wings directed the flow of escaping gasoline under the wing and onto the fuselage. Warren II, p. 180; Blair, p. 457.

9. Warren II, p. 177.

10. Blair, p. 445, Huston, *Blue*, p. 215, and MacDonald, *Airborne*, p. 153 agree with this negative assessment.

11. Weigley 1981, p. 649. The 30th Division mentioned here—the American "Old Hickory"—was part of Simpson's Ninth Army; it led the attack across the Rhine to the south of Wesel.

12. See also Breuer, *Rhine*, pp. 99–104, and Crookenden, p. 144.

13. Warren II, pp. 191, 193.

14. The official USAF history states that of the grand total of 2,926 parachute planes, tow planes, and gliders—British and American—dispatched for VARSITY, 2,861 "accomplished their mission successfully." Craven and Cate, p. 774. A postwar Air Forces study credits VARSITY with "flawless execution."

USAFETO, "Organization, Equipment, and Tactical Employment of the Airborne Division," Study # 16, n.d. (after Nov. 1945).

15. Gavin, 1979, p. 309.

16. 53rd TCW, "Report on Operation VARSITY," April 1945, p. 15.

17. "Report on Operation VARSITY," pp. 13–14. The glider pilots themselves, however, were not happy about having been landed at the same time as the paratroopers, and claimed that their casualties would have been less if the previous sequencing—first paratroopers, then gliders—had been followed.

18. Gavin, 1947, p. 137.

19. Warren II, p. 184; IX TCC, "Final Phases," p. 40.

# 22. Cleaning Up
## The Final Missions and the Return Home

### Repatriations

The collapse of effective German resistance in April 1945 had an entirely different impact on troop carrier than on other elements of the Army Air Forces. For fighters and bombers, there were fewer tanks and AA emplacements to strafe, or factories to smash, or cities to level. The Allies began to forbid bombers to attack bridges and railroad marshalling yards. Some sort of viable transport system would be needed in postwar Germany to prevent massive starvation. For troop carrier, on the other hand, the period between a winding-down war and a disorganized peace provided us with a new mission. The same flexibility that allowed us to shift from fighting to freighting now gave us the chance to alleviate some of the suffering inflicted on the world by the Nazis.

Our main task now, for most of April and May, was to remove people from wherever the ruthless Nazi system had dumped them, and start them on their way back to their own homes. We were now in the business of helping empty concentration camps, prisoner of war camps, slave labor settlements. Our "cargo" now became the survivors of the Nazis' crimes against humanity. We also brought back our own soldiers unlucky enough to be wounded during the last few weeks of fighting.

We were accomplishing what no other sort of outfit could. A bomber might be able to move some of these DPs (displaced persons) once they were on a large and well-serviced airfield; a C-47 could pick them up from any decently level field anywhere in Europe—and deliver them near their homes a few hours later. This was our opportunity to eliminate the delay, worry, and discomfort thousands of POWs and DPs otherwise would have endured if they had had to be moved by truck or by rail over bad roads or in worn-out railroad cars.

It was hard, tiring work, with flights almost every day for every plane. Sometimes we flew two missions a day. Practically all loads were overloads. My guess is I spent more time away from our "Tent City" Melun airbase than I spent on it.

One of us came within an ace of being able to fly back his own brother, a recently liberated POW.

> My brother Sam had been taken prisoner in Africa, flown to Italy by the Italians and imprisoned there. Later he escaped and was taken in by farmers in the Italian hills. On his birthday he was recaptured by the Germans and, along with other POWs, forced to walk all the way to Germany. His prison camp was liberated by Russian troops, and he was taken to Hildesheim to wait for transportation to a rehabilitation camp in Rheims [France]. Sam used to sit on a hill above the field and watch the C-47s landing and loading up. What he didn't know was that the 81st TCS had been assigned to ferry back the POWs in Hildesheim. After the war, when we were back home and I showed him pictures of my plane, he realized from the name on the plane, *Dark Beauty*, and its other markings, that he had seen my plane! Here we were, probably only yards away from each other, and not aware of the other's presence. (Hal Friedland, radio operator)

As long as any fighting continued, we usually loaded up on the outward flight with some sort of freight—often jerricans of gas—to be delivered to the fast-moving American armored units; coming back, we had human cargo.

> April 18th: We just got back from Germany—brought a bunch of Frenchmen that the Germans had been using as slave labor. Some had been there for five years. They were sure a happy bunch when we landed in France. As soon as we cut the engines they gave a big cheer. At another air strip in Germany there was a group of American POWs that were waiting transport to France. Some had on German clothing. We have been flying back a lot of wounded people from Germany. Some are really pitiful—I saw three fellows that were truly nothing but skin and bones. A lot of these got airsick.
>
> April 28th: In one German town everybody was running around looking for a place to stay—Czechs, Poles, Russians. A lot of the GIs here were high on wine. The town was full of convoys moving through. We met the batch we had to carry at the burgomeister's house. There were a couple of accordions in the crowd and a lot of them were dancing.
>
> May 8: We just heard Churchill's announcement about the official end of the war in Europe. No one celebrated too much. There are still the Japs to go, and the war's end is still far off. The Colonel gave us a couple of quarts of German liquor; don't know what it is, but it tastes bad.
>
> May 12: We have been flying liberated POWs from Germany. We should be getting the last of them soon. Yesterday we flew over Munich—

and it is *scratched!* like other big cities. Somebody told me the bombers must have been trying to get that famous Munich Beer Hall. (Ken De Blake, radio operator, from his wartime letters home)

For us in the plane crews, there was a strange mixture of satisfaction and sorrow in these repatriation missions. The men and women involved were no longer stories or pictures in *Stars and Stripes,* but people on our own planes— often vermin-ridden, skeleton-thin, obscenely smelly people. It was hard for us to cope with thoughts of what they must have gone through.

Whenever we transported back a batch of repatriated slave laborers, the first thing they did when we landed was make a dash for the edge of the runway where they could relieve their bladders. And I remember a French woman and her baby we were repatriating from Germany; was the baby's father a German soldier? I was told to advise the woman to try nursing the baby on take-off and landing so the changing air pressure on his inner ear would hurt less as he swallowed. But how can you do that when you can't speak the language? (Jerome Loving, crew chief)

Johnny Harris (crew chief) saw some DPs running as hard as they could toward his plane, frantic at the thought they might be left behind; but they were so weak they collapsed on the runway and had to be carried aboard. He remembers both regretting there was no nurse to help them on the way back and resenting the vomit and other filth they left behind on his plane.

Rather than trying to express emotions that embarrassed us, we found refuge in the funny or ironic situations these missions often involved.

We were picking up ex-POWs (French and Russian) off a large green field in Germany. There were thousands of them there. We made them leave their bulky packages behind in order to get more of them on the plane. Each time we flew them to their destination they would get a ceremonious greeting. But they often were too drunk: they had been sneaking wine and booze aboard. Once when we got to Paris some of them were so drunk they had to be stretchered out of the plane. Not to mention the couple of inches of puke in the area around the cargo door. On the way, one of the pilots in our flight radioed that he couldn't keep up with us—his plane wouldn't do more than 120 mph. We suggested to him that he probably had some stowaways aboard. Sure enough, he turned up seven Frenchmen hiding in the latrine. He got them out, made them lie down on the floor in the area between the wings, and the plane's speed went right up to our indicated 150 mph. (Art Feigion, pathfinder pilot)

Med-evac: a medical technician and a nurse offer drinks to litter patients. (Courtesy Smithsonian Institution)

Headed home: repatriated Dutch slave laborers land at Le Bourget, near Paris, on the first leg of their trip home.

One story that went the rounds of the Squadron those days concerned a plane of Soviet slave laborers we took from France to eastern Germany—where they were to be transported by truck back to Russia. They had been paid some nominal wage all the years they had been laborers on French farms; some of them had saved up their money and now had thick rolls of francs. Suspecting these francs would be seized by the government as soon as they got to Russia, they were desperate to buy any commodity a GI might sell them. They still had a lot of money when they got on board the planes and would immediately begin to negotiate with the crew members.

Never was a language barrier more vexatious. On one of our planes, a Russian pointed to the crew chief's watch, and the crew chief held up nine fingers (it was 9:00 a.m.). The Russian whipped nine 1,000-franc notes ($180, those days) from his roll and handed them over to the startled crew chief. It was an offer too good to be refused.

> A lot of those repatriation missions were heart-rending. I remember one in particular—but mostly because we had to land and take off in such a short field. It couldn't have been more than about three football fields in length. We dropped in there, using full flaps—and using all the pilots' skill. We landed OK and taxied around back to the other end of the field. There the people were standing; looked like hundreds of them, pathetically keen to be taken out of Germany and back to France. We let them pile on, along with the pitiful bags and luggage they had—all their possessions, I guess. They jammed themselves into every seat, and some of them were on the floor with their baggage. We could barely squeeze through them to get from the back of the plane up to the cockpit. The pilots began to worry about whether we could get of that field with that much of a load. Then down we went to try to take off from that tiny and very muddy field. God was with us that day. We barely cleared the tree-tops at the end of the field. (Johnny Hirtreiter, assistant crew chief)

Several of us feel that this great repatriation effort was troop carrier's finest hour, a matter for greater pride than any of our combat missions. In addition to gathering up American and British POWs, we expedited the joyous homecomings of Polish, Czech, French, Greek, Belgian, and Dutch victims of Nazi cruelty. Total POWs repatriated in the ETO by all of IX TCC amounted to more than 69,000 in April and 184,000 in May. By June this gigantic homecoming was over: only 20,000 were transported that month.[1] Impressive statistics: but we remember what is difficult to add up—the anxious faces, the hot tears, the grimy clothes, the pathetic baggage.

In all this confusion and hurry, there was no way of knowing just who we were flying eastward from France, and from eastern Europe back to Britain or France. It is just as well for our consciences that this was the case. Did we repatriate any of those Russians captured by the Nazis early in the war, who—on pain of death—had put on German uniforms and worked on garrison duty in Normandy and South France? After we so obligingly gave them a lift on their way back to Russia, were they branded as traitors? On May 28, at Col. Williams' staff meeting, 436th TC Group planes were ordered not to fly over territories assigned by the Allies for Red Army occupation.[2] This was our first sign of the sort of Soviet suspicion and hostility that helped bring about the Cold War of the late 1940s and 50s.

One topic that was beyond anybody's capacity to handle was the Nazi death camps. Many of us, in the course of our repatriation missions, saw these camps—usually after the worst of the carnage they held had been cleaned up. The Holocaust is such a well-studied tragedy that it is difficult to remember how stunned Americans were when it first came to public attention. Even Jewish fellows among us had trouble taking in the enormity revealed when the German extermination camps were liberated. What was particularly agonizing was the evidence that huge numbers of Germans, especially those living around the death camps, must have at least known about, and tolerated, the liquidation of all those millions of Jews, non-Jewish Poles and Russians, gypsies, and political prisoners of all nationalities. Now we had to face up to the newspaper pictures we saw after the British liberated Belsen, the Americans liberated Buchenwald, and the Russians liberated Auschwitz.

We still tend to avoid the subject during Squadron reunions.

Ellery Bennett, Rex Selbe, Jesse Coleman, and Art Feigion remember arriving in one of these camps shortly after it was opened up, but their recollections tend to be mercifully skimpy. Art Feigion remembers that he once was stuck in Nuremberg for three days and visited a death camp; when he saw those "stripe-suited prisoners from Buchenwald" he didn't even know what they were.

> We all had to go to Buchenwald and Dachau to pick up survivors and take them back to Paris and other cities. On our plane, somehow they found out that we had extra K-rations aboard. We passed it out and they would try to eat; but right away they would just have to pass the barf-bucket. They couldn't stand it; they were just so weak the food would make them sick. (Ellery Bennett, pilot)

> Once I had the experience of evacuating some concentration camp victims from Germany back to England. They were terribly emaciated. One of them

died en route. The picture I have in my mind of these people remains with me to this day. (Rex Selbe, pilot)

———————

Minutes for Group Staff Meeting. Monday morning, April 16, 1945.
Colonel Williams: Major Rowerdink [436th Group Operations Officer] just came back from the front and he is going to tell us a little about one of those "Murder Factories."

Major Rowerdink: This factory is 19 miles south of Gotha. I visited it the first day after it was captured. This factory is scattered around Ohrdruf for 100 kilometers and is the main center of the concentration camp. There were 5500 prisoners here in six months, 4700 of them murdered. In the building in the rear were 70 bodies ready for burning. They beat them with pipe and their heads were bashed in. In the middle of the square was a place to hang the people who refused to work. This camp was manned by SS troopers. . . . The table on which they beat the prisoners was right alongside this gallows. . . .

About a quarter of a mile from the main camp 50 or 100 bodies were lying there burning. . . . Some people we talked to had been in the concentration camp for five years. . . . I actually saw bodies burning on the railroad tracks. Most of these prisoners were Poles, Russians and French. Three American officers were reported there. . . .

When the Grave Registrar came around, the Americans made all the inhabitants of the town come up to the camp and pick up the charred bodies piece by piece. A soldier stood behind each one and if they hesitated, they got a swift kick. . . . These prisoners were not criminals, they were just political opposers.[3]

## Adding up "points"

Not a single one of us in the 81st Troop Carrier Squadron was destined to be shipped to the Pacific to help fight the war against Japan. But until "The Bomb" was dropped on Hiroshima on August 6, 1945, we had no way of knowing the end of the war in Europe would mean the end of compulsory military service. During the spring and early summer of 1945—and even as late as July, when most of us had returned to the States or were on our way—we believed that many of us, perhaps the majority, would finish our service obligations in the Pacific. Certainly the big brass in troop carrier, including Lewis Brereton and Paul Williams, believed that airborne forces would be used to overcome the expected fanatical Japanese defense of their main islands.

It would have been entirely possible for Washington to have ruled that each and every man in the 53rd TCW was to be sent to the Pacific. But political pressure on the War Department was strong to spare at least some ETO veterans a kind of "double jeopardy" in Asia. After much bickering between political and military leaders, a compromise was reached: some ETO soldiers would be sent to the Pacific, others not. Only a few weeks after VARSITY, rumors began to circulate that some of us—older men, men with the most combat credit, those serving the most months away from home, those with children—might be sent to Germany as part of an army of occupation, or be allowed to fulfill their service duty stateside, or perhaps even (ah, Heaven!) be returned to civilian life. A system of "points" was drawn up: one point for every month in uniform, one for every month's service overseas, five for participating in each major campaign, five for every combat decoration, and twelve points for every child up to three. Because troop carrier had been in several campaigns, and because of all the Air Medals we got, many of us had more than the eighty-five points needed to be eligible for a discharge.

Announcement of the "points" system completely changed the mood at Melun. "Thoughts of home, civilian life, and other dreams of similar nature [were] foremost in our minds."[4]

It now looked as though the fortunate ones among us—and not necessarily the most worthy—would soon be on their way back to home and family, while others would be forced to see an entirely different and perhaps even bloodier war through to another bitter end. Up to then we had been a tightly knit, deeply committed unit intent on finishing an important job. Soon we would become a collection of individuals, each with slightly different prospects for "getting the hell out of it!" Anxiously, we all began to add up our individual points, and to try to get some idea of how many points would be needed to keep from being sent to the Pacific. This changing mood represented a problem for our commanding officers, especially those responsible for morale. They responded by denying any problem existed.

> With the end of the month comes the realization that our job is half completed. VE day has come. VJ is still to come. Everyone in the squadron has been given a physical check-up and everyone is ready to go, if and when the time comes.[5]

> Now that Hitler and Company have thrown in the towel we are prepared to join the surge that is sweeping up to, and eventually over, the islands of Japan. Judged from past successes in the European Theater of Operations, all members of the 436th Troop Carrier Group feel highly con-

fident that, whatever the future holds, we will be in there pitching, bringing added credit to ourselves and the United States Army Air Forces.[6]

Such official "two down and one to go!" sloganizing (Mussolini and Hitler, next Emperor Hirohito!) hardly reflected our real feelings. Not that we were in an "every man for himself" situation. But the esprit that had helped bind the Squadron together obviously was beginning to weaken.


## Last missions

There was one job no one ever had to command us to do: help handle wounded soldiers.

The pace of medical evacuation flights speeded up tremendously in April. Under ideal conditions plane and medical crews would land, take on the wounded, and get them airborne in as little as twenty minutes. But sometimes there weren't enough flight nurses, surgical technicians, and ambulance truck crews to do the job as quickly as needed. Those of us among the plane crews—and many others, when such work was on our own base—would hang around, trying to look helpful, only too glad to pitch in with the delicate work of hoisting litters in and out of ambulances and planes.[7]

> Whenever they brought in wounded, some of us would go up on the flight line and help unload those fellows. A few of us, I remember, couldn't handle that; they couldn't stand being near wounded people. Some of these had arms gone, legs gone, the sides of their faces shot away, holes in their bellies and more of that sort of thing. But somehow I was able to cope with this; I helped unload many of those poor fellows into ambulances. And I always felt fortunate I was in the Air Forces and not in the front lines like those boys were. (John Merril, glider mechanic)
>
> ———
>
> I helped unload quite a few wounded soldiers. I'll never forget one fellow who came in on a stretcher; he had a head wound that looked as though he had been shot right in the forehead; but the poor fellow actually tried to get off his stretcher and walk. The Flight Surgeon pushed him back down. The way the Flight Surgeon shook his head made me realize this poor man was about out of time. (Grover Benson, flight chief)

On each "med-evac" plane we had one nurse and at least one medical technician. They usually were part of the 806th Medical Air Evacuation Squad-

Ambulances with wounded soldiers draw up to Squadron planes.

Litter patients loaded on a C-47.

ron, based first at Melun and later at Villacoublay. When we flew large numbers of planes in a single mission we were supposed to have a flight surgeon along, too; but this was rarely the case. The pressure of work that spring was just too great for the small number of flight surgeons we had. During April alone, the 806th MAES evacuated 17,287 patients.[8] Usually we ferried twelve litter patients or eighteen walking wounded per plane; but in a pinch a plane could accommodate twenty-four litter patients.

Such an evacuation flight, for most of these patients, was the very first time they had ever been in an airplane. The nurses, on the other hand, were perfectly at home in a C-47; many of them had been airline stewardesses before the war. (Those were the days when to hold down such a job you had to be a registered nurse.) We, the plane crews, can testify what a great comfort it was for wounded men to have a nurse along. Several times I overheard patients anxiously questioning the nurses about how they thought their wives and girl friends would react to the news of their wounds. All the arguments about how the U.S. should not expose women to the risks of combat or to airplane accidents went out the window when we saw the difference nurses made.

When there were only walking wounded on your plane, as soon as the nurse came aboard the atmosphere brightened perceptibly. On such flights there would be a lot of respectful kidding. Ken De Blake, a radio operator, wrote home about one flight when:

> These fellows were all in high spirits even though shot up or in casts. The nurse on our flight kidded the co-pilot about not having enough gas to get us to England. One of the evacuees said "If you guys are out of money, we guys will pitch in and buy you some gas."

"Regulations" stated that when patients flew over water—as when we were ferrying them back to Britain—nurses were supposed to put "Mae West" life jackets on them; but of course many were in too much pain to be handled that way. Another flight problem we encountered was the rule that when we had litter patients with chest wounds we were not supposed to fly above 3,000 feet; the thinner air up there made patients breath harder. But complying often meant flying through low clouds and turbulent air, equally bad for wounded men. Pilots with litters on board also were forbidden to bank their planes at more than a twenty-degree angle; this made for vexatiously slow approaches to a landing field. Sometimes heated arguments on handling the plane would break out between nurse and pilot.

Ellery Bennett, flying back at one time with a very severely wounded batch of soldiers ("seventeen men with sixteen legs") was continually harrassed by the nurse (a major) to fly lower—and "Do something about this bumpy ride!" Finally Bennett yelled out "Major, if you can fly the ship better, come up here and I'll go back and take care of the wounded!" When Bennett's ship got back she reported him to David Brack, who said only "Well, Bennett, at least I'm glad you know which end of the plane you belong in."

If the wounded were litter cases, often the groans of distress in the cabin would be hard to take. Sometimes the agony on those litters was so intense I would have to close the door between them and the crew compartment and try to concentrate on working my radios. One thing that the cabin door could not keep out, however, was the smell of gangrene. Even today, I have only to close my eyes and call up a memory of a med-evac mission, and the sensation of that overpowering, disgustingly sweet smell fills my head.

> I can still smell the odor of rotten flesh. I will never forget the sight of some of those boys on stretchers with bandages covering every part of their bodies. I used to think: "Another batch of kids scarred for life." And I remember what great morale builders the flight nurses were as they went from one to the other doing what they could to help. (Jerome Loving, crew chief)

By now our pilots were so proficient at landing on tiny fields that they began to take greater and greater chances. Was that designated landing strip nothing but wet grass, making your brakes virtually useless in stopping? Were there high trees just this side of the optimum landing spot, making it necessary for you to plunk your plane down quickly in a "power off" landing? Was there no radio truck on the field to give you landing directions? Did that concrete runway you were told you could land on turn out to be full of bomb craters? No matter: it would make a better story in the mess hall that evening.

> Landing on small fields with C-47s was something like landing on an aircraft carrier. When either coming over trees at a steep angle or dragging the aircraft in at a low level, the technique required you to come in at the lowest possible speed with full flaps and literally dump the plane on a spot at the edge of the field. This wasn't easy, when wallowing in prop wash from planes preceding you or landing with high cross winds or turbulence. You had to be pretty good with rudder controls or the plane would dip a wing and plow in.
>
> In my opinion, Duane Smith was one of the finest and most daring pilots in the Squadron. Once I was flying co-pilot with him in *Buzz Buggy*. We had to check out a pasture in France which Patton's forces had designated for a supply dump. That pasture turned out to be narrow and pretty short. We made contact with a radio truck on the field and began our approach. The field was sopping wet. Smitty landed near the edge; but be-

cause of the slippery grass he didn't dare to brake the plane. We were zooming toward the end of the field and a row of high trees; it looked like curtains for us. What I hadn't noticed was a plowed field about a hundred feet wide between the end of the pasture and the trees. We slammed into the mud in that field and slewed around about 90 degrees to the right. The mud piled up against the wheels and stopped us just before we reached those trees. An Army half-track had to tow us out; the mud was over the top of the plane's wheels. (Rex Selbe, pilot)

## Tag ends

Grant Howell, one of our teletype operators, was the first person in the Squadron to know the war in Europe was really about to end. He happened to be on duty in the Group message center the morning of May 7. There had been false alarms on April 23 and again on May 6. But this was the real thing: at around 6:00 a.m. we got a TWX that Germany was going to surrender, unconditionally.

President Truman and Prime Minister Churchill designated the following day, May 8, as "VE-Day," Victory in Europe. The immediate problem for each of us in the 81st TCS was how to find some appropriate and memorable way of celebrating. David Brack sent a plane to Germany to bring back some bottled cheer, but his good intentions fell flat when the enlisted men discovered they had received bottles of very questionable wine while the officers got schnapps or cognac.

Crew members, in any case—and the mechanics who supported them—had little time for celebrating. During all of May we flew heavy schedules, almost up to our very high performance of the previous month. All we could do to mark VE-Day was to shoot off huge batches of red, white, and blue flares. Group HQ officers objected strenuously to this wasteful display, but everybody's face was saved after we came up with the clever idea that those must have been "liberated" German flares.

VE-Day was much the same as any other: up at 6:30 and take-off at 8:30. We went to R-16, Hildesheim in Germany; it was gasoline as usual. Major Farley flew the ship for a change; he is sure a fine flyer. This was a long day. We got back to base at 6:40 p.m. But we had beautiful weather, and this helped some. We had lunch at R-55 [another German airstrip] with the medics. A cheese sandwich and two slices of pineapple. We got into R-16, but had to circle for quite a while: about thirty ships were taking off while we were in the landing pattern. We unloaded and took off for R-55. Seems we were the only ship to come that way, though an ATC plane landed right after we did. Major Farley and I looked over a Focke-Wulf 109 that had been strafed. We finally got loaded up with twenty-four litter patients, twenty-two Americans, one French, and one British. We took them to A-80 [Rheims in France].

When we got back to base all our guys were celebrating by shooting off flares everywhere. And all the announcers on the radio were celebrating the war's end. (Pat Bowen, crew chief; diary entry for May 8, 1945)

On VE-Day Group HQ threw a party that lasted until 5:00 a.m. the next morning. But we crew members, the first few nights after VE-Day, would drink all we could, tumble into our cots for a few hours sleep, and be rousted out early for the next morning's flights. Glider pilots and others not needed just then could go to Paris, the real place to celebrate. "That was a wild day and night," Thayer Bonecutter (glider pilot) reports. Those lucky enough to be strolling along the Champs Elysées on VE-Day evening can never forget the joyous jam-packed crowds of people and how

Every person in uniform was a hero and everyone wanted to shake your hand, buy you a drink, or give you a kiss. I was standing up near the Arc de Triomphe when I heard the crowd noise rise even higher. As I looked down toward the Place de la Concorde, I saw with amazement what appeared to be a huge truck with very bright lights driving right through the crowd. Then I detected the familiar sound of a pair of engines and I could see that it was a C-47 with its landing lights on. That plane was flying down between the buildings with its props less than thirty feet above the crowd. Approaching the Arc de Triomphe with props in low pitch and motors roaring, it pulled up, shining the lights on the Arc, and then disappeared into the darkness. The war in Europe was over—and the city of Paris had received one final salute from troop carrier.[9]

We in the 81st TCS had been held together not only by conventional military discipline but also by the satisfaction of functioning well both as fighters and freighters. But now combat in Europe was history;[10] and our efficient supply-evac missions would soon taper off to an end. European highways were beginning to be cleared up; and whatever locomotives and freight cars could be assembled were being put back on the tracks. Trucks and trains could handle freight much more cheaply. Troop carrier was increasingly irrelevant to postwar Europe. Our realization of this reduction in our status was reflected in our deteriorating morale and discipline. Sloppy dress, filthy planes, increased disregard for military convention (like using "Sir" for officers and addressing NCOs by their rank), and incidents of pilferage, all indicated that our solidarity and sense of

"Where are the propellers?" 81st TCS pilots and crewmen examining one of the dreaded German Me 262 jet fighters on our base.

In a ceremony at Chartres, Colonel Williams and Captain Robert Sanctuary receive the French Legion of Honor.

purpose were cracking up. One day in Villaroche two of our men beat each other up so badly that a French doctor on the spot had to patch them up before turning them over to our own medics. Surveying the problem of troop carrier morale (in all theaters) just after the war, Col. Samuel T. Moore stated:

> It is to be remarked that morale was highest when transport crews were busy in close support of ground forces. The close contacts with embattled forces, and frequent praise from ground force commanders for their aid, conveyed a sense of battle participation denied to most airmen. Morale touched high peaks at such times.[11]

The increase in venereal disease represented a massive headache for Group Headquarters. It was Colonel Adriel Williams, our Group CO, and not David Brack, our Squadron CO, who bore primary responsibility for moving all the 436th Group squadrons to the U.S. in good shape; when large numbers of us, especially officers, spent time in hospitals "taking the cure" it reflected badly on Williams. For the first time since figures on VD were compiled, there were more new cases of VD in the 436th TCG than in other 53rd Troop Carrier Wing groups.

Williams tried to jar his squadrons back into some semblance of good order with tough inspections, increasing penalties for disregarding "military courtesy," and threatening court-martial for anyone caught appropriating government property. He ordered all squadron orderly room clerks to make sure each man, before he received his liberty pass, had his "pro-kit" (prophylactic medicine) with him; he also insisted that all squadron COs "chew ass" on every man returning from VD hospitalization. He appropriated all "private" motorcycles on the base, U.S. as well as European, and turned these over to the Group motor pool. Officers he caught in Melun "without proper uniform" were kicked out of the officers club there; and additional guards were posted around the base in an increasingly vain attempt to prevent local French women from strolling through the tent areas looking to trade or sell things (including their bodies). These women also were known to be pilfering soldiers' belongings during lunch time when the men were at chow and most tents unoccupied.

However, not all aspects of the relaxed discipline during that May and June were bad for Squadron morale. We acquired a human mascot, fourteen-year-old Freddie, one of those countless homeless boys of obscure origin wandering around Europe and hoping against hope to be taken to the States.[12] And now that there was no danger from enemy planes or ground fire, many of us who had never flown were able to go on milk run trips and get first-hand looks at German towns and bases. If you couldn't be properly assigned to a flight by Operations, you could easily get an unauthorized trip by begging a pilot you happened to know, or—if you were a plane or glider mechanic—by trading places with the regular crew chief. Only the very few who were deathly afraid of flying turned down such an opportunity to see a bit more of Europe.

One notable passenger we carried those days was a French cousin of Hal Friedland (radio operator). Jacques Friedland, who had fought with the Maquis in south France, showed up one day looking very dashing in his Maquis uniform, complete with kepi (box hat). He was a real charmer, readily accepted by the men in our Squadron; and he was able to spend several nights on the base.

Meanwhile, during the month of May, there was an enormous amount of planning and work at Melun that somehow had to be accomplished before we could move out. We had to strip the Squadron of everything not essential to our moving, and put everything else in good order. Records, equipment, tools, planes—all had to shape up in a few weeks, that is, before our "air echelon" left for the States. In this air echelon would be crew members and others judged to be both essential to the Squadron's functioning and without enough points to rule out a second tour of duty.

Now we had to jettison some of the more bulky, more dangerous, or more illegal souvenirs we had been hoarding. Several of us had second thoughts about taking back pairs of live artillery shells we once believed would look classy on a bookshelf. Johnny Hirtreiter (assistant crew chief) also thought better about carting home two German 30-caliber machine guns he had stripped from a crashed JU-88; these simple but efficient guns—"masterpieces of engineering," he thought—might make trouble if spotted by Army inspectors checking baggage in the States. He was even more reluctant to surrender a battery-operated lamp that was a souvenir from his trip over on the *Queen Mary*. But such items, and much, much more, now went into the base dump.

Many glider pilots, a few plane pilots, and almost all our glider mechanics (including Del Montgomery) were transferred to other troop carrier outfits or to infantry units destined to function as part of the army of occupation in Germany. The split-up of the Squadron had already begun.

I was shipped up to Nuremberg. We got there late in the evening, about chow time. This quartermaster outfit was located in a bombed-out factory. The captain came out and said "Before you fellows even get off the truck I have to tell you I can't use you! You have too much rank." He explained that in his outfit even a corporal didn't have to do any work besides taking charge of three truck drivers. But he explained that any one of us willing to drive trucks could join in. We were tired of being moved around; and I figured this was as good a place as any. So I got off that truck. This was my introduction to another nice bunch of fellows. I drove a truck out of Nuremberg all over Germany. It was sad but interesting; I now could see what the

Air Forces had done. In Nuremberg itself there was hardly anything left. Frankfurt was practically leveled. It was one horrible sight after another. (John Merril, glider mechanic)

———

A batch of us were sent to Germany and served as security guards. We went to a town called Erlangen not far from Nuremberg where that banty rooster Hitler started his monkeyshines. I had mixed feelings about the hard times the Germans were having. We saw farmers plowing with milk cows. We saw old women wearing high top shoes out near the forest picking up pieces of dead branches for their fireplaces. We saw little kids walking along with beer mugs as big as syrup pitchers and drinking out of them on their way home. (Russell Charlesworth, glider mechanic)

While we were packing up, and waiting to learn what was to be done with our Squadron—and with each of us individually—one of us, who had been a POW in Germany since September 1944, visited the Squadron in Melun. This was our former Squadron Glider Officer, Darlyle Watters. Darlyle, as we saw in Chapter 16, had been captured by Germans during the Holland invasion when his glider—which was being towed by David Brack—was cut off while still far short of the LZ. He and John Webster (captured the day before Watters) had to endure eleven appalling months as POWs. After being released Darlyle was sent to Camp Lucky Strike, near Le Havre in France; and after a few days there he caught a ride back to Melun and to a joyful reception by his Squadron buddies. They were able to tell Darlyle he had been put in for a Distinguished Flying Cross. But they also had some shocking news for him.

> I finally learned the real circumstances under which I was cut off from Brack's plane back on that fateful day of September 19. The man who had been Brack's co-pilot sought me out. He told me that the tow rope had come loose not because it had been hit or had broken, but because Brack had *ordered* him to cut the glider off. The tow-rope release handle in the plane was on the co-pilot's side, up over his head. At the time Brack's plane, severely hit by flak, was full of smoke in the cargo section. But both of the plane's engines were still working—as I remembered seeing myself back then. The co-pilot had not seen any fire in those engines; he asked Brack to repeat the order, and Brack again told him to cut me off. Afterward, as everybody knows, Brack managed to bring his plane safely back to Brussels. [See Chapter 10]
>      I was in pretty bad physical shape. In prison camp my weight had gone down by fifty pounds. The news of how Brack might—just might—have pulled us in the glider all the way to the LZ, or to safety in Belgium—hit

me hard. Meanwhile, no word from Brack himself. But a couple of days later he saw me walking along one of the camp roads. I can still see his face the moment he caught sight of me—he turned beet red. He stopped his jeep and said he wanted to show me something. Then he drove me out to the flight line and showed me all the patches on his plane's flooring. And he explained that when he landed in Brussels the plane was such a wreck he was told the plane would have to be junked. Only three wires were left of the braided cables that went back to the elevators.

Then he drove me back to his tent, went in, and came out with two bottles of wine. He handed them to me. I was so upset by this I can't remember what was said next. I never saw or heard from Brack again. (Darlyle Watters, Squadron Glider Officer)

The disappearance of our former sense of purpose and self-management brought an even greater relaxation of discipline and of the drive to work hard. Officers over at Group or at Wing might be beset with anxieties about how we were getting along in the 81st TCS; but that was *their* problem. During those balmy spring days, we in the Squadron were having what amounted to a lively and exceedingly interesting month-long vacation—with plenty of time for delicious slothful relaxing. By mid-June, much of the work needed for preparing to move was done or nearly done. Our planes were flying less and less; in June we ferried only 1,583 evacuees and patients, compared to 4,444 in April. Walking along TARFU Boulevard, the main activity you could spot some days was sunbathing: dozens of cots outside our tents with us in them, soaking up that beautiful June sun.

In a way, the most exciting flying on the base that late spring was done by Germans. Several German turbo-jet fighters, the once-dreaded ME-262s, touched down at Melun on their way to a Navy carrier at Le Havre and eventual study by Army Air Forces designers at Wright Field in Dayton, Ohio. To Johnny Harris (crew chief) the strange, menacing sound of those jet engines was "like an old-fashioned electric fan with its cage being hit by its fan blades."

It was becoming easier and easier to get a day pass to Paris; Group ran a shuttle truck there three times a week. Officers, on the other hand, wrote out their own passes to Paris and used their own jeeps to get there. Now that it was warm and parks in Paris were showing their wonderful colors, even those of us with no need for the sexier things Paris had to offer were glad to get the chance to stroll around and get another look at the sights. These last looks meant a great deal.

And free time to take a stroll around Melun, with its sidewalk cafés now operating, was practically yours for the asking. In Melun you could sip a *vin blanc* and nibble a bit of that delicious French bread. One wonderful Sunday in

June, George Doerner, Grant Howell, and I took the Squadron shuttle into Melun, rented a rowboat, and went out for a little excursion on the Seine River. The
weather was so warm we stripped off our shirts and undershirts. We rowed up to
where Army engineers had constructed a "Bailey Bridge" across the river to
replace the bridge our bombers had knocked out. Then we turned and let the
boat drift us back downstream. It was so relaxing we turned around and did the
same thing again. You could feel tensions of the last two years ooze away.

France was a land that fascinated but also slightly repelled us. Rex Selbe
(pilot) was surprised to find French people not at all ashamed of or dejected by
the Nazis' six-week conquest of their country back in May–June of 1940. The
language barrier, furthermore, was just too great for us to be able to develop
close friendships. One afternoon early in June the enlisted men had a Red
Cross–sponsored dance on our base with French girls from nearby towns; but
even for those with a smattering of French, talking with these girls was too
painful to make pursuing the acquaintance attractive. Only two men in the entire
436th Group, so far as I know—none in our Squadron—eventually married
French girls.[13]

Already a few of us were comparing the French unfavorably with the Germans. This was especially the case among those who had flown to Germany and
brought back—after visiting German towns that had been spared bombing—
impressions of how polite, clean, and industrious those Germans were.[14] But
when we talked of the slim possibility of one day returning to Europe, it was
Britain or Holland we had in mind.

Three or four of our officers, it is true, managed to enjoy some pleasant get-
togethers with older French people. One relatively wealthy family in Melun was
particularly kind to a few officers, inviting them into their home for Sunday
dinners.

> What was great was that when a group of us would go over they would give
> us a typical French meal—the kind that starts in the afternoon and lasts
> three or four hours. I remember that in between courses we all would sing
> "Un petit verre de vin"; and their children would play the piano for us. The
> kids also loved to try out their English on us. We would come back with
> our fractured French. Of course we would bring along with us some of the
> goodies we could get from the PX, especially chocolates. (Joseph Konecny,
> Squadron Engineering Officer)

And Mme. Montzon-Brachet, the aged owner of the Château Grégy in the
town of Brie-Comte-Robert, invited Charles Hastings and three other officers
who knew a little French to join her for Sunday tea; Hastings reports that he was

also able to get something more enjoyable: a luxurious hot bath with "several soakings and soapings."

By far the most chic "French connection" belonged to Colonel Adriel Williams.

> Once when we were on a field near Rheims it became obvious we would have to stay awhile for the ground crews to lay out some needed landing strips. So Captain Wilson [co-pilot] was all for getting into Rheims and treating ourselves to a case of champagne. We borrowed an Army jeep and scooted over there to where the Mumm company [a famous champagne winery] was. At the door we were met by a Frenchman named Jacques Barot. He may have been just about the homeliest person I have ever seen; but he gave us a wonderfully warm welcome. In fact he hugged me; and practically from that time on, all the rest of his life, we remained truly close friends. And he supplied me and the Group HQ people—and as much of our other people as I could manage—with Mumm's Cordon Rouge champagne, for the rest of the war! Incidentally, he invited me and all the people in our Group Staff over for the very first party his family had had since the Germans took over France. They had promised themselves to not have any celebrations at all until their Liberation. (Adriel Williams, Group Commander)

## Splitting up

By the Fourth of July we were ready to go our separate ways—depending on how many points we had. IX TCC was already beginning to split up: some groups were transformed into Air Transport Command units, others ordered to assist in helping the military occupation of Germany, and still others—those who had the longest service in Europe—"redeployed to the Zone of the Interior" (the U.S.) for discharge. But our 53rd TCW was "slated for direct redeployment to the Pacific," that is, after only one month's furlough in the U.S.[15] Not everybody low on points took the prospect of being redeployed to the Pacific calmly.

> The outfit fragmented fast when the war was over. They tried to shanghai me to go to the Pacific. That didn't work, and they sent me to England. I was AWOL for three months, chasing women and getting drunk. Finally I learned they would let me go home. I was still AWOL—my buddies packed my bag and I got on that ship an hour before it left. There were 150 of us—all troublemakers. It took until November 1945 until I got out. (Jack McGlothlin, glider mechanic)

I was Personnel Equipment Officer and had to stay at Melun after the other glider pilots left so we could write up and return everything we could. Most of the stuff was written off as "lost in combat." But then came an order knocking me off Col. Williams' plane as it was about ready to go back to the States. The only way I could stay on that plane was to sign an agreement to go to the Pacific. Williams said, "Sign it, Earl; I can change it in the States." But I said, "Colonel, I've fought my war! I have a wife and four daughters waiting at home for me. I owe it to them to get out and go home if I can."

The Group Adjutant told me I would be transferred to Germany and another outfit, with no certainty of where I'd go next. I told him I'd go AWOL before I'd go to Germany! He cut a new order for me right then and there and added my name on the list of those going back to the States by ship. (Earl Goodwin, glider pilot)

At the Squadron level we had little of the sort of tough control needed to get us through the vast and complex transition from France to the States and perhaps to the Pacific.

David Brack did not have the temperament for grappling with the multitude of managerial decisions that had to be made in the face of the growing disinterest—or outright opposition—of some people in the Squadron. In any case, our Squadron CO was on his way out of our lives. He would be the first man to be discharged. In 1942, when he had left his civilian job as airline pilot, he had been given a firm promise that once his tour of duty in Europe ended he could wind up his military career and go back to civilian life. Soon after VE-Day Brack began to make plans for leaving the Squadron behind. Francis Farley, our Operations Officer, would be our new Squadron CO; and Jack Wallen, leader of "A" flight, would become Operations Officer.

I remember the day Col. Brack left the Squadron. He turned his ship back over the base and buzzed our tents so close he was right down on the deck. I thought he was going to lift the tent roofs right off. (Ken De Blake, radio operator)

At the time we began to split up few of us were inclined to blame David Brack for wanting to shake the French dust off his boots as quickly as possible. So did all of us.

I was an airline pilot before the war, and all airline pilots in troop carrier were going to be turned loose as soon as we got back to the States. We knew we weren't going to the Pacific. What happened after I left France would be entirely up to Major Farley. He took my job as acting Squadron commander until he got back to the States. I did indeed think, until they dropped the bomb, that it was possible the Squadron would be sent to the Pacific. (David Brack, Squadron Commander)

Only later, when we began to talk about the regrettable lack of ceremony in the way the Squadron ended, did we wonder if David Brack could have handled the break-up in France more satisfyingly. Of course no one could have predicted that by the end of August the Squadron would inactivate; so far as our Squadron commanders knew, something called the "81st Troop Carrier Squadron" would resurface soon in the Philippines. All the same, we miss very much not having had some sentimental leave-taking, some big Squadron bash, some sort of formal parade and speech-making that only Brack could have provided. About the only ritual we had was a "Service of Remembrance" on April 17 commemorating those who had died; but this was for the entire 436th TC Group. And, in a ceremony at Chartres on June 6, the high-ranking officers of the 436th TC Group, Colonel Williams and several others in Group HQ, and the 436th TCG squadron commanders, received the French Legion of Honor or the Croix de Guerre "for outstanding achievements in operations leading to the liberation of France."

It was precisely when we were beginning to leave "Tent City" in Melun that the atom bomb got its first top secret test, in the New Mexico desert near Alamagordo, on July 16. The sixteen planes of our air echelon had started leaving Melun on July 10; and the main echelon began to pull out on July 15. Our planes retraced the southern route across the Atlantic we had used in the other direction back in December 1943: Marrakesh, Ascension Island, South America, Puerto Rico or Cuba, Florida.

Once back in the States, the crews and passengers on the air echelon got their promised thirty-day furlough. When they reported back to the various bases near their homes they got the news about how the bomb dropped on Hiroshima would affect them. In a few more weeks, on September 2, 1945, they were able to celebrate "VJ-Day" (Victory over Japan). Most of our air echelon people had already been discharged; in fact, they were released from military service as soon as they reported back from their thirty-day furloughs. A few, however, had to serve four or five additional months on U.S. bases.

In South Carolina they stripped our plane of a lot of its equipment and even took some of our personal bags away from us. They re-issued us ODs [woolen olive drab uniforms]—and God! was it hot. It was kind of comical: they were stripping the guys on the line of almost everything that looked to be GI, even watches. From Charleston we were shipped to Baer Field, then to another station, and finally we got our thirty-day furlough.

When I came back from leave I was shipped to several different bases. Often the permanent party there [that is, men who had been assigned to one base all during the war] gave us a bad time; we had to pull of lot of detail [clean-up work]. Once we were even set to work putting together a communications course, mostly for Morse code. I remember being sent on detached service to Sioux Falls, where I became part of a crew flying bombardment personnel either to their discharge stations or to their next assignment.

November 8, 1945, was the day I was discharged; I was quite happy for that; but between the time we left France and then, things hadn't moved nearly fast enough for me. At first I thought I would want to stay in the service. But they didn't need me; and now I'm glad. (Ken De Blake, radio operator)

Considering the enormous number of men involved in this vast redeployment, and the complexity of the change, transferring home our air echelon was handled with remarkable efficiency. About the most vivid negative recollection of fellows in our air echelon is the exasperation some of them experienced when their barracks bags—which had had to travel by ship from France—were sent to the wrong stations and lost. Ironically, most of the air echelon men became civilians sooner than did those in the main echelon—though the main echelon men had more points.

The Squadron's main echelon was made up of those scheduled to take the slow route to the States, by ship, because they would arrive last and thus have the most protection against early transfer to the Pacific. On July 15, 1945, the main echelon went from Melun to Camp Lucky Strike or to Camp New York or to one of the other dozen or so transhipment camps near Rheims in France for soldiers headed back. There we waited for a ship with space for us at our transatlantic port, Antwerp in Belgium. Meanwhile we could visit Rheims, sample its famous champagne, and marvel at its strikingly flamboyant Gothic cathedral.

A few of us—the "rear echelon"—were left behind at Melun for two nights in order to break down the tents and pull together the cots and other GI property troop carrier did not want to leave behind. "Tent City" was now almost entirely without MPs; this meant the neighboring French people would soon drift in, trying to scrounge useful things from the enormous mass of unwanted items we as individuals—or our various Group departments—had discarded. And some of the French, it was all too obvious, took advantage of the turmoil to steal what they could.

Because I could speak a little French, I was put in charge of the enlisted men in this rear echelon "detail," doing the last-minute dismantling and clean-up. This work involved me in some half-comic, half-sad confrontations with our French neighbors. Dozens of them would start picking through stockpiles not only of discards but also of equipment we planned to ship with us. I would shout, "No, no! Don't touch! Come back tomorrow! Tomorrow!" But they would retreat only a short distance or stand there defiantly. Because we were considerably out-numbered it took some rather silly pushing and shoving to clear the French off the base. We certainly could sympathize. After five years of deprivation and German occupation, they believed themselves entitled to anything they could scrounge, especially from those rich Americans. It was a relief to get on a truck the next day and to leave Melun behind.

At the transhipment camps, where the main echelon and rear echelon people waited to go to Antwerp and the long journey home, we were quartered hit-or-miss in areas among other troop carrier outfits and even fellows from entirely different branches of the service. Our sense of disorientation at no longer being clearly under the control of our own Squadron officers was very unpleasant; on the other hand, everybody's uppermost thoughts were so exclusively focused on the fact that we were truly going back to the States—and on the hope that we were not going to the Pacific—that any complaints we might have at the moment seemed mighty trivial. Most remaining semblances of military discipline among those of us in the 81st TCS at Camp Lucky Strike now vanished. The mood we were in would not permit anything else. The only orders we wanted to hear were, "This is it, men! Let's get on board that ship!"

> We were waiting at Camp Lucky Strike to be shipped to Antwerp and to home. That camp was really deep in soldiers. There could have been thousands of us there waiting for ships. The camp was nothing but mud and dust. One day Henry Brewer and I were walking along when he overheard what some German prisoners were saying about us. These were POWs who were being set to work loading supplies and stuff on trucks. I must admit they were a healthy-looking, strong batch of fellows. In that warm weather they were stripped to the waist, and a lot of them were built like prize fighters. Now, Brewer could understand German—though he hated Germans more than anybody—and he found that they were laughing and joking about what a poor-looking and undisciplined batch of Sad Sacks we were. They laughed about how they could ever have lost the war to a sad-looking bunch of people like us. (Jesse Coleman, Squadron Flight Surgeon)

We made the ride from the Rheims area to the Antwerp docks in trains so old they could have been in railroad museums—understandable, in view of the havoc Allied bombers had wreaked on French rolling stock. Many of us with cameras hurried to get photos of the cattle cars used to carry our heavy baggage. Some of these cars were the famous "Forty and Eights"—freight cars that still carried the sign "40 hommes ou 8 chevaux" (forty men or eight horses) used to transport those of our fathers who had served in France during World War I. We did not ride in those cattle cars, but rather in decrepit passenger cars where at least we had wooden benches to sit on.

Finally after a few days at Camp Top Hat or Camp Lucky Strike, we were put on board ship: in my case, the *Joseph W. Gale*. This was no *Queen Mary* that could travel from Europe to New York in five days. This was a World War II "Liberty Ship," one of those prefabricated vessels turned out amazingly quickly in American shipyards and, up to VE-Day and later, set to work carrying oil, coal, food, and military supplies to Europe. Now ships like this were refitted to "bring the boys home!" It took us three whole days just to go from Antwerp harbor up the long Scheldt estuary and reach the Atlantic Ocean. Our voyage from Antwerp to New York took fifteen days.

Enlisted men were berthed in bunks with almost as little room between them as the litters for wounded patients on our C-47s. Officers also were crowded together, but in cabins. All told there were 753 of us (plus a crew of eighty-two) on a ship never designed to transport passengers. But comfort was a minor consideration; nobody bitched too seriously, since we all understood the reason we were on that slow boat was that troop carrier expected that the longer it took us to get back and go through our promised month's furlough, the less our chances would be of winding up fighting Japan. So we put up with the enormously boring daily routine of chow, reading, gambling, chow, ships drill, some more reading, chow, some more gambling, and back to sleep. To relieve the tedium there were old movies, a boxing tournament, and the daily "Gale's Tales" shipboard newspaper.

In sharpest contrast to our detailed recollections of the trip to Britain on the *Queen Mary* eighteen months before, few of us have any clear memories of our experiences or thoughts while sailing home. I remember some bull sessions about whether or not we would get sent to the Pacific and other bull sessions about our chances for jobs. There was also some questioning about what the GI Bill would do in financing college and getting home mortgages.

During the entire trip we were all half depressed, almost numb. This was partly because of the way our Squadron was breaking up—not even with a whimper, let alone a bang—and partly because it was hard for us to take in the fact that our lives would soon change for the better or the worse—but in any case in ways impossible to predict. While we were soldiers we had despised being moved around like pawns; now that we were about to take sole charge of our own destinies, we began to realize that a life in which somebody else made the

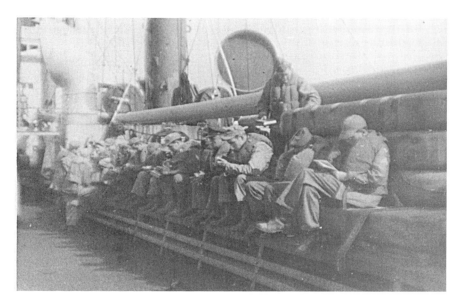

Dullsville at sea: the 81st's "main echelon" tries to while away the time on the long trip
back from Antwerp to New York.

Welcome home! A ship meets us in New York harbor, with sirens, flags, and a WAC
band.

important decisions had something to recommend it. It was then that several fellows—perhaps to their own surprise—began to think seriously about a career in the military service.

We soldiers of World War II were very much civilians in uniform, influenced by the anti-militarist bias that remains a part of American culture. At that time, it was hard for us to admit to ourselves that acquaintances made during miliary service—even though made with some pretty interesting and mostly decent fellows from all parts of our country—would mean anything important to us.

> After VE-Day, as we totted up "points" and wondered whether it was the Pacific or the States that lay ahead, it began to dawn on us that the 81st had become "home"—that redeployment would shatter associations and friendships and routines that had become our pattern of life. (Grant Howell, teletype operator)

Most of us didn't even exchange home addresses. The plane and glider mechanics, it is true, had passed around a sign-up sheet; but they put down only their names and home towns—no street addresses—as if they were not even contemplating writing Christmas cards. Crew members who together faced death in the sky, who sweated mightily together month after month with jerricans of gasoline and wounded patients, faded abruptly out of each others' lives.

The strange mood was complicated by the announcement on the ships's loudspeaker, on August 7, that some new and terrible weapon had been used against Japan—something called an "atomic bomb." There were no riotous celebrations on board, no rejoicing at all—we had no idea what "The Bomb" was or that it might end the war. Not even the very satisfying welcome we got on August 10 in Staten Island harbor—banners flying, a welcoming ship coming out to greet us with a "Well Done!" sign and a brass band of WACs, fire-fighting ships sending up huge jets of water—snapped us out of this mood.

In my case, however, this mood would last only one more hour. Down on my bunk I heard a rumor that there was a woman trying to get on board. I would have paid more attention if I had known that it was my wife.

Dotty, who during the war worked as a newspaper reporter in nearby Bayonne, New Jersey, had learned that some members of the 81st TCS were scheduled to land soon at Staten Island, New York. She investigated the shipping news, discovered when our ship would arrive, and decided that with a little journalistic trickery she could get aboard that ship. She showed up at the dock about an hour after we did.

Dotty got by the MP at the Staten Island docks entrance by waving her press card and mumbling something about interview assignments. But she was foiled from getting on the ship by another MP, who insisted he had no authority to allow a civilian on board. So she paced up and down the dock, peering up at the ship's railing, where more and more soldiers congregated, whistling at this attractive dame in a fetching black dress and a romantic floppy hat. She was trying to spot me; but, very boorishly, I had just joined a chow line on the other side of the ship. My thoughts—as I have been vainly trying to convince her ever since—were not on food but on my dear wife, supposedly only a few miles away in Bayonne. Running through my head were phrases from the scores of explicitly passionate love letters I had been mailing her during the nineteen months we had been separated; I refused to get interested in some crazy broad trying to get on the ship.

Showing the enterprise of a born reporter, Dotty spotted a public relations officer and dragged him over to the ship. She convinced him that as a reporter for the *Bayonne Times* (which she certainly was) she had been sent there to interview men from New Jersey for their home-town newspapers. This affable officer, probably glad of having something useful to do for a change, swept aside the MP at the gangway and hauled Dotty on board.

She was immediately surrounded by a flock of GIs, all anxious to get as close as possible to the first non-uniformed American woman they had seen since leaving the States. The noise level of all that whistling and kidding was fierce. Dotty kept looking around, but I was still nowhere in sight. She began to yell out as loud as she could, "Anybody from New Jersey? Any New Jersey soldiers?"

Near the throng around Dotty stood Louis Kramer, up on a hatch, smiling down at all this hubbub and banter. Hearing her ask to interview men from New Jersey, he said to one of the 81st people there "Go get Wolfe!" Dotty looked up at him and said "Which Wolfe?" "Marty Wolfe!" said Kramer. "Yes, yes, get Marty Wolfe!" screamed Dotty.

Not for nothing was Louis Kramer our Squadron Intelligence Officer. He stared hard at Dotty, comprehension dawning.

"Are you his wife?" he demanded.

There was nothing for her to do but admit it. And Kramer, demonstrating that that he was a gentleman as well as an officer, ordered somebody to dig up this guy Marty and bring him to Kramer's cabin. Then he broke up the crowd around Dotty and escorted her, also, down to his cabin.

So here in Captain Kramer's cabin, unbelievably! is Dotty, not in my dreams but in the flesh! I don't waste time: big clinch! Says Dotty to Kramer, when she can catch her breath,

"How did you ever guess I was Marty's wife?"

This gives Kramer the chance to deliver one of the better exit lines of all of World War II.

"Oh," says he, getting ready to leave us in the cabin, "I censored most of Marty's letters to you!"

### Notes

1. IX TCC, "History of HQ, IX TCC," n.d. (after June 1945), p. 6.
2. 436th TCG, hist. narr. for May 1945, minutes of staff meeting.
3. 436th TCG, hist. narr. for May 1945.
4. HQ, 436th TCG, hist. narr. for April.
5. 81st TCS, hist. narr. for May 1945.
6. 436th TCG, hist. narr. for May, 1945.
7. During World War II our 436th Group evacuated more patients than any other group: about 41,000. "The Carrevac" (newspaper of the I TCC, Malden, Missouri), Sept. 26, 1945.
8. From a sketch history of the 806th MAES, reprinted in the "Newsletter No. 7" of the 79th TCS.
9. From a letter by R. J. Redfern in "Silent Wings," a newsletter for glider pilots of World War II, June 1986.
10. Officially, "combat operations"—that is, missions over potentially dangerous geography that counted as "combat credit"—ceased as of 2400 hours, April 23, 1945.
11. Moore, Ch. 2, p. 48.
12. Freddie accompanied us all the way to Antwerp, Belgium, our port of embarkation from Europe, where we had to leave him, sobbing his heart out on the docks.
13. Corporal Gatewood Etheridge of the 79th TCS married a girl who had worked many months for the French Resistance; and Bernard Burg, our Group Dental Officer, also married a French girl.
14. This preference for Germans over French after VE-Day was common throughout the American Army. See Kennett, p. 217.
15. IX TCC, "History of HQ, IX TCC," n.d. (after June 1945), pp. 7, 9.

# 23. Thinking Back
## How It Looks to Us Now

### Judging troop carrier

Troop carrier has always had an image problem. Its effective span of existence was short, less than five years.[1] During that period its obligations were numerous and complex. Newspapers and magazines of the day usually had to begin a report on one of its missions with an ABC of troop carrier components and methods. Before the world could form a picture of this new military technique, it vanished, made obsolete in the short run by the atom bomb and in the long run by helicopters.

For us troop carrier veterans it is understandable, though exasperating, to find persons old enough to remember World War II who know nothing about troop carrier. Such people find it hard to believe that long ago and far away there were slow-moving, unarmed planes flying close to the ground in rigid formations, delivering entire regiments of airborne troopers behind enemy lines. It is even more difficult to make younger people believe there were such things as glider assaults: "combat gliders" sounds to them like a contradiction in terms, about as absurd as "combat water skiers."

> Later, whenever I talked to people about troop carrier, I found that they didn't know the first thing about it. It was kind of disappointing to have the bomber groups get all the main glory. In the movies I saw there was very little about troop carrier. But I know that every one of us who went through all that flak felt that he was doing an important job. I think we did a hell of a lot more than we got credit for. (Johnny Hirtreiter, assistant crew chief)

Even during the war we were troubled by what we felt was the undervaluation of troop carrier's contribution and its potential. It is easy to find evidence of this in Squadron records. Our Squadron diarist found it necessary to proclaim that the campaigns of 1944 demonstrated that, finally, "Troop carrier came into its own and distinguished itself as a major factor in the art of modern warfare."[2]

But this was only wishful thinking. Deep down, we realized that troop carrier was—and was destined to remain—a stepchild of the armed forces.

Compounding this image problem was the tendency to confuse troop carrier with the Air Transport Command, a branch of the Air Forces that did not drop paratroopers nor tug gliders into combat. The most humiliating case of such confusion involves Dwight Eisenhower himself. On August 10, 1944, he was addressing a parade of 101st Airborne Division soldiers during an awards ceremony. Referring to the fact that both airborne troopers and plane crews now would be under FAAA commanders, Eisenhower said, "It's through this [combined] command that we hope all the airborne troops and the Air Transport Command will become brothers. . . . I am proud of you and what the Air Transport Command has done." [3]

Among World War II historians there is a different sort of troop carrier image problem. Most who deal with airborne operations tend to confuse the indecisive impact of airborne units in specific battles on the one hand with the quality of troop carrier performance on the other. They conclude that elite paratrooper and glider units would have been put to better use if they had gone into battle on the ground, and that troop carrier should have been restricted to freighting: supplying forward armored operations and evacuating wounded soldiers.

Judgments that "vertical envelopment" failed to decide the course of a single major battle [4] of course make troop carrier veterans uncomfortable; but, since several experts on World War II have reached this conclusion, we have to admit they are right. We must continue to insist, however, on the important *contribution* troop carrier made to the Allied victories in Normandy, southern France, the Battle of the Bulge, and across the Rhine. Troop carrier veterans, I believe, also can be proud of their role during the Eindhoven and Nijmegen phases of the Holland invasion: the misuse of airborne forces at Arnhem was mainly the fault of the RAF and the commanders of the British First Airborne Division.

What concerns me more is that some World War II historians leave their readers with the feeling that if troop carrier had performed better, airborne infantry on the ground would have scored even greater successes. To a large extent this feeling is based on the the airborne fiascos in Sicily and the scattered drop on D-Day in Normandy; this negative judgment about the Normandy drop is mistakenly applied to the remainder of the troop carrier assault missions after D-Day in Normandy. But by far the greater number of troop carrier sorties for the ETO must be judged as highly praiseworthy.

I believe the evidence assembled in this book supports the following generalizations:

1. After the first paratrooper drop in Normandy, almost all troop carrier

pilots delivered their paratroopers and their gliderborne troopers skillfully and bravely.

2. In all its functions—supply, evacuation, glider tow, and paratrooper drops—troop carrier performance improved dramatically between June 1944 and June 1945. This improvement was won partly through combat experience gained by pilots and aircrews. But in part this better performance depended on troop carrier leaders making far-reaching changes in tactical deployment; the change from nighttime to daytime operations is only one example.

3. Troop carrier gave good value as an extremely flexible weapon. It is important to understand the worth of this flexibility even though several of the operations for drops ahead of fast-moving Allied armor were canceled. As we have seen, during the late summer and fall of 1944 several FAAA operations were planned to speed the pace of Allied breakthrough in central and eastern France, Belgium and finally in Germany. All were canceled except MARKET and VARSITY. Because fast-moving armor, time after time, made "forward vertical envelopment" unnecessary, some military historians state that FAAA should not have continued to plan them—nor should troop carrier have wasted resources training for them, but should have confined its work to freighting. But determined Wehrmacht leaders were showing themselves capable of redeploying enough of their diminishing strength to threaten the Allies with the real possibility of extended, deadly, attrition warfare. The rapidity of the Allied advances in the period before the Holland invasion (and after February 1945) could not have been predicted at FAAA headquarters with any degree of assurance. By the same token, troop carrier planners could not anticipate that Americans would capture the Remagen bridge before the Germans could demolish it, or that Stalin's "meat grinder" offensives on the eastern front would be so successful. Five airborne divisions in reserve—and planes capable of delivering them—gave Eisenhower and Brereton a trump card with which to smash, if necessary, any defensive lines the Germans might set up, in the Alps or anywhere else. After the Holland invasion this trump card was played only once, at the time of the drop across the Rhine; but this does not mean it had no value.

At the end of March 1945, American forces were about 200 miles from Berlin. The Russians were closer, about fifty miles away, and apparently ready to sacrifice thousands upon thousands more of their soldiers to capture that great prize, so necessary was it for them to avenge themselves on the Germans—and to extend the westward influence of Communism in the postwar world. FAAA *probably* could have taken Berlin for the Allies with an airborne operation. The 101st, the 82nd, and the 17th Airborne Divisions were standing by, ready to launch Operation ECLIPSE against Berlin; and troop carrier was ready to ferry them.[5] James Gavin, like many other military leaders turned historian, believes that for political reasons America should have made that attempt.[6] But on March 28, a month before Hitler's suicide, Eisenhower had already assured Stalin that Berlin would be left to the Russians to conquer; and Marshall and Bradley, dreading the huge cost in American lives a vertical envelopment of Berlin might entail—with street-by-street fighting against fanatical Nazi defenders—backed Eisenhower's decision. The American armies turned south into Bavaria and Saxony. ECLIPSE was canceled.[7] This episode, also, demonstrates not that the combat features of troop carrier were unnecessary but that the possibility of mounting an airborne assault provided the Allies with a potent and flexible option.

### "A good outfit"

For its size, a troop carrier squadron may well have been the most complex military unit ever sent to an overseas theater of war. Among the 260 or so enlisted men alone we had more than forty-five different "primary duty specializations"— a large array of skills in engineering, electronics, communications, and management. In addition, our officers represented more than a dozen primary duty specializations plus their "collateral duties" like censoring mail, supervising the mess hall, arranging transport, and so on. Bomber and fighter squadrons, also, had plane, management, and engineering specialists, but they did not have the large number of specialists needed to fly and maintain gliders.

In spite of its structural complexity and its manifold assignments, the 81st TCS functioned smoothly and successfully. In many sections of this book I have tried to explain why this could happen.

Given that troop carrier *as a whole* worked well, can one say that all troop carrier squadrons must have had about the same sort of governance, the same esprit de corps, the same kind of experiences as did the 81st TCS? Unfortunately there is very little evidence we can use to answer that question. Since this book is the first detailed account of *any* troop carrier squadron, we are in no position to make the kind of comparisons that would show whether the 81st TCS was typical or exceptional. There are indeed monthly "historical narratives" for other squadrons written during the war; but they give only limited information on internal relationships and squadron management.[8] If veterans of the other fifty-nine troop carrier squadrons in the ETO read this book, probably they would find dozens of examples in which structures and relationships inside their squadrons differed from ours. This is even more likely for troop carrier squadrons in the MTO, the Pacific, and the CBI.

This is not to say the 81st TCS was "exceptional" in the usual sense of that word. It is gratifying, of course, that Adriel Williams, our Group Commander, called us "best in the ETO!" But we had no real heroes; and there were the usual "goofballs" and "fuck-ups," plus a few examples of dead wood, among us. And like other pilots in other squadrons, some in our squadron also "flinched" during the first D-Day mission and dropped their troopers off target.

Certainly one of the reasons the 81st TCS worked well is the decent quality and the almost endless quantity of the supplies provided us. We were truly in a position of "military affluence." We suffered only one serious shortage (self-sealing gas tanks) and a few minor ones (watches and sunglasses for certain crew members, penicillin for enlisted men with VD). The aircraft we flew, both planes and gliders, were superb instruments capable of sustaining scores of bullet and flak holes and still accomplishing their missions. We received new aircraft engines and parts—and entire new planes and gliders—just about as fast as we needed them. So far as gliders were concerned, we were an example of what today's conservationists condemn as "a throw-away society." HQ IX Troop Carrier Command might agonize over the hundreds of CG-4As left to rot or be vandalized after a mission; but as long as we got all the brand-new gliders we needed, this was no concern of ours. There was no "patch-and-make-do" in *this* man's army![9]

Another form of military affluence we enjoyed concerns personnel: the very large pool of relatively well-educated, highly trained specialists on which we could draw. The outstanding example here is the crews added to the Squadron or those that arrived as replacements for crews we lost. Our Squadron increased from twelve planes when we went overseas to twenty-seven when we were at full strength; and the number of our glider pilots increased proportionately. While the new crews may have lacked some of the advantages enjoyed by our more experienced flyers, they were just as well trained and well endowed physically— as their performance demonstrated.

Only a "people of plenty" like our American society could have furnished a raw recruit like me with five weeks of basic (infantry) training, five months of intensive electronics and communications schooling, and six months of "transition training" as a crew member in a C-47—before I went overseas. We were all very conscious of what such extensive training meant to us as a squadron. Bill Westcott, a pilot, credits the small number of accidents and casualties we suffered to this first-rate training program, another feature of "military affluence."

At the time, of course, what we talked about was not the plenty, but the perceived shortages. There was always bitching to be heard about the occasional lack of Cokes and chocolate at the PX. But whatever the complaints we made to each other, we remained very conscious of the huge amount of supplies available. Appreciation of our relatively affluent situation was driven home by the sight of hardships among civilians around us in Europe and by our realization of how much more we were paid than were British soldiers.

One obvious reason we believe the 81st TCS was "a good outfit" is our feeling that, in general, when we were given an order, the order seemed rational—that is, justifiable in terms of tasks we recognized as useful for the war effort. Squadron management was not "chicken," not a matter of unquestioning obedience to peremptory orders. Our superiors did not seem motivated by some unreasoning need to maintain discipline, but rather by the need to improve performance in our technically demanding jobs.

I believe that a less obvious but important reason for our positive feelings about our Squadron is that we did not make sharp distinctions between the one-third of our people who were combat personnel and the non-flying soldiers who supported them. Perhaps such a cleavage could have existed if the crews had been made up entirely of officers; but there were enlisted men in the planes, too, risking their necks during combat along with the pilots and navigators. By the same token, there were few hard and fast separations between aircrew radio men and crew chiefs, on the one hand, and the ground radio men and mechanics on the other. We were all technicians in uniform. Pappy Harris, our Line Chief, was an officer (warrant officer); but he dressed and he worked like a top mechanic. David Brack and several other pilots praised Pappy's work to the skies—and accepted him as their social equal. Another example of this absence of sharp cleavages is the vivid memory that Grant Howell, a teletype operator, holds of George Doerner, an aircrew radio operator; in this recollection, George is standing beneath his plane, his fist poked up through a deadly looking flak hole in the wing. Grant and George, both before and after our combat operations began, were good friends.

Perhaps these positive feelings would have changed if more combat crew members had been killed. In that case—perhaps—Squadron flying personnel might have harbored bitter resentments against those at less risk. But our casualties, though deeply felt, were not numerous. As Charles Hastings says, "We lost dearly but not severely."

A final reason that we look back at the 81st TCS as "a good outfit" lies in the nature of the relations between Squadron and Group. In several chapters we saw that the Squadron, for most of its internal functions, was just about autonomous. However, when orders concerning flying duties came down from Group HQ they tended to be accepted without question, partly because of our high regard for Adriel Williams. Occasionally some officer in the 81st TCS might deplore Williams' indignant forays into Squadron affairs aimed at restoring military decorum and discipline. One of them remembers calling Williams (behind his back) "West Point Willy." But all our airplane pilots had to respect Williams for personally leading us into each and every combat operation during the entire war. And the glider pilots, as we have seen, tended to look for support and understanding more to Williams than to Brack.

World War II histories dealing with infantry often explain good military performance through concepts of "kinship for the duration," that is, on peer pressure inducing soldiers to act bravely in order to "not fail your buddies." [10] This consideration, of course, did exist in the 81st TCS, especially among our pilots; but I believe it was relatively unimportant. We did feel pressure similar to this; but basically it came not from inside the Squadron but from our feelings of responsibility toward the airborne troopers, feelings that were powerfully reinforced when we suffered the stinging indictments levelled at us after the first Normandy mission.

## How our experiences changed our lives

Basically there were three ways you could sever your ties with the 81st TCS. You could try for a regular appointment in the postwar Air Force—though you might have to take a reduction in rank to get one, since the military now needed far fewer officers and men. Or you could become a civilian, sign up for duty in the active reserves, and hope to stick it out long enough to qualify for a pension. Or you could take the $300 discharge money and run.

Most of us did run—hardly daring to believe our good fortune; we actually were going to enter the civilian world of which we had been dreaming for at least three years—without exposure to the war in the Pacific!

David Brack, as we have seen, thankfully jumped back into the left-hand seat of a DC-3 as an Eastern Airlines pilot. But several other high-ranking officers in the 81st TCS remained in military service or reentered it during the Berlin Airlift crisis or the Korean War; they got regular or reserve commissions and stayed on, serving their twenty years or more, and retired as colonels or lieutenant colonels. This was the case for John Bohan, Art Feigion, Lake Stroup, Whitman Peek, James Rike, George Rankin, Oliver Semmes, Julian Hoshal, Henry Zimmerman, and probably others whose post-World War II experiences are unknown to us. These were not necessarily posts in the Air Force: Hal Read, our wire chief, was tapped to go to OCS (Officers Candidate School) while still at Melun; then he took an infantry commission (in the Third Army) and worked for several years with the occupation forces in Germany. When he retired from his regular commission he stayed in the reserves and eventually became a major general. Only a few of us who were not officers reenlisted; but John Hiles—who could never get George Rankin or Cecil Elder to value his work as a radio mechanic—reenlisted in the Air Force in 1948, became a crew radio operator, and participated in the Berlin Airlift of that year. And Johnny Harris stayed in the Air Force, switched from engineering to communications work, became manager of a radio station in Korea (1957), and in 1966 got the assignment of setting up a broadcasting network in Thailand.

When asked "How did our service with the wartime 81st TCS change our lives?" practically all of us respond that as a group we were better off for the experience materially as well as intellectually. Pressed for details, we mention such things as increased engineering and flying skills (supposedly making for more rapid job advancement) or the GI Bill subsidies (home mortgages, business loans, and college tuition grants and allowances). As a group we seem to feel that the war did indeed push us up the social and economic ladder. But this would be hard to prove, since as a group we were above average in many respects *before* the war. If the war had never happened, and we had begun our careers or our college education in 1942 rather than 1946, many of us just might have ended up even further ahead.

Some of us, especially those who had had some college before the war, used the GI Bill to go on and finish degrees and even tackle graduate school. This was the case for Ed Vosika, who went on to get his M.D. Many others became professionals through the GI bill: engineers, dentists, doctors, teachers, accountants. This group, one might say, indeed benefited from the war in the sense that they might not have been able to afford graduate school. But this supposition, too, is debatable. Many of these same men were highly motivated; they likely would have found ways to get their graduate degrees even if there had never been a Second World War.

One surprising feature of our postwar experiences is that not many of us who had previously never attended college subsequently began a college career courtesy of the GI Bill. It is hard to understand why. One reason may be that back in those days, when a college education was so much more rare than it is today, few of us had relatives or friends with college degrees who could reassure us that we had the stuff to make it through that strange academic environment. George Doerner and Hal Burrows, for example, both tell us that they were fearful of being unable to make the grade in college studies and had to be talked into it by we older men who knew that such fellows would be able to breeze through and benefit enormously.

Others insisted that college would be a waste of time. They were frantic to "get on with our lives," that is, get a job, get married, settle down, raise a family. Few took advantage of the allowances offered by the federal government to unemployed veterans that we called "The Fifty-two Twenty Club"—that is, $20 per week for fifty-two weeks. There was little of the "postwar restlessness" and "flashback syndrome" among us that are such well-discussed features of

Vietnam veterans.[11] Those who had worked before the war and whose jobs had been saved for them by their firms went immediately—and thankfully—back to those jobs. Thayer Bonecutter returned to AT&T; Grant Howell picked up again as editor of the *Royal Oak* (Michigan) *Tribune*; Pat Bowen got back his job in Trans World Airlines; Carlisle Jordan returned to Delta Airlines and compiled a record of forty years of perfect attendance; Emmett Pate went back to the Vulcan Rivet and Bolt Corporation, compiling a record total of forty-five years there; Pappy Harris went back to the Chesapeake and Potomac Telephone Company; George Rankin to ALCOA (between World War II and his service in Korea and Vietnam); and Joseph Konecny to his job in a branch of Union Carbide.

Several of us could not get decent jobs quickly and were pretty bitter about it.

> After the war it was a bitch. 4-Fs bossed me. The smart bastards who had been draft dodgers had the jobs people like me . . . should have had. [Eventually] I went into business for myself. (Charles Hastings)

The largest number of us ended up in the world of business. Louis Kramer started a retail fabric and decorating firm. Bull Ryman became a roofer and a sheet metal worker. Cliff Fearn went into an auto dealership. Jack McGlothlin worked for a construction firm. Hal Friedland got a job with a poultry distribution company. Bert Schweizer went into a ladies' apparel firm. Leo Promis worked as salesmen. David Neumann set up a dry cleaning establishment. Dan Bonica started out with RCA but later began a TV repair business.

One clear trend in this postwar transition of ours was the drift away from farming. Several of us who had been farm boys before the war left farming altogether. Others moved off farms but took jobs connected with agriculture, for example selling farm machinery or animal feed. This was the case for Bob Lough and Ben Obermark. A few kept their farms but got their main income from jobs in nearby towns. Don Skrdla returned to his family ranch in Nebraska.

Only a handful of us took advantage of "veterans preference" for getting civil service jobs. Both Ken De Blake and Darlyle Watters ended up employed by the Michigan State government; and Bob Tangeman worked for the federal postal service. Johnny Hirtreiter now works for the New York State Environmental Conservation Administration. George Trumbo worked for a while in a Veterans' Administration hospital but eventually became a salesman for a beauty products firm.

The general rule for postwar jobs has been: fairly high positions for our high-ranking officers; decent jobs and professions for the rest of us. Only a few of us ended up in unusual or truly noteworthy jobs: George Doerner (who played trumpet in our 436th dance band) toured with the Tommy Dorsey orchestra after he finished college; and he then formed up his own dance band (which he still has); Bob MacInnes studied for the priesthood but then had a long career in the CIA; and Hal Burrows, even before he finished college, competed in professional tennis tours and later became a tennis pro for the Richmond, Virginia, Country Club. Hal also served one term as state legislator for Virginia. He and Earl Goodwin, who has for many years been a state representative in Alabama, are the only ones in our Squadron I know of who did anything in political life beyond the local level.

When speaking about *economic* change, then, there is no simple answer to the question: How did the war affect our lives? However, there is near-unanimity concerning one *social* change: everybody agrees the 81st TCS taught us the value of being able to work beside and to get along with a whole batch of different sorts of people. Not only did we learn to appreciate good qualities to be found in fellows from far-away parts of the United States—who might have funny accents and manners—but also we became more tolerant of people from ethnic minorities in our outfit: the Italians, Jews, Poles, Czechs, and others from central Europe. This did not mean we became politically more liberal. To judge from the talk at our veterans' reunions recently we remain what most of us were before the war: either middle-of-the-road or decidedly conservative.

For people familiar with the problems that today beset Vietnam veterans, it may seem strange how few of us are bitter about the effects of the war on our careers, our social affairs, and our general outlooks on life. Many of us do mention terribly upsetting experiences: a newly empty bunk in our barracks, a dead trooper in our glider, a dying man in a plane litter. Those who talk about such haunting memories are likely to admit that for a few years after the war they had nightmares—sometimes truly ghastly nightmares that bounced them right out of their beds—but they seem to have overcome these traumas with little permanent damage. More serious were the long-lasting and painfully disruptive weeks and months suffered by those among us in POW camps or hiding out with the Dutch Underground. But even these fellows do not entirely reject their wartime experiences. Rather, they balance their worst recollections with aspects of their life in the 81st TCS that they remember in a very positive fashion.

### Forgotten fields

When troop carrier began it was an entirely new branch of the military, with no tradition to build on. Today it is gone, and our veterans' groups have no branch of contemporary military service with which we can closely identify. One possible connection might be with today's MAC (Military Airlift Command) and the

Rapid Deployment Units; but the absence of gliders in such outfits rules out close fellow-feeling.

Few of us expected troop carrier would disappear so completely and so quickly. In 1947 James Gavin was writing enthusiastically about "the future of the airborne arm," that is, how tow plane and glider tactics could be improved and how "independent airheads" behind enemy lines could be established and protected. But by 1950 it was becoming obvious that troop carrier was an idea whose time had passed. Our 81st TCS officers who stayed in the service and who expected their good troop carrier records would get them interesting posts and promotions in a peacetime troop carrier outfit were in for a rude shock.

Some of the optimistic predictions about the future of troop carrier being made between 1945 and 1949 make for strange reading today. Toward the end of the war IX Troop Carrier Command staff officers were given the job of critiquing ETO airborne performance—with the aim of improving its effectiveness against Japan. They speculated about "the coming of age of aerial re-supply" and based their expectations of troop carrier's role in the next few years on its splendid performances in the past—not taking into account the possibility of new military technology making airborne armadas as vulnerable as flights of geese. Their demands for change boiled down to matters of detail and did not touch on the possibility that the tactic of "vertical envelopment" itself might no longer be feasible.

Other writers, in troop carrier and in the country's newspapers and magazines, seemed to find it inconceivable that the vast and successful plane-glider combinations troop carrier had fielded could not be put to some important peacetime use. They called up visions of large "glider trains," and "great aerial freight convoys" with gliders being towed to inexpensively maintained local airstrips and, after being landed and unloaded, "snatched" up in the air again for additional use.[12] At least the planners for later military uses for troop carrier could excuse themselves on the grounds that helicopters (and, later, ground-to-air missiles) were things of the future. But those who dreamed that "glider trains" would become a standard feature of our country's transportation system seem now to have been not much more practical than writers of science fiction. In a study on the future of airborne operations which Matthew Ridgway authorized, contributors stated that technological progress could make gliders a standard feature of the American transportation system:

> If and when commercial air transport companies become interested in this arm of transportation, it is believed that we will see a rapid and progressive development of the glider. . . . I am convinced that a glider, like a rail freight car or passenger car, should be designed in accordance with the locomotive or power-craft which is to haul or tow it.[13]

And, in this study, Ridgway himself proclaimed that "the future of airborne operations is limitless," and recommended that the postwar military establishment should include five airborne divisions.

I do not mean to imply that the entire experience of wartime troop carrier was wiped off the books as a World War II "freak" with no lasting benefit for our nation. The later career of our Group Commander, Adriel Williams, shows how at least some of the expertise in rapid transportation of elite troops, and rapid evacuation of soldiers in trouble, could be applied in later conflicts. After troop carrier inactivated, Williams served in several stateside posts; but in 1953 he was sent to Japan where he first became an advisor on air transport of combat troops to the French fighting in Indochina, and later served in Vietnam. He became such a recognized expert in airlifting troops by fixed-wing planes and by helicopters that his colleagues called him "Mr. Troop Carrier." He played an important part in developing the Air Rescue and Recovery Service in Vietnam— especially the "Jolly Green Giants" (rescue helicopters) that earned our country's admiration and gratitude; and in 1965 he became Vice Commander of the Eastern Transport Air Force.

Partly because of its image problem, partly because of the way it ended so suddenly, troop carrier veterans have a difficult time explaining the significance of our wartime experience—even to ourselves. One road toward clearer understanding is to talk over at least some of these problems at our reunions. But we have a long way to go: in the 81st TCS the first of our reunions took place only in 1985—just forty years after most of us returned to the States and were discharged. By 1985 many of us were retired or approaching retirement. We were therefore not only able to take the time to attend such reunions, but we also became more interested than ever in exploring what our service had meant to us and our country.

During the intervening forty years several of us have given at least one unmistakable proof of how interested we were in such retrospective assessment. As individuals—or sometimes with our wives and children—we traveled to Melun and Membury, our chief European bases, to walk once again the streets of those and neighboring towns, poke into unforgettable pubs and cafés, and plant our feet on airfield grounds where we had spent the most gripping months of our young lives.

I returned to Le Muy (southern France) and to Melun once and to Membury twice. My first trip to the neighborhood of our British base was partly to prove to my wife and daughter that at Chilton Foliat there were indeed such wonderful things as thatch-roof cottages, a wood-paneled pub, and swans in brooks under an ancient stone bridge—idyllic scenes with which I had been boring them for years. The beautiful Anglican church of Chilton Foliat was still there, though it

When he visited Membury in 1978, John Hiles (radio operator) was astonished to find several of the main wartime buildings on our base still standing, including the control tower and the officers' club. The large structure pictured above is the parachute riggers' tower; it has since been torn down.

What remained of our Membury airbase control tower in 1990: home for a small specialty oil and lubricants company.

now looked rather deserted and a bit shabby; but nobody in town seemed to remember that only three miles away there once had been hundreds of troop carrier gliders and planes, and thousands of airmen and airborne troopers.

> Ten years after 1945, my wife and I, travelling a half-remembered road from Hungerford to Membury, found the Squadron area. An empty hut and a bunker remained, and some hardstand. At Melun, even the gendarme who volunteered to accompany us couldn't find the field. There was only a road lined with Lombardy poplars that looked vaguely familiar. Such a road, I remembered, ran behind our Squadron area. But there was nothing else. (Grant Howell)

---

> In one of our trips to Europe recently we tried to find the airfield we had used near Melun; but no luck! We drove all around that territory and couldn't find it. We asked some people living there where the airfield had been. But they didn't seem to know much about it at all. They did remember that Germans had had an airfield around there! That was the field we in the 436th had taken over. (Joe Konecny)

---

> In 1950 my wife and I set out during a leave of absence in my old 1939 Ford station wagon to revisit the sites of campaigns. I had my wartime maps with me; but even so I couldn't locate the DZs at Eindhoven or Wesel. But at Bastogne the DZs were visible, or at least the one of them that was roughly triangular. We then went from Dunkirk to London, and visited Swindon where we saw the Jeffrey family who had befriended me during the war. After a three-hour walk from Swindon to Membury I was exhausted. I climbed up above the embankment to the airstrip. There was little of the airfield remaining. The hardtop runways were cracking up. The Operations shack was a shambles. Fields had become pasture land.
>
> I stopped at the crossroads where the Hare and Hounds pub still stood. But it was closed. (Bill Westcott)

### Notes

1. Our 436th Troop Carrier Group formally inactivated on November 15, 1945. In 1954, it is true, the French tried an equivalent of troop carrier tactics when they planted a garrison inside Viet Minh territory at Dienbienphu and tried to maintain it with C-47s and French paratroopers; but, as everyone knows, this operation failed disastrously.

2. 81st TCS hist. narr. for Dec. 1944. Cf. the 436th TCG hist. narr. for Aug. 1944: "Often the part played by troop carrier units in the winning of battles and campaigns remains generally unnoticed by the public."

3. Critchell, p. 110. Even Army correspondents sometimes made the same irritating mistake: see *Yank*, October 22, 1944, p. 10, and McVay, pp. 12–15.

4. Weigley 1981, p. 317; MacDonald, *Airborne*, p. 159.

5. Plans for Operation ECLIPSE were ready even before the Battle of the Bulge was over: see FAAA, "Operation ECLIPSE: Outline Airborne Plan," Dec. 31, 1944.

6. Thus the title of his 1979 history of European airborne warfare, *On to Berlin*. See pp. xiii–xiv.

7. Ambrose, *Eisenhower*, pp. 628–31.

8. We can guess, of course, that the experiences of the other three squadrons in the 436th TCG must have been pretty similar. A history of the 79th TCS, one of our sister squadrons at Membury, is being written by Roger Airgood; but it seems this will not provide the material needed to make close comparisons. An interesting book of one soldier's personal recollections exists for the 60th TCG: Robert Miley, *But Never A Soldier*, 1984 (privately printed); but the 60th TCG, one of the first troop carrier groups to go overseas, fought its war in North Africa, Italy, and the Balkans. W. L. Brinson's *Three One Five Group* (on the 315th TCG) deals only with combat. I have been told a history of the 439th Troop Carrier Group will soon be published.

9. To keep this matter of "throw-away gliders" in perspective, we should point out that CG-4As cost only about $15,000 each—possibly some $75,000 in today's dollars. "Super-Stallion" Sikorsky helicopters—the kind that can carry fifty-five men—cost over $20,000,000 each in 1987.

10. Studs Terkel, p. 5.

11. This is true of World War II veterans in all branches of the service: see Kennett, pp. 233–34.

12. For an early example, see the *Stars and Stripes* article of November 16, 1944, "Troop Carrier 'Routine' a Prelude to Air Freight Lines of Future."

13. HQ XVIII Corps (Airborne). Ridgway papers, CBAMHI, May 18, 1945.

# Appendix 1
# 81st Troop Carrier Squadron Casualties

## Killed In Action

T/Sgt Cloyd Clemons, crew chief. From Glouster, Ohio. Killed March 24, 1945 (Operation VARSITY)

2nd Lt Willard R. Cooke, Jr, pilot. From Galveston, Texas. Killed March 24, 1945 (Operation VARSITY).

1st Lt Eugene R. Davis, Jr., navigator. From Norfolk, Virginia. Killed March 24, 1945 (Operation VARSITY).

F/O Emory A. Fry, glider pilot. From Greensboro, North Carolina. Killed September 19, 1944 (Operation MARKET-GARDEN).

Capt William M. Frye, Jr., pilot. From Kelly Lake, Minnesota. Killed March 24, 1945 (Operation VARSITY).

F/O Raymond D. Gephart, glider pilot. From Lakeville, Minnesota. Killed March 24, 1945 (Operation VARSITY).

F/O Joseph C. Graves, glider pilot. From Amarillo, Texas. Killed June 7, 1944 (killed when the Germans shelled the hospital where he was placed after being wounded in Operation NEPTUNE).

F/O Edward M. Griffen, glider pilot. From Charlotte, North Carolina. Killed September 19, 1944 (Operation MARKET-GARDEN).

F/O John J. Hampton, glider pilot. From Dallas, Texas. Killed March 24, 1945 (Operation VARSITY).

2nd Lt John G. Kearns, glider pilot. From South Orange, New Jersey. Killed March 24, 1945 (Operation VARSITY).

Lt Kenneth N. Okeson, pilot. From Wakefield, Nevada. Killed September 19, 1944 (Operation MARKET-GARDEN).

F/O George G. Pittman, glider pilot. From Etna Green, Indiana. Killed March 24, 1945 (Operation VARSITY).

S/Sgt Benjamin L. Smith, radio operator. From New Bern, North Carolina. Killed March 24, 1945 (Operation VARSITY).

Captain Charles W. Stevenson, pilot. From Akron, Ohio. Killed September 19, 1944 (Operation MARKET-GARDEN).

## Prisoners Of War

2nd Lt  Howard C. Johnson, navigator
T/Sgt  Clinton H. Perry, crew chief
S/Sgt  Warren S. Runyan, radio operator
T/Sgt  Willis W. Shumake, crew chief
1st Lt  Darlyle M. Watters, glider pilot
1st Lt  John W. Webster, pilot

# Appendix 2
# The Roster, February 1945

Who made up the 81st Troop Carrier Squadron? This question is more complicated than it might seem. All during the existence of our Squadron, some men were entering or leaving. Many of these men really "belonged" to other outfits for most of their service time. To list all the men who ever figured on our Squadron rolls, therefore, would give a distorted picture. Perhaps the most representative roster we have was one "cut" (mimeographed) for general orders when we were about to move from our Membury base in Britain to our Melun base in France. This roster does not include men who had been killed in the invasions of Normandy and Holland or had been made prisoners of war or who been transferred to other outfits. It also does not include glider pilots who transferred into the Squadron for the double-glider tow across the Rhine (Operation VARSITY). The following orders are divided into advanced, main, and rear echelons: "advanced," to get our Melun "Tent City" started up, and "rear," to close down our Membury base. It is as good a snapshot as we can get of our Squadron's make-up at one particular time; however, the microfilm of this document is in poor condition, which may have caused me to misspell some names. Note that enlisted men have MOS (military occupation specialization) numbers; for example, crew radio operators were MOS #2756. Officers have only their serial numbers.

| Rank | Name | Serial Number | MOS |
|------|------|--------|-----|
| "Advanced Echelon—Will proceed o/a 12 February 1945" | | | |
| Major | Harold W. Walker | AC | O 542 960 |
| Capt | James W. Knott | AC | O 363 913 |
| Capt | George J. Rankin | AC | O 857 477 |
| 1st Lt | Oliver M. Semmes | AC | O 582 391 |
| 2d Lt | Clifford J. Fearn | AC | O 542 662 |
| W/O | Edwin R. Harris | AC | W 213 036 7 |
| M/Sgt | Edmund L. Utterback | 18 046 136 | 750 |
| T/Sgt | Cecil R. Elder | 38 124 744 | 542 |
| T/Sgt | Harold N. Read | 31 290 311 | 261 |
| S/Sgt | Dante P. Bonica | 32 618 541 | 754 |
| S/Sgt | Harry C. Brewer | 32 918 440 | 511 |
| S/Sgt | Robert J. Farnham | 12 167 896 | 685 |

| Rank | Name | Serial Number | MOS |
|---|---|---|---|

"Advanced Echelon—Will proceed o/a 12 February 1945"

| Rank | Name | Serial Number | MOS |
|---|---|---|---|
| S/Sgt | Charles J. Ferro, Jr. | 18 122 694 | 559 |
| S/Sgt | Thomas V. Healy | 32 629 330 | 620 |
| S/Sgt | Thomas M. Hubbard | 33 281 831 | 754 |
| S/Sgt | Joseph N. Koelbl | 39 515 327 | 854 |
| S/Sgt | Simon (NMI) Kriegel | 32 294 896 | 685 |
| S/Sgt | Francis (NMI) Lester | 32 585 978 | 631 |
| S/Sgt | Leonard C. Lewis | 34 300 757 | 687 |
| S/Sgt | Wilbur H. Nolte | 18 162 800 | 559 |
| S/Sgt | Grady L. Pace | 38 385 419 | 559 |
| S/Sgt | Edward G. Smith | 36 349 178 | 754 |
| S/Sgt | Ray C. Thomas | 13 118 087 | 821 |
| S/Sgt | Clifton H. Thompson | 6 148 379 | 750 |
| S/Sgt | George R. Trumbo, Jr. | 15 116 992 | 673 |
| Sgt | Henry A. Bailey, Jr. | 38 383 523 | 559 |
| Sgt | Walter E. Baum | 32 570 984 | 849 |
| Sgt | Stewart F. Bowers | 34 669 690 | 060 |
| Sgt | Roy (NMI) Christian | 38 340 655 | 559 |
| Sgt | Leonard T. Cookson | 19 059 136 | 750 |
| Sgt | Cyril H. Dusek | 38 246 215 | 060 |
| Sgt | Robert J. Harrison | 39 613 993 | 849 |
| Sgt | Patrick L. Hart | 13 134 895 | 849 |
| Sgt | Lewis B. Hoagland | 32 749 873 | 620 |
| Sgt | Duane E. Lodge | 37 654 504 | 502 |
| Sgt | Gerald E. O'Shea | 39 116 915 | 405 |
| Sgt | Russell E. Pope | 31 266 581 | 620 |
| Sgt | Hayes M. Purdom | 13 108 174 | 555 |
| Sgt | Leo P. Spielbusch | 37 499 687 | 405 |
| Sgt | Kenneth C. Worthley | 39 407 283 | 835 |
| Cpl | Mitchell (NMI) Adda | 33 669 567 | 2756 |
| Cpl | Billie J. Anthis | 38 327 417 | 2756 |
| Cpl | Antonio F. Balzofiore | 31 173 109 | 747 |
| Cpl | Howard S. Bennett | 31 321 991 | 2750 |
| Cpl | Alton H. Benson, Jr. | 11 068 492 | 070 |
| Cpl | Clinton C. Burrow | 35 563 420 | 809 |
| Cpl | Anthony (NMI) Campisi | 12 147 263 | 747 |
| Cpl | William C. Chastain | 14 139 999 | 747 |
| Cpl | Howard R. Clifton | 38 434 929 | 2756 |
| Cpl | Barney (NMI) Davis | 36 654 487 | 559 |
| Cpl | Edson S. Dearden | 31 261 786 | 2750 |
| Cpl | Albert J. DeProspo | 32 909 668 | 2750 |
| Cpl | Ralph L. Dyer | 13 144 359 | 2756 |
| Cpl | Alfred H. Eggen | 16 056 720 | 2756 |
| Cpl | David (NMI) Eisendorf | 36 343 158 | 747 |
| Cpl | Will E. Elrod | 34 645 278 | 405 |

| Rank | Name | Serial Number | MOS |
|------|------|--------------|-----|

"Advanced Echelon—Will proceed o/a 12 February 1945"

| Rank | Name | Serial Number | MOS |
|------|------|--------------|-----|
| Cpl | Orville T. Etling | 36 482 585 | 835 |
| Cpl | James S. Halsey | 16 151 541 | 2756 |
| Cpl | Howard L. Harman | 37 601 390 | 559 |
| Cpl | Millard F. Howsare | 33 282 940 | 747 |
| Cpl | Walter P. Leddy | 36 590 764 | 2750 |
| Cpl | Jack J. McGlothlin | 19 124 362 | 559 |
| Cpl | Harry G. Mahnke | 36 298 155 | 405 |
| Cpl | John L. Merril | 37 667 644 | 559 |
| Cpl | Jules (NMI) Quebedeaux | 33 282 940 | 747 |
| Cpl | Preston L. Riddle | 18 231 581 | 559 |
| Cpl | Jesse H. Shoemaker, Jr. | 35 596 263 | 405 |
| Cpl | Donald T. Smith | 37 470 563 | 835 |
| Cpl | Robert E. Tangeman | 35 567 252 | 747 |
| Cpl | William J. Walter | 32 762 655 | 620 |
| Pfc | Fred L. Mattacks | 36 479 196 | 2750 |
| Pfc | Jeff D. Monroe | 39 294 012 | 590 |
| Pfc | Ernest A. Philipp | 37 111 357 | 559 |
| Pfc | John K. Redmond | 42 000 596 | 2750 |
| Pfc | Warren S. Vivian | 36 568 190 | 405 |
| Pvt | Hubert (NMI) Buttery | 33 733 934 | 345 |
| Pvt | J. D. Calhoun | 15 353 761 | 2756 |
| Pvt | James L. Hall | 33 534 905 | 144 |
| Pvt | Leonard M. Holcomb | 6 929 401 | 747 |
| Pvt | Wilson (NMI) Knight | 34 826 489 | 345 |

"Main Echelon—Will Proceed o/a 16 February 1945"

| Rank | Name | Serial Number | MOS |
|------|------|--------------|-----|
| Lt Col | David W. Brack | AC | O 402 316 |
| Major | Francis E. Farley | AC | O 664 990 |
| Capt | David L. Britt | AC | O 814 015 |
| Capt | Jesse L. Coleman | MC | O 471 118 |
| Capt | William N. Frye | AC | O 800 341 |
| Capt | Joseph A. Konecny | AC | O 855 005 |
| Capt | Robert A. MacInnes | AC | O 814 102 |
| Capt | Whitman R. Peek | AC | O 660 798 |
| Capt | Curtis C. Steffens | AC | O 542 920 |
| Capt | Edward J. Vosika | AC | O 677 345 |
| Capt | John F. Wallen | AC | O 729 276 |
| Capt | Robert D. Waterman | AC | O 677 621 |
| Capt | Roscoe D. Wilkins, Jr. | AC | O 677 380 |
| Capt | Richard A. Wilson | AC | O 677 927 |
| Capt | Gregory F. Wolf | AC | O 799 910 |
| 1st Lt | James C. Ackerman | AC | O 757 145 |
| 1st Lt | Stuart J. Anderson | AC | O 806 770 |

| Rank | Name | | Serial Number |
|------|------|---|---------------|

"Main Echelon—Will proceed o/a 16 February 1945"

| Rank | Name | | Serial Number |
|------|------|---|---------------|
| 1st Lt | Judson (NMI) Ball | AC | O 802 448 |
| 1st Lt | Joseph (NMI) Berryman | AC | O 679 813 |
| 1st Lt | William H. Bishop | AC | O 679 815 |
| 1st Lt | Leonard E. Braden | AC | O 680 844 |
| 1st Lt | Henry B. Brewer | AC | O 739 386 |
| 1st Lt | Theodore W. Burns | AC | O 694 119 |
| 1st Lt | Leo E. Byrum, Jr. | AC | O 677 975 |
| 1st Lt | Russell E. Carle | AC | O 806 404 |
| 1st Lt | Chauncey D. Clapp | AC | O 542 735 |
| 1st Lt | Jack S. Clarke | AC | O 857 946 |
| 1st Lt | Robert A. Clement | AC | O 694 123 |
| 1st Lt | William B. Collins, Jr. | AC | O 542 301 |
| 1st Lt | Edward E. Coombs | AC | O 182 236 7 |
| 1st Lt | Eugene R. Davis, Jr. | AC | O 814 029 |
| 1st Lt | Elmer E. Doremus, Jr. | AC | O 806 416 |
| 1st Lt | Lloyd V. Drouhard | AC | O 695 244 |
| 1st Lt | Robert J. Eads | AC | O 538 446 |
| 1st Lt | Donald C. Gessling | AC | 0 693 669 |
| 1st Lt | Samuel H. Green | AC | O 542 851 |
| 1st Lt | Henry R. Griffen, Jr. | AC | O 697 847 |
| 1st Lt | Edward (NMI) Kozlowski | AC | O 697 877 |
| 1st Lt | Louis G. Kramer | AC | O 581 972 |
| 1st Lt | James R. Lott | AC | O 677 077 |
| 1st Lt | Thomas J. McCann | AC | O 542 770 |
| 1st Lt | Douglas W. Mauldin | AC | O 705 748 |
| 1st Lt | Desle O. H. Miller | AC | O 862 901 |
| 1st Lt | Donald J. Skrdla | AC | O 537 875 |
| 1st Lt | Duane (NMI) Smith | AC | O 677 908 |
| 1st Lt | Norman S. Strand | AC | O 205 666 7 |
| 1st Lt | Lake W. Stroup, Jr. | AC | O 676 814 |
| 1st Lt | Arthur C. Swasey | AC | O 677 612 |
| 1st Lt | Earl R. Wangerin | AC | O 698 495 |
| 2d Lt | Gale R. Ammerman | AC | O 542 661 |
| 2d Lt | Melvin S. Banks | AC | O 755 747 |
| 2d Lt | Ellery A. Bennett, Jr. | AC | O 704 873 |
| 2d Lt | Thayer W. Bonecutter | AC | O 542 733 |
| 2d Lt | Floyd H. Brockenbush | AC | O 714 642 |
| 2d Lt | Guy W. Brown | AC | O 887 238 |
| 2d Lt | Wayne H. Bryant | AC | O 671 206 |
| 2d Lt | Robert E. Carney | AC | O 542 774 |
| 2d Lt | Adelore J. Chevalier | AC | O 199 825 2 |
| 2d Lt | Herbert J. Christie | AC | O 542 596 |
| 2d Lt | Willard R. Cooke, Jr. | AC | O 721 103 0 |
| 2d Lt | John R. Cooke | AC | O 779 102 |

| Rank | Name | | Serial Number |
|------|------|------|--------|

"Main Echelon—Will proceed o/a 16 February 1945"

| Rank | Name | | Serial Number |
|------|------|------|--------|
| 2d Lt | Clyde W. Devore | AC | O 285 726 3 |
| 2d Lt | Robert D. Dopita | AC | O 204 129 |
| 2d Lt | James J. DiPietro | AC | O 199 828 5 |
| 2d Lt | Richard G. Farnsworth | AC | O 542 738 |
| 2d Lt | Clifford J. Fearn | AC | O 542 662 |
| 2d Lt | Jacob A. Feigion | AC | O 689 951 |
| 2d Lt | Joseph M. Garcia | Inf | O 129 804 7 |
| 2d Lt | Louis P. George | AC | O 887 239 |
| 2d Lt | Julian B. Hoshal | AC | O 543 302 |
| 2d Lt | John J. Howarth | AC | O 706 401 |
| 2d Lt | Martin (NMI) Jacobson | AC | O 705 960 |
| 2d Lt | Winston A. Johnson | AC | O 765 994 |
| 2d Lt | Richard J. Kennan | AC | O 206 700 5 |
| 2d Lt | Paul J. Klokowski | AC | O 542 790 |
| 2d Lt | William B. Lindsey | AC | O 708 716 |
| 2d Lt | Robert E. Lough | AC | O 206 668 6 |
| 2d Lt | Bob (NMI) Mc Lucas | AC | O 816 905 |
| 2d Lt | Henry (NMI) Marquis | AC | O 206 786 5 |
| 2d Lt | Glenn G. Miller | AC | O 199 828 3 |
| 2d Lt | Lester H. Olsfield | AC | O 784 828 |
| 2d Lt | Ferdinand A. Oliverio | AC | O 887 240 |
| 2d Lt | Claude E. Pauley, Jr. | AC | O 718 238 |
| 2d Lt | J. M. Pearce | AC | O 206 227 7 |
| 2d Lt | Lee E. Personius | AC | O 782 345 |
| 2d Lt | Lloyd Peterson | AC | O 778 549 |
| 2d Lt | Glenn A. Poppaw | AC | O 766 051 |
| 2d Lt | John D. Prairie | AC | O 199 824 4 |
| 2d Lt | Samuel (NMI) Prisuta | AC | O 206 229 4 |
| 2d Lt | James E. Pritchett | AC | O 830 920 |
| 2d Lt | Albert G. Rostenbach | AC | O 766 413 |
| 2d Lt | Sherman B. Ryman | AC | O 199 827 0 |
| 2d Lt | Rexford L. Selbe | AC | O 699 779 |
| 2d Lt | James B. Sorensen | AC | O 199 826 6 |
| 2d Lt | Otis E. Smith, Jr. | AC | O 719 777 |
| 2d Lt | William (NMI) Tieber | AC | O 715 865 |
| 2d Lt | William E. Warner | AC | O 776 458 |
| 2d Lt | Richard E. Weaver | AC | O 721 270 |
| 2d Lt | William S. Westcott | AC | O 199 826 8 |
| 2d Lt | Kenneth D. Wilson | AC | O 748 867 |
| 2d Lt | Harold H. Wist | AC | O 784 646 |
| 2d Lt | John C. Wyse | AC | O 704 397 |
| 2d Lt | Robert E. Yoakum | AC | O 778 646 |
| 2d Lt | Henry W. Zimmerman | AC | O 766 139 |
| 2d Lt | Edgar E. Zoerb | AC | O 777 890 |

| Rank | Name | Serial Number | MOS |
|------|------|---------------|-----|

"Main Echelon—Will proceed o/a 16 February 1945"

| Rank | Name | Serial Number | MOS |
|------|------|---------------|-----|
| F/O | Richard G. Edwards | AC | T 131 995 |
| F/O | Hensley B. Garlington | AC | T 126 891 |
| F/O | Raymond D. Gephart | AC | T 122 446 |
| F/O | Earl (NMI) Goodwin | AC | T 123 825 |
| F/O | Paris L. Guy | AC | T 122 345 |
| F/O | Richard S. Hall, Jr. | AC | T 122 927 |
| F/O | John H. Hampton | AC | T 122 455 |
| F/O | Joseph W. Hickey | AC | T 132 015 |
| F/O | Otto C. Hinnant, Jr. | AC | T 121 334 |
| F/O | Hershel (NMI) Hollingsworth | AC | T 126 900 |
| F/O | Anthony (NMI) Kolka | AC | T 125 125 |
| F/O | Henry N. La Bruce | AC | T 134 098 |
| F/O | William C. Lane | AC | T 125 127 |
| F/O | Theodore E. Merta | AC | T 441 |
| F/O | Vaughn M. Olson | AC | T 132 160 |
| F/O | Freddie I. Peat | AC | T 122 722 |
| F/O | George G. Penman | AC | T 126 100 |
| F/O | John J. Randall | AC | T 131 881 |
| F/O | Harold L. Reddick | AC | T 131 882 |
| F/O | Robert R. Reed | AC | T 125 102 |
| F/O | David R. Reese | AC | T 121 457 |
| F/O | James C. Rike | AC | T 125 137 |
| F/O | Richard V. Robinson | AC | T 121 378 |
| F/O | James H. Schlessler | AC | T 124 288 |
| F/O | James L. Sindledecker | AC | T 121 098 |
| F/O | John J. Sweeney | AC | T 737 0 |
| F/O | John H. Taylor | AC | T 737 3 |
| F/O | Carroll L. Wendlun | AC | T 132 067 |
| F/O | Robert M. Winjum | AC | T 132 070 |
| F/O | Arthur W. Youngberg | AC | T 125 787 |
| 1st Sgt | Luman H. Fason | 34 702 615 | 502 |
| M/Sgt | Robert C. Atkinson, Jr. | 31 162 354 | 750 |
| M/Sgt | Grover W. Benson | 15 054 661 | 750 |
| M/Sgt | George L. Heck, Jr. | 35 474 885 | 750 |
| M/Sgt | Carlisle A. Jordan | 34 265 683 | 750 |
| M/Sgt | Lillard H. Mount | 18 073 767 | 750 |
| M/Sgt | Vernon L. Sawvell | 37 111 832 | 750 |
| T/Sgt | Raymond B. Aliff | 15 320 399 | 2750 |
| T/Sgt | George E. Bednar | 39 094 764 | 2750 |
| T/Sgt | Adolph (NMI) Bogotch | 12 043 808 | 2750 |
| T/Sgt | Howard K. Bowen | 35 612 568 | 2750 |
| T/Sgt | Cloyd (NMI) Clemons | 35 412 496 | 2750 |
| T/Sgt | Leonard J. Dudzinski | 36 590 102 | 2750 |
| T/Sgt | Harold I. Gerry | 37 419 185 | 2750 |

| Rank | Name | Serial Number | MOS |
|------|------|--------------|-----|
| \"Main Echelon—Will proceed o/a 16 February 1945\" | | | |
| T/Sgt | John B. Harris, Jr. | 14 159 745 | 2750 |
| T/Sgt | Joseph J. Heck | 15 334 215 | 685 |
| T/Sgt | Earl R. Hein | 39 571 324 | 2750 |
| T/Sgt | Vernon I. Hunsaker | 39 190 115 | 2750 |
| T/Sgt | Elmer F. Jespersen | 39 530 263 | 559 |
| T/Sgt | Clarence W. Johnsman | 35 410 767 | 636 |
| T/Sgt | Clayton L. Johnson | 35 454 232 | 2750 |
| T/Sgt | William A. Johnson | 16 098 339 | 2750 |
| T/Sgt | Cater (NMI) Jones | 18 173 505 | 2750 |
| T/Sgt | Clarence W. Long | 13 143 233 | 2750 |
| T/Sgt | John R. McDonald | 14 149 707 | 2750 |
| T/Sgt | Erwin V. Martens | 32 756 209 | 2750 |
| T/Sgt | Delma H. Montgomery | 18 077 875 | 559 |
| T/Sgt | Richard B. Nice | 36 433 874 | 2750 |
| T/Sgt | Bernard F. Obermark | 37 377 179 | 2750 |
| T/Sgt | Edward T. Trimble | 11 037 147 | 2750 |
| T/Sgt | Albert I. Wade | 37 285 192 | 2750 |
| S/Sgt | Julius R. Alsdorf | 37 668 655 | 2756 |
| S/Sgt | Willis J. Baxter | 37 916 453 | 2756 |
| S/Sgt | Irving (NMI) Bornstein | 31 159 721 | 502 |
| S/Sgt | George E. Britt | 34 304 033 | 559 |
| S/Sgt | Harold M. Burrows, Jr. | 33 632 594 | 2756 |
| S/Sgt | Kenneth G. Callahan | 11 014 907 | 2756 |
| S/Sgt | Carl S. Dennis | 34 313 933 | 2756 |
| S/Sgt | George D. Doerner | 34 766 194 | 2756 |
| S/Sgt | Henry S. Downe, Jr. | 12 162 738 | 849 |
| S/Sgt | Ellington E. Franklin | 14 177 909 | 2756 |
| S/Sgt | Harold (NMI) Friedland | 32 761 066 | 2756 |
| S/Sgt | Lawson T. Holmes | 37 606 169 | 2756 |
| S/Sgt | Michael (NMI) Hrycaj | 32 056 691 | 826 |
| S/Sgt | Charles J. Knight | 36 124 410 | 2756 |
| S/Sgt | Jerome A. Loving | 17 070 163 | 2750 |
| S/Sgt | Daniel L. Mackison | 33 238 140 | 747 |
| S/Sgt | Richard R. Minder | 32 672 982 | 2756 |
| S/Sgt | Lee (NMI) Muhleman | 15 322 334 | 014 |
| S/Sgt | George A. Olmstead, Jr. | 32 668 452 | 2756 |
| S/Sgt | Thomas B. Rohan | 39 257 427 | 2756 |
| S/Sgt | James F. Ryley | 12 148 520 | 2756 |
| S/Sgt | Ralph W. Salisbury | 12 121 605 | 2756 |
| S/Sgt | James J. Sheehan | 32 405 257 | 2756 |
| S/Sgt | John L. Sheldon | 39 612 687 | 2756 |
| S/Sgt | Benjamin L. Smith | 34 316 821? | 2756 |
| S/Sgt | Lewis P. Thomas | 16 086 308 | 2756 |
| S/Sgt | Raymond (NMI) Thompson | 35 566 817? | 2750 |

| Rank | Name | Serial Number | MOS |
|------|------|---------------|-----|

"Main Echelon—Will proceed o/a 16 February 1945"

| Rank | Name | Serial Number | MOS |
|------|------|---------------|-----|
| S/Sgt | Howard C. Walch | 11 110 521? | 2756 |
| S/Sgt | Bennett G. Wing | 18 108 608 | 2756 |
| S/Sgt | Martin B. Wolfe | 32 560 865 | 2756 |
| Sgt | Robert J. Bates | 15 334 700 | 405 |
| Sgt | Melvin N. Boring | 33 572 813 | 060 |
| Sgt | Warren A. Boston | 11 100 848 | 747 |
| Sgt | Donald L. Bullock | 35 791 422 | 685 |
| Sgt | Clyde E. Burkett | 33 567 891 | 573 |
| Sgt | Fury (NMI) Dallacroce | 35 741 374 | 747 |
| Sgt | Kenneth E. De Blake | 36 459 644 | 2756 |
| Sgt | Joseph E. Dees | 38 336 157 | 349 |
| Sgt | Francis W. Donovan | 35 266 712 | 521 |
| Sgt | William L. Dooms | 38 445 872 | 559 |
| Sgt | Joseph P. Feltz | 32 590 565 | 747 |
| Sgt | Roy L. Frost, Jr. | 35 092 765 | 620 |
| Sgt | Randolph P. Graves | 38 438 749 | 060 |
| Sgt | John A. Hirtreiter | 32 840 475 | 747 |
| Sgt | Maurice H. Jackson | 37 472 893 | 060 |
| Sgt | Arnold W. Jacobson | 37 298 402 | 552 |
| Sgt | Ralph A. Johnson | 37 122 372 | 405 |
| Sgt | Thomas P. Leach | 35 628 550 | 060 |
| Sgt | Jack (NMI) Mc Coy | 35 096 578 | 275 |
| Sgt | James V. Mc Gee | 32 451 573 | 552 |
| Sgt | Gilbert J. Meyer | 36 339 245 | 754 |
| Sgt | Joseph A. Raybits | 13 155 537 | 502 |
| Sgt | Elmo D. Reed, Jr. | 18 232 272 | 559 |
| Sgt | John H. Russ | 33 188 638 | 502 |
| Sgt | Tazewell G. Sanderson | 38 426 562 | 559 |
| Sgt | Vincent E. Southworth | 32 445 911 | 060 |
| Sgt | James E. Stone | 35 679 574 | 747 |
| Sgt | Albert F. York | 32 572 077 | 747 |
| Sgt | Ernell J. Zifka | 36 816 308 | 2756 |
| Cpl | George (NMI) Adams | 37 418 610 | 2750 |
| Cpl | J. G. Anderson | 38 396 551 | 405 |
| Cpl | Lawrence L. Anzelde | 16 146 030 | 747 |
| Cpl | Marvin R. Burress | 18 077 989 | 2756 |
| Cpl | Nick (NMI) Chizmadia, Jr. | 12 134 304 | 747 |
| Cpl | Salvatore (NMI) Cuccia | 32 789 675 | 060 |
| Cpl | Michael A. Fiondella | 31 330 783 | 650 |
| Cpl | Ira A. Grandy | 19 146 493 | 650 |
| Cpl | Roy A. Grant | 31 174 270 | 2750 |
| Cpl | Rodney W. Ilger | 35 599 901 | 2756 |
| Cpl | James R. Krammes | 35 092 441 | 060 |
| Cpl | Stanley P. Lukaszeski | 32 760 027 | 405 |

| Rank | Name | Serial Number | MOS |
|------|------|--------|-----|

**"Main Echelon—Will proceed o/a 16 February 1945"**

| Rank | Name | Serial Number | MOS |
|------|------|--------|-----|
| Cpl | Milton K. Olmsted | 36 650 656 | 014 |
| Cpl | Bert (NMI) Schweizer II | 37 414 025 | 405 |
| Cpl | Albert J. Thebidault | 31 307 322 | 060 |
| Cpl | Howard V. Vailhancourt | 37 546 119 | 060 |
| Cpl | John O. Vecchiono | 33 577?399 | 657 |
| Cpl | William W. Warren | 14 142 061 | 747 |
| Pfc | Clifford (NMI) Barker | 35 389 911 | 657 |
| Pfc | Joseph P. Baynock | 33 466 492 | 635 |
| Pfc | Frank J. Budny | 36 621 672 | 055 |
| Pfc | Alfred R. Carifa | ?? ?03 020 | 405 |
| Pfc | Francis W. Carroll | 32 918 345 | 055 |
| Pfc | Calvin (NMI) Daw | 36 851 324 | 590 |
| Pfc | Chester S. Herman | 33 618 603 | 435 |
| Pfc | John L. Hiles | 39 201 096 | 754 |
| Pfc | Joseph N. Hitchon | 33 596 326 | 559 |
| Pfc | Grant W. Howell | 36 854 498 | 237 |
| Pfc | Lawrence B. Imorogno | 31 326 374 | 345 |
| Pfc | Albert S. Krouse | 32 441 345 | 590 |
| Pfc | Fulton H. Krupsaw | 33 737 977 | 620 |
| Pfc | Arthur (NMI) Martin | 34 354 621 | 747 |
| Pfc | Francis J. Cates | 31 262 165 | 345? |
| Pfc | William A. Schwanzer | 32 401 767 | 590 |
| Pfc | Michael C. Vasalauskas | 31 310 935 | 590 |
| Pvt | Richard L. Fisher | 36 441 399 | 590 |
| Pvt | Raymond P. Radford | 37 613 792 | 590 |
| Pvt | Philip J. Rehill | 33 580 821 | 345 |

**"Rear Echelon—Will Proceed o/a 20 February 1945"**

| Rank | Name | Serial Number | MOS |
|------|------|--------|-----|
| Capt | Walter B. Ditto | AC O 574 414 | |
| 1st Lt | Vito A. Capuco | AC O 860 360 | |
| M/Sgt | William L. Norton | 36 355 379 | 750 |
| T/Sgt | Charles (NMI) Maguire | 32 299 874 | 824 |
| S/Sgt | Vincent R. Angolemmo | 32 625 700 | 620 |
| S/Sgt | Howard (NMI) Broadbent | 39 035 639 | 559 |
| S/Sgt | Emil B. Kruppa | 18 232 216 | 559 |
| S/Sgt | George W. Manderscheid | 18 220 973 | 559 |
| S/Sgt | David Newmann | 32 795 196 | 620 |
| S/Sgt | Harry I. Pressley | 33 241 243 | 747 |
| S/Sgt | William T. Sullivan, Jr. | 34 447 674 | 687 |
| S/Sgt | Diego T. Vella | 11 087 920 | 747 |
| Sgt | Henry C. Allai | 37 437 328 | 055 |
| Sgt | Trinidad T. Alvarado | 39 405 510 | 559 |
| Sgt | Marion S. Ashby | 35 092 496 | 620 |

| Rank | Name | Serial Number | MOS |
|------|------|---------------|-----|
| \multicolumn{4}{l}{"Rear Echelon—Will proceed o/a 20 February 1945"} | | | |
| Sgt | Fraser E. Burg | 17 106 696 | 747 |
| Sgt | Manuel A. Carrasco | 39 852 597 | 849 |
| Sgt | Russell L. Charlesworth | 38 410 948 | 559 |
| Sgt | Thomas F. Clohosey, Jr. | 12 094 509 | 239 |
| Sgt | Wade J. Greene | 34 498 013 | 756 |
| Sgt | Matthew J. Korkowski | 33 287 175 | 552 |
| Sgt | David (NMI) Markowitz | 32 871 436 | 821 |
| Sgt | Benjamin F. Mullen, Jr. | 34 607 997 | 835 |
| Sgt | Earl C. Owens | 38 327 589 | 559 |
| Sgt | Emmett F. Pate | 14 163 680 | 747 |
| Sgt | Leopold E. Promis | 11 100 169 | 754 |
| Sgt | Leroy W. Ratliff | 38 132 395 | 747 |
| Sgt | Horacio R. Romo | 38 257 537 | 552 |
| Sgt | Frank L. Ruffini | 35 602 644 | 095 |
| Sgt | James B. Vallely | 33 570 073 | 237 |
| Sgt | Jack R. Vest | 15 383 146 | 747 |
| Sgt | Earl S. Wenzel | 37 653 397 | 747 |
| Cpl | Edgar A. Baer | 33 622 377 | 2750 |
| Cpl | Duane J. Burdick | 36 850 763 | 060 |
| Cpl | Cosimo S. Calcagino | 12 214 679 | 650 |
| Cpl | Robert E. Carr | 37 492 190 | 620 |
| Cpl | George F. Castle | 32 445 846 | 747 |
| Cpl | Howard C. Hatcher | 34 361 919 | 747 |
| Cpl | Amado (NMI) Hernandez | 38 358 153 | 060 |
| Cpl | Harvey E. Mall | 36 742 530 | 555 |
| Cpl | Earl A. Oliver | 35 666 630 | 756 |
| Cpl | Arthur D. Rouse | 37 611 785 | 2750 |
| Cpl | Cleo R. Rutherford | 37 514 012 | 747 |
| Cpl | Harry J. Slowik | 32 380 940 | 747 |
| Cpl | Gerald F. Witherell | 12 186 526 | 747 |
| Cpl | Chauncey V. Young | 37 462 616 | 237 |
| Pfc | George D. Adams | 34 587 512 | 590 |
| Pfc | Peter (NMI) D'Addario | 32 850 924 | 590 |
| Pfc | Leon K. Dobson | 36 407 881 | 559 |
| Pfc | Joseph F. Luna | 20 801 477 | 756 |
| Pfc | David M. Mihay | 31 329 421 | 590 |
| Pfc | Armand L. Munoz | 39 285 836 | 620 |
| Pfc | Theodore F. Slattery | 1 723 855 | 055 |
| Pfc | Harry J. Strazzinski | 36 814 058 | 237 |
| Pvt | Wyatt D. Hall | 18 218 099 | 559 |
| Pvt | Joseph W. Lane | 32 759 553 | 657 |
| Pvt | Fred I. Youngblood | 35 459 781 | 756 |
| Cpl | John H. Morgan | 35 398 088 | 853 |
| Cpl | Anthony J. Scotto di Covello | 32 824 965 | 055 |
| Pvt | Paul J. Swain | 16 110 359 | 559 |

# Appendix 3
# Time Line: Airborne History and the 81st TCS

| | |
|---|---|
| May 10, 1940 | German "silent wings" operation captures Belgian Eben Emael fortress |
| August 1940 | First jumps of the U.S. Parachute Test Platoon |
| June 22, 1940 | France surrenders; the Blitzkrieg is over |
| March 1941 | First invitations go out for a design for an American combat glider |
| May 20, 1941 | Operation MERKUR, German airborne conquest of Crete |
| December 7, 1941 | Pearl Harbor |
| January 1942 | Three regiments of U.S. paratroopers authorized; the 82nd is reborn as an airborne division |
| July 1942 | The first troop carrier cadres are formed up from ATC units |
| July 30, 1942 | Two airborne divisions authorized |
| August 1, 1942 | 53rd TCW activates |
| November 1942 | Graduates of glider pilot schools are made Flight Officers |
| November 8, 1942 | TORCH: Invasion of North Africa with a small airborne component |
| February 27, 1943 | Cadre of 436th TCG forms up at Dunnellon, Florida |
| April 1, 1943 | 81st TCS activates at Dunnellon, Florida |
| April 18, 1943 | We get our first airplane (Baer Field) |
| May 1, 1943 | The entire 436th arrives at Alliance, Nebraska |
| June 6, 1943 | First Squadron bivouac, Alliance |
| July 1943 | Mussolini overthrown |
| July 1943 | Glider pilots begin to join the Squadron |
| July 9, 1943 | HUSKY: Airborne invasion of Sicily |
| August 1, 1943 | Entire 436th begins move to Laurinburg-Maxton |
| September 9, 1943 | The Salerno invasion; Italy surrenders |
| September 12, 1943 | Skorzeny rescues Mussolini from an Italian prison |
| September 13, 1943 | Successful 82nd Airborne drop at the Salerno beachhead |
| September 14, 1943 | Airborne fiasco at Avellino, Italy |
| October 1943 | Navigators begin to join the Squadron |
| October 3–5, 1943 | First large-scale maneuvers, Tullahoma, Tennessee |
| October 31, 1943 | Our first double glider tow |

| | |
|---|---|
| November 3, 1943 | First men move to Baer Field to pack supplies |
| December 7, 1943 | Two-day "demonstration maneuver" begins |
| December 14, 1943 | Entire Squadron at Baer Field |
| December 24, 1943 | Air echelon begins to leave for overseas |
| January 1944 | Anzio beachhead campaign |
| January 5, 1944 | 81st TCS air echelon begins to arrive at Bottesford, England |
| January 22, 1944 | Sea echelon of the 81st TCS boards the *Queen Mary* |
| March 1, 1944 | Squadron moves from Bottesford to Membury |
| June 4, 1944 | Air Marshal Sir Trafford Leigh-Mallory addresses the 436th at Membury |
| | Allies enter Rome |
| June 5–6, 1944 | Normandy invasion begins: a paratroop drop |
| June 6, 1944 | Our first glider mission. First loss: Joseph Graves hospitalized in France; killed July 7 when hospital is shelled. Brewer and Fearn captured but soon manage to escape |
| June 10, 1944 | First 81st supply mission lands in France |
| July 16, 1944 | Brereton made head of the FAAA |
| July 18, 1944 | Twelve of our planes leave for Italy, for the invasion of southern France |
| July 24, 1944 | Our armored infantry breaks out at St.-Lô |
| August 1, 1944 | Planes in Britain begin to practice with Polish paratroopers |
| August 14, 1944 | Eisenhower orders the FAAA to supply 2,000 tons daily to the ground forces in east France and Belgium |
| August 15, 1944 | DRAGOON begins; paratroop drop on the Riviera (from Ciampino) |
| | Glider mission (from Voltone) |
| August 15–September 15 | Heavy schedules of supply-evac missions |
| | Our busiest month |
| August 16, 1944 | First stoppage of Patton's tanks for lack of fuel |
| August 16, 1944 | Re-supply mission to the Riviera |
| August 23, 1944 | Our twelve planes return to Membury from Italy |
| | We are awarded the Presidential Citation Medal |
| August 25, 1944 | Paris is liberated |
| September 17, 1944 | Invasion of Holland begins: a paratrooper drop at Eindhoven |
| September 18, 1944 | A glider tow to Eindhoven area (Zon). Webster's plane is shot down and he is taken prisoner. |
| September 19, 1944 | Bad weather wrecks mission number three; most planes have to abort; Stevenson's and Vosica's planes shot down; Stevenson and Okeson are killed; Watters is a POW; Fry is killed; Griffen is killed in the English Channel |
| September 20, 1944 | A re-supply mission to the Nijmegen area |
| September 23, 1944 | A glider mission |
| September 25, 1944 | A re-supply mission |

| | |
|---|---|
| October 6, 1944 | Air Medals awarded (for Normandy) |
| November 1944 | We begin ferrying the 17th ABD to France |
| November 7, 1944 | Farr, Obergfell, and Brooks return to Membury, courtesy of the Dutch Underground |
| November 15–December 15 | Very bad weather; few missions |
| December 10, 1944 | The Germans attack out of the Ardennes |
| December 21, 1944 | Bastogne surrounded |
| December 23-27 | Pararack re-supplies (Bastogne) |
| February 14–19, 1945 | The Squadron moves to Melun (Villaroche), France |
| March 24, 1945 | Glider mission across the Rhine (Wesel). Frye's plane shot down, and he, Cooke, Davis, Clemons, and Smith are killed; glider pilots Kearns, Pittman, Gephart and Hampton are killed |
| March 30–April 23 | A heavy schedule of supply and evac missions |
| April 12, 1945 | President Roosevelt dies |
| April and May 1945 | Huge volumes of freight and people moved these months |
| April 17, 1945 | Service of Remembrance for the 436th men KIA |
| April 23, 1945 | All of troop carrier is taken off combat status |
| May 8, 1945 | V-E Day |
| June 14, 1945 | Last date any 436th plane flies a tactical mission |
| July 12, 1945 | Our air echelon leaves for the States |
| July 15, 1945 | Ground-sea echelon leaves Melun for Camp New York and Camp Top Hat (Antwerp) |
| July 28, 1945 | S.S. *Joseph W. Gale* sails for the States |
| August 6, 1945 | Hiroshima bombed |
| August 10, 1945 | S.S. *Joseph W. Gale* arrives in New York; we are transferred to Camp Shanks |
| November 15, 1945 | The 436th Troop Carrier Group inactivates |

# Glossary

| | |
|---|---|
| AA | Antiaircraft |
| AEAF | Allied Expeditionary Air Force |
| ATC | Air Transportation Command |
| ATS | Auxiliary Territorial Service (British women soldiers) |
| AWOL | Absent without leave |
| BOQ | Bachelor officers quarters |
| CBAMHI | Carlisle Barracks Army Military History Institute |
| CBI | China-Burma-India war theater |
| CG | Commanding general |
| CO | Commanding officer |
| COSSAC | Chief of Staff, Supreme Allied Commander |
| DP | Displaced person (i.e., moved from his homeland by the Nazis, or who had fled because of the war) |
| DS | Detached service |
| DZ | Drop zone (for paratroopers and supplies) |
| EM | Enlisted man (i.e., not officers) |
| ETO | European theater of operations |
| FAAA | First Allied Airborne Army |
| FO | Flight officer (glider pilot rank) |
| GI | Government issue (supplies); enlisted man; "chicken" (according to strict regulation) |
| IFF | Identification, friend or foe (radar) |
| IP | Initial point (at which a formation turns into its final course for its objective) |
| KP | Kitchen police (mess hall work) |
| LST | Landing ship, tanks |
| LZ | Landing zone (for gliders) |
| MOS | Military occupation specialization |
| MP | Military police |
| MTO | Mediterranean theater of operations |
| NAAFI | Navy, Army, and Air Force Institute (British canteens) |
| NCO | Non-commissioned officer (corporal, sergeant) |
| NMI | No middle initial |
| O | Officers |
| OCS | Officers candidate school |

| | |
|---|---|
| OD | Olive drab (wool uniform); officer of the day (in charge of base security for the day) |
| OSS | Office of Strategic Services |
| PCT | Parachute combat team (usually a temporary arrangement) |
| PFAB | Parachute field artillery battalion |
| PIR | Parachute infantry regiment |
| POE | Port of embarkation (by sea or land) |
| POL | Petrol, oil, and lubricants |
| PX | Post exchange (base store) |
| R & R | Rest and rehabilitation (individuals); rest and replacements (for units); "remove and replace" (for engineering parts) |
| ROTC | Reserve officers training corps (college military classes) |
| SHAEF | Supreme Headquarters, Allied Expeditionary Forces |
| SOP | Standard operating procedure |
| TCC | Troop carrier command (theater command) |
| TCG | Troop carrier group |
| TCS | Troop carrier squadron |
| TCW | Troop carrier wing |
| TD | Temporary duty |
| TO | Table of organization; technical orders |
| TS | Tough shit! |
| TWX | Teletype message |
| USO | United Service Organizations (civilian volunteers) |
| VD | Venereal disease |
| WAC | Women's Army Corps (U.S.) |
| ZI | Zone of the Interior (i.e., the U.S.) |

# Sources

## Published Sources

Adleman, Robert, and George Walton. *The Champagne Campaign*. Boston: Little, Brown & Co., 1969.

———. *The Devil's Brigade*. Philadelphia: Chilton Books, 1966.

Ambrose, Stephen A. *Pegasus Bridge: June 6, 1944*. New York: Simon & Schuster, 1985.

———. *The Supreme Commander: The War Years of General Dwight D. Eisenhower*. Garden City: Doubleday, 1970.

Andrews, Allen. *The Air Marshals: The Air War in Western Europe*. New York: William Morrow & Co., 1970.

Anstey, E. C. "Airborne Invasion." *Cavalry Journal*, Nov.–Dec. 1944, pp. 32–33.

Army Air Forces. *Official Guide to the Army Air Forces*. n.p., 1944.

Blair, Craig. *Ridgway's Paratroopers: The American Airborne in World War II*. New York: The Dial Press, 1985.

Borge, Jacques, and Nicolas Viasnoff. *The Dakota: The DC-3 Story*. New York: VILO, 1980.

Bradley, Omar N. *A Soldier's Story*. New York: Henry Holt, 1951.

Bradley, Omar N., and Clay Blair. *A General's Life: An Autobiography by General of the Army Omar N. Bradley*. New York: Simon & Schuster, 1983.

Brereton, Lewis Hyde. *The Brereton Diaries*. New York: William Morrow & Co., 1946.

Breuer, William B. *Drop Zone Sicily: Allied Airborne Strike, July 1943*. Novato, California: Presidio Press, 1983.

———. *Operation Torch: The Allied Gamble to Invade North Africa*. New York: St. Martin's Press, 1985.

———. *Storming Hitler's Rhine: The Allied Assault, February–March 1945*. New York: St. Martin's Press, 1985.

Brinson, W. L. *Three One Five Group: An Account of the Activities of the 315th Troop Carrier Group, United States Army Air Forces, 1942–1945*. Lakemont, Georgia: Copple House Books, 1984.

Burgett, Donald R. *Currahee!* Boston: Houghton Mifflin, 1967.

Clark, Mark W. *Calculated Risk*, New York: Harper & Bros., 1950.

Collier, Richard. *The Freedom Road*, New York: Atheneum, 1984.

Comeau, M. G. *Operation Mercury*. London: Tandem Books, 1972.

Cornett, Jack. "Airborne Invasion—Normandy." *Military Review*, Nov. 1944, pp. 21–24.

Craven, Wesley Frank, and James Lea Cate, eds. *The Army Air Forces in World War II,
vol. II: Europe, From Argument to V-E Day, January 1944–May 1945*. Chicago:
The University of Chicago Press, 1949.

Critchell, Lawrence. *Four Stars of Hell*. NY: The Declan X. McMullen Co., 1947.

Crookenden, Napier. *Airborne at War*. New York: Charles Scribner's Sons, 1978.

Dank, Milton. *The Glider Gang*. Philadelphia: J. B. Lippincott, 1977.

Devlin, Gerard M. *Paratrooper!* New York: St. Martin's Press, 1979.

———. *Silent Wings*. New York: St. Martin's Press, 1985.

Eisenhower, Dwight D. *Crusade in Europe*. New York: Doubleday & Co., 1948.

———. *At Ease*. Garden City, New York: Doubleday & Co., 1967.

Eisenhower, John S. D. *The Bitter Woods*. New York: G. Putnam's Sons, 1969.

Ellis, L. F. *Victory in the West*. Vol. II. London: HMSO, 1968.

Farrar-Hockley, Anthony. *Airborne Carpet: Operation Market Garden*. New York: Ballantine Books, 1969.

Gavin, James M. *Airborne Warfare*. New York: Infantry Journal Press, 1947.

———. *On to Berlin*. New York: Bantam Books, 1979.

Greenfield, Kent Roberts. *Command Decisions*. Washington, D.C.: Office of the Chief
of Military History, 1960.

Gregory, Barry, and John Batchelor. *Airborne Warfare, 1918– 1945*. New York: Exeter
Books, 1979.

Howarth, David. *D-Day: The Sixth of June, 1944*. New York: McGraw Hill, 1959.

Huston, James A. *Airborne Operations* (typescript). Washington, D.C.: Office of the
Chief of Military History, 1950.

———. *Out of the Blue: U.S. Army Airborne Operations in World War II*. West Lafa-
yette, Indiana: Purdue University Studies, 1972.

Infield, Glenn B. *Skorzeny: Hitler's Commando*. New York: St. Martin's Press, 1981.

Keegan, John. *Six Armies in Normandy*. New York: Viking, 1982.

Kennett, Lee. *G.I.: The American Soldier in World War II*. New York: Charles Scribner's
Sons, 1987.

Kiriakopoulos, G. C. *Ten Days to Destiny*. New York: Franklin Watts, 1985.

Koskimaki, George E. *D-Day with the Screaming Eagles*. 2nd ed. New York: Vantage
Press, 1970.

Longmate, Norman. *The G.I.'s: The Americans in Britain, 1942–1945*. London: Hutch-
inson, 1975.

MacDonald, Charles. *Airborne*. New York: Ballantine Books, 1970.

———. *A Time for Trumpets: The Untold Story of the Battle of the Bulge*. New York:
William Morrow & Co., 1985.

McKee, Alexander. *The Race for the Rhine Bridges: 1940–1944–1945*. New York: Stein
& Day, 1971.

McVay, John N. "The Troop Carrier Command." *Military Review*, May 1945,
pp. 12–15.

Marshall, S. L. A. *Bastogne: The First Eight Days*. n.p., Infantry Journal, 1946.

———. *Night Drop: The American Airborne Invasion of Normandy*. Boston: Little,
Brown & Co., 1962.

Moore, Samuel T. "Tactical Employment in the U.S. Army of Transport Aircraft and
Gliders," (typescript, pages numbered within chapters). n.p., 1953.

Mrazek, James E. *The Glider War*. New York: St. Martin's Press, 1975.

101st Airborne Division. *History of the 101st Airborne Division*. Fort Campbell, Kentucky: n.d. (after 1964).

Rapport, Leonard, and Arthur Northwood, Jr. *Rendezvous with Destiny: A History of the 101st Airborne*. Madelia, Minnesota: for the 101st Airborne Division, 1948; enlarged ed., 1972.

Ridgway, Matthew B. *Soldier: The Memoirs of Matthew B. Ridgway, as told to Harold H. Martin*. New York: Harper & Brothers, 1956.

Robichon, Jacques. *The Second D-Day*. New York: Walker & Co., 1969.

Ruppenthal, Roland G. *Logistical Support of the Armies, the European Theater of Operations* ("United States Army in World War II"). 2 vols. Washington, D.C.: Office of the Chief of Military History, 1953, 1959.

Rust, Kenn C. *The 9th Air Force in World War II*. Fallbrook, California: Aero Publishers, 1967.

Ryan, Cornelius. *A Bridge Too Far*. New York: Popular Library, 1974.

Saunders, Hilary St. George. *The Red Beret: The Story of the Parachute Regiment at War, 1940–1945*. London: Michael Joseph, 1950.

Turkel, Studs. *The Good War: An Oral History of World War II*. New York: Pantheon Books, 1984.

U.S. Army Air Forces, HQ, IX Troop Carrier Command. *Tactical and Non-tactical Operations during the Final Phase of the War in Europe*, mimeo., HQ: IX TCC, June 1945.

Urquhart, R. E., *Arnhem*. Derby, Connecticut: Monarch Books, 1960.

Warren, John C. *Airborne Missions in the Mediterranean, 1942–1945* ("USAF Historical Studies," no. 74). Air University: USAF Historical Division, 1955 (referred to above as "Warren I").

———. *Airborne Operations in World War II, European Theater* ("USAF Historical Studies," no. 97). Air Unversity: USAF Historical Division, 1956 (referred to above as "Warren II").

Weigley, Russell F. *The American Way of War: A History of U.S. Military Strategy and Policy*. New York: Macmillan, 1973.

———. *Eisenhower's Lieutenants: The Campaigns of France and Germany, 1944–45*. Bloomington: Indiana University Press, 1981.

Wilt, Alan F. *The French Riviera Campaign of August 1944*. n.p., Southern Illinois University Press, 1981.

## Main Wartime Troop Carrier Mimeographed Reports

Army Air Forces, Air Intelligence Contact Unit. "Report on Returnees." Various dates, 1944–45.

USAFETO. "Organization, Equipment, and Tactical Employment of the Airborne Division." Study no. 16, n.d. (Nov. 1945?).

War Department. "Employment of Airborne and Troop Carrier." October 1943.

FAAA. "Supply by Air, Belgium." n.d.

———. "Operation TALISMAN." Sept. 13, 1944.

———. "Supply by Air, France and Holland." Nov. 20, 1944.

———. "ECLIPSE: Outline Airborne Plan." Dec. 31, 1944.

————. "History of HQ, FAAA, 2 August 1944–20 May 1945." Dec. 4, 1945.

IX TCC. "Report on Operation Neptune." n.d. (after July 1944).

————. "History of HQ, IX TCC." n.d. (after June 1945).

————. "Final Stages of Airborne Operations in the ETO." n.d. (after Nov. 1945).

————. "Operation Market: Air Invasion of Holland." Jan. 1945.

————. "Operation Varsity." March 28, 1945.

53rd TCW. "Historical Record: Rear Echelon, for the month of August 1944. " n.d.

————. "Report on MARKET-GARDEN." n.d. (after Sept. 1944).

————. "Ever First! The 53rd Troop Carrier Wing" (printed souvenir brochure). n.d. (after May 1945).

————. "D-Day." July 10, 1944.

————. "Historical Report of Advanced Headquarters for period 18 July 1944 to 24 August 1944: Operation DRAGOON." Sept. 10, 1944.

————. "Report on MARKET." Oct. 20, 1944.

————. "Report on Operation VARSITY." April 1945.

436th TCG. "Historical Data of the 436th TCG, April and May, 1945." n.d. (after June 1945).

Kerney, Captain John E. "Combat" (a short history of the 436th TCG in combat). n.d. (after June 1945).

Lester, Frank, and Grant Howell. "TARFU History" (a short history of the 81st TCS). n.d. (after June 1945).

# Index

A "Q" before a page number indicates a firsthand account by the soldier involved.

# The Author

During World War II, Martin ("Marty") Wolfe was a radio operator in a troop carrier plane. After the war ended, the G.I. Bill gave him the chance to earn a Ph.D. and then spend his entire career teaching economic history, first at Wayne State University in Detroit, Michigan, and then–for thirty-two years–at the University of Pennsylvania in Philadelphia. While teaching, he coped with the "publish or perish!" rule (for college professors who want promotions) by writing books and articles on French economic history.

Dr. Wolfe still does some work on economic history, particularly on the history of American and European foreign aid. He has also served as president of his local chapter of the Society for International Development, an organization that works for better understanding of foreign aid problems.

His current devotion to airborne troop carrier history was sparked by the tremendous uplift he gained from seeing his former war buddies at 81st TCS reunion meetings. Marty currently shares his enthusiasm for troop carrier history with many devoted British World War II history buffs, who in 1992 elected him honorary president of the British club known as BOTNA–"Buddies of the Ninth (U.S. Army Air Force) Association."